H21 416736 2

-0 OCT. 1986

333 .322'

DOMESDAY
BOOK
AS   6/86

Yorkshire,
part two
26.00
(2 vols, 1
set)

DOMESDAY BOOK

Yorkshire

History from the Sources

DOMESDAY BOOK

A Survey of the Counties of England

LIBER DE WINTONIA

Compiled by direction of

KING WILLIAM I

Winchester
1086

DOMESDAY BOOK

general editor

JOHN MORRIS

30

Yorkshire

edited by
Margaret L. Faull and Marie Stinson

(Part Two)

PHILLIMORE
Chichester
1986

1986
Published by
PHILLIMORE & CO. LTD.
London and Chichester
Head Office: Shopwyke Hall,
Chichester, Sussex, England

ISBN 0 85033 530 2 (case)
ISBN 0 85033 531 0 (limp)

© Mrs. Susan Morris, and the editors, 1986:
    Dr. Margaret L. Faull: place name identification, personal
                    name regularisations, index of persons,
                    index of places, and maps.
    Ms. Marie Stinson: appendix, biographies of landholders,
                    text translation
    Dr. Faull and Ms. Stinson: notes

*Printed in Great Britain by
Titus Wilson & Son Ltd.,
Kendal*

YORKSHIRE

(Part One)
Introduction

The Domesday Survey of Yorkshire

(to Landholder XXIV [23], Hugh son of Baldric)

(Part Two)

The Domesday Survey of Yorkshire

(Landholder XXXV [24], Erneis de Burun to
the Summary)
Bibliography and Abbreviations
Appendix
Notes
Index of Persons
Index of Places
Maps and Map Keys

.XXXV. TERRA ERNEIS DE BVRVN.

WESTREDING: SIRACHES WAP

Ⓜ In *BINGHELEIA*.ħɓ Gofpatric . iiii . car træ
ad glđ.Tra . ē ad . ii . car . Ernegis de buruntħ.
7 waſt.ē.T.R.E. ual . iiii . liɓ . Silua paſt . ii . leu
lg.7 i.laꞇ.Toꞇ Ⓜ.iiii.lev lg.7 ii.laꞇ.
Infra hanc meꞇā contineꞇ ħ Soca . Beldune.
Cotingelei . Helguic . Muceltuoit . Mardelei . Ha
teltun . Simul ad glđ.viii . caruc . Tra . ē ad . iiii . car.
Waſte funt oɱs.

Ⓜ In *COPEMANTORP*.ħɓ Gofpatric . ii . car 7 ii . ɓo
ad glđ . Tra ad . i . car . Ibi hꞇ Ernegis ɱ . ii . car.
7 iii.uiłł 7 ii.borđ.cū . i . car . T.R.E. ual xx.fot.ɱ xl . fot.

Ⓜ In *ACASTRA* ħɓ Grim . v . bou træ ad glđ . Nꞓ hꞇ
Vlric de Ernegis.7 waſt.ē. *BORGESCIRE WAP*.

Ⓜ In *DVNESFORDE* ħɓ Gofpatric . iii . car træ ad glđ.
Tra ad . ii . car . Rannulf ħo Ernegis hꞇ.fʒ waſt.ē.
T.R.E. ual xx . fot . ɱ . iii . fot . Ibi . vi . aꞓ p̃ti.

Ⓜ In *BRANTVNE* 7 *GRAFTVNE* . ħɓ Gofpatric . vii.
car tre ad glđ . Tra ad.iiii . car . Ernegis hꞇ.7 Waſta
funt . T.R.E. ual . xxx . fot.

LAND OF ERNEIS DE BURUN

WEST RIDING

SKYRACK Wapentake

1 M. In BINGLEY Gospatric had 4 carucates of land taxable. There is
land for 2 ploughs. Erneis de Burun has (it). Waste.
Value before 1066 £4.
  Woodland pasture, 2 leagues long and 1 wide.
  The whole manor, 4 leagues long and 2 wide.
Within this boundary is contained this jurisdiction: BAILDON, 2 c.;
COTTINGLEY, 2 c.; ELDWICK, 1 c.; MICKLETHWAITE, 1 c.; MARLEY, 1 c.;
and 'HALTON', 1 c. Together 8 carucates taxable. Land for 4
ploughs. All waste.

2 M. In COPMANTHORPE Gospatric had 2 carucates and 2 bovates
taxable. Land for 1 plough. Now Erneis has there 2 ploughs; and
  3 villagers and 2 smallholders with 1 plough.
Value before 1066, 20s; now 40s.

3 M. In ACASTER (Selby) Grimr had 5 bovates of land taxable. Now
Wulfric has (it) from Erneis. Waste.

'BURGHSHIRE' (CLARO) Wapentake

4 M. In (Upper and Lower) DUNSFORTH Gospatric had 3 carucates of
land taxable. Land for 2 ploughs. Ralph, Erneis' man, has (it)
but it is waste.
Value before 1066, 20s; now 3s.
  Meadow, 6 acres.

5 2 In BRANTON (Green) and GRAFTON Gospatric had 7 carucates of
M. land taxable. Land for 4 ploughs. Erneis has (them). Waste.
Value before 1066, 30s.

ꟾ In *CATHALE* . ħɓ Goſpatric . III . car̄ ad glđ . Tra
ad . II . car̄ . Ernegis ħt ibi . I . car̄ . 7 v . uiłł . 7 III .
borđ cū . II . car̄ . Dimiđ leu̅ lḡ . 7 dim lat̄ . T.R.E . uat
xxx . ſoł . m̄ ſimiłit̄ .

ꟾ In *HVLSINGOVRE* ħɓ Goſpatric IIII . car̄ tre 7 III . bŏ
ad glđ . Tra ad . II . car̄ . Ibi ħt Ernegis . I . car̄ . 7 IX .
uiłł 7 III . borđ . cū . III . car̄ . Silua paſt . II . q̊ɀ lḡ .
7 I . lat̄ . T.R.E . uat xxx . ſoł . m̄ L . ſoł .

Š In eađ uilla ſunt . x . bou tre ad glđ . ſoca in **Chena**
.II. resburg . Ernegis ħt 7 colit̄ .

ꟾ In *RIPESTAIN* 7 *HOMPTONE* ħɓ Turgot 7 Archil
II . car̄ ad glđ . Tra . e̅ ad . I . car̄ . T.R.E . uat . xx . ſoł . m̄
v . ſoł 7 IIII . den .

Š In *FLATESBI* IIII . car̄ tre ad glđ . Tra ad . II . car̄ . Soca
in **BVRG** . Ibi ħt Ernegis . I . car̄ . 7 v . uiłł . 7 II . borđ .
cū . I . car̄ . Dim leu̅ lḡ . 7 dim lat̄ . T.R.E . uat xxx . ſoł .
m̄ . xx.v . ſoł .

6 M. In '(Little) CATTAL' (OLD THORNVILLE HALL) Gospatric had 3
carucates taxable. Land for 2 ploughs. Erneis has there 1 plough;
and
    5 villagers and 3 smallholders with 2 ploughs.
    ½ league long and ½ wide.
Value before 1066, 30s; now the same.

7 M. In HUNSINGORE Gospatric had 4 carucates and 3 bovates of land
taxable. Land for 2 ploughs. Erneis has there 1 plough; and
    9 villagers and 3 smallholders with 3 ploughs.
    Woodland pasture, 2 furlongs long and 1 wide.
Value before 1066, 30s; now 50s.

8 S. In the same vill there are 10 bovates of land taxable.
Jurisdiction in KNARESBOROUGH. Erneis has (it); it is cultivated.

9 2 In (Great and Little) RIBSTON and HOPPERTON Thorgautr and
M. Arnketill had 2 carucates taxable. Land for 1 plough.
Value before 1066, 20s; now 5s 4d.

10 S. In FLAXBY 4 carucates of land taxable. Land for 2 ploughs.
Jurisdiction in (Ald)BOROUGH. Erneis has there 1 plough; and
    5 villagers and 2 smallholders with 1 plough.
    ½ league long and ½ wide.
Value before 1066, 30s; now 25s.

ⲙ̄ In *ARGHENDENE* 7 *LOTES* ħƀ Gamel . v . car̄ ꞇre

ad glđ . T́ra ad . ii . car̄ 7 dim̄ . Idē ħꞇ De Ernegis . 7 coliꞇ́.

T.R.E . ual . xl . iii . foł . m̄ . vi . foł.

ⲙ̄ In *COPEGRAVE* . ħƀ Goſpatric . vi . car̄ ꞇre ad glđ.

Tŕa . ē ad . iii . car̄ . Ibi ħꞇ Turſten ħō Ernegis . i . car̄.

7 vii . uiłł cū . i . car̄ . Ibi . ē æcclá . Vna lev̄ lḡ . 7 ḍim̄ laꞇ.

328 d

T.R.E . ual . xx . foł . m̄ . xvi . foł.

ⲙ̄ In *BIRNEBEHA¯* . ħƀ Goſpatric . iii . car̄ 7 vi . boủ

ad glđ . Tŕa . ē ad . ii . car̄ . Ernegis ħꞇ . 7 waſta . ē . T.R.E.

ual xxiii . foł.

In *WIPELEI* 7 *BEMESLAI* . ħƀ Goſpatric . i . car̄ ꞇre

ad glđ . Tŕa . ē ad dim̄ car̄ . Ernegis ħꞇ 7 waſt . ē.

ⲙ̄ In *BEVRELIE* 7 *DACRE* . ħƀ Goſpatric . vi . car̄ ꞇræ

ad glđ . Tŕa ad . iiii . car̄ . Ernegis ħꞇ 7 waſta . ē . T.R.E.

ual . l . foł . Silua paſt́ . ii . lev̄ lḡ . 7 ii . laꞇ . Toꞇ . iiii.

lev̄ lḡ . 7 iii . laꞇ.

ⲙ̄ In *LITELBRAN* . ħƀ Goſpatric . iiii . car̄ ꞇræ ad glđ.

Tŕa . ē ad . ii . car̄ . Ibi ħꞇ Ernegis . i . car̄ . 7 iii . uiłł . cū . i . car̄.

Dimid lev̄ lḡ . 7 dim̄ laꞇ . T.R.E . ual xx . foł . m̄ ſimiliꞇ.

Picot tenet de Ernegis.

Ƀ H́ p̄tinet ad ipſū ⲙ̄ . Michelbran . i . car̄ ꞇre ad glđ.

Waſta . ē . ſʒ xvi . den̄ redđ.

ⲙ̄ In *NEVSONE* ħƀ Earne . ii . car̄ ꞇre ad glđ . Tŕa ad

. i . car̄ . Joħs ħō Ernegis ħꞇ . ſʒ waſt . ē . Silua paſt́

iiii . ac̄s . lḡ . 7 iiii . laꞇ . Dim̄ lev̄ lḡ . 7 dim̄ laꞇ . T.R.E.

ual . xx . foł.

11 M. In ARKENDALE and LOFTUS (Hill) Gamall had 5 carucates of land
taxable. Land for 2½ ploughs. The same man has (it) from
Erneis and it is cultivated.
Value before 1066, 43s; now 6s.

12 M. In COPGROVE Gospatric had 6 carucates of land taxable. Land
for 3 ploughs. Thorsteinn, Erneis' man, has there 1 plough; and
7 villagers with 1 plough.
A church is there.
1 league long and ½ wide.
Value before 1066, 20s; now 16s.   328 d

13 M. In BRIMHAM (Hall) Gospatric had 3 carucates and 6 bovates
taxable. Land for 2 ploughs. Erneis has (it). Waste.
Value before 1066, 23s.

14 M. In WHIPLEY (Hall) and BEAMSLEY Gospatric had 1 carucate of land
taxable. Land for ½ plough. Erneis has (it). Waste.

15 2 In BEWERLEY and DACRE Gospatric had 6 carucates of land taxable.
M. Land for 4 ploughs. Erneis has (it). Waste.
Value before 1066, 50s.
Woodland pasture, 2 leagues long and 2 wide.
The whole, 4 leagues long and 3 wide.

16 M. In 'LITTLE' BRAHAM Gospatric had 4 carucates of land taxable.
There is land for 2 ploughs. Erneis has there 1 plough; and
3 villagers with 1 plough.
½ league long and ½ wide.
Value before 1066, 20s; now the same.
Picot holds (it) from Erneis.

17 B. This belongs to the same manor: 'GREAT' BRAHAM, 1 carucate of
land taxable. Waste, but it pays 16d.

18 M. In NEWSOME (Farm) Earne had 2 carucates of land taxable. Land
for 1 plough. John, Erneis' man, has (it) but it is waste.
Woodland pasture, 4 acres long and 4 wide.
½ league long and ½ wide.
Value before 1066, 20s.

§ In WEDREBI.suɴ.II.caɼ ꞌꞌtre ad glƌ.Soca in Che
nareſburg.Ṫra ad.I.caɼ.Ibi hɼ Ernegis.I.ſochm.
7 IIII.uiłł.cū.II.caɼ.Silua paſt dĩ leᵛ lḡ.7 dim łt.
§ In BERGHEBI 7 DISTONE.7 GEMVNSTORP.
Soca in Holſingoure.Simul ad glƌ.VIII.caɼ
7 dim.Ṫra.ē ad.IIII.caɼ.Ibi hɼ Ernegis.I.ſochm
7 IIII.uiłł 7 II.borƌ.cū.II.caɼ.T.R.E.uał xxvIII.

.III. ſoł.m̊.v.ſoł.   IN CRAVE.

In MERDELAI.Heldetone.Cotingelai.Colinga
7 B uuorde.Hageneuuorde.Simul ad glƌ.vI.caɼ 7 dim
ꞌtræ.Ṫra ad.III.caɼ.Ernegis hɼ.7 waſta ſuɴ.

      ESTREDING. CAVE HVNDRET.

In COTEVVID.hƀ Grim.I.caɼ ꞌꞌtre ad glƌ.Ṫra ad
dim caɼ.Ernegis hɼ 7 waſta.ē.Silua paſt.II.
q̃z lḡ.7 II.łaɼ.

In STEFLINGEFLED.hƀ Grim.II.caɼ ad glƌ.Ṫra ad.II.
caɼ.Ibi Hunfrid hō Ernegis.II.caɼ.7 7 II.uiłł.
7 I.borƌ.T.R.E.uał.x.ſoł.m̊ xv.ſoł.

★
.XXXVI. TERRA OSBERNI DE ARCHES.

      WESTREDING EINESTI WAP

.IIII. In STIVETONE.hƀr Archil Goduin 7 Goduin
7 Æluuin.vI.caɼ træ ad glƌ.Ṫra.ē ad vI.caɼ.Nc̄
ibi hɼ Osƀn de arcis.I.caɼ.7 II.uiłł 7 IIII.borƌ.
cū.I.caɼ.7 III.ac̄s p̃ti.Vna leᵛ lḡ.7 dimiƌ łaɼ.
T.R.E.uał xx.ſoł.m̊ xL.ſoł.

19 S. In WETHERBY there are 2 carucates of land taxable. Jurisdiction in KNARESBOROUGH. Land for 1 plough. Erneis has there
> 1 Freeman and 4 villagers with 2 ploughs.
> Woodland pasture, ½ league long and ½ wide.

20 S. In BARROWBY (Grange), 3 c.; (Kirk and North) DEIGHTON, 4 c.; and INGMANTHORPE (Hall), 1½ c. Jurisdiction in HUNSINGORE. Together 8½ carucates taxable. There is land for 4 ploughs. Erneis has there
> 1 Freeman, 4 villagers and 2 smallholders with 2 ploughs.
> Value before 1066, 28s; now 5s.

In CRAVEN

21 3 In MARLEY, 1 c.; 'HALTON', 2 c.; COTTINGLEY, 2 c.; CULLINGWORTH,
M. 2 c.; and HAINWORTH, ½ c. Together 6½ carucates of land taxable.
& B. Land for 3 ploughs. Erneis has them. Waste.

EAST RIDING

CAVE Hundred

1 M. In (West) COTTINGWITH Grimr had 1 carucate of land taxable. Land for ½ plough. Erneis has (it). Waste.
> Woodland pasture, 2 furlongs long and 2 wide.

2 M. In STILLINGFLEET Grimr had 2 carucates taxable. Land for 2 ploughs. Humphrey, Erneis' man, has there 2 ploughs; and
> 2 villagers and 1 smallholder.
> Value before 1066, 10s; now 15s.

(36) **LAND OF OSBERN DE ARCHES** 329 a

WEST RIDING

AINSTY Wapentake

1 4 In STEETON (Hall) Arnketill, Godwine, Godwine and Alwine had 6
M. carucates of land taxable. There is land for 6 ploughs. Now Osbern de Arches has there 1 plough; and
> 2 villagers and 4 smallholders with 1 plough.
> Meadow, 3 acres.
> 1 league long and ½ wide.
> Value before 1066, 20s; now 40s.

.III.
🖳 In *APLETONE* . ħbr Fardan Aluin⁹ 7 Tone . xii . car
tre ad glđ . Tra . ē ad xii . car . Ibi hōēs Osɓni . ii . hñt
nc̄ . vii . uiłł cū . v . car . 7 feđ molđ . 7 xx . ac̄s p̃ti.
Silua paſt . i . lev lg̃ 7 dim lat . Tot . ii . lev lg̃ . 7 i . lat
T.R.E . uał . iiii . liɓ . m̂ . xxx . ii . ſoł.

.v.
🖳 In *COLETONE* . ħbr Archil Goduin 7 Goduin Tor
7 Vłſtan . iiii . car 7 dim ad glđ . Tra . ē ad . iiii . car.
De hac tra ſuꝗ . ix bou in ſoca de Rodouuelle.
Nc̄ . ii . hōēs Osɓni hñt ibi . v . borđ . cū . i . car.
Silua paſṭ dim lev lg̃ . 7 dim lat . Tot . i . leu lg̃ . 7 dim
lat . T.R.E . uał xl . ſoł . m̂ xii . ſoł.
In *TORP* . ſunt . ii . bou tre ad glđ . Osɓn⁹ ħt 7 waſt . ē.
§ In *OSSETONE* ē ſoca de Merſtone . iiii . car tre
ad glđ . Tra . ē ad . ii . car . Osɓn⁹ ħt 7 waſt . ē

🖳 In *CADRETONE* ħbr . v . taini . ii . car ad glđ.
Tra ad . ii . car . Ibi Fulco hō Osɓni ħt . iiii . uiłł.
7 i . borđ cū . ii . car . 7 vi . ac̄s p̃ti . Silua paſtił
i . lev lg̃ . 7 iiii . q̃ꝝ lat . Tot . i . lev lg̃ . 7 dim lat.
T.R.E . uał xvi . ſoł . m̂ xvii . ſoł.
In *HORNITONE* ħt iđ Osɓn⁹ . i . bou tre ad glđ.
.III.
🖳 In *TORP* ħbr Orm Goduin 7 Tor . iii . car tre ad
glđ . Tra . ē ad . iii . car . Ibi ħt nc̄ Osɓn⁹ . iii . car.
7 vi . uiłł 7 vii . borđ . cū . ii . car . Ibi pɓr 7 æccła.
7 feđ molđ . Vna lev lg̃ . 7 dim lat . T.R.E . uał
iiii . liɓ . m̂ . x . ſoł miň.

329 a

2 3 In APPLETON (Roebuck) Farthegn, Alwine and Tonni had 12
M. carucates of land taxable. There is land for 12 ploughs. 2 men
of Osbern now have there
  7 villagers with 5 ploughs.
  A mill site; meadow, 20 acres; woodland pasture, 1 league
    long and ½ wide.
The whole, 2 leagues long and 1 wide.
Value before 1066 £4; now 32s.

3 5 In COLTON Arnketill, Godwine, Godwine, Thorr and Wulfstan
M. had 4½ carucates taxable. There is land for 4 ploughs. 9 bovates
of this land are in the jurisdiction of RODOUUELLE. Now 2 men
of Osbern have there
  5 smallholders with 1 plough.
  Woodland pasture, ½ league long and ½ wide.
The whole, 1 league long and ½ wide.
Value before 1066, 40s; now 12s.

4 In (Palla)THORPE there are 2 bovates of land taxable. Osbern has
it. Waste.

5 S. In OXTON is a jurisdiction of (Long)MARSTON. 4 carucates of land
taxable. There is land for 2 ploughs. Osbern has it. Waste.

6 2 In CATTERTON 5 thanes had 2 carucates of land taxable. Land
M. for 2 ploughs. Fulco, Osbern's man, has there
  4 villagers and 1 smallholder with 2 ploughs.
  Meadow, 6 acres; woodland pasture, 1 league long and 4
    furlongs wide.
The whole, 1 league long and ½ wide.
Value before 1066, 16s; now 17s.

7 In HORNINGTON (Manor) the same Osbern has 1 bovate of land
taxable.

8 3 In THORP (Arch) Ormr, Godwine and Thorr had 3 carucates of
M. land taxable. There is land for 3 ploughs. Osbern now has there 3
ploughs; and
  6 villagers and 7 smallholders with 2 ploughs.
  There, a priest and a church.
  A mill site.
  1 league long and ½ wide.
Value before 1066 £4; now 10s less.

ⓂIn *WALETONE* h̄br.vi.taini.ix.car̄ ⁷⁷ tre ad glđ.

Tra.ē ad ix.car̄.Ibi h̄t Osb̄n.i.car̄.7 un hō ei

i.car̄.7 vi.uilt.cū.ii.car̄.7 xiiii.ac̄s p̄ti.V̄na

lev̄ lḡ.7 i.lat̄.Ibi filua modica.T.R.E.ual iiii.lib̄.

.iii. m̊.xxx.fot.

ⓂIn *BILETONE* h̄br vii.taini.ix.car̄ ⁷⁷ træ ad glđ.

Tra.ē ad.ix.car̄.Ibi h̄t nc̄ Osb̄n.viii.uilt cū.iiii.

car̄.7 ii.ac̄s p̄ti.Silua minuta.i.lev̄ lḡ.7 iii.q̂ƶ lat̄.

Tot̄.i.lev̄ lḡ.7 i.lat̄.T.R.E.ual.iii.lib̄.m̊.xv.fot.

ⓂIn *MERSETONE* h̄b Æluuin.xxiii.car̄ ⁷⁷ træ ad

gld.Tra.ē ad totid car̄.De his fuȷ.xi.car̄ in foca.

329 b

in Tocvi 7 Wileftorp.iacet.Nc̄.ii.hōes Osb̄ni

h̄nt ibi.i.car̄ 7 dim̄.7 ix.uilt cū.iii.car̄.Silua

paft.ii.lev̄ lḡ.7 i.lat̄.Tot̄.ii.lev̄ lḡ.7 ii.lat̄.

T.R.E.ual.vi.lib̄.m̊ xlii.fot 7 iiii.den.

ⓂIn *WANDESLAGE* h̄b Eluuin.vi.car̄ ⁷⁷ tre ad glđ.

Tra.ē ad.vi.car̄.Nc̄ id h̄t de Osb̄no.Ipfe.i.car̄.

7 v.uilt 7 ii.bord cū.ii.car̄.7 vii.ac̄s p̄ti.Silua paft

iiii.q̂ƶ lḡ.7 ii.lat̄.Tot̄.i.lev̄ lḡ.7 dim̄ lat̄.T.R.E.

ual.xl.fot.m̊ xxx.vi.fot.

ⓂIn *POPLETONE*.h̄b Ernuin.iii.car̄ ⁷⁷ træ 7 dim̄ ad

glđ.Tra.ē ad totid car̄.Ibi Herm̄frid hō Osb̄ni h̄t

iii.uilt cū.i.car̄.T.R.E.ual.xx.fot.m̊ viii.fot.

In altera *POPLETONE* h̄b Ode.ii.car̄ 7 dim̄ ad glđ.

Tra.ē ad totid car̄.H̄ fuit tra S Elurilde.Ibi h̄t Osb̄n

.i.car̄.7 ii.uilt cū.i.car̄.Silua paft.i.lev̄ lḡ.7 iii.q̂ƶ

lat̄.T.R.E.ual xl.fot.m̊.xxviii.fot.

9 6   In WALTON 6 thanes have 9 carucates of land taxable. There is
M.   land for 9 ploughs. Osbern has there 1 plough; and
      1 of his men (has) 1 plough; and
      6 villagers with 2 ploughs.
      Meadow, 14 acres.
      1 league long and 1 wide.
      There, a little woodland.
  Value before 1066 £4; now 30s.

10 3   In BILTON 7 thanes had 9 carucates of land taxable. There is land
M.   for 9 ploughs. Osbern now has there
      8 villagers with 4 ploughs.
      Meadow, 2 acres; underwood, 1 league long and 3 furlongs wide.
      The whole, 1 league long and 1 wide.
  Value before 1066 £3; now 15s.

11 M.   In (Long) MARSTON Alwine had 23 carucates of land taxable.
  There is land for as many ploughs. Of these 11 carucates are in
  jurisdiction which lies in TOCKWITH and WILSTROP (Hall). Now 2   329 b
  of Osbern's men have there 1½ ploughs; and
      9 villagers with 3 ploughs.
      Woodland pasture, 2 leagues long and 1 wide.
      The whole, 2 leagues long and 2 wide.
  Value before 1066 £6; now 42s 4d.

12 M.   In (Hutton) WANDESLEY Alwine had 6 carucates of land taxable.
  There is land for 6 ploughs. Now the same man has (it) from
  Osbern. He (has) 1 plough; and
      5 villagers and 2 smallholders with 2 ploughs.
      Meadow, 7 acres; woodland pasture, 4 furlongs long and
        2 wide.
      The whole, 1 league long and ½ wide.
  Value before 1066, 40s; now 36s.

13 M.   In (Upper) POPPLETON Earnwine had 3½ carucates of land taxable.
  Land for as many ploughs. Ermenfrid, Osbern's man, has
      3 villagers with 1 plough.
  Value before 1066, 20s; now 8s.

14   In another (Nether) POPPLETON Oddi the Deacon had 2½ carucates
  taxable. There is land for as many ploughs. This land was of St.
  Everilda's. Osbern has there 1 plough; and
      2 villagers with 1 plough.
      Woodland pasture, 1 league long and 3 furlongs wide.
  Value before 1066, 40s; now 28s.

ⓂIn *Ascam*. ħƀr Eldred 7 Suartcol. vi. car̄ træ
ad glđ. Tra. ē ad. vi. car̄. Ibi hȳ Osƀn̄ m̄. i. car̄. 7 v.
uilt. 7 ii. borđ cū. ii. car̄. 7 vii. ac̄s p̄ti. Silua past̄
iiii. q̄ʒ lḡ. 7 ii. lat̄. Tot̄. i. lev̄ lḡ. 7 dim̄ lat̄. T.R.E.
ual iiii. liƀ. m̄ xxx. fol.

ⓂIn *Scarchetorp*. ħƀ Ernuin. iii. car̄ træ ad glđ.
Tra. ē ad. iii. car̄. Ibi hō Osƀni Erm̄frid hȳ. i. uilt
7 iiii. borđ. 7 iii. ac̄s p̄ti. Silua past̄ dim̄ lev̄ lḡ.
7 iiii. ac̄s lat̄. Tot̄. i. lev̄ lḡ. 7 dim̄ lat̄. T.R.E. ual
x. fol. 7 viii. den. m̄. vi. fol.

ⓂIn *Hesdesai*. ħƀ Ragenot. ii. car̄ træ 7 ii. boū
ad glđ. Tra. ē ad totid̄ car̄. Ibi Eldred de Osƀno
hȳ. ii. borđ cū. i. car̄. Silua past̄. iii. q̄ʒ lḡ. 7 iii. lat̄.
T.R.E. ual. x. fol 7 viii. den. m̄. iiii. fol.

ⓂIn *Cnapetone* ħƀ Æluuin̄. ii. car̄ trē ad gld. Tra
ē ad. ii. car̄. Nc̄ iđ hȳ de Osƀno. Ibi. i. fochs. ē cū
. i. car̄. 7 iii. ac̄ p̄ti. Silua past̄. iii. q̄ʒ lḡ. 7 ii. lat̄.
T.R.E. ii. fol 7 ii. den. m̄ similit.

ⓂIn *Rvfort*. ħƀr Aluuin 7 Aldulf. iiii. car̄ træ ad
glđ. Tra. ē ad. iiii. car̄. Nc̄ Ofƀn̄ hō Osƀni hȳ ibi. i. c̄.
7 iii. uilt 7 v. borđ cū. i. car̄. 7 iii. ac̄s p̄ti. Silua past̄
dim̄ lev̄ lḡ. 7 dim̄ lat̄. Tot̄. i. lev̄ lḡ. 7 i. lat̄. T.R.E.
ual. xl. fol. m̄. xxx. fol. *BORGESCIRE WAPENT.*

ⓂIn *Monechetone* ħƀr. v. taini. viii. car̄ træ
ad glđ. Tra. ē ad totid̄ car̄. Ibi Hugo hō Osƀni hȳ
x. uilt cū. iiii. car̄. 7 iiii. ac̄s p̄ti. 7 dim̄ pifcariā.
Silua past̄. i. lev̄ lḡ. 7 iii. q̄ʒ lat̄. Tot̄. i. lev̄ ḡ.
7 dimiđ lat̄. T.R.E. ual. xl. fol. m̄. xxv. fol.

15 2 In ASKHAM (Richard) Aldred and Svartkollr had 6 carucates of
M. land taxable. There is land for 6 ploughs. Osbern now has there 1
plough; and
   5 villagers and 2 smallholders with 2 ploughs.
   Meadow, 7 acres; woodland pasture, 4 furlongs long and 2 wide.
   The whole, 1 league long and ½ wide.
Value before 1066 £4; now 30s.

16 M. In SCAGGLETHORPE Earnwine had 3 carucates of land taxable.
There is land for 3 ploughs. Ermenfrid, Osbern's man, has there
   1 villager and 4 smallholders.
   Meadow, 3 acres; woodland pasture, ½ league long and
      4 acres wide.
   The whole, 1 league long and ½ wide.
Value before 1066, 10s 8d; now 6s.

17 M. In HESSAY Ragenot had 2 carucates and 2 bovates of land taxable.
There is land for as many ploughs. Aldred has there from Osbern
   2 smallholders with 1 plough.
   Woodland pasture, 3 furlongs long and 3 wide.
Value before 1066, 10s 8d; now 4s.

18 M. In KNAPTON Alwine had 2 carucates of land taxable. There is land
for 2 ploughs. Now the same man has (it) from Osbern.
   There is there 1 Freeman with 1 plough.
   Meadow, 3 acres; woodland pasture, 3 furlongs long and 2 wide.
Value before 1066, 2s 2d; now the same.

19 2 In RUFFORTH Alwine and Aldwulf had 4 carucates of land taxable.
M. There is land for 4 ploughs. Now Osbern, Osbern's man, has there
   1 plough; and
   3 villagers and 5 smallholders with 1 plough.
   Meadow, 3 acres; woodland pasture, ½ league long and ½ wide.
   The whole, 1 league long and 1 wide.
Value before 1066, 40s; now 30s.

'BURGHSHIRE' (CLARO) Wapentake
20 5 In (Nun) MONKTON 5 thanes had 8 carucates of land taxable.
M. There is land for as many ploughs. Hugh, Osbern's man, has there
   10 villagers with 4 ploughs.
   Meadow, 4 acres; ½ fishery; woodland pasture, 1 league long
      and 3 furlongs wide.
   The whole, 1 league long and ½ wide.
Value before 1066, 40s; now 25s.

Ꝏ In CHIRCHEBI . ħb Norman . II . car̄ tre ad glđ.

Tra ad . II . car̄ . Osbn̊ hī nc̄ . 7 ualet . xx . den.

Ꝏ In CVCHESLᴀGE ħb Baret . XIII . car̄ tre ad glđ.

Tra . ē ad totiđ car̄ . Osbn̊ hī nc̄ 7 wasī . ē . Ibi ſunt

II . æcclæ . 7 III . ac̄ pti . T.R.E. ual . III . lib . m̊ . XXI . den.

★ Ꝏ In HANBRETONE ħbr . III . taini . v . car̄ tre

ad glđ . Tra . ē ad . vi . car̄ . Osbn̊ hī 7 wasī . ē.
III.

Ꝏ In altera HANBRETONE ħbr Turchil Gamel Heltor.

VI . car̄ træ 7 dim̄ ad glđ . Tra . ē ad . VI . car̄ . Ibi Joħs

ħo Osbni hī . II . car̄ . 7 v . uiłł cū . I . car̄ . Ibi pbr 7 æcła

7 I . molđ . II . ſoł 7 . I . piſcar̄ . III . ſoł . Toī dim̄ lev lḡ . 7 dim̄

laī . T.R.E. ual . IIII . lib . m̊ . XLV . ſoł.

Ꝏ In HOMPTONE . ħb Gamel . I . car̄ tre ad glđ . Tra

ad . I . car̄ . Osbn̊ hī 7 waſta . ē . T.R.E. ual . x . ſoł.

Ꝏ In SOSACRA ħb Norman . I . car̄ tre ad glđ . Tra

ad . I . car̄ . Osbn̊ hī 7 waſta . ē . T.R.E. ual . x . ſoł.

✝ BARCHESTON WAPENTAC.

Ꝏ In STVTVNE ħb Torchil . I . car̄ tre 7 dim̄ ad glđ.

Tra . ē ad totiđ car̄ . Ibi . II . ħoēs Osbni ħnt . II . uiłł.

7 II . borđ cū . I . borđ . cū . I . car̄ . 7 x . ac̄s pti . Silua

paſt . I . q̊z 7 dim̄ lḡ . 7 tntđ laī . T.R.E. ual . xxx . ſoł.
.IIII . m̊ . x . ſoł.

Ꝏ7 In TOGLESTVN 7 Neuueton 7 Ogleſtorp . ħbr . IIII.
7 B

taini . VII . car̄ træ 7 VII . bo ad glđ . Nc̄ hī Fulco

ħo Osbni ibi . I . car̄ . 7 v . uiłł cū . I . car̄ . 7 VIII . ac̄s pti.

Toī . I . lev lḡ . 7 I . laī . T.R.E. ual . XL . ſoł . m̊ . xx . ſoł.

21 M. In KIRBY (Hall) Northmann had 2 carucates of land taxable. Land   329 c
for 2 ploughs. Osbern has (it) now.
Value 20d.

22 M. In WHIXLEY Barthr had 13 carucates of land taxable. There is land
for as many ploughs. Osbern has it now. Waste.
2 churches there.
Meadow, 3 acres.
Value before 1066 £3; now 21d.

23 2 In (Kirk) HAMMERTON 3 thanes had 6 carucates of land taxable.
M. There is land for 6 ploughs. Osbern has it. Waste.

24 3 In another (Green) HAMMERTON Thorketill, Gamall and Halldorr
M. had 6½ carucates of land taxable. There is land for 6 ploughs.
John, Osbern's man, has there 2 ploughs; and
5 villagers with 1 plough.
There, a priest and a church.
1 mill, 2s; 1 fishery, 3s.
The whole, ½ league long and ½ wide.
Value before 1066 £4; now 45s.

25 M. In HOPPERTON Gamall had 1 carucate of land taxable. Land for 1
plough. Osbern has it. Waste.
Value before 1066, 10s.

26 M. In SUSACRES Northmann had 1 carucate of land taxable. Land for
1 plough. Osbern has it. Waste.
Value before 1066, 10s.

A marginal mark indicates that the entry for Cattal (25W27 below) should be inserted here.

BARKSTON (Ash) Wapentake
28 M. In STUTTON Thorketill had 1½ carucates of land taxable. There is
land for as many ploughs. 2 of Osbern's men have there
2 villagers and 2 smallholders with 1 smallholder with 1 plough.
Meadow, 10 acres; woodland pasture, 1½ furlongs long and
as wide.
Value before 1066, 30s; now 10s.

29 4 In TOULSTON, NEWTON (Kyme) and OGLETHORPE (Hall) 4 thanes
M. had 7 carucates and 7 bovates of land taxable. Now Fulco,
& B. Osbern's man, has there 1 plough; and
5 villagers with 1 plough.
Meadow, 8 acres.
The whole, 1 league long and 1 wide.
Value before 1066, 40s; now 20s.

.v.

ⓂⒷ In *NEVTON* 7 Ogleſtun ħbr.v.taini.iii.car træ

ad glđ.Tra.ē ad.iiii.car.Ibi Fulco hō Osbni hŧ

.i.car.7 vii.uiłł.cū.ii.car.7 xvi.aċs p̄ti.7 ſeđ.i.

molđ.Toŧ Ⓜ.vi.q̊ꝥ łḡ.7 tntđ laŧ.T.R.E.ual.lx.ſoł.

m̄ xx.ſoł. *IN CRAVE.*

Ⓜ In *SIGLESDENE*.ħbr.v.taini.viii.car træ ad glđ.

ⓂⒷ In *HEBEDENE*.7 Torp ħb Dringlel.iiii.car træ

7 ii.bou ad glđ.

ⓂⒷ In *BRINESHALE* 7 Drebelaie ħb Dringhel.ii.car

7 ii.bov ad glđ.

Has tras hŧ Osbn de archis.ſʒ uuaſte ſunt om̄s.

✝ Ṡ In *CATALE* ſuꝥ.v.car tre ad glđ.Tra.ē ad.ii.car.

Soca.ē in Burg.Ⓜ.regis.Osbn hŧ 7 waſt.ē.

329 d

TERRA ODONIS ARBALISTARII.

ESTREDING.

Ⓜ In *BVCHETORP*.ħb Forne.iiii.car træ 7 dim̄ ad glđ.

Tra.ē ad totiđ car.Ibi hŧ Odo arbaliſt.i.car.7 iii.

uiłł cū.i.car.7 viii.aċs p̄ti.T.R.E.ual.xx.ſoł.m̄ x.ſoł.

Ⓜ In *BARCHETORP*.ħb Forne.ii.car træ ad glđ.Tra

ad.ii.car.Odo hŧ 7 waſta.ē.T.R.E.ual.x.ſoł.

Ṡ In *AIVLFTORP*.ſoca de poclinton.iiii.car tre ad glđ.

Tra ad totiđ car.Odo hŧ 7 waſta.ē.

Ⓜ In *FRIDAGSTORP*.ħbr Forne 7 Game.xiii.car træ ᴠɪɪɪ. 7 dim̄

ad glđ.Tra ad totiđ car.Odo hŧ.7 waſta.ē.T.R.E.xx.ſoł.

30 5 In NEWTON (Kyme) and TOULSTON 5 thanes had 3 carucates of
M. land taxable. There is land for 4 ploughs. Fulco, Osbern's man,
& B. has there 1 plough; and
>7 villagers with 2 ploughs.
>Meadow, 16 acres; 1 mill site.
>The whole manor, 6 furlongs long and as wide.
>Value before 1066, 60s; now 20s.

CRAVEN

31 5 In SILSDEN 5 thanes had 8 carucates of land taxable.
M.

32 M. In HEBDEN and THORPE Drengr had 4 carucates and 2 bovates of
& B. land taxable.

33 M. In BURNSALL and DREBLEY Drengr had 2 carucates and 2 bovates
& B. taxable.
>Osbern de Arches has these lands but they are all waste.

A marginal mark indicates that the following entry should be inserted after 25W26 above.

27 S. In CATTAL there are 5 carucates of land taxable. There is land
for 2 ploughs. The jurisdiction is in (Ald)BOROUGH, the King's
manor. Osbern has it. Waste.

(37) **LAND OF ODO THE CROSSBOWMAN** 329 d

EAST RIDING

1 M. In BUGTHORPE Forni had 4½ carucates of land taxable. There is
land for as many ploughs. Odo the Crossbowman has there 1
plough; and
>3 villagers with 1 plough.
>Meadow, 8 acres.
>Value before 1066, 20s; now 10s.

2 M. In BARTHORPE (Grange) Forni had 2 carucates of land taxable.
Land for 2 ploughs. Odo has it. Waste.
>Value before 1066, 10s.

3 S. In YOULTHORPE, a jurisdiction of POCKLINGTON, 4 carucates of land
taxable. Land for as many ploughs. Odo has it. Waste.

r. 4 2 In FRIDAYTHORPE Forni and Gamall had 13 carucates/18½
M. carucates of land taxable. Land for as many ploughs. Odo has it.
Waste.
>Value before 1066, 20s.

Ⓜ In SIXTEDALE hƀr Game 7 Orm . IIII . car̄ tre 7 II .
bou̇ ad glđ . Odo h̄ 7 waṡt . ē . T.R.E . ual . XLV . ſoł .

Ⓑ In FRIDAGTORP ſuꝗ . v . car̄ tre ad gld . ꝑtinentes
ad Sixtedale . inland . Tṙa . ē ad . v . car̄ . Waſta . ē .

Ⓜ In REDRESTORP . ħƀ Orm . II . car̄ tre ad gld . Tṙa
ad . II . car̄ . Odo h̄ . 7 waſta . ē . T.R.E . ual . xx . ſoł .

Ⓜ In SCRADIZTORP . ħƀr Orm 7 Forne . III . car̄ tre
ad glđ . Tṙa ad . III . car̄ . Ibi h̄ Odo . IIII . uiłł cū . I . car̄ .
Dim̄ leṽ lḡ . 7 dim̄ laṫ . T.R.E . ual . x . ſoł . m̊ . v . ſoł .

Ⓜ In SVAVETORP ħƀ Forne . IX . car̄ tre ad glđ . Tṙa . ē
ad . IX . car̄ . Odo h̄ 7 waſta . ē . T.R.E . ual xx . ſoł

Ⓜ In SCARPENBEC ħƀ Forne . v . car̄ 7 vI . bō tre and glđ .
Tṙa ad totiđ car̄ . Ibi h̄ Odo . I . car̄ . 7 xx . vII . uiłł .
cū . vI . car̄ . 7 I . molđ . II . ſolidoꝣ . Vna leṽ lḡ . 7 I . laṫ .
T.R.E . ual . III . liƀ . m̊ . IIII . liƀ .

Ⓜ In GRIMESTON h̄ Odo . IIII . car̄ tre 7 dim̄ ad glđ
Tṙa ad totiđ car̄ . H̄ ređđ . III . ſoł . Ibi ſuꝗ . vIII . aē p̄ti

Ⓜ In CHILLON ħƀr Forne 7 Game . vII . car̄ træ ad glđ .
Tṙa ad totiđ car̄ . Odo h̄ 7 waſta . ē . T.R.E . ual . xx . ſoł .

XXXVIII. TERRA ALBERICI DE COCI.

Ⓜ In CHICHELTONE ħƀr Suuen 7 Artor . v . car̄ træ
7 v . bou̇ ad glđ . Tṙa ad . IIII . car̄ . Alberic⁹ de coci
h̄ ibi . II . car̄ . 7 IIII . uiłł . 7 XIII . borđ . hn̄tes . III . car̄
T.R.E . ual . LXX ſoł . m̊ . XL . ſoł .

Ⓜ In CATEBI ħƀ Suuen . II . car̄ 7 I . bou̇ ad glđ . Tṙa
ad I . car̄ . Ibi h̄ Albic⁹ . I . car̄ . 7 IIII . uiłł 7 II . borđ
7 II . ſoch cū . I . car̄ . T.R.E . ual XL . ſoł . m̊ . xx . ſoł .

5 2 In THIXENDALE Gamall and Ormr had 4 carucates and 2 bovates
M. of land taxable. Odo has it. Waste.
Value before 1066, 45s.

6 B. In FRIDAYTHORPE 5 carucates of land taxable belonging to
THIXENDALE. *Inland*. There is land for 5 ploughs. Waste.

7 M. In RAISTHORPE Ormr had 2 carucates of land taxable. Land for 2
ploughs. Odo has it. Waste.
Value before 1066, 20s.

8 2 In *SCRADIZTORP* Ormr and Forni had 3 carucates of land taxable.
M. Land for 3 ploughs. Odo has there
4 villagers with 1 plough.
½ league long and ½ wide.
Value before 1066, 10s; now 5s.

9 M. In SWAYTHORPE Forni had 9 carucates of land taxable. There is
land for 9 ploughs. Odo has it. Waste.
Value before 1066, 20s.

10 M. In SKIRPENBECK Forni had 5 carucates and 6 bovates of land
taxable. Land for as many ploughs. Odo has there 1 plough;
27 villagers with 6 ploughs.
1 mill, 2s.
1 league long and 1 wide.
Value before 1066 £3; now £4.

11 M. In (Hanging) GRIMSTON Odo has 4½ carucates of land taxable.
Land for as many ploughs. This pays 3s.
There are there 8 acres, meadow.

12 2 In KILHAM Forni and Gamall had 7 carucates of land taxable.
M. Land for as many ploughs. Odo has it. Waste.
Value before 1066, 20s.

(38)   **LAND OF AUBREY OF COUCY**

[WEST RIDING]

1 2 In HICKLETON Sveinn and Arnthorr had 5 carucates and 5 bovates
M. of land taxable. Land for 4 ploughs. Aubrey of Coucy has there 2
ploughs;
4 villagers and 13 smallholders who have 3 ploughs.
Value before 1066, 70s; now 40s.

2 M. In CADEBY Sveinn had 2 carucates and 1 bovate taxable. Land
for 1 plough. Aubrey has there 1 plough; and
4 villagers, 2 smallholders and 2 Freemen with 1 plough.
Value before 1066, 40s; now 20s.

.XXXVIIII. TERRA GOSPATRIC.

WEST REDING;

ⓂIn MARTONE ħɓ Gofpatric xii . car̄ træ ad glđ.
Tra ad.vi.car̄.Idē ipſe ħꝛ nc̄ ibi.i.car̄.7 ii.uiłł
7 ii.borđ.cū.ii.car̄.Vna lev lḡ.7 i.lat̄.T.R.E.uat xl.
ſol.m̄.xx.ſol.

In CADRETONE ħꝛ Gofpatric dim car̄ tre ad gld
In ALVERTONE ſimilit dim car̄ tre ad gld.In his.Tra ad.i.c̄.
In TORP ħꝛ.i.car̄ træ ad glđ.Ħ v ſol reddit.

ⓂIn TORNBVRNE ħꝛ Gofpatric.iii.car̄ tre ad gld.
Tra ad.i.car̄.Dim lev lḡ.7 dim lat̄.Waſta.ē.

ⓂIn STANLEIA ħꝛ.Go.viii.car̄ tre ad glđ.Tra ad.iiii.
car̄.Nc̄.ē ibi.i.car̄ 7 i.uiłłs.Dim lev lḡ.7 dim lat̄.
T.R.E.uat.xx.ſol.m̄.x.ſol.

In FARNEHA.Goſp.iii.car̄ tre ad gld.Tra ad.i.car̄.
Nc̄ ibi pɓr 7 æccła.7 i.car̄.T.R.E.uat x.ſol.m̄.v.ſol.

ⓂIn CLARETONE Goſp.iii.car̄ træ ad gld.Tra ad.i.car̄
7 dim.Idē ibi nc̄ ħꝛ.ii.car̄ 7 i.uiłł.T.R.E.x.ſol.m̄ ſimił.

ⓂIn LAVRETONE Goſp.ii.car̄ 7 dim ad gld.Tra
ad.i.car̄.Ibi m̄.i.uiłł.7 i.borđ.T.R.E.xx.ſol.m̄.iiii.ſol.

ⓂIn CHIRCHEBI Goſp.v.car̄ tre ad gld.Tra ad.iii.
car̄.Ibi m̄ ħꝛ.i.car̄.7 viii.uiłł cū.i.car̄.Silua mi
nuta.i.lev lḡ.7 i.lat̄.Tot̄ Ⓜ.i.lev 7 dim lḡ.7 tntđ
lat̄.T.R.E.uat xxx.ſol.m̄.xx.ſol.

(39)   **LAND OF GOSPATRIC**   330 a

WEST RIDING

1 M. In MARTON Gospatric had 12 carucates of land taxable. Land for 6 ploughs. Now the same man has there 1 plough; and
    2 villagers and 2 smallholders with 2 ploughs.
    1 league long and 1 wide.
Value before 1066, 40s; now 20s.

2 In *CADRETONE* Gospatric has ½ carucate of land taxable.

3 In ALLERTON (Mauleverer) likewise ½ carucate of land taxable. In these there is land for 1 plough.

4 In THORPE (Hill) he has 1 carucate of land taxable. This pays 5s.

5 M. In THORNBOROUGH Gospatric has 3 carucates of land taxable. Land for 1 plough.
    ½ league long and ½ wide. Waste.

6 M. In STAVELEY Gospatric has 8 carucates of land taxable. Land for 4 ploughs. Now there is there 1 plough and
    1 villager.
    ½ league long and ½ wide.
Value before 1066, 19s; now 10s.

7 In FARNHAM, Gospatric, 3 carucates of land taxable. Land for 1 plough.
    Now there a priest and a church; 1 plough.
Value before 1066, 10s; now 5s.

8 M. In CLARETON, Gospatric, 3 carucates of land taxable. Land for 1½ ploughs. Now the same man has there 2 ploughs; and
    1 villager.
Value before 1066, 10s; now the same.

9 M. In LAVERTON, Gospatric, 2½ carucates taxable. Land for 1 plough.
    Now 1 villager and 1 smallholder.
Value before 1066, 20s; now 4s.

10 M. In KIRKBY (Malzeard), Gospatric, 5 carucates of land taxable. Land for 3 ploughs. Now he has there 1 plough; and
    8 villagers with 1 plough.
    Underwood, 1 league long and 1 wide.
    The whole manor, 1½ leagues long and as wide.
Value before 1066, 30s; now 20s.

II

Ⓜ In *Torp*. Gosp. vii. car træ and gld. Tra ad. iii. car.
Ipse ibi nc. i. car. 7 iii. uitt 7 ii. bord cu. i. car. Silua
minuta dim lev lg. 7 iiii. q̷ lat. Tot. i. lev lg. 7 dim
lat. T.R.E. uat xx. sot. m̃. x. sot.

Ⓜ In *Stolleia* Gosp. ii. car tre 7 dim ad gld. Tra ad. i.
car. Wast. ē.

Ⓜ In *Wincheslaie*. Gosp. iii. car tre ad gld. Tra
ad. ii. car. Ipse ht nc f̷ non colit. Silua minuta ibi.
Tot. i. lev 7 dim lg. 7 tntd lat. T.R.E. uat. xx. sot. m̃. x. st

Ⓜ In *Asserle*. Gosp. v. car træ ad gld. Tra ad. iii. car.
Ipse ibi nc. i. car. 7 i. uitt 7 ii. bord. cu. i. car. T.R.E.
uat. xx. sot. m̃ x. sot.

Ⓜ In *Brameleia*. ii. car tre ad gld. Tra ad. i. car.

Ⓜ In *Carlesmore*. ii. car tre ad gld. Tra ad. i. car.

Ⓜ In *Cotesmore*. ii. car tre ad gld. Tra ad. i. car.

Ⓜ In *Svatvne*. ii. car tre ad gld. Tra ad. i. car.

Ⓜ In *Popletone*. iii. car tre ad gld. Tra ad. ii. car.

Ⓜ In *Birnebeha*. iii. car tre 7 ii. bou ad gld. Tra ad. ii. c

Ⓜ In *Advlfestorp*. iiii. car tre ad gld Tra ad. ii. car.

Ⓜ In *Chirchebi*. vi. car tre ad gld. Tra ad. iii. car.

330 b

Ⓜ In *Beristade*. i. car ad gld. Tra ad dim car.

In *Scheltone*. i. car ad gld. Tra ad dim car

Ⓜ In *Hevvorde*. i. car tre ad gld. Tra ad dim car.

Ⓜ In *Svndreslanwic*. i. car 7 dim ad gld. Tra ad. i. car.

11 2 In (Grewel)THORPE, Gospatric, 7 carucates of land taxable. Land
M. for 3 ploughs. Now he has there 1 plough; and
    3 villagers and 2 smallholders with 1 plough.
    Underwood, ½ league long and 4 furlongs wide.
    The whole, 1 league long and ½ wide.
    Value before 1066, 20s; now 10s.

12 M. In STUDLEY (Royal), Gospatric, 2½ carucates of land taxable.
Land for 1 plough. Waste.

13 M. In WINKSLEY, Gospatric, 3 carucates of land taxable. Land for 2
ploughs. Now the same man has (it) but does not cultivate it.
    Underwood there.
    The whole, 1½ leagues long and as wide.
    Value before 1066, 20s; now 10s.

14 M. In AZERLEY, Gospatric, 5 carucates of land taxable. Land for 3
ploughs. Now the same man has there 1 plough; and
    1 villager and 2 smallholders with 1 plough.
    Value before 1066, 20s; now 10s.

15 M. In BRAMLEY (Grange), 2 carucates of land taxable. Land for 1
plough.

16 M. In CARLESMOOR, 2 carucates of land taxable. Land for 1 plough.

17 M. In KEX MOOR, 2 carucates of land taxable. Land for 1 plough.

18 M. In SWETTON, 2 carucates of land taxable. Land for 1 plough.

19 M. In *POPLETONE*, 3 carucates of land taxable. Land for 2 ploughs.

20 M. In BRIMHAM (Hall), 3 carucates and 2 bovates of land taxable.
Land for 2 ploughs.

21 M. In ADDLETHORPE, 4 carucates of land taxable. Land for 2 ploughs.

22 M. In KIRBY (Hill), 6 carucates of land taxable. Land for 3 ploughs.

23 M. In BIRSTWITH, 1 carucate taxable. Land for ½ plough.   330 b

24 In SKELTON, 1 carucate taxable. Land for ½ plough.

25 M. In *HEUUORDE*, 1 carucate of land taxable. Land for ½ plough.

26 M. In (Old) SUNDERLANDWICK, 1½ carucates taxable. Land for 1
plough.

ᕏ In SNECHINTONE . I . car tre ad gld . Tra ad dim car.
Ħ oīa habuit 7 habet Gofpatric ; fȝ m̃ wafta funt.

ᕏ In ASCVID . Gofp . II . car tre ad gld . Tra . e ad . I . car.
Ipfe ibi hť nc . IIII . uilł . cū . I . car . T.R.E. uał . xx . fol.

ᕏ In WIDETVN . Gofp . II . car tre 7 dim ⌐ m̃ . x . sł:
ad gld . Tra ad . II . car . Ibi m̃ . II . uilł 7 I . bord . cū . I . c.
7 VII . fol reddit:

.II.
ᕏ In WARTLE . Ligulf 7 Saxulf ħbr . v . car tre
ad gld . Nc hť Gofp 7 wast . e . T.R.E. uał ; xxv . fol.
Dim lev lg . 7 dim lat.

ᕏ In TORP . Gofp . VI . car træ ad gld . Tra ad . III . car.
Ipfe ibi nc . I . car . 7 I . uilł 7 III . bord . Dim lev lg.
7 dim lat . T.R.E. uał xxx ; fol . m̃ . x . fol.

ᕏ In TORENTONE . Gofp . VI . car tre ad gld . Tra ad . III.
car . Ipfe ibi nc . I . car . 7 VII . uilł cū . III . car . Vna
lev lg . 7 dim lat . T.R.E. uał . xx . fol . m̃ fimilit.

ᕏ In BVRTVN . ħb Archil . IIII . car tre 7 II . bou ad glď.
Tra ad ; II . car . Ibi hť Gofp m̃ ; I . car . 7 VII . uilł
cū . II . car . 7 IIII ; acs p̃ti . Silua modica ; II ; qȝ lg . 7 II ; lt.
T.R.E. uał xvi . fol . m̃ VIII . fol.

ᕏ In BRATFORTONE . Gofp . I . car tre ad gld . Tra ad dim
car . Ipfe ibi m̃ hť ; I ; uilł cū dim car . Valet . II . fol 7 dim.

ᕏ In VLVESTONE . Gofp . VI ; car tre ad gld . Tra ad . III . car.
Ibi funt m̃ . IIII . uilł . fȝ n̄ aran̄ . Vna lev lg . 7 dim lat.
T.R.E. uał xx . fol . m̃ . x . fol:

§ In BVRTONE . |IIII . car⁊ foca in burg ᕏ regis . Tra ad . II.
car . Wast . e . Gofp tenet.

27 M. In SNAINTON, 1 carucate of land taxable. Land for ½ plough. Gospatric had and has all these, but now they are waste.

28 M. In ASKWITH, Gospatric, 2 carucates of land taxable. There is land for 1 plough. Now the same man has there
    4 villagers with 1 plough.
Value before 1066, 20s; now 10s.

29 M. In WEETON, Gospatric, 2½ carucates of land taxable. Land for 2 ploughs.
    Now there 2 villagers and 1 smallholder with 1 plough.
It pays 7s.

30 2 In WEARDLEY Ligulfr and Saksulfr had 5 carucates of land taxable.
M. Now Gospatric has (it). Waste.
Value before 1066, 25s.
    ½ league long and ½ wide.

31 M. In (Lang)THORPE, Gospatric, 6 carucates of land taxable. Land for 3 ploughs. Now the same man has there 1 plough; and
    1 villager and 3 smallholders.
    ½ league long and ½ wide.
Value before 1066, 30s; now 10s.

32 M. In THORNTON (Bridge), Gospatric, 6 carucates of land taxable. Land for 3 ploughs. Now the same man has there 1 plough; and
    7 villagers with 3 ploughs.
    1 league long and ½ wide.
Value before 1066, 20s; now the same.

33 M. In (Hum)BURTON Arnketill had 4 carucates and 2 bovates of land taxable. Land for 2 ploughs. Now Gospatric has there 1 plough;
    7 villagers with 2 ploughs.
    Meadow, 4 acres; brushwood, 2 furlongs long and 2 wide.
Value before 1066, 16s; now 8s.

34 M. In BRAFFERTON, Gospatric, 1 carucate of land taxable. Land for ½ plough. Now the same man has there
    1 villager with ½ plough.
Value 2½s.

35 M. In OULSTON, Gospatric, 6 carucates of land taxable. Land for 3 ploughs.
    Now there are there 4 villagers, but they do not plough.
    1 league long and ½ wide.
Value before 1066, 20s; now 10s.

36 S. In (Hum)BURTON, 4 carucates, jurisdiction in (Ald)BOROUGH, the King's manor, and 2 carucates *inland*. Land for 2 ploughs. Waste. Gospatric holds (it).

ⓂIn _BICRETONE_. h̄b Archil. VIII. car̄ træ ād gld. Tra ad. IIII.
car̄. Ibi h̄t Gofp n̄c. IIII. uilt. cū. I. car̄ 7 dim̄. Silua
paſt dim̄ lev̄. Tot̄. I. lev̄ l̄g. 7 I. lat̄. T.R.E. ual xL : ſot̄.
m̊. x. ſot.

ⓂIn _ALDEFELT_. h̄b Archil. II. car̄ træ ad gld̄ : Tra ad. I. car̄.
Nc̄ h̄t Gofp. 7 ual x. ſot. T.R.E. ual ſimilit̄.

ⓂIn _MIDDELTVN_. Gofp. IIII car̄ tre ad gld̄. Tra ād. II. car̄.
Ipſe h̄t ibi. I. car̄. 7 IIII. uilt 7 III. bord. cū. II. car̄. Ibi æccta
7 p̄br. 7 VI. ac̄ p̄ti. T.R.E. ual. xx. ſot. m̊. x. ſot.

ⓂIn _SLIDEMARE_. Gofp. IX. car̄ træ ad gld̄. Tra ad. V. car̄.
Ipſe h̄t 7· waſt. ē. T.R.E. ual. xL. ſot. Ibi. c. ac̄s p̄ti.

In _NERESFORDE_. Gofp dim̄ car træ ad gld. Idē ipſe h̄t. 7 waſta. ē.

330 c

XL. TERRA TAINORV̄ REGIS.

WESKEDING; SIRACHES WAPENT̄.

ⓂIn _CARLETVN_ h̄b Wiga. VI. car̄ tre ad gld. Tra. ē
ad. II. car̄. Nc̄ h̄t Vlchil ibi. II. car̄. 7 VII. uilt
7 V. bord. cū. IIII. car̄. Silua paſt. I. lev̄ 7 dimit̄.
Tot̄. I. lev̄ l̄g. 7 I. lat̄. T.R.E. ual xL. ſot. m̊ xx. ſot.

★r ⓂIn _CANBESFORD_ h̄b Crucan. I. car̄ tre ad gld̄.
Tra ad dim̄ car. Nc̄ h̄t Ernuin. 7 waſt. ē. Ibi Silua
paſt. I. lev̄ 7 dim̄. Tot̄. I. lev̄ 7 dim̄ l̄g. 7 dim̄ lat̄
T.R.E. ual. x. ſot.

37 M. In BICKERTON Arnketill had 8 carucates of land taxable. Land for
3 ploughs. Now Gospatric has there
    4 villagers with 1½ ploughs.
    Woodland pasture, ½ league.
    The whole, 1 league long and 1 wide.
Value before 1066, 40s; now 10s.

38 M. In ALDFIELD Arnketill had 2 carucates of land taxable. Land for 1
plough. Now Gospatric has (it).
Value 10s; value before 1066 the same.

39 M. In 'MIDDLETON', Gospatric, 4 carucates of land taxable. Land for 2
ploughs. The same man has there 1 plough; and
    4 villagers and 3 smallholders with 2 ploughs.
    There, a church and a priest.
    Meadow, 6 acres.
Value before 1066, 20s; now 10s.

40 M. In SLEDMERE, Gospatric, 9 carucates of land taxable. Land for 5
ploughs. The same man has (it). Waste.
Value before 1066, 40s.
    There, meadow, 100 acres.

41 In 'KNARESFORD', Gospatric, ½ carucate of land taxable. The same
man has (it). Waste.

(40)   **LAND OF THE KING'S THANES**   330 c

WEST RIDING

SKYRACK Wapentake

1 M. In CARLTON Wicga had 6 carucates of land taxable. There is land
for 2 ploughs. Now Ulfketill has there 2 ploughs; and
    7 villagers and 5 smallholders with 4 ploughs.
    Woodland pasture, 1½ leagues.
    The whole, 1 league long and 1 wide.
Value before 1066, 40s; now 20s.

r   2 M. In CAMBLESFORTH Grucan had 1 carucate of land taxable. Land
for ½ plough. Now Earnwine the Priest has (it). Waste.
    There, woodland pasture, 1½ leagues.
    The whole, 1½ leagues long and ½ wide.
Value before 1066, 10s.

ⓜ **In** *DEREVVELLE*. Alſi 7 Chetelber h̄br . IIII . car⁊
træ ad gld . Tra ÷ ad . II . car⁊. Nc̄ h̄t Alſi ibi . II . car⁊.
7 v . uiłł 7 x . borđ . cū . III . car⁊. Silua paſt . I . lev⁊
7 III . q̊⁊. Tot . I lev⁊ 7 I . q̊⁊ l̄g . 7 I . lev⁊ lat̄. T.R.E. uał
XL . ſoł . m̄ . XXX.II . ſoł.

ⓜ **In** 7 MEDELTONE
WANBELLA . h̄b Tor . II . car⁊ tre⁊ 7 I . bou⁊ ad gld.
Tra ad . I . car⁊. 7 dim̄. Dimid carucata . ē ſoca
Ibi h̄t nc̄ ipſe . I . car⁊. 7 v . uiłł. 7 III . borđ. 7 II . ſoch̄
cū . II . car⁊. Silua paſt . v . q̊⁊ . Tot . v . q̊⁊ l̄g . 7 v . lat̄.
T.R.E. uał . XL . ſoł . m̄ . XX . ſoł.

ⓜ⁊ **In** *MERELTONE* 7 Bereuuitis. IIII . h̄b Suuen . v . car⁊
7 B⁊ tre⁊ ad gld . Tra ad . III . car⁊. Ibi h̄t nc̄ ipſe . I . car⁊.
7 IX . uiłł cū . III . car⁊. Silua paſt una lev̄. Tot Ⓜ
I . lev⁊ l̄g . 7 I . lat̄. T.R.E. uał . XXX . ſoł . m̄ XV . ſoł.

ⓜ⁊ **In** *WATE* . cū . III . berevv⁊ . h̄b Vlſi . VII . car⁊ tre⁊
7 B 7 v . bou⁊ ad gld . Tra ad . IIII . car⁊. Ipſe h̄t ibi nc̄
. I . car⁊. 7 I . uiłł 7 III . borđ. 7 II . ac̄s p̄ti . Silua paſt⁊
I . lev⁊ 7 dim̄ . Tot Ⓜ . I . lev⁊ 7 dim l̄g . 7 I . lev⁊ lat̄.
T.R.E. uał . XXX . ſoł . m̄ . XV . ſoł.

ⓜ **In** 7 BRANTONE cū
MEDELTONE 7 Berevv⁊ . IIII . h̄b Artorᵖᵇʳ VI . car⁊ træ⁊⁊

Iₐ *BILINGELIE.* II.bou⁊
dim car ad gld 7 dim̄ ad gld . Tra ad . v . car⁊. Ipſe h̄t ibi m̄ . II . car̄.
Vał. x. ſoł. 7 III . uiłł. 7 I . borđ . cū . II . car⁊. 7 VI . ac̄s p̄ti . Silua
Artor j
Id tenuit q̃ tenet paſt . I . lev⁊ 7 dim̄ . Tot . Ⓜ . II . lev̄ l̄g . 7 I . lat̄.

ⓜ **In** *ERNVLFESTORP* . h̄b Vlchil . v . car⁊ træ ad gld.
Tra ad . III . car⁊. Ibi h̄t nc̄ Ernuinᵖᵇʳ dim caȓ . 7 I . uiłł
7 III . borđ. 7 IIII . ſoch̄ . h̄ntes . II . car⁊ 7 dim . Silua
paſt . II . lev⁊. Tot Ⓜ . II . lev̄ l̄g . 7 x . q̊⁊ lat̄. T.R.E.
uał XL . ſoł . m̄ . XX . ſoł.

3 2 In DARFIELD Alsige and Ketilbjorn had 4 carucates of land taxable.
M. There is land for 2 ploughs. Now Alsige has there 2 ploughs; and
5 villagers and 10 smallholders with 3 ploughs.
Woodland pasture, 1 league and 3 furlongs.
The whole, 1 league and 1 furlong long and 1 league wide.
Value before 1066, 40s; now 32s.

4 M. In WOMBWELL and (West) MELTON Thorr had 2 carucates and 1
bovate of land taxable. Land for 1½ ploughs. ½ carucate is
jurisdiction. Now the same man has there 1 plough; and
5 villagers, 3 smallholders and 2 Freemen with 2 ploughs.
Woodland pasture, 5 furlongs.
The whole, 5 furlongs long and 5 wide.
Value before 1066, 40s; now 20s.

5 M. In (West) MELTON with 4 outliers, Sveinn had 5 carucates of land
& B. taxable. Land for 3 ploughs. Now the same man has there 1 plough;
9 villagers with 3 ploughs.
Woodland pasture, 1 league.
The whole manor, 1 league long and 1 wide.
Value before 1066, 30s; now 15s.

6 M. In WATH (upon Dearne) with 3 outliers, Wulfsige had 7 carucates
& B. and 5 bovates of land taxable. Land for 4 ploughs. Now the same
man has there 1 plough; and
1 villager and 3 smallholders.
Meadow, 2 acres; woodland pasture, 1½ leagues.
The whole manor, 1½ leagues long and 1 league wide.
Value before 1066, 30s; now 15s.

7 2 In (West) MELTON and BRAMPTON (Bierlow) with 4 outliers,
M. Arnthorr the Priest had 6[½] carucates and 2 bovates of land
taxable. Land for 5 ploughs. Now the same man has there 2
ploughs; and
3 villagers and 1 smallholder with 2 ploughs.
Meadow, 6 acres; woodland pasture, 1½ leagues.
The whole manor, 2 leagues long and 1 wide.

8 In BILLINGLEY ½ carucate taxable.
Value 10s.
The same man, Arnthorr, held (it) who holds (it).

9 M. In ARMTHORPE Ulfketill had 5 carucates of land taxable. Land for
3 ploughs. Now Earnwine the Priest has there ½ plough; and
1 villager, 3 smallholders and 4 Freemen who have 2½ ploughs.
Woodland pasture, 2 leagues.
The whole manor, 2 leagues long and 10 furlongs wide.
Value before 1066, 40s; now 20s.

§ In *WITELAIE*. ħƀr Ragenald 7 Wige . ii . car̄ tre ad
gld . ſoca p̄tiñ ad Eſnoit . Tra ad . i . car̄ . Ibi ħⱦ Elric̄
ii . uiłł 7 vi . bord . cū . ii . car̄ . Silua paſt . i . leu̇ . Toⱦ ⱺ
. i . leu̇ lḡ . 7 i . laⱦ . T.R.E. uaⱡ xl . ſoⱡ . m̄ . xx . ſoⱡ .

In *MVLEDE* . ħƀr . iii . taini . i . car̄ træ ad gld . Tra ad dim̄
car̄ . Ipſi idē ħ̄nt de rege . 7 waſta . ē .

330 d

★ . ⱺ In *BADETORPES* ħƀ Turchil dim̄ car̄ træ ad gld .
Tra ad . ii . bō . Ipſe ibi ħⱦ dim̄ car̄ . 7 ualet . iii . ſoⱡ .

ⱺ In *ACVM* . ħƀ Vlchel . ii . car̄ træ ad gld . Tra ad . i .
.II. car̄ . Ipſe ibi ħⱦ dim̄ car̄ . Silua . x . q̃ȝ . iiii . ſoⱡ ualet .

ⱺ In *VSEBVRNE* ħƀr Macus 7 Orm . iii . car̄ træ
ad gld . Nc̄ ħⱦ Malcolun ibi . iii . uiłł ħ̄ntes . ii . car̄ .
7 iiii . ac̄s p̄ti . T.R.E. xx . ſoⱡ . m̄ . v . ſoⱡ .

ⱺ In *HOMTONE* ħƀ Chetel . i . car̄ tre 7 dim̄ ad gld .
Tra ad . i . car̄ . Ipſe ħⱦ ibi dim̄ car̄ . 7 ualet . x . ſoⱡ .

ⱺ In *ALVERTONE* ħƀ Vlchil . i . car̄ træ 7 dim̄ ad gld .
Tra ad . i . car̄ . Ipſe ħⱦ ibi dim̄ car̄ . 7 ualet . x . ſoⱡ .

ⱺ In *LOTHVSE* ħƀr . iii . tani . iiii . car̄ tre ad gld .
Tra ad . ii . car̄ . Ipſi adhuc ħ̄nt . 7 colunt eā . v . ſoⱡ

ⱺ In *SCOTONE* Ramechil . ii . car̄ træ ad gld ⸿redⱡ .
Tra ad . i . car̄ . Ipſe ħⱦ ibi . i . car̄ 7 i . uiłł . Valet . x . ſoⱡ

ⱺ In *TORP* . Rauenchil 7 Torchil . ii . car̄ træ ad gld .
Tra ad . i . car̄ . Ipſi ħ̄nt adhuc . ſȝ waſt . ē

. ii . ⱺ In *LAVRETON* . Vlchil | 7 Vluric . iii . car̄ træ ad gld . Tra ad
. ii . car̄ . Ipſi ibi ħ̄nt . i . car̄ . Valet . xi . ſoⱡ .

10 S. In WHITLEY Ragnaldr and Wicga had 2 carucates of land taxable. The jurisdiction belongs to SNAITH. Land for 1 plough. Alric has there
>2 villagers and 6 smallholders with 2 ploughs.
>Woodland pasture, 1 league.
>The whole manor, 1 league long and 1 wide.

Value before 1066, 40s; now 20s.

11 In *MULEDE*, 3 thanes had 1 carucate of land taxable. Land for ½ plough. The same men have (it) from the King. Waste.

12 M. In (Bishop)THORPE Thorketill had ½ carucate of land taxable. Land for 2 oxen. The same man has there ½ plough. Value 3s.

330 d

13 M. In ACOMB Ulfketill had 2 carucates of land taxable. Land for 1 plough. The same man has there ½ plough.
>Woodland, 10 furlongs.

Value 4s.

14 2 M. In (Little) OUSEBURN Maccus and Ormr had 3 carucates of land taxable. Maelcolumban now has there
>3 villagers who have 2 ploughs.
>Meadow, 4 acres.

Value before 1066, 20s; now 5s.

15 M. In HOPPERTON Ketill had 1½ carucates of land taxable. Land for 1 plough. The same man has there ½ plough. Value 10s.

16 M. In ALLERTON (Mauleverer) Ulfketill had 1½ carucates of land taxable. Land for 1 plough. The same man has there ½ plough. Value 10s.

17 3 M. In LOFTUS (Hill) 3 thanes had 4 carucates of land taxable. Land for 2 ploughs. The same men still have and cultivate it. It pays 5s.

18 M. In SCOTTON, Rafnketill, 2 carucates of land taxable. Land for 1 plough. The same man has there 1 plough; and
>1 villager.

Value 10s.

19 M. In (*Scotton*) *THORPE*, Rafnketill and Thorketill, 2 carucates of land taxable. Land for 1 plough. The same men still have (it), but it is waste.

20 2 M. In LAVERTON, Ulfketill and Wulfric, 3 carucates of land taxable. Land for 2 ploughs. The same men have there 1 plough. Value 11s.

ᛗ In *WIDETONE*. Alured.ɪ.car̄ tre ad gld.Tra ad
dim̄ car̄.Ipſe ht̄ 7 waſt̄.ē.T.R.E.ual.v.ſoł 7 ɪɪɪɪ.d̄.

ᛗ In *WIDETONE*.Vlchil.ɪɪ.car̄ tre 7 dim̄ ad gld.Tra
ad.ɪ.car̄.Ipſe ibi ht̄.ɪɪɪ.uiłł 7 ɪɪ.car̄.Valet.v.ſoł.

ᛗ In *ASERLA* Orm.dim̄ car̄ træ ad gld.Tra ad dim̄
car̄.Idē ipſe ht̄.7 waſt̄.ē.

ᛗ In *RITONE*.Ligulf.ɪɪɪ.car̄ træ ad gld.Tra ad.ɪɪ.car̄.
Ipſe ht̄ ibi dim̄ car̄.7 vɪɪ.uiłł.7 pḃrm.Vna leu lḡ.
7,ɪ.lat̄.T.R.E.ual.xvɪ.ſoł.m̄ x.ſoł.

ÆSTREDING. HASE HVNDRET.

ᛗ In *VMLOVEBI*.ḣḃ Eſcul.ɪɪ.car̄ træ ad gld.Tra ad.ɪ.
car̄.Nc̄ ht̄ Turchil.ibi.ɪ.car̄.7 vɪɪ.uiłł.7 ɪɪ.bord.
cū.ɪ.car̄.Valet xx.ſoł.

ᛗ In *TIBETORP*.Game.ɪɪ.car̄ tre 7 ɪɪ.boū ad gld.Tra
ad.ɪ.car̄.Ipſe ht̄ ſub rege.7 waſt̄.ē.

ᛗ In *DALTON*.Autbert.ɪ.car̄ tre ad gld.Tra ad dim̄
car̄.Ipſe ht̄ ibi.ɪ.car̄ 7 ɪ.uiłł.Valet.x.ſoł.

ᛗ In *BRVNHĀ*.Morcar.Turuet 7 Turchil.ḣḃr xɪ.
car̄ tre ad glđ.Tra ad.vɪ.car̄.Vna car̄.ē ſoca
in Poclinton.Forne ht̄ de rege 7 waſt̄.ē.

ᛗ In *BODELTON*.Carle.ɪ.car̄ tre ad gld.Tra ad dim̄
car̄.Idē ipſe ht̄ ibi.ɪ.car̄.7 ɪɪ.ac̄s p̄ti.Valet.ɪɪɪɪ.ſoł.

ᛗ In *FLANEBVRG*.Clibert.ɪ.car̄ 7 dim̄ ad gld.Tra ad.ɪ.
car̄.Idē ipſe ht̄ 7 waſt̄.ē. · ⌠ht̄ m̄ 7 waſt̄.ē

ᛗ In *HVGHETE*.Ingrede.vɪɪɪ.car̄ ad gld.Tra ad.ɪɪɪɪ.car̄.Ernuin

21 M. In WIDDINGTON (Hall), Alfred, 1 carucate of land taxable. Land
for ½ plough. The same man has (it). Waste.
Value before 1066, 5s 4d.

22 M. In WEETON, Ulfketill, 2½ carucates of land taxable. Land for 1
plough. The same man has there
  3 villagers and 2 ploughs.
Value 5s.

23 M. In AZERLEY, Ormr, ½ carucate of land taxable. Land for ½ plough.
The same man has (it). Waste.

24 M. In (East) RIGTON, Ligulfr, 3 carucates of land taxable. Land for 2
ploughs. The same man has there ½ plough.
  7 villagers.
  A priest.
  1 league long and 1 wide.
Value before 1066, 16s; now 10s.

EAST RIDING

HESSLE Hundred

1 M. In ANLABY Skuli had 2 carucates of land taxable. Land for 1
plough. Now Thorketill has there 1 plough; and
  7 villagers and 2 smallholders with 1 plough.
Value 20s.

2 M. In TIBTHORPE, Gamall, 2 carucates and 2 bovates of land taxable.
Land for 1 plough. The same man has (it) under the King. Waste.

3 M. In (North) DALTON, Authbjorn, 1 carucate of land taxable. Land
for ½ plough. The same man has there 1 plough; and
  1 villager.
Value 10s.

4 M. In (Nun)BURNHOLME Morcar, Thorfrothr and Thorketill had 11
carucates of land taxable. Land for 6 ploughs. 1 carucate is
jurisdiction in POCKLINGTON. Forni has (it) from the King. Waste.

5 M. In BOLTON, Karli, 1 carucate of land taxable. Land for ½ plough.
The same man has there 1 plough.
  Meadow, 2 acres.
Value 4s.

6 M. In FLAMBOROUGH, Clibert, 1½ carucates taxable. Land for 1
plough. The same man has it. Waste.

7 M. In HUGGATE, Ingirithr, 8 carucates taxable. Land for 4 ploughs.
Now Earnwine the Priest has (it). Waste.

★ Ⓜ In MARTONE . Clibert . II . car̃ træ ad glđ Tra ad . I.

car̃ . Idē ipſe hĩ 7 waſta . ē.

Ⓜ In HILGRETORP . Clibert dim̃ car̃ træ ad gld . Tra

ad . II . bou . Idē ipſe hĩ ibi . VI . uiłł . cũ . I . car̃ . Valet

Ⓜ In FRESTINTORP . hɓ Garle . I . car̃ tre   £x . ſol.

ad glđ . Tra ad dim̃ car̃ . Vĩtred hĩ nē ibi . I . car̃.

7 ualet . v . ſol.

Ⓜ In HELMESWELLE . Norman . x . car̃ tre ad gld.

Tra ad . v . car̃ . Idē ipſe hĩ 7 waſt . ē . Vna leu lg̃.

.II. Ⓜ 7 dim̃ lat̃.

7 ʙ In CHILLVN 7 Grenzmore 7 Arpen hɓ Ernuin^pɓr . XL.

car̃ tre ad glđ . Tra ad . xx . car̃ . Idē ipſe hĩ nē

7 waſt̃ . ē . T.R.E. ual . xv . liɓ.

Ⓜ In LOGETORP |7 Aſa^Norman . II car̃ tre ad gld . Tra ad . ii . car̃.

Ibi hĩ Game . VI . uiłł . cũ . I . car̃ . 7 æcclam . Valet . VIII . ſol.

Ⓜ In RODESTAN . Ligulf . VIII . car̃ tre ad gld . Tra ad

. IIII . car̃ . Ibi hĩ Vĩtred . I . car̃ . 7 v . uiłłi cũ . I . car̃.

Valet . x . ſol.

Ⓜ In BRITESHALE^7 Sudtone Vlchil . III . car̃ tre 7 dim̃ ad glđ.

Tra ad . II . car̃ . Idē ipſe hĩ ibi dim̃ car̃ . 7 II . borđ.

Valet . II . ſol.

Ⓜ In GRIMSTONE Godrida 7 Auduid . hɓr . IIII . car̃

tre ad gld . Nē Oſuuard 7 Rodmund hñt de rege.

7 waſt̃ . e.

.II. Ⓜ In CHIRCHEBI . Haregrin^7 Siuuard.I.c' . VI . bou tre ad gld . Tra ad

una car̃ . Idē ipſi hñt adhuc . 7 ualet . II . ſol.

Ⓜ In THORF Aregrin . I . car̃ tre ad glđ . Tra ad dim̃ car̃.

Idē ipſe hĩ 7 waſt . ē.

8 M. In MARTON, Clibert, 2 carucates of land taxable. Land for 1 plough. The same man has (it). Waste.

9 M. In HILDERTHORPE, Clibert, ½ carucate of land taxable. Land for 2 oxen. The same man has there
 6 villagers with 1 plough.
Value 10s.

10 M. In FRAISTHORPE Karli had 1 carucate of land taxable. Land for ½ plough. Uhtred now has 1 plough there.
Value 5s.

11 M. In ELMSWELL, Northmann, 10 carucates of land taxable. Land for 5 ploughs. The same man has (it). Waste.
 1 league long and ½ wide.

12 2 M. & B. In KILHAM, GRANSMOOR and HARPHAM Earnwine the Priest had 40 carucates of land taxable. Land for 20 ploughs. The same man has (it) now. Waste.
Value before 1066 £15.

13 M. In LOWTHORPE, Northmann and Asa, 4 carucates of land taxable. Land for 2 ploughs. Gamall has
 6 villagers with 1 plough.
 A church.
Value 8s.

14 M. In RUDSTON, Ligulfr, 8 carucates of land taxable. Land for 4 ploughs. Uhtred has there 1 plough; and
 5 villagers with 1 plough.
Value 10s.

15 M. In BIRDSALL and SUTTON (Grange), Ulfketill, 3½ carucates of land taxable. Land for 2 ploughs. The same man has there ½ plough; and
 2 smallholders.
Value 2s.

16 2 M. In (Hanging) GRIMSTON, Guthrithr and Authvithr had 4 carucates of land taxable. Now Osweard and Rothmundr have (it) from the King. Waste.

17 2 M. In KIRBY (Underdale), Arngrimr, 6 bovates, and Siward, 1 carucate of land taxable. Land for 1 plough. The same men still have (them).
Value 2s.

18 M. In (Pains)THORPE, Arngrimr, 1 carucate of land taxable. Land for ½ plough. The same man has (it). Waste.

Ⓜ In *GHERVENZBI*. Game. $\overset{\text{iii}}{\text{vi}}$. car̄ træ ad glđ . Tra

ad . I . car̄ 7 dim̄ . Ipfe nē hᵗ ibi . II . uitꞁos cū . II . car̄ .

Valet . VIII . fot.

Ⓜ In *TVRALZBI* Game cū matre & frē . ħƀ . IIII . car̄

tre ad glđ . Tra ad . II . car̄ . Idē ipfe hᵗ . 7 locat eā .

Valet . V . fot.

In *WARRAN* . hᵗ Chilƀt . I . car̄ tre de rege . quæ

redd . X . fot . Tra ad dim̄ car̄ .

Ⓜ In *HESLERTONE* Gofpatric . III . car̄ tre 7 dim̄ ad

glđ . Tra ad . I . car̄ 7 dim̄ . Vᵗred hᵗ m̄ 7 wast̄ . ē

Ⓜ In alia *HESLERTONE* Ofuuard . . V . car̄ træ ad glđ

Tra ad . II . car̄ 7 dim̄ . Idē ipfe hᵗ 7 waft . ē.

Ⓜ In *WALCHINTONE* Gamel ħƀ . I . car̄ tre ad gld . Tra ad

dimid car̄ . Idē ipfe hᵗ . 7 waft . ē . T.R.E . uat . V . fot

Ⓜ In *CLIVE* . Norman . I . car̄ træ ad gld . Tra ad dim̄ car̄ . Ibi m̄ fuᴎ

IIII . uitꞁ . 7 I . bord . cū . I . car̄ . T.R.E . uat . X . fot . m̄ . VIII . fot.

Ⓜ In *WATON* . Tored . III . car̄ ad gld . Idē ipfe hᵗ . Tra ad . II . car̄ . †

331 b

NORT REDING

Ⓜ In *WILTVNE* . ħƀ Altor . III . car̄ træ 7 VI . bou ad gld .

Tra ad . II . car̄ . Ibi hᵗ Maldred ibi . I . car̄ . 7 VIII . uitꞁ

7 X . bord cū . III . car̄ . 7 VI . aᶜs p̄ti . T.R.E . uat XX . fot . m̄ fimit.

Ƨ In Wiltune 7 Lefighebi . I . car̄ tre ad gld . Tra ad dim̄

car̄ . foca p̄tiꞁ ad Wiltune.

19 M. In GARROWBY (Hall), Gamall, 3[6] carucates of land taxable.
Land for 1½ ploughs. Now the same man has there
  2 villagers with 2 ploughs.
Value 8s.

20 3 In THORALBY (Hall) Gamall, with his mother and brother, had 4
M. carucates of land taxable. Land for 2 ploughs. The same man has
(it) and lets it.
Value 5s.

21 In WHARRAM (Percy) Ketilbjorn has 1 carucate of land from the
King which pays 10s. Land for ½ plough.

22 M. In (East) HESLERTON, Gospatric, 3½ carucates of land taxable.
Land for 1½ ploughs. Now Uhtred has (it). Waste.

23 M. In another (West) HESLERTON, Osweard, 5 carucates of land
taxable. Land for 2½ ploughs. The same man has (it). Waste.

24 M. In WALKINGTON Gamall had 1 carucate of land taxable. Land
for ½ plough. The same man has (it). Waste.
Value before 1066, 5s.

25 M. In (North) CLIFFE, Northmann, 1 carucate of land taxable. Land
for ½ plough.
  Now there are there 4 villagers and 1 smallholder with 1 plough.
Value before 1066, 10s; now 8s.

26 M. In WATTON, Thorthr, 3 carucates taxable. The same man has (it).   Ψ
Land for 2 ploughs.

The East Riding continues below, at 29E 27, after the entries for the North Riding, 29N 1–13.

NORTH RIDING   331 b

1 M. In WILTON Halldorr had 3 carucates and 6 bovates of land taxable.
Land for 2 ploughs. Madalred has there 1 plough; and
  8 villagers and 10 smallholders with 3 ploughs.
  Meadow, 6 acres.
Value before 1066, 20s; now the same.

2 S. In WILTON and LAZENBY, 1 carucate of land taxable. Land for ½
plough. The jurisdiction belongs to WILTON.

ↂ In ORMESBI . IIII . taini ħbr XII . car̅ tre ad gld . T̅ra
ad . VIII . car̅ . Ibi ħt Orme . I . car̅ . 7 II . uiłł 7 XVI . bord .
cū . III . car̅ . Ibi p̅br 7 eccła . Vna lev̅ lḡ . 7 I . lat̅ . T.R.E.
uał . IIII . liƀ . m̊ . XL . fol .   T̅ra ad . I . car̅ .

§ In VPESHALE . II . car̅ tre ad gld . foca ptiñ ad Ormeſbi .

In CHILDALE . ħƀ Ligulf . VI . car̅ træ ad gld . T̅ra
ad . III . car̅ . Ibi ħt Orme . I . car̅ . 7 VIII . bord . cū . II .
car̅ . Ibi p̅br 7 æccła . Duas lev̅ lḡ . 7 I . lat̅ . T.R.E.
uał . XVI . fol . m̊ . XX . fol .

ↂ In MARTVNE . Archil . III . car̅ tre ad głd . T̅ra ad
II . car̅ . Idē ipſe ħt ibi . I . car̅ . 7 XIIII . uiłł 7 VI . bord .
cū . III . car̅ . T.R.E. uał . XL . fol . m̊ . XX . fol .

ƀ In Tolleſbi . IIII . car̅ træ ad głd . ptiñ ad Martune .
T̅ra ad . II . car̅ . Waſta . e̅ .

ↂ In STOCHESLAGE . ħƀ Hauuart . VI . car̅ træ ad gld .
T̅ra ad . III . car̅ . Ibi ħt Vc̅tred . I . car̅ . 7 VIII . uiłł
cū . IIII . car̅ . Ibi p̅br 7 æccła . 7 I . molt̅ . X . fol . 7 VIII .
ac̅ pti . Vna lev̅ lḡ . 7 dim lat̅ . T.R.E. uał XXIIII . liƀ .
m̊ . VIII . liƀ .

§ In Codeſchelf . Turoldeſbi . Englebi . Broctune . Tametun .
Cherchebi . Dragmalebi . Buſchebi 7 ał Buſchebi .
Simul ad głd . XXX . IIII . carucate . T̅ra ad . XVI . car̅ .
Ibi funt nc̅ . IX . fochi . 7 XVIII . uiłłi . hn̅tes . X . car̅ .

In STEMANESBI . II . car̅ tre ad gld . T̅ra ad . I . car̅ .
Vc̅tred ħt 7 wast . e̅ .

ↂ In LILINGE . Vłf . XIIII . bou ad gld . T̅ra ad . I . car̅ .
Game ħt ibi wast . e̅ .

3 4   In ORMESBY 4 thanes had 12 carucates of land taxable. Land forr
M.   8 ploughs. Ormr has there 1 plough; and
      2 villagers and 16 smallholders with 3 ploughs.
      There, a priest and a church.
      1 league long and 1 wide.
      Value before 1066 £4; now 40s.

4 S.   In UPSALL (Hall), 2 carucates of land taxable. The jurisdiction
belongs to ORMESBY. Land for 1 plough.

5   In KILDALE Ligulfr had 6 carucates of land taxable. Land for 3
ploughs. Ormr has there 1 plough; and
      8 smallholders with 2 ploughs.
      There, a priest and a church.
      2 leagues long and 1 wide.
      Value before 1066, 16s; now 20s.

6 M.   In MARTON (in Cleveland), Arnketill, 3 carucates of land taxable.
Land for 2 ploughs. The same man has there 1 plough; and
      14 villagers and 6 smallholders with 3 ploughs.
      Value before 1066, 40s; now 20s.

7 B.   In TOLLESBY, 4 carucates of land taxable belong to MARTON (in
Cleveland). Land for 2 ploughs. Waste.

8 M.   In STOKESLEY Havarthr had 6 carucates of land taxable. Land
for 3 ploughs. Uhtred has there 1 plough; and
      8 villagers with 4 ploughs.
      There, a priest and a church.
      1 mill, 10s; meadow, 8 acres.
      1 league long and ½ wide.
      Value before 1066 £24; now £8.

9 S.   In SKUTTERSKELFE (Hall), 2 c. and 2 bovates; THORALDBY (Farm),
2 c.; INGLEBY (Greenhow), 7 c.; (Little) BROUGHTON, 8 c.; TANTON,
1½ c.; KIRKBY, 3 c.; DROMONBY (Hall), 3 c.; (Great) BUSBY, 5 c.;
another (Little) BUSBY, 3 c. Together 34½ carucates taxable. Land
for 16 ploughs.
Now there are there 9 Freemen and 18 villagers who have 10
ploughs.

10   In STEMANESBI, 2 carucates of land taxable. Land for 1 plough.
Uhtred has it. Waste.

11 M.   In (East) LILLING, Ulfr, 14 bovates taxable. Land for 1 plough.
Gamall has it. Waste.

In NEVVEHVSV . Torber 7 Vĉtred . II . car̄ 7 dīm ad glđ

Tra ad . I . car̄ . Ipſi hn̄t m̄ . II . car̄ . 7 VI . uiħ 7 . I . borđ

cū . I . car̄ . 7 XII . aĉs p̄ti . T.R.E . uaɫ . III . ſoɫ . m̄ . V . ſoɫ.

ⓂIn HOBI . Sasforđ 7 Siuuard . II . car̄ tre ad glđ . Tra

ad . I . car̄ . Ibi nc̄ in dn̄io dim car̄ . 7 VI . uiħ cū . I . car̄.

T.R.E . uaɫ . IIII . ſoɫ . m̄ . III . ſoɫ . ITĒ IN ESƀEDING.

✝ ⓂIn SIVVARDBI . Clibert . I . car̄ 7 dim ad gld . Tra ad . I . car̄.

Idē ipſe hƀ . 7 waſt . ē . T.R.E . vaɫ . X . ſoɫ.

.II. ⓂIn CHERENDEBI . Chilbert . XIII . car̄ ad gld . Tra ad

VII . car̄ . Ibi . II . cenſores hn̄t . IX . uiħ . cū . III . car̄.

de rege teneſ . Vna lev̄ lḡ . 7 I . laɫ.

331 c

★ ⓂIn ACLVN . Siuuard ħƀ . IX . car̄ tre 7 dīm . Nc̄ duo hōes

Tra ad . IIII . car'

hn̄t de rege . Ipſi ibi . II . car̄ . 7 æcc̄lam . Valet . X . ſoɫ.

.II. ⓂIn Ledlinghe . Sprot Colbrand . Odfrid . Ghilebrid.

ħƀr . V . car̄ tre ad gld . Tra ad . III . car̄ . Nc̄ duo hōes de

WESTRƀ Ⓜ 7 rege hn̄t . Ipſi ibi . V . uiħ . 7 V . borđ . T.R.E . XL . ſoɫ . m̄ XXX . s̄

7 ŜIn EDESHALE . Baret . IIII . car̄ træ ad gld . Tra ad . II . car̄.

Soca . ē in Eſnoid . Ibi . ē nc̄ . I . car̄ in dn̄io . 7 V . ſochi

7 XII . borđ . 7 IIII . ac̄ p̄ti . T.R.E . uaɫ . IIII . liƀ . m̄ . X . ſoɫ.

12 In NEWSHAM, Thorbjorn and Uhtred, 2½ carucates taxable. Land
    for 1 plough. Now the same men have there 2 ploughs; and
        6 villagers and 1 smallholder with 1 plough.
        Meadow, 12 acres.
    Value before 1066, 3s; now 5s.

13 M. In HUBY, Saexfrith and Siward, 2 carucates of land taxable. Land
    for 1 plough. Now in lordship there ½ plough; and
        6 villagers with 1 plough.
    Value before 1066, 4s; now 3s.

Also in the EAST RIDING

This is a continuation of the East Riding section of the holdings of the King's Thanes from above, before 29N1.

† 27 M. In SEWERBY, Clibert, 1½ carucates taxable. Land for 1 plough.
    The same man has (it). Waste.
    Value before 1066, 10s.

28 2 In CARNABY, Ketilbjorn, 13 carucates taxable. Land for 7 ploughs.
   M.   2 tributaries have there 9 villagers with 3 ploughs. They hold
            from the King.
        1 league long and 1 wide.

29 M. In ACKLAM Siward had 9½ carucates of land. Land for 4 ploughs.   331 c
    Now 2 men have (it) from the King. The same men (have) there
    2 ploughs.
        A church.
    Value 10s.

30 4 In LEAVENING Sprottr, Kolbrandr, Odfrid and Gillebride had 5
   M. carucates of land taxable. Land for 3 ploughs. Now 2 men have
    (them) from the King. The same men (have) there
        5 villagers and 5 smallholders.
    Value before 1066, 40s; now 30s.

WEST RIDING

25 M. In HENSALL, Barthr, 4 carucates of land taxable. Land for 2
  & S. ploughs. The jurisdiction is in SNAITH. Now there is in lordship 1
    plough;
        5 Freemen and 12 smallholders.
        Meadow, 4 acres.
    Value before 1066 £4; now 10s.

⊕ In *WIRTLEIE*. Vlſi 7 Elric ħbr . IIII . car træ ad glđ
Tra ad . II . car . Nc̄ Elric de rege tenet . ſed waſta . ē.
T.R.E. uał . XL . ſoł . Silua paſt . I . lev̄ lḡ . 7 I . laī . Toī
II . lev̄ lḡ . 7 II . laī.

⊕ In *BADETORP*. Baſin dimiđ car ad gld . Tra ad . II . bō
Nc̄ ħī ibi Landri . dim̄ car . T.R.E. uał xx . ſoł . m̄ . VI . ſoł.

⊕ In *ACASTRE* . ħb Cħetel . VI . bou tre ad gld . Tra ad dim̄
car . Nc̄ Landricus ħī ibi . III . uiłł cū dim̄ car . T.R.E.
uał . XII . ſoł . m̄ . V . ſoł 7 IIII . den̄

⊕ Ibidem ħb Torchil . V . bō tre ad gld . Tra ad . II . bō
Nc̄ Tona tenet de rege . 7 ualet . II . ſoł.

⊕ In *DVNESFORDE* . ħb Turbern . III . car træ ad gld . Tra
ad . II . car . Iſđē ħī 7 waſta . ē . T.R.E. uał XVI . ſoł.

⊕ In *BRANTVNE* . ħb Turbern . IIII . car træ ad gld . Tra ad
II . car . Iſđē ħī de rege . 7 waſta . ē . T.R.E. uał xx . ſoł.

⊕ In *GRAFTONE* . ħb Torbern . II . car tre ad gld . Tra ad
. I . car . Iſđē ħī 7 wast . ē . T.R.E. uał . x . ſoł.

⊕ In *STOLLAI*. Eſnebern ħb . VII . bō træ ad gld . Tra ad dim̄ car .
Iſđē ħī nc̄ de rege . ſʒ waſta . ē . T.R.E. uał x . ſoł.

⊕ In *WIPELEIE*. ħb Archil dim̄ car træ ad gld . Tra ad . II . bou.
Iſđē ħī . 7 wast . ē . T.R.E. uał . II . ſoł 7 VIII . den̄ .   . II . s.

⊕ In *RIPELEIE*. Ramechil 7 Archil . I . car tre 7 dim̄ ad gld.
Tra ad . I . car . Ipſi ħn̄t adhuc . T.R.E. uał . XIII . ſoł . Wasī . ē.

26 2 In WORTLEY Ulfr and Alric had 4 carucates of land taxable. Land
    M. for 2 ploughs. Now Alric holds it from the King, but it is waste.
        Value before 1066, 40s.
            Woodland pasture, 1 league long and 1 wide.
            The whole, 2 leagues long and 2 wide.

27 M. In (Bishop)THORPE, Basing, ½ carucate taxable. Land for 2 oxen.
        Now Landric has there ½ plough.
        Value before 1066, 20s; now 6s.

28 M. In ACASTER (Selby) Ketill had 6 bovates of land taxable. Land
        for ½ plough. Now Landric has there
            3 villagers with ½ plough.
        Value before 1066, 12s; now 5s 4d.

29 M. In the same place Thorketill had 5 bovates of land taxable. Land
        for 2 oxen. Now Tonni holds (it) from the King.
        Value 2s.

30 M. In (Upper and Lower) DUNSFORTH Thorbjorn had 3 carucates of
        land taxable. Land for 2 ploughs. The same man has (it). Waste.
        Value before 1066, 16s.

31 M. In BRANTON (Green) Thorbjorn had 4 carucates of land taxable.
        Land for 2 ploughs. The same man has (it) from the King. Waste.
        Value before 1066, 20s.

32 M. In GRAFTON Thorbjorn had 2 carucates of land taxable. Land
        for 1 plough. The same man has (it). Waste.
        Value before 1066, 10s.

33 M. In STUDLEY (Royal) Snaebjorn had 7 bovates of land taxable.
        Land for ½ plough. Now the same man has (it) from the King,
        but it is waste.
        Value before 1066, 10s.

34 M. In WHIPLEY (Hall) Arnketill had ½ carucate of land taxable. Land
        for 2 oxen. The same man has (it). Waste.
        Value before 1066, 2s 8d.   [Now] 2s.

35 2 In RIPLEY, Rafnketill and Arnketill, 1½ carucates of land taxable.
    M. Land for 1 plough. The same men still have (them).
        Value before 1066, 13s.
            Waste.

ᴍ In CHESVIC . Vlchil . IIII . car̄ tre ad gld . Tra ad . II . car̄.
Nc̄ iſdē 7 vxor ei hn̄t ibi . I . car̄ 7 I . uilt . 7 II . ac̄s p̄ti . T.R.E.
ual . VIII . ſol . m̄ . v . ſol.

ᴍ In RISTONE . Archil . II . car̄ træ ad gld . Tra ad . I . car̄.
Iſdē ht̄ nc̄ 7 waſt . ē . T.R.E. ual . x . ſol.

ᴍ In BILLETONE . Archil . III . car̄ tre 7 dim̄ ad gld . Tra
ad . II . car̄. Iſdē ht̄ nc̄ 7 waſt . ē . T.R.E. ual . x . ſol.

331 d

IN CRAVE

ᴍ In RILESTVN . Almunt . IIII . car̄ tre ad gld . Dolfin ht̄.

ᴍ In HERLINTONE . Almunt . I . car̄ tre ad gld . Dolfin ht̄.

ᴍ In APLETREVVIC . I . car̄ tre 7 dim̄ ad gld . Dolfin ht̄.

★ 7 B In BRINSHALE 7 Torp . Hardul . III . car̄ 7 dim̄ ad gld .
Hardulf ht̄ iſdem de rege.

ᴍ In HERLINTVN . Norman . III . car̄ tre ad glđ . Iſdē ht̄.

ᴍ In RILISTVNE . Rauenchil . I . car̄ 7 dim̄ ad gld . Iſdē ht̄.

ᴍ In APLEK̃EVVIC . Chetel . II . car̄ 7 dim̄ ad gld . Orme ht̄.

ᴍ In HOLEDENE . Chetel . II . car̄ tre ad gld . Orme ht̄.

★ ᴍ Ibidē . Goſpat 7 Vlchil . IIII . car̄ tre ad gld . Idē ipſi hn̄t.

ᴍ In CHILESEIE . Gamel . VI . car̄ træ ad gld . Vlf ht̄.

ᴍ In HEVVRDE . Goſpatric . I . car̄ ad gld . Idē ipſe ht̄.

ᴍ In CVNESTVNE . Archil . III . car̄ ad gld . Chetel ht̄.

In

36 2 In (Dun)KESWICK, Ulfketill, 4 carucates of land taxable. Land
M. for 2 ploughs. Now the same man and his wife have there 1
plough; and
1 villager.
Meadow, 2 acres.
Value before 1066, 8s; now 5s.

37 M. In RIGTON, Arnketill, 2 carucates of land taxable. Land for 1
plough. Now the same man has (it). Waste.
Value before 1066, 10s.

38 M. In BILTON, Arnketill, 3½ carucates of land taxable. Land for 2
ploughs. Now the same man has (it). Waste.
Value before 1066, 10s.

In CRAVEN   331 d
39 M. In RYLSTONE, Almund, 4 carucates of land taxable. Dolgfinnr
has (it).

40 M. In HARTLINGTON, Almund, 1 carucate of land taxable. Dolgfinnr
has (it).

41 M. In APPLETREEWICK, 1½ carucates of land taxable. Dolgfinnr has (it).

42 M. In BURNSALL and THORPE, Heardwulf, 3½ carucates taxable. The   *r*
& B. same Heardwulf has (it) from the King.

43 M. In HARTLINGTON, Northmann, 3 carucates of land taxable. The
same man has (it).

44 M. In RYLSTONE, Rafnketill, 1½ carucates taxable. The same man
has (it).

45 M. In APPLETREEWICK, Ketill, 2½ carucates taxable. Ormr has (it).

46 M. In *HOLEDENE*, Ketill, 2 carucates of land taxable. Ormr has (it).

47 2 In the same place, Gospatric and Ulfketill, 4 carucates of land   *r*
M. taxable. The same men have (them).

48 M. In KILNSEY, Gamall, 6 carucates of land taxable. Ulfr has (it).

49 M. In *HEUURDE*, Gospatric, 1 carucate taxable. The same man has (it).

50 M. In CONISTONE, Arnketill, 3 carucates taxable. Ketill has (it).

51   In ....

TERRA ROGERII PICTAVENSIS.

In GHIGELESVVIC hƀ Fech. IIII. car ad gld.

Stranforde. Rodemele. Chirchebi. Litone. He Berew.

adiacent fupdicto. M. Roger pictauenfis. hƭ nc.

In Cuningeftone. II. car. Wttts tenuit. ſʒ Rog pict hƭ.

In Bernulfefuuic. Gamel xII. car ad gtd. Bereng de

todeni tenuit. ſʒ m̊. e in caftellatu. Rog pictauenfis.

In Preftune hƀ Vlf. III. car ad gld. 7 I. æcclam.

Stainforde. Wiclesforde. Helgefelt. Neuhufe. Padehale.

Ghiseburne. Hortone. Cheuebroc. Croches. ad gld.

In CHETELEVVELLE. hƀ Vlf. I. car ad gld. Huburgheha.

Stamphotne.

In Anele. hƀ Bû. III. car tre ad gld. Setel. ad gtd.

In WITREBVRNE. hƀ Torfin. III. car træ ad gld. Leuetat.

Flatebi. Geregraue. Neutone. Hortune. Selesat.

Ibide. Torfin. hƀ. II. car tre ad gld.

In Rodemare. hƀ Carle. II. car ad gld. Winchelefuurde

Helgeflet.

In Erneforde hƀ Almund. II. car ad gld. Wincheles

uuorde. Caretorp.

In Paſtorme. Gameltorp. hƀ. II. car. Eluuinetorp. dim c.

In Otreburne. Gamelbar. III. car ad gld.

In Gheregraue Gamel hƀ. vIII. car ad gld.

In Carlentone 7 Lodrefdene. x. car ad gtd. Gamel hƀ.

In Braifuelle hƀ Vlchil 7 Archil. vI. car ad gld

In Stoche. hƀ Archil. IIII. car ad gld.

In Broftune. IIII. taini. xII. car ad gld.

In Collinghe. Archil. II. car 7 II. bo ad gld.

LAND OF ROGER OF POITOU

1 M. In GIGGLESWICK Feigr had 4 carucates taxable. STAINFORTH, 3 C.;
RATHMELL, 2 C.; KIRKBY (Malham), 2 C.; and LITTON, 6 C. These
outliers appertain to the said manor. Roger of Poitou now
has (it).

2 In CONISTON (Cold) 2 carucates. William of Percy held (it), but
Roger of Poitou has (it).

3 M. In BARNOLDSWICK, Gamall, 12 carucates taxable. Berenger of
Tosny held (it), but now it is in the castlery of Roger of Poitou.

4 M. In (Long) PRESTON Ulfr had 3 carucates taxable.
1 church.
STAINFORTH, 3 C.; WIGGLESWORTH, 1 C.; HELLIFIELD, 1½ C.;
NEWSHOLME, ½ C.; PAINLEY, 1 C.; GISBURN, 2 C.; HORTON, 1½ C.;
KELBROOK, 6 bovates; CROOKS (House), 2 bovates; taxable.

5 M. In KETTLEWELL Ulfr had 1 carucate taxable. HUBBERHOLME, ½ C.;
STARBOTTON, ½ C.

6 M. In ANLEY Bui had 3 carucates of land taxable. SETTLE, 3 C. taxable.

7 M. In WINTERBURN Thorfinnr had 3 carucates of land taxable.
LEUETAT, 3 C.; FLASBY, 4 C.; GARGRAVE, 2 C.; (Little) NEWTON, 2 C.;
HORTON (in Ribblesdale), 2 C.; and SELSIDE, 1 C.

8 M. In the same place Thorfinnr had 2 carucates of land taxable.

9 M. In RATHMELL Karli had 2 carucates taxable. WIGGLESWORTH, 10
bovates; HELLIFIELD, 2½ C.

10 M. In ARNFORD Almund had 2 carucates taxable. WIGGLESWORTH, 2 C.;
CARETORP, 2 C.

11 M. In PAYTHORNE Gamalbarn had 2 carucates. ELLENTHORPE, ½
carucate.

12 M. In OTTERBURN, Gamalbarn, 3 carucates taxable.

13 M. In GARGRAVE Gamall had 8 carucates taxable.

14 M. In CARLETON and LOTHERSDALE, 10 carucates taxable. Gamall
had (it).

15 2 In BRACEWELL Ulfketill and Arnketill had 6 carucates taxable.
M.

16 M. In STOCK Arnketill had 4 carucates taxable.

17 4 In BROUGHTON, 4 thanes, 12 carucates taxable.
M.

18 M. In COWLING, Arnketill, 2 carucates and 2 bovates taxable.

Ⓜ In Torentune. ħƀ Alcolm . III . car̄ ad gld.

Ⓜ In Eurebi ħƀ Alcolme . III . car̄ ad gld.

Ⓜ In alia Eurebi Alcolme . II . car̄ 7 VI . ƀō ad gld.

Ⓜ In Eleſlac. Goſpatric 7 Chetel . VIII . car̄ ad gld.

Ⓜ In Neutone. Goſpat̄ . IIII . car̄ ad gld

Ⓜ In Hetune . Suartcol . ỈIIII . car̄ ad gld.

★ Ⓜ In Stamton ħƀ Stam . III . car̄ ad gld.

Ⓜ In Martun . Archil 7 Orm 7 Ernebrand . VI . car̄ ad gld.

Ⓜ In Venetorp. Vĕtred 7 Archil . II . car̄ ad gld

Ⓜ In Airtone . Arnebrand . IIII . car̄ ad gld.

Ⓜ In Scotorp. Archil 7 Orm . III . car̄ ad gld.

Ⓜ In Caltun. Goſpat 7 Glunier . IIII . car̄ ad gld . Erneis habuit.

Ⓜ In Lanclif Feg . III . car̄ ad gld̄ . ⌐ ɧ m̄ . ē in caſtełł Roḡ

Ⓜ In Stacuſe. Archil . III . car̄ ad gld̄.

In Eſtune . Archil 7 Vĕtred . VI . car̄ ad gld̄.

332 b

Ⓜ In Borelaie . Suartcol . II . car̄ ad gld.

Ⓜ In Arneclif. Torfin . IIII . car̄ ad gld.

Ⓜ In Hocheſuuic. Gamel . III . car̄ ad gld.

Ⓜ In GRETLINTONE . ħƀ comes Toſti . IIII . car̄ træ ad gld.
In Bradeforde , Widitun . Baſchelf . Mitune.
Hamereton . Slateborne . Badreſbi . Neutone . Boge
uurde . Eſintune . Radun . Sotleie.

Hæ træ adiacent in Gretlintone.

Ⓜ In LANESDALE . 7 COGREHA . ħƀr Vlf 7 Machel
II . car̄ ad gld.

332 a, b

19 M. In THORNTON (in Craven) Alcolm had 3 carucates taxable.

20 M. In EARBY Alcolm had 3 carucates taxable.

21 M. In another EARBY, Alcolm, 2 carucates and 6 bovates taxable.

22 2 M. In ELSLACK, Gospatric and Ketill, 8 carucates taxable.

23 M. In (Bank) NEWTON, Gospatric, 4 carucates taxable.

24 M. In HETTON, Svartkollr, 4 carucates taxable.

25 M. In (Little) STAINTON Steinn had 3 carucates taxable.

26 3 M. In (East and West) MARTON, Arnketill, Ormr and Arnbrandr, 6 carucates taxable.

27 2 M. In INGTHORPE (Grange), Uhtred and Arnketill, 2 carucates taxable.

28 M. In AIRTON, Arnbrandr, 4 carucates taxable.

29 2 M. In SCOSTHROP, Arnketill and Ormr, 3 carucates taxable.

30 2 M. In CALTON, Gospatric and Gluniairnn, 4 carucates taxable. Erneis had (it), but now it is in Roger's castlery.

31 M. In LANGCLIFFE, Feigr, 3 carucates taxable.

32 M. In STACKHOUSE, Arnketill, 3 carucates taxable.

33 In ESHTON, Arnketill and Uhtred, 6 carucates taxable.

34 M. In BORDLEY, Svartkollr, 2 carucates taxable.　　　　　332 b

35 M. In ARNCLIFFE, Thorfinnr, 4 carucates taxable.

36 M. In HAWKSWICK, Gamall, 3 carucates taxable.

37 M. In GRINDLETON Earl Tosti had 4 carucates of land taxable. (West) BRADFORD, 2 c.; WADDINGTON, 2 c.; BASHALL (Eaves), 4 c.; (Great) MITTON, 4 c.; HAMMERTON (Hall), 2 c.; SLAIDBURN, 4 c.; BATTERSBY (Barn), 2 c.; NEWTON, 4 c.; *BOGEUURDE*, 2 c.; EASINGTON, 3 c.; RADHOLME (Laund), 2 c.; *SOTLEIE*, 3 c. These lands appertain to GRINDLETON.

38 2 M. In 'LONSDALE' [L] and COCKERHAM [L] Ulfr and Machelm had 2 carucates taxable.

III

꘎In *Estvn* . Cliber . Machern 7 Ghilemichel ħƀr . vi . car̆
ad gld . In Ellhale . ii . car̆ . In Scozforde . ii . car̆ .

꘎In *Biedvn* . ħƀ comes Tofti . vi . car̆ ad gld . Nc̄ hr̄ Roğ

★ pictau . 7 Ernuin fub eo . In jaiant . Fareltun . preftun .

★ Bereuuic . Hennecaftre . Eureshaim . Lefuenes .

332 c

Hic est Fevdvm Rotƀti de
Bruis qđ fuit datū poftq̈ liber
de Wintonia fcript fuit . Videlicet .

In Ouftredinc . In *Bortona* . & in
Soca ei tenet hic Rotƀt . xliiii . car
rucatas trǣ . Hoc eft In *Harpein* .

7 in Grentefmor . 7 in Hafchetorp . 7
in Tirnū . 7 in Foxohole . 7 in Tuenc .
Et in eodē Tuenc͗ tenet ipfe . x . car̆ .

7 in Rodeftein . viii . car̆ . Et in duabʒ
Hafelintonis . x . car̆ . 7 . vi . bouat .

7 in Scameftona . v . car̆ .

In Burnous . 7 in Tipetorp . xxxii .
car̆ . 7 . ii . bou . ſʒ pars ifti trǣ eft
de feudo Rotƀti foffart .

In Brentingehā . 7 in Caua . 7 in
Hodhū . ix . car̆ . 7 . i . bou .

In Cliue . ii . bou . In Chelingewic .
. xvi . car̆ . In Milletona . vi . bou .

In Bridefhala . ii . car̆ . In Geruezbi .
. vi . car̆ . In Eduardeftorp . iiii . car̆ .

39 3 In ASHTON (Hall) [L] Clibert, Machern and Gillemicel had 6
M. carucates taxable. In ELLEL [L], 2 carucates; in SCOTFORTH [L],
2 carucates.

40 M. In BEETHAM [W] Earl Tosti had 6 carucates taxable. Now Roger
of Poitou has (it) and Earnwine the Priest under him.
In YEALAND (Conyers and Redmayne) [L], 4 c.; FARLETON [W],
4 c.; PRESTON (Richard) [W], 3 c.; BORWICK [L], 2 c.; HINCASTER
[W], 2 c.; HEVERSHAM (Head) [W], 2 c.; and LEVENS [W], 2 c.

[42]   **THIS IS THE HOLDING OF ROBERT OF BRUS**   332 c
which was given after the Book of WINCHESTER was written,
namely:

EAST RIDING

1   In BURTON (Agnes) and its jurisdiction, this Robert holds 44
carucates of land. This is in HARPHAM, in GRANSMOOR, in
HAISTHORPE, in THORNHOLME, in FOXHOLES and in THWING.

2   And in this same THWING he holds 10 carucates; in RUDSTON, 8
carucates; in two (East and West) HESLERTONS, 10 carucates and
6 bovates; and in SCAMPSTON 5 carucates.

3   In (Kirk)BURN, and TIBTHORPE, 32 carucates and 2 bovates, but
part of that land is of Robert Fossard's holding.

4   In BRANTINGHAM, (North) CAVE and HOTHAM, 9 carucates and 1
bovate.

5   In (South) CLIFFE, 2 bovates; in KILNWICK (Percy), 16 carucates;
and in MILLINGTON, 6 bovates.

6   In BIRDSALL, 2 carucates; in GARROWBY (Hall), 6 carucates; and in
EDDLETHORPE, 4 carucates.

In Torgrimeſtorp . I . caꝛ . 7 . VI . bõ .

In Friebia . II . caꝛ . In Grimetona .

. IIII . caꝛ . 7 . II . bõ . In Berguetorp .

. III . caꝛ .

In *WESTRĘDINC* . tenẹt jdē Robt⁹

in Aluretona . VI . caꝛ . tꝛæ .

In Widetona . I . caꝛ . In Vſebruna

. XII . caꝛ . In Hopretone . IIII . caꝛ .

In Doneforde . II . caꝛ . 7 dĩ . In

Brantona . III . caꝛ . 7 . IIII . bou . In

Graſtona . IIII . caꝛ . 7 . VI . bõ . In Torp

. II . caꝛ . In Scotona . II . caꝛ . In So

teſac . I . caꝛ . In Lauretona . IIII . caꝛ .

7 dĩ . In Haſerlai . VI . caꝛ . tꝛæ

332 d

In Ledelai . II . caꝛ . In Rodum .

. VI . bou . In Hoſeforde . II . caꝛ

In Torp . II . caꝛ . In Carletona

. VI . caꝛ . In Gamesford . I . caꝛ .

In Nortreding . tenet Idem

Rotbt⁹ In Apeltona . VI . caꝛ . tꝛæ

In Hornebia . II . caꝛ . In Werchef

hala . III . caꝛ . In Gerou . III . caꝛ .

In Otrintona . VI . caꝛ . In Herleſia .

. VI . caꝛ . In Welberga . VI . caꝛ .

In Leuetona . VI . caꝛ . In Alia Leue

tona . IIII . caꝛ . In Mortona . III . caꝛ

7   In THORNTHORPE, 1 carucate and 6 bovates.

8   In FIRBY, 2 carucates; in (North) GRIMSTON, 4 carucates and 2 bovates; and in BURYTHORPE, 3 carucates.

WEST RIDING

The same Robert holds:

1   In ALLERTON (Mauleverer), 6 carucates of land.

2   In WIDDINGTON (Hall), 1 carucate; in (Great) OUSEBURN, 12 carucates; and in HOPPERTON, 4 carucates.

3   In (Upper and Lower) DUNSFORTH, 2½ c.; in BRANTON (Green), 3 carucates and 3 bovates; in GRAFTON, 4 carucates and 6 bovates; in (*Scotton*) *THORPE*, 2 carucates; in SCOTTON, 2 carucates; in SUSACRES, 1 carucate; in LAVERTON, 4½ carucates; and in AZERLEY, 6 carucates of land.

4   In LEATHLEY, 2 carucates; in RAWDON, 6 bovates; and in HORSFORTH   332 d 2 carucates.

5   In (Grewel)THORPE, 2 carucates; in CARLTON, 6 carucates; and in CAMBLESFORTH, 1 carucate.

NORTH RIDING

The same Robert holds:

1   In APPLETON (Wiske), 6 carucates of land.

2   In HORNBY, 2 carucates; in (Low) WORSALL, 3 carucates; and in YARM, 3 carucates.

3   In (South) OTTERINGTON, 6 carucates; in (East) HARLSEY, 6 carucates; and in WELBURY, 6 carucates.

4   In (Kirk) LEAVINGTON, 6 carucates; in another (Castle) LEAVINGTON, 4 carucates; and in MORTON (Grange), 3 carucates.

In Bordelbia . II . car' . In Erneclive.
.II . car' . In Englebia . VI . car' . In
Buſchebia . II . car' . In Cratorna.
7 in Foxtun . IX . car̃ . In Hiltona
.III . car' . In Tormozbia . I . car' . 7
dim̃ . In Martona . IIII . car̃ . In
Niueham . II . car' . 7 . II . bõ . In Toleſbi
.III . car' . In Achelũ . II . car' . In Foi
teſbi . VIII . car' . In Tametona . II . car̃.
7 dim̃ . In Goltona . I . car' . In Ber
golbi . I . car' . In Torp . VI . car'.
In Mortona . III . car' . In Nietona
.IIII . car' . 7 . VI . bõ . In Vpeſale.
.III . car' . In Ouſtorp . III . car'
In Childala . VI . car' . In Ormesbia
.XII . car' . In Laiſinbia . I . car'.
7 dim̃ . In Giſeborne . I . car'.
In Eſteintona . I . bõ . In Morhusũ
dim̃ . car' . In Caltorna . I . car' . In
Crambun . IIII . car' . In Niehusũ.
.X . bõ . In Edmundrebia . II . car̃.
7 dim̃ . In Hotun . III . car' . In Gal
metona . dim̃ . car' . In Brunetona

333 a
.XIIII . bõ . In Torentona . XI . bõ.
In Wicam . dim̃ . car' . In Caimtona.
.II . car' . tr̃æ.

5 In 'BORDELBY' (MOUNT GRACE), 2 carucates; ARNCLIFFE (Hall), 2 carucates; INGLEBY (Arncliffe), 6 carucates; (Little) BUSBY, 2 carucates; CRATHORNE and FOXTON, 9 carucates; HILTON, 3 carucates; THORNABY, 1½ carucates; MARTON (in Cleveland), 4 carucates; NEWHAM (Hall), 2 carucates and 2 bovates; TOLLESBY, 3 carucates; ACKLAM, 2 carucates; FACEBY, 8 carucates; TANTON, 2½ carucates; GOULTON (Grange), 1 carucate; *BERGOLBI*, 1 carucate; (Nun)THORPE, 6 carucates.

6 In MORTON (Grange), 3 carucates; in NEWTON, 4 carucates and 6 bovates; in UPSALL (Hall), 3 carucates; and in (Pinchin)THORPE (Hall), 3 carucates.

7 In KILDALE, 6 carucates; in ORMESBY, 12 carucates; in LAZENBY, 1½ carucates; and in GUISBOROUGH, 1 carucate.

8 In 'STAINTON', 1 bovate; MOORSHOLM, ½ carucate; CAWTHORN, 1 carucate; CRAMBE, 4 carucates; NEWSHAM, 10 bovates; AMOTHERBY, 2½ carucates; (Low) HUTTON, 3 carucates; GANTHORPE, ½ carucate; BROMPTON, 14 bovates; THORNTON (Dale), 11 bovates.   333 a

9 In WYKEHAM, ½ carucate; in CAYTON, 2 carucates of land.

In *HARPEIN* tenet Rotb̄t⁹ de Bruis
.VIII . cař . tr̄æ . q̄s Cambiauit erga
Regē . Et In Grentefmora . II . cař.
Et jn Efchedala . XII . cař . 7 . II . b̄o .
Scilic̄ . Danebia . VI . cař . 7 in Cr̄u
becliua . III . cař . 7 in duab₃ Hane
chetonis . II . cař . 7 in Laclum . x . b̄o

CLAMORES DE EVŘVIC SCIRE:
IN NORT ŘEDING.

In Langeb̄ge Wapentac cal̄upniat͛ Hugo comes
fup Willelm̄u de . pci . I . carucatā tr̄æ . In Figelingæ.
dice₂s eā ptinere ad Witebi . S₃ teftimoniū n̄ habet.
In Manefhou Wapent̄ cal̄uniat Rad̄ pagenel . VI .
bou tre In Stainegrif . de tra Vlf . f; h̄oes qui iurauer̄
dicunt . ēē . S̄ Petri eboracenfis.
Teftant͛ qđ terrā Hauuard in euruicfcȳre . tenuit
Wilłs malet . ānteq̄ caftellū captū fuiffet.
Dicunt qđ . VII . cař tr̄æ Sprot in Hotone emit Wilłs
malet . x . markas argenti.
Terrā Tuřulf 7 Turchil 7 Turften | hoc . ē . III . M̄ de . IIII .
In Hotune
cař tr̄æ tenuit Nigel foffard injufte . f; dimifit 7 funt
in manu regis. *ÆSŘEDING*
Duas cař tre in Cliue quæ fuer̄ Bafin . ifdē Nigell⁹ reliqt̄.
Duas cař tr̄æ In Elretone . quæ fuer̄ Bar 7 Vlf . Nigel reliqt̄:
In Middeltun . ifdē Nigel tenuit . I . cař tre quæ fuit Mule
grim . f; m̄ dimifit.

10 In HARPHAM Robert of Brus holds 8 carucates of land which he has exchanged with the King. In GRANSMOOR, 2 carucates; and in ESKDALE(side), 12 carucates and 2 bovates, namely in DANBY, 6 carucates; in CRUNKLY (Gill), 3 carucates; in two HANGTONS ('HANGTON' and HANGTON Hill), 2 carucates; and in LEALHOLM, 10 bovates.

CLAIMS OF YORKSHIRE

In the NORTH RIDING

In LANGBARGH Wapentake

1 Earl Hugh claims against William of Percy 1 carucate of land in FYLING (Old Hall), saying it belongs to WHITBY, but he has no testimony.

MANESHOU (RYEDALE) Wapentake

2 Ralph Paynel claims 6 bovates of land in STONEGRAVE from Ulfr's land, but the men who have sworn say that it is St. Peter's of York.

3 They testify that William Malet held Havarthr's land in Yorkshire before the castle was taken.

4 They say that William Malet bought 7 carucates of Sprottr's land in (Sand) HUTTON for 10 marks of silver.

5 Nigel Fossard wrongfully held the land of Thorulfr, Thorketill and Thorsteinn in (Sheriff) HUTTON; this is 3 manors of 4 carucates of land; but he has given (them) up and they are in the King's hands.

EAST RIDING

1 The same Nigel has relinquished 2 carucates of land, 1 manor, in (South) CLIFFE, which were Basing's.

2 In ELLERTON Nigel has relinquished 2 carucates of land which were Barn's and Ulfr's.

3 In MIDDLETON (on the Wolds) the same Nigel held 1 carucate of land which was Mulagrimr's, but now he has given (it) up.

¶ Socā de dim̄ car̄ træ 7 iii . parte . i . bouatæ . In ead uilla.
7 ꝑtinet ad drifeld ꝋ regis : ifd Nigel ufq; m̄ p uī retinuit.
Similit̄ Hamelin detinuit ufq; nc̄ p uī . ii . car̄ træ 7 v . bou
in ead uilla . cū foca ad drifeld ꝑtinentē.

¶ In ead uilla Ricard de furdeual ten̄ . iii . car̄ tre 7 v . bou.
quæ fuer̄ Eldid . cui tra non fuit delibata Roḃto comiti.

¶ In ead etiā uiila tenet ifd Ricard . vi . bou træ . de qbʒ ptiñ
foca ad drifelt . fed reddita ufq; m̄ non eſt.

¶ In Dalton ifdē Nigel tenuit . ii . car̄ tre . 7 i . bou . ꝗ terra
fuit Norman . Hanc etiā m̄ dimittit.

¶ In Naborne dimifit Roḃt malet . ii . car̄ træ . quæ fuer̄
Turchil . 7 Goisfr̄ de belcāpo de eod Roḃto tenebat.

¶ In Crogun dimifit Nigel foffard . ii . car̄ tre . ꝗ fuer̄ Milne
grim . H̄ eſt in Torefhov Wapent . nc̄ ē in manu regis.

¶ In Burton ꝋ S Joħis de beureli . tenuit Nigel . i . car foffard
træ ꝗ fuit Morcar . 7 foca . ē in Welletone . m̄ reliquit.

¶ In Ballebi . funt . iiii . bou tre quæ fuer̄ Orme 7 Bafin.
7 habuer̄ ibi aulas . Eps dunelmenfis ufqʒ m̄ tenuit.
f; nemo clamat nē . nec uicecomes nec eps.

¶ Terr̄a Norman filij Vlf in Brentinghā quā habet
foffard
Nigel . dicunt homines qui jurauer̄ qd Wiłłs malet
habuit in dn̄io . Similit̄ dn̄t de tra Vlf diaconi.
quā habuit in Caue . Nigel h̄t eā . fed Wiłłs malet habuit.

¶ Tres bou tre & dim quas clamat Rad de mortemer
in Lont . teſtim̄ hōum ꝗ jurauer̄ fuer̄ Aluuini ante
cefforis Giflebti Tifon . non Eddiuæ cuj tr̄a habet
Rad de mortemer.

4　In the same vill the same Nigel has until now detained by force the jurisdiction of ½ carucate and the third part of 1 bovate of land belonging to (Great) DRIFFIELD, the King's manor.

5　Likewise Hamelin has until now detained by force 2 carucates and 5 bovates of land in the same vill, with the jurisdiction belonging to (Great) DRIFFIELD.

6　In the same vill Richard of Sourdeval holds 3 carucates and 5 bovates of land which were Aldgyth's, whose land was not delivered to Count Robert.

7　In the same vill also, the same Richard holds 6 bovates of land, of which the jurisdiction belongs to (Great) DRIFFIELD, but until now it has not been returned.

8　In (North) DALTON the same Nigel held 2 carucates and 1 bovate of land, which was Northmann's. This also he is now giving up.

9　In NABURN Robert Malet has given up 2 carucates of land which were Thorketill's. Geoffrey of Beauchamps held (it) from the same Robert.

10　In CROOM (House) Nigel Fossard has given up 2 carucates of land which were Mylnugrimr's. This is in 'THORSHOWE' Wapentake. Now it is in the King's hands.

11　In (Cherry) BURTON, a manor of St. John of Beverley, Nigel Fossard held 1 carucate of land which was Morcar's. The jurisdiction is in WELTON. He now relinquishes (it).

12　In BELBY (House) are 4 bovates of land which were Ormr's and Basing's. They had halls there. The Bishop of Durham held (them) until now, but no one now claims (them), neither the Sheriff nor the Bishop.

13　The men who have sworn say that William Malet had in lordship the land of Northmann, son of Ulfr, in BRANTINGHAM, which Nigel Fossard has. Likewise, concerning the land of Ulfr the Deacon which he had in (North) CAVE, they say that Nigel has it, but William Malet had it.

14　The 3½ bovates of land which Ralph of Mortemer claims in LUND were, on the testimony of the men who have sworn, Alwine's, Gilbert Tison's predecessor, not Eadgifu's, whose land Ralph of Mortemer has.

¶ De oṁi tra Afæ teſtant qd̄ Roƀti malet debeat

eſſe. eo qd̄ ipſa habuit trā ſuā ſeparatā 7 liberā

a dominatu 7 poteſtate Bernulſi mariti ſui. etiam

cū ſimul. eeɴ. ita ut ipſe de ea nec donā

tionē nec uenditionē facere. nec forisfacere

poſſet. Poſt eoʒ ū ſeparationē. ipſa cum

ƀṁi terra ſua receſſit. & eā ut dña poſſedit.

Hōes autē de comitatu tā de illa quā de

tota terra ej Willelmū malet ſaiſitū uider.

donec inuaſū eſt caſtellum. Hoc atteſtant

de oṁi tra Afæ quā habuit in Euruicſcire.

¶ Socā quā Clamat Giſlebt tiſon in Birland.

dn̄t. ee. debere epi dunelm in Houeden.

¶ Quattuordeci boū træ quas clam eps dunelm

ſup Roƀt malet in Bellebi. dicuɴ fuiſſe Mule

7 Egbrand 7 Baſin 7 Orm. cū ſaca 7 ſoca. 7 hanc

trā habuit Wilłs malet.

¶ Terrā quā Ernuin pƀr clamat in Aƈtun.

dn̄t qa ipſius. ee. debet. ſed Nigel foſſard

clamat regē aduocatū de hac tra ad op comitis.

★ ¶ De. vii. car træ in Nort duſelt quas hɫ Nigel.

dn̄t fuiſſe ſaiſitū Willelmū malet. 7 habuiſſe

terrā 7 ſeruitiū donec fraƈtū eſt caſtellū.

¶ Duas car tre quas hɫ Nigel in Sud duſelt.

dn̄t ꝑtinere regis dñio in Poclinton. Reliq̄s

uero. vi. carucatas Ibidē habuit Wilłs

malet quādiu tenuit caſtellū de Euruic.

7 hōes ſeruitiū reddebant ei.

15 Concerning all Asa's land they testify that it ought to be Robert Malet's because she herself had her land separate and free from the control and power of Bjornulfr her husband, even when they were together, so that he could make neither gift nor sale of it, nor forfeit it. Indeed after their separation she herself withdrew with all her own land and possessed it as lady. Moreover the men of the county saw William Malet in possession both of that (land) and the whole of her land, until the castle was attacked. This they attest concerning all the land of Asa which she had in Yorkshire.

16 They say that the jurisdiction which Gilbert Tison claims in BURLAND (House) ought to be the Bishop of Durham's in HOWDEN.

17 The 14 bovates of land which the Bishop of Durham claims over Robert Malet in BELBY (House) they say belonged to Muli, Egbrand, Basing and Ormr with full jurisdiction. William Malet had this land.

18 The land which Earnwine the Priest claims in AUGHTON they say ought to be his, but Nigel Fossard claims the King as warrantor of this land to the use of Count Robert.

19 Concerning 7 carucates of land in NORTH DUFFIELD which Nigel has, they say William Malet was in possession (of them) and had the land and service until the castle was destroyed.

20 The 2 carucates of land which Nigel has in SOUTH DUFFIELD they say belong to the King's lordship in POCKLINGTON. But the remaining 6 carucates in the same place William Malet had as long as he held the castle of York and men rendered service to him.

Tres car̄ tre in Cliue.7 tres car̄ in Anſgotebi.
Nigel eaṡ tenet . ſed dn̄t qui jurauer̄ q̄ia
Wiłłs malet habuit hanc tr̄a in dn̄io . quādiu
in Euruicſcire tr̄a tenuit.

In Santune . VII . car̄ tre 7 dim hoc . ē medie
tatē uillæ teſtant Willelmū malet in dn̄io
h̄abuiſſe. 7 inde ſaiſitū fuiſſe.

Totā terr̄a Norman filij malcolūbe quā
habuit in Eſtreding; teſtatur om̄is comitatus
Willelmū malet tenuiſſe in ſuo dn̄io . quādiu
In Euruicſcire terr̄a tenuit.

Socā quā clam̄ ep̄s dunelm̄ de . v . car̄ tre 7 II.
bouatis . dicun̄t uere jacuiſſe in Welletone . ſed
canonici de Beureli clamant de ea donū regis . W.
& confirmatiōnē . Similit de|unius car̄ terræ
in Neutone . quā clamat ep̄s dunelm̄ ad Welle
tone . dicunt q̇a T.R.E. ſic fuerit . ſ; clerici eodē
modo clamant de rege.

★ Socā duarū bou in Lanulfeſtorp quas h̄t Wiłłs
de p̄ci . Archiepi dn̄t eſſe debere.

★ Totā uillā Scorneſbi . . eſt . VI . car̄ tre . teſtant
fuiſſe . W . malet . 7 in dn̄io eā poſſediſſe.

★ Similit . XIIII . bou træ in Lanulfeſtorp . 7 in dōnī
ton terr̄a Norman 7 Alden . teſtant Wiłłi
malet fuiſſe 7 eas in dn̄io tenuiſſe.

De tr̄a Sonulfi in Grimeſton quā Nigel tenet
7 Wiłł de p̄ci clamat . neſciuṅ quis eoꝝ habe debeat.

Eandē tr̄a Ernuin clam̄.

21 The 3 carucates of land in CLIFFE and the 3 carucates in OSGODBY, Nigel holds them, but they say who have sworn, that William Malet had this land in lordship as long as he held land in Yorkshire.

22 In SANCTON they testify that William Malet had in lordship and was in possession of 7½ carucates of land, that is half of the vill.

23 The whole county testifies that William Malet held in his lordship all the land which Northmann, son of Maelcolumban, had in the East Riding, as long as he held land in Yorkshire.

24 The jurisdiction which the Bishop of Durham claims of 5 carucates and 2 bovates of land, they say to have lain truly in WELTON. But the Canons of Beverley claim this as King William's gift and confirmation. Likewise concerning the jurisdiction of 1 carucate of land in *NEWTON* (GARDHAM) which the Bishop of Durham claims to WELTON, they say it was so before 1066, but the clerics, in the same way, now claim (it) of the King.

25 The jurisdiction of 2 bovates in *IANULFESTORP* which William of Percy has, they say ought to be the Archbishop's.

26 The whole vill of SCOREBY (Manor), that is 6 carucates of land, they testify was William Malet's and that he possessed it in lordship. Likewise the 14 bovates of land in *IANULFESTORP* and in DUNNINGTON, the land of Northmann and Halfdan, they testify was William Malet's and he held them in lordship.

27 Concerning Sunnulfr's land in GRIMSTON which Nigel holds and William of Percy claims, they do not know which of them ought to have it. Earnwine the Priest claims the same land.

⨍ Sex bou̅ tr̃ in Rudetorp quas clam̃ archieps

teſtant̃ Gislebti. e̅e̅. debere.

⨍ Sex car̃ tre Vlchil In̄ Aluuintone. quas h̅t̅

Wilts de p̅ci. teſtant̃ ad op̃ Rob̅ti malet. q̃a

pat̃ ſuus habuit. ſic̃ ſupiores terras.

⨍ Terr̃a. IIII. car̃ in Coldrid qu̅a tenet Wilt̅s de

p̅ci de q̃ p̅tinet ſoca in Cliftune. teſtant̃ qui jura

u̅eru̅nt non ſolu̅ illas. IIII. car̃. ſed etia̅ tota̅ villa̅

Coldrid Wilt̅m malet| It̃ d̅n̅io tenuiſſe 7 de ea ſaiſitu̅ fuiſſe.

⨍ In Logetorp clam̃ Ricard de. Surdeual tr̃a

Norman 7 Aſæ. ſed d̅n̅t q̃ jurauer̃ regis. e̅e̅. deb̅e.

⨍ In Scarpinberg 7 Scardiztorp h̅t̅ Odo baliſt̃

tr̃a Orm 7 Bunde. ſ; hoꝫ q̃ jurauer̃ teſtim

regis debet. e̅e̅.

⨍ In Riſbi habuit Gam. IIII. car̃ tre q̃s uendidit

Ældredo archiepo. T.R.W. De hae tra jacuit ol̃i̅m̃ soca̅

in Welleton. ſed Thomas Arc̅h h̅t̅ b̅reu̅e regis. W.

p̃ qu̅e c̅ceſſit ipſa̅ ſoca q̃eta̅ S̃ Joh̅i de Beureli.

Similit̃ de. IIII. car̃ tre in Walchinton p̅tineb̅

ſoca ad Welleton. ſ; rex. W. donauit ea̅ q̃eta̅

Eldr̅edo archiepo. teſtante Wapent̃ qui breu̅e

regis inde uidit 7 audiuit. *IN WESKEDING.*

⨍ Ho̅es de Barcheſton Wapent̃ 7 de Siraches

Wapent̃ p̃hibent Osb̅no de arcis teſtimoniu̅.

q̅d Gulb̅tus Anteceſſor ej̃ habuit om̅em Tor

noure. neſciunt cuj̃ dono. Ideſt. IIII. Maneria̅

VIII. caruc̃ tr̃æ. Sed om̅is Tornoure ſedet infra

meta̅ caſtelli Ilb̅ti. ſcd̅m p̃m̃a menſura̅. 7 ſcd̅m

nouiſſima̅ me̅nſura̅ ſedet extra.

28 The 6 bovates of land in THORPE (le Street) which the Archbishop   373 c
claims, they testify ought to be Gilbert Tison's.

29 The 6 carucates of land of Ulfketill in ELVINGTON, which William
of Percy has, they testify (were) for Robert Malet's use because
his father had them, just like the lands above.

30 The land, 4 carucates, in WHELDRAKE, which William of Percy
holds and of which the jurisdiction belongs in CLIFTON, those who
have sworn testify that William Malet held in lordship and was in
possession of not only those 4 carucates but also the whole vill
of Wheldrake.

31 In LOWTHORPE Richard of Sourdeval claims the land of Northmann
and Asa, but those who have sworn say that it ought to be the
King's.

32 In SKIRPENBECK and *SCARDIZTORP* Odo the Crossbowman has the
land of Ormr and Bondi, but the men who have sworn testify
that it ought to be the King's.

33 In RISBY Gamall had 4 carucates of land which he sold to
Archbishop Aldred after 1066. The jurisdiction of this land
formerly lay in WELTON, but Archbishop Thomas has King
William's writ through which he granted that same jurisdiction
with exemption to St. John's of Beverley.
Likewise the jurisdiction of 4 carucates of land in WALKINGTON
belonged to WELTON, but King William granted it, with exemption,
to Archbishop Aldred, as those of the wapentake testify who saw
and heard the King's writ thereon.

WEST RIDING

1 The men of BARKSTON (Ash) Wapentake and of SKYRACK Wapentake
cite testimony to Osbern de Arches that Wulfbert, his predecessor,
had all THORNER, they do not know by whose gift, that is 4
manors, 8 carucates of land. But all Thorner is situated within
the bounds of Ilbert's castle, according to the first measurement,
and, according to the most recent measurement, it is situated
outside (it).

Has tras phibeſ habuiſſe Wiłłm malet . ii . cð)
★ Terrā Gamel in Ladon . ii . caŕ . 7 In Ogleſtorp
.i . caŕ de tra Grim 7 Aſger . ſ; Soca jacuit ad
Bramehā.　　　In Heſeleuuode . xii . bouat
de tra Gamel . f . Oſmundi . 7 i . caŕ de tra Archil
7 friſ ej in ead uilla . Hæc p̄diĉta uilla . ē infra
metā Ilb̄ti ſcđm p̄mā menſurā . 7 ſcđm nouiſſimā
extra. ꝼ Atq; Omēm Stantun ut dn̄t habuit
Wiłłs malet . iii . caruc tre 7 . i . moliñ . 7 in Tate
caſtre . ii . caŕ 7 ii . bou . 7 i . culturā de tra Torchil.
In Mileforde . ii . caŕ de tra Vlſtan . Hæc uilla
eſt infra metā Ilb̄ti ſic ſup̄diĉtū eſt de alijs . 7 In
Neuhuſe . ii . caŕ de tra Chetel . In Togleſtun . i . caŕ
de tra Torchel . ſimilit infra fines Ilb̄ti . In Ridre
ii . caŕ de tra Chetel 7 frm ej . 7 hæc . ē infra metā
Ilb̄ti . ſic ſup̄ de alijs diĉtū . ē . In Saxehale . ii . caŕ
de tra chetel infra metā caſtelli . In Lede . ii . caŕ
ſoca q̄ jacet ad Heſeleuuode . In Neutone . ii . caŕ
de tra Ligulf 7 Torn.
De his om̄ib; dn̄t fuiſſe Willelmū malet ſaiſitū.
ꝼ Scđm teſtimon eoꝗ h̄t Giſleb̄t de gand . i . caŕ
de tra Vlf . in Berchine.
373 d
ꝼ Dn̄t n̄ habuiſſe Duneſtan trā Turchil in Tate
caſtre . T . R . E .
ꝼ Dn̄t trā Ligulf jacuiſſe Wardā 7 Riſton . In Con
tone trā Ricardi de Surdeual.
ꝼ Hoēs de Strafordes Wapent teſtificant ad op̄ Wiłłi
de Warenna . ii . caŕ de tra Siuuardi in Cliftune . quā
clamaƀ Roger de buſli.

2   They cite that William Malet had these lands: in YEADON,
     Gamall's land, 1 manor, 2 carucates; in OGLETHORPE (Hall), 2
     manors, 1 carucate, of Grimr's and Asgeirr's land, but the
     jurisdiction lay in BRAMHAM; in HAZELWOOD (Castle), 3 manors,
     12 bovates, of Gamall son of Asmundr's land; and 1 carucate of
     Arnketill's and his brother's land in the same vill. This said vill
     is within Ilbert's boundary according to the first measurement,
     and according to the most recent, outside (it).

3   And, as they say, William Malet had the whole of STUTTON, 3
     manors, 3 carucates of land and 1 mill; in TADCASTER, 2 manors,
     2 carucates and 2 bovates and 1 arable holding of Thorketill's
     land; in (North) MILFORD (Hall), 1 manor, 2 carucates, of
     Wulfstan's land. This vill is within Ilbert's boundary as is
     stated above of the others. In NEUHUSE, 1 manor, 2 carucates
     of Ketill's land; in TOULSTON, 1 carucate of Thorketill's land,
     likewise within Ilbert's borders; in RYTHER, 2 manors, 2
     carucates of Ketill's and his brother's land; this is within Ilbert's
     boundary as is stated above of the others. In SAXEHALE, 1 manor,
     2 carucates of Ketill's land within the castle boundary; in LEAD,
     2 carucates, the jurisdiction of which lies in HAZELWOOD (Castle);
     in NEWTON (Kyme), 1 manor, 2 carucates of Ligulfr's and Thorn's
     land. They say that William Malet was in possession of all these.

4   According to their testimony Gilbert of Ghent has 1 carucate of
     Ulfr's land in BIRKIN.

5   They say that Dunstan did not have Thorketill's land in TADCASTER   373 d
     before 1066.

6   They say that Ligulfr's land lay in WEARDLEY and (East) RIGTON
     and Richard of Sourdeval's land in COMPTON.

7   The men of STRAFFORTH Wapentake testify to William de
     Warenne's use 2 carucates of Siward's land in CLIFTON which
     Roger de Busli claimed.

⌐Quattuor boů tre in Cliftune de tra Brune.q̃s habebat
Wilłs de Warenna.teſtant̃ ad opus regis in dñio.

⌐Sex cař træ in Berneborc teſtant̃ ad oṕ Wiłłi de Warene.
quæ ṕtiñ ad Coningeſborc.

⌐Ad oṕ ejđ Wiłłi teſtificant̃.xv.ac̃s tre in Wiſeleuuinc.
ħ jacet ad barneburg.7 om̃e qđ illud ṕtinet.

⌐Dñt qđ Nigełł foſſard debet habe in Sandale.vii.boů
tre de tra Aluuini.unde ſoca ṕtiñ ad Coningeſburg.
7 in eađ uilla.i.æccłam. ſetecoł. de qua jacet ſoca in Coningeſburg.

⌐Dñt qđ Nigełł iſđ habe debet.iii.boů de tra Vlchel.
7 ſoca.ē in Coningeſburg.7 in Branuuode.i.boů de tra
Vlchil.ſimilit̃ ſoca.ē in Coningeſburg.

⌐In Tudeforde 7 Steinforde ħt Nigełł.i.boů tre 7 iii.toftes
de tra Vlchel.ſoca jacet ad Coningeſburg.
7 in Fiſcelac tra Norman.i.toftã 7 quartã parte.i.bouatæ.
Soca ad Cuningeſburg.

⌐Fulco de Luſorijs ħt in Loureſhale.ii.boů de tra
Vlfmer.ſoca jacet ad Heſtorp tra Nigel.
7 in Scireſtorp.i.cař de tra Suen.ſoca jacet ad Cuninges⌐burg.

⌐Roger de Buſli.i.car træ in Cathalai.de tra Alſi.

⌐Goisfriđ Alſelin
in Loureſhale.iiii.boů de tra Tochi.Soca jacet ad Eſtorp.

⌐Duo mareſcalli ſaiſier tra normanni.
& tenuer.Neſciuɲ hões de Wapent quonã modo.
nec ad cuj opus.Sed uider eos tenentes.

⌐Nigełł foſſard in Wadeuurde .i.m̃ xiiii.boů tre
de tra Siuuardi.

In Stemeshale .i.m̃ .i.cař de tra Siuuardi.

⌐Goisfriđ Alſelin in Wadeuorde
x.caruc tre 7 dim̃ de tra Tochi.
Sed iſtã tra tenet Roger de Buſli.neſciuɲ quonã modo.

8   4 bovates of land in CLIFTON of Brunn's land, which William de Warenne had, they testify to the use of the King in lordship.

9   6 carucates of land in BARNBROUGH, which belong to CONISBROUGH, they testify to the use of William de Warenne.

10   To the use of the same William they testify 15 acres of land in WILSIC (Hall). This lies in BARNBROUGH and all that belongs to it.

11   They say that Nigel Fossard ought to have in (Kirk) SANDALL 7 bovates of land of Alwine's land, whose jurisdiction belongs to CONISBROUGH; and in the same vill 1 church of Sotakollr's, whose jurisdiction lies in CONISBROUGH.

12   They say that the same Nigel ought to have 3 bovates of Ulfketill's land; the jurisdiction is in CONISBROUGH; and in (Kirk) BRAMWITH 1 bovate of Ulfketill's land; the jurisdiction likewise is in CONISBROUGH.

13   In TUDWORTH (Green) and STAINFORTH Nigel has 1 bovate of land and 3 plots of Ulfketill's land; the jurisdiction lies in CONISBROUGH; and in FISHLAKE, 1 plot and the fourth part of 1 bovate of Northmann's land; the jurisdiction (is) in CONISBROUGH.

14   Fulk of Lisors has in LOVERSALL 2 bovates of Wulfmaer's land; the jurisdiction lies in HEXTHORPE, Nigel's land; and in *STREETTHORPE* (EDENTHORPE), 1 carucate of Sveinn's land; the jurisdiction lies in CONISBROUGH.

15   Roger de Busli, 1 carucate of land in CANTLEY, of Alsige's land.

16   Geoffrey Alselin, 4 bovates of Toki's land in LOVERSALL. The jurisdiction lies in HEXTHORPE.

17   2 marshalls seized Northmann's land and held it. The men of the wapentake do not know in what way or for whose use, but they saw them holding it.

18   Nigel Fossard, in WADWORTH, 1 manor, 14 bovates, of Siward's land; and in STANCIL, 1 manor, 1 carucate, of Siward's land.

19   Geoffrey Alselin, in WADWORTH, 10½ carucates of Toki's land, but Roger de Busli holds this land, they do not know in what way.

⌐In Haltune h̄r rex vi . boū t̄re . de terra Godife.

⌐De calūniis Nigelli in Eftorp . dixer̄ fuiffe in die . R.E.
fic̄ nunc eft.

⌐Terrā Suen de Hadeuuic dn̄t Aldred archiep̄m
emiffe poft mort̄e. E.R. 7 eā quietā habuiffe.

⌐Sup̄ æccłam ⅏ MARIÆ quæ . ē in filua Morelege . h̄t
rex medietat̄e elemofinæ trium fefto₄ ⅏ MARIÆ . q̄
jacet ad Wachefeld . Om̄e aliud h̄t Ilbertus . 7 p̄br
qui æcclæ feruit . judicio hōum de Morelege Wapent́ .

⌐Homines de   Aneftig Wapent́ teftifi
cant ad opus Wiłłi   malet in Stiuetune 7 Cole
tune 7 Cadretune . iii . car̄ t̄ræ 7 v . boú de t̄ra Archeł.
has tenet Osb̄n de arcis.

374 a

⌐In Hagendebi dn̄t Wiłłm malet habuiffe . iii . car̄
t̄ræ de t̄ra Archel filij Vlf . q̄ ten Wiłłs de pci.
Vna ex iftis carucatis jacet ad focā in Helage.

⌐Similit́ teftant́ ad op⁹ Wiłłi . iiii . caruc̄ 7 dimidiā
de t̄ra Norman filij Malcolūbe . quā ten Osb̄n de
7 In Coletune 7 Stiuetune . xiii . boū de t̄ra   ⌐arcis.
Goduine filij Edric quas ten̄ ifd Osb̄nus . teftant́
ad opus Wiłłi malet.

7 In Afchā . i . car̄ t̄ræ q̄ fuit Vlf diac̄ . q̄ tenet Osb̄n
de arcis . dn̄t deb̄e hab̄e Wiłłm malet.

7 In Coletune . vii . boū de t̄ra Vlftan p̄bri tenet
ifd Osb̄n . 7 dn̄t qd Wiłłs malet hab̄e debet.

⌐In Torp . i . car̄ t̄ræ 7 In Mulehale dimid̄ carucata
de t̄ra Norman q̄ tenet Landricus . teftantur
Wiłłi malet . ēē . debere.

20 In (Great) HOUGHTON, 1 manor, the King has 6 bovates of Godhyse's land.

21 Concerning Nigel's claims in HEXTHORPE, they say that as it was in King Edward's day so it is now.

22 They say that Archbishop Aldred bought Sveinn of ADWICK (le Street)'s land after the death of King Edward and had it with exemption.

23 Concerning St. Mary's Church which is in MORLEY Wood, the King has half of the alms of the three festivals of St. Mary because it lies in WAKEFIELD. Ilbert and the priest who serves the church have all the other [half] in the judgement of the men of MORLEY Wapentake.

24 The men of AINSTY Wapentake testify 2 manors to William Malet's use in STEETON (Hall), COLTON and CATTERTON, 3 carucates and 5 bovates of Arnketill son of Wulfstan's land. Osbern de Arches holds these.

25 They say that William Malet had in 'HAGGENBY' 3 carucates of Arnketill son of Ulfr's land, which William of Percy holds. One of those carucates lies in the jurisdiction of HEALAUGH.

374 a

26 Likewise they testify to the use of the same William, 4½ carucates of Northmann son of Maelcolumban's land, which Osbern de Arches holds.

27 In COLTON and STEETON (Hall) they testify to the use of William Malet 13 bovates of Godwine son of Eadric's land, which the same Osbern holds.

28 They say that William Malet ought to have 1 carucate of land in ASKHAM (Richard), which was Ulfr the Deacon's, which Osbern de Arches holds.

29 They say that William Malet ought to have 7 bovates of Wulfstan the Priest's land in COLTON which the same Osbern holds.

30 They testify that 1 carucate of land in (Palla)THORPE and ½ carucate in *MULEHALE* of Northmann's land which Landric holds, ought to be William Malet's.

In Horninctune . x . boú trǽ de t̃ra Aldene.

7 in ead uilla . v . boū de terra Ode 7 Aluuine.

H̃ tenet Wilłs de p̃ci . ſ; hões de Wapent d̃nt

q̃d malet debet eas habere.

In Scachertorp 7 in duab; Popletunis . vi . car̃ trǽ

7 dim̃ de tr̃a Ernuin   Catenaſe . q̃ teñ Osb̃n

de arcis . teſtant̃ ad op̃ malet . 7 d̃nt q̃d Ernuin

pb̃r debet hab̃e de Rob̃to malet.

Ita teſtificant̃ . q̃d Wilłm malet uider̃ ſaiſitū

7 tenentẽ . 7 hões de tr̃a ſeruitiū ſibi fecer̃ . 7 hões

ej fuer̃ . ſed neſciunt quom̃ habuit.

In Bodeltune h̃t Wilłs de p̃ci . v . car̃ de tr̃a

Ligulf . Soca p̃tiñ ad Hailaga tr̃a Goisf̃r alſelin.

De xii . boú terre in Waletune de tr̃a Goduini.

p̃tiñ ſoca ad Hailage tr̃a . G . Alſelini.

Wilłs de p̃ci aduocat pares ſuos in teſtimoniū.

q̃d uiuente Wilło malet 7 uicecomitatū tenente

in Euruic ꞓ fuit ipſe ſaiſitus de Bodetone 7 eā tenuit.

Osb̃n de arcis confirmat q̃d Gulb̃t anteceſſor

ſuus habuit Apeltone 7 om̃s alias tr̃as quietas.

Vlchil ſuabrodre In Stiuetone . ii . car̃ . in Hornin

tone dim̃ car̃ . In Oxetone . i . car̃ . In Torp . vii . boú.

In Coletone . vii . boú.

Com̃ Rob̃t h̃t . Nigel foſſard de eo tenet.

Hões de Borcheſcire Wap̃ teſtificant̃ ad op̃ Rad̃

Pagenel . iiii . boú trǽ in Monechetone . de terra

Merleſuen . q̃ teñ Osb̃n de arcis.

31 In HORNINGTON (Manor) 10 bovates of Halfdan's land, and in the same vill 5 bovates of Oddi's and Alwine's land. William of Percy holds these, but the men of the wapentake say that Malet ought to have them.

32 In SCAGGLETHORPE, 1 manor, and in the two (Upper and Nether) POPPLETONS, 1 manor, 6½ carucates of land, of Earnwine Catenase's land which Osbern de Arches holds, they testify to the use of Malet, and they say that Earnwine the Priest ought to have (them) of Robert Malet.
Likewise they testify that they saw William Malet in possession and holding (them) and men performed service to him in respect of the land and were his men, but they do not know in what manner he had it.

33 In BOLTON (Percy) William of Percy has 5 carucates of Ligulfr's land. The jurisdiction belongs to HEALAUGH, Geoffrey Alselin's land.

34 Concerning 12 bovates of land in WALTON, of Godwine's land, the jurisdiction belongs to HEALAUGH, Geoffrey Alselin's land.

35 William of Percy calls on his peers to witness that while William Malet was alive and held the Sheriffdom in York, he was in possession of BOLTON (Percy) himself, and held it.

36 Osbern de Arches confirms that his predecessor Wulfbert had APPLETON (Roebuck) and all the other lands with exemption.

37 Ulfketill Sveinnbrothir, in STEETON (Hall), 2 carucates; in HORNINGTON (Manor), ½ carucate; in OXTON, 1 carucate; in (Palla)THORPE, 6 bovates and in COLTON, 7 bovates. Count Robert has (them). Nigel Fossard holds from him.

38 The men of 'BURGHSHIRE' (CLARO) Wapentake testify to the use of Ralph Paynel 4 bovates of land in (Nun)MONKTON of Merlesveinn's land, which Osbern de Arches holds.

Omēm trā quā calūniabat Drogo sup S Johēm.

teſtificata . ē ad op ipſi S Johis p hōes de Treding;

7 p donū regis W . qd dedit S Johi Tpr Ӕldredi

archiepi . De hoc hnt canonici ſigillū regis Edw .

7 regis Witti .

374 b

Homines de heldernesse qui jurauer teſtiſi

cati ſunt ad op Witti malet tras has infra no

tatas ; ita qd uider eas ſaiſire in manu ejd Witti ;

7 uider eū habentē 7 tenentē . uſq; dani cepuᷓ

illū ; ſ; de hoc breue regis uel ſigillū non uider;

ⓜ In Branzbortune xi . car tre ; ɋ fuer Aldeuuif

7 Vlf 7 frīs ej ; 7 Vlchel.

ⓜ In Luuetotholm ; i . car tre ɋ fuit Luuetote;

ⓜ In Chenuthefholin . i . car trӕ que fuit Cnut;

ⓜ In Catefos . vi . car tre ɋ fuit Cnut.

ⓜ In Riſun . vii . car tre 7 dim que fuit Cnut

Ḃ In Catinuuic . iiii . car trӕ ɋ fuit Aldeuuif

ⓜ In Aluuardebi . iiii . car trӕ ɋ fuit Frane . F ; Tor.

ⓜ In Lābetorp . i . car trӕ ɋ fuit Echefrid

ⓜ In Sprotclie ; vi . car trӕ quӕ fuit Turſtane;

ⓜ In Chaingehā . viii . car trӕ quӕ fuit Turuert.

ⓜ In Preſtune . xvi . car trӕ ɋ fuit Frane 7 frīs ej ;

ⓜ In Andrebi . ii . car trӕ quӕ fuit Rauenchil

ⓜ In Waxham . v . car trӕ quӕ fuit Brandulf;

ⓜ In Redmӕre . i . car trӕ quӕ t Rauenchil.

ⓜ In Holmetune ; viii . car trӕ t Ode pbri ; Adeſtan. 7 Siuuard.

ⓜ In Vtriſun . ii . car trӕ quӕ t Turgod;

ⓜ In Torp ; iii ; car trӕ quӕ t Grinchel;

39   All the land which Drogo claimed against St. John's is testified to the use of St. John's by the men of the riding through King William's gift which he gave to St. John's in Archbishop Aldred's time. Concerning this, the Canons have the seal of King Edward and King William.

[EAST RIDING]

[HOLDERNESS]

34   The men of HOLDERNESS who have sworn testify to the use of William Malet these lands noted below because they saw them held in possession in the same William's hand, and saw him having and holding [them] until the Danes seized him, but concerning this they have not seen the King's writ or seal.

35 4 In BRANDESBURTON 11 carucates of land which were Aldwif's,
M. Ulfr's and his brother's and Ulfketill's.

36 M. In *LUUETOTHOLM* 1 carucate of land which was Lovettot's.

37 M. In *CHENUTHESHOLM* 1 carucate of land which was Knutr's.

38 M. In CATFOSS (Hall) 6 carucates of land which was Knutr's.

39 M. In RISE 7½ carucates of land which was Knutr's.

40 B. In CATWICK 4 carucates of land which was Aldwif's.

41 M. In ELLERBY 4 carucates of land which was Frani's, Thor's son.

42 M. In LANGTHORPE (Hall) 1 carucate of land which was Ecgfrith's.

43 M. In SPROATLEY 6 carucates of land which was Thorsteinn's.

44 M. In KEYINGHAM 8 carucates of land which was Thorfrothr's.

45 7 In PRESTON 16 carucates of land which were Frani's and his
M. brother's.

46 M. In *ANDREBI* 2 carucates of land which was Rafnketill's.

47 M. In WAXHOLME 5 carucates of land which was Brandulfr's.

48 M. In REDMERE 1 carucate of land which was Rafnketill's.

49 5 In HOLMPTON 8 carucates of land which were Oddi the Priest's,
M. Aethelstan's and Siward's.

50 M. In RYSOME (Garth) 2 carucates of land which was Thorgautr's.

51 M. In '(Nor)THORPE' 3 carucates of land which was Grimketill's.

ᴔ In Sotecotes: ɪ . car trǽ quæ ꝼ Ode diaconi.

Hanc trā ħt Drogo:

Ħ tra jacet in Hailaga. In Bodeltone . v . car trǽ.

In Hagedebi . ɪ . car . Acaſtre . ɪ . boū . Wlſintone . ɪɪ . car
7 dim inland . 7 ɪɪɪɪ . boū ſoca . Has tenet Wiłłs de ꝑci.

In Waletone . xɪɪ . boū trǽ : In Ruforde . ɪ . car . has tenet
Osbn de arcis : In Aſcham : ɪ . car trǽ . Hanc ħt Alanⁱ.

379 a

N Geldo ciuitatis eboracenſis ſunt quater xx . 7 ɪɪɪɪ . car trǽ
quæ T.R.E . geldaƀ unaꝗꝗ quantū una dom ciuitatis.

De his ħt Archieps . vɪ . carucat in firma aulæ ſuæ.

In Oſboldeuuic . vɪ . car . In Mortune . ɪɪɪɪ . car.

In Stochetun . ɪɪɪ . car . Ibiđ . ɪɪɪ . car . In Sābure . ɪɪɪ . car.

In Heuuorde . ɪɪɪ . car . Ibiđ . ɪɪɪ . car . In Fuleforde . x . car.

In Cliftune . vɪɪɪ . car 7 dim . Ibiđ . ɪx . car 7 dim . Ibiđ xxx . vɪɪ . ac̄ ꝑti.

In Roudeclif . ɪɪ . car . Ibiđ . ɪ . car . In Ouertune . v . car.

In Scheltun . ɪɪɪ . car 7 dim . Ibiđ . ɪɪ . car 7 vɪ . bō . Ibiđ . ɪɪ . car 7 vɪ . bō.

In Mortun . ɪɪɪ . car . In Wichintun . ɪɪɪ . car . In circuitu urƀ ɪɪɪ . car.

Torfin 7 Turchil tenuer̄.

374 b, 379 a

52 M. In SOUTHCOATES 1 carucate of land which was Oddi the Deacon's. Drogo has this land.

[WEST RIDING]

40 This land lies in HEALAUGH: in BOLTON (Percy) 5 carucates of land; in 'HAGGENBY' 1 carucate; ACASTER (Selby) 1 bovate; OUSTON (Farm) 2½ carucates *inland* and 4 bovates jurisdiction. William of Percy holds these.

41 In WALTON 12 bovates of land; in RUFFORTH 1 carucate. Osbern de Arches holds these.

42 In ASKAM (Bryan) 1 carucate of land. Count Alan has it.

[THE SUMMARY]

[NORTH RIDING]

1 In the City of YORK'S tax are 84 carucates of land which each paid as much tax as one city house before 1066. Of these the Archbishop has 6 carucates in the revenue of his hall.

2 The Archbishop, in OSBALDWICK, 6 carucates. In MURTON, 4 carucates.

3 The Archbishop, in STOCKTON (on the Forest), 3 carucates. In the same place, 3 carucates. In SANDBURN (House), 3 carucates.

4 In HEWORTH, 3 carucates. Count Alan, in the same place, 3 carucates; Count Alan, in (Gate) FULFORD, 10 carucates.

5 The Archbishop, in CLIFTON, 8½ carucates. Count Alan, in the same place, 9½ carucates. The Archbishop, in the same place, 37 acres of meadow.

6 Saexfrith had, in RAWCLIFFE, 2 carucates. The King, in the same place, 1 carucate. Count Alan, in OVERTON, 5 carucates.

7 The Archbishop, in SKELTON, 3½ carucates. The King, in the same place, 2 carucates and 6 bovates. Count Alan, in the same place, 2 carucates and 6 bovates.

8 Arnketill had, in *MORTUN*, 3 carucates. The Archbishop, in WIGGINTON, 3 carucates. In the circuit of the city, 3 carucates. Thorfinnr and Thorketill held (them).

SIRACHES WAPENTAC.

In OTELAI. Pouele. Gifele. Hauoceforde 7 alia Hauocheford.

Beldone. Merfintone. Burgelei. Illecliue: LX. car 7 VI. bo.

Itē In GEREBVRG WAPENT fuꝫ He BEREW in Otelai

Stube Fernelie. Mideltun. Timbe. Dentun. Eftone.

Cliftun Bicherun.   Int totū. xx.   H arcħ

In Ritun. III. car. In Warde. IIII. car. Dimidia ex his. ē Gos ᵖᵃᵗʳⁱᶜ·

In CHIPESCH. 7 Ledeftun. Alretun. Preftun. Suillintun.

Ingereforde. Sceltun. Caldecotes. Coletun. Offetorp.

Maneftun. Bereuuith. Chidal. Potertun. plintun. Chipetun.

Int tot. LX. IX. car træ 7 dimid.

In Gereford. VII. car. In Suillintun. IX. car. In Stretun. V. car.

In Scipene 7 Stretun. IIII. car. In Chidal 7 ptilintun. III. car.

In Cudford. II. car. In Halletun. VI. car. In Sacrofft. VIII. car.

In Tornoure. VIII. car. In Bretebi 7 Watecrost. II. car.

In Alretun. VI. car. In Cipetun 7 Coletun. IIII. car 7 dim.

In Scadeuuelle. VI. car. In Neuhufū. VIII. car. In Torp. IIII. car.

In Ledes. X. car 7 VI. bo. In Hedingelei. VII. car. In Mortun. II. car.

In Snitertun. VIII. car. In Wodehufū. IIII. car. In Berdefei. II. car.

In Redelefdene. I. car. In Hareuuode 7 Niuuehale. X. car.

In Chefing. V. car. In Stochetun 7 Niuuehale. VI. car 7 VI. bo.

In Locthufun. II. car. In Stubufhū. I. car. In Aluuoldelei. V. car.

[WEST RIDING]

SKYRACK Wapentake

1 The Archbishop, in OTLEY, a manor, POOL, GUISELEY, HAWKSWORTH, another ('Little') HAWKSWORTH, BAILDON, MENSTON, BURLEY (in Wharfedale) and ILKLEY, 60 carucates and 6 bovates.

2 Also in *GEREBURG* Wapentake there are these outliers in OTLEY: STUBHAM, FARNLEY, MIDDLETON, (Nether) TIMBLE, DENTON, *ESTONE*, CLIFTON and *BICHERUN*. In all 20 .... The Archbishop (has) them.

3 In (East) RIGTON, 3 carucates. In WEARDLEY, 4 carucates. Half of these are Gospatric's.

4 Ilbert, in KIPPAX, LEDSTON, ALLERTON (Bywater), (Great and Little) PRESTON, SWILLINGTON, GARFORTH, SKELTON (Grange), COLDCOTES, COLTON, AUSTHORPE, MANSTON, BARWICK (in Elmet), KIDDAL (Hall), POTTERTON, PARLINGTON, GIPTON. In all, 69½ carucates of land.

5 Ilbert, in GARFORTH, 7 carucates. The same Ilbert, in SWILLINGTON, 9 carucates; Ilbert, in STURTON (Grange), 5 carucates.

6 Ilbert, in SHIPPEN (House) and STURTON (Grange), 4 carucates; Ilbert, in KIDDAL (Hall) and PARLINGTON, 3 carucates.

7 Ilbert, in *CUFFORTH* (COWTHWAITE), 2 carucates; Ilbert, in HALTON, 6 carucates; Ilbert, in SEACROFT, 8 carucates.

8 Ilbert, in THORNER, 8 carucates; Ilbert, in BIRKBY (Hill) and 'WHEATCROFT', 2 carucates.

9 Ilbert, in (Chapel) ALLERTON, 6 carucates; Ilbert, in GIPTON and COLTON, 4½ carucates.

10 The King, in SHADWELL, 6 carucates. Ilbert, in (Temple) NEWSAM, 8 carucates; Ilbert, in THORPE (Stapleton), 4 carucates.

11 Ilbert, in LEEDS, 10 carucates and 6 bovates; Ilbert, in HEADINGLEY, 7 carucates. The King, in MORTON, 4 carucates.

12 Ilbert, in *SNITERTUN*, 8 carucates. The King, in WOTHERSOME, 4 carucates; the King, in BARDSEY, 2 carucates.

13 The King, in RIDDLESDEN, 1 carucate; the King, in HAREWOOD and *NEWHALL*, 10 carucates.

14 The King, in (East) KESWICK, 5 carucates; the King, in STOCKTON and *NEWHALL*, 6 carucates and 6 bovates.

15 The King, in LOFTHOUSE, 2 carucates; the King, in STUB HOUSE, 1 carucate; the King, in ALWOODLEY, 5 carucates.

In Wich [Rex] . vi . car . In Brahop [G.tison] . viii . car . In Carletun [Ro.mat] . iii . car.

★ In Horfeford [Rex] . vi . car . In Roudun [Rex] . iii . car . In Ladun [Rex] . iiii . car.

In Bingelei 7 Beldun . Heluuic Mardelei Cotingelei Hatelton.

Muceltuit [Erneis] . xii . car . In Illiclei [W.pci] . iii . car . In Adele [co.Mor'.] . i . car 7 dim.

In Ardinton [co.Morit'.] . iii . car 7 ii . bo 7 dim . In Cucheric [co.Morit'] . iii . car.

In Burgedurun [co.Morit'] . ii . car . In Echope [co.morit'.] . i . car.

In BARCHESTON. WAPENTAC.

In Screþurne cū Bereuuit . c . car træ . iiii . min [Arcĥ]

In Olefchel . cū Bereuuicĥ [Arcĥ] . xiii . car una bouata min.

In Cliford [co.Mor'] . vi . car . In Brahā . 7 Monuchetone . Togeleftun.

Niuueton . Ogleftorp [co.Morit'] . xviii . car . In Hefeleuuode [W.pci] . iii . car.

379 b

In Saxhale [W.pci.] . iiii . car . In Stutun [W.pci.] . i . car 7 dim . Ibid [o.Arcĥ] . i . car 7 dim.

In Saxtun Stouetun Grimeftun Touetun 7 Chirchebi :

xv . car . 7 ii . bo [Ilbt] . In Led . ii . c . In Burtun Brettan 7 Torp [id] :

iii . car 7 vi . bo . In Hunchilhufes [Ilbt] . i . c . In Barcheftun [id] . i . c.

In Fentun [id] . iii . bo . In Rie [id] . ii . c . In Hameltun [id] . iii . car.

In Berchige [id] . i . c . In Carletun [Rex] . vi . c . In Cābesford [Ernuin] . i . car.

In Niuuetun [Ilbt] . iii . c . In Toglefton Neuton 7 Ogleftorp [o.arcis] .

★ vii . c 7 vi . bo . In Grimeftun [Ilbt] . i . c 7 v . bo . Neuhufe [Ilb] . ii . car.

In Chirchebi . dim car . In Mileford [Ilbt] . ii . c . In Drac Ermenia

Camelesford 7 Berlai [Ra.Pag'.] . v . car 7 i . bo.

379 a, b

16 The King, in WIKE, 6 carucates. Gilbert Tison, in BRAMHOPE, 8 carucates. Robert Malet, in (East) CARLTON, 3 carucates.

17 The King, in HORSFORTH, 6 carucates; the King, in RAWDON, 3 carucates; the King, in YEADON, 4 carucates.

18 Erneis, in BINGLEY, BAILDON, ELDWICK, MARLEY, COTTINGLEY, 'HALTON' and MICKLETHWAITE, 12 carucates. William of Percy, in ILKLEY, 3 carucates. The Count of Mortain, in ADEL, 1½ carucates.

19 The Count of Mortain, in ARTHINGTON, 3 carucates and 2½ bovates; the Count of Mortain, in COOKRIDGE, 3 carucates.

20 The Count of Mortain, in BURDEN (Head), 2 carucates; the Count of Mortain, in ECCUP, 1 carucate.

BARKSTON (Ash) Wapentake

1 The Archbishop, in SHERBURN (in Elmet) with its outliers, 100 carucates of land, less 4.

2 The Archbishop, in ULLESKELF with its outliers, 13 carucates less 1 bovate.

3 The Count of Mortain, in CLIFFORD, 6 carucates; the Count of Mortain, in BRAMHAM, MONK HAY (Stile), TOULSTON, NEWTON (Kyme) and OGLETHORPE (Hall), 18 carucates. William of Percy, in HAZELWOOD (Castle), 3 carucates.

4 William of Percy, in SAXHALE, 4 carucates; William of Percy, in STUTTON, 1½ carucates. Osbern de Arches, in the same place, 1½ carucates.   379 b

5 Ilbert, in SAXTON, STUTTON, GRIMSTON (Grange), TOWTON, and KIRKBY (Wharfe), 15 carucates and 2 bovates; the same, in LEAD, 2 carucates; the same, in BURTON (Hall), BRAYTON and THORPE (Willoughby), 3 carucates and 6 bovates; Ilbert, in HUNCHILHUSES, 1 carucate; Ilbert, in BARKSTON, 1 carucate.

6 The same, in (Church and Little) FENTON, 3 bovates; the same, in RYTHER, 2 carucates; the same, in HAMBLETON, 3 carucates.

7 The same, in BIRKIN, 1 carucate. The King, in CARLTON, 6 carucates. Earnwine, in CAMBLESFORTH, 1 carucate.

8 Ilbert, in NEWTON ('Wallis'), 3 carucates. Osbern de Arches, in TOULSTON, NEWTON (Kyme) and OGLETHORPE (Hall), 7 carucates and 7 bovates. Ilbert, in GRIMSTON (Grange), 1 carucate and 5 bovates; Ilbert, NEUHUSE, 2 carucates.

9 Ilbert, in KIRKBY (Wharfe), ½ carucate; Ilbert, in (North) MILFORD (Hall), 2 carucates. Ralph Paynel, in DRAX, (Little) AIRMYN, CAMBLESFORTH and BARLOW, 5 carucates and 1 bovate.

In Fareburne . 11 . c 7 dim
In Ledeshā . 11 . c.
In Tatecastre . viii . car
In Niuueton . 111 . c.

In Coningeſburg cū Berew . q̄t xx 7 xi . c træ 7 111 . bō ÷7 xv ﹒ac

In Laſtone . Trapun . Dunintone . Titelanſtan . Aneſtan

Torp Wales Hotone . Neuhalle ꞏ liiii . car træ.

In Wadeuurde . xii . c . In Stantone . 1 . car 7 dim.

In Dadeſlei Stainton 7 Elgebi . viii . c . In Wincreſlei . 1111 ﹒c.

In Maltebi 7 Elgebi . 1111 . c 7 dim . In Brinesford . 1 . c 7 111 . bō

Ibid . 111 . car 7 v . bō . In Tineſlauue . viii . car 7 1 . bō.

Ibid . vii . bō . In Greſseburg . 111 . c . In Grimeſhou . 111 . c 7 dim.

In Mecheſburg . v . c . In Neuhalle Hotun Denegebi . vi . car.

In Adeuuic . 11 . c 7 dim . In Barneburg 7 Bilhā . vi . car.

In Eclesfeld . 1111 . c . In Wade Suintone 7 Wintreuuorde . vii . c 7 11 . bō.

In Hoiland . 11 . c . In Wanbuelle 7 Medeltone 7 Toftes . 11 . c.

Ibid . 11 . c 7 1 . bō . Ibid . 1111 . c 7 11 . bō . In Rodemeſc . 1111 . car.

In Icheltone . v . c 7 v . bō . Ibid . 1 . car 7 v . bō . In dereuueld . 11 . c.

10 Ilbert, in FAIRBURN, 2½ carucates.

11 Ilbert, in LEDSHAM, 2 carucates.

12 William of Percy, in TADCASTER, 8 carucates.

13 Osbern de Arches, in NEWTON (Kyme), 3 carucates.

[STRAFFORTH Wapentake]

1 William de Warenne, in CONISBROUGH with its outliers, 91 carucates of land and 3 bovates and 15 acres.

2 Roger de Busli, in LAUGHTON (en le Morthen), THROAPHAM, DINNINGTON, (South) ANSTON, (North) ANSTON, THORPE (Salvin), WALES, (Slade) HOOTON and NEWHALL (Grange), 54 carucates of land.

3 Roger de Busli, in WADWORTH, 12 carucates; Roger de Busli, in STAINTON, 1½ carucates.

4 Roger de Busli, in DADSLEY, STAINTON and HELLABY, 8 carucates; the same, in WICKERSLEY, 4 carucates.

5 The same Roger, in MALTBY and HELLABY, 4½ carucates; Roger de Busli, in BRINSWORTH, 1 carucate and 3 bovates.

6 William of Percy, in the same place, 3 carucates and 5 bovates. Roger de Busli, in TINSLEY, 8 carucates and 1 bovate.

7 The King, in the same place, 7 bovates. Roger de Busli, in GREASBROUGH, 3 carucates; Roger de Busli, in GRIMESHOU, 3½ carucates.

8 Roger de Busli, in MEXBOROUGH, 5 carucates; Roger de Busli, in NEWHILL, HOOTON (Roberts) and DENABY, 6 carucates.

9 Roger de Busli, in ADWICK (upon Dearne), 2½ carucates; Roger de Busli, in BARNBROUGH and BILHAM (House), 6 carucates.

10 Roger de Busli, in ECCLESFIELD, 4 carucates; Roger de Busli, in WATH (upon Dearne), SWINTON and WENTWORTH, 7 carucates and 2 bovates.

11 The same Roger, in HOYLAND (Nether), 2 carucates; the same Roger, in WOMBWELL, (West) MELTON and TOFTES, 2 carucates.

12 The King, in the same place, 2 carucates and 1 bovate. Walter of Aincourt, in the same place, 4 carucates and 2 bovates; Walter of Aincourt, in RAWMARSH, 4 carucates.

13 Count Aubrey, in HICKLETON, 5 carucates and 5 bovates; the same Aubrey, in the same place, 1 carucate and 5 bovates. The King, in DARFIELD, 4 carucates.

In Medeltone. viii . c̄ . In Widuntorp . ii . c̄ . In Catebi. iii . car.

Ibid̄ . ii . c̄ 7 i . bō . In Sproteburg 7 Cuzeuuorde 7 Ballebi . viii . c̄   r

Ibid̄ . i . c̄ . In Merelton Hoiland Torp Winteuuorde 7 Brantone.

v . car 7 dim . In Wat Mideltone Winteuuord 7 Eldebge.

vii . car 7 v . bō . In Medeltone . i . c̄ 7 v . bō .

In Brantone Tor 7 Eldebge . iii . c̄ 7 i . bō . In Bingeliẹ dim̄ c̄ .

In Winte uuorde . i . car 7 ii . bō . In haltone . ii . car 7 dim .

In Bilingelei . v . c̄ . In Bodetone . ii . c̄ 7 dim . Ibid̄ . ii . c̄ 7 dim .

In Goldetorp 7 Dermefc op . iiii . c̄ 7 vi . bō . In Marra . iiii , c̄ 7 dim .

Ibid̄ . v . bō . In Eftorp Donecaftre Ballefbi Scitelefuuorde

Wermesford Iuurefhale Ouftrefeld Alceflei Alchelie.

xxii . c̄ 7 dim . In Brantone 7 Cantelie . xiiii . c̄ 7 i . bō 7 dim .

In Einuluestorp . v . car . In Branuuet . i . c̄ 7 dim .

In Barnebi . ii . c̄ 7 ii . bō . Ibid̄ . i . c̄ 7 i . bō . Ibid̄ . i . c̄ 7 i . bō .

In Sandale . vi . c̄ 7 v . bō . In Hotone . iii . car 7 vi . bō .

In Eilintone Bradeuuelle 7 Donecaftre . iii . car 7 vi bō .

In Triberge . iiii . c̄ . In Daltone . ii . c̄ 7 vi . bō . In Rodreha . v . c̄ .

In Chibereuuorde . vi . c̄ . In Sinitun . iii . car 7 vi . bō .

379 b

14   Roger de Busli, in (High) MELTON, 8 carucates; the same Roger, in WILDTHORPE, 2 carucates; Roger de Busli, in CADEBY, 3 carucates.

r 15   Count Aubrey, in the same place, 2 carucates and 1 bovate. In SPROTBROUGH, CUSWORTH and BALBY, 8 carucates.

16   The King, in the same place, 1 carucate; the King, in (West) MELTON, HOYLAND (Nether), THORPE (Hesley), WENTWORTH and BRAMPTON (Bierlow), 5½ carucates; the King, in WATH (upon Dearne), (West) MELTON, WENTWORTH and *ELDEBERGE*, 7 carucates and 5 bovates; the King, in (West) MELTON, 1 carucate and 5 bovates.

17   The King, in BRAMPTON (Bierlow), THORPE (Hesley) and *ELDEBERGE*, 3 carucates and 1 bovate; the King, in BILLINGLEY, ½ carucate.

18   The King, in WENTWORTH, 1 carucate and 2 bovates. Roger de Busli, in (Little) HOUGHTON, 2½ carucates.

19   Roger de Busli, in BILLINGLEY, 5 carucates; the same, in BOLTON (upon Dearne), 2½ carucates. William of Percy, in the same place, 2½ carucates.

20   Roger de Busli, in GOLDTHORPE and THURNSCOE, 4 carucates and 6 bovates; the same, in MARR, 4½ carucates.

21   The Count of Mortain, in the same place, 5 bovates; the Count of Mortain, in HEXTHORPE, DONCASTER, BALBY, *SHUTTLEWORTH* (LITTLEWORTH), WARMSWORTH, LOVERSALL, AUSTERFIELD, AUCKLEY and AUCKLEY, 22½ carucates. Geoffrey Alselin, in BRANTON and CANTLEY, 14 carucates and 1½ bovates.

22   Earnwine, in ARMTHORPE, 5 carucates. Roger de Busli, in (Kirk) BRAMWITH, 1½ carucates.

23   The Count of Mortain, in BARNBY (Dun), 2 carucates and 2 bovates. William of Percy, in the same place, 1 carucate and 1 bovate. Roger de Busli, 1 carucate and 1 bovate.

24   The Count of Mortain, in (Long) SANDALL, 6 carucates and 5 bovates; the Count of Mortain, in HOOTON (Levitt), 3 carucates and 6 bovates.

25   William of Percy, in (Old) EDLINGTON, BRAITHWELL and DONCASTER, 3 carucates and 6 bovates.

26   William of Percy, in THRYBERGH, 4 carucates; William of Percy, in DALTON, 2 carucates and 6 bovates. The Count of Mortain, in ROTHERHAM, 5 carucates.

27   Roger de Busli, in KIMBERWORTH, 6 carucates. Gilbert Tison, in SWINTON, 3 carucates and 6 bovates.

In Honepol .III. c̄ . In Fricelei 7 Stodfald . VI . bō . In Hotun . x . c̄

In Brochesuuorde 7 picheburne . v . c̄ 7 dim̄ . Ibid̄ . II . c̄ 7 dim̄ .

In Tateuuic . XII . c̄ . In Haltune . VI . c̄ . In Ternusch Claitone

Dictenebi 7 Stofald ꝛ VI . c̄ 7 v . ac̄s 7 dim̄ . Ibid̄ . VI . bō .

In Guldetorp . I . c̄ 7 II . bō . In Widesthā 7 Handesuuord . IX . c̄ 7 dim̄ .

In Tretone . III . c̄ . In HACTONE . II . c̄ 7 VI . bō . In Walis . I . car̄ .

In Estone . II . c̄ 7 . II . bō . In Ollei . IIII . c̄ . In Brantone . VI . c̄ .

In Watelag Donecaſtre Adeuuic Scineſtorp Langetouet

Benelei 7 Sandalie ꝛ xv . car̄ . In Aldeuuorde . II , car̄ .

379 c

In Hallun̄ . XXIX . car̄ . In Atecliue . III . c̄ . In Scafeld . III . car̄ .

In Sceuelt . I . car̄ . In Vghil 7 Wihale 7 Wadelei . I . c̄ 7 VI . bō .

In Ermeſhale 7 Frichelie . Torp 7 Chirchebi ꝛ XI . car̄ træ .

_I_OSGOTGROS WAPENTAC.

In Archeſei . II . car̄ 7 VI . bō . In Beneſlei . II . c̄ 7 II . bō

In Adeuuic . VII . car̄ . 7 II . bō . Ibid̄ . II . bō . In Nortone . v . car̄ .

In Scalchebi . v . c̄ . In Canſale . II . c̄ 7 dim̄ .

In Scanhalle . IIII . c̄ . In Burg . III . c̄ . In Austhū . IIII . car̄ .

28 Roger de Busli, in HAMPOLE, 3 carucates; Roger de Busli, in FRICKLEY and STOTFOLD, 6 bovates. The Count of Mortain, in HOOTON (Pagnell), 10 carucates.

29 Roger de Busli, in BRODSWORTH and PICKBURN, 5½ carucates. The Count of Mortain, in the same place, 2½ carucates.

30 The Count of Mortain, in TODWICK, 12 carucates; the Count of Mortain, in (Great) HOUGHTON, 6 carucates; the Count of Mortain, in THURNSCOE, CLAYTON, DEIGHTONBY (Fields) and STOTFOLD, 6 carucates and 5½ acres. William of Percy, in the same place, 6 bovates.

31 The King, in GOLDTHORPE, 1 carucate and 2 bovates. The Count of Mortain, in WHISTON and HANDSWORTH, 9½ carucates.

32 The Count of Mortain, in TREETON, 3 carucates; the Count of Mortain, in AUGHTON (Hall), 2 carucates and 6 bovates; the Count of Mortain, in WALES, 1 carucate.

33 The Count of Mortain, in ASTON, 2 carucates and 2 bovates; the Count of Mortain, in ULLEY, 4 carucates; the Count of Mortain, in BRAMPTON (en le Morthen), 6 carucates.

34 The Count of Mortain, in WHEATLEY, DONCASTER, ADWICK (le Street), SCINESTORP, LANGTHWAITE, BENTLEY and (Kirk) SANDALL, 15 carucates. Roger de Busli, in HOLDWORTH, 2 carucates.

35 The Countess Judith, in HALLAM, 29 carucates; the same Countess, 379 c in ATTERCLIFFE, 3 carucates; the same Countess, in SHEFFIELD, 3 carucates.

36 The King, in (Walder)SHELF, 1 carucate. Roger de Busli, in UGHILL, WORRALL and WADSLEY, 1 carucate and 6 bovates.

37 Ilbert, in (South) ELMSALL, FRICKLEY, (Moor)THORPE and (South) KIRKBY, 11 carucates of land.

OSGOLDCROSS Wapentake

1 Roger de Busli, in ARKSEY, 2 carucates and 6 bovates; Roger de Busli, in BENTLEY, 2 carucates and 2 bovates.

2 Roger de Busli, in ADWICK (le Street), 7 carucates and 2 bovates. The Count of Mortain, in the same place, 2 bovates. Ilbert, in NORTON, 5 carucates.

r 3 Roger de Busli, in SCAWSBY, 5 carucates. Ilbert, in CAMPSALL, 2½ carucates.

4 Ilbert, in SKELLOW, 4 carucates; Ilbert, in BURGH(wallis), 3 carucates; Ilbert, in OWSTON, 4 carucates.

In Neuhuſe 7 Sutone . II . c̄ . In Scalebro . III . c̄ . In hanepol . I . c̄

In Iſtop . III . c̄ 7 dim bō . In Torp . VI . car 7 III . bō.

In Badeſuuorde Vptone 7 Rogartorp . IX . car 7 V . bō.

In Smedetone . IIII . car̄ . In Wilmereſlege . VI . car̄.

In Stapleton . IIII . c̄ . In Darnitone . VI . c̄ . In Aſele . dim c̄.

In Aceuurde . VI . c̄ . In Hoctun . VI . c̄ . In Ferie . V . car.

In Fredeſtan 7 preſton Harduic 7 Oſle . XVI . car.

In Weldale 7 Friſtone . VII . c̄ . In Notingelai . IIII . car̄.

In Begale . IIII . c̄ . In Ghelintune . II . c̄ . In Ermeſhale . VIII . c̄.

In Ruhale . IIII . c̄ . In Chelintune 7 Egeburg . IIII . car̄.

In Tateſhale . XVI . c̄ . 7 in elemoſina . II . car træ

In Edeſhale . IIII . c̄ . In Witelai . II . c̄ . In Maneſtorp . II . c̄.

I**STANCROS WAPENTAC.**
n Chineſlei . III . car . In Hilmeuuord . IIII . c̄ . In Barnebi . II . c̄.

In Silcheſtone . I . car 7 dim . In Adelingesſluet . VI . car̄.

In Breſelie 7 Indelie . VI . c̄ . In Roreſtun . IIII . c̄.

In Dodeſuuorde . V . c̄ . In Caltorn . III . c̄ . In Silcſton . III . c̄.

In Pengeſton . I . car 7 II . bō . In Dertun . I . c̄ . In Berg . III . c̄.

In Cezeburg . II . c̄ 7 dim . In Holand . II . c̄.

5   Ilbert, in 'NEWSHAM' and SUTTON, 2 carucates; Ilbert, in SKELBROOKE, 3 carucates; Ilbert, in HAMPHALL (Stubbs), 1 carucate.

6   Ilbert, in (Walden) STUBBS, 3 carucates and ½ bovate; Ilbert, in THORPE (Audlin), 6 carucates and 3 bovates.

7   Ilbert, in BADSWORTH, UPTON and ROGERTHORPE (Manor), 9 carucates and 5 bovates.

8   Ilbert, in (Kirk and Little) SMEATON, 4 carucates; Ilbert, in WOMERSLEY, 6 carucates.

9   Ilbert, in STAPLETON, 4 carucates; Ilbert, in DARRINGTON, 6 carucates; Ilbert, in HESSLE, ½ carucate.

10   Ilbert, in ACKWORTH, 6 carucates; Ilbert, in (Glass) HOUGHTON, 6 carucates; Ilbert, in FERRY (Fryston), 5 carucates.

11   Ilbert, in FEATHERSTONE, PURSTON (Jaglin), (West) HARDWICK and NOSTELL (Priory), 16 carucates.

12   Ilbert, in WHELDALE and (Water) FRYSTON, 7 carucates; Ilbert, in KNOTTINGLEY, 4 carucates.

13   Ilbert, in BEAL, 4 carucates; Ilbert, in KELLINGTON, 2 carucates; Ilbert, in (North) ELMSALL, 8 carucates.

14   Ilbert, in ROALL (Hall) and EGGBOROUGH, 4 carucates; Ilbert, in KELLINGTON and EGGBOROUGH, 4 carucates.

15   The King, in TANSHELF, 16 carucates. In alms, 2 carucates of land.

16   The King, in HENSALL, 4 carucates; the King, in WHITLEY, 2 carucates. Ilbert, in MINSTHORPE, 2 carucates.

STAINCROSS Wapentake

1   Ilbert, in KINSLEY, 3 carucates; Ilbert, in HEMSWORTH, 4 carucates. The King, in BARNBY (Hall), 2 carucates.

2   The King, in SILKSTONE, 1½ carucates. Geoffrey of La Guerche, in ADLINGFLEET, 6 carucates.

3   Ilbert, in BRIERLEY and (South) HIENDLEY, 6 carucates; Ilbert, in ROYSTON, 4 carucates.

4   Ilbert, in DODWORTH, 5 carucates; Ilbert, in CAWTHORNE, 3 carucates; Ilbert, in SILKSTONE, 3 carucates.

5   In PENISTONE, 1 carucate and 2 bovates. In DARTON, 1 carucate. Ilbert, in BARUGH, 3 carucates.

6   Ilbert, in KEXBROUGH, 2½ carucates; Ilbert, in (High) HOYLAND, 2 carucates.

In Sactun . xii . c . In Sceptun 7 Carleton xviii . car.

In Wircefburg . v . c 7 dim . In Pillei . ii . c . In Wirlei . iiii . c.

In Wirlei . i . c . In Tancreflei . i . car 7 dim . ⌐iii . c

In Turgefland . iiii . c 7 dim . In Stanburg . ii . c . In Hunefcelf⸴

In Turoluefton 7 Berceworde . vi . c . In Cūbreuuorde . i . car.

In Denebi . iii . c . In Scemeltorp . iii . c . In Claitone . iii . c.

In Bretone . i . c 7 dim . In Ofpring 7 Berceuuorde . ii . car.

In Holande . i . car 7 i . bō . In Dertone . iiii . c . In Norton . vi . c.

In Creuesford 7 Berneflai . v . c . In Ceuet . i . car 7 dim .

In Hindelei . iiii . car . Ibid 7 Rihelle . iiii . car.

AGEBRVGE WAPENTAC.

In Warnesfeld 7 Bereuuic . ix . car . In Medelai . viii . c.

In Witeuude . viii . c . In Attone . iii . c . In Weftrebi . vi . c.

In Normtone . x . car . In Snitehale . vi . c . In Waleton . vii . c.

In Scroftune . iiii . c . In Sandale . vi . c . In Flocheton . iii . c.

In Denebi . iii . c . In Amelai . iii . c . In Tornil . iiii . c.

In Witelei . v . c . In Leptone . iii . c . In Heptone . iii . c.

In Daltone . ii . c . In Almaneberie . iiii . c . In Ferlei . iii . c.

7 The King, in SACTUN, 12 carucates. Ilbert, in SHAFTON and CARLTON, 18 carucates.

8 Ilbert, in WORSBOROUGH, 5½ carucates. The Count of Mortain, in PILLEY, 2 carucates. The King, in WORTLEY, 4 carucates.

9 The Count of Mortain, in WORTLEY, 1 carucate; the Count of Mortain, in TANKERSLEY, 1½ carucates.

10 Ilbert, in THURGOLAND, 4½ carucates; Ilbert, in STAINBOROUGH (Castle), 2 carucates; Ilbert, in HUNSHELF (Hall), 3 carucates.

11 Ilbert, in THURLSTONE and (Ing)BIRCHWORTH, 6 carucates; Ilbert, in (Upper) CUMBERWORTH, 1 carucate.

12 Ilbert, in (Upper and Lower) DENBY, 3 carucates; Ilbert, in SKELMANTHORPE, 3 carucates; Ilbert, in CLAYTON (West), 3 carucates.

13 Ilbert, in (Monk) BRETTON, 1½ carucates; Ilbert, in OXSPRING and (Rough)BIRCHWORTH, 2 carucates.

14 Ilbert, in HOYLAND (Swaine), 1 carucate and 1 bovate; Ilbert, in DARTON, 4 carucates; Ilbert, in NOTTON, 6 carucates.

15 In KERESFORTH (Hall) and BARNSLEY, 5 carucates. Ilbert, in CHEVET, 1½ carucates.

16 Ilbert, in (Cold) HIENDLEY, 4 carucates; Ilbert, in the same place and in RYHILL, 4 carucates.

AGBRIGG Wapentake

1 The Archbishop, in WARMFIELD and its outlier, 9 carucates. Ilbert, in METHLEY, 8 carucates.

2 Ilbert, in WHITWOOD, 8 carucates; Ilbert, in ACKTON, 3 carucates; Ilbert, in 'WESTERBY', 6 carucates.

3 The King, in NORMANTON, 10 carucates. Ilbert, in SNYDALE, 6 carucates. The King, in WALTON, 8 carucates.

4 Ilbert, in CROFTON, 4 carucates. The King, in SANDAL (Magna), 6 carucates. Ilbert, in FLOCKTON, 3 carucates.

5 Ilbert, in (Upper) DENBY, 3 carucates. In EMLEY, 3 carucates. Ilbert, in THORNHILL, 4 carucates.

6 Ilbert, in (Lower) WHITLEY, 5 carucates; Ilbert, in LEPTON, 3 carucates; Ilbert, in (Kirk)HEATON, 3 carucates.

7 Ilbert, in DALTON, 2 carucates; Ilbert, in ALMONDBURY, 4 carucates; Ilbert, in FARNLEY (Tyas), 3 carucates.

In Hanelei 7 Melthā.ɪɪɪɪ.c̄ . In Scipelei 7 Sciuelei.ɪɪɪ.c̄.

In Wachefeld. ˣ xʟ . car̄ 7 ɪɪɪ . bō træ . 7 tcia pars . ɪ . bō.In Crigeston.ɪ.c̄ʼ

In Bretone . ɪ . car̄ 7 dɪm̄ . In Horberie . ɪɪ . car̄ 7 vɪɪ . bō . In Etone . ɪ . car̄.

In Oſſeſet . ɪɪɪ . c̄ 7 dɪm̄ . In Stanlei . ɪɪɪ . c̄ . In Schelintone . ɪɪɪ . car̄.

In duabʒ Holne 7 Alſtaneſlei 7 Tohac . ɪɪ.c̄.In Cūʒreuuorde.ɪ . car̄.

In Bertone.ɪɪɪ . c̄ . In Croſland.ɪ.c̄.In Hoptun . ɪɪ . c̄ . In Odresfeld.vɪ.c̄.

In Cheteuuorde 7 Heppeuuord Vluedel Fugeleſtun 7 Toſtenland. vɪ . c̄.

★ In Bradelie.ɪɪ.c̄.In Lillai.ɪɪ.c̄.In Gudlageſargo dim c̄ . In Corneſbi.ɪɪ.c̄.

In altero Croſland . ɪɪ . car̄.

MORELEI WAPENTAC.

In Morelei.vɪ.car̄ . In Erdeſlau.v.car̄ 7 ɪɪɪ.bō. In Beſtone.vɪ.car̄.

In Rodouuelle 7 Carlentone Loℱthuſe Torp 7 Mildentone.xxɪɪɪɪ.car̄.

In Hunſlet.vɪ.c̄.In Riſton 7 Ermelai . vɪ . c̄.In Bramelei.ɪɪɪɪ.car̄.

In Cauerlei 7 Ferſellei.ɪɪɪ.c̄ . In Podecheſai.vɪɪɪ.c̄.In Tuinc.ɪɪɪɪ.c̄.

In Dreſlingtone.ɪɪɪɪ.c̄ . In Gomeſhale 7 duabʒ Bereuu.xɪɪɪɪ.car̄.

In Bodeltone.ɪɪɪɪ.c̄.In Bradeford 7 vɪ.Bereuu.xv.c̄.In Bollinc.ɪɪɪɪ.c̄.

In Celeſlau Torenton Alreton Claiton 7 Wibeteſe.x.car̄.

In Scipelei.ɪɪɪ.c̄. In Birle.ɪɪɪɪ.c̄. In Wich.ɪɪɪɪ.c̄. In Hetun.vɪ.c̄.

8   Ilbert, in HONLEY and MELTHAM, 4 carucates. In SHEPLEY and SHELLEY, 3 carucates.

9   The King, in WAKEFIELD, 40 carucates 3 bovates of land and the   379 d
third part of 1 bovate; the King, in CRIGGLESTONE, 1 carucate and 2 bovates.

10   The King, in (West) BRETTON, 1½ carucates; the same, in HORBURY, 2 carucates and 7 bovates; the same, in (Earls)HEATON, 1 carucate.

11   The same, in OSSETT, 3½ carucates; the same, in STANLEY, 3 carucates; the same, in SHITLINGTON, 3 carucates.

12   The King, in the two HOLMES (HOLME and YateHOLME), AUSTONLEY and (Upper)THONG, 2 carucates; the same, in (Lower) CUMBERWORTH, 1 carucate.

13   The same, in (Kirk)BURTON, 3 carucates; the same, in (North) CROSLAND, 1 carucate. Ilbert, in (Upper) HOPTON, 2 carucates; Ilbert, in HUDDERSFIELD, 6 carucates.

14   The King, in CARTWORTH, HEPWORTH, WOOLDALE, FULSTONE and THURSTONLAND, 6 carucates.

15   Ilbert, in BRADLEY, 2 carucates; Ilbert, in LINDLEY, 2 carucates; Ilbert, in GOLCAR, ½ carucate; Ilbert, in QUARMBY, 2 carucates.

16   Ilbert, in another (South) CROSLAND, 2 carucates.

MORLEY Wapentake

1   Ilbert, in MORLEY, 6 carucates; Ilbert, in (East) ARDSLEY, 5 carucates and 3 bovates; Ilbert, in BEESTON, 6 carucates.

2   Ilbert, in ROTHWELL, CARLTON, LOFTHOUSE, THORPE (on the Hill) and MIDDLETON, 24 carucates.

3   Ilbert, in HUNSLET, 6 carucates; Ilbert, in REESTONES and ARMLEY, 6 carucates; Ilbert, in BRAMLEY, 4 carucates.

4   Ilbert, in CALVERLEY and FARSLEY, 3 carucates; Ilbert, in PUDSEY, 8 carucates; Ilbert, in TONG, 4 carucates.

5   Ilbert, in DRIGHLINGTON, 4 carucates; Ilbert, in GOMERSAL and its two outliers, 14 carucates.

6   Ilbert, in BOLTON, 4 carucates; Ilbert, in BRADFORD and its six outliers, 15 carucates; Ilbert, in BOWLING, 4 carucates.

7   Ilbert, in CHELLOW (Grange), THORNTON, ALLERTON, CLAYTON and WIBSEY, 10 carucates.

8   Ilbert, in SHIPLEY, 3 carucates; Ilbert, in (North) BIERLEY, 4 carucates; Ilbert, in WYKE, 4 carucates; Ilbert, in (Cleck)HEATON, 6 carucates.

In Cliftone . XII.c. In Mirefeld. VI.c. In Deuſberie. III.c. In Bathelie. V.c.

In Liureſech . IIII.c. In Horteſheue. II.c. In Elont. III.c. In Oure. III.c.

In Huperun. II.c. In Vfrun. II.c. In Scelf . I.car. In Stanland. II.c.

In Linlei.dim car. In Fecheſbi. I.car. In Raſtric. I.c. In Egleſhil. III.c.

In Fernelei. III.c. In Erdeſlau. IIII.c 7 v.bõ. In Greland. dim car.

In Etun. I.car. H̃ om̃a de Soca Wachefeld.

ANNESTI WAPENTAC.

In Badetorpes.v.car 7 VII.bõ.Ibid.II.car 7 I.bõ. In Torp.xpicerce.II.c.

In Copeman Torp. II . car 7 II.bõ. Ibid. III . car 7 VI. bõ 7 Ibid.I.car.

In Acaſtre. IIII.c. In alio Acaſtre.VI.bõ.Ibid.I.c 7 II.bõ.Ibid. v.bõ.

Ibid. XI. bõ. In Apleton.XII.c. In Badetone. VIII.c. In Stiueton. VI.c.

Ibid. I.car. In Torp . II . c.Ibid.II.bõ.Ibid. VI.bõ.In Oſitone.IIII.c.

In Coletone. IIII . c 7 dim. In Viſitone.III.c.In Malchetone. IIII . c.

In Hagendebi 7 Hailaga. III.c.In Hornitone.III.car.Ibid.I.bõ.

9 Ilbert, in CLIFTON, 12 carucates; Ilbert, in MIRFIELD, 6 carucates. The King, in DEWSBURY, 3 carucates. Ilbert, in BATLEY, 5 carucates.

10 Ilbert, in LIVERSEDGE, 4 carucates; Ilbert, in HARTSHEAD, 2 carucates; Ilbert, in ELLAND, 3 carucates; Ilbert, in (South)OWRAM, 3 carucates.

11 The King, in HIPPERHOLME, 2 carucates. In (North)OWRAM, 2 carucates. In SHELF, 1 carucate. In STAINLAND, 2 carucates.

12 In (Old) LINDLEY, ½ carucate. In FIXBY, 1 carucate. In RASTRICK, 1 carucate. In ECCLESHILL, 3 carucates.

13 In FARNLEY, 3 carucates. In (West) ARDSLEY, 4 carucates and 5 bovates. In GREETLAND, ½ carucate.

14 In (Hanging) HEATON, 1 carucate. All these of WAKEFIELD's jurisdiction.

AINSTY Wapentake

1 Hugh son of Baldric, in (Bishop)THORPE, 5 carucates and 7 bovates. The King, in the same place, 2 carucates and 1 bovate. Richard son of Arnfastr, in (Middle)THORPE Christ Church, 2 carucates. Robert Malet, in the same place, 1 carucate.

2 Erneis, in COPMANTHORPE, 2 carucates and 2 bovates. Count W., in the same place, 3 carucates and 6 bovates.

3 Robert Malet, in ACASTER (Malbis), 4 carucates. Count Alan, in another ACASTER (Selby), 6 bovates. Robert Malet, in the same place, 1 carucate and 2 bovates. Erneis, in the same place, 5 bovates.

4 The King, in the same place, 11 bovates. Osbern de Arches, in APPLETON (Roebuck), 12 carucates. William of Percy, in BOLTON Percy), 8 carucates. Osbern de Arches, in STEETON (Hall), 6 carucates.

5 Earnwine, in the same place, 1 carucate. William of Percy, in (Palla)THORPE, 2 carucates. Osbern de Arches, in the same place, 2 bovates. The Count of Mortain, in the same place, 6 bovates. Osbern de Arches, in OXTON, 4 carucates.

6 Osbern de Arches, in COLTON, 4½ carucates. William of Percy, in OUSTON (Farm), 3 carucates; William of Percy, in 'MALKTON', 4 carucates.

7 William of Percy, in 'HAGGENBY' and HEALAUGH, 3 carucates; William of Percy, in HORNINGTON (Manor), 3 carucates. Osbern de Arches, in the same place, 1 bovate.

In Cadretone . ii . c . In Mileburg xpicerce . viii . c . In Torp . iii . car.

In Hailaga 7 duab3 Wicheles . xviii . c . In Walitone . ix . car.

In Biletone . ix . c . In Merſtone 7 Wiulestorp . xxiii . car.

In Wandeslage . vi . c . In Aſchā . vi . c . In Popletone . ii . car 7 dim.

In alia popletone . viii . c . Ibid . iii . car 7 dim . In Scachertorp . iii . c

In Monechetone xpi cerce . ix . car . In Eſdeſai . ii . car 7 ii . bō.

Ibid . i . car 7 vi . bō . In Cnapetone xpicerce . iii . c . Ibid . ii . car.

In Acun . xiiii . c 7 dim . Ibid . ii . car . In Ruford . iiii . car.

In xpicerce iuxta urbē . dim car 7 iii . crofte . In Mulhede . i . c.

In Bithen . i . bō . In Coletorp . iiii . c . In Bichretone . viii . car.

In Aſchā . viii . c . Juxta ciuitatē . xv . car træ . 7 lx . ac p̄ti.

I*BARGESCIRE WAPENTAC.*

n Monuchetone . viii . car . In Tuadestorp . i . c . In Torp . vii . c

Ibid . i . car . In Widetone . i . car . In Chirchebi . vi . c.

In Vſeburne . xii . c . In alia Vſeburne . viii . c . In dunesford . iii . c

8 Osbern de Arches, in CATTERTON, 2 carucates. Richard son of Arnfastr, in BILBROUGH Christ Church, 8 carucates. Osbern de Arches, in THORP (Arch), 3 carucates.

9 Geoffrey Alselin, in HEALAUGH and the two WIGHILLS (WIGHILL and WIGHILL Park), 18 carucates. Osbern de Arches, in WALTON, 9 carucates.

10 Osbern de Arches, in BILTON, 9 carucates; Osbern de Arches, in (Long) MARSTON and WILSTROP (Hall), 23 carucates.

11 Osbern de Arches, in (Hutton) WANDESLEY, 6 carucates; Osbern de Arches, in ASKHAM (Richard), 6 carucates; Osbern de Arches, in (Upper) POPPLETON, 2½ carucates.

12 The Archbishop, in another (Nether) POPPLETON, 8 carucates. Osbern de Arches, in the same place, 3½ carucates; Osbern de Arches, in SCAGGLETHORPE, 3 carucates.

13 Richard son of Arnfastr, in (Moor) MONKTON Christ Church, 9 carucates. Osbern de Arches, in HESSAY, 2 carucates and 2 bovates.

14 There also Richard son of Arnfastr, in the same place, 1 carucate and 6 bovates; Richard son of Arnfastr, in KNAPTON Christ Church, 3 carucates. Osbern de Arches, in the same place, 2 carucates.

15 The Archbishop, in ACOMB, 14½ carucates. The King, in the same place, 2 carucates. Osbern de Arches, in RUFFORTH, 4 carucates.

16 Richard son of Arnfastr, in Christ Church near the city, ½ carucate and 3 crofts. The King, in MULHEDE, 1 carucate.

17 In BITHEN, 1 bovate. William of Percy, in COWTHORPE, 4 carucates. Gospatric, in BICKERTON, 8 carucates.

18 Count Alan, in ASKHAM (Bryan), 8 carucates. The Archbishop, near the city, 15 carucates of land and 60 acres of meadow.

'BURGHSHIRE' (CLARO) Wapentake

1 Osbern de Arches, in (Nun) MONKTON, 8 carucates. Ralph Paynel, in THORPE (Underwood), 1 carucate. Hugh son of Baldric, in THORPE (Hill), 7 carucates.

2 Gospatric, in the same place, 1 carucate. The King, in WIDDINGTON (Hall), 1 carucate. Osbern de Arches, in KIRBY (Hall), 6 carucates.

3 The King, in (Great) OUSEBURN, 12 carucates; the King, in another (Little) OUSEBURN, 8 carucates. Erneis, in (Upper and Lower) DUNSFORTH, 3 carucates.

Ibid̃ . iii . c̃ . [Rex ⁊] In Brantun . iiii . c̃ . [Erneis ⁊] Ibid̃ . v . c̃ . [Rex. ⁊] In Martone . xii . car . [Gofpatric ⁊]

In Graftone . iii . c̃ . [Arch ⁊] Ibid̃ . iii . c̃ . [Erneis ⁊] Ibid̃ . vi . c̃ . [Rex. ⁊] In Torneburne . iii . car . [Gofpatric. ⁊]

380 a

In Cucheslage . xiii . car . [O. arcis ⁊] Ibid̃ . v . c̃ . [Gofpat' ⁊] In Eleuuic . iiii . c̃ . [Rex ⁊] In Catala . v . c̃ . [O. arcis t ⁊]

In Ambretone . vi . c̃ . [O. arcis ⁊] In alia Ambretone . viii . c̃ . [O. arcis ⁊] In alia Catala . iii . c̃ . [Erneis ⁊]

In Hulfingoure . iiii . c̃ ⁊ iii . bõ . [co. Morit' ⁊] Ibid̃ . v . c̃ ⁊ iii . bõ . [Erneis ⁊] In Godesburg . viii . c̃ . [Ra . Pagenel ⁊]

In Ripeftam . iiii . c̃ . [Ra . Pag' ⁊] Ibid̃ . i . c̃ ⁊ dim . [Rex ⁊] Ibid̃ . i . car̃ . [Erneis ⁊] Ibid̃ . i . car̃ ⁊ dim . [W. pei ⁊]

In Homptone . iii . c̃ . [Rex ⁊] Ibid̃ . i . c̃ . [Erneis ⁊] Ibid̃ . i . c̃ . [O. arcis ⁊] In Alureton . iii . c̃ ⁊ dim . [Rex ⁊]

Ibid̃ . i . car̃ ⁊ dim . [Gofpat' ⁊ ⁊] In Flatesbi . iiii . c̃ . [Erneis ⁊] In Clareton . ii . car̃ . [Rex ⁊]

Ibid̃ . iii . c̃ . [Gofp' ⁊] In Archedene . i . c̃ . [Rex ⁊] Ibid̃ . iiii . c̃ . [Erneis ⁊] In Locthufun . iiii . c̃ . [⁊]

Ibid̃ . i . car̃ . [Erneis ⁊] In Burg . xx . car̃ . [Rex ⁊] In Minefcip . viii . c̃ . [Rex ⁊]

In Stanlei . viii . c̃ . [Gofpat' ⁊] In Hilton . vi . c̃ . [Rex ⁊] In Copegraue . vi . car . [Erneis ⁊]

In Burton . vi . c̃ . [Rex ⁊] In Farnehā . iii . c̃ . [Rex ⁊] Ibid̃ . iii . c̃ . [Gofp' ⁊] In Torp . ii . c̃ [Rex ⁊]

In Walchingehā . iii . c̃ . [Rex ⁊] In Ferefbi . vi . c̃ . [Rex ⁊] In Scrauinge . vi . c̃ [Rex ⁊]

In Chenarefburg . vi . c̃ . [Rex ⁊] In Scotone . iiii . c̃ . [G. tifon ⁊] In Scotone . ii . c̃ . [Rex ⁊]

4   The King, in the same place, 3 carucates. Erneis, in BRANTON (Green), 4 carucates. The King, in the same place, 5 carucates. Gospatric, in MARTON, 12 carucates.

5   The Archbishop, in GRAFTON, 3 carucates. Erneis, in the same place, 3 carucates. The King, in the same place, 6 carucates. Gospatric, in THORNBOROUGH, 3 carucates.

6   Osbern de Arches, in WHIXLEY, 13 carucates. Gospatric, in the same place, 5 carucates. The King, in ELWICKS, 4 carucates. Osbern de Arches, in CATTAL, 5 carucates.   380 a

7   Osbern de Arches, in (Kirk) HAMMERTON, 6 carucates; Osbern de Arches, in another (Green) HAMMERTON, 8 carucates. Erneis, in another '(Little) CATTAL' (OLD THORNVILLE HALL), 3 carucates.

8   The Count of Mortain, in HUNSINGORE, 4 carucates and 3 bovates. Erneis, in the same place, 5 carucates and 3 bovates. Ralph Paynel, in GOLDSBOROUGH, 8 carucates.

9   Ralph Paynel, in (Great and Little) RIBSTON, 4 carucates. The King, in the same place, 1½ carucates. Erneis, in the same place, 1 carucate. William of Percy, in the same place, 1½ carucates.

10   The King, in HOPPERTON, 3 carucates. Erneis, in the same place, 1 carucate. Osbern de Arches, in the same place, 1 carucate. The King, in ALLERTON (Mauleverer), 3½ carucates.

11   Gospatric, in the same place, 1½ carucates. Erneis, in FLAXBY, 4 carucates. The King, in CLARETON, 2 carucates.

12   Gospatric, in the same place, 3 carucates. The King, in ARKENDALE, 1 carucate. Erneis, in the same place, 4 carucates. The King, in LOFTUS (Hill), 4 carucates.

13   Erneis, in the same place, 1 carucate. The King, in ALDBOROUGH, 20 carucates; the King, in MINSKIP, 8 carucates.

14   Gospatric, in STAVELEY, 8 carucates. The King, in 'HILTON', 6 carucates. Erneis, in COPGROVE, 6 carucates.

15   The King, in BURTON (Leonard), 6 carucates; the King, in FARNHAM, 3 carucates. Gospatric, in the same place, 3 carucates. The King, in (*Scotton*) THORPE, 2 carucates.

16   The King, in WALKINGHAM (Hill), 3 carucates; the King, in FERRENSBY, 6 carucates; the King, in SCRIVEN, 6 carucates.

17   The King, in KNARESBOROUGH, 6 carucates. Gilbert Tison, in SCOTTON, 4 carucates. The King, in SCOTTON, 2 carucates.

In Baretone . vi . c̃ . In Sofacre . ii . c̃ . In Stanlei . iiii . car̃.

★ In Cheitone . ii . c̃ . In Merchefeld . v . c̃ . In Afmundrebi . ii . c̃.

In Aldefeld ii . c̃ . Ibid . dim car . Ibid . ii . bõ . In Cludun . i . c̃ 7 dim .

In Stollei . ii . c̃ 7 dim . Ibid . vii . bõ . Ibid . xiii . bõ.

In Wichingeflei . iii . car . In Lauretone . ii . c̃ 7 dim . Ibid . iii . c̃ 7 dim .

In Chirchebi . v . car . In Torp . v . c̃ . In Torp . ii . c̃ . In Aferle . v . c̃ 7 dim .

Ibid . dim car . In Bramelie . ii . c̃ . In Calefmor . ii . c̃ . In Sualun . ii . c̃

In Chetesmor . ii . c̃ . In popletone . i . c̃ . Ibid . iii . c̃ . In Wipelie . dim c̃.

In Birnebehã . iii . c̃ 7 ii . bõ . Ibid . ii . bõ . Ibid . dim c̃ . Ibid . i . c̃ 7 dim.

In Ripelie . iiii . c̃ 7 dim . Ibid . i . car 7 dim . In Higrefeld . ii . c̃.

In Beurelie . iii . c̃ . In Dacre . iii . car̃ . In Befthaim . iiii . car.

In Foftun . iii . c̃ . In Elefuuorde Cliftone 7 Timble . v . car 7 dim.

In Beriftade . i . c̃ . Ibid . i . c̃ . In Felgefclif . iii . c̃ . In Rodun . ii . car̃.

380 a

18 The King, in BREARTON, 6 carucates. Osbern de Arches, in SUSACRES, 2 carucates. The King, in (South) STAINLEY, 4 carucates.

19 The King, in CAYTON, 2 carucates. William of Percy, in MARKENFIELD (Hall), 5 carucates; William of Percy, in AISMUNDERBY, 2 carucates.

20 Gospatric, in ALDFIELD, 2 carucates. The King, in the same place, ½ carucate. The Archbishop, in the same place, 2 bovates. William of Percy, in CLOTHERHOLME, 1½ carucates.

21 Gospatric, in STUDLEY (Royal), 2½ carucates. The King, in the same place, 7 bovates. William of Percy, in the same place, 13 bovates.

22 Gospatric, in WINKSLEY, 3 carucates; the same Gospatric, in LAVERTON, 2½ carucates. The King, in the same place, 3½ carucates.

23 Gospatric, in KIRKBY (Malzeard), 5 carucates; the same Gospatric, in (Grewel)THORPE, 5 carucates; the same Gospatric, in (Grewel)-THORPE, 2 carucates; the same Gospatric, in AZERLEY, 5½ carucates.

24 The King, in the same place, ½ carucate. Gospatric, in BRAMLEY (Grange), 2 carucates; the same Gospatric, in CARLESMOOR, 2 carucates; the same Gospatric, in SWETTON, 2 carucates.

25 The same Gospatric, in KEX MOOR, 2 carucates. The King, in POPLETONE, 1 carucate. Gospatric, in the same place, 3 carucates. Erneis, in WHIPLEY (Hall), ½ carucate. The King, in the same place, 1½ carucates.

26 Gospatric, in BRIMHAM (Hall), 3 carucates and 2 bovates. Gilbert Tison, in the same place, 2 bovates. Erneis, in the same place, ½ carucate.

27 Ralph Paynel, in RIPLEY, 4½ carucates. The King, in the same place, 1½ carucates. Berenger of Tosny, in HEATHFIELD, 2 carucates.

28 Erneis, in BEWERLEY, 3 carucates; Erneis, in DACRE, 3 carucates. The King, in BESTHAIM, 4 carucates.

29 The King, in FEWSTON, 3 carucates; the King, in 'ELSWORTH', CLIFTON and TIMBLE, 5½ carucates.

30 The King, in BIRSTWITH, 1 carucate. Gospatric, in the same place, 1 carucate. The King, in FELLISCLIFFE, 3 carucates; the King, in ROWDEN, 2 carucates.

In Chenehalle [Rex] . I . c . In Bemeslai [Erneis] . dim c . Ibid [Rex] . VI . bo . Ibid [G.tison] . VI . bo.

★ In Nacefeld [W.pci] . III . c . In Ediha [Rex] . I . c . Ibid [G.tison] . I . c . In Afcuid [Gofpat'] . II . car.

Ibid [W.pci] . III . c . Ibid [B.todeni] . I . car . In Weſtone [B.todeni] . v . c . In Ledelai [W.pci] . III . c 7 VII . bo.

Ibid . II . car 7 dim . Ibid . I . c . In Widitun [Rex] . v . c 7 dim . Ibid [Goſp'] . II . c 7 dim.

In Cheſuic [Rex] . IIII . c . In Cherebi . IIII . c . In Berghebi [Erneis] . III . c . Ibid [W.pci] . I . car.

In Cherchebi [W.pci] . III . c . In Waltone 7 Todoure [W.pci] . IIII . c . In Sidingal [Rex] . VI . c.

In Arduluestorp [Gofpat'] . IIII . c . Ibid . I . car . In Riſton [Rex] . II . c . Ibid [G.tison] . II . car.

In Stainburne [Rex] . v . c . In Becui [G.tison] . III . c . In Roſert [Rex 7 G.tison] . III . c.

In Billeton [Rex] . III . c 7 dim . Ibid [G.tison] . III . c 7 dim . In Rofellinton [W.pci] . II . c 7 II . bo.

Ibid [G.tison] . I . car 7 VI . bo . In Plontone [W.pci] . II . c . Ibid [G.tison] . II . c . In Litelbra [Erneis] . IIII . car.

In Michelbra [W.pci] . IIII . c . Ibid [G.tison] . IIII . c . Ibid [Erneis] . I . c . In Spoford [W.pci] . III . car.

In Caldeuuelle [W.pci] . II . c . In Neuſone [Erneis] . II . c . In Lintone [W.pci] . VIII . c 7 dim.

31 The King, in KILLINGHALL, 1 carucate. Erneis, in BEAMSLEY, ½ carucate. The King, in the same place, 6 bovates. Gilbert Tison, in the same place, 6 bovates.

32 William of Percy, in NESFIELD, 2 carucates. The King, in ADDINGHAM, 1 carucate. Gilbert Tison, in the same place, 1 carucate. Gospatric, in ASKWITH, 2 carucates.

33 William of Percy, in the same place, 3 carucates. Berenger of Tosny, in the same place, 1 carucate; Berenger of Tosny, in WESTON, 5 carucates. William of Percy, in LEATHLEY, 3 carucates and 7 bovates.

34 The King, in the same place, 2½ carucates. Gilbert Tison, in the same place, 1 carucate. The King, in WEETON, 5½ carucates. Gospatric, in the same place, 2½ carucates.

35 The King, in (Dun)KESWICK, 4 carucates. William of Percy, in KEARBY (Town End), 4 carucates. Erneis, in BARROWBY (Grange), 3 carucates. William of Percy, in the same place, 1 carucate.

36 William of Percy, in KIRKBY (Overblow), 3 carucates; William of Percy, in WALTON (Head) and 'TIDOVER', 4 carucates. The King, in SICKLINGHALL, 6 carucates.

37 Gospatric, in ADDLETHORPE, 4 carucates. The King, in the same place, 1 carucate; the King, in RIGTON, 2 carucates. Gilbert Tison, in the same place, 2 carucates.

38 The King, in STAINBURN, 5 carucates. Gilbert Tison, in BECKWITH (House), 3 carucates. The King and Gilbert Tison, in ROSSETT (Green), 3 carucates.

39 The King, in BILTON, 3½ carucates. Gilbert Tison, in the same place, 3½ carucates. William of Percy, in RUDFARLINGTON, 2 carucates and 2 bovates.

40 Gilbert Tison, in the same place, 1 carucate and 6 bovates. William of Percy, in PLOMPTON (Hall), 2 carucates. Gilbert Tison, in the same place, 2 carucates. Erneis, in 'LITTLE' BRAHAM, 4 carucates.

41 William of Percy, in 'GREAT' BRAHAM, 4 carucates. Gilbert Tison, in the same place, 4 carucates. Erneis, in the same place, 1 carucate. William of Percy, in SPOFFORTH, 3 carucates.

42 William of Percy, in CALDEUUELLE, 2 carucates. Erneis, in NEWSOME (Farm), 2 carucates. William of Percy, in LINTON, 8½ carucates.

In Wedrebi . III . c . Ibid . II . c . In Distone . XII . car . Ibid . IIII . car.

In Germundftorp . I . c 7 dim . Ibid . I . c⁷ 7 dim . In Coletorp . III . car.

In RIPVN Leuu S Wilfridi . In Torp . IIII . c . In Estuuic . In Nith.

In Weftuuic . In Monuchetone . In Chilingale . In Torentone.

In Sallai . In Euestone . In Wiueshale In Chenaresford . In Stollai,

In Grentelai . In Erleshold . In Merchintone . In Stanlai 7 Sud

tunen . In Nordftanlai 7 Sclenneford.

In Neresford . dim car . In Castelai . II . car.

HALICHELDE WAPENTAC.

In Nonneuuic . v . car . In Suthauuic . In Gherindale.

In Scheltone . In Hogra . In Hadeuuic . In Hafhundebi .

In Hotone . In Merchinton 7 Stanlai . In Hauuic . H arch

In HOTONE . XII . car . In Norton . In Sudton . In Hogram.

In Hulme . In Torp . H eps dun ad Hoton

In Scheltone . I . car . In Torp . In Chirchebi . In Torenton . In Burton . H Gofp

In Adelingeftorp . vi . c . In Mildebi . vi . c 7 dim . In Brantone . IIII . c

43 William of Percy, in WETHERBY, 3 carucates. Erneis, in the same place, 2 carucates. Ralph Paynel, in (Kirk and North) DEIGHTON, 12 carucates. Erneis, in the same place, 4 carucates.

44 The Count of Mortain, in INGMANTHORPE (Hall), 1½ carucates. Erneis, in the same place, 1½ carucates. William of Percy, in COWTHORPE, 3 carucates.

45 The Archbishop, in RIPON, St. Wilfrid's Territory; the Archbishop, in (Little)THORPE, 4 carucates. In 'EASTWICK', 2 carucates. In NIDD, 5 carucates.

46 In WESTWICK, 4 carucates. In (Bishop) MONKTON, 8 carucates. In KILLINGHALL, 1 carucate. In (Bishop) THORNTON, 2 carucates.

47 In SAWLEY, 2 carucates. In EAVESTONE, 2 carucates. In WILSILL, 2 carucates. In 'KNARESFORD', 1½ carucates. In STUDLEY (Roger), 4 carucates.

48 In (High) GRANTLEY, 2½ carucates. In 'HERLESHOW' (HOW HILL), 3 carucates. In MARKINGTON, 4½ carucates. In ('East') STAINLEY and SUTTON (Grange), 8 carucates. In NORTH STAINLEY and SLENINGFORD, 6½ carucates.

49 In 'KNARESFORD', Gospatric, ½ carucate. Eburhard, a man of William Percy's, in CASTLEY, 2 carucates.

HALIKELD Wapentake   380 b
1 The Archbishop, in NUNWICK, 5 carucates. In *SUTHAUUIC*, 5 carucates. In GIVENDALE, 11 carucates.

2 In SKELTON, 8 carucates. In SUTTON (Howgrave), 2 carucates. In (Copt) HEWICK, 2 carucates. In *HASHUNDEBI*, 2 carucates.

3 In HUTTON (Conyers), 2 bovates. In MARKINGTON and (South) STAINLEY, 1 carucate. In (Bridge) HEWICK, 3 carucates. These (are) the Archbishop's.

4 The Bishop of Durham, in HUTTON (Conyers), 12 carucates. In NORTON (Conyers), 6 carucates. In SUTTON (Howgrave), 3 carucates. In HOWGRAVE, 2 carucates.

5 In HOLME, 6 carucates. In *TORP*, 1 carucate. These (are) the Bishop of Durham's at HUTTON (Conyers).

6 Gospatric, in SKELTON, 1 carucate. In (Lang)THORPE, 6 carucates. In KIRBY (Hill), 6 carucates. In THORNTON (Bridge), 6 carucates. In (Hum)BURTON, 6 carucates. These (are) Gospatric's.

7 The King, in ELLENTHORPE (Hall), 6 carucates; the King, in MILBY, 6½ carucates; the King, in BRAMPTON (Hall), 4 carucates.

In *CVNDEL* . $\overset{co.Mor'}{\text{XII}}$. c . In Nortone . In Ledebi . In Brantone.

In Goindel . In Stanlei . In Danefeld . In Caldeuuelle H̄ om̄a ad

CRAVESCIRE.

In *BODELTONE* . vi . car . In Haltone . In Embefie . In Dractone.

In Schibeden . In Scipton . In Snachehale In Torederebi.

In Odingehen . In Bedmeslei . In Holme . In Geregraue.

In Staintone . In Otreburne . In Scotorp . In Malgon . In Anlei .

In Coningefton . In hælgefeld . In hanelif . Ī om̄ia ad Bodeltone.

380 c

LANGEBERGE WAPENTAC.

In *FIGLINGE* . i . car træ . Ibid . i . car . In Nortfigelinge . v . c.

In Ghinipe . iii . c . In Witebi . x . car . In Prestebi . ii . car.

In Normanebi . ii . c . In Snetune . v . c . In Vlgeberdefbi . iii . c.

In Sourebi . iiii . c . In Breche . i . car . In Baldebi . i . c . In Flore . ii . c.

In Staxebi . ii . c 7 vi . bō . Ibid . ii . bō . In Neuhā . iiii . c . In Lid . ii . c.

8   The Count of Mortain, in CUNDALL, 12 carucates. In NORTON (le Clay), 7 carucates. In LECKBY (Palace), 6 carucates. In BRAMPTON (Hall), 2 carucates.

9   In CUNDALL, 2 carucates. In (North) STAINLEY, 1 carucate. In (East) TANFIELD, 1 carucate. In *CALDEUUELLE*, 4 carucates. All these belong to CUNDALL.

CRAVEN

1   In BOLTON (Abbey), 6 carucates. In HALTON (East), 6 carucates. In EMBSAY, 6 carucates. In DRAUGHTON, 3 carucates.

2   In SKIBEDEN, 3 carucates. In SKIPTON, 4 carucates. In (Low) SNAYGILL, 6 carucates. In THORLBY, 10 carucates.

3   In ADDINGHAM, 2 carucates. In BEAMSLEY, 2 carucates. In HOLME (House), 3 carucates. In GARGRAVE, 3 carucates.

4   In (Little) STAINTON, 3 carucates. In OTTERBURN, 3 carucates. In SCOSTHROP, 3 carucates. In MALHAM, 3 carucates. In ANLEY, 2 carucates.

5   In CONISTON (Cold), 3 carucates. In HELLIFIELD, 3 carucates. In HANLITH, 3 carucates. All these (belong) to BOLTON (Abbey).

[NORTH RIDING]

LANGBARGH Wapentake   380 c

1   William of Percy, in FYLING (Old Hall), 1 carucate of land. Earl Hugh, in the same place, 1 carucate; Earl Hugh, in FYLING (Thorpe), 5 carucates.

2   Earl Hugh, in GNIPE (Howe), 3 carucates; Earl Hugh, in WHITBY, 10 carucates; Earl Hugh, in 'PRESTBY', 2 carucates.

3   The King, in NORMANBY, 2 carucates. Earl Hugh, in SNEATON, 5 carucates; Earl Hugh, in UGGLEBARNBY, 3 carucates.

4   Earl Hugh, in 'SOWERBY', 4 carucates; Earl Hugh, in 'BRECK', 1 carucate; Earl Hugh, in *BALDEBI*, 1 carucate; Earl Hugh, in FLOWER(gate), 2 carucates.

5   Earl Hugh, in (High) STAKESBY, 2 carucates and 6 bovates. The Count of Mortain, in the same place, 2 bovates. Earl Hugh, in NEWHOLM, 4 carucates. The Count of Mortain, in LYTHE, 2 carucates.

In Dunefla .III. c . Ibiđ . I . car . In Hotone . III . c . In Egetune . III . c.

In Grif . VI . c . In Barnebi . IIII . c . In Goldeburg . II . c.

In Aluuardebi . VI . c . In Michelbi . IIII . c . In Neutone . III . c.

In Grimesbi . II . c . In Bergesbi . V . c . In Rozebi . III . c . Ibiđ . I . car.

In Vgetorp . IIII . c . In Rofcheltorp . I . c . In Afuluebi . III . car.

In Arnodeftorp . I . car 7 II . bõ . In Ildreuuelle . IIII . c 7 VI . bõ.

Ibiđ . I . car 7 II . bõ . In Scetune . III . c . In Boilebi . I . c . Ibiđ . II . c.

In Efingeton . VIII . c . In Liuretun . VI . c . In Loctehusū . IIII . c.

In alia Loctehusū . IIII . c . In Crūbeclif Lelun 7 Danebi . XII . c.

In Steintun . VII . bõ . Ibiđ . I . bõ . In Morehufun . III . c 7 dim . Ibiđ dim c .

In alia Morehusū . I . car . In Torp . I . car 7 dim . Ibiđ . II . c 7 dim.

In Chiltun . I . car . Ibiđ . III . car . In Brotune . XII . c . In Sceltun . XIII . c.

In Chigefburg Mideltune 7 Hotun . XXV . c . Ibiđ . I car.

Ibiđ . III . c 7 II . bõ . Ibiđ . VI . bõ . In Roudcliue . II . c.

6   The King, in DUNSLEY, 3 carucates. Berenger of Tosny, in the same place, 1 carucate. The Count of Mortain, in HUTTON (Mulgrave), 3 carucates; the Count of Mortain, in EGTON, 3 carucates.

7   The Count of Mortain, in (Mul)GRAVE (Castle), 6 carucates. The King, in (East and West) BARNBY, 4 carucates. The Count of Mortain, in GOLDSBOROUGH, 2 carucates.

8   The Count of Mortain, in ELLERBY, 6 carucates; the Count of Mortain, in MICKLEBY, 4 carucates; the Count of Mortain, in NEWTON (Mulgrave), 3 carucates.

9   The Count of Mortain, in GRIMESBI, 2 carucates; the Count of Mortain, in BORROWBY, 5 carucates; the Count of Mortain, in RO··BY, 3 carucates. The King, in the same place, 1 carucate.

10   The King, in UGTHORPE, 4 carucates. Earl Hugh, in 'ROSKELTHORPE', 1 carucate. The Count of Mortain, in AISLABY, 3 carucates.

11   William of Percy, in ARNODESTORP, 1 carucate and 2 bovates; William of Percy, in HINDERWELL, 4 carucates and 6 bovates.

12   Earl Hugh, in the same place, 1 carucate and 2 bovates. The Count of Mortain, in SEATON (Hall), 3 carucates. The King, in (Old) BOULBY, 1 carucate. Earl Hugh, in the same place, 2 carucates.

13   Earl Hugh, in EASINGTON, 8 carucates; Earl Hugh, in LIVERTON, 6 carucates; Earl Hugh, in (South) LOFTUS, 4 carucates.

14   The King, in another LOFTUS, 4 carucates. Hugh son of Baldric, in CRUNKLY (Gill), LEALHOLM and DANBY, 12 carucates.

15   The Count of Mortain, in 'STAINTON', 7 bovates. The King, in the same place, 1 bovate. The Count of Mortain, in MOORSHOLM, 3½ carucates. The King, in the same place, ½ carucate.

16   The Count of Mortain, in another (Little) MOORSHOLM, 1 carucate; the Count of Mortain, in (Kilton) THORPE, 1½ carucates; the King, in the same place, 2½ carucates.

17   The Count of Mortain, in KILTON, 1 carucate. The King, in the same place, 3 carucates. The Count of Mortain, in BROTTON, 12 carucates; the Count of Mortain, in SKELTON, 13 carucates.

18   The Count of Mortain, in GUISBOROUGH, 'MIDDLETON' and HUTTON (Lowcross), 25 carucates. The King, in the same place, 1 carucate.

19   Robert Malet, in the same place, 3 carucates and 2 bovates. Earl Hugh, in the same place, 6 bovates; Earl Hugh, in RAWCLIFF (Banks), 2 carucates.

In Tocstune. II . c̃ . In Tornetun . II . c̃ . In Vpelider . x . car̃.

In Merich . x . car̃ . Ibid . vIII . c̃ . Ibid . II . c̃ . In Weſtlid . III car̃.

Ibid . IIII . c̃ . Ibid . II . c̃ . Ibid . Ix . car̃ . In Wiltune . IIII . c̃ 7 dim.

Ibid . IIII . c̃ 7 dim . In Leſingebi . III . c̃ 7 vI . bõ . Ibid dim⁊ car̃.

In Lachenebi . I . c̃ 7 v . bõ . Ibid . II . car̃ . In Astun . Ix . car̃.

In Normanebi . vII . c̃ . Ibid . dim⁊ c̃ . Ibid dim⁊ car̃.

In Ormeſbi . xII . c̃ . In Vpeshale . IIII . c̃ . In Bernodebi . vI . car̃.

In Torp . III . c̃ . Ibid . III . c̃ . In Ergun . II . c̃ . In Atun . III . car̃.

Ibid . II . c̃ . Ibid . vI . c̃ . In Neuuetun . vI . c̃ . In Mortun . III . c̃.

In Torp . vI . c̃ . In Atun . II . c̃ . In alia Atun . II . c̃ . In Eſebi . II . car̃.

In Badresbi . II . c̃ . In Childaļe . vI . car̃.

In Martun . v . car̃ . Ibid . IIII . c̃ 7 dim . In Neuhã . II . c̃ 7 II bõ.

Ibid . vI . bõ . In Tolleſbi . vI . c̃ . Ibid . III . c̃ . In Aclun . III . car̃.

20   The Count of Mortain, in TOCKETTS (Farm), 2 carucates. The King, in THORNTON (Fields), 2 carucates. Earl Hugh, in UPLEATHAM, 10 carucates.

21   The Count of Mortain, in MARSKE (by the Sea), 10 carucates. William of Percy, in the same place, 8 carucates. Earl Hugh, in the same place, 2 carucates. The King, in *WESTLID* (KIRKLEATHAM), 3 carucates.

22   William of Percy, in the same place, 4 carucates. Earl Hugh, in the same place, 2 carucates. The Count of Mortain, in the same place, 9 carucates. The King, in WILTON, 4½ carucates.

23   The Count of Mortain, in the same place, 4½ carucates. The King, in LAZENBY, 3 carucates and 6 bovates. Earl Hugh, in the same place, ½ carucate.

24   Earl Hugh, in LACKENBY, 1 carucate and 5 bovates. The Count of Mortain, in the same place, 2 carucates; the Count of Mortain, in ESTON, 9 carucates.

25   The Count of Mortain, in NORMANBY, 7 carucates. Robert Malet, in the same place, ½ carucate. William of Percy, in the same place, ½ carucate.

26   The King, in ORMESBY, 12 carucates; the King, in UPSALL (Hall), 4 carucates. The Count of Mortain, in BARNABY, 6 carucates.

27   Robert Malet, in (Pinchin)THORPE (Hall), 3 carucates. The King, in the same place, 3 carucates; the King, in AIRY (Holme), 2 carucates. Robert Malet, in (Little) AYTON, 3 carucates.

28   The King, in the same place, 2 carucates. The Count of Mortain, in the same place, 6 carucates. The King, in NEWTON, 6 carucates; the King, in MORTON (Grange), 3 carucates.

29   The King, in (Nun)THORPE, 6 carucates. Robert Malet, in (Little) AYTON, 2 carucates. The King, in another (Great) AYTON, 2 carucates; the King, in EASBY, 2 carucates.

30   The King, in BATTERSBY, 2 carucates; the King, in KILDALE, 6 carucates.

31   Robert Malet, in MARTON (in Cleveland), 5 carucates. The King, in the same place, 4½ carucates; the King, in NEWHAM (Hall), 2 carucates and 2 bovates.

32   Robert Malet, in the same place, 6 bovates. The King, in TOLLESBY, 6 carucates. Robert Malet, in the same place, 3 carucates. The King, in ACKLAM, 3 carucates.

Ibid. viii . c. Ibid. i . c. In Colebi . i . c. In Himelintun . iii . car.

In Steintun . ii . c. Ibid . ii . car. In Torentun . iii . c. Ibid . i . car.

In Maltebi . iii . c. In Englebi . vi . c. In Bereuuic . iii . car.

In Turmozbi . i . c 7 dim. Ibid . i . car 7 dim. Ibid . iii . car.

In Steinesbi . iii . c. In Toneſtale . iii . c. In Tametun . iiii . car.

Ibid . ii . c. In Semer . xi . c. In Berguluesbi . i . c. In Hiltun . vi . c.

In Mideltun . viii . c. In Foſtun . iii . c. In Turoldeſbi . iii . car.

In Stocheslag . vi . c. In Englebi . vii . c. In Camiſedale . v . car.

Ibid . iii . car. Ibid . i . c. In Broſtun . viii . c. In alia Broctun . v . c.

Ibid . iiii . c. In Cherchebi . iii . c. In Dragmalebi . iii . c In Hotun . vi . c.

In . ii . Buſchebi . ix . c 7 dim. Ibid . dim c. In Carletun . viii . c.

In Feizbi . viii . c. In Blatun 7 Wirueltun . xvi . car 7 iii . bō.

Ibid . vi . c. In Rontun . viii . car.

DIC WAPENTAC

In Waleſgrif . x . car. In Norfel . v . c. In Aſgozbi . iiii . c.

33 Earl Hugh, in the same place, 8 carucates. Robert Malet, in the same place, 1 carucate. Earl Hugh, in COULBY, 1 carucate; Earl Hugh, in HEMLINGTON, 3 carucates.

34 Earl Hugh, in STAINTON, 2 carucates. Robert Malet, in the same place, 2 carucates. Earl Hugh, in THORNTON, 3 carucates. Robert Malet, in the same place, 1 carucate.

35 Earl Hugh, in MALTBY, 3 carucates; Earl Hugh, in INGLEBY (Hill), 6 carucates; Earl Hugh, in BARWICK, 3 carucates.

36 The King, in THORNABY, 1½ carucates. Robert Malet, in the same place, 1½ carucates. Earl Hugh, in the same place, 3 carucates.

37 Earl Hugh, in STAINSBY (Hall), 3 carucates. The King, in TUNSTALL (Farm), 3 carucates; the King, in TANTON, 4 carucates.

38 The Count of Mortain, in the same place, 2 carucates; the Count of Mortain, in SEAMER, 11 carucates. The King, in *BERGULUESEBI*, 1 carucate. The Count of Mortain, in HILTON, 6 carucates.

39 The Count of Mortain, in MIDDLETON (upon Leven), 8 carucates; the Count of Mortain, in FOXTON, 3 carucates. The King, in THORALDBY (Farm), 3 carucates.

40 The King, in STOKESLEY, 6 carucates; the King, in INGLEBY (Greenhow), 7 carucates; the King, in *CAMISEDALE*, 5 carucates.

41 The Count of Mortain, in the same place, 3 carucates. Hugh son of Baldric, in the same place, 1 carucate. The King, in (Little) BROUGHTON, 8 carucates. The Count of Mortain, in another (Great) BROUGHTON, 5 carucates.

42 The King, in the same place, 4 carucates; the King, in KIRKBY, 3 carucates; the King, in DROMONBY (Hall), 3 carucates. The Count of Mortain, in HUTTON (Rudby), 6 carucates.

43 The King, in the two BUSBYS (Great BUSBY and Little BUSBY), 9½ carucates. Robert Malet, in the same place, ½ carucate. The Count of Mortain, in CARLTON, 8 carucates.

44 The King, in FACEBY, 8 carucates. The Count of Mortain, in *BLATEN (Carr)*, GOULTON (Grange), WHORLTON and CRATHORNE, 16 carucates and 3 bovates.

45 The King, in the same place, 6 carucates; the King, in (East) ROUNTON, 8 carucates.

DIC (PICKERING LYTHE) Wapentake
1 The King, in FALSGRAVE, 10 carucates; the King, in NORTHFIELD (Farm), 5 carucates; the King, in OSGODBY, 4 carucates.

In Torneslag. Steintun. Brinitun 7 Scalebi.^{Rex} xiiii. car.

In Cloctune.iiii.c. Ibid^{or}.i.c.$^{W.pci.}$ Ibid.ii.bõ.$^{co.Mor'}$ In Stemainesbi.ii.c 7 dim.$^{co.Mor}$

★ In Ledbeztun. Scagestorp.$^{Grisetorp.}$ Roudelueftorp$^{Etestorp.}$ 7 Fuielac ✓ xviii.c.^{Rex}

380 d

In Chiluertesbi.ii.c.$^{W.pci.}$ In Caitun.iiii.c.^{Rex} In Bortun 7 Depedale.xii.c.^{Rex}

In Semer.vi.c.$^{W.pci}$ In Torp 7 Iretune.iiii.c 7 dim.$^{W.pci}$ In Ildegrip.i.car.$^{W.pci.}$

In Atun.vi.c.$^{W.pci}$ Ibid.ii.car.$^{B.todeni.}$ In alia Atune 7 Neuuetone 7 Presteton.xxii.c.$^{7 Hotun.}$ ^{Rex}

In Martun Wichã 7 Roftun.x.c.^{Rex} In Sudfeld 7 Eurelag.vi.car.$^{W.pci}$

In Hageneise.iiii.car.$^{W.pci}$

In Bruntun.ix.car.^{Rex} Ibid·vi.c.$^{B.todeni}$ In Neuton.i.c.$^{B.tod}$ In paruo Merfc.ii.c.$^{B.tod.}$

In Picheringe Bartun Blandebi Neuton 7 Eftorp.xxxvii.car.$^{Rex.}$

In Ouduluefmerfc Alueftun Edbriztun Farmanefbi. Chinetorp.

Afchelefmerfc Wiltune Rozebi Chiluefmerfc Maxudefmerfc.xxxvii.c.$^{Rex\ 7\ vi.bõ}$

In Snechintun.v.c.$^{B.tod}$ Ibid.iii.c 7 dim.^{Rex} Ibid.i.c 7 dim.$^{W.pci.}$ In Truzftal.ii.c.$^{Rex.}$

In Alureftain.iii.c.^{Rex} In Loctemerfc.i.c 7 dim.$^{co.Mor.}$ Ibid.i.car 7 dim.$^{Rex.}$

In Chigomerfc.i.c 7 ii.bõ.$^{co.Mor'.}$ Ibid.i.car 7 ii.bõ.$^{Rex.}$ In Torentun.v.c 7 dim.^{Rex}

2   The King, in THIRLEY (Cotes), STAINTON(dale), BURNISTON and SCALBY, 14 carucates.

3   The King, in CLOUGHTON, 4 carucates. William of Percy, in the same place, 1 carucate. The Count of Mortain, in the same place, 2 bovates; the Count of Mortain, in STEMAINESBI, 2½ carucates.

4   The King, in LEBBERSTON, 'SCAWTHORPE', GRISTHORPE, ROUDELUESTORP, ETERSTORP and FILEY, 18 carucates.

5   William of Percy, in KILLERBY (Hall), 2 carucates. The King, in CAYTON, 4 carucates; the King, in 'BURTON (Dale)' and (High, Middle and Low) DEEPDALE, 12 carucates.   380 d

6   William of Percy, in SEAMER, 6 carucates; William of Percy, in 'THORPE(field)' and IRTON, 4½ carucates; William of Percy, in HILLGRIPS, 1 carucate.

7   William of Percy, in (East) AYTON, 6 carucates. Berenger of Tosny, in the same place, 2 carucates. The King, in another (West)AYTON, 'NEWTON', PRESTON (Hill) and HUTTON (Buscel), 22 carucates.

8   The King, in MARTIN (Garth), WYKEHAM and RUSTON, 10 carucates. William of Percy, in SUFFIELD and EVERLEY, 6 carucates.

9   William of Percy, in HACKNESS, 4 carucates.

10 The King, in BROMPTON, 9 carucates. Berenger of Tosny, in the same place, 6 carucates; Berenger of Tosny, in NEWTON, 1 carucate; Berenger of Tosny, in 'LITTLE MARISH', 2 carucates.

11 The King, in PICKERING, BARTON (le Street), (High) BLANDSBY, NEWTON and EASTHORPE (House), 37 carucates.

12 The King, in OUDULUESMERSC, ALLERSTON, EBBERSTON, FARMANBY, KINGTHORPE (House), ASCHELESMERSC, WILTON, ROXBY (Hill), CHILUESMERSC and MAXUDESMERSC, 37 carucates and 6 bovates.

13 Berenger of Tosny, in SNAINTON, 5 carucates. The King, in the same place, 3½ carucates. William of Percy, in the same place, 1½ carucates. The King, in TROUTSDALE, 2 carucates.

14 The King, in ALLERSTON, 3 carucates. The Count of Mortain, in LOFT MARISHES, 1½ carucates. The King, in the same place, 1½ carucates.

15 The Count of Mortain, in CHIGOMERSC, 1 carucate and 2 bovates. The King, in the same place, 1 carucate and 2 bovates; the King, in THORNTON (Dale), 5½ carucates.

Ibiđ . ı . car . In Liedtorp . ııı . c̃ 7 dim . In Elrebrune . ı . c̃ . In Dalbi . ıı . c̃.

In Chetelestorp . ı . c̃ 7 dim . Ibiđ . ı . car . In Lochetun . v . car.

In Leuuecen . ıı . c̃ 7 vı . bõ . In Mideltun . v . c̃ . In Aslachebi . ıııı . car.

In Wereltun . ı . c̃ 7 dim . In Bartun . dim c̃ . In Caltorn . ı . car.

In Croptun . v . c̃ . In Lestinghã . ıı . c̃ . Ibiđ . ı . c̃ . In Baschesbi . ı . c̃.

In Apeltun . ıı . c̃ . In Siuenintun . ııı . c̃ . In Martun . v . car.

I MANESHOV WAPENTAC.

In Tornentun . ıııı . car . In Cherchebi 7 alia Cherchebi . vıı . car.

In Abetune . vı . c̃ 7 dim . Ibiđ . dim̉ car . In Salescale . vı . bõ.

In Ritun . ıı . c̃ 7 dim . In Neuhuse 7 Andebi . ııı . c̃ 7 vı . bõ . In Wich . ı . c̃.

In Andebi . ıı . c̃ 7 dim . Ibiđ . ı . c̃ 7 dim . In alia Wich . ıı . car.

Ibiđ . dim car . Ibiđ . vı . bõ . In Maltun . ı . c̃ . Ibiđ . xı . c̃ 7 dim.

Ibiđ . ı car̉ 7 dim . In Broctun . vııı . c̃ 7 ıı . bõ . Ibiđ . ı . car.

In Suintun . xı . c̃ . In Apletun . v . c̃ . In Saletun . ıx . c̃ . I.

16 Berenger of Tosny, in the same place, 1 carucate; Berenger of Tosny, in *LIEDTORP*, 3½ carucates. The King, in ELLERBURN, 1 carucate; the King, in (Low) DALBY, 2 carucates.

17 The King, in 'KETTLETHORPE', 1½ carucates. The Count of Mortain, in the same place, 1 carucate. The King, in LOCKTON, 5 carucates.

18 The King, in LEVISHAM, 2 carucates and 6 bovates; the King, in MIDDLETON, 5 carucates; the King, in AISLABY, 4 carucates.

19 The King, in WRELTON, 1½ carucates; the King, in BARTON (le Street), ½ carucate; the King, in CAWTHORN, 1 carucate.

20 The King, in CROPTON, 5 carucates. The Abbot, in LASTINGHAM, 2 carucates. Berenger of Tosny, in the same place, 1 carucate. The King, in *BASCHESBI*, 1 carucate.

21 The Abbot, in APPLETON (le Moors), 2 carucates. Berenger of Tosny, in SINNINGTON, 3 carucates; Berenger of Tosny, in MARTON, 5 carucates.

MANSHOWE (RYEDALE) Wapentake

1 The King, in THORNTON (Riseborough), 4 carucates. Berenger of Tosny and the Abbot from him, in KIRBY (Misperton) and another KIRBY (Misperton), 7 carucates.

2 The King, in (Great and Little) HABTON, 6½ carucates. The Count of Mortain, in the same place, ½ carucate. The King, in *SALESCALE*, 6 bovates.

3 The King, in RYTON, 2½ carucates; the King, in NEWSHAM and AMOTHERBY, 3 carucates and 6 bovates; the King, in WYKEHAM, 1 carucate.

4 The King, in AMOTHERBY, 2½ carucates. The Count of Mortain, in the same place, 1½ carucates. The King, in another WYKEHAM (Hill), 2 carucates.

5 The Archbishop, in the same place, ½ carucate. Ralph Paynel, in the same place, 6 bovates. The Archbishop, in (Old) MALTON, 1 carucate. The King, in the same place, 11½ carucates.

6 The Count of Mortain, in the same place, 1½ carucates. The King, in BROUGHTON, 8 carucates and 2 bovates. Berenger of Tosny, in, the same place, 1 carucate.

7 The King, in SWINTON, 11 carucates; the King, in APPLETON (le Street), 5 carucates. The Archbishop, in SALTON, 9 carucates.

In Bragebi . vi . c̄ . In Berg . iii . c̄ . Ibid . ii . c̄ . In alia Berg . dim car.
^{Arch̄} ^{Arch̄} ^{Rex} ^{Arch̄}

Ibid . i . car 7 dim . In Micheledestun . viii . c̄ . In alia Edestun . iii . c̄ .
^{Rex} ^{B. tod.} ^{B. tod.}

In Holm . i . c̄ 7 dim . Ibid . i . car 7 dim . In Siuerintune . ii . car̄ .
^{Rex} ^{B. tod.} ^{B. todeni}

In Nageltune . iiii . c̄ . Ibid . ii . car .
^{Arch̄} ^{B. tod}

In Wellebrune . i . car . Ibid . i . car . In Winbeltun . i . car .
^{B. tod.} ^{Rex} ^{Arch̄}

In Waleton . i . bo . In Spantune . vi . c̄ 7 dim . Ibid . i . car̄ .
^{B. tod.} ^{B. tod. 7 abb de eo} ^{Rex 7 ab de eo.}

In Apeltun . ii . c̄ . In Normanebi . iii . c̄ . Ibid . iii . c̄ . In Bartun . viii . c̄ .
^{Abb de rege} ^{Rex} ^{Abb de rege} ^{co . Mor̄.}

In Osuualdescherce . i . c̄ . Ibid . i . car . In Neutun . iiii . c̄ . Ibid . ii . c̄ .
^{B. tod.} ^{co . Mor̄.} ^{Arch̄} ^{Rex}

In Gellinge . iiii . c̄ . In Neutune . ii . c̄ . In Sprostune . v . car .
^{Ra . Mortem̄.} ^{Rex} ^{Rex}

In Fademore . v . c̄ . In Scaltun . iiii . c̄ . In Grif . ii . c̄ . Ibid . ii . car .
^{co . Mor̄.} ^{Ro . Mal.} ^{co . Mor̄.} ^{Rex}

In Tilstune . i . c̄ . Ibid . iii . c̄ . In Elmeslac . iii . c̄ 7 dim . Ibid . vii . c̄ .
^{Rex} ^{co . Mor̄.} ^{Rex} ^{co . Mor̄.}

In Pochelac . i . c̄ . Ibid . i . car . In Bodlun . iiii . c̄ . In Harun . v . car .
^{Arch̄} ^{co . Morit̄.} ^{co . Morit̄.} ^{co . Morit̄.}

Ibid . i . car 7 dim . Ibid . ii . bo . In Ricalf . ii . c̄ . In Nonnintune . vi . c̄ .
^{Rex} ^{B. tod.} ^{Rex.} ^{Ra . Paḡ.}

8   The Archbishop, in BRAWBY, 6 carucates; the Archbishop, in (Great) BARUGH, 3 carucates. The King, in the same place, 2 carucates. The Archbishop, in another (Little) BARUGH, ½ carucate.

9   The King, in the same place, 1½ carucates. Berenger of Tosny, in GREAT EDSTONE, 8 carucates; Berenger of Tosny, in another (Little) EDSTONE, 3 carucates.

10   The King, in (North) HOLME (House), 1½ carucates. Berenger of Tosny, in the same place, 1½ carucates; Berenger of Tosny, in SINNINGTON, 2 carucates.

11   The Archbishop, in NAWTON, 4 carucates. Berenger of Tosny, in the same place, 2 carucates.

12   Berenger of Tosny, in WELBURN, 1 carucate. The King, in the same place, 1 carucate. The Archbishop, in WOMBLETON, 1 carucate.

13   Berenger of Tosny, in 'WALTON', 1 bovate; Berenger of Tosny and the Abbot from him, in SPAUNTON, 6½ carucates. The King and the Abbot from him, in the same place, 1 carucate.

14   The Abbot from the King, in APPLETON (le Moors), 2 carucates. The King, in NORMANBY, 3 carucates. The Abbot from the King, in the same place, 3 carucates. The Count of Mortain, in BARTON (le Street), 8 carucates.

15   Berenger of Tosny, in OSWALDKIRK, 1 carucate. The Count of Mortain, in the same place, 1 carucate. The Archbishop, in (East) NEWTON, 4 carucates. The King, in the same place, 2 carucates.

16   Ralph of Mortemer, in GILLING (East), 4 carucates. The King, in (West) NEWTON (Grange), 2 carucates; the King, in SPROXTON, 5 carucates.

17   The Count of Mortain, in FADMOOR, 5 carucates. Robert Malet, in SCAWTON, 4 carucates. The Count of Mortain, in GRIFF (Farm), 2 carucates. The King, in the same place, 2 carucates.

18   The King, in STILTONS (Farm), 1 carucate. The Count of Mortain, in the same place, 3 carucates. The King, in HELMSLEY, 3½ carucates. The Count of Mortain, in the same place, 7 carucates.

19   The Archbishop, in POCKLEY, 1 carucate. The Count of Mortain, in the same place, 1 carucate; the Count of Mortain, in BEADLAM, 4 carucates; the Count of Mortain, in HAROME, 5 carucates.

20   The King, in the same place, 1½ carucates. Berenger of Tosny, in the same place, 2 bovates. The King, in RICCAL (House), 2 carucates. Ralph Paynel, in NUNNINGTON, 6 carucates.

Ibid̃ ^{co. Morit'} vi. car. In Steinegrif ^{Arcĥ}. vi. bõ. Ibid̃ ^{Ra. Paǧ.}. v. c 7 ii. bõ. In Neiſſe ^{Ra. pag'.}. iii. c̃.

In Holm ^{Ra. paǧ.}. i. c. In Ampreforde. iii. c. In Coltun ^{Arcĥ} ^{Rex}. i. c. In Coletun ^{Arcĥ}. dim c.

Ibid̃ ^{co. Moŕ}. i. c 7 dim. In Caluetun ^{co. Mor'.}. iii. c. In Selungesbi ^{co. Mor'.} xiiii. c.

In Fritun ^{co. Morit'}. dim c.

BOLESFORD WAPENTAC.

In Hotun ^{B. tc̃d}. v. car 7 dim. Ibid̃ ^{Rex}. viii. c 7 dim. In Ilderſchelf ^{B. toĩ.}. iiii. c̃.

In Dalbi ^{B. 7 abb̃ de eõ.}. iii. c̃. In Scacheldene. dim c. Ibid̃ ^{co. Mor'}. i. car 7 dim.

In Bolemere 7 Stidnun ^{co. Mor'}. xv. c. In Hotune ^{co. Mor'.}. xi. c̃. Ibid̃ ^{Rex}. iiii. c.

In Wellebrune ^{co. Mor'.}. iii. c 7 dim. In Gameltorp ^{co. Mor'\}. ii. car 7 dim.

Ibid̃ ^{Rex.}. dim c. In Teurintune ^{co. Mor'.}. vi. c 7 iii. bõ. Ibid̃ ^{B. toĩ}. ii. bõ.

Ibid̃ ^{co. Alan}. i. c 7 dim. In Wicĥgastorp ^{co. Mor'.}. i. c. Ibid̃ ^{Rcx}. i. c̃. Ibid̃ ^{B. toĩ}. i. car.

In Ildingeſlei ^{Rex.}. ii. c. In Coningeſtorp ^{cõ. Morit'}. iii. c. In Martun ^{co. Mor'}. vi. car.

In Farlintun 7 Fornetorp ^{co. Mor'}. vii. c. Ibid̃ ^{B. toĩ}. i. c. In Corlebroc ^{co. Mor'}. ix. car.

In Scoxebi ^{co. Mor'}. viii. c. In Lilinge ^{Rex}. iii. c. Ibid̃ ^{co. Mor'.}. ii. bõ. In Torentun ^{co. Mor'.}. iii. car.

21 The Count of Mortain, in the same place, 6 carucates. The Archbishop, in STONEGRAVE, 6 bovates. Ralph Paynel, in the same place, 5 carucates and 2 bovates; Ralph Paynel, in (East) NESS, 3 carucates.

22 Ralph Paynel, in (South) HOLME. 1 carucate. The Archbishop, in AMPLEFORTH, 3 carucates. The King, in COULTON, 1 carucate. The Archbishop, in COULTON, ½ carucate.

23 The Count of Mortain, in the same place, 1½ carucates; the Count of Mortain, in CAWTON, 3 carucates; the Count of Mortain, in SLINGSBY, 14 carucates.

24 The Count of Mortain, in FRYTON, ½ carucate.

BOLESFORD (BULMER) Wapentake
1 Berenger of Tosny, in (Low) HUTTON, 5½ carucates. The King, in the same place, 8½ carucates. Berenger of Tosny, in HENDERSKELFE, 4 carucates.

2 Berenger and the Abbot from him, in DALBY, 3 carucates. The King, in SCACKLETON, ½ carucate. The Count of Mortain, in the same place, ½ carucate.

3 The Count of Mortain, in BULMER and STITTENHAM, 15 carucates; the Count of Mortain, in (Sheriff) HUTTON, 11 carucates. The King, in the same place, 4 carucates.

4 The Count of Mortain, in WELBURN, 3½ carucates; the Count of Mortain, in GANTHORPE, 2½ carucates.

5 The King, in the same place, ½ carucate. The Count of Mortain, in TERRINGTON, 6 carucates and 3 bovates. Berenger of Tosny, in the same place, 2 bovates.

6 Count Alan, in the same place, 1½ carucates. The Count of Mortain, in WIGANTHORPE (Hall), 1 carucate. The King, in the same place, 1 carucate. Berenger of Tosny, in the same place, 1 carucate.

7 The King, in HILDENLEY (Hall), 2 carucates. The Count of Mortain, in CONEYSTHORPE, 3 carucates; the Count of Mortain, in MARTON (in the Forest), 6 carucates.   381 a

8 The Count of Mortain, in FARLINGTON and *FORNETORP*, 7 carucates. Berenger of Tosny, in the same place, 1 carucate. The Count of Mortain, in CORNBROUGH (House), 9 carucates.

9 The Count of Mortain, in SKEWSBY, 8 carucates. The King, in (West) LILLING, 3 carucates. The Count of Mortain, in the same place, 2 bovates; the Count of Mortain, in THORNTON (le Clay), 3 carucates.

Ibid . ii . car . Ibid . ii . c . In Cranbon . iiii . c . Ibid . iiii . c . In Bartun . vi . c.

In Heretun . xii . c . In Claxtorp . iii . c . Ibid . i . c . In Hotun . i . car.

In Dic . ii . c . In Hamelfech . iiii . c . In Suton . iii . c . In Holtebi . vi . c.

In alia Hamelfech . iiii . c 7 ii . bo . In Wardhille . iii . c . Ibid . ii . car.

In Careltun . iii . c . In Witeuuelle . ix . c 7 dim . In Lilinge . i . c 7 vi . bo.

Ibid . i . c 7 ii . bo . In Strenfhale . v . c . In Touetorp . iii . c . Ibid . i . car.

In Edrezuic . iii . c . In Huntindune . v . c . Ibid . ii . c . 7 vi . bo . ibid . i . c 7 ii . bo

In Flaxtune . ii . c 7 dim . Ibid . vi . bo . Ibid . i . c 7 dim . In Hobi . vi . c.

In Quennebi . viii . c . In Foftun . viii . c . In Stiuelinctun . x . car.

In Molfcebi . iii . c . In Mortun . ii . c 7 dim . Ibid . ii . car.

In Torp Cheleftuit Sutune 7 Carebi . xvii . c.

In Eifinceuuald . xii . c . In Rafchel . viii . c . In Coteburun . iii . c.

In Neuton 7 Torefbi . ix . c . In Ingulueftuet . viii . c.

In Haxebi . vi . c 7 i . bo . In Tolletune . In Alne . In Loietun . In Mitune

10 Count Alan, in the same place, 2 carucates. In the same place, 2 carucates. The Count of Mortain, in CRAMBE, 4 carucates. The King, in the same place, 4 carucates. The Count of Mortain, in BARTON (le Willows), 8 carucates.

11 The King, in HARTON, 12 carucates; the King, in CLAXTON, 3 carucates. The Count of Mortain, in the same place, 1 carucate. The King, in (Sand) HUTTON, 1 carucate.

12 The King, in DIC, 2 carucates. The Count of Mortain, in (Upper) HELMSLEY, 4 carucates. The King, in SUTTON (on the Forest), 3 carucates; the King, in HOLTBY, 6 carucates.

13 The Archbishop, in another (Gate) HELMSLEY, 4 carucates and 2 bovates; the Archbishop, in WARTHILL, 3 carucates. The Count of Mortain, in the same place, 2 carucates.

14 The Archbishop, in CARLTON (Farm), 3 carucates. The Count of Mortain, in WHITWELL (on the Hill), 9½ carucates. The King, in (East) LILLING, 1 carucate and 6 bovates.

15 The Count of Mortain, in the same place, 1 carucate and 2 bovates. In STRENSALL, 5 carucates. In TOWTHORPE, 3 carucates. The Count of Mortain, in the same place, 1 carucate.

16 In EARSWICK, 3 carucates. The Count of Mortain, in HUNTINGTON, 5 carucates. The King, in the same place, 2 carucates and 6 bovates. Count Alan, in the same place, 1 carucate and 2 bovates.

17 The King, in FLAXTON, 2½ carucates. The Archbishop, in the same place, 6 bovates. Count Alan, in the same place, 1½ carucates. The King, in HUBY, 6 carucates.

18 The King, in WHENBY, 8 carucates. Count Alan, in FOSTON, 8 carucates. The Archbishop, in STILLINGTON, 10 carucates.

19 The King, in MOXBY (Hall), 3 carucates. The Archbishop, in MURTON (Farm), 2½ carucates. The King, in the same place, 2 carucates.

20 In THORPE (Hill), KELSIT (Grange), SUTTON (on the Forest) and (Cold) KIRBY, 17 carucates.

21 The King, in EASINGWOLD, 12 carucates; the King, in RASKELF, 8 carucates. In 'CORBURN', 3 carucates.

22 Ralph Paynel, in NEWTON (upon Ouse) and TORESBI, 9 carucates. William of Percy, in 'INGLETHWAITE', 8 carucates.

23 The Archbishop, in HAXBY, 6 carucates and 1 bovate. In TOLLERTON, 8 carucates. In ALNE, 8 carucates. In YOULTON, 4 carucates. In MYTON (on Swale), 2 bovates.

In Turolueſtorp 7 Wibedſtune . In Hilprebi . H̃ archi.

In Ilprebi . IIII . c . In Mitune . IIII . c 7 dim . Ibid . III . c 7 II . bõ.

In Aldeuuerc . VIII . c . In Bradfortune . VI . c . Ibid . I . c . In Stilſbi . II . c.

In Muletorp . III . c . In Hipton . VI . c . In Boſciale . II . bõ 7 dim.

I GERLESTRE WAPENTAC.

In Turmozbi . I . c 7 dim . Ibid . dim c . Ibid . IIII . c . In Creic . VI . car.

In Baſcheſbi . VI . car 7 I . bõ . In Carletun . IIII . c 7 dim . In Torp . III . c.

In Vlueſtun . VI . c . In Begeland . VI . c . In Bernebi . IIII . c 7 dim.

In Sezai . V . c . In Horenbodebi . III . c . In Topecliue cũ Berew . XXVI . c.

In Bergebi . VIII . c . In Rainingeuuat . IIII . c . In Catune . VI . car.

In Carletun . IIII . c . In Hotune . VI . c . In Bracheberc . VI . c . In Treſc . VI . c.

In Neuhuſe . II . c 7 dim . In Sorebi . V . c . In Cheniuetune . IIII . c . Ibid . II . c.

In Cheluintun . VIII . c . Ibid 7 in Vpſale 7 Hundulſtorp . XIII . car.

24 In THOLTHORPE and WIDE OPEN (Farm), 7 carucates. In HELPERBY, 6 carucates. These (are) the Archbishop's.

25 The Archbishop, in HELPERBY, 4 carucates; the Archbishop, in MYTON (on Swale), 4½ carucates. The King, in the same place, 3 carucates and 2 bovates.

26 The Count of Mortain, in ALDWARK, 8 carucates. The King, in BRAFFERTON, 6 carucates. The Count of Mortain, in the same place, 1 carucate; the Count of Mortain, in STEARSBY, 2 carucates.

27 The Count of Mortain, in (Low) MOWTHORPE (Farm), 3 carucates. Count Alan, in SHIPTON, 6 carucates. In BOSSALL, 2½ bovates.

GERLESTRE (BIRDFORTH) Wapentake

1 The King, in THORMANBY, 1½ carucates. Gamall held, in the same place, ½ carucate. Robert Malet, in the same place, 4 carucates. The Bishop of Durham, in CRAYKE, 6 carucates.

2 The Archbishop, in BAXBY, 6 carucates and 1 bovate; the Archbishop, in CARLTON (Husthwaite), 4½ carucates. Gospatric, in THORPE (le Willows), 3 carucates.

3 Gospatric, in OULSTON, 6 carucates. Robert Malet, in (Old) BYLAND, 6 carucates; Robert Malet, in *BERNEBI*, 4½ carucates.

4 The Bishop of Durham, in SESSAY, 5 carucates; the Bishop of Durham, in *HORENBODEBI*, 3 carucates. William of Percy, in TOPCLIFFE with 4 outliers, 26 carucates.

5 William of Percy, in *BERGEBI*, 8 carucates; William of Percy, in RAINTON, 4 carucates; William of Percy, in CATTON, 6 carucates.

6 The King, in CARLTON (Miniott), 4 carucates; the King, in (Sand) HUTTON, 6 carucates. The Count of Mortain, in BRECKENBROUGH, 6 carucates. The King, in THIRSK, 8 carucates.

7 The King, in NEWSHAM, 2½ carucates; the King, in SOWERBY, 5 carucates. The Bishop of Durham, in KNAYTON, 4 carucates. The King, in the same place, 2 carucates.

8 The King, in (North) KILVINGTON, 8 carucates. The Count of Mortain, in the same place, in UPSALL and in HUNDULFTHORPE (Farm), 13 carucates.

ALVRETVN WAPENTAC.

★ In Aluretune Bretebi . Sourebi Cherchebi Landemot Griftorentun ꞉

<small>Rex ·· Smideſ · 7 Smideſ · Cotun · Bergebi · Romundebi 7 Laforde</small>

XL . II . car træ . In Neuhuſe Herſelaige Weſthuſe Manneſbi

<small>Rex</small>

★ Sigeſtun . Coleſbi . Werlegeſbi . Timbelli Eindrebi . Laiforde Leche

Cheniueton . Leiſinghi . Raueneſtorp Dineſhale Torentun . Croxebi

Runtune Otrintune Romundebi . Bruntun . Irebi ꞉ LXXV . car

In Otrintune . VI . c . In Romundrebi . v . c 7 1 . bõ . In Hotune . VI . c.

In Smidetune . v . c . In Griſebi . VI . c . In duab Wirceſhel . VII . c.

In Apletun . VI . c . In Lentune . VI . c . In alia Lentune . IIII . car.

★ In Larun . III . c . In Welleberg . VI . c . In duab Erleſeie . IX . car.

★ In Di&tune . VI . c . In Winetune . In Foſtune In Bruntune . H eps duñ

In Mortune . III . c . In Englebi . VI . c . In Lernedif . I . c . In Bordalebi . II . c.

In Elrebec . v . c . In Aſmundrelac . v . c . In Silftune . III . c . In alia . III . c.

In Sourebi . II . c . In Croxebi . I . c . In Torentune . v . c . In Lece . III . c.

ALLERTON Wapentake

1　The King, in
(North)ALLERTON, BIRKBY, SOWERBY (under Cotcliffe), KIRBY
(Wiske), LANDMOTH, THORNTON (le Beans), (Great) SMEATON,
(Little) SMEATON, (East) COWTON, BORROWBY, ROMANBY, YAFFORTH,
42 carucates of land. The King in
NEWSHAM (Grange), (West) HARLSEY, 'WESTHOUSE', MAUNBY, (Kirby)
SIGSTON, COWESBY, WARLABY, THIMBLEBY, AINDERBY (Steeple),
YAFFORTH, LEAKE, KNAYTON, LAZENBY (Hall), RAVENSTHORPE
(Manor), (Over) DINSDALE (Grange), THORNTON (le Street), CROSBY
(Grange), (West) ROUNTON, (North) OTTERINGTON, ROMANBY,
BROMPTON, IRBY (Manor), 75 carucates.

2　The King, in (South) OTTERINGTON, 6 carucates; the King, in
ROMANBY, 5 carucates and 1 bovate; the King, in HUTTON
(Bonville), 6 carucates.

3　The King, in (Little) SMEATON, 5 carucates. The Bishop of Durham,
in GIRSBY, 6 carucates. The King, in two (High and Low)
WORSALLS, 7 carucates.

4　The King, in APPLETON (Wiske), 6 carucates; the King, in (Kirk)
LEAVINGTON, 6 carucates; the King, in another (Castle) LEAVINGTON,
4 carucates.

5　The King, in YARM, 3 carucates; the King, in WELBURY, 6
carucates; the King, in two (East and West) HARLSEYS, 9
carucates.

6　The Bishop of Durham, in DEIGHTON, 6 carucates. In WINTON, 6
carucates. In FOXTON, 2 carucates. In BROMPTON. These (are) the
Bishop of Durham's.

7　The King, in MORTON (Grange), 3 carucates; the King, in INGLEBY
(Arncliffe), 6 carucates; the King, in ARNCLIFFE (Hall), 1 carucate;
the King, in 'BORDELBY' (MOUNT GRACE), 2 carucates.

8　The King, in ELLERBECK, 5 carucates; the King, in OSMOTHERLEY,
5 carucates; the King, in (Over) SILTON, 3 carucates. The Count
of Mortain, in another (Nether) SILTON, 3 carucates.

9　The King, in SOWERBY (under Cotcliffe), 2 carucates; the King,
in CROSBY (Grange), 1 carucate. Robert Malet, in THORNTON (le
Moor), 5 carucates. The Count of Mortain, in LEAKE, 3 carucates.

In Capuic . v . c̄ . In Mortun . vi . c̄ . In Đal . i . c̄ 7 dim . Ibid . i . c̄ 7 dim .
In Halmbi . i . c̄ 7 dim . Ibid . i . c̄ 7 dim .

ALANI COMITIS.

In *GELLINGES* . iiii . car træ . In Herford . In Neuton.

In Cudtone . In alia Cudtone . In Argun . In Hale.

In Stapledun . In Forfed . In Bereford.

In *MOLTVN* . In Barton . In Aplebi . In Cliue . In Cartune.

In Bereford . In Vlfeton . In Gerlinton . In Witcliue . In Torp.

In Mortham . In Eghifton . In Bringhale . In Scacreghil.

In Beringhā . In Latton . In Latone . In duab Steinueges.

In Manefeld . In Hotune . In Midelton . In Naton . In Staplendun.

In Beringhā . In Latone . In Steinuuege . In Dirnefhale.

In Sineton . In Langeton . In Caldeuuelle . In Aldeburne . In Cartun.

In Clesbi . In Croft . In Torp . In Stradford . In Indrelag . In Afebi.

In Brunton . In Schirebi . In Neutone . In Boletone . In Chipeling.

10   The King, in KEPWICK, 5 carucates. Robert Malet, in MURTON, 6 carucates. The King, in DALE (Town), 1½ carucates. Robert Malet, in the same place, 1½ carucates.

11   The King, in HAWNBY, 1½ carucates. Robert Malet, in the same place, 1½ carucates.

[LAND] OF COUNT ALAN 381 b

1   In GILLING, 4 carucates of land; in HARTFORTH, 3 carucates; in NEWTON (Morrell), 6 carucates.

2   In (South) COWTON, 3 carucates; in another (North) COWTON, 3 carucates; in ERYHOLME, 6 carucates; in (Low) HAIL, 2½ carucates.

3   In STAPLETON, 3 carucates; in FORCETT, 8 carucates; in BARFORTH (Hall), 3 carucates.

4   In MOULTON, 16 carucates; in BARTON, 2½ carucates; in EPPLEBY, 7 carucates; in CLIFFE (Hall), 3 carucates; in CARLTON, 2 carucates.

5   In BARFORTH (Hall), 1 carucate; in OVINGTON, 3 carucates; in GIRLINGTON (Hall), 3 carucates; in WYCLIFFE, 12 carucates; in THORPE (Hall), 3 carucates.

6   In MORTHAM (Tower), 3 carucates; in EGGLESTONE (Abbey), 3 carucates; in BRIGNALL, 12 carucates; in SCARGILL, 3 carucates.

7   In BARNINGHAM, 4 carucates; in (West) LAYTON, 3 carucates; in (East) LAYTON, 3 carucates; in the two STANWICKS, 4 carucates.

8   In MANFIELD, 16 carucates; in HUTTON (Magna), 6 carucates; in MIDDLETON (Tyas), 6 carucates; in KNEETON (Hall), 8 carucates; in STAPLETON, 5 carucates.

9   In BARNINGHAM, 2 carucates; in (East) LAYTON, 3 carucates; in STANWICK, 4 carucates; in (Over) DINSDALE (Grange), 3 carucates.

10   In (Great) SMEATON, 6 carucates; in (Great) LANGTON, 9 carucates; in CALDWELL, 6 carucates; in ALDBROUGH, 8 carucates; in CARLTON, 2 carucates.

11   In CLEASBY, 6 carucates; in CROFT, 14 carucates; in *TORP*, 2 carucates; in STARTFORTH, 6 carucates; in *INDRELAG* (RICHMOND), 5 carucates; in EASBY, 6 carucates.

12   In BROMPTON (on Swale), 10 carucates; in SKEEBY, 6 carucates; in *NEUTONE*, 6 carucates; in BOLTON (upon Swale), 6 carucates; in KIPLIN, 8 carucates.

^{vii.c'⁊ dim̄}   ^{v.c'}   ^{iiii.c'}   ^{x.c'}   ^{viii.c'}
In Langeton . In Tirnecofte . In Solberge . In Mannebi . In Chirchebi.

In Mortune . In Alreton . In Eiford . In Eindrebi . In Warlauesbi.

★ In Danebi . In Cotune . In Lontone . In Mideton . In Rumoldefcerce.

In Hundredeftoith . In Lertinton . In Codrefton . In Rochebi.

In Broctune . In Neuhufon . In Dalton . In alia Dalton . In Rauenefuet.

In Maffenebi . In Dirdefton . In Scortone.

EIVSDĒ COMITIS.

In *CATRICE* . x . car ⁊ . In Chiluordebi . v . c ⁊ . In Endrebi . In Tuneftale.

In Endrebi . In Tuneftale . In Cherchebi . In Fleteha̅ . In Hafe.

In duabʒ Fencotes . ix . c ⁊ . In Scurueton . xii . c ⁊ . In Langetorp.

In Acheforde . In Hornebi . In Eltebi . In Apleton . In Burg.

In Corburne . In Hipleuuelle . In Scotune . In Vdrefuuelle.

In Indrelage . In Dune . In Elreton . In Mange . In Grinton.

In Freminton . In Rie . In Denton . In Burg . In Fors . In Afcric.

13 In (Little) LANGTON, 7½ carucates; in THRINTOFT, 5 carucates; in SOLBERGE, 4 carucates; in MAUNBY, 10 carucates; in KIRBY (Wiske), 8 carucates.

14 In MORTON (upon Swale), 11 carucates; in ELLERTON (on Swale), 9 carucates; in YAFFORTH, 8 carucates; in AINDERBY (Steeple), 9 carucates; in WARLABY, 6 carucates.

15 In DANBY (Wiske), 10 carucates; in (East) COWTON, 6 carucates; in LONTON, 1 carucate; in MICKLETON, 6 carucates; in ROMALDKIRK, 1 carucate.

16 In HUNDERTHWAITE, 1 carucate; in LARTINGTON, 3 carucates; in COTHERSTONE, 6 carucates; in ROKEBY (Hall), 3 carucates.

17 In BROUGHTON (House), 5 carucates; in NEWSHAM, 7 carucates; in DALTON, 8 carucates; in another DALTON, 4 carucates; in RAVENSWORTH, 12 carucates.

18 In MELSONBY, 11 carucates; in DIDDERSTON (Grange), 4 carucates; in SCORTON, 16 carucates.

[LAND] OF THE SAME COUNT

19 In CATTERICK, 10 carucates; in KILLERBY (Hall), 5 carucates; in AINDERBY (Mires), 2½ carucates; in TUNSTALL, 3 carucates and 6 bovates.

20 In AINDERBY (Mires), 2½ carucates; in TUNSTALL, 2 carucates; in KIRKBY (Hall), 3 carucates; in (Kirkby) FLEETHAM, 8 carucates; in ASKE (Hall), 6 carucates.

21 In the two (Great and Little) FENCOTES, 9 carucates; in SCRUTON, 14 carucates; in LANGTHORNE, 3 carucates.

22 In HACKFORTH, 6 carucates; in HORNBY, 8 carucates; in HOLTBY (Hall), 3 carucates; in (East) APPLETON, 12 carucates; in BROUGH (Hall), 9 carucates.

23 In COLBURN, 5 carucates; in HIPSWELL, 3 carucates; in SCOTTON, 8 carucates; in HUDSWELL, 6 carucates.

24 In *INDRELAGE* (RICHMOND), 1 carucate; in DOWNHOLME, 3 carucates; in ELLERTON (Abbey), 2 carucates; in MARRICK, 5 carucates; in GRINTON, 1 carucate.

25 In FREMINGTON, 1 carucate; in REETH, 6 carucates; in *DENTON*, 3 carucates; in BROUGH (Hill), 3 carucates; in FORS (Abbey), 4 carucates; in ASKRIGG, 10 carucates.

In Werton [vi.c'] . In Torenton [vi.c'] . In Echescard [iii.c'] . In Crochesbi [i.c'] . In Turodesbi [vi.c'],

In Burton [vi.c'] . In Chirprebi [i.c'] . In Bodelton [vi.c'] . In alia Bod [vi.c'] . In Toresbi [i.c'].

In Ridemare [v.c'] . In Preston [iii.c'] . In Witun [xii.c'] . In Toresbi [ii.c'] . In Witun [v.c'] . In Scalstun [iii.c'].

In duabʒ Wentreslage [vii.c'] . In Carleton [vi.c'] . In Melmerbi [vi.c'] . In Aculestorp [iii.c'].

In Caldeber [ʒ.c'] . In Coureha [iiii.c'] . In Medelai [v.c'] . In Leborne [vii.c' 7 dim] . In Ernebi [ix.c'].

In Speningetorp [viii.c' 7 dim] . In Danebi [iiii.c'] . In Belgebi [vi.c'] . In Bernedan [v.c'] . In Gerdeston [iii.c'].

In Hauochesuuelle [vi.c'] . In alia In Bertone [vi.c' / xii.c'] . In Tornenton [vi.c'] . In Aschā [iiii.c'].

In Ellintone [vi.c'] . In Siuuartorp [i.c'] . In Sutone [i.c'] . In Federbi [iii.c'] . In Ilcheton [ii.c'].

In Maisan [xii.c'] . In Tuislebroc [iii.c'] . In Suinton [iii.c'] . In Sudton [i.c'] . In Clifton [iii.c'].

In Welle [viii.c'] . In Burton [iii.c'] . In Opetune [iiii.c'] . In Achebi [iiii.c'] . In Fredebi [v.c'] . In Bedale [vi.c'].

In Echescol [x.c'] . In Borel [v.c'] . In Torreton [vi.c'] . In Wadles [iii.c'] . In Torp [iiii.c'] . In Torneton [iiii.c'].

In Thirne [iii.c'] . In Rocuid [vi.c'] . In Hotune [v.c'] . In Finegal [vi.c'] . In Riteuuic [ii.c'] . In Neuton [xii.c'].

In Hunton [xii.c'] . In Eslinton [vi.c'] . In Brunton [xiii.c'] . In Crachele [xii.c'] . In Tanefeld [v.c'].

26 In WORTON, 6 carucates; in THORNTON (Rust), 6 carucates; in AYSGARTH, 3 carucates; in CROOKSBY (Barn), 1 carucate; in THORALBY, 6 carucates.

27 In (West) BURTON, 6 carucates; in CARPERBY, 9 carucates; in (Castle) BOLTON, 6 carucates; in another (West) BOLTON, 6 carucates; in THORESBY, 1 carucate.

28 In REDMIRE, 5 carucates; in PRESTON (under Scar), 3 carucates; in (East) WITTON, 12 carucates; in THORESBY, 2 carucates; in (West) WITTON, 5 carucates; in (West) SCRAFTON, 3 carucates.

29 In the two WENSLEYS, 7 carucates; in CARLTON, 6 carucates; in MELMERBY, 6 carucates; in AGGLETHORPE, 3 carucates.

30 In CALDBERGH, 5 carucates; in COVERHAM, 4 carucates; in MIDDLEHAM, 5 carucates; in LEYBURN, 7½ carucates; in HARMBY, 9 carucates.

31 In SPENNITHORNE, 8½ carucates; in DANBY, 4 carucates; in BELLERBY, 6 carucates; in BARDEN, 5 carucates; in GARRISTON, 3 carucates.

32 In (East) HAUXWELL, 6 carucates; in another (West) HAUXWELL, 6 carucates; in (Constable) BURTON, 12 carucates; in THORNTON (Steward), 6 carucates; in *ASCHAM*, 4 carucates.

33 In (High) ELLINGTON, 6 carucates; in 'SWARTHORPE', 1 carucate; in (High) SUTTON, 1 carucate; in FEARBY, 3 carucates; in ILTON, 2 carucates.

34 In MASHAM, 12 carucates; in 'TWISLEBROOK', 3 carucates; in SWINTON, 3 carucates; in (High) SUTTON, 1 carucate; in CLIFTON (on Ure), 3 carucates.

35 In WELL, 8 carucates; in (High) BURTON, 4 carucates; in *OPETUNE*, 4 carucates; in *ACHEBI*, 4 carucates; in FIRBY, 5 carucates; in BEDALE, 6 carucates.

36 In AISKEW, 10 carucates; in BURRILL, 5 carucates; in THORNTON (Watlass), 6 carucates; in (Thornton) WATLASS, 3 carucates; in THORP (Perrow), 4 carucates; in *THORNTON* (COWLING), 4 carucates.

37 In THIRN, 3 carucates; in ROOKWITH, 6 carucates; in HUTTON (Hang), 5 carucates; in FINGALL, 6 carucates; in RUSWICK, 2 carucates; in NEWTON (le Willows), 12 carucates.

38 In HUNTON, 12 carucates; in HESSELTON, 6 carucates; in (Patrick) BROMPTON, 13 carucates; in (Great) CRAKEHALL, 12 carucates; in (East) TANFIELD, 5 carucates.

VIII.c'. ⁊   .III.c'.   .v.c'.   .IIII.c'.   VI.c'.
In alia Tan. In Vpſale. In Hograue. In Sutone. In Wat.

.VI.c'.   .v.c'.   IX.c'.   .III.c'.
In Malmerbi. In Mideltune. In Cherdinton. In Gernuic.

.VI.c'.   .IIII.c'.   .VIII.c'.   .XII.c'.   .VIII.c'.
In Normanebi. In Caretorp. In Brennigſton. In Eſton. In Atchilebi.

.VI.c'.   III.c'.   .III.c'.   .VI.c'.   .XII.c'.
In Neutone. In Cheneteſbi. In Ounesbi. In Suanebi. In Picale.

.II.c'.   .III.c'.   .VI.c'.   .VI.c'.
In Erleueſtorp. In Seuenetorp. In Senerebi. In Andrebi.

.III.c'.   III.c'.   .IIII.c'   IX.c'.
In Hou. In Baldrebi. In Afebi. In Reineton.

Comes. A. ħt jn ſuo caſtellatu. cc. Maner⁊. uñ minᵍ. De his ſꝛ
uuaſti. c ⁊ VIII. ⁊ de his teñ hões ſui. CXXXIII. Ꝏ. In oṁibȝ ſꝛ ad glꝺ
mille ⁊ c. ⁊ LIII. car⁊ træ⁊. Tra octingent⁊ ⁊ LIII . car⁊. Pciu. q̃t xx. liƀ.
Præt caſtellariā ħt. XLIII. Ꝏ. Ex his ſꝛ. IIII. waſti. In oṁibȝ
ſꝛ ad glꝺ. CLXI. car⁊ træ⁊. ⁊ v. bõ. Tra. CLXX. car⁊ ⁊ dim⁊. De his
teñ ſui hões. x. Man. Appciantᴶ. cx. liƀ. ⁊ XI. ſoł ⁊ VIII. den⁊.

381 c

I H‍ASE HVNDRET.

G.ᵗⁱ̃a ⁊⁊   Rᴀ.Morᵗ ⁊   G.tiſon   ⁊
n HASE. VII. car⁊ træ. Ibid. I. car. In Crachetorp. III. c.

Rex   G.tiſon ⁊   ⁊   co.Moritᵖ
In Vnlouebi. III.c ⁊ I. bõ. Ibid. III. c ⁊ dim. Ibid. v. bõ.

Fᴀ.Morᵗ   G.tiſon   ⁊   ⁊   Rᴀ.M rᵗ ⁊
Ibid. II. bõ. In Aluengi. XXII. c ⁊ dim. Ibid. x. car.

39 In another (West) TANFIELD, 8 carucates; in UPSLAND, 3 carucates; in HOWGRAVE, 5 carucates; in SUTTON (Howgrave), 4 carucates; in WATH, 6 carucates.

40 In MELMERBY, 6 carucates; in MIDDLETON (Quernhow), 5 carucates; in KIRKLINGTON, 9 carucates; in YARNWICK, 3 carucates.

41 In *NORMANEBI*, 6 carucates; in CARTHORPE, 4 carucates; in BURNESTON, 8 carucates; in THEAKSTON, 12 carucates; in EXELBY, 8 carucates.

42 In NEWTON ('Picot'), 6 carucates; in GATENBY, 3 carucates; in *OUNESBI*, 3 carucates; in (Low) SWAINBY, 6 carucates; in PICKHILL, 12 carucates.

43 In ALLERTHORPE (Hall), 2 carucates; in *SEUENETORP*, 3 carucates; in SINDERBY, 6 carucates; in AINDERBY (Quernhow), 6 carucates.

44 In HOWE, 3 carucates; in BALDERSBY, 3 carucates; in *ASEBI*, 4 carucates; in RAINTON, 9 carucates.

45 Count Alan has in his castlery 200 manors less 1. Of these 108 are waste; and of these his men hold 133 manors. In all there are 1,153 carucates of land taxable. Land for 853 ploughs. Value £80. Besides the castlery he has 43 manors. Of these 4 are waste. In all there are 161 carucates and 5 bovates of land taxable. Land for 170½ ploughs. Of these his men hold 10 manors.
They are appraised at £110 11s 8d.

EAST RIDING

HESSLE Hundred

1 Gilbert Tison, in HESSLE, 7 carucates of land. Ralph of Mortemer, in the same place, 1 carucate. Gilbert Tison, in *CRACHETORP*, 3 carucates.

2 The King, in ANLABY, 3 carucates and 1 bovate. Gilbert Tison, in the same place, 3½ carucates. The Count of Mortain, in the same place, 5 bovates.

3 Ralph of Mortemer, in the same place, 2 bovates. Gilbert Tison, in (Kirk) ELLA, 22½ carucates. Ralph of Mortemer, in the same place, 10 carucates.

Ibid . iiii . c . Ibid . ii . car . In Ferebi . x . c . Ibid . dim car.

Ra . Mort'. ⁊ Ra . Mort' ⁊ Ra . mort'. ⁊ bō.
In Walbi . i . c . In Mitun . i . c ⁊ dim . In Ripinghā . i . c ⁊ ii.

Ra . mort' ⁊ Ra . mor'. ⁊ ⁊ G . tiſn
In Totſled . i . c . In Vlfardun dim c . In Wereſa . xiiii . c.

Ra . mort' ⁊ Ra . mort' ⁊ cō . Morit' ⁊ i . bō ⁊ dim.' ⁊
Ibid . i . c ⁊ vi . bō . In Neſse . vi . c ⁊ i . bō . In Spellinton . iii . c

G . tiſon ⁊ ⁊ Ra . mortem' ⁊ Ra . mort'
In Lont . i . c ⁊ dim . Ibid . ii . c ⁊ dimid . In Briſtun . ii . car.

G . tiſon ⁊ cō . Mor'. ⁊ G . tiſon ⁊ ⁊
In Bonnebi . i . c ⁊ iii . bō . Ibid . v . bō . In Bubuid . viii . c ⁊ dim.

Ra . Mort' ⁊ cō . Morit' ⁊ Ra . mort' ⁊ ⁊
Ibid . i . c ⁊ iii . bō . In Wilgetot . v . bō . Ibid . ii . car ⁊ dim.

G . tiſon ⁊ Rex ⁊
Ibid . vii . bō . In Wilgardi . ii . c.

IWELLETON HVNDRET.

Eſps dun' ⁊ ii . c' ix . c'
In Welleton . xxvi . car . In Brendinghā . In Walchinton.

⁊ ⁊ ⁊
In Lont . xviii . c . In Brentinghā . ii . c ⁊ vii . bō . H oā eſps dun

H . F . bald ⁊ c ⁊ 9 ⁊ H . F . bald ⁊
In Cotinghā . xiiii . c ⁊ ii . part . i . car . In Wideton . v . car.

Arch ⁊ ⁊ ⁊ x . c' ⁊ vii . c'
In Schitebi . xiiii . c ⁊ tcia pars . i . c . In Elgendon . In Walbi.

viii . c' ⁊ i . bō ii . c' vi . c'
In Walchinton . In Benedlage . In Rasbi . H oma Arch

cō . Morit' ⁊ ⁊ Ro . mat ⁊ ⁊
In Brentinghā . i . c ⁊ vi . bō ⁊ dim . Ibid . ii . c ⁊ vii . bō ⁊ dim.

Rex . ⁊ oald ⁊
In Walchinton . i . c . In Pileford . ii . c.

4 The Count of Mortain, in the same place, 4 carucates. Hugh son of Baldric, in the same place, 2 carucates. Ralph of Mortemer, in (North) FERRIBY, 10 carucates. The Count of Mortain, in the same place, ½ carucate.

5 Ralph of Mortemer, in WAULDBY, 1 carucate; Ralph of Mortemer, in 'MYTON', 1½ carucates; Ralph of Mortemer, in RIPLINGHAM, 1 carucate and 2 bovates.

6 Ralph of Mortemer, in TOTFLED, 1 carucate; Ralph of Mortemer, in WOLFRETON, ½ carucate. Gilbert Tison, in WRESSLE, 14 carucates.

7 Ralph of Mortemer, in the same place, 1 carucate and 6 bovates; Ralph of Mortemer, in NEWSHOLME, 6 carucates and 1 bovate. The Count of Mortain, in SPALDINGTON, 3 carucates and 1½ bovates.

8 Gilbert Tison, in LUND, 1½ carucates. Ralph of Mortemer, in the same place, 2½ carucates; Ralph of Mortemer, in BREIGHTON, 2 carucates.

9 Gilbert Tison, in GUNBY, 1 carucate and 3 bovates. The Count of Mortain, in the same place, 5 bovates. Gilbert Tison, in BUBWITH, 8½ carucates.

10 Ralph of Mortemer, in the same place, 1 carucate and 3 bovates. The Count of Mortain, in WILLITOFT, 5 bovates. Ralph of Mortemer, in the same place, 2½ carucates.

11 Gilbert Tison, in the same place, 7 bovates. The King, in WILLERBY, 2 carucates.

WELTON Hundred

1 The Bishop of Durham, in WELTON, 26 carucates. In BRANTINGHAM, 2 carucates. In WALKINGTON, 9 carucates.

2 In LUND, 18 carucates. In BRANTINGHAM (Thorpe), 2 carucates and 7 bovates. The Bishop of Durham (has) all these.

3 Hugh son of Baldric, in COTTINGHAM, 14 carucates and 2 parts of 1 carucate; Hugh son of Baldric, in (Little) WEIGHTON, 5 carucates.

4 The Archbishop, in SKIDBY, 14 carucates and the third part of 1 carucate. In ELLOUGHTON, 10 carucates. In WAULDBY, 7 carucates.

5 In WALKINGTON, 8 carucates and 1 bovate. In BENTLEY, 2 carucates. In RISBY, 6 carucates. The Archbishop (has) all these.

6 The Count of Mortain, in BRANTINGHAM, 1 carucate and 6½ bovates. Robert Malet, in the same place, 2 carucates and 7½ bovates.

7 The King, in WALKINGTON, 1 carucate. Hugh son of Baldric, in PILLWOODS (Farm), 2 carucates.

CAVE HVNDRET.

In Caue . XXIIII . car . In alia Caue . VII . c 7 II . bo . $\Big/$ [Ro. mat] [Ro. mat] [co. Morit']

Ibid . I . c 7 VI . bo . Ibid . VI . c 7 II . bo . Ibid . II . bo . In Euertorp. [Arch] [co. Morit'] [H.F. bald] [v.c']

In Droueton . IIII . c . In Hundeslege . II . c 7 dimid . Ibid . II . c 7 dim. [Ro. mat] [Eps Dun] [H.F. bald]

In Niuuebold . XXVIII . c 7 II . bo . In Torp . III . c . In Hode . III . car. [Arch] [Ro. mat] [Eps dun]

Ibid . I . c . Ibid . V . c 7 dim . Ibid . III . c . In Cliue . III . c 7 dim . Ibid . II . car. + N. [Rex] [co. morit'] [Ro. mat] [Eps dun] [Rex]

In Setton . IIII . c . Ibid . IIII . c . In Fulcartorp . I . c 7 dim . Ibid . II . car. [Rex] [co. Morit'] [co. Morit'] [Ra. mort']

Ibid . III . c . In Gripetorp . II . c . Ibid . II . c . In Ladon . II . c 7 V . bo. [G. jvon] [G. tfion] [Ra. mort'] [co. morit']

Ibid . I . c 7 III . bo . In Actun . VI . c . In Elreton . II . c . Ibid . II . car. + N [G. ti on] [co. Morit'] [Rex]

In Coteuuid . II . c . In alia Coteuuid . II . c 7 VI . bo . Ibid . I . car. [co. morit'.] [co. Morit'] [Erneis]

★ In Midelborne . VI . c . In Tornetun . VI . c . In Lugufled . I . c 7 dim . Ibid . I . c. [Ra. mort'.] [Ra. mort'.] [eps dun] [Ro. mat.]

HOVEDEN HVNDRET.

In Houeden . XV . car . In Hidon . In Duuestorp . In Portinton. [Eps Dun] [I. c'] [I. c' 7 dim'] [I. c' 7 dim']

CAVE Hundred

1 Robert Malet, in (South) CAVE, 24 carucates; Robert Malet, in another (North) CAVE, 7 carucates and 2 bovates.

2 The Archbishop, in the same place, 1 carucate and 6 bovates. The Count of Mortain, in the same place, 6 carucates and 2 bovates. Hugh son of Baldric, in the same place, 2 bovates. The Count of Mortain, in EVERTHORPE, 5 carucates.

3 Robert Malet, in DREWTON, 4 carucates. The Bishop of Durham, in HUNSLEY, 2½ carucates. Hugh son of Baldric, in the same place, 2½ carucates.

4 The Archbishop, in (North and South) NEWBALD, 28 carucates and 2 bovates. Robert Malet, in (Kettle)THORPE, 3 carucates. The Bishop of Durham, in HOTHAM, 3 carucates.

5 The King, in the same place, 1 carucate. The Count of Mortain, in the same place, 5½ carucates. Robert Malet, in the same place, 3 carucates. The Bishop of Durham, in (South) CLIFFE, 3½   **+N** carucates. The King, in the same place, 2 carucates.

6 The King, in SEATON (Ross), 4 carucates. The Count of Mortain, in the same place, 4 carucates; the Count of Mortain, in FOGGATHORPE, 1½ carucates. Ralph of Mortemer, in the same place, 2 carucates.

7 Gilbert Tison, in the same place, 3 carucates; Gilbert Tison, in GRIBTHORPE, 2 carucates. Ralph of Mortemer, in the same place, 2 carucates. The Count of Mortain, in LAYTHAM, 2 carucates and 5 bovates.

8 Gilbert Tison, in the same place, 1 carucate and 3 bovates. The Count of Mortain, in AUGHTON, 6 carucates; the Count of Mortain,   **+N** in ELLERTON, 2 carucates. The King, in the same place, 2 carucates.

9 The Count of Mortain, in (East) COTTINGWITH, 2 carucates; the Count of Mortain, in another (West) COTTINGWITH, 2 carucates and 6 bovates. Erneis, in the same place, 1 carucate.

10 Ralph of Mortemer, in MELBOURNE, 6 carucates; Ralph of Mortemer, in THORNTON, 6 carucates. The Bishop of Durham, in YOKEFLEET (Grange), 1½ carucates. Robert Malet, in the same place, 1 carucate.

HOWDEN Hundred

1 The Bishop of Durham, in HOWDEN, 15 carucates. In HIVE, 1 carucate; in OWSTHORPE, 1½ carucates; in PORTINGTON, 1½ carucates.

★ In Birland. In Cheuede. In Estrinton. In Chelpin. In Lugufled.

In Cotes. In Saltenierfc. In Laxinton. In Schilton. In Berneheld.

In Ballebi. IIII . c 7 vi . bō. In Torp. In Cledinton. In Afchilebi.

In Baruebi. In Babetorp. In Bracheneholm. In Achetorp. In Boletorp.

In Bardulbi. In Richale. Ħ oma eps dun ad Houed.

In Ballebi dim c. In Afchilebi. i . c. In Brachenelholm. v . bō. In Cliue. iii . c.

In Achetorp. dim c. In Suddufeld. vii . c 7 v . bō. In Dufeld vii . c 7 ii . bō

Ibid . i . c. In Schipeuuic. v . c. In Brachenelholm. ii . bō. In Antgotebi. iii . c.

In Hamiburg. iii . c. In Bardulbi . i . c. Ibid \ i . c. In Cotinuui . i . c 7 ii . bō

In Richale . ii . c. In Turgisbi . iii . c

I WICSTVN HVNDRET.
In Wicftun. xxiiii. car. In Epton. vi . c. In Oueton. iii . c 7 dim. In Cliue. i . c
In Holme. viii . c. In Gudmundhā. i . c 7 dim. Ibid . i . c 7 v . bō. Ibid . i . c 7 ii . bō

2   In BURLAND (House), 1 carucate; in CAVIL, 2 carucates and 2 bovates; in EASTRINGTON, 6 carucates; in KILPIN, 3 carucates and 2 bovates; in YOKEFLEET, ½ carucate.

3   In COTNESS (Hall), ½ carucate; in SALTMARSHE, 6 carucates; in LAXTON, 1 carucate; in SKELTON, 3 carucates and 2 bovates; in BARNHILL (Hall), 1 carucate.

4   In BELBY (House), 4 carucates and 6 bovates; in THORPE (Lidget), 1½ carucates; in KNEDLINGTON, 6 carucates; in ASSELBY, 5 carucates.

5   In BARMBY (on the Marsh), 6 carucates; in BABTHORPE, 1 carucate; in BRACKENHOLME, 1 carucate and 6 bovates; in HAGTHORPE, 1 carucate; in BOWTHORPE, 4 carucates.

6   In BARLBY, 1 carucate; in RICCALL, 1 carucate. The Bishop of Durham (has) all these at HOWDEN.

7   The King, in BELBY (House), ½ carucate. The Count of Mortain, in ASSELBY, 1 carucate. Gilbert Tison, in BRACKENHOLME, 5 bovates. The Count of Mortain, in CLIFFE, 3 carucates.

8   Gilbert Tison, in HAGTHORPE, ½ carucate. The Count of Mortain, in SOUTH DUFFIELD, 7 carucates and 5 bovates; the Count of Mortain, in (North) DUFFIELD, 7 carucates and 2 bovates.

9   Gilbert Tison, in the same place, 1 carucate. Hugh son of Baldric, in SKIPWITH, 5 carucates. Earnwine, in BRACKENHOLME, 2 bovates. The Count of Mortain, in OSGODBY, 3 carucates.

10   The Bishop of Durham, in HEMINGBROUGH, 3 carucates. The King, in BARLBY, 1 carucate. The Bishop of Durham, in the same place, 1 carucate. Ralph Paynel, in (West) COTTINGWITH, 1 carucate and 2 bovates.

11   The Archbishop, in RICCALL, 2 carucates. Ralph Paynel, in THORGANBY, 3 carucates.

WEIGHTON Hundred

1   The King, in (Market) WEIGHTON, 24 carucates; the King, in SHIPTON(thorpe), 6 carucates. The King or Robert Malet, in HOUGHTON, 3½ carucates. The King, in (North) CLIFFE, 1 carucate.

2   Gilbert Tison, in HOLME (upon Spalding Moor), 8 carucates; Gilbert Tison, in GOODMANHAM, 1½ carucates. The King, in the same place, 1 carucate and 5 bovates. The Count of Mortain, in the same place, 1 carucate and 2 bovates.

In S.ntun . xv . c . In Houeton . iiii . c 7 dim . Ibid dim c . In Cliue . i . c.

In Gudmundhū . iiii : c . Ibid . v . c 7 vi . bō . Ib.d . ii . c . Ibid dim car.

381 d

In Efttorp . vii . c 7 ii . bō . Ibid . ii . c 7 vi . bō . In Lodenefburg . vii . c 7 dim.

In Toletorp . iii . c . In Erfeuuelle . i . c . In Torpi . iiii . c . In Cleuinge . iii . c.

In Clinbicote . ii . c 7 dim . Ibid . ii . c . Ibid . i . c . In Burton . xvii . car.

SNECVLFCROS HVNDRET.

In Midelton . v . c 7 vi . bō . Ibid . xii . c 7 i . bō 7 tcia pars . i . bō.

In Brachen : vi . c . In Watun . iii . c . Ibid . xiii . c . In Chileuuid . v . car.

Ibid . v . c . In Bafetuuic . iii . c . Ibid . iii . c . In Locheton . ix . c 7 dim . Ibid . ii . c7 7 dim.

In Ach . vi . bō . Ibid . vi . bō . In Piche . iiii . bō . Ibid . ii . bō . In Scogerbud . i . c.

Ibid dim c . In Eton . ix . c . 7 ii . bō . In Torp . i . c . In Steintorp . i . c . In Eton . vi . c.

Ibid . vi . c 7 vi . bō . In Lachinfeld . iii . c 7 v . bō . Ibid . i . c 7 ii . bō . In Neuton . i . c

3   Gilbert Tison, in SANCTON, 15 carucates. The King, in HOUGHTON, 4½ carucates. Gilbert Tison, in the same place, ½ carucate. The King, in (North) CLIFFE, 1 carucate.

4   The Archbishop, in GOODMANHAM, 4 carucates. The Count of Mortain, in the same place, 5 carucates and 6 bovates. William of Percy, in the same place, 2 carucates. In the same place, ½ carucate; no one has it.

5   William of Percy, in EASTHORPE, 7 carucates and 2 bovates. The   381 d
Count of Mortain, in the same place, 2 carucates and 6 bovates. The Archbishop, in LONDESBOROUGH, 7½ carucates.

6   The Archbishop, in TOWTHORPE, 3 carucates. The King, in HARSWELL, 1 carucate; the King, in TORPI, 4 carucates; the King, in CLEAVING (Grange), 3 carucates.

7   The Archbishop, in KIPLING COTES, 2½ carucates. The Count of Mortain, in the same place, 2 carucates. William of Percy, in the same place, 1 carucate. The Archbishop, in (Bishop) BURTON, 17 carucates.

SNECULFCROS Hundred

1   The Archbishop, in MIDDLETON (on the Wolds), 5 carucates and 6 bovates. The Count of Mortain and his men, in the same place, 12 carucates, 1 bovate and the third part of 1 bovate.

2   Erneis, in BRACKEN, 6 carucates. The King, in WATTON, 3 carucates. The Count of Mortain, in the same place, 13 carucates. The King, in KILNWICK, 5 carucates.

3   The Count of Mortain, in the same place, 5 carucates; the Count of Mortain, in BESWICK, 3 carucates. The King, in the same place, 3 carucates. The Count of Mortain, in LOCKINGTON, 9½ carucates. The Archbishop, in the same place, 2½ carucates.

4   The Archbishop, in AIKE, 6 bovates. The Count of Mortain, in the same place, 6 bovates. William of Percy, in PERSENE, 4 bovates. The Bishop of Durham, in the same place, 2 bovates; the Bishop of Durham, in SCORBOROUGH, 1 carucate.

5   William of Percy, in the same place, ½ carucate. Hugh son of Baldric, in ETTON, 8 carucates and 2 bovates; Hugh son of Baldric, in TORP, 1 carucate. The Count of Mortain, in STEINTORP, 1 carucate. The Archbishop, in ETTON, 8 carucates.

6   The Count of Mortain, in the same place, 6 carucates and 6 bovates. William of Percy, in LECONFIELD, 3 carucates and 5 bovates. The Count of Mortain, in the same place, 1 carucate and 2 bovates; the Count of Mortain, in NEUSON, 1 carucate.

InRageneltorp.iii.c.Ibid.iiii.c 7 dim. In Burton.xiiii.c 7 ii.bo.Ibid.i.c. + x

Neuton In Neuton.iii.c.In Molecroft.iii.c. In Gerdene.vi.c. In Delton.xii.c.

.i.c. In Hougon.xii.c.In Scornefbi.vi.c.In.Lanulfeftorp.ii.c.In Doniton.ii.c.

Ibid.v.c 7 vi.bo.In Grimefton.ii.c.Ibid.i.c. In Beureli.i.c træ qeta.

DRIFELT HVNDRET.

In DRIfeld.xxxii.c 7 dim. In Elmefuuelle.ii.c.In Calgeftorp.ii.bo.

Ibid.iiii.c 7 dim.In Cheldale.vi.c.In Auguftburne.vi.c.In Weftburne.v.c.

In Sudburne.vii.c.In Tibetorp.viii.c 7 dim.In Schirne 7 Cranzuic.ii.c 7 dim

In Drifeld.vi.bo. In Rotefse.ii.c.In Schirne.vi.c.In Neffeuuic.ix.c.

In Cranzuic 7 Hotune.viii.c 7 iii.bo.Ibid.ii.c.In Bagenton.xiii.c.Ibid.xi.c.

In Sundrelanuuic.i.c 7 dim.Ibid.i.c 7 dim.In Tibetorp.iii.c 7 ii.bo.In Torp.ii.c.

WARTRE HVNDRET.

In Wartre.xx.car.Ibid.iiii.c.In Naborne.iiii.c.Ibid.ii.c.

7   The Archbishop, in RAVENTHORPE, 3 carucates. The Count of
Mortain, in the same place, 4½ carucates. The Archbishop, in
(Cherry) BURTON, 14 carucates and 2 bovates. The King, in the
same place, 1 carucate.   *++N*

8   The Archbishop, in *NEWTON* (GARDHAM), 1 carucate. The Bishop of
Durham, in *NEWTON* (GARDHAM), 3 carucates. The Archbishop, in
MOLESCROFT, 3 carucates. The Bishop of Durham, in GARDHAM,
6 carucates. The Archbishop, in (South) DALTON, 12 carucates.

9   The Bishop of Durham, in HOLME (on the Wolds), 12 carucates.
William of Percy, in SCOREBY (Manor), 6 carucates; William of
Percy, in *IANULFESTORP*, 2 carucates. The Archbishop, in
DUNNINGTON, 4 carucates.

10   William of Percy, in the same place, 5 carucates and 6 bovates.
The Count of Mortain, in GRIMSTON, 2 carucates. William of
Percy, in the same place, 1 carucate. St. John's, in BEVERLEY,
1 carucate of land, with exemption.

DRIFFIELD Hundred

1   The King, in (Great) DRIFFIELD, 32½ carucates; the King, in
ELMSWELL, 2 carucates. The Archbishop, in KELLEYTHORPE, 2
bovates.

2   The King, in the same place, 4½ carucates; the King, in (Great)
KENDALE, 6 carucates; the King, in EASTBURN, 6 carucates; the
King, in (Kirk)BURN, 5 carucates.

3   The King, in SOUTHBURN, 7 carucates; the King, in TIBTHORPE,
8½ carucates; the King, in SKERNE and CRANSWICK, 2½ carucates.

4   The Count of Mortain, in (Great) DRIFFIELD, 6 bovates; the
Count of Mortain, in ROTSEA, 2 carucates. Hugh son of Baldric,
in SKERNE, 6 carucates. The Count of Mortain, in NESWICK (Hall),
9 carucates.

5   The Count of Mortain, in CRANSWICK and HUTTON (Cranswick),
8 carucates and 3 bovates. Hugh son of Baldric, in the same
place, 2 carucates. The Count of Mortain, in BAINTON, 13
carucates. Hugh son of Baldric, in the same place, 11 carucates.

6   The King, in (Old) SUNDERLANDWICK, 1½ carucates. Gospatric,
in the same place, 1½ carucates. The King, in TIBTHORPE, 3
carucates and 2 bovates; the King, in *TORP*, 2 carucates.

WARTER Hundred

1   The King, in WARTER, 20 carucates. William of Percy, in the
same place, 4 carucates. Robert of Tosny, in NABURN, 4
carucates. The King, in the same place, 2 carucates.

In Dalton . vi . c . Ibid . iii . c 7 v . bō . Ibid . xxii . c . 7 i bō . In Brunhā . xi . car.

In Wetuuanghā . xiii . c 7 dim . In Hughete . viii . c 7 dim . Ibid . viii . car.

In Holde . v . c . Ibid . i . c . In Chileuuic . xvi . c . In Metelbi . viii . c . In Torp . iii . c.

In Lapuṅ . xi c . In Geuedale . viii . c . In alia Geuedale . iiii . c . Ibid . ii . c.

In Grintorp . iiii . c . In Milleton . xv . c . Ibid . iii . c . In Fuletorp . i . c 7 ii . bō

Ibid . i . c 7 iii . bō . Ibid . i . c 7 iii . bō . In Eslinton . iiii . c . Ibid . v . c . Ibid . iii . c.

In Languelt . i . c 7 dim . Ibid . dim car.

POCLINTON HVNDRET.

In Poclinton . xiii . car . In Belebi . iii . c . In Haiton . ix . c 7 dim . Ibid . ii . c 7 dim.

In Brunebi . i . c 7 dim . Ibid . iiii . c . Ibid . ii . c . Ibi . ii . c 7 dim . In Waplinton . ii . c.

In Aluuarestorp . vi . c . In Rudtorp . iii . c . In Euringhā . iii . c . In Sudton . vi . c.

Ibid . vi . c . In Caton . xl . c . In Chelchefeld . ii . c 7 i . bō . Ibid . i . c 7 vii . bō.

2   The Count of Mortain, in (North) DALTON, 6 carucates. The King, in the same place, 3 carucates and 5 bovates. Robert of Tosny, in the same place, 22 carucates and 1 bovate. The King, in (Nun)BURNHOLME, 11 carucates.

3   The Archbishop, in WETWANG, 13½ carucates. The King, in HUGGATE, 8½ carucates. Earnwine, in the same place, 8 carucates.

4   The King, in HAWOLD, 5 carucates. The Archbishop, in the same place, 1 carucate. The King, in KILNWICK (Percy), 16 carucates; the King, in MELTONBY, 8 carucates; the King, in (Ouse)THORPE (Farm), 3 carucates.

5   The King, in YAPHAM, 11 carucates; the King, in (Great) GIVENDALE, 8 carucates; the King, in another (Little) GIVENDALE, 4 carucates. The Archbishop, in the same place, 2 carucates.

6   The King, in GRIMTHORPE (Manor), 4 carucates; the King, in MILLINGTON, 15 carucates. The Archbishop, in the same place, 3 carucates; the Archbishop, in (Water) FULFORD, 1 carucate and 2 bovates.

7   Count Alan, in the same place, 1 carucate and 3 bovates. Erneis, in the same place, 1 carucate and 3 bovates. The Archbishop, in HESLINGTON, 4 carucates. Count Alan, in the same place, 5 carucates. Hugh son of Baldric, in the same place, 3 carucates.

8   Count Alan, in LANGWITH (Lodge), 1½ carucates. Hugh son of Baldric, in the same place, ½ carucate.

POCKLINGTON Hundred

1   The King, in POCKLINGTON, 13 carucates; the King, in BIELBY, 3 carucates; the King, in HAYTON, 9½ carucates. William of Percy, in the same place, 2½ carucates.

2   The King, in BURNBY, 1½ carucates. The Archbishop, in the same place, 4 carucates. Robert Malet, in the same place, 2 carucates. William of Percy, in the same place, 2½ carucates. The King, in WAPLINGTON (Hall), 2 carucates.

3   The King, in ALLERTHORPE, 6 carucates. Gilbert Tison, in THORPE (le Street), 3 carucates. The Archbishop, in EVERINGHAM, 3 carucates. The Count of Mortain, in SUTTON (upon Derwent), 6 carucates.

4   William of Percy, in the same place, 6 carucates. Earl Hugh, in (High and Low) CATTON, 40 carucates. Count Alan, in KELFIELD, 2 carucates and 1 bovate. Hugh son of Baldric, in the same place, 1 carucate and 7 bovates.

★ In Steflingefeld.ii.bō.Ibid.ii.bō.Ibid.ii.c.Ibid.i.c7 dim.In Afcri.iiii.c.

In Morebi.i.c.Ibid.i.c.In Difton.iiii.c:In Chetelftorp.iiii.c.In Wilton.xv.c.

In Coldrid.vi.c7 vi.bō.In Aluuinton.vi.c.In Bodelton.i.c.Ibid.iiii.c7 dim.

In Frangefos.viii.c.In Geutorp.iiii.c.In Auiltorp.iiii.c.Ibid.ii.car.

In Greneuuic.iii.c.In Balchetorp.iiii.c.In Bernebi.vii.c7 ii.bō.Ibid.vi.bō.

HVNTOV. HVNDRET.

In Flaneburg.xv.car.In Sluuardbi.i.c7 dim.Ibid.vi.c7 dim.

Ibid.i.c7 dim.In Marton.v.c.Ibid.iii.c.Ibid.i.c.In Bredinton.xiii.c.

Ibid.v.c.In Hilgertorp.ii.c7 dim.Ibid.iii.c7 dim.In Wiuleftorp.ii.c.

Ibid.ii.c.In Bafingebi.viii.c.In Freftintorp.i.c.Ibid.vii.c.Ibid.i.car.

In Eleburne dim c.In Efton.vi.c.In Bouintorp.viii.c7 dim.Ibid.v.c7 dim.

In Gerendele.iiii.c.Ibid.viii.c.In Ricton.iii.c.Ibid.v.c.In Benton.vi.c.

381 d

5   The King, in STILLINGFLEET, 2 bovates. Count Alan, in the same place, 2 bovates. Erneis, in the same place, 2 carucates. Hugh son of Baldric, in the same place, 1½ carucates. Count Alan, in ESCRICK, 4 carucates.

6   Count Alan, in MOREBY (Hall), 1 carucate. Hugh son of Baldric, in the same place, 1 carucate. Count Alan, in DEIGHTON, 4 carucates; Count Alan, in CHETELSTORP, 4 carucates. The Archbishop, in (Bishop) WILTON, 15 carucates.

7   William of Percy, in WHELDRAKE, 6 carucates and 6 bovates; William of Percy, in ELVINGTON, 6 carucates. The King, in BOLTON, 1 carucate. The Archbishop, in the same place, 4½ carucates.

8   The King, in FANGFOSS, 8 carucates. The Archbishop, in GOWTHORPE, 4 carucates. Odo the Crossbowman, in YOULTHORPE, 4 carucates. The Archbishop, in the same place, 2 carucates.

9   The Archbishop, in GREENWICK, 3 carucates; the Archbishop, in BELTHORPE, 4 carucates; the Archbishop, in BARMBY (Moor), 7 carucates and 2 bovates. The King, in the same place, 6 bovates.

HUNTHOW Hundred

1   Earl Hugh, in FLAMBOROUGH, 15 carucates; Earl Hugh, in SEWERBY, 1½ carucates. The Count of Mortain, in the same place, 6½ carucates.

2   The King, in the same place, 1½ carucates; the King, in MARTON, 5 carucates. The Archbishop, in the same place, 3 carucates. The Count of Mortain, in the same place, 1 carucate. The King, in BRIDLINGTON, 13 carucates.

3   The Count of Mortain, in the same place, 5 carucates. The King, in HILDERTHORPE, 2½ carucates. The Count of Mortain, in the same place, 3½ carucates. The King, in WILSTHORPE, 2 carucates.

4   Drogo, in the same place, 2 carucates. The King, in BESSINGBY, 8 carucates; the King, in FRAISTHORPE, 1 carucate. The Count of Mortain, in the same place, 7 carucates. Hugh son of Baldric, in the same place, 1 carucate.

5   The King, in AUBURN, ½ carucate; the King, in EASTON, 6 carucates; the King, in BOYNTON, 8½ carucates. The Count of Mortain, in the same place, 5½ carucates.

6   The Archbishop, in GRINDALE, 4 carucates. The King, in the same place, 8 carucates. The Archbishop, in REIGHTON, 3 carucates. The King, in the same place, 5 carucates. The Count of Mortain, in BEMPTON, 6 carucates.

In Spetton.IIII.c.Ibid.VI.c.In Bocheton.v.c 7 VI.bo.Ibid.III.c 7 VI.bo.
Ibid.II.c 7 dim.In Fleuston.XIIII.c.In Stacstone.VI.c.In Foxhole.VII.c.

TVRBAR HVNDRET.

In Hundemanebi.XXIIII.c.In Ricstorp.IIII.c.In Mustone.IIII.c.
In Scloftone.III.c.In Neuton.VII.c.In Flotemanebi.v.c 7 VII.bo
Ibid.I.bo.In Muston.II.c.In Neuton.IIII.c.In Fordun.v.c.
In Ledemare.I.c.In Burton.XVI.c.In Fulcheton.IX.c.In Chelc.v.c.
In alia Chelch.II.c.In Ergone.I.c.Ibid.I.c.In Bringeha.III.c 7 dim.
Ibid.dim c.In Estolf.I.c.In Fodstone.v.c.In Chemelinge.v.c.
In Nadfartone.XXIII.c.Ibid.VI.bo.In Pochetorp.v.c.Ibid.I.car.
★ In Helmesuuelle.x.c.In Gartune.IX.c.Ibid.XXV.car.

BVRTON HVNDRET.

In Burton.XII.car.In Grenzmore.IIII.c.Ibid.II.c.In Arpen.II.c.
Ibid.VIII.c.In Chillon.XXX.c.Ibid.XI.c.Ibid.VII.c.

7 The King, in SPEETON, 4 carucates. The Count of Mortain, in the   382 a
same place, 6 carucates. The King, in BUCKTON, 5 carucates and 6
bovates. The Count of Mortain, in the same place, 3 carucates
and 6 bovates.

8 Earl Hugh, in the same place, 2½ carucates. The King, in FLIXTON,
14 carucates; the King, in STAXTON, 6 carucates; the King, in   •
FOXHOLES, 8 carucates.

TURBAR Hundred
1 Gilbert of Ghent, in HUNMANBY, 24 carucates; Gilbert of Ghent,
in *RICSTORP*, 4 carucates; the same Gilbert, in MUSTON, 4 carucates.

2 The same Gilbert, in *SCLOFTONE*, 3 carucates; the same Gilbert, in
(Wold) NEWTON, 7 carucates; the same Gilbert, in (East and West)
FLOTMANBY, 5 carucates and 7 bovates.

3 The Archbishop, in the same place, 1 bovate. The King, in
MUSTON, 2 carucates; the King, in (Wold) NEWTON, 4 carucates;
the King, in FORDON, 5 carucates.

4 The King, in *LEDEMARE*, 1 carucate; the King, in BURTON
(Fleming), 16 carucates; the King, in FOLKTON, 9 carucates. The
Archbishop, in (Great) KELK, 5 carucates.

5 The King, in another (Little) KELK, 2 carucates; the King, in
ARGAM, 1 carucate. The Count of Mortain, in the same place, 1
carucate; the Count of Mortain, in BRIGHAM, 3½ carucates.

6 The King, in the same place, ½ carucate; the King, in *ESTOLF*, 1
carucate. William of Percy, in FOSTON (on the Wolds), 5 carucates.
The Archbishop, in GEMBLING, 5 carucates.

7 William of Percy, in NAFFERTON, 23 carucates. The King, in the
same place, 6 bovates. William of Percy, in POCKTHORPE, 5
carucates. The Count of Mortain, in the same place, 1 carucate.

8 The King, in ELMSWELL, 9 carucates. The Archbishop, in GARTON
(on the Wolds), 9 carucates. The Count of Mortain, in the same
place, 25 carucates.

BURTON Hundred
1 The King, in BURTON (Agnes), 12 carucates; the King, in
GRANSMOOR, 4 carucates. Earnwine, in the same place, 2 carucates.
The King, in HARPHAM, 4 carucates.

2 Earnwine, in the same place, 8 carucates; Earnwine, in KILHAM,
30 carucates. The King, in the same place, 11 carucates. Odo the
Crossbowman, in the same place, 7 carucates.

In Roreſton.ix.c.Ibid.iii.c. In Logetorp.i.c7 dim. Ibid.v.c7 dim.

In Thirnon.vii.c.In Aſcheltorp.iiii.c.Ibid.ii.c.In Torp.iii.c.

In Cherendebi.xiii.c.ln Caretorp.v.c.Ibid.iiii.c.Ibid.iii.c.

In Rodeſtain.viii.c.Ibid.viii.c.Ibid.viii.c.In Tuuenc.xvii.c7 ii.bo.

In Suauetorp.ix.c.In Fornetorp.iiii.c.Ibid.xiiii.c.In Butruid.xii.c.

In Langetou.ix.c.Ibid.vi.c.In Buitorp.v.c.In Bruneton.iii.c.

In Galmeton.viii.c.In Binneton.vi.c.In Widlaueſton.v.car.

SCARD HVNDRET.

In Lanton.xviii.car.In Cheretorp.ii.c7 v.bo.In Briteſhale

7 Sudton.xiii.c7 dim.Ibid.iii.c7 dim.Ibid.ii.c7 dim.

In Wellon.v.c7 v.bo.Ibid.i.c7 iii.bo.In Suton.ii.c7 vi.bo.

Ibid dim c.Ibid.iiii.c.Ibid.i.c7dim.In Norton.i.c7 i.bo.

Ibid.i.c.Ibid.iii.c.In Sendriton.ix.c.In Warran.xii.car.

3   The Archbishop, in RUSTON (Parva), 9 carucates. The King, in the same place, 3 carucates. The Archbishop, in LOWTHORPE, 1½ carucates. The King, in the same place, 5½ carucates.

4   The King, in THORNHOLME, 7 carucates; the King, in HAISTHORPE, 4 carucates. The Archbishop, in the same place, 2 carucates. The Count of Mortain, in THORPE (Hall), 3 carucates.

5   The King, in CARNABY, 13 carucates; the King, in (Low) CAYTHORPE, 5 carucates. The Archbishop, in the same place, 4 carucates. The Count of Mortain, in the same place, 3 carucates.

6   The King, in RUDSTON, 8 carucates. The Count of Mortain, in the same place, 8 carucates. Ralph Paynel, in the same place, 8 carucates. The King, in THWING, 17 carucates and 2 bovates.

7   Odo the Crossbowman, in SWAYTHORPE, 9 carucates. The King, in *FORNETORP* and OCTON, 4 carucates. The Count of Mortain, in the same place, 14 carucates; the Count of Mortain, in BUTTERWICK, 12 carucates.

8   The Archbishop, in LANGTOFT, 9 carucates. The King, in the same place, 6 carucates; the King, in BOYTHORPE, 5 carucates; the King, in (Potter) BROMPTON, 3 carucates.

9   The King, in GANTON, 8 carucates. The Count of Mortain, in BINNINGTON, 6 carucates. The King, in WILLERBY, 5 carucates.

SCARD Hundred

1   Hugh son of Baldric, in LANGTON, 18 carucates; the same Hugh, in KENNYTHORPE, 2 carucates and 5 bovates. The Count of Mortain, in BIRDSALL and SUTTON (Grange), 13½ carucates. The King, in the same place, 3½ carucates. The Archbishop, in the same place, 2½ carucates.

2   Ralph of Mortemer, in WELHAM, 5 carucates and 5 bovates. Hugh son of Baldric, in the same place, 1 carucate and 3 bovates. The King, in SUTTON (Grange), 2 carucates and 6 bovates.

3   The Archbishop, in the same place, ½ carucate. Ralph of Mortemer, in the same place, 4 carucates. Hugh son of Baldric, in the same place, 1½ carucates. The King, in NORTON, 1 carucate and 1 bovate.

4   Ralph of Mortemer, in the same place, 1 carucate. Hugh son of Baldric, in the same place, 3 carucates. Berenger of Tosny, in SETTRINGTON, 9 carucates. The Count of Mortain, in WHARRAM (le Street), 12 carucates.

In Bocheton . xxII . c 7 vi . bõ . Ibid . III . c . In Grimſton . IIII . c 7 II . bõ.

Ibid . III . c . 7 dim . Ibid . II . c . 7 II . bõ . In Difgelibi . vIII . c . Ibid . II . c.

In Touetorp . vI . c . Ibid . III . c . In Bredale . vI . c . Ibid . x . bõ.

In Wentrigehã . xx . c . In Linton . IIII . c . In Scameſton . IIII . c.

Ibid . v . c 7 dim . In Torp . v . c . Ibid . vI . bõ . In Redlinton . II . c.

Ibid . II . c 7 II . bõ . Ibid . v . c . In Scachetorp . II . c 7 dim . Ibid . I . c.

I HACLE HVNDRET.

n Menniſtorp . vI . c . Ibid . II . c . In Geduualeſtorp . IIII . c . G . maminot

In Bergetorp . III . c . Ibid . II . c . In Chirchebi . vI . c . In Thorf . v . c . Ibid

In Vnchelfſbi . IIII . c . Ibid . II . c . In Grimeſton . IIII . c 7 dim . Ibid . II . c 7 dim.

In Aclun . vI . c 7 dim . Ibid . II . c 7 dim . In Gheruenzbi . III . c.

Ibid . III . c . In Ledlinge . v . c . In alia Ledlinge . vII . c . In Huſon . vI . c

In Bugetorp . IIII . c 7 dim . Ibid . IIII . c 7 dim . In Turalzbi . IIII . c.

5 Berenger of Tosny, in BUCKTON (Holms), 22 carucates and 6 bovates. Hugh son of Baldric, in the same place, 3 carucates. The King, in (North) GRIMSTON, 4 carucates and 2 bovates.

6 The Archbishop, in the same place, 3½ carucates. Hugh son of Baldric, in the same place, 2 carucates and 2 bovates. Berenger of Tosny, in DUGGLEBY, 8 carucates. The King, in the same place, 2 carucates.

7 The King, in TOWTHORPE, 6 carucates. The Count of Mortain, in the same place, 3 carucates. Hugh son of Baldric, in BURDALE, 6 carucates. The King, in the same place, 10 bovates.

8 Ralph of Mortemer, in WINTRINGHAM, 20 carucates; the same Ralph, in LINTON, 4 carucates; the same Ralph, in SCAMPSTON, 4 carucates.

9 The King, in the same place, 5½ carucates; the King, in THORPE (Bassett), 5 carucates. The Count of Mortain, in the same place, 6 bovates. The King, in RILLINGTON, 2 carucates.

10 The Count of Mortain, in the same place, 2 carucates and 2 bovates. Berenger of Tosny, in the same place, 5 carucates; Berenger of Tosny, in SCAGGLETHORPE, 2½ carucates. The Count of Mortain, in the same place, 1 carucate.

ACKLAM Hundred

1 Berenger of Tosny, in MENETHORPE, 6 carucates. The King, in the same place, 2 carucates; the King, in EDDLETHORPE, 4 carucates.

2 Berenger of Tosny, in BURYTHORPE, 3 carucates. The King, in the same place, 2 carucates; the King, in KIRBY (Underdale), 6 carucates; the King, in (Pains)THORPE, 5 carucates. Geoffrey Maminot, in the same place, 1 carucate.

3 Berenger of Tosny, in UNCLEBY, 4 carucates. The King, in the same place, 2 carucates; the King, in (Hanging) GRIMSTON, 4½ carucates. Odo the Crossbowman, in the same place, 4½ carucates.

4 The King, in ACKLAM, 6½ carucates. The Count of Mortain, in the same place, 2½ carucates. The King, in GARROWBY (Hall), 3 carucates.

5 The Count of Mortain, in the same place, 3 carucates. The King, in LEAVENING, 5 carucates. The Count of Mortain, in another LEAVENING, 7 carucates; the Count of Mortain, in HOWSHAM, 8 carucates.

6 The Archbishop, in BUGTHORPE, 4½ carucates. Odo the Crossbowman, in the same place, 4½ carucates. The King, in THORALDBY (Hall), 4 carucates.

In Scarpenbec.IX.c.Ex his ħt com morit.III.c 7 II.bŏ.In Screnghā.XII.c.

In Scradiztorp.III.c.In Barchetorp.VI.c.Ibid.II.c.

In Lepinton.VIII.c.In Sudeniton.VI.c.In Chirchan.VIII.car.

In Warron.IX.c.In Fridagstorp.VI.c 7 III.bŏ.Ibid.I.c.Ibid.I.c 7 dim.

Ibid.VII.c 7 dim.In Sixtendale.V.c 7 VI.bŏ.Ibid.IIII.c 7 II.bŏ.

In Redrestorp.III.c.Ibid.II.c.Ibid.I.car.

TORESHOV HVNDRET.

In Schiresburne.III.car.Ibid.VI.c.Ibid.IX.c.In Neuton.XVI.c

In Eslerton.III.c 7 dim.Ibid.II.c.Ibid.III.c.Ibd.I.c 7 dim.

In alia Eslerton.V.c.Ibid.V.c.In Cnapetone.VI.car.

In Wifretorp.XVIII.c.In Ludton.VIII.c.In Elpetorp.XII.c

In Turgislebi.VIII.c.In alia Turgislebi.IIII.c.In Turodebi.VI.c.

In Chirchebi.XVI.c 7 dim.Ibid.I.c 7 dim.In Muletorp.VI.c.

7   Odo the Crossbowman, in SKIRPENBECK, 9 carucates. Of these the
     Count of Mortain has 3 carucates and 2 bovates. Hugh son of
     Baldric, in SCRAYINGHAM, 12 carucates.

8   Odo the Crossbowman, in *SCRADIZTORP*, 3 carucates. The Count
     of Mortain, in BARTHORPE (Grange), 6 carucates. Odo the
     Crossbowman, in the same place, 2 carucates.

9   The Count of Mortain, in LEPPINGTON, 8 carucates; the Count of
     Mortain, in *SUDCNITON*, 6 carucates; the Count of Mortain, in
     KIRKHAM, 8 carucates.

10   The King, in WHARRAM (Percy), 9 carucates. The Archbishop, in
     FRIDAYTHORPE, 6 carucates and 3 bovates. The King, in the same
     place, 1 carucate. The Count of Mortain, in the same place, 1½
     carucates.

11   Odo the Crossbowman, in the same place, 7½ carucates. The
     Count of Mortain, in THIXENDALE, 5 carucates and 6 bovates. Odo
     the Crossbowman, in the same place, 4 carucates and 2 bovates.

12   The King, in RAISTHORPE, 3 carucates. Odo the Crossbowman, in
     the same place, 2 carucates. Hugh son of Baldric, in the same
     place, 1 carucate.

'THORSHOWE' Hundred   382 b

1   The Archbishop, in SHERBURN, 3 carucates. The Count of Mortain,
     in the same place, 6 carucates. Hugh son of Baldric, in the same
     place, 9 carucates. Ralph Paynel, in NEWTON, 18 carucates.

2   The King, in (East) HESLERTON, 3½ carucates. The Count of
     Mortain, in the same place, 2 carucates. Hugh son of Baldric, in
     the same place, 3 carucates. Berenger of Tosny, in the same place,
     1½ carucates.

3   The King, in another (West) HESLERTON, 5 carucates. The Count
     of Mortain, in the same place, 5 carucates. Ralph of Mortemer, in
     KNAPTON, 6 carucates.

4   The Archbishop, in WEAVERTHORPE, 18 carucates; the Archbishop,
     in (East and West) LUTTON, 8 carucates; the Archbishop, in
     HELPERTHORPE, 12 carucates.

5   Ralph of Mortemer, in THIRKLEBY (Manor), 8 carucates. The
     Count of Mortain, in another THIRKLEBY (Manor), 4 carucates.
     The King, in *TURODEBI*, 6 carucates.

6   The Count of Mortain, in KIRBY (Grindalythe), 16½ carucates.
     The King, in the same place, 1½ carucates. The Archbishop, in
     (Low) MOWTHORPE, 6 carucates.

Ibid̃ . 11 . c̃ . In Slidemare . 1x . c̃ . Ibid̃ . 1x . c̃ . In Coletun . dim c̃.

In Crogun . 1111 . c̃ . Ibid̃ . 1 . c̃ . Ibid̃ . 111 . c̃ . In Cottun . 1x . c̃.

In Colnun . v1 . c̃ . Ibid̃ . v1 . car.

In Patrictone . xv . c̃ . 7 11 . bō . In Wifeſtede . v11 . c̃ 7 dim̃.

In Halſam . v11 . c̃ . 7 11 . bō . 7 11 . partes . 1 . bō . In Torp . 111 . car.

In Torueleſtorp . 11 . c̃ 7 v1 . bō . In Suine . v11 . c̃ . 7 v11 . bō.

In Scirlai . In Mereflot . In Sprotelai . In Danetorp . H̃ Arc̃h

In Waghene . 11 . c̃ 7 v1 . bō . In Vela . In Tichetone . In Aſch.

In Weluuic . In Wideton . In *VTH HVND* ⸗ In Estorch.

In Grimeſton . In Monneuuic . In Otringehā . *IN MITH* H⁊

In Billetone . In Santriburtone . In Neutone . In Flintone.

In Danetorp . In Witforneuuinc . In Rutha . In Sutone.

In Sotecote . In Dripold . *IN NORTHVND.*

In Coledun . 1x . c̃ . In Riſon . In Siglestone . In Cotingeuuic.

In Brantiſburtune . In Leuene.

7 The Count of Mortain, in the same place, 1 carucate. The King, in SLEDMERE, 9 carucates. The Count of Mortain, in the same place, 9 carucates. The Archbishop, in COWLAM, ½ carucate.

8 The King, in CROOM (House), 4 carucates. Berenger of Tosny, in the same place, 1 carucate. Hugh son of Baldric, in the same place, 3 carucates. The Archbishop, in COTTAM, 9 carucates.

9 The King, in COWLAM, 6 carucates. Berenger of Tosny, in the same place, 6 carucates.

[HOLDERNESS]

10 The Archbishop, in PATRINGTON, 15 carucates and 2 bovates. In WINESTEAD, 7½ carucates.

11 In HALSHAM, 7 carucates, 2 bovates and 2 parts of one bovate. In (*Welwick*) THORPE (THORPE HILL), 3 carucates.

12 In 'THARLESTHORPE', 2 carucates and 6 bovates. In SWINE, 7 carucates and 7 bovates.

13 In (North) SKIRLAUGH, 9 bovates. In MARFLEET, 1 bovate. In SPROATLEY, 1 bovate. In DANTHORPE, 1 carucate. The Archbishop (has) them.

14 The Archbishop, in WAWNE, 2 carucates and 6 bovates. In WEEL, 2 carucates. In TICKTON, 1½ carucates. In ESKE, 2 carucates. In STORK(hill), 1 carucate.

SOUTH Hundred

1 In WELWICK, 4 carucates. In WEETON, 2 carucates and 5 bovates.

2 In GRIMSTON, 2 carucates. In MONKWITH, 2 carucates. In OTTRINGHAM, 6½ carucates.

MIDDLE Hundred

1 In BILTON, 3 carucates. In BURTON (Constable), 5 carucates. In (West) NEWTON, 3 carucates. In FLINTON, 6 bovates.

2 In DANTHORPE, 1 carucate. In WITHERNWICK, 1 carucate. In ROUTH, 1 carucate and 7 bovates. In SUTTON (on Hull), 1 carucate and 1 bovate.

3 In SOUTHCOATES, 1 carucate. In DRYPOOL, 1 carucate.

NORTH Hundred

1 The Archbishop, in (Great) COWDEN, 9 carucates. In RISE, ½ carucate. In SIGGLESTHORNE, 8 carucates. In CATWICK, 1 carucate.

2 In BRANDESBURTON, 1 carucate. In LEVEN, 6 carucates.

IN HELDRENESSE.

In BROSTEWIC . IIII . car tre . In Pagele . In Sutone . In Holm.

In Niuueton . In Nothele . In Scachelinge . In Camerinton.

In Torn . In Holme . In Dic . In Sprotele . In Prestune.

In Chilneffe . XIII . c 7 dim . In Tunestal . In Roffe . 7 tcia pars . I . c

In Heldeuuefton . In Osteuuic . In Afteneuuic . In Tansterne.

In Redeuuic . In Rigeborch . In Vmeltun . In Fostun . In Flentun.

In Wiuestad . In Widforneffei . XVIII . c 7 VI . bo . In Andrebi . In Bortun.

In Danetorp . In Fitlinge . In Sprotele . In Grimefton . In Washa.

In Tuneftal . In Thorne . In Holun . In Redmar . In Mapletone.

In Rolueftun . V . c 7 II . bo . 7 II . part . I . bo . In Arnestorp . In Coldun.

In Widforneuuic . In Torchilebi . In Widetun . In Mereflet . In Coningefbi.

In Rute . Ibid . I . c . In Horneffei . XXVII . c . In Bortun . In Torp

In Riftun . In Schirelai . In Schereltun . In Cletun . XXVIII . c 7 I . bo 7 dim.

In Hefinton . XV . c . In Gartun . In Ringeburg . In Aldenburg . IX . c

HOLDERNESS

1. In BURSTWICK, 4 carucates of land. In PAULL, 1 carucate. In SUTTON (on Hull), 2 carucates. In (Paull) HOLME, 1 carucate.

2. In NEWTON (Garth), 1 carucate. In NUTHILL, 2 carucates. In SKECKLING, 2 carucates and 2 bovates. In CAMERTON (Hall), 6 carucates.

3. In THORN(gumbald), 2 carucates. In (Paull) HOLME, 1 carucate. In (Lelley) DYKE, 4 carucates. In SPROATLEY, 1 carucate. In PRESTON, 1 carucate and 3 bovates.

4. In KILNSEA, 13½ carucates. In TUNSTALL, 7 carucates. In ROOS, 3 carucates and the third part of 1 carucate.

5. In HILSTON, 2 carucates. In OWSTWICK, 5 carucates and the third part of 1 carucate. In ELSTRONWICK, 4 carucates. In TANSTERNE, 1 carucate.

6. In ETHERDWICK, 2 carucates. In RINGBROUGH, 1 carucate. In HUMBLETON, 1 carucate. In FOSTUN, 3 carucates. In FLINTON, 4½ carucates.

7. In WINESTEAD, ½ carucate. In WITHERNSEA, 18 carucates and 6 bovates. In ANDREBI, 2 carucates. In BURTON (Pidsea), 7 carucates.

8. In DANTHORPE, 2 carucates and 6 bovates. In FITLING, 6 carucates. In SPROATLEY, 5 bovates. In GRIMSTON, 4 carucates. In WAXHOLME, 6 bovates.

9. In TUNSTALL, 1 carucate. In (Ow)THORNE, 5 bovates. In HOLLYM, 1 carucate. In REDMERE, 3 bovates. In MAPPLETON, 13 carucates.

10. In ROLSTON, 5 carucates, 2 bovates and two parts of 1 bovate. In ARNESTORP, 1½ carucates. In (Little) COWDEN, 3 carucates.

11. In WITHERNWICK, 6 carucates. In THIRTLEBY, 4 carucates. In WYTON, 4 carucates. In MARFLEET, 2 carucates. In CONIS(ton), 4 carucates.

12. In ROUTH, 3 carucates. St. John's, in the same place, 1 carucate. In HORNSEA, 27 carucates. In (Hornsea) BURTON, 2 carucates. In (Sou)THORPE, 1½ carucates.

13. In (Long) RISTON, 2 carucates and 6 bovates. In (North) SKIRLAUGH, 6 bovates. In (High) SKIRLINGTON, 5 carucates. In CLEETON, 28 carucates and 1½ bovates.

14. In EASINGTON, 15 carucates. In GARTON, 6 carucates. In RINGBROUGH, 2 carucates. In ALDBROUGH, 9 carucates.

.I.c⁷ dim   .I.c⁷   II.bo   VII.c⁷.   II.c⁷

In Niuuetone . In Schirelai . In Totele . In Wagene . In Melfe.

II.c⁷ 7 v.bo.   II.c⁷   IIII.c⁷   III.c⁷   II.c⁷.

In Benicol . In Rugeton . In Schirle . In Duuetorp . In Meretone.

III.c⁷   VI.c⁷   I.c⁷ 7 dim   .I.c⁷   II.c⁷ 7 II.bo

In Foisham . In Biuuich . In Niuuetun . In Ringeborg . In Waisha.

dim c⁷   v.c⁷ 7 vI.bo   7   IIII.c⁷   vI.bo.

In Otrengha . In Totele . In Caingeha . VIII.c . In Otringeha . In Halsha.

v.c⁷ 7 II.bo   v.c⁷ 7 II.bo   II.c⁷   .I.c⁷ 7 dim   .VIII.c⁷.

In Neuhufon . In Rimefuuelle . In Washa . In Redmar . In Vimetun.

.v.c⁷   .II.c⁷   III.c⁷   III.c⁷   XII.7 c⁷ dim   .vI.c⁷

In Niuueton . In Rifon . In Torp . In Lefsete . In Biuuorde . In Dodintone.

.v.c⁷ 7 II.bo   .II.c⁷   XII.c⁷.   .VIII.c⁷   .II.c⁷ 7 dim

In Wincheton . In Chelinge . In Frotingha . In Benestun . In Vlfram.

.IIII.c⁷   v.c⁷ 7 vI.bo   .I.c⁷.   XII.c⁷ 7 dim   vI.c⁷   vI.c⁷.

In Chilinge . In Begun . In Argun . In Bortun . In Settun . In Catefofs.

.v.c⁷.   .I.c⁷   III.c⁷   v.c⁷ 7 dim   .II.c⁷   III.c⁷

In Catinuuic . In Chenucol . In Riston . In Rifon . In Wadlande . In Haifeld.

.I.c⁷.   .I.c⁷   II.c⁷ 7 II. partes.   7   .IIII.c⁷   .II.c⁷

In Widforneuuic . In Lanbetorp . In Heifeld . I.c In Aluuardebi . In Vieburg.

IIII.c⁷   III.c⁷ 7 II.bo   .I.c⁷   XII.c⁷ 7 I.bo   .I.c⁷   v.bo

In Gagenestad . In Sutone . In Bileton . In Prefton . In Sotecote . In Dripold.

.II.c⁷   .I.c⁷   IIII.c⁷   III.c⁷ 7 v.bo

In Carletun . In Meretune . In Sprotele . In Koife.

15   In (East) NEWTON, 1½ carucates. In (South) SKIRLAUGH, 1 carucate. In TOTLEYS (Farm), 2 bovates. In WAWNE, 7 carucates. In MEAUX, 2 carucates.

16   In BENNINGHOLME (Hall), 2 carucates and 5 bovates. In ROWTON (Farm), 2 carucates. In (South) SKIRLAUGH, 4 carucates. In DOWTHORPE (Hall), 3 carucates. In MARTON, 2 carucates.

17   In FOSHAM, 3 carucates. In BEWICK (Hall), 6 carucates. In (East) NEWTON, 1½ carucates. In RINGBROUGH, 1 carucate. In WAXHOLME, 2 carucates and 2 bovates.

18   In OTTRINGHAM, ½ carucate. In TOTLEYS (Farm), 5 carucates and 6 bovates. In KEYINGHAM, 8 carucates. In OTTRINGHAM, 4 carucates. In HALSHAM, 6 bovates.

19   In (Great and Little) NEWSOME, 5 carucates and 2 bovates. In RIMSWELL, 5 carucates and 2 bovates. In WAXHOLME, 2 carucates. In REDMERE, 1½ carucates. In HOLMPTON, 8 carucates.

20   In (Out) NEWTON, 5 carucates. In RYSOME (Garth), 2 carucates. In '(Nor)THORPE', 3 carucates. In LISSETT, 3 carucates. In BEEFORD, 12½ carucates. In DUNNINGTON, 6 carucates.

21   In 'WINKTON', 5 carucates and 2 bovates. In (Nun)KEELING, 2 carucates. In (North) FRODINGHAM, 12 carucates. In BARMSTON, 8 carucates. In ULROME, 2½ carucates.

22   In (Nun)KEELING, 4 carucates. In BEWHOLME, 5 carucates and 6 bovates. In ARRAM, 1 carucate. In (Brandes)BURTON, 12½ carucates. In SEATON, 6 carucates. In CATFOSS (Hall), 6 carucates.

23   In CATWICK, 5 carucates. In *CHENUCOL*, 1 carucate. In (Long) RISTON, 3 carucates. In RISE, 5½ carucates. In WASSAND (Hall), 2 carucates. In (Great) HATFIELD, 3 carucates.

24   In WITHERNWICK, 1 carucate. In LANGTHORPE (Hall), 1 carucate. In (Little) HATFIELD, 3 carucates and 2 parts of 1 carucate. In ELLERBY, 4 carucates. In OUBROUGH, 2 carucates.

25   In GANSTEAD, 4 carucates. In SUTTON (on Hull), 3 carucates and 2 bovates. In BILTON, 1 carucate. In PRESTON, 12 carucates and 1 bovate. In SOUTHCOATES, 1 carucate. In DRYPOOL, 5 bovates.

26   In (West) CARLTON, 2 carucates. In MARTON, 1 carucate. In SPROATLEY, 4 carucates. In ROOS, 3 carucates and 5 bovates.

NOTES ON THE TEXT AND TRANSLATION

BIBLIOGRAPHY and ABBREVIATIONS used in the Notes

AN ... Anglo-Norman.

Arnold ... *Symeonis Monachi Opera Omnia; Historia Regum*, ed. T. Arnold (*Rolls Series* [75], London 1885).

AS ... Anglo-Scandinavian.

ASC ... 'The Anglo-Saxon Chronicle', in *English Historical Documents: ii, 1042-1189*, ed. D. C. Douglas & G. W. Greenway (London 1953) 110-203.

b. ... berewick (i.e. outlier).

Barlow ... F. Barlow, *William Rufus* (London 1983).

Barlow, *Edward* ... F. Barlow, *Edward the Confessor* (London 1970).

Barlow, *Church* ... F. Barlow, *The English Church, 1000-1066* (London 1963).

Boldon Book ... *Domesday Book, Supplementary Volume, 35: Boldon Book: Northumberland and Durham*, ed. D. Austin (Chichester 1982).

c. ... about.

Chibnall ... *The Ecclesiastical History of Orderic Vitalis: ii-iv*, ed. M. Chibnall (Oxford 1969-73).

d. ... daughter.

DB ... Domesday Book.

DB Cheshire ... *Domesday Book, 26: Cheshire*, ed. P. Morgan (Chichester 1978).

DB Herts ... *Domesday Book, 12: Hertfordshire*, ed. J. Morris (Chichester 1976).

DB Leics ... *Domesday Book, 22: Leicestershire*, ed. P. Morgan (Chichester 1979).

DB Norf ... *Domesday Book, 33: Norfolk*, ed. P. Brown (Chichester 1984).

DB Staffs ... *Domesday Book, 24: Staffordshire*, ed. J. Morris (Chichester 1976).

DF ... *Domesday Book or the Great Survey of England of William the Conqueror A.D. MLXXXVI: Facsimile of the Part relating to Yorkshire*, introduction by H. James (Southampton 1862).

DG ... H. C. Darby & G. R. Versey, *Domesday Gazetteer* (Cambridge 1977).

DGNE ... *The Domesday Geography of Northern England*, ed. H. C. Darby & I. S. Maxwell (Cambridge 1962).

Douglas ... D. C. Douglas, *William the Conqueror* (London 1969).

Douglas *Companions* ... D. C. Douglas, 'The companions of the Conqueror', *History* xxvii (1943), 129-47.

DTL ... G. Fellows Jensen, 'On the identification of Domesday tenants in Lincolnshire', *Nomina* (1986, forthcoming).

EPNS ... English Place-Name Society volumes.

ER ... East Riding of Yorkshire.

EYC ... *Early Yorkshire Charters* (*Yorkshire Archaeological Society Record Series*).

Faull ... M. L. Faull, 'The use of place-names in reconstructing the historic landscape: illustrated by names from Adel township', *Landscape History* i (1979), 34-43.

Forssner ... T. Forssner, *Continental-Germanic Personal Names in England in Old and Middle English Times* (Uppsala 1916).

Forstemann ... E. Forstemann, *Altdeutsches Namenbuch, Band i, Personennamen* (2nd edn., Bonn 1900).

Freeman ... E. A. Freeman, *The History of the Norman Conquest of England; iii-v* (Oxford 1876).

Galbraith ... V. H. Galbraith, *The Making of Domesday Book* (Oxford 1961).

Greenway ... D. E. Greenway, *Charters of the Honour of Mowbray* (*British Academy Records of Social and Economic History* new series i, 1972).

Jensen ... G. Fellows Jensen, 'The Domesday Book account of the Bruce fief', *English Place-Name Society Journal* ii (1969-70), 8-17.

JMcND ... John McNeal Dodgson (personal communications).

Jones ... G. R. J. Jones, 'The cultural landscape of Yorkshire: the origins of our villages', *Annual Report of the Yorkshire Philosophical Society* (York 1966), 45-57.

Kapelle ... W. E. Kapelle, *The Norman Conquest of the North* (London 1979).

Le Patourel ... J. le Patourel, *The Norman Empire* (Oxford 1976).

LVY ... M. W. Beresford, 'The lost villages of Yorkshire', *Yorkshire Archaeological Journal* xxxviii (1955), 44-70, 215-40, 280-309.

m. ... manor.

m. ... married.

ME ... Middle English.

NR ... North Riding of Yorkshire.

OE ... Old English.

OEB ... G. Tengvik, *Old English Bynames* (Uppsala 1938).

OF ... Old French.

OG ... Old German.

ON ... Old Norse.
OS ... Old Saxon.
OS ... Ordnance Survey.
PNDB ... O. von Feilitzen, *The Pre-Conquest Personal Names of Domesday Book* (*Nomina Germanica* iii, Uppsala 1937).
PNER ... A. H. Smith, *The Place-Names of the East Riding of Yorkshire and York* (*EPNS* xiv, Cambridge 1937).
PNL ... E. Ekwall, *The Place-Names of Lancashire* (Manchester 1922).
PNNR ... A. H. Smith, *The Place-Names of the North Riding of Yorkshire* (*EPNS* v, Cambridge 1928).
PNOE ... M. Redin, *Studies on Uncompounded Personal Names in Old English* (Uppsala 1919).
PNRB ... A. L. F. Rivet & C. Smith, *The Place-Names of Roman Britain* (London 1979).
PNW ... A. H. Smith, *The Place-Names of Westmorland* (*EPNS* xlii-xliii, Cambridge 1967).
PNWR ... A. H. Smith, *The Place-Names of the West Riding of Yorkshire* (*EPNS* xxx-xxxvii, Cambridge 1961-3).
PRO ... Public Record Office.
s. ... soke (i.e. jurisdiction).
s. ... son.
s.a. ... under the year of.
Sanders ... I. J. Sanders, *English Baronies* (Oxford 1960).
Serle ... E. Serle, 'Women and the legitimisation of succession at the Norman Conquest', *Proceedings of the Battle Conference on Anglo-Norman Studies* iii (1980), 159-70.
Skaife ... R. H. Skaife, *Domesday Book for Yorkshire* ([Leeds] 1896).
s.n. ... under the name.
sp ... without heirs.
SPN ... G. Fellows Jensen, *Scandinavian Personal Names in Lincolnshire and Yorkshire* (Copenhagen 1968).
Stenton ... F. M. Stenton, *Anglo-Saxon England* (3rd edn., Oxford 1971).
Taylor & Taylor ... H. M. Taylor & J. Taylor, *Anglo-Saxon Architecture* (Cambridge 1965).
Thorpe ... *Florentii Wigorniensis Monachi Chronicon ex Chronicis*; i, ed. B. Thorpe ([*English Historical Society* xiii], London 1848).
VCH ... *Victoria History of the County of Yorkshire*, ed. W. Farrer (London 1907-25) (unless otherwise stated references are to volume ii).
VCH Lancs ... *Victoria History of the County of Lancaster*, ed. W. Farrer & J. Brownbill (London 1906-11).
Whitelock ... D. Whitelock, 'The dealings of the kings of England with Northumbria in the 10th and 11th centuries', in D. Whitelock, *History, Law and Literature in 10th-11th Century England* (London 1981), 70-88.
WR ... West Riding of Yorkshire.
WYAS ... *West Yorkshire: An Archaeological Survey to A.D. 1500*, ed. M. L. Faull & S. A. Moorhouse (Wakefield 1981).
YASI ... Yorkshire Archaeological Society Inventory (housed at the headquarters of the Yorkshire Archaeological Society, Claremont, Clarendon Road, Leeds).

It should be noted that all abbreviations in Domesday Book have been represented in the notes by a full stop, rather than a reproduction of the form of contraction actually used, except where the form of the abbreviation is itself relevant.

It is not possible in a work of this size even to attempt to provide a full critical discussion of the Yorkshire section of Domesday Book. The editors are currently working on such a full study, but in this volume have necessarily confined themselves simply to an outline of some of the material available, both in the Appendix and in the notes, including the details on place-names and their locations. We should like to acknowledge the assistance of the many people who have supplied us with information and advice during the course of the preparation of this work, and in particular the following. Professor J. McN. Dodgson, University College, London, the General Editor of this series after the death of Dr. John Morris, for his assiduous attention to detail in the amendment of errors in his reading of the manuscript and notes and for extensive advice on the form and identification of personal-names and place-names. Professor Dodgson's name does not appear on the title page of this volume, and we would like here to record our thanks to him and our appreciation of the time and effort he has contributed to this undertaking over the past years. Mr. I. S. Maxwell, joint editor of DGNE, for reading through all the notes and providing valuable comments on the identifications of various places. Mr. I. S. Moxon, School of Classics, University of Leeds, for assistance with the translation and for writing 29W30 note. We should also like to extend our thanks to Mrs. P. Newton, the typesetter, for her skill and accuracy in preparing the manuscript for publication, and to Mrs. R. Savage, who saw the work through the press.

APPENDIX

1. BACKGROUND.

The earldom of Northumbria was the complex descendant of the old Anglian kingdom of Northumbria, which lay roughly between the Humber and the Tweed. It had its own ruling house and its own history of cultural development and political expansion in competition with other Anglian kingdoms (Stenton and Whitelock cover the whole period). This process was effectively halted by the influx of Scandinavian settlers, broadly the Danes from the east in the ninth century and the Norwegians from the west in the 10th century. This led to a long period of political turmoil in Yorkshire. The Danes seized power from the Angles and established themselves in York. They were subsequently challenged by simultaneous Norse incursions from the west and Saxon expansionism from the south. By the mid-10th century the efforts of the revived West Saxon monarchy had proved successful, and thereafter Northumbria became an earldom under the English kings. But English rule could never be taken for granted. The area was strongly Scandinavian and developed a lasting tradition of regional separatism. Eric Bloodaxe, the last Viking king, was expelled in 954, but in 1014 the Anglo-Scandinavian nobility of Northumbria and the Danelaw supported the invasion of the Danish king Sveinn, although they were less enthusiastic about his son Knutr. In 1066 and after there was the very real possibility that Northumbria would act as a base for a Scandinavian bid to seize the throne. Harold Godwinson was accepted as king only with reluctance and possibly without serious intent, for the people of Yorkshire showed considerable support for Harold Hardrada after his initial success at Fulford. With this background William of Normandy had no reason to believe that Northumbria would willingly accept his rule and every reason to believe the opposite.

By the 11th century it was clear that an independent kingdom of Northumbria was not politically viable, and it is unlikely that this was the object of the Northumbrian nobility. Their prime objective was to preserve and extend their own power within an earldom where the earl undoubtedly counted for more than the king. They were hostile to interference from the English monarchy and well aware of the opportunities presented by conflicting claims to the English crown in 1066. It did not take a genius to recognise that one battle did not permanently win a kingdom, and only a political fool would have been blind to Northumbria's pivotal position between Scotland, Scandinavia and England with all the opportunities for political manoeuvering which this represented. It should not be thought, however, that there was no room for political intrigue on the part of the English (or Scottish) king. There was ample opportunity to exploit the internal conflicts within the Northumbrian ruling class which were an integral part of the political complexity of the earldom throughout the 11th century.

Throughout most of the 11th century Northumbrian politics can be summarised as the attempts of various factions to take and hold the effectively vice-regal position of earl. The English king was involved in these disputes insofar as he wished to see his own supporter in power and not a representative of the opposition. In the late 10th century, therefore, the English kings re-established the descendants of the old Northumbrian ruling house as earls of Northumbria, with the additional safeguard of at times splitting the earldom into northern and southern sections divided by the river Tees. Under the Scandinavian king Knutr, however, the ascendancy of the Bamburgh line was challenged primarily by southern Northumbrian Danish interests. This has been seen as the background to the famous blood-feud which lasted from 1016 to 1073.

Around 1000 the House of Bamburgh was represented by Earl Waltheof. His son and successor Uhtred supported Aethelred against Knutr, but met with opposition from the Danish faction in York, represented by a thane called Thorbrandr and his followers (Kapelle chapter 1 for details and useful genealogical tables). Despite Uhtred's eventual submission to Knutr he was killed by Thorbrandr with Knutr's connivance. This led to some twenty years of confusion. The Bamburgh line continued to hold power beyond the Tees where Uhtred's brother and his two sons, Aldred and Eadwulf succeeded him in turn as Earl. Aldred avenged his father's murder by killing Thorbrandr, but was himself killed by Thorbrandr's son Karli. Meanwhile Knutr's nominees for the earldom, first Eric, then Siward – a man of obscure Scandinavian origins – were attempting to take control of the earldom from the south. Siward finally established control over the whole of Northumbria in 1041 by the expedient of killing Eadwulf (Arnold ii, 198), and attempted to unite the two factions by marrying Aldred's daughter. The result was that two main lines of claimants to the earldom traced their origins back to Waltheof, the distinction being between the older line and the newer line represented by Siward and his descendants. Because of the murder of Aldred, Siward's line also became direct participants in the blood-feud against the descendants of Thorbrandr.

Siward ruled successfully until his death in 1055, apparently untroubled by either Northumbrian factions (who may have regarded him as a representative of the Bamburgh line following his marriage and who anyway had first-hand experience of his military prowess) or Edward the Confessor. But his only surviving son was too young to succeed him. Whereupon King Edward and his council, under the dominant influence of the House of Godwine, instead of appointing any of the representatives of the ancient line gave the earldom to Tosti Godwinson. Tosti was unwelcome as an outsider and maintained his rule only with the support of extensive armed forces (Kapelle 88). Unlike Siward he was not successful in the all-important question of relations with Scotland, and it can be assumed that there was internal opposition to his rule. Tosti responded to this in the traditional manner of murdering his opponents. In 1064 he killed Gamall son of Ormr and Ulfr son of Dolgfinnr in particularly underhand circumstances. The following year he had Gospatric, the senior representative of the Northumbrian line, killed at the royal court (Arnold ii, 178). In response the Northumbrian nobility, led by Gamalbarn, Dunstan son of Aegelnothes and Gluniairnn son of Eardwulf, in alliance with Mercia, successfully deposed Tosti. Morcar, the younger brother of Edwin, Earl of Mercia, was appointed in his place – presumably the price of Mercian support. Morcar gave the northern part of the earldom to Asulfr (also known to historians as Oswulf) son of the former Earl Eadwulf (Arnold ii, 178), which was probably also part of the agreement.

This was the position when Edward the Confessor died in 1066. Not surprisingly the claims to the throne made by the House of Godwine were not received with any enthusiasm. Outright hostility met Tosti on his initial incursions (Arnold ii, 180). Harold only obtained northern support with difficulty, through his physical presence and his marriage with Edith, sister of Earls Edwin and Morcar (Chibnall ii, 139 and editor's comment). Earls Edwin and Morcar naturally opposed Harold Hardrada's invasion, but sections of the Yorkshire nobility were prepared to support the Norwegian king after his victory at Fulford, until he in his turn, and Tosti with him, were defeated and killed by Harold's forces at Stamford Bridge.

After Duke William's victory at Hastings sections of the northern nobility submitted to him at Barking (Chibnall ii, 195). These were Earls Edwin and Morcar who, however, probably had little influence in Northumbria, and Siward and Aldred, representatives of the Bamburgh line. These two were probably grandsons of Earl Uhtred and so brothers or half-brothers of the later Earl Gospatric. The Siward in question was probably Sigvarthbarn, i.e. Siward Barn 'child of Siward' (Chibnall ii, 195, editor's comment; Freeman iv, 21; Kapelle 18). Then or later Waltheof, Earl Siward's son, made Earl of Northampton and Huntingdon by Edward the Confessor (Stenton 599), did likewise (Chibnall ii, 197). It is highly likely that these lords submitted more from military weakness than any real acceptance of the Norman king, indeed the most serious challenges to his rule came from Northumbria in the following years. Significantly there is no record of Asulfr, Earl in northern Northumbria, coming to terms with King William.

Outright opposition in Northumbria was partly the result of King William's own ineptitude. He not only failed to make an effective alliance with the ancient line but also sent Kofsi to Northumbria as Earl early in 1067. Kofsi had been associated with Tosti's unpopular rule and had maintained himself by piracy along the Northumbrian coast after 1065 (Kapelle 106), before he too submitted to the King at Barking (Chibnall ii, 195). Most likely he had been instructed to overthrow Asulfr's *de facto* rule. This he attempted to do, with the predictable result that Asulfr killed him in March 1067. Asulfr retained power until the following autumn when he was himself killed by a robber (Arnold ii, 198-9). King William then decided to accept a representative of the Northumbrian house and accordingly sold the earldom to Gospatric son of Madalred, the senior member of the line (Arnold ii, 199). Presumably the King felt he was giving office to someone acceptable to the northerners but who, unlike Asulfr, had not openly opposed him.

This was a far from auspicious beginning to Norman rule. The main objective of the Northumbrian nobility was to minimise English interference in order to preserve their own power. Not surprisingly there was already opposition to royal taxation policy (Kapelle 107-8). Equally unsurprisingly Gospatric was more committed to his Northumbrian peers than to the English king. By 1068 Edgar Aetheling, who was emerging as a credible alternative candidate to the throne, had fled to Scotland accompanied by the powerful thane Merlesveinn (ASC s.a.1067) and Edwin and Morcar escaped from their 'honourable captivity' to organise a rising in the Midlands (Chibnall ii, 217). The Northumbrian nobility decided to support this. Unfortunately for them King William moved rapidly, effectively put paid to the trouble in the Midlands, and marched on York where he had at least one castle built (Orderic says one: Chibnall ii 219; ASC 'D' and Simeon say two: ASC s.a. 1068; Arnold ii, 186). Gospatric was able to flee to Scotland, but the people of York had little option but to submit. They included Arnketill, 'the most powerful of the Northumbrian nobles', who gave his son to King William as a hostage, and Bishop Alwine of Durham (Chibnall ii, 219). This first attempt at a rising had thus led nowhere but to an extension of Norman power in the North.

For all this there remained no reason why the North should accept Norman rule. Whatever claims he made for legitimacy, William of Normandy really held the English crown by conquest. It was both theoretically possible and perfectly justified for the English to drive him and his Norman barons out by the same method. It is thus inappropriate to describe the Northumbrian risings as rebellions, for a rebellion implies an accepted legitimacy. Rather they were manifestations of the wish of sections of the English ruling class to restore their own position against that section of the Norman ruling class which was currently occupying the country and increasingly consolidating its position at their expense. So far Norman power had penetrated only minimally into Northumbria, but any attempt to extend it could expect to meet with resistance, which is exactly what happened.

In January 1069 King William, once more ignoring the native nobility, sent Robert de Commines north as Earl. As before the result was predictable. Despite having been warned by Bishop Alwine, de Commines persisted in entering Durham, where he was ambushed and killed (Arnold ii, 187). This was the signal for another burst of resistance to Norman rule. Robert son of Richard, one of the custodians of York castle, was caught away from that secure base and killed (Chibnall ii, 223), after which the main body of Northumbrian nobles – Gospatric, Merlesveinn, Arnketill, the sons of Karli, along with Edgar Aetheling, prepared to attack York (Chibnall ii, 223). The castellan, William Malet, sent a desperate message to King William, who once more had to march rapidly north. He relieved the castle, built a second one (Chibnall ii, 223) – if he had not done so already – and entrusted the governance of the North to one of his chief barons, William fitz Osbern (Chibnall ii, 223), who remained there for a short time.

The 1069 rising was more serious than that of the previous year, for it was bound up with the invasion plans of Sveinn, King of Denmark. Although King William had put down the early stages of resistance, he was aware of the dangers from Scandinavia and ordered his lieutenants in Yorkshire to prepare themselves against this contingency. The Danish fleet arrived in September 1069 (Arnold ii, 187), at which point the rising was renewed. The Northumbrians were once again led by Gospatric, Merlesveinn, Arnketill and the four sons of Karli, joined by Earl Waltheof, Sigvarthbarn, Alwine son of Northmann and an unidentified *Elnocinus*, with Edgar Aetheling in attendance (Arnold ii, 187; Chibnall ii, 227, 229). Despite William Malet's assurance that York could hold out for a year (Chibnall ii, 227), the Danes and Northumbrians advanced on York, took the castles, killed most of the garrison and captured the castellans, William Malet with his family, and Gilbert of Ghent (Arnold ii, 188).

This was the greatest threat to Norman rule during King William's reign. Risings occurred all over England and the new ruling class were under immense pressure. Militarily, however, neither the Danes nor the Northumbrian ruling class seemed able to exploit their position. Their actions were ineffective throughout the autumn and by Christmas they were, to say the least, out-generalled by the Normans. King William came north, made an agreement with the Danes whereby they would return to their ships in the Humber, and marched on York. From there he devoted the Christmas festival to starting the infamous Harrying of the North (Arnold ii, 188). The object of the policy seems to have been to make the North a wasteland, incapable of mounting any serious threat to the southern part of the country, and there is no reason to doubt either the thoroughness of the action or its lasting effects. Those warned in advance retreated before the onslaught – if they could, which effectively meant the ruling class. The peasantry, whose interests were not considered by any of the warring parties, Normans, Northumbrians or Danes, were left to take the brunt of the devastation. Simeon recounts how the Bishop of Durham and the nobility fled to Lindisfarne taking with them their greatest treasure, the body of St. Cuthbert. This was possibly not so much to gain the saint's protection, for Cuthbert, although he had a reputation for being a most irascible saint and not lightly to be meddled with, proved singularly ineffective on this occasion, but more in case anyone stole him to profit from his miracles elsewhere (Arnold ii, 189). King William advanced as far as the Tees, where both Waltheof and Gospatric submitted to him (Chibnall ii, 233), returned through Yorkshire, devastating as he went, and continued his destructive journey south-west into Cheshire.

The main Northumbrian resistance had been broken. There was little material basis in either supplies or manpower for renewed opposition. The chief people were not too bady affected, Edgar Aetheling returned to Scotland accompanied by Merlesveinn, Sigvarthbarn and Alwine son of Northmann and others, and Bishop Alwine subsequently joined them in their exile (Arnold ii, 190). For most of them active resistance was at an end except for the bishop and Sigvarthbarn who later joined Hereward in Ely where they were captured and afterwards imprisoned (Arnold ii, 195). Bishop Alwine died the same year, 1071, at Abingdon (Arnold ii, 195), but Sigvarthbarn remained imprisoned in Normandy until released by Robert Curthose on King William's death (Barlow 50).

Northumbria did not remain entirely quiet, but the involvement of the native Northumbrian ruling class in risings against Norman rule was effectively at an end. For reasons of convenience King William restored Gospatric to his earldom in 1070, in which capacity he actively opposed Malcolm of Scotland, who had naturally seized this opportunity to wreak further damage by extensive raiding (Arnold ii, 191-2). Despite this Gospatric was replaced as Earl after King William's successful Scottish campaign of 1072 which was concluded by his agreement with King Malcolm by which all English exiles were expelled from Scotland (Kapelle 120-6). Gospatric went first to Flanders and afterwards to Scotland, where King Malcolm made him Earl of Dunbar and gave him lands in Lothian (Arnold ii, 199).

One possible reason why the Norman king felt able to dispossess Gospatric was that he had a new nominee who was himself of the Bamburgh ruling house. Waltheof was the son of the Earl Siward who had died in 1055, and was thus a genuine representative of the line, even though via the outsider Siward. The new Earl was high in King William's favour and married to his niece Judith (Chibnall ii, 263). As he had not been as involved in the northern risings as many Northumbrians, the King presumably felt that he was reliable. But if Waltheof was innovative in showing a new attitude to the Normans, he was traditional in other ways. The sons of Karli, who had been involved in the 1069 rising, had possibly made their peace with King William, but whether or not, they seem to have been living in Yorkshire. In pursuance of the ancient blood-feud (very possibly re-vitalised by more recent political disagreements, for its existence had not prevented both parties from collaborating in the 1069 rising), Waltheof had four of the six killed treacherously at Settringham in 1073 (Arnold ii, 200). This finally avenged the murder of his grandfather by their grandfather and in fact ended the vendetta – possibly because Waltheof himself did not long survive his enemies. In 1075 he joined the revolt of the Norman earls. His motives for doing so are not clear and he appears to have mobilised little support in Yorkshire or the further North. Possibly his own position there was not very strong, possibly the northerners had neither the capacity nor the wish to engage in a conspiracy which, despite Danish intervention during which York was sacked, was essentially a dispute within the Norman ruling class from which they could expect to gain little. Waltheof abandoned the rebellion in its early stages and sought a reconciliation with the King. It did him no good, however, for he was executed at Winchester in 1076 (Arnold ii, 207).

Waltheof was not only the last English Earl of Northumbria, he was also the last representative of the top ranks of the English ruling class. All others were either dead, in exile or in prison. King William's conquest was indeed built on the destruction of the native ruling class (Le Patourel passim). After Waltheof's death the political problems in the North took on a new dimension. The rule of Bishop Walcher of Durham, who attempted to combine episcopal and comital functions, was a turning point. Walcher was an outsider, a Norman associate though not himself Norman, but he died in the traditional Northumbrian manner, killed in the course of internal faction fights (Arnold ii, 210). Thereafter the political problems of royal government in the North were mainly those of finding a nominee strong enough to rule a traditionally turbulent region – for example Aubrey of Coucy, whom Simeon caustically dismissed as incompetent (Arnold ii, 199), was a dramatic failure in this respect – and how to prevent such a person, Norman though he might be, from using his position as a base from which to attack the royal government – as was to be the case with Aubrey's successor Robert of Mowbray in the reign of William Rufus (Barlow 346-59).

2. THE CHURCH IN THE NORTH.

York

Before the Norman Conquest York was both an archdiocese and an independent province. It was established in 735 (Stenton 109), and as an archdiocese its boundaries originally extended far into the South. There was a particular connection with the bishopric of Worcester, which at times was held in pluralism with York (for example Barlow *Church* 88). In 1070 through deposition in one case and death in the other the archbishoprics of Canterbury and York were both vacant. Lanfranc, William I's firm supporter and new Archbishop of Canterbury, wished both to extend the power of his see and also reduce the potential for separatism which an independent metropolitan see gave the North. Largely through what are now known to be forged documents, and with the political co-operation of the Pope, Lanfranc's claim to primacy was upheld. York was not only brought into dependence on Canterbury but also lost authority over the sees of Lichfield, Dorchester (later Lincoln) and Worcester. It retained thereafter only Durham and, for the time being, the Scottish dioceses (Stenton 664-5).

Within the archdiocese of York there were four minsters of which three were in Yorkshire: York itself, Ripon and Beverley. Ripon had been established in the mid-seventh century by Bishop Wilfrid, and was originally a monastic house. Beverley was founded by St. John of Beverley, Archbishop of York 705-18, who died there in 721, and was also originally monastic (VCH iii, 2-5). All three foundations had a troubled history between the ninth and 11th centuries, but by the 11th century they all functioned as houses of secular canons and served as local centres of the archdiocese (Barlow *Church* 229). St. Peter's, York, although a house of secular canons, nevertheless operated under a rule which was monastic in tone, but it was in a poor condition when Archbishop Thomas was installed, with only three out of the seven canons in residence (Barlow *Church* 228-9).

In the years following the Norman Conquest there was a revival of monasticism in the North. Selby was founded around 1070; Whitby was refounded under the patronage of the Percy family; and St. Mary's, York, which had its origins in the pre-Conquest monastery of St. Olaf, was refounded by Count Alan of Brittany (VCH iii, 95-108). Abbot Stephen, first Abbot of St. Mary's, tells of persecution of the new foundation at Whitby by the Percies and his consequent move with some followers to Lastingham, where he established himself as abbot (VCH iii, 102). Eventually he moved to the new foundation of St. Mary, but it should be noted that the Abbot of York held land in Lastingham and its environs from Berenger of Tosny.

Durham
St. Cuthbert might have been a useful saint to own, but the history of his diocese is far from untroubled. Its early history reads like a travelogue, with the saint's body and its attendant foundation moving from place to place, mainly fleeing from disturbances of various kinds, until the diocese was finally established in Durham in 995 (Barlow *Church* 229). The foundation was of secular canons called the Clerks of St. Cuthbert, under the dean. They were, however, married men, living in their own houses, owning hereditary estates and having a history of discord with their bishop (Barlow *Church* 229-30). The institution was reformed by Bishop William of St. Calais, who drove out the old canons and established a fully monastic house following the Benedictine rule (Freeman iv, 673-4).

The bishops themselves had an equally troubled history. Bishop Alric (1042-56) was a monk of Peterborough, opposed by the canons as an outsider imposed on them by the Earl (Barlow *Church* 85). He was succeeded by his brother Alwine, also a monk of Peterborough, who equally disagreed with his see, and who was integrally involved in the Northumbrian resistance to Norman rule (see above). His successor Bishop Waltheof (1071-80) attempted to combine the dual functions of Bishop and Earl, and met the kind of end a Northumbrian earl might expect (see above). William of St. Calais, bishop in 1086, was a religious reformer and church builder, but also a politician who suffered from his involvement in the political complexities of William Rufus' reign.

3. BIOGRAPHIES OF TENANTS

Norman
Although it is a useful shorthand to use the term 'Norman' as a collective description of all the non-English post-Conquest landholders, it is important to remember that not all of them originated from within the duchy. Duke William's expedition of 1066 attracted investors, mercenaries and plunderers from a wide area of northern Europe. Brittany and Flanders were well represented, but there were also people from Maine, Picardy, Poitou, Anjou, Burgundy and Sicily (Douglas 191).

The tenants-in-chief are listed here in the order in which they appear in DB. Their tenants are listed under the fee in which they held the most land (although it is rare for any tenant to be mentioned outside of that fee). Their first mention in this fee is the reference given, even though this may not be their first mention in DB. Other mentions of them in the text are listed in the Index of Persons. People who held land in the City of York and nowhere else are listed first.

C2. BISHOP WALCHER. His name is Old Germanic Walcher (Forssner 240). He was a Lotharingian and Bishop of Durham 1071-80. He was a friend of Earl Waltheof and encourager of monasticism in the diocese. He was appointed Earl of Northumberland after the execution of Waltheof, but got caught up in internal factional disputes amongst the Northumbrian nobility, as a result of which he was killed at Gateshead in May 1080 (Arnold ii, 201-5, 207-10).

C4. NIGEL OF MUNEVILLE. His name is derived from Muneville in the Saint-Sauveur canton of the arrondissement of Coutances of the department of La Manche, France (which has been used in this edition), or from Muneville-sur-Mer in the Brehal canton of the same arrondissement (Tengvik 99). He was the son of Ralph de Muneville and Avicia his wife. He married Emma the d. and co-heiress of William de Arcis of Folkestone. His d. and heiress Matilda m. Riwallon de Avranches (VCH 191; for his descendants see Sanders 45).

C9. BISHOP OF COUTANCES. Little evidence of his origin except his surname. He was confirmed in his bishopric only after a charge of simony had been disproved in 1049. He was present at Hastings and thereafter very active in King William's government. He was about the seventh richest man in England outside the royal family. Nevertheless he joined the 1088 rebellion, and although he was pardoned and restored to his possessions, he spent much of the rest of his life in his diocese. He died in 1093 (J. Le Patourel 'Geoffrey of Montbray, Bishop of Coutances, 1049-1093', *English Historical Review* lix, 1944, 129-61).

C14. GILBERT MAMINOT. His surname is the Old French Christian name *Maminot*, derived ultimately from that of St. Maximus, with the addition of the diminutive suffix *-ot* (Tengvik 222). On the form of his Christian name see 9W17 note. This Gilbert Maminot was probably Gilbert Maminot, Bishop of Lisieux, 1077-1100 (Freeman iv, 656). He was originally from Courbépine. Orderic stresses his medical skill and says he was a man of great learning and eloquence, but he was worldly and cared little for his episcopal duties (Chibnall iii, 19-21). He was with King William at his death and officiated at his funeral (Freeman iv, 704, 713). Skaife 4 says that the Yorkshire tenant was the nephew of the Bishop and says he held a barony based on Deptford near London. This seems to be a confusion with the Bishop's son, Hugh, who inherited West Greenwich, which estate eventually descended to the Say family (Sanders 97-8).

C19. HUBERT OF MONT-CANISY. His surname is derived from Mont-Canisy in the Tourgeville-en-Huge commune of the department of Calvados, France (Tengvik 100). He was also a tenant-in-chief in Suffolk.

1Y1. KING WILLIAM. King William was born in 1027, illegitimate son of Robert II, Duke of Normandy, and Herleva, hence his by-name 'William the Bastard'. Despite his bastardy he succeeded his father as Duke in 1035, but had a very troubled early period before his position was established at the Battle of Mortemer in 1054. He m. Matilda d. of Baldwin V of Flanders *c.*1051, although papal dispensation for the union was not given until 1059. He claimed the English throne by designation from Edward the Confessor and claimed that Harold Godwinson had given him his oath to promote his succession. He enlisted papal approval for his invasion of 1066 and defeated the English forces at Hastings. Between 1066-70 he repressed various English risings and in 1072 led a successful expedition to Scotland. In 1075 he overcame a revolt of the Norman earls, and in 1082 imprisoned his half-brother Odo of Bayeux for disloyalty. He had extensive problems in Normandy and with his eldest son Robert in the latter part of his reign. He died in 1087 and was buried in Caen. The children of the marriage included Robert Duke of Normandy, William II of England and Henry I of England (Douglas).

2A1. ARCHBISHOP THOMAS. Archbishop Thomas (1070-1100) was a native of Bayeux where he became a canon in the cathedral. A learned man, he studied in France, Germany and Spain, and became Treasurer of Bayeux (Freeman iv, 339-40). As a canon of Bayeux he was doubtless associated with Odo of Bayeux, King William's half-brother. He was a reputable archbishop, but had to concede the primacy to Archbishop Lanfranc (see above). He composed the epitaph engraved on King William's tomb (Barlow 51).

2B4. CANONS OF ST. PETER'S. Secular canons of the minster in York dedicated to St. Peter.

2W6. WILLIAM OF VERLY. His surname is derived from Verly in the department of Aisne, France; the modern form of the name is Varley (Tengvik 118).

2W7. ST. WILFRID'S TERRITORY. Land belonging to Ripon Minster, dedicated to St. Wilfrid, also a house of secular canons, associated with the archbishopric of York.

2E1. ST. JOHN'S, BEVERLEY. Land belonging to Beverley Minster, dedicated to St. John of Beverley, also a house of secular canons, associated with the archbishopric of York.

3Y1. BISHOP WILLIAM. On the form of Bishop William's name see 1W63 note. William of St. Calais, Bishop of Durham 1080-96, was educated at Bayeux under Odo of Bayeux, and was later his protégé. He became Prior of St. Calais in Maine and Abbot of St. Vincent-des-Pres near Le Mans. He received his bishopric in 1080 as the reward for diplomatic missions for King William. At the start of the reign of William Rufus he was pre-eminent in the government. He was, however, partially associated with the 1088 conspiracy headed by Odo of Bayeux, which led to his famous trial and subsequent exile. He was reconciled with William Rufus in 1091 and thereafter associated with the government until his death, although not so closely as before. He was a prominent supporter of the King in his dispute with Archbishop Anselm. He died in January 1096 (Barlow passim).

3Y11. ST. CUTHBERT'S. The community established around Durham Cathedral, once a foundation of secular canons, but reformed into a Benedictine priory by Bishop William.

4N1. EARL HUGH. He was the son of Richard of Goz, and nephew of King William (Skaife 48). He was an important noble in Normandy, holder of the hereditary Vicomté of Avranchin (Douglas 93). As one of Duke William's trusted advisers, he was left in Normandy to assist Duchess Matilda in 1066, and according to the Whitby Cartulary arrived in England in 1067 (Douglas 186). He was given the Earldom of Chester in 1070/1 and was prominent in the wars against the Welsh (Freeman iv, 487, 490). He was one of the greatest landholders in England. He founded the Abbey of St. Sever in Normandy and restored St. Werburgh's in Chester (Skaife 48-9), where he took the monastic habit shortly before his death (Freeman iv, 491). Possibly this was to atone for his lifestyle which, according to Orderic, was notorious for extravagance, sexual excesses and gluttony (Chibnall ii, 261, 263). He prepared to go on Odo of Bayeux's expedition in 1082, but suffered no adverse consequences (Chibnall iv, 41). He was succeeded by his son Richard, who died in the White Ship disaster (Skaife 49).

5N1. COUNT (ROBERT) OF MORTAIN. He took his name from Mortagne in the department of La Manche, France (Tengvik 101), but the form used here is that by which he is usually known to historians. The name survives in modern English as Mortyn, Morten and Mortan (Tengvik 101). Robert of Mortain, whose name derives from his pre-Conquest county in France, was the half-brother of King William. He was present at Hastings (Douglas *Companions* 133) and became the largest landholder in England after the King, his estates being especially extensive in the south-west where he held most of Cornwall. He m. Matilda d. of Roger of Montgomery and sister of Roger of Poitou (Skaife 51), and had a reputation for despoiling the Church (Freeman iv, 169). He joined the 1088 rebellion, was banished and his lands confiscated. He did not return to England. He died in 1090 and was buried in the Abbey of Grestain (Skaife 51). His lands were restored to his son William as part of the settlement between William Rufus and Robert Curthose (Freeman v, 85); however, it appears that the Yorkshire lands were not restored (VCH 155). Count William lost the whole of his English fee in 1106 (VCH 155).

5N1. NIGEL FOSSARD. His surname is the Old French Christian name *Fossard*, derived perhaps ultimately from Latin *fossa* 'ditch' (Tengvik 218). He was one of the two sub-tenants who between them held almost the whole of the Count of Mortain's Yorkshire lands. He was a liberal benefactor to St. Mary's Abbey and Holy Trinity, York. Little else is known about him (Skaife 2-3). Sanders 66 gives his date of death as 1120. The family held the barony (and presumably the castle) of Mulgrave. The forfeiture of Robert of Mortain led to the Fossards becoming tenants-in-chief, possibly as early as 1088, but certainly by 1106 (VCH 155).

5N9. RICHARD OF SOURDEVAL. His surname is derived from Sourdeval in the arrondissement of Mortain of the department of La Manche, France, or else Sourdeval in the department of Calvados, France (Tengvik 115). He is sometimes known in modern historical writings as Richard de Surdeval. He was the other of the two main tenants of Robert of Mortain in Yorkshire, and like the Fossards the Sourdevals became tenants-in-chief by 1088 or 1106 (VCH 155). He was succeeded by ds., co-heiresses, one of whom married Ralph Paynel (EYC vi, 4).

5W38. ALFRED. Said to be the Count of Mortain's butler. He held other lands from the Count in Nottinghamshire and Northamptonshire and had a son living in 1130 (VCH 155).

6N1. COUNT ALAN. Alan the Red was a son of Eudo of Penthiévre in Brittany, a younger branch of the ducal house. Traditionally he led the Breton contingent at Hastings (Douglas *Companions* 145). His extensive lands would suggest that he played a leading role in the campaign. He was one of the greatest landholders in England, including the extensive estates in Norfolk and Suffolk granted to him after the rebellion of Earl Ralph (VCH 157). It is possibly significant here that Earl Ralph de Gael was himself a Breton. He was constantly in attendance on William I (Douglas 268) and founded St. Mary's Abbey, York, on the previous foundation of St. Olaf (see above). He was probably unmarried, as was his brother and successor, but for the matrimonial plans of the brothers with King Malcolm's daughter Edith and Harold Godwinson's daughter Gunnhildr, an ex-nun, see Searle, and Barlow 310-16. He died c.1093 and was succeeded by his brother, Alan the Black, and he by their brother Stephen. Alan the Red was buried in Bury St. Edmund's (Skaife 73).

6N5. ENISANT MUSARD. His name is Breton, with a by-name derived from *musardus* 'stupid' (DB Norfolk 1-4, 14). He held land in Cambridgeshire and Norfolk from Count Alan. It is thought that he held the Constable's fee of 81 knights in Richmond, although there is no evidence that he himself was Constable of Richmond. He was dead by 1130. The bulk of his holdings passed to Roald the

Constable and Richard de Rolles, who may have married his two daughters (and presumably co-heiresses). His lands constituted the Constable's holding in the early 12th century (EYC v, 81-4).

6N7. BODIN. Bodin and his brother Bardulf were said to be illegitimate sons of Eudo de Penthiévre, and therefore half-brothers of Count Alan. Bodin later became a monk in St. Mary's, York, accompanied by an endowment from his brother (who may possibly have been his heir) (VCH 157).

6N27. PICOT. Skaife 73 suggests that he was probably from Loucelles near Caen. He also held land from Count Alan in Lincolnshire. He was still alive c.1115-8, but dead by 1130. He was succeeded by Roger de Lacell', his son (EYC v, 182-3). He was the founder of the Lascelles family which continued with heirs male until 1294, when 4 co-heiresses split the estate (VCH 159).

6N35. HEREWIG. Also the Count's tenant in Lincolnshire, Norfolk, and Nottinghamshire. He made donations to St. Mary's, York (VCH 159).

6N57. WIUHOMARCH. An Old Breton personal-name (PNDB s.n. *Wimarc*). He also held lands from the Count in Norfolk (VCH 159). He was the holder of the Steward's fee, originally of 15 knights. He apparently continued as Steward under Earls Alan the Black and Stephen. He died before 1130, when his Yorkshire lands were divided between his two sons. By the end of the 12th century the sub-tenants of the Steward's fee held directly of the lord of the honour, and not of the Steward (EYC v, 17-19). He was the founder of the family of Thornton, of Thornton Steward (EYC v, 1).

6N59. ODO. *Odo Camerarius*, presumably the Count's chamberlain. He held the Chamberlain's fee, the original service of which was 11 knights, and apparently continued as Chamberlain under the following two Earls. He was dead by 1130. He was succeeded by his son Robert, also called 'Chamberlain', who founded Denny Priory in Cambridgeshire (EYC v, 167-9).

6N87. RIBALD. Probably the 'Ribald, brother of Count Alan' who gave land to St. Mary's, York, before 1112 for the souls of his wife Beatrice and Count Alan. His wife was the d. of Ivo Taillebois of Lincolnshire. There were three sons, the eldest of whom married Agatha d. of Robert of Brus (Skaife 82-3). He held a large fee from Count Alan in Norfolk (VCH 158). He was the founder of the family of the lords of Middleham (EYC v, 1).

6N128. ROBERT. Identified as Robert de Mosters, the Count's tenant in Nottinghamshire and Lincolnshire (but not Cambridgeshire). He was the founder of the Musters family (EYC v, 1).

7E1. ROBERT OF TOSNY. In DB his name is given in the form *de Todeni*, by which he is sometimes known to historians. His name derives from Tosny in canton Gaillon of the Louviers arrondissement of the department of Eure, France (Tengvik 116). Skaife describes him as a younger son of Ralph lord of Tosny. He held lands in various counties, but his chief estates were in Lincolnshire and Leicestershire (Skaife 92). He was lord of the Honour of Belvoir and was succeeded by his son William who died sp. The lands were inherited by his d. Alice, and through her went first to the de Albini family and later, in the 14th century, to the Roos family of Helmsley (Sanders 12).

8E1. BERENGER OF TOSNY. Son of the above. He also had lands in Lincolnshire, Oxfordshire and Nottinghamshire (Skaife 92). His estate was later known as the Honour of Settrington. He died sp. and his lands descended with those of the Honour of Belvoir to Alice his niece and her husband, Roger Bigod. Unlike the Honour of Belvoir, the Honour of Settrington remained in the Bigod family. His heirs general recovered Barnoldswick, which Roger of Poitou was holding in 1086 (VCH 160-1).

8E1. THE ABBOT OF YORK. St. Mary's Abbey, York, re-established from the pre-Conquest St. Olaf's by Count Alan (see above).

9W1. ILBERT DE LACY. His surname derives from Lassy in the canton of Conde sur Noireau in the arrondissement of Vire of the department of Calvados, France, modern forms of the name being Lacy, Lacey, Lassey and Lassy (Tengvik 94). He is usually known in modern historical writings as Ilbert de Laci or de Lacy, the latter form being used in this edition. He was probably a vassal of Odo of Bayeux, from whom he held a moderately substantial fee in Lincolnshire and the south Midlands.

He and his brother Walter – an important lord in the Welsh marches – were in the second rank of Norman lords who owed their position to their military skill. Ilbert de Lacy was not associated with Odo of Bayeux's fall in 1082 or 1088. Instead his position advanced as he was granted the Honour of Pontefract in Yorkshire and later held his former mesne fees in chief. His main religious foundation was the Collegiate Chapel of St. Clement within Pontefract Castle which was the *caput* of his fee. He was succeeded, probably by 1095, by his son and heir, Robert. Despite some vicissitudes in the 12th century the family continued to add to its possessions and were the forebears of the Earls of Lincoln. See further W. E. Wightman, *The Lacy Family in England and Normandy, 1066-1194* (Oxford 1966).

9W4. RALPH. Identified as the Ralph le Grammaire who gave tithes to St. Clement's and was ancestor of a long line (VCH 165). He was probably the ancestor of the Gramary family (WYAS 422).

9W11. ROBERT. Identified as Robert de Somerville who granted land to St. Clement's Chapel (VCH 165). Skaife 98 suggests an origin in Somerveio near Bayeux, where he says the bishops had a castle. For the later history of the fee see WYAS 494.

9W17. GILBERT. Farrer identifies him as the ancestor of the Stapleton family (VCH 165), who certainly held land in the township in the Middle Ages (WYAS 540).

9W19. WILLIAM. Assumed to be the father of Ascelin de Dai, whose son held tenements in Ackton in 1166 (VCH 165). In 1166 Ackton was divided between Henry and Ralph de Day and Peter de Toulston (WYAS 295).

9W24. HUGH. Farrer merely observes that he cannot be connected with the local family of Ria or Ryther (VCH 165).

9W27. HUMPHREY. It is thought that he might have originated from Villy in the department of Calvados, France (VCH 165). The association is prompted by the fact that Lassy is situated in this same department (see above under 9W1, s.n. Ilbert de Lacy).

9W37. WILLIAM. Identified as William le Peytevin who made donations to St. Clement's (VCH 165).

9W40. ALFRED. He may have been the ancestor of the family of Hay of Aughton in the East Riding. Roger his son still held lands there in 1166 (VCH 164).

9W42. HEREWIG. Possibly the same as *Herveus* who held lands in Oxfordshire from the Bishop of Bayeux; these became part of the Lacy fee after the Bishop's banishment (VCH 165).

9W44. ROBERT. The predecessor of Gerard de Rainville and the Rainville family (VCH 165). Skaife 103 thinks they originated from Rainville near Caen.

9W46. RALPH. As Ralph Pincerna made donations to St. Clement's Chapel. It is thought that the lands escheated, though no date is available for this (VCH 165). William son of Aldelin held the land in 1166 (WYAS 538).

9W53. MALGER. It seems that his lands had escheated by the time of Henry I (VCH 165).

9W54. RALPH. He made donations to St. Clement's Chapel from the holding, and it was still held by his descendants in 1166 according to Farrer (VCH 165). WYAS 370-1, however, would suggest otherwise.

9W56. GERBODO. He made donations to St. Clement's and also possibly to Nostell Priory, and may have been the ancestor of William Fitz Gerbodo and Robert his brother, who made donations to Roche Abbey (Skaife 105). Farrer, however, is of the view that his lands had escheated, and the township was certainly held by Sveinn son of Alric in the 12th century (WYAS 352).

9W57. HAMELIN. The fee seems to have escheated by the early 12th century when the vill was held by Robert de Fryston (WYAS 372).

9W99. ROGER. Identified as Roger le Peytevin through his donations to St. Clement's (VCH 165). It is possible, however, that the estate was resumed into the demesne by the end of the 11th century, and it seems that Roger le Peytevin was not holding there by 1166 (WYAS 561).

10W1. ROGER DE BUSLI. His surname may be derived from Bully-en-Brai in the Neufchatel canton of the arrondissement of Dieppe in the department of Seine-Inferieure, France, although the absence of early forms of the place-name preclude conclusive identification (Tengvik 78). He is usually known in modern historical writing as Roger de Busli, the form used in this edition in view of the uncertainty as to the origins of his surname. Roger de Busli was lord of the lands which became known as the Honour of Tickhill. His estate included other lands in Derbyshire, Leicestershire, Lincolnshire and Nottinghamshire. He founded Blythe Abbey around 1088 and died *c.*1098-1100. As his s. and heir was under age, his kinsman Robert of Belleme claimed the wardship. Possibly the son was dead by 1102 since, when Henry I seized Belleme's land in that year, he retained the honour himself and later granted it to the Count of Eu. The honour is sometimes called the Honour of Blythe, but by the mid-12th century the *caput* was firmly established at Tickhill Castle and the honour known by that name (Sanders 147; Skaife 116; VCH 166).

10W33. FULCO. Farrer identifies him as the Fulk of Lisors of the Claims (CW14). Fulk of Lisors' name is derived from either Lisores in the Livarot canton of the arrondissement of Lisieux of the department of Calvados, France, or Lisors in the Lyons canton of the department of Eure, France (Tengvik 95), the latter being used in this edition as preferred by Tengvik. On the form of his name see 13N15 note. Fulk of Lisors was the founder of the Lisours family. He died sometime after 1088. His s. and heir Robert m. Albreda d. of Robert de Lacy of Pontefract, and from them was derived the second house of Lacy after the death sp. of the last of the elder line in 1193 (VCH 167).

10W41. COUNTESS JUDITH. She was the daughter of King William's sister Adelaide and her second husband Lambert, Count of Lens. She married Earl Waltheof of Northumbria *c.*1070-2 (Freeman iv, 301, 524). According to Orderic (Chibnall ii, 321), she was the chief accuser of her husband. This may be an attempt by Orderic to share the blame for one of King William's more disreputable deeds. Countess Judith kept Waltheof's lands after his death, but may well have had her other estates by direct grant to herself (Freeman iv, 601). The lands descended to the children of the marriage, all girls. The eldest married David of Scotland (Freeman iv, 601) and Hallam passed to the Scottish crown via this marriage (VCH ii, 167).

11E1. ROBERT MALET. His surname is a nick-name, OF *malet* 'evil', a diminutive of *mal* 'evil'; its modern forms are Mallet and Mallett (Tengvik 350-1). Robert Malet was the son of William Malet (see below under CN3). He inherited little of his father's Yorkshire property, although he did retain the Honour of Eye in Suffolk and other lands in Lincolnshire (VCH 169). He was Sheriff of Suffolk (Douglas 297) and active in repressing the Revolt of the Earls in 1075 (Freeman iv, 579). He was Chamberlain to Henry I, but Farrer says that he supported Duke Robert and was killed in Tinchebrai in 1106. His estates were forfeited and although his nephew, the Earl of Chester, obtained Eye (Skaife 123), his Yorkshire estates were dispersed amongst other landholders (VCH 169). Eleanor Serle (228), however, notes that despite his loyalty in 1075, he was not only not rewarded but actually lost lands to others, and that by 1086 he was no longer Sheriff of Suffolk. When he died in 1106 his heir was not allowed to inherit in England, and she quotes the ASC for 1110 as saying his heir was deprived of his lands but no reason was given for this. This conflicts with Barlow (151) who notes that he was a favourite of William I and Henry I, but not William Rufus. His removal as Sheriff is not surprising: Sheriffs did not necessarily have life tenure in the office and the holder changed very often in Yorkshire, for example. If Robert Malet died at Tinchebrai, it is not particularly surprising that his heir was not allowed to inherit.

12W1. WILLIAM DE WARENNE. His surname is probably derived from La Varenne, on the Varenne (now the Arques) in the department of Seine-Inferieure, although alternative possibilities are a derivation from Old French *warenne* 'warren', i.e. a locational surname, or from the Old French personal name Warin; the modern forms of the name are Warren and Warrin (Tengvik 119-20). He is usually known in modern historical writing as William de Warenne, the form used in this edition. William de Warenne was the younger son of a moderately important Norman family from near Rouen (EYC viii, 1). He was a distant cousin of Duke William and was amongst the select group of men whom the Duke established as the main supporters of his rule in Normandy, where he gained extensive lands through service to the duke (L. E. Loyd, 'The origin of the family of Warenne', *Yorkshire Archaeological Journal* xxxi (1934), 97-113). He was a prominent supporter of Duke William's bid for the English throne and is one of the few people known to have been at Hastings (Douglas *Companions* 137). He remained loyal to King William throughout his reign, fighting against Hereward and being active in the suppression of the Revolt of the Earls (Freeman iv, 470, 479). He was one of the main landholders in England, his main estates being in Sussex and East Anglia. He married Gundreda, sister of Gerbod, Earl of Chester, and founded the first Cluniac priory in England at Lewes c.1078-82. He was created Earl of Surrey by William II and died fighting for him during the 1088 rebellion. He was succeeded by his son William (EYC viii, 2-5) and by a long line of earls who were commonly known as the Earls Warenne (EYC viii, 238-41).

13W1. WILLIAM OF PERCY. His surname is probably derived from Percy in the arrondissement of Saint-Lo in the department of La Manche, France, although it should be noted that there are three other places called Percy in Calvados; the modern form of the surname is Percy. This is one of the earliest examples of a surname becoming a Christian name (Tengvik 105-6). William of Percy's parentage is unknown, but he seems to have had early connections with Hugh, Earl of Chester. The tradition in the Whitby Cartulary is that they came to England together in 1067 (VCH 154) and he was one of Hugh's few sub-tenants in Yorkshire. He was connected with Yorkshire as early as 1070 (EYC xi, 1) and was present on the Scottish campaign of 1072 (see above C10). He founded a castle at Topcliffe (EYC xi, 1), though the principal family seat was at Spofforth (Skaife 129). He refounded Whitby Abbey where his brother Serlo became prior and his nephew the first abbot. His wife was Emma d. of Hugh de Port (EYC xi, 1), who was an important landholder in Hamoshire and the Midlands. He joined the First Crusade with Robert Curthose and died in Palestine. His eldest son Alan succeeded him (EYC xi, 1-2). The estate shows considerable extension in the early 12th century (EYC xi, 3).

13W2. MALGER. He was probably the founder of the Vavasour family of Hazlewood (VCH 170), and was probably the same Malger who witnessed Percy charters between 1100-1115 (EYC xi, 32).

13W6. ROZELIN. This Rozelin is probably the same man who held land from the Earl of Chester in Lincolnshire. He was the ancestor of the Normanville family. His descendants seem to have given Bolton Percy to Picot's descendants in return for Bolton-on-Dearne (EYC xi, 286).

13W7. PICOT. Little is known about him. He witnessed Percy charters up to 1114 and was succeeded by his son or grandson Robert. His descendants possibly exchanged Bolton-on-Dearne for Bolton Percy and established the family of Percy of Bolton Percy (EYC xi, 104). Skaife (129) regards him as a brother of William of Percy, but Farrer (EYC xi, 104) says there is no evidence for this, though it may be possible. It should be noted that if he was William of Percy's brother, his sibling was not overgenerous, for he held only two manors worth no more than 35s. altogether.

13W13. FULCO. Farrer identifies him as Fulco the Steward, son of Reinfred, who was an important vassal of Osbern de Arches. He also held lands in Lincolnshire from William of Percy (VCH 170).

13W16. EBURHARD. Eburhard also held lands from William of Percy in Lincolnshire and witnessed various Percy charters. He was succeeded by his s. Hugh, and was the founder of the Leathley family (EYC xi, 137-8; VCH 170).

13E1. WILLIAM OF COLLEVILLE. There are three places in Normandy called Colleville from which his surname might be derived, although the Colleville in the Valmont canton of the arrondissement of Yvetot in the department of Seine-Inferieure, France, is perhaps the most likely candidate; the modern forms of the surname are Colville, Colvile, Colvill, Colwell and Colwill (Tengvik 83). This entry is one of the few instances in DB where the surname of the mesne tenant is given. Despite this, however, nothing further is known of him (EYC xi, 190), and his immediate descendants cannot be traced. It is assumed that he is probably the ancestor of the Colevile family of North Yorkshire (VCH 171).

13E5. OSBERN. Farrer identifies him as Osbert the Sheriff of Lincoln, where he also held lands (VCH 170).

13E15. HUGH. It has been suggested that he too may have been a brother of William of Percy (Skaife 138 reports Ellis' view but does not himself seem to hold it). There is no evidence for this family connection and for a brother the provision of one manor worth 15s. is very meagre. This Hugh cannot be identified further. His lands were regranted by the Percies in the reign of Henry I (VCH 170).

14E1. DROGO DE BEVRERE. He took his name from La Beuvriere, in the canton of Bethune in the department of Pas-de-Calais, France (Tengvik 73), but is usually known to historians in the form used in this edition. Drogo himself is thought to have been Flemish, an able soldier who was given a substantial estate, largely in Yorkshire, but including lands in Lincolnshire. According to the Meaux Chronicle he married a relation of King William, but then killed her and (with some unlikely details in the Meaux Chronicle about obtaining the King's licence by deceit), made his escape abroad and never came back. He was the tenant of all Holderness except for the lands of the Archbishop and St. John's of Beverley (VCH 172). The lands had subsequently been granted by 1087 to Odo of Champagne, husband of Adelaide, the King's sister. From them they descended to the Earls of Albemarle (EYC iii, 26).

14E30. RAINER. This man also occurs as Drogo's sub-tenant in Kettleby, Lincolnshire (Skaife 146).

14E33. FRANCO. He was an ancestor of the baronial family of Fauconberg. He is mentioned in the Meaux Chronicle as Franco Falconberg de Rice (Skaife 147). Possibly the same as the Franco described as Drogo's man in Norfolk (Freeman v, 790).

14E52. ROGER. Probably Roger de Montbegon, vassal of Roger of Poitou in Lincolnshire and Lancashire who also held land from Ivo Taillebois in Lincolnshire. The identity is derived from Ernald de Montbegon who held Sproatley and Newsham of the Earl of Albemarle during Stephen's reign (VCH 172).

15E1. RALPH OF MORTEMER. His surname is derived from Mortemer in the Neufchatel en Brai canton of the department of Seine-Inferieure; its modern forms are Mortimer and Mortimore (Tengvik 102). On his Christian name see 9W4 note. He was a younger son of the Roger of Mortemer who lost much of his land to William de Warenne following the Battle of Mortemer in 1054 (Douglas 100). Around 1074-1086 he succeeded to the family estate, his brothers having died sp. This included the Yorkshire lands, but the main concentration was in the Welsh marches around the chief seat, Wigmore (Skaife 150). Despite his involvement with the 1088 rebellion he became a close associate of William Rufus and assisted him in Normandy in 1090 (Barlow 69, 82, 273-4). He died at St. Victor-en-Caux around 1100-1104. His wife was Millicent and there were two sons and one d. who m. Stephen, Earl of Albemarle, William I's nephew (Skaife 150). Farrer adds that the immediate descent is obscure and that some part of the inheritance went to the Vescy family (VCH 173), although it appears that his s. and heir Hugh did succeed him. Their descendants were the Mortimers of Wigmore.

16E1. RALPH PAYNEL. His surname, in the form *Pagenel* in DB, is derived ultimately from Latin *Paganus*, OF *Pagen* 'pagan'; its modern forms are Paynel, Pagnel, Pennell, Pannell and Painell (Tengvik 223). He is usually known in modern historical writing as Paynel, the form used in this edition. On his Christian name see 9W4 note. The family was Norman from the department of La Manche, it held lands from the Abbey of Mont St. Michel and was possibly also connected with the Belleme family. He was granted almost the whole of Merlesveinn's land which extended across the country from the south-west to the north. Like the Percy family, the Paynels extended their lands after 1086 by marriage and through further grants. Ralph Paynel was Sheriff of Yorkshire from c.1088 to c.1093. He opposed the rebellion of 1088 and was very active against the Bishop of Durham (Barlow 72, 82-3). He was William Rufus' justiciar in Yorkshire after he had been Sheriff (Barlow 190) and by this time was considered to be of baronial standing because of the lands he had accumulated (Barlow 188). He refounded Holy Trinity, York, between 1070-1100, and gave it to Marmoutier Abbey. He was dead by 1124 at the latest. It is probable that he married twice, first a d.

or sister of Ilbert de Lacy, secondly a d. and co-heiress of Richard of Sourdeval. The Sourdeval lands were subsequently held by younger sons. He was succeeded by his s. and heir William, who founded Drax Priory (EYC vi, 1-4).

17W1. GEOFFREY OF LA GUERCHE. His surname is derived from La Guerche in the arrondissement of Vitre in the department of Ille-et-Villaine, France (Tengvik 120). In DB it is given in the Norman French spelling of *La Wirce*. On the form of his Christian name see 6N60 note. Geoffrey of La Guerche was the son and heir of Silvester, lord of La Guerche and Pouencé near Rennes. His father was Chancellor of Brittany and Bishop of Rennes, 1075-96. In Yorkshire Geoffrey of la Guerche had only one manor, but he had extensive and valuable property in Lincolnshire, Leicestershire and Warwickshire as well. These Midland estates were derived from his marriage with Aelfgifu d. of Leofwine who had held them pre-1066 (Greenway xxi); this was quite unusual (see Serle). He accompanied William Rufus on his Norman campaign of 1091 (Barlow 279) and is last heard of in Brittany in 1093, where he probably died soon afterwards (Greenway xx). As he had no heirs his fee escheated (i.e. returned to the chief lord). Henry I granted it to Nigel d'Aubigny (VCH 174) and it later became part of the Mowbray fee (Greenway xx).

18W1. GEOFFREY ALSELIN. On his Christian name see 6N60 note. His surname is derived from the OG and OF Christian name Alselin (Tengvik 213). Geoffrey Alselin's parentage and birthplace are not known, neither is the date of his death. His Yorkshire fee was small, but he held extensive lands in the Midlands (Skaife 155). On his death his lands seem to have been divided between his d. and heiress who m. Robert de Caux, and his nephew (VCH 174). Sanders is probably thinking of this when he notes that the estate was divided in the reign of Henry I. It was in the hands of the Bardolf and Everingham families at the end of the 13th century (Sanders 76).

19W1. WALTER OF AINCOURT. His surname is derived from Aincourt in the Magny canton of the arrondissement of Mantes in the department of Seine-et-Oise, France; the modern forms of the name are Deincourt and D'Eyncourt (Tengvik 66). Walter of Aincourt's Yorkshire estate was negligible, but he had other lands in Derbyshire, Nottinghamshire and Lincolnshire. Blankney near Sleaford was his principal residence and the head of his descendants' barony. Information about his family connections and political importance are largely derived from his son William's epitaph, once in Lincoln Cathedral. This describes Walter as related to Bishop Remegius of Lincoln. William, his son, died whilst being brought up at William II's court and is said to have been of royal stock (Barlow 133-4, citing F. M. Stenton, *The First Century of English Feudalism* (Oxford 1932), 32, where the text is given). It is not clear whether the royal stock was on the paternal or maternal side. Walter of Aincourt was in attendance on William Rufus in 1088-9 (Barlow 95). His date of death is unknown, but he was succeeded by his s. Hugh (Skaife 156).

20E1. GILBERT OF GHENT. Sometimes referred to in modern historical writing as Gilbert or Gislebert de Gand, the form in which his name is given in DB. His surname derives from Ghent in Flanders (Tengvik 89). On the form of his Christian name see 9W17 note. Gilbert of Ghent is said to have been a younger son of Ralph, lord of Alost near Ghent; and the brother-in-law of Queen Matilda's sister (Skaife 157). In 1068 he was castellan of York castle with William Malet and Robert son of Richard, and was captured there by the Danes in the following year (Freeman iv, 204, 258, 268). Although his Yorkshire estate was not remarkably large, he was the greatest tenant-in-chief in Lincolnshire and had other lands in the Midlands. Before his death around 1095 William Rufus had augmented his Yorkshire property with lands around Bridlington (VCH 175). He m. Alice d. of Hugh de Montfort, lord of Montfort-sur-Risle. Alice inherited her father's estate which passed to her elder son. The younger, Walter, retained the English lands, founded Bridlington Priory and m. a d. of Count Stephen of Richmond, from which union the later Earls of Lincoln were descended (Skaife 157). In medieval England the family name took the form of *Gant*.

21E1. GILBERT TISON. His surname is a nick-name, OF *tison* 'firebrand' (Tengvik 382). On the form of his Christian name see 9W17 note. Gilbert Tison's family and birthplace are unknown. He was a moderate landholder in Nottinghamshire and Lincolnshire in addition to his Yorkshire estate. He died sometime between 1124-30 and was succeeded by his son Adam. By this time, and possibly as early as 1115-18, the Yorkshire lands had become a mesne fee of the Honour of Mowbray. There is no connection between this Gilbert Tison and the family of a similar name associated with Alnwick in Northumberland (EYC xii, vi, ix, 3-5).

22W1. RICHARD SON OF ARNFASTR. Probably the son of Arnfastr (*Herfast*) Bishop of Elmham/Thetford, 1070-86 (Skaife 162, who cites a charter to Thetford Priory which mentions

Bishop Arnfastr and Richard his son). The Bishop was a royal chaplain of no exceptional learning according to some (Freeman iv, 342). He was, however, a creditable royal official, being the first person to be styled 'chancellor'; but a discreditable bishop (Douglas 292, 327). Of Richard himself little is known. He presumably had no descendants and his lands passed to Ralph Paynel in the reign of William Rufus (VCH 176).

23N1. HUGH SON OF BALDRIC. There seems no reason to dispute his Norman origins. He made gifts to the Abbey of Préaux near Lisieux (which presumably was a local connection). Baldric was a common Norman name and there are several possibilities for his family connections (EYC ix, 70-2). Although he had some lands in the south of the country his main holdings were in Lincolnshire and Yorkshire. His Yorkshire fee was the most extensive. His association with Yorkshire dates from 1069/70 when he replaced William Malet as Sheriff of York (see above C10). He clearly held the office until late in the 1070s (Arnold ii, 201). He was obviously a trusted official of King William, being given the task of escorting Edgar Aetheling to Normandy on his reconciliation with the King (Freeman iv, 567-70). At some point he was also Sheriff of Nottingham (VCH 177-9). Clay (EYC ix, 72-3) regards it as certain that Hugh was not in possession of his English lands after King William's death, but is less certain about whether Hugh himself was dead. He notes that only lands which probably comprised his daughter's *maritagium* (marriage endowment) were inherited by her and her family, the rest being regranted. A Hugh son of Badric, who may be the same man, witnessed a charter of Robert of Normandy in Normandy in 1089 (EYC ix, xii). It may be, therefore, that he forfeited his English lands on account of his support for Robert (EYC ix, 72-3). His Yorkshire lands went to Robert de Stuteville and after his forfeiture in 1106 to Nigel d'Aubigny and became part of the Mowbray fee (VCH 177-9). For his association with the foundation of Selby Abbey see Freeman iv, 789-802.

24W1. ERNEIS DE BURUN. He is usually known in modern historical writing in the form used in this edition. It is possible that he derived his surname from Buron in the department of Calvados, France, although the absence of early forms of the place-name precludes certainty (Tengvik 78). The modern form of the surname is Byron. Very little is known about this man and almost nothing before he became Sheriff of Yorkshire sometime in the 1080s – certainly by 1086, although he may have succeeded Hugh son of Baldric as early as 1080. He himself was succeeded in office by Ralph Paynel around 1088. He is last heard of in 1088 when he acted with Ivo Taillebois to seize Durham castle in the course of the action against the Bishop of Durham. He was succeeded by his son Hugh, who was alive *c.*1089-93. Thereafter there is no information on the fee until 1115-8 when Geoffrey fitz Pain, ancestor of the Trussebut family, held all his Lincolnshire lands and presumably his Yorkshire ones as well (EYC x, 1). For his part in the foundation of Selby Abbey see Freeman iv, 789-802.

24W4. RALPH. A tenant of this name also held under Erneis de Burun in Lincolnshire (Skaife 172).

24W18. JOHN. A tenant of this name also held under Erneis de Burun in Lincolnshire (Skaife 173).

25W1. OSBERN DE ARCHES. His surname is probably derived from Arques in the Saint-Omer canton of the department of Pas-de-Calais, France (Tengvik 68-9), but he is usually known in modern historical writing as Osbern de Arches, the form used in this edition. Osbern de Arches is said to have been a younger son of Godfrid, Viscount of Arques, near Dieppe (Skaife 174). His chief holdings were in Yorkshire, though he did have land in Lincolnshire also. There are some writs addressed to *Osbert* Sheriff of Yorkshire during the reign of Henry I and gifts to Selby Abbey by the same person at this time. This may be Osbern de Arches, but there is no conclusive evidence. He was dead by 1115 and was succeeded by his son William, although after this the lands were incorporated as a mesne fee into William d'Aubigny's land (VCH 181-2). His son William was the founder of Nun Monkton Priory (Skaife 174).

25W6. FULCO. He has been identified as the Fulk fitz Reinfrid who was Steward of William of Percy (see above 13W1, and VCH 182).

26E1. ODO THE CROSSBOWMAN. DB *Odo Balistarius*. 'Odo the Gunner' would also have been possible. The term *ballista* was applied to any kind of powered missile weapon, not only a crossbow, and in Middle English the term 'gun' is older than the introduction of gunpowder for these arms. Little is known about Odo himself. He held land in both Yorkshire and Lincolnshire (VCH 182) and seems to have been the most important of King William's military technicians, if his lands are anything to go by (see Barlow 126 for explanation of the various terms used and where similar technicians can be found holding land in 1086). His manor of Skirpenbeck later became a barony but his immediate descendants are obscure. By 1115-8 his Lincolnshire lands (and presumably also those in Yorkshire) had passed to Amfrey de Chauncy who may well have been the son of Odo's sister. The lands were divided between Amfrey's grandsons around 1130 (Sanders 78; VCH 183).

27W1. AUBREY OF COUCY. His surname derives from Coucy-le-Chateau in the Laon arrondissement of the department of Aisne, France (Tengvik 83). In England in the Middle Ages the family name took the form *de Curci* or *de Curcy* (WYAS 928). Aubrey of Coucy's association with Yorkshire was not great nor was his estate large. He was appointed Earl of Northumbria after Walcher, Bishop of Durham, had been killed. Simeon of Durham says of him caustically that he had too little strength to cope with difficult circumstances and so returned to his native land (Arnold ii, 199). The withdrawal to Normandy is not in doubt. Although he is still said to hold his Yorkshire lands, elsewhere in DB the past tense 'held' is applied to his holdings. In 1087 he was the man sent to announce to Robert Curthose that King William was dead (Barlow 50) and was captured later in the course of the conflicts between William Rufus and Duke Robert (Barlow 161). There is no contemporary evidence about his Yorkshire lands after his withdrawal, but they were probably granted to Guy de Balliol by William Rufus (VCH 183).

30W1. ROGER OF POITOU. DB gives his surname in the latinised form *Pictavensis* 'of Poitou'; this is equivalent to Old French *peytevin*; the modern form of the surname is Petwin (Tengvik 134-5). He is sometimes known in modern historical writing as Roger le Peitevin, the form which the family name took in medieval England (WYAS 941). Roger of Poitou was a member of one of the most powerful Anglo-Norman families. He was the third son of Roger of Montgomery who had vast possessions in both England and Normandy. As a younger son he was provided for by marriage to Almodis, the sister and heiress of the Count of La Marche in Poitou – hence his name. He became Count of La Marche (by right of his wife) in 1091 (Barlow 91). During the reign of William I he was given a large estate in Lancashire as well as lands in the south-east, but the Lancashire lands were resumed in the 1080s and his Yorkshire lands given in their place. He was initially involved in the 1088 conspiracy, but was soon detached by William Rufus, after which he was very active against the Bishop of Durham. In return William II extended his holdings to include most of Lancashire and may have made him an earl (Barlow 77-95, 167). By the 1090s he seems to have switched his support to Robert of Normandy (Barlow 133) although he did not finally lose his English estates until he openly supported Robert against Henry I in 1102. He returned to La Marche, where he died some time after 1123. His heirs continued to hold La Marche, but the English property was given to Stephen, Count of Blois. (For further details see J. F. A. Mason, 'Roger de Montgomery and his sons, 1067-1102', *Transactions of the Royal Historical Society*, 5th series, 13 (1963), 1-28.)

31E1. ROBERT OF BRUS. His surname is derived either from Brix in the arrondissement of Valognes in the department of La Manche, France (there are traces of the old castle located between Cherbourg and Valognes) or from Le Brus in the department of Calvados, France (Tengvik 76-7). He is sometimes referred to in modern historical writing as Robert of Bruce (the modern form of the name) or Robert de Bruis (the form in which he is entered in DB), but as his holding is generally known as the Brus fee, he is called 'of Brus' in this edition.
  The account of the Brus fee, created about 1106, was added to the DB manuscript sometime between 1120-1129. It seems likely that the account was compiled after reference either to the original returns for the places concerned or to a local draft, rather than to DB itself (see Jensen). The creation of the fee was part of the continuing process by which the great lordships were established in Yorkshire. It should be noted that there is no comparable record of the Rumilly and Balliol fees created by William Rufus.
  Robert of Brus himself was one of Henry I's 'new men'. He received the fee around 1106 when there had been somewhat of a shake-out of the older Anglo-Norman baronage following Henry I's Norman Campaign. He received the more famous Lordship of Annandale from David of Scotland around 1124 (Kapelle 206, 287). Robert of Brus was succeeded by heirs male until 1272 when the estate was divided between the four sisters and co-heiresses of Peter III (Sanders 77).

31E3. ROBERT FOSSARD. Son of Nigel Fossard (see above, including notes on the name). No land in Kirkburn or Tibthorpe is recorded as part of the holding of Nigel Fossard in either DB proper or the Summary, so this must be an addition to the Fossard fee some time after 1086.

CN3. WILLIAM MALET. Father of Robert Malet (see above, 11E1, for details and origin of name). William Malet came from Graville Ste. Honorine near Le Havre. He was possibly in England before 1066, but was certainly at Hastings and was believed to have been entrusted with the burial of

Harold's body (Douglas 217; Freeman iii, 466, 514). He was put in charge of the castle in York in 1068 with Robert son of Richard and Gilbert of Ghent, but was captured there with his family by the Danes the following year (Freeman 204, 258, 268). He was possibly made Sheriff in 1068, and was certainly in office by mid-1069 (Arnold ii, 188). It was probably at this time that he obtained his Yorkshire lands. His direct connection with Yorkshire seems to end at the point of his capture. He was certainly replaced as Sheriff by Hugh son of Baldric (see above C10) and his son, Robert Malet, inherited little of his property in the county. He was certainly dead by 1086 and probably died in 1071. Entries in DB Norfolk have been held to mean that he died fighting against Hereward in Ely, although it has been suggested the *maresc* ('marsh') is a mistranscription of *eurvik* ('York') (DB Norfolk i, 1.197; ii, 35.16; 1.197 note and reference cited there). His widow continued to hold land in her own right. Skaife (123) gives his wife as Hesilia, d. of Gilbert Crispin, but see Serle for other family connections. See also Freeman iv, 787-790.

CE9. GEOFFREY OF BEAUCHAMPS. His surname, given in the latinised form *de Belcampo* in DB, is derived from Beauchamps in the La Haye-Paisnel canton of the arrondissement of Avranches in the department of La Manche, France; it survives in modern English in the surnames Beauchamp, Beacham, Beachem, Beecham (Tengvik 70-1). On the form of his Christian name see 6N60 note.

English

Pre-Conquest English landholders cannot be categorised as neatly as their post-Conquest successors. Norman fees were often built up from the estates of more than one previous landholder, consequently any one English thane might be the predecessor of several Norman lords. If this makes for complexity in the first instance, the range of personal names used cannot but add to it. The English were on the whole much more imaginative than the Normans (who seem to have run out of inspiration after William and Robert), but nevertheless they had their fair share of Gamalls, Ormrs and Ligulfrs. In general it is a reasonable assumption that a named thane whose land goes to a certain new lord – for example Thorr's land to Count Alan – is the same thane throughout that section. But it still has to be borne in mind firstly, that it may not be the same Thorr; secondly, that there is no reason to believe that this Thorr is the same as another Thorr whose land might go to another Norman lord; but thirdly, that it is quite possible that it is the same Thorr. The matter is complicated, and the complexities cannot be unravelled here. The arrangement of names used is that which is hoped will be most useful given that the matter cannot be examined in detail. The English landholders who were of the upper aristocracy – kings, queens, earls – are listed first, followed by Gospatric as the only post-Conquest tenant-in-chief, followed by the remainder in alphabetical order. All names will have a reference to the text included. This will be either the most useful reference or the reference where the identity can be certain, and thus not necessarily the first occasion on which the person is cited in the text. For example, although Merlesveinn is mentioned elsewhere, the reference given for him is that of Ralph Paynel's fee, since Paynel took over almost all of Merlesveinn's land. Other references will be found in the Index of Persons, although this should be used with care as it simply lists the number of occasions on which the name is found, and in no way indicates that persons with the same name are in fact the same person.

KING EDWARD (C1a). Edward the Confessor, King of England 1042-66, was born around 1105, the son of Aethelred *unraed* 'ill-advised' and Emma of Normandy. On Knutr gaining the throne in 1016 he went into exile in Normandy, returning in 1041 during the reign of his younger half-brother Harthaknutr, whom he succeeded in 1042. He had an undistinguished, but largely peaceful reign, characterised by the ascendency of the House of Godwine, Earl of Wessex. He married Edith, d. of Earl Godwine, but the union produced no children. As a childless king he promised the throne to both Sveinn of Denmark and William of Normandy and also invited representatives of Aethelred's line, Edward and his son Edgar Aetheling, to come to England. He died in January 1066 soon after and possibly as a result of the Northumbrian rising which ousted Earl Tosti. After his death a cult of his sanctity developed and he was canonised in 1161 (Barlow *Edward* passim).

KING HAROLD (4E1). On the form of his name see 9W119 note. King Harold was the second son of Earl Godwine of Wessex and Gytha his wife, and thus brother-in-law of Edward the Confessor. On Godwine's death in 1053 he relinquished the Earldom of East Anglia and succeeded his father as Earl of Wessex. As the chief nobleman at court he obtained other earldoms for his brothers in order to extend the power of their house and probably with a view to his succeeding the childless King Edward. Possibly because he saw his brother Tosti as a rival in this matter, he concurred in his exile in 1065. He was a renowned soldier, particularly famous for his Welsh campaigns. Norman sources allege that he promised to support William of Normandy's claim to the English throne, but on King Edward's death in 1066 he took the throne himself. He married *more Danico* Eadgifu 'Swan-neck' which union produced several children, and later another Eadgifu, sister of Earls Edwin and Morcar, to whom at least one son was born after his death. He successfully defeated the invasion of Harold Hardrada, but was defeated and killed at Hastings by William of Normandy. He is mentioned in the text only as Earl Harold since King William did not recognise his reign (Barlow *Edward* passim).

EADGIFU (15E1). The sister of Earls Edwin and Morcar, previously m. to Gruffyth ap Llywelyn. She was m. to King Harold as the price of northern support in 1066. She was in London at the time of the Battle of Hastings and was sent to Chester for safety by her brothers (Arnold ii, 181). She had at least one son, Ulfr (and possibly two: Freeman iv, 754), who was captured by King William, possibly on his march to Chester in 1070 (Freeman iv, 315). Ulfr was imprisoned in Normandy during King William's lifetime, but was released after his death by Robert Curthose (Barlow 50). Nothing further is heard of Eadgifu herself.

EARL SIWARD (4N1). On the form of his name see 1N36 note. A man of obscure Danish origin, Siward established himself fully as Earl of Northumbria by 1041, and held the office until his death in 1055 in the wake of his successful Scottish campaign. He married into the House of Bamburgh and the later Earl Waltheof was his only surviving son (see history above).

EARL TOSTI (1Y3). Tosti was the third son of Earl Godwine of Wessex and Gytha his wife, and thus brother-in-law to Edward the Confessor and brother of King Harold. He m. Judith the half sister of Baldwin of Flanders – a highly distinguished international marriage. He was given the Earldom of Northumbria in 1055 but was neither successful nor popular, and was expelled by an aristocratic rising in 1065 after which he went into exile. On Edward the Confessor's death he joined Harold Hardrada's invasion of England and was killed at Stamford Bridge (see history above and Barlow *Edward* passim).

EARLS MORCAR AND EDWIN (1Y1, 1Y2). On the form of Edwin's name see C36 note. These were brothers, sons of Earl Aelfgar of Mercia. Edwin succeeded his father as Earl of Mercia in 1062 (Stenton 575) and Morcar gained the Earldom of Northumbria as the price of Mercian support in the 1065 rising (see history above). They compelled King Harold to marry their sister as the price of their support in 1066, which they gave him, though their combined forces were defeated by Harold Hardrada at Fulford. After the Battle of Hastings they submitted to King William, but around 1069 they began to organise resistance in the Midlands. This came to nothing and, after a brief reconciliation with the King, they again went into opposition. Edwin was killed by his own followers en route to Scotland, but Morcar joined Hereward in Ely where he was captured in 1071 (Arnold ii, 195). He was imprisoned during King William's lifetime, briefly released on his death, but reincarcerated by William Rufus in Winchester where he presumably died (Barlow 50).

EARL WALTHEOF (10W41). On the form of his name see C27 note. Waltheof was the son of Earl Siward of Northumbria, but was too young to succeed him in 1055. He was later made Earl of Northamptonshire and Huntingdonshire by King Edward. Although he submitted to King William after the Battle of Hastings, he joined the rising in 1069, but rapidly capitulated. He was restored to the King's favour, married his niece Judith, and was made Earl of Northumbria in 1072. He associated himself, however, with the Revolt of the Earls in 1075, for which he was executed in 1076 (see history above). His wife retained his lands alongside her own (see Countess Judith) and their children inherited them.

EARL KOFSI (6N36). Kofsi was an adherent of Earl Tosti during his tenure of the Earldom of Northumbria and went into exile on his expulsion in 1065. He submitted to King William after the Battle of Hastings and was appointed Earl of Northumbria in 1067, but was killed after only a few weeks by Asulfr the *de facto* Earl (see history above).

GOSPATRIC (28W1). Gospatric should not be confused with the Earl of Northumbria of the same name. The Yorkshire Gospatric was the son of Arnketill, a leading Yorkshire thane, who was involved in both the 1068 and 1069 risings. Arnketill submitted to King William at York in 1068, where he also surrendered his son, Gospatric, as a hostage (see history above). For this reason, if no other, Gospatric was not associated with his father's involvement in the subsequent rising, and managed to retain some part of his own and his father's pre-1066 estate. He was the only thane who was a tenant-in-chief in 1086, although not all of his lands continued to be held in chief, most being depressed to mesne tenancies or freeholds from the Crown. Of his sons, Uhtred of Allerston is identifiable, granting land in that vill to Whitby Priory (the land had belonged to Gospatric before 1066), and Simon de Mohaut and his descendants who held Bingley (also Gospatric's before 1066) as a mesne tenancy (VCH 183-5; WYAS 252).

AETHELWULF (13E14). He seems to have come to terms with William of Percy since he held Elvington and also Stainton-le-Vale in Lincolnshire. Both of these were part of the land William de Murers held from the Percies in the 12th century (VCH 170).

ALRIC (9W70). Alric retained some land under Ilbert de Lacy. He was succeeded by his son Sveinn, who made various donations to Pontefract Priory. Sveinn received an extensive lordship in Cumberland from Henry I, and his sons Adam and Henry also held lands in Cumberland and Lancashire. Adam founded Bretton Priory around 1156 (EYC iii, 317; Skaife 107).

ALWINE (21E1). His lands seem to have gone to Gilbert Tison and possibly to William of Percy. He was succeeded by his son Uhtred, and this Uhtred's son Northmann attested Gilbert Tison's charter by which he gave lands in Kirk Ella and Gunby, both of which had been held by Alwine before the Conquest, to Selby Abbey (VCH 272).

ASKETILL (6N34). He obtained the land of Thorketill and Ulfketill in Ainderby Steeple, and also held land from Count Alan in Cambridgeshire and Norfolk. He witnessed charters up to around 1097, in one of which he described himself as *Asquitellus de Furnellis*. He was dead by 1130 and was succeeded by his son or grandson, Robert. He was the ancestor of the Furneaux family who held a fee of 8 knights from the Earls of Richmond (EYC v, 174-5; VCH 159).

ARNGRIMR (1N101). He is identified by both Skaife and Farrer as the Arngrimr who retained land in Painsthorpe, Huntington and Kirby Underdale. He appears to have become a monk in St. Mary's Abbey, York, to which he gave most of his land, and this gift was confirmed by William I (Skaife 20; VCH 185).

ARNKETILL (6N62). Father of Gospatric (see above) he held land in what became Count Alan's fee and elsewhere, and is probably the Arnketill who had a house in York (see above C3).

BARTHR (9W20). He had a considerable estate before 1066, most of which went to Ilbert de Lacy, although he retained some manors as an under-tenant. He was succeeded by his son Gamall, who, with his son Richard, made grants to Selby Abbey. The lands later descended to the de Ruhale family (EYC iii, 284-5; Skaife 23; VCH 186).

BASING (14E52). According to the Meaux Chronicle Basing was the lord of Wawne after 1066 (VCH 269). It is to be noted, however, that he was not lord of Wawne before 1066.

BJORNULFR (6N53). He retained all his land, except Ainderby Mires, as an under-tenant of Count Alan. All these lands, however, became part of Ribald's fee at a later date (VCH 158).

BJORNULFR (13E11). A man of substance before 1066 and possibly the owner of a house in York (see above C10). This is also the Bjornulfr mentioned in the Claims (CE15) in respect of his wife Asa. A Gamall son of Bjornulfr witnessed a charter of William of Percy around 1150 (EYC xi, 32), but there is nothing to connect him directly with this Bjornulfr.

DOMNALL (6N113). He replaced Knutr at Clifton-on-Ure and gave to St. Mary's land in Ruswick. A Garnegan son of Domnall attested a charter of Robert Brus around 1130 (VCH 158).

DUNSTAN (9W113). He is identified by Skaife (112) as the Dunstan son of Aegelnothes who was one of the leaders of the rising against Tosti in 1065, and the same Dunstan who had a house in York. However, there is nothing to establish this identity with any precision, although it may be correct.

EARNWINE THE PRIEST (29W2). Skaife (185) thinks that Earnwine was one of King Edward's chaplains, though he gives no evidence for this except the circumstantial fact that he had estates in Bedfordshire, Lincolnshire, Nottinghamshire and the City of Lincoln. He has been identified as the son of Earnwine Catenase (VCH 150) though possibly on flimsy evidence, and also as the Earnwine whose land went to Bishop Walcher of Durham after 1066 (Skaife 2), again rather insubstantially.

FORNI SON OF SIGULFR (29E4). He seems to have been in possession of the manor of Nunburnholme by the early 12th century (VCH 286). He has been identified as the father of one of Henry I's mistresses, and as a minister of King Henry in the 1120s, particularly in Northumberland. He was granted a small estate in Yorkshire, but more importantly the Barony of Greystoke in Cumberland. He was the ancestor of the Greystoke family (Kapelle 207).

GAMALL (6N103). Farrer identifies him as the Gamall whose sons succeeded at Danby and the same man who held Barden and West Hauxwell before 1066. He regards him as the same Gamall who held part of Kilham and Fridaythorpe with Forni (not Forni Sigulfrson), since an Ulfr Fornisson gave land in Skirpenbeck (held by Forni before 1066) along with land and the church in Hauxwell near Richmond to St. Mary's Abbey. He concludes that Ulfr succeeded to some of his father's land, and also to the land of Gamall, who may have been a kinsman. In this case it is to be wondered what became of the sons. Since Barden, West Hauxwell and Danby all became part of the 'butler's' fee of Richmond later, there seems no reason to doubt the initial identification. The connection between the ER lands and the WR lands is furthered by the observation that the Egglescliffe family held Hauxwell, Barden and Danby in the 13th century and their under-tenant in Barden and Danby took his name from the manor of Kilham. Farrer also identifies this Gamall with Gamall son of Osbert of Collingham, but there is much less reason for this association to be accepted (VCH 158, 183).

GAMALL (8N2). Farrer thinks that this man may be the Gamall son of Ormr who was killed by Earl Tosti in York in 1064 (VCH 160; Arnold ii, 178). The Ormr who built St. Gregory's, Kirkdale (see Ormr below) may have been his son (Skaife 93).

GAMALL (9W142). He seems to have been succeeded by his son Leysingr whose lands were divided between his two sons Hugh and Henry de Elland. The Elland family was descended from Hugh (WYAS 243).

GAMALL SON OF OSBERT (23E2). A man of considerable estate before 1066 much of which went to Hugh son of Baldric. He was one of the few pre-1066 lords who had full jurisdiction, market rights and all customary dues, even though this only accrued to him in Cottingham (see above C36).

GAMALL (24W11). He retained the manor of Arkendale and seems to have held lands in Lincolnshire also (VCH 180).

GLUNIARNN (24W11). It is possible that this is the same Gluniarn son of Eardwulf who was one of the leaders of the rising against Tosti in 1065 (see above and Skaife 26).

GRIMR (24E1). This man seems to have held land in Lincolnshire also (VCH 180).

HUGH SON OF NORTHMANN (4N3). Ellis identifies him with the man who held a considerable fee of the Earl in Cheshire, and thinks he is the Hugh de Lamare who gave lands to the monks of St. Florent in 1086. Farrer, however, is not convinced of this identification (VCH 154).

KARLI (20E21). This Karli is assumed to be the Karli son of Thorbrandr who was involved in the famous blood feud, and whose sons were active in the risings of 1069 (see above and VCH 175).

KNUTR (14E33). Farrer quotes Ellis as saying that this is the Knutr son of Karli son of Thorbrandr, although he does not say that he accepts the identification (VCH 171). Earl Waltheof had the sons of Karli killed at Settringham (see above), but two of them are said to have escaped, Sumarlithi because he happened to be absent, and Knutr because of his good character (VCH 145).

MERLESVEINN (16E1). Merlesveinn had extensive possession all over England before 1066. He was Sheriff of Lincolnshire at the time of King Edward's death and after Stamford Bridge King Harold left him in control in the North (Freeman iv, 186). He had a house in York (see above C1a) and wide estates in Yorkshire, where he was one of the few thanes to have full jurisdiction, market rights and all customary dues (C36). It can be assumed that he submitted to King William in 1066 but soon fled to Scotland with Edgar Aetheling to mount opposition to the Norman king. He was one of the leaders of the 1069 risings after which he returned to Scotland. Nothing further is known of him (see history above).

MURDAC (14E3). This was possibly the same Murdac who had a house in York before 1066 (see above C14). Farrer notes that the name was the surname of 'a family of some importance in the county' in the 12th century (VCH 171).

ORMR (23N17). This is probably the Ormr son of Gamall whose inscription still remains on the outside of the church of St. Gregory, Kirkdale (see 23N19 note). Scaife (93) goes further and thinks that the Gamall in question was the Gamall son of Ormr who was killed by Earl Tosti in 1064.

SIGVARTHBARN (17W1). Sigvarthbarn was probably a senior member of the house of Bamburgh and possibly a brother or half-brother of Earl Gospatric. Although he submitted to King William in 1066, he was amongst the leaders of the risings of 1069. After they had proved unsuccessful he first fled to Scotland but then joined Hereward in Ely where he was captured in 1071 (see history above). He was imprisoned in Normandy during King William's lifetime, but was released by Robert Curthose along with Duncan, future king of Scots (Barlow 50).

SUMARLITHI (1N92). Skaife (20) thinks he was one of the sons of Karli who escaped being killed with his brothers at Settringham. See Knutr above.

THORBRANDR (8N1). It is assumed that this Thorbrandr was the eldest son of Karli, and that he was killed at Settringham on the orders of Earl Waltheof in pursuit of the famous blood feud. In this case he was doubtless one of the four sons of Karli who were active in the 1069 risings (see above and VCH 145, 160).

THORGAUTR (7E1). Farrer identifies this man as the *lageman* of Lincoln, since Robert of Tosny received these two manors in Yorkshire and also the lands of Thorgautr the Lageman in Lincoln, and Berenger his son the lands of the same Englishman in Oxfordshire and Nottinghamshire (VCH 145-6). The name is not common in Yorkshire and he may well be the Thorgautr Lagr who is said to have had full jurisdiction, market rights and all customary dues (see above C36), one of the few thanes to have had such privileges.

TOKI (18W1). All his land in Yorkshire went to Geoffrey Alselin. He may be the Toki son of Ottarr who also held full jurisdiction, market rights and all customary dues, and was one of the few thanes to have done so (see above C36).

UHTRED (5N11). He was the tenant under Richard of Sourdeval of Roxby, a soke of Seaton Hall, formerly held by Uhtred before 1066 with many other places. Farrer thinks he was Uhtred son of Thorketill of Cleveland who gave lands to Whitby Priory, and probably the same as the Uhtred of Cleveland named in the 11th century by Robert of Brus. He seems to have been the predecessor, if not the ancestor, of the Ivo de Seton who held lands there in the reign of Henry II (VCH 154).

UHTRED (6N3). He succeeded his father Ulfr at Middleton and Kneeton and gave the church at Middleton to St. Mary's Abbey, York (VCH 158).

4. TEXT, CLAIMS AND SUMMARY

The Yorkshire section of Domesday Book presents a host of interpretative questions, not a few of which stem from the fact that it is composed of three separate sections: the text proper (sometimes referred to as the *breves*), the Claims and the Summary. A full discussion of these, including an investigation of the manifold discrepancies between them, is bound up with wider questions on the interpretation of the whole of Domesday Book and cannot be pursued in detail here. However, a brief review of some of the opinions advanced to date provides a useful introduction to the subject.

The three sections: text, Claims and Summary, are stylistically distinct. The text is arranged tenurially, lands being listed and described under the name of each tenant-in-chief; the Claims section deals with matters of dispute and is arranged geographically by riding; the Summary is also arranged geographically by riding and wapentake, places being listed with the name of the current landholder rubricated (written in red) above them.

Since the text and the Summary are essentially concerned with listing lands and their holders they are generally considered together, the chief points at issue being their relationship and their chronology. I. S. Maxwell summed the matter up most concisely: the Summary could be derived from the text; the text from the Summary; both from different sources; and both from the same source. Because there is not an accurate correlation of place-names between text and Summary, he concludes that it is 'manifestly impossible either that the Summary was derived from the Text, or that the Text was derived from the Summary'. However, he also noted certain peculiarities of spelling which made him conclude that both Summary and text were derived from the same source, although for unknown reasons some entries were deleted from either the text or the Summary (DGNE 460-1).

R. Welldon Finn, on the other hand, argued that they cannot have had a common origin 'for in addition to their statistical differences they show a marked disparity of name form' as well as other serious discrepancies. He concluded that the Summary was very probably written by an English person and predated the text, which was probably written by a foreigner (R. Welldon Finn, *The Making and Limitations of the Yorkshire Domesday* (York 1972), 16).

V. H. Galbraith also considered the issue, although not as a special subject of enquiry. He was of the opinion that both text and Summary were produced in the course of making the survey, and that the Summary, 'a unique Domesday Book document', was part of the original returns which were sent to Winchester and abbreviated there into the text of Domesday Book as we know it. He suggested that the Summary was retained by the abbreviator because of its usefulness in locating the wapentakes and manors mentioned in the text (Galbraith 177).

S. P. J. Harvey took the matter further in her discussion of the Domesday Book 'satellites'. She argued that for Domesday Book to have been completed as rapidly as it is generally thought to have been (i.e. by the end of the reign of William I), it must have been based on existing English administrative and fiscal records, some of which at least were tenurially arranged. She regarded the Yorkshire Summary as one such document, drawing attention to the fact that there is a marked tendency for the order in which the lands of each tenant-in-chief are listed in the main text to follow the order found in the Summary and that, whereas in the text some of the lands described as 'waste' do not have a carucage figure (i.e. number of carucates) entered there, a carucage figure is given for them in the Summary (S. P. J. Harvey, 'Domesday Book and its predecessors', *English Historical Review*, lxxxvi (1971), 753-73). Her further investigation of the Yorkshire section of Domesday Book, including an assessment of place-name and other evidence, confirmed her opinion that the word 'Summary' was a misnomer and that the document clearly predated the survey of 1086. She argued that it was inserted in Domesday Book because of the still unstable state of the county after the devastation of 1069-70, but was not intended to be a permanent part of the record (S. P. J. Harvey, 'Domesday Book and the Anglo-Norman governance', *Transactions of the Royal Historical Society*, 5th series vol. 25 (1975), 175-93).

Sections entitled 'Claims' are an unusual feature of Domesday Book as a whole. Their significance both in understanding the purpose of the survey and the method of its compilation has been noted, but has not aroused the same measure of controversy as that found in the interpretation of the text and Summary.

V. H. Galbraith (73) pointed out that separate sections entitled 'Claims' are appended only to Yorkshire, Lincolnshire and Huntingdonshire – although they are broadly similar to other differently entitled sections elsewhere in the survey. He regarded the Claims as contemporary with the Survey and an integral part of the process of compilation, indeed the presence of Claims for both Yorkshire and Lincolnshire is a factor in his suggestion that these two counties may have formed a separate circuit of their own (ibid. 177). In both *The Making of Domesday Book* and *Domesday Book, its Place in Administrative History* (Oxford 1974), Galbraith stressed the extent to which the method of compilation of Domesday Book was bound up with existing judicial procedures, drawing attention particularly to the use of the sworn inquest and the county-court session as the scene of the proceedings. He pointed out that it was inevitable that, during the course of the taking and recording of evidence, disputes would surface as to who should be holding certain lands. One of the purposes of Domesday Book being to pass final judgement on such questions, he regards the Claims as showing the process of determination of disputes, which could well have been regarded as settling the matter. Since these judgements were incomprehensible without the rest of the text, he argued that they were included as an appendix to the original returns and were retained when the final abridgement was made (Galbraith 73-4).

R. Welldon Finn, however, being concerned with the correlation of the various sections of the Yorkshire section of Domesday Book, took a rather more complex view. He noted that either the clerks did not take the Claims into consideration when compiling the text, or that the Claims were actually later than the text (R. Welldon Finn, *The Making and Limitations of the Yorkshire Domesday* (York 1972), 22-4). He preferred the latter interpretation, suggesting that as the survey proceeded various claims were settled and the results inserted in the text, but that for some cases local judgements were held to be unsound, and consequently expert assessors were subsequently dispatched to resolve these (R. Welldon Finn, *The Domesday Inquest* (London 1961), 96-7). Whilst this does not wholly conflict with Galbraith's view, it does introduce yet another stage into the process of the compilation of Domesday Book, and with this putative stage, a number of other problems of harmonisation arise, which together leave much scope for future controversy.

5. TECHNICAL TERMS

Domesday Book as a broad social and economic description of the country necessarily contains many technical terms. These are not defined in the text, as contemporaries would have been well aware of what was being described. Unfortunately they are not as clear to later historians, although much of our comprehension of 11th-century conditions is dependent on an interpretation of what they mean. Once more a full discussion of such a subject is impossible here, but these few introductory remarks may be of use to the general reader.

The kinds of landed interest described are the manor, soke, berewick and *inland*. The key institution is the manor, for although not all manors had berewicks, *inland* or soke attached to them, where these are found it is always in relation to a manor. Interpretation of the manor – especially the Danelaw manor which had many features which were not found elsewhere – is not easy. This is partly because it denoted both a legal interest and a social and economic unit, partly because the institution itself developed during the Middle Age, partly, and not least, because of the kinds of landed interest which could be subsumed within the overall designation 'manor'. It also has to be remembered that there was no necessary identity between manor and vill; any vill might contain land belonging to more than one manor, and any manor might extend beyond one vill.

The word 'manor' is derived from *manere* meaning 'to stay' or 'to abide', and it can be assumed that the compilers of Domesday Book had in mind an existing unit of landholding, dependent on one chief place, although mention of the actual dwelling place, a hall or halls usually, is not always made. This was the *manerium*, the chief seat, possession of which carried title to all the other lands associated with it. Broadly the lands associated with a complex manor were of two kinds: those which the lord held in direct ownership, and those which the lord did not own, but over which she or he exercised judicial superiority or jurisdiction.

The lands held in direct lordship were the lands around the chief seat itself and the berewicks and *inland* of the manor. Stenton regarded berewicks and *inland* as substantially the same, the main point about them being that they were directly within the lord's ownership. They were of varying sizes and were often geographically separate from the cluster of lands around the *manerium* itself. The word 'berewick', meaning a barley-farm, carries the connotation of an outlying settlement for supplementary food provision. *Inland* also, despite what its name might seem to suggest, could also be far distant from the main seat.

Sokelands had a much looser association with the manor, the essential point about them being that the lord of the manor did not own the land within the sokes, rather she or he simply had jurisdictional right over the land. Sokes, often large in area and with a close association with the wapentake, probably originated in the influx of substantial numbers of free, colonising, warrior-peasants in the period of the Danish invasions. These owned their own land and gave general allegiance to the ruler. They came within the ambit of the manor by the king's granting of his jurisdictional rights over these otherwise unattached peasants to a thane, earl, lady, religious foundation or the like. The lord's rights, however, remained those of jurisdiction not ownership. Sokemen (the word can apply equally to men and women) rendered rent, dues and services, but the land was their own. The strength of the legal or jurisdictional bond is emphasised by the fact that the word 'sokeman' means one who owed suit to a court (Stenton 515). The jurisdictional authority of the lord soon became territorialised in that sokemen could not remove their land into another's jurisdiction, and in this sense the soke developed from lordship over people into lordship over land, but at this period nevertheless an indirect judicial superiority and in no way outright control of the land.

The complex manor contained these two basic landed interests: the manorial lands themselves, including berewicks and *inland*, and soke. These two kinds of interest were not found in coherent blocks, but were interspersed one with another across the extent of the manor. It was impossible to indicate *the* soke and *the* inland, for example, as if they could be identified by their location alone. Also, because large manors were a feature of the Danelaw, the manors themselves were far from being continuous stretches of land. Lands belonging to another lordship might be found interspersed among component parts of a manor, and detached elements, away from the main territorial block, and to all appearances in the midst of another manorial complex, were quite common (for much of this see F. M. Stenton, *Types of Manorial Structure in the Northern Danelaw*, Oxford Studies in Social and Legal History (Oxford 1910)).

Manors were described in terms of their extent, productive capacity, population and level of production, and value. The first two of these, extent or carucage (the number of carucates which comprised the holding) and the productive capacity, have an air of artificiality about them. Carucages are often expressed on a duodecimal basis and all too often the ratio of 2:1 is found for carucates to the number of plough teams they could support. Essentially the carucage figure was a statement of geld liability rather than an accurate description of the situation on the ground, or as I.

S. Maxwell so concisely expressed it 'the carucate in Yorkshire implied not what was real but what was rateable' (DGNE 23, 107, 184).

The word 'carucate', however, is obviously associated with *caruca* 'plough' and some measure in terms of basic agricultural capacity seems to be implied by this. Later medieval farming treatises accepted the theory that the carucate was the area which an eight-ox plough team could plough in one year, and it was composed of bovates, the area which one ox could plough in one year. The arithmetic would thus give eight bovates to the carucate. However, the physical extent of the component bovates would depend on terrain and soil type at least, not to mention the condition of the stock, and consequently the bovate cannot be reduced to a standard number of customary acres (the size of the acre itself, although carefully measured, varied from place to place). In the middle ages the bovate varied in size between around six to 30 customary acres (J. A. Shepherd, 'Field systems of Yorkshire', in *Studies of Field Systems in the British Isles*, ed. A. R. H. Baker and R. A. Butler (Cambridge 1973), 173). Where bovate figures are given in Yorkshire Domesday Book (acres are rarely mentioned) roughly eight bovates to the carucate is often found; there are, however, significant exceptions to this (if the addition in the text is accurate) especially in the East Riding.

Population was described as appurtenant to a manor, but the basic social and economic unit was not the manor but the vill. As has been noted elsewhere (see Introduction to Index of Places), the vill was not necessarily a single settlement but could be a complex of settlements spread over a wide area, belonging wholly to one manor or shared between several. Within the vill there were various groups of people who were involved more or less directly with the cultivation of the soil. The main categories described are *liber homo* 'Freeman'; *socmannus* 'freeman', often found referred to in historical writings as 'sokeman'; *villanus* 'villager' often found as 'villein'; *bordarius* 'smallholder', often found as 'bordar'; and *censor* 'tributary' or rent-payer. Exactly what kinds of social and economic status and legal standing are conveyed by these words is not made apparent in Domesday Book. However, the broad distinctions established in the later Middle Ages between free persons and (unfree) villeins must not be read back into 11th-century conditions. Anglo-Saxon society was slave-owning, but where slaves are found (there are none mentioned in Yorkshire Domesday Book) they are stated explicitly to be such, *servus* being the word used. It would be unwise to assume personal unfreedom unless it is specifically stated, especially since there is much evidence to suggest that the villein of the 11th century was personally free and only degraded later (P. Vinogradoff, *Villeinage in England* (Oxford, 1892; reprint, 1968), 218-20). The distinction is probably much more to do with the amounts of land held and the duties, differing in their degree of burdensomeness, owed from it to the lord, than with freedom or unfreedom as such. The range of dues owed can be illustrated by the tributaries who, it can be assumed, paid a money rent only, and the bordars or smallholders who held little land and possibly owned no plough teams. The significance of the rent types for the later history of the peasantry lies in the ability of medieval lords to increase the burdens laid on sections of the peasantry and later to enforce the legal distinction between free people and serfs (R. H. Hilton 'Freedom and villeinage in England', *Past and Present*, 31 (1965) 3-19).

Distinctions in social and economic standing were not only found amongst the peasantry. The thanage, the chief landholding class, showed considerable internal wealth differentiation. This is not only discernible from the statements concerning their lands, but also perceptible in their differing relationships with the king, and the internal divisions of authority. Traditionally thanes acknowledged the king as their lord by making a payment to him when they entered into their inheritance. It is noticeable that by the late 11th century a distinction is being made between those thanes who held more than six manors and who paid a large sum on inheritance which went directly to the king, and those with less than six, who paid a much smaller sum into the general shire revenues, not all of which went to the king. Possibly in connection with this internal stratification is the listing in Domesday Book of those major thanes who held full jurisdiction, market rights and all customary dues. Above the thanes the king, the earl and the archbishop all had specific rights, particularly those relating to jurisdiction and punitive fines. In addition the king, as representing public authority, was owed the three traditional dues: military service in the field, construction work on bridges and construction work on fortresses and defences (Stenton 289-91), although the earl and sheriff would have actually organised and enforced these.

NOTES

C1a   SHIRES. Divisions within the city. The meaning could be expressed as 'wards' or 'districts'.
THE ARCHBISHOP. In this and most subsequent entries the rights and holdings referred to are those of the office of archbishop of York, as opposed to individual archbishops. For clarity, entries relating to the holdings of the Archbishop in the time of King Edward have been recorded in the Index of Persons under the name of Archbishop Aldred, who was archbishop in 1066 (on the form of his name see 1N16 note). Entries relating to holdings of the Archbishop in the time of King William have been indexed under the name of Archbishop Thomas, who was archbishop in 1086.
LAID WASTE FOR THE CASTLES. DB *Vastata in castellis*. Latin *in* normally means 'in' or 'into', but it can also mean 'for' or 'for the purpose of'. In this case what is meant is that the buildings of one ward of the city were destroyed for the purpose of clearing space for the erection of castles. There were two castles, one on the site now occupied by Clifford's Tower, the other on the opposite bank of the river.
INHABITED DWELLINGS. There are several words used to describe accommodation in York: *mansio*, *domus* and *hospitium*, translated as 'dwelling', 'house' and 'lodging' respectively. *Mansio* and *domus* are roughly similar – indeed in the entry relating to William of Percy (C7) they are used interchangeably – but *mansio* carries, nevertheless, the implication of less permanency of occupation, the distinction possibly being between staying somewhere for whatever length of time, and living there all the time. *Hospitium* is a guest-house or lodging, and is thus more clearly connected with temporary residence.

C1a.C2   THE CANONS. As this section is dealing with the situation within York, these must be the Canons of St. Peter's of York, not of St. John's of Beverley.

C1b   THE ARCHBISHOP. Although this sentence follows the paragraph mark, logically it fits better as the last sentence of the preceding paragraph. As the first two paragraphs deal with the land of the Archbishop of York, they have both been given the number 1, subdivided as 1a and 1b.
BOTH LARGE AND SMALL. *Inter* literally means 'among', but the sense requires that *inter magnas et parvas* be translated as 'both large and small'. The same phrase occurs in C21 below.

C2   UNLESS AS ONE OF THE HOUSES OF THE BURGESSES. DB *nisi sicut una burgensium*. The *una* 'one' here can only refer to the house which is the subject of the paragraph. By gender it cannot refer to the burgesses. Thus the sense of the sentence is 'one of the houses of the burgesses', although the word 'house' is understood and not written.
ON ACCOUNT OF THAT HOUSE. DB *propter ea*. The *ea* refers to the house. The principle is as in the preceding note.
BESIDES THIS HOUSE. DB *praeter hanc*. Here *hanc* refers to the house. The principle is as in the preceding note.
BISHOP OF DURHAM. This would seem to imply that the Bishopric was considered to be synonymous with St. Cuthbert. The variation in vocabulary is perhaps designed to emphasise this point.
THE CHURCH OF ALL SAINTS. All Saints, Ousegate, or Pavement (VCH 191 note 3).
UHTRED. The regularised West Saxon form for DB *Vctred* would be OE *Uhtraed* (PNDB 398), which has here been regularised to the OE Northumbrian form *Uhtred*.
EARNWINE. DB *Ernui* could represent either OE *Earnwine* or *Earnwig*, as the frequent confusion of OE *-wig* and *-wine* in AN, and of Latin *-wi(us)* and *-win(us)*, renders correct identification of the forms *Arnui*, *Ernui* and *Ernuin* impossible (PNDB 244), so the form *Earnwine* has been adopted for consistency throughout.
WHO LIVE IN IT. DB *in ea manent*. Presumably *ea* refers to the house which is the main subject of the paragraph.

C3   THE CHURCH OF ST. CRUX. *Sancta Crux* meant 'holy cross', but such churches were often known as St. Crux in the Middle Ages. The York church of St. Crux stood at the corner of the Shambles and Pavement. It was demolished in 1883 and the stones were used to build the parish hall of All Saints, Pavement.
DRENGS. From ON *drengr* 'man'. A dreng was someone who combined a considerable landholding with light personal service (*Boldon Book* 84).

C10   BJORNULFR. DB *Bernulf* could represent either ON *Bjornulfr* (SPN 55-6) or OE *Beornwulf* (PNDB 200); in view of the Anglo-Scandinavian complexion of eleventh-century Yorkshire society, the ON forms of personal names have been chosen in all such cases in this edition, so *Bjornulfr* is used throughout.

C

GAMALBARN. SPN 95 suggests that this Gamalbarn is probably identical with the Gamalbearn mentioned by Florence of Worcester as one of the leaders of the 1065 Northumbrian insurrection (Thorpe 223; see further Appendix).

OTBERT. DB *Otbert* could represent either OG *Odbert* or OG *Otbert* (PNDB 333). *Otbert* has been preferred here as being closer to the DB form.

THE CHURCH OF ST. MARY. In Castlegate, called in later records *ecclesia S. Mariae ad portam castri* (VCH 192 note 9).

THE CHURCH OF ST. CUTHBERT. At Peasholme Green, just inside the walls. Part of the fabric of the present church is probably pre-Conquest in date (Taylor & Taylor 697). The rectory of St. Cuthbert's was subsequently appropriated to the Prior and Convent of the Holy Trinity, York (VCH 192 note 10).

C11   ALDWULF. The regularised West Saxon form for DB *Aldulf* would be OE *Ealdwulf* (PNDB 240), which has here been regularised to the OE Northumbrian form *Aldwulf*.

HEDNED. The DB form *Hedned* is anomalous. It is probably the OS personal name *Hethinn* (SPN 137) with the Norman French suffix *-et* (PNDB 125-6; 94, para. 97).

THE CHURCH OF ST. ANDREW. This subsequently came into the possession of the Dean and Chapter of York (VCH 192 note 12).

C13   THE CHURCH OF ST. MARTIN. In Coney St., and now known as St. Martin-le-Grand.

C15   LODGING HOUSES. DB *mansiones ad hospitia*. *Hospitium* is a lodging house, *mansio* a dwelling house probably connected somewhat with non-permanent residence. The use of both words here, and in C16, seems rather tautologous, but the sense of both entries, *mansiones ad hospitia* and *mansiones in hospitia*, seems best rendered by 'lodging houses' in both cases.

A MOIETY. This is rather a loose term, but it means approximately one half.

C16   BRUNN. DB *Brun* could represent either ON *Brunn* (SPN 66) or OE *Brun(a)* (JMcND). The ON form is used throughout this edition.

LODGING HOUSES. See C15 note.

C17   THREE DWELLINGS. Only 2 previous owners are named. Normally where the number of buildings and the previous owners are not identical, the details of multiple ownership are also given.

C18   ALHMUND. The regularised West Saxon form for DB *Alchemont* would be OE *Ealhmund* (PNDB 243), which has here been regularised to the OE Northumbrian form *Alhmund*.

THE CHURCH OF THE HOLY TRINITY. In Micklegate.

C21; 23-5   THE CANONS. As these entries deal with the situation in York and with places in or close to York, these must be the canons of St. Peter's of York, not of St. John's of Beverley.

C22   CARUCATE. See Appendix.

THE KING'S 3 WORKS. See Appendix.

AT REVENUE FOR. This means that the land is given over to tenants whose rent, whether in money, produce or both, is used to meet the expenses of the Archbishop's household.

THE KING'S POOL. Formed by the River Fosse, which enters the Ouse, not far from the castle (VCH 193 note 16).

C23   VILLAGERS, SMALLHOLDERS, VILLS. See Appendix.

C23-25   THE CANONS. See C21 note.

SANDBURN HOUSE. DG 533 Sandburn. The full modern name is Sandburn House.

C26   HEWORTH. This entry is repeated in 23N36.

C27   WALTHEOF. DB *Waltef* should represent ON *Valthjofr/*AS *Waeltheof*, but the form *Waltheof* has been used in this edition, that being the form in which the name of Earl Waltheof is usually cited in modern historical writings, and because it is impossible to distinguish when the reference in the DB entries is definitely to the Earl and when not.

C28   (GATE) FULFORD. The two DB vills of *Fuleford* (Gate Fulford) and *Fuleforde* ('Water' Fulford) were later amalgamated, and there is now only one township and settlement called simply Fulford. Gate Fulford Hall (SE 608 492) has been used as the vill centre for Gate Fulford and Fulford Hall (SE 608 484) as the centre for 'Water' Fulford. These 10 carucates are also recorded in the record proper of the lands of Count Alan (6W5).

C30   CLIFTON. This entry partly repeated in the lands of Count Alan (6W6). The waste and the meadow belonging to St. Peter's are omitted there.

THE CANONS. See C21 note.

C31   SAEXFRITH. The regularised West Saxon form for DB *Saxford* would be OE *Seaxfrith* (PNDB 357), which has here been regularised to the OE Northumbrian form *Saexfrith*.

C32   OVERTON. This entry is substantially repeated in the lands of Count Alan (6W2), but also see C33 note below.

IN ALL, 1 LEAGUE LONG. Measurements following the words 'in all' are usually those of the whole manor. There is an error here, however, as the dimensions given are the same as those given for the woodland. As there was clearly more to the manor than woodland, either the extent of the woodland, or the extent of the manor, is wrong. There is no way of determining which is correct.

C33   SKELTON. This entry substantially repeated in the lands of Count Alan (6W2). There, however, the entries for Overton and Skelton are combined. Furthermore only the lands which Count Alan himself holds are entered; consequently the lands in Skelton held by St. Peter's and the tributary are omitted.

TRIBUTARY. See Appendix.

C34   *MORTUN*. A lost vill. PNNR 15 places *Mortun* in Overton township, but DG 529 places it in Skelton township. The DG location has been followed in this edition.

C35   THERE [IS] 1 CARUCATE. The text literally reads *sunt ad geldum* 'there are 1 carucate'. In the text there is quite a wide gap between the stroke for '1' and the following word (DF II), and it is possible that it was originally thought that the number should have been more than 1.

C36   FULL JURISDICTION, MARKET RIGHTS AND ALL CUSTOMARY DUES. DB *soca et saca et tol et taim et omnes consuetudines* 'full jurisdiction, market rights and all customary dues'. This formula, which often included *infangtheof*, is not usually taken as being intended to define specific jurisdictional limits, but as a general expression of the remit of the private jurisdictional powers of lords within their own estates. Soke and sac are both related to the exercise of ordinary justice, toll was a payment made to the lord on the sale of cattle or other goods transacted within the lordship and team was the right to exercise jurisdiction related to the disputed possession of stock on the estate. *Infangtheof*, the right of jurisdiction over thieves taken within the lordship with the stolen goods in their possession, is omitted here, the formula being completed with the vaguer expression 'all customary dues' (see Stenton 498).

ULFR FENISC. *Fenisc* is a by-name from Old West Scandinavian *fjonski* 'from Fjon, Fünen (in Denmark)' (OEB 135).

THORGAUTR LAGR. *Lagr* is a by-name meaning 'the short' (SPN 182-3).

EDWIN. The regularised West Saxon form for DB *Eduin* should be *Eadwine*, but the modern form Edwin has been used throughout this edition, as it is not always possible to be certain that the individual concerned is not Earl Edwin (see 6N128 note).

KOFSI. SPN 176 suggests that the DB entries probably refer to the man who was appointed Earl of Northumbria by William the Conqueror (Arnold 198; see further Appendix).

C37   IN THE DEMESNE MANORS. DB *in dominicis maneriis*. The phrase presumably means in the King's own manors, that is the lands held in direct lordship, *dominicis maneriis* being a description given as a whole. The purpose of this section, comprising three parts, written in smaller characters at the foot of the column (DF II), is to distinguish between the rights, forfeits, etc., of the King, the Earl and the Archbishop. The phrase cannot mean the manors of other lords, partly because this seems to be a more developed feudal usage, distinguishing between demesne manors and subinfeudated manors, than would be appropriate for the pre-Conquest period under discussion, and partly because the situation with regard to other lords has been established in C36. Were the manors of other lords at issue the phrase would have been more likely to read *in maneriis dominorum* 'in the manors of the lords'.

NEITHER HAD THE KING. Possibly because of the physical compression of this paragraph into a small space at the foot of the column, the meaning has also been somewhat compressed. As this sentence stands, it seems to suggest that all the King had in the Earl's manors was some kind of right with regard to the spiritual jurisdiction, but that this (whether by right or by practice is not clear) in fact belonged to the Archbishop.

C39   OUTLAWED. DB *exulatus fuerit*. *Exsulare* meant 'to be exiled', but in medieval Latin it could also carry the sense of being outlawed. In this case, however, it is not so, although it is conceivable that a distinction is being made between outlawry, and exile imposed by the Sheriff or Earl.

IF THEY WISH. DB *si voluerint*, literally 'if they will have wished'.

C40   WHO HAVE. DB *habuerint, habuerit*, literally 'they/he shall have had'.

FOR THE LANDS. DB *Terrarum*, literally 'of the lands', in the phrase *relevatio terrarum*.

3 MARKS OF SILVER. The mark was a figure of account, not a coin. It represented the payment of 13s 4d in whatever coins were available

L1   LANDHOLDERS IN YORKSHIRE. The list of landholders in other counties normally carries the title 'here are listed those holding lands in ...' and the names then follow in nominative case. This form is kept on the few occasions when the heading itself has been omitted. In the Yorkshire section, however, not only is there no title, but the listing takes the form of the first entry being 'land of the King', and the others then follow in the same form, with 'land' being understood and all the names in the genitive.

L4   THE ABBOT OF YORK. The text does not contain a section for the holdings of the Abbot and some of his lands were certainly not surveyed. For example the earlier Summary records the Abbot as holding 2 carucates of land in Appleton le Moors (SN, D21), 2 carucates in Lastingham (SN, D20) and 1 carucate held from the King in Spaunton (SN,Ma13), none of which are recorded in the main text, but which were given by the King to St. Mary's Abbey (VCH 201 note 27).

1Y1   MOXBY (HALL). DG 529 Moxby. The full modern name is Moxby Hall, with the site of the mill and moat and of Moxby Priory nearby.
MURTON (FARM). DG 529 reports Murton, in Sutton in the Forest township. The full modern name of the vill centre is Murton Farm.
THORPE (HILL). DG 536 Thorpe. The full modern name is Thorpe Hill. The vill was subsequently amalgamated with Sutton on the Forest.
KELSIT (GRANGE). DG 526 Kelsit. The full modern name is Kelsit Grange.

1Y2   BIRKBY. On the depopulated vill centre see LVY 295.
SOWERBY (UNDER COTCLIFFE). The DB vill of *Sourebi* is now represented by the township of Sowerby under Cotcliffe. There is now no settlement of the name, the vill centre at SE 412 936 having been depopulated (LVY 306), although the name survives in Sowerby Grange (SE 415 939), a second Sowerby Grange (SE 400 930) and Sowerby House (SE 407 940).
(LITTLE) SMEATON. The vill centre (NZ 346 035) of Little Smeaton township was subsequently depopulated (LVY 305).
LANDMOTH. On the shrunken vill centre see LVY 302.
NEWSHAM (GRANGE). DG 530 Newsham. The full modern name is Newsham Grange.
'WESTHOUSE'. DG 538 identifies with Westhouse between Yafforth and Northallerton (DG map 62, J4); not on either modern 6 in. or 1st ed. 6 in. OS map (sheet 55), so here given as lost.
WARLABY. DB *Werlegesbi* (DF III); DG 538, PNNR 276 erroneously *Wergeleshi*.
LAZENBY (HALL). DG 526 Lazenby. The full modern name is Lazenby Hall in Lazenby township.
(OVER) DINSDALE (GRANGE). DG 531 Over Dinsdale. The full modern name is Over Dinsdale Grange.
IRBY (MANOR). DG 525 Irby. The full modern name is Irby Manor. On the shrunken vill centre see LVY 301.
(WEST) HARLSEY. DB *Heressaie* (DF III); DG 538 erroneously *Herelsaie*. The vill centre of West Harlsey township is now depopulated (LVY 299) and located at SE 415 981, to the north-east of Harlsey Castle (SE 414 980).
(KIRBY) SIGSTON. DG 534 Sigston. The DB vill of *Sighestun* is now represented by the township of Kirby Sigston. The site of the depopulated settlement of Kirby Sigston is at SE 417 947 (LVY 305), adjacent to the now-isolated parish church.
LEAKE. There is now no settlement of the name. Leake church is isolated with a few earthworks adjacent which may represent the original vill centre, especially as the Tithe Award shows *Old Leake Green* on the opposite side of the road from the church (LVY 302). The present church has a Norman tower (N. Pevsner, *Yorkshire: the North Riding* (Harmondsworth, 1966), 226), and the pre-Danish Anglo-Saxon cross built into the wall of the church (W. G. Collingwood, 'Anglian and Anglo-Danish sculpture: addenda to the North Riding', *Yorkshire Archaeological Journal*, 23 (1915), 256-8) suggests that this has been the ecclesiastical centre since at least before the Norman Conquest.
KNAYTON. Occurs twice in this entry, once as *Chennieton* and once as *Keneuetun* (given erroneously in DG 526 as *Keneueton*).
RAVENSTHORPE (MANOR). DG 532 Ravensthorpe. The full modern name is Ravensthorpe Manor at SE 4951 8512. LVY 304 places the depopulated vill centre at SE 481 866, but does not say whether there are any earthworks.
CROSBY (GRANGE). DG 519 Crosby. The full modern name is Crosby Grange; a grange of Rievaulx Abbey located at the site of the now-deserted settlement (LVY 297).

(NORTH) OTTERINGTON. On the shrunken vill centre see LVY 304.
(NORTH) KILVINGTON. PNNR 200, 205 ascribes DB *Cheluintun* (SN,Bi8) and
Chelvinctune (5N72; 5N75) to South Kilvington and *Chelvintun* (1Y2) to North Kilvington,
whereas DG 531 ascribes all these forms entirely to North Kilvington. The entry in the
Summary (SN,Bi8), referring to land held there by the King and the Count of Mortain,
makes it obvious that it combines the two entries in the text relating to the King's land
(1Y2) and the holding of the Count of Mortain (5N72; 75), so that all entries must relate
to the same place, i.e. North Kilvington. On the depopulated vill centre see LVY 301.

1Y3   NORTHFIELD (FARM). DG 531 Northfield. The full modern name is Northfield Farm.
NORTHFIELD. This place-name with *B'* for *berwicus* 'outlier' written above Falsgrave.
OSGODBY, 4 CARUCATES. '4 carucates' written above the line.
'SCAWTHORPE'. DG 533 reports Scawthorpe, but the name appears on neither the
modern 6 in. nor the 1st ed. 6 in. OS map (sheet 94) and PNNR 105 gives no forms
subsequent to the DB entry, so the name has been treated here as lost.
ETERSTORP. Lost in Gristhorpe township (DG 521; PNNR 104).
RODEBESTORP. Lost in Gristhorpe township (DG 532; PNNR 104).
FILEY. DB *Fiuelac* (DF III). Farley erroneously *Fucelac*. The name is in miniscules and is a
mistake made in transcribing miniscules.
'BURTON (DALE)'. DG 517 reports Burton Dale, but the name occurs on neither the
modern 6 in. nor the 1st ed. 6 in. OS map (sheets 93, 94), so it is treated here as lost.
(HIGH, MIDDLE AND LOW) DEEPDALE. Deep Dale is a dale running north-south
from High Deepdale (TA 040 857) through Middle Deepdale (TA 045 853) to Low
Deepdale (TA 042 841). As it is impossible to be certain which, if any, of these three
settlements was the original vill centre, all three have been used in this edition.
'NEWTON'. DG 530 identifies DB *Neuuetun* with Newton in West Ayton, whereas PNNR
54 identifies it as Newton located in Stonegrave. The DG location has been adopted here.
The name occurs on neither the modern 6 in. nor the 1st ed. 6 in. OS map (sheets 77, 93),
so it has been given here as lost.
PRESTON (HILL). DG 532 Preston. The full modern name is Preston Hill; which lies
just to the north of Hutton Buscel. On the depopulated vill centre see LVY 304.
MARTIN (GARTH). DG 528 reports DB *Martune* as lost in Hutton Buscel, but it is in fact
Martin Garth (DGNE 477-8; personal communication 13.4.85 I. S. Maxwell), which is in
the eastern part of Wykeham township (near Scarborough), just to the west of the
boundary with Hutton Buscel township. Cf. 1N43 note.
STAINTON(DALE). DG 534 Stainton Dales. The modern name is Staintondale.

1Y4   (HIGH) BLANDSBY. DG 516 Blandsby. The full modern name is High Blandsby.
EASTHORPE (HOUSE). DG 520 Easthorpe. The full modern name is Easthorpe House,
adjacent to the probable site of the vill centre (LVY 298).
IS 16 LEAGUES LONG. Literally *ht.* for *habet* 'has' 16 leagues long.
BROMPTON, 3 CARUCATES. '3 carucates' written above the line.
ODULFESMARE, CHILUESMARES, ASCHILESMARES, MAXUDESMARES. All lost in
Pickering Marishes (DG 531, 515, 518, 528). This is an extensive low-lying area of
marshland in the south of Pickering Lythe wapentake, as is indicated by the elements Old
French *mareis* and OE *mersc* 'marsh' in the name Marishes and the four lost DB vill names
in the various forms occurring in DB (see also SN,D12 note).
FARMANBY, ROXBY (HILL). DG 533 Roxby. The full modern name is Roxby Hill. It has
been suggested that the earthworks at SE 826 828, adjacent to the site of *Roxby Hall,* may be
those of the original vill centre and that the church of the now-lost *Farmanby,* which was
subsequently linked with Roxby, may be that at SE 838 831 in Thornton Dale village
(which is not recorded in DB), which serves Ellerburn parish (LVY 305). Although not on
the modern map, the name *Farmanby* does appear on the 1st ed. 6 in. OS map, sheets 91,
92, as an area name centred at SE 854 858 to the north-east of Thornton Dale village. This
area on the 1st ed. map is divided into small numbered areas, and a note at the bottom of
sheet 91 states 'NOTE. The portions numbered 2 to 33 belong to the Township of
Thornton Dale in the Parish of Thornton Dale, those numbered 34 to 72 belong to the
Township of Farmanby in the parish of Ellerburn, those numbered 73 to 78 belong to
both these Townships, but the portions belonging to each cannot be shewn by distinct
boundaries, and the portions numbered 79 to 81 belong to the Townships of Thornton
Dale, Farmanby and Ellerburn in the parishes of Thornton Dale and Ellerburn'. This
suggests that by the 19th century the territories of Thornton Dale and *Farmanby* townships
had become inextricably intertwined, explaining why *Farmanby* was eventually absorbed
into Thornton Dale and disappeared as a separate township.

KINGTHORPE (HOUSE). DG 526 Kingthorpe. The full modern name is Kingthorpe House (at SE 835 858). The location of the original vill centre has not been ascertained (LVY 301).
CHIGOGEMERS. Lost in Thornton Dale (DG 518).
IN ALL 16 LEAGUES LONG. See C32 note.

1Y5   HEMINGBROUGH. This land is assigned to the Bishop of Durham in the Summary (SE, How10).
2 PLOUGHS CAN PLOUGH. *arare* 'to plough' written above the line.

1Y6   SHIPTON(THORPE). DG 479 Shipton. The full modern name is Shiptonthorpe.
NOW THE KING HAS. Between *modo* and *ht.* for *habet* 'he has' 2 letters are written above the line (DF III). Presumably these are an abbreviation, but it is difficult to determine either what they are, or what they might mean. Possibly for this reason, Farley omits them altogether.
JURISDICTION. The entries for both Goodmanham and Houghton, written in much tighter lettering, appear to have been added afterwards. Possibly this accounts for the somewhat curtailed and yet tautologous form. The repetition of the word *soca* 'jurisdiction' is necessary to make the status of the land clear.
CARUCATE. The abbreviation of *carucata* 'carucate' to *car.* is possibly due to shortage of space, although such an abbreviation is found elsewhere in the text. Where the abbreviation takes this form it is identical with the abbreviation often used for *caruca* 'plough'. To make the distinction between the two clear, when *car.* means carucate it is often followed by *tre.* for *terrae* 'of land'. However, even when *tre.* does not follow *car.* (as in this case), the meaning is often clear from the context. Here it is quite apparent, since it would be absurd to find soke (legal jurisdiction) levied over a thing (a plough) rather than over an area of land (a carucate).
HOUGHTON. Robert Malet is said to hold 4½ carucates in Houghton as soke of Market Weighton (11E7). However, the land is said to be the King's in the Summary (SE,Wei3).
HOUGHTON. The depopulated vill centre of Houghton lies to the south-west of Sancton at SE 890 390 (LVY 63).

1Y7   *TORP.* DG 481 ascribes the *Rud(e)torp* forms (21E12, CE28 and SE,P3) to Thorpe le Street and the *Torp/Torpi* forms (1Y7 and SE, Wei6) to a lost *Torp* in Thorpe le Street. PNER 229 places all these forms together under Thorpe le Street, pointing out that there were apparently two DB manors in the neighbourhood – *Torp* in Weighton Hundred (SE,Wei6) and *Rud(e)torp* in Pocklington Hundred (SE,P3). The two vills were subsequently amalgamated to form the township of Thorpe le Street, but whether the present township centre at SE 837 440 was originally in *Torp* or in *Rud(e)torp* is impossible to determine. The DG ascriptions, presumably arbitrary, have been followed in this edition.
TURODEBI. Lost in Kirby Grindalythe (DG 482; PNER 125).
HOTHAM, SEATON (ROSS). These entries added in small lettering in the margin. They are probably part of the 8 carucates jurisdiction (soke) belonging to Warter, but since no amounts of land are given for Duggleby and *Turodebi*, it is impossible to be absolutely sure of this. However, their position in the margin, almost immediately after Duggleby, implies the intention to make them an integral part of this entry.

1Y8   (LITTLE) DRIFFIELD. DG 475 identifies DB *Drigelinghe* with Little Driffield, as was first suggested by Skaife 11, whereas Farrer (VCH 197) suggested an identification with Brigham, which appears elsewhere in DB as *Bringeham* (5E53; SE,Tu5). The identification with Little Driffield seems more likely in view of the stated relationship with Great Driffield, but the DB form of the name (this being the only time it is mentioned) is certainly anomalous, and is the only time that it takes this form in any of the documented sources (PNER 153-4; 153 note 1).
JURISDICTION. The extent of the jurisdiction (soke land) in each vill entered above the relevant place names.
(GREAT) KENDALE. DG 475 Kendale. The full modern name is Great Kendale.
EASTBURN. The vill centre of Eastburn had been depopulated by the early 17th century (LVY 60).
(KIRK)BURN. DB reports Kirkburn as *Westburne*, while the account of the Bruce fee reports it as *Burnous* (31E3). The 'west' of the DB form is in relation to Eastburn, in the ecclesiastical parish of Kirkburn; the second element of the name being from OE *burna* and *hus*, i.e. 'house by the stream'. The *kirkja* element does not appear in the name until the later 13th century (PNER 166-7).
50 CARUCATES. The individual amounts add up to only 49 carucates.

1Y9   AND ANOTHER ½ WHICH WAS JOLI'S. Added above the line over '2½ carucates'. It is not clear whether the '2 ploughs' refers to the 2½ carucates originally entered, or to 3, including Joli's.

JOLI. DB *Iole* (DF IV). Farley erroneously *Lole*.

1Y10   JURISDICTION. See 1Y8 note.

GRIMTHORPE (MANOR). DG 473 Grimthorpe. The full modern name is Grimthorpe Manor, the settlement of the name now being represented by only the manor-house and the mill (LVY 62).

WAPLINGTON (HALL). DG 482 Waplington. The full modern name is Waplington Hall. The site of the depopulated vill centre is now represented by fishponds, manor-house, park and farm (LVY 69).

BARMBY (MOOR). DG 467 reports Barmby on the Moor, a form by which it has been known in some documents (PNER 184), but the form given on the modern 2½ in. OS map is Barmby Moor, which has therefore been used here.

(OUSE)THORPE (FARM). DG 478 Ousethorpe. The full modern name is Ousethorpe Farm, the vill centre now being represented only by the farm, mill and moat centred at SE 813 511 (not SE 820 515 as given in LVY 66).

55½ CARUCATES. The total given for the sokelands is 55½ carucates. The individual extents given in carucates add up to 54½ carucates. For the addition to be correct, therefore, the 6 bovates in Barmby Moor must be the equivalent of 1 carucate, or the term 'half' is very loosely used.

KILNWICK (PERCY). On the depopulated vill centre see LVY 64.

1Y11   HILDERTHORPE. The site of the depopulated original vill centre of Hilderthorpe has now been absorbed into the suburbs of Bridlington (LVY 63).

WILSTHORPE. The earthworks of the depopulated vill centre are still visible, although there has been some cliff-edge erosion (LVY 70).

JURISDICTION. The extent of the jurisdiction (sokeland) in each vill has been entered above the place-names. For most of the entries the scribe has failed to indicate whether the amounts are carucates or bovates, but they must all be carucates, since the final total given is 58½ caruates and the numbers add up to 58½.

EASTON. On the shrunken vill centre see LVY 61.

ELESTOLF. Lost in Brigham (DG 471).

1Y12   HENSALL. This entry written in very small, tight lettering at the foot of the column. Accordingly the text is very abbreviated, presumably in the interests of space.

1Y13   *SANTONE* and WOOLLEY. This entry is written as the previous one (see 1Y12 note). 8 PLOUGHS. There is a *II* written above the total 8.

SANTONE. DG 505 reports DB *Santone* as Santon, and locates it (DG map 61,I12) just to the south of Woolley, but no such place appears on the modern 2½ in. OS map and PNWR i, 289 gives no forms subsequent to the DB entry, so the name has been treated here as lost. The 12 carucates of land here assigned to *Santone* and Woolley are allocated in the Summary solely to *Sactun*, indicating that it was somewhere in the general area of Woolley, although it could as easily have become part of Darton township (WYAS 567).

1Y14   TAXABLE. *ad gld.* for *ad geldum* 'taxable' written above the line.

JURISDICTION. As 1Y8 note.

ONE TRIBUTARY. This was probably Geoffrey Bainard (VCH 198 note 9).

1Y15   WARLEY. The DB name *Werlafeslei* is split between two lines with the second half of the name beginning with a lower case *f* rather than a capital and this, combined with the fact that DB states that there are nine outliers to Wakefield and then names only eight, has caused the supposition that two places were named, and the identification of the second half of the name, *feslei*, with Halifax. Other early recordings of the name of Warley (this is the only entry in DB; Warley does not occur in the Summary) show that the whole of the name must apply to Warley (see further PNWR iii, 104, 122). While the addition in Domesday Book is not always correct, the inaccuracies normally arise from adding up reasonably numerous entries of individually small amounts of land. An error in the number of outliers attached to a manor is only found here. In the Middle Ages Warley township contained a large number of settlements, and it is impossible to be certain which was the main vill centre (WYAS 551). The grid reference given in the index is that for Warley Town.

WADSWORTH. There is no main settlement called Wadsworth in Wadsworth township, and the grid reference for the vill centre given in the index is that for Old Town (see further WYAS 547).

CRUTTONSTALL. DG 497 reports DB *Crumbetonestun* as Heptonstall, but it is in fact Cruttonstall (PNWR iii, 172; WYAS 367). The vill may have ceased to exist as the result of the creation of Erringden township, although Cruttonstall vill was probably larger than the subsequent Erringden township (WYAS 367). The grid reference for the vill centre given in the index is that of Erringden Grange.

LONGFIELD. Although the township, Langfield, retains the *a* spelling of DB *Langefelt*, the main settlement is known as Longfield.

STANSFIELD. It seems likely that the name Stansfield has always referred to the township area, rather than to an individual settlement, notwithstanding the existence of Stansfield Hall. The grid reference given in the index for the vill centre is that for Cross Stone in the centre of the township (WYAS 523).

JURISDICTION. See 1Y8 note. The amounts are given in carucates and bovates. If the final total of 30 carucates is correct, then 23 bovates make 2½ carucates, which makes a carucate here 9.2 bovates on average. It is always possible that the addition is not correct.

(WEST) BRETTON. It seems likely that the DB entry refers to only part of West Bretton township and that the moiety held by Ilbert de Lacy was ignored (WYAS 556).

(EARLS)HEATON. The DB vills of Earlsheaton and Hanging Heaton were subsequently amalgamated to form the township of Soothill, containing the hamlet divisions of Nether Soothill (containing the settlement of Earlsheaton) and Upper Soothill (containing the settlement of Hanging Heaton), whose boundaries preserve those of the DB vills (WYAS 510-11).

STANLEY. On the probable extent of the DB vill of Stanley see WYAS 21.

SHITLINGTON. It would appear that DB refers to only part of Shitlington vill (WYAS 502). Medieval Shitlington contained four hamlet divisions – Middle Shitlington, Nether Shitlington, Over Shitlington (whose main settlements were Middlestown, Netherton and Overton respectively) and Midgley (WYAS 502). The grid reference given for the vill centre in the index is that for Middlestown. In 1929 the name was euphemised to Sitlington (the form in which it is given in DG 507), although the derivation of the name is in fact 'Scytel's *tun*' (PNWR ii, 206).

CARTWORTH. In the Summary Cartworth, Fulstone, Hepworth, Thurstonland and Wooldale are listed separately (SW,Ag14), but in the text here their combined carucage appears under the name of Cartworth alone, suggesting that in 1086 it formed the administrative centre for an 11th-century estate on the south-eastern side of the Holme Valley (WYAS 338).

(LOWER) CUMBERWORTH. DG 500, 510 reports DB *Cumbreuu(o)rde* of 1Y15 and SW,Ag12 as Upper Cumberworth and DB *Combre-*, *Cumbreuuorde* of 9W88 and SW,St11 as Lower Cumberworth, but the correct identification is in fact the reverse (WYAS 353-5). Upper Cumberworth is located in the township of Cumberworth, and Lower Cumberworth in the township of Cumberworth Half; the respective territories of the two townships were inextricably intermixed (see WYAS 354, fig. 3).

(NORTH) CROSLAND (LOCKWOOD). This entry refers to North Crosland, the 'north' element of the name first appearing in documentary sources mid-13th century to distinguish this from South Crosland (PNWR ii, 265). The vill of North Crosland subsequently came to be known as Lockwood, the name North Crosland only surviving as that of one of the two hamlet divisions which made up the township (WYAS 437).

THE OTHER (YATE)HOLME. Usually thought to be Yateholme (DG 513), although there is no satisfactory evidence for this (WYAS 402, which see also for the likely boundary between the two vills). Only the name Yateholme survives now at SE 114 049, the nearest settlement being the single building at Yateholme Cote (SE 113 047).

(UPPER)THONG. DG 504 and PNWR ii, 312 both identfy DB *Thoac* with Quick, but it is in fact Upperthong (WYAS 543). The morphology of the DB name (< *Thoanc* < *Thoang* < *Thwang*) supports this identification (cf. PNWR ii, 286, 288).

THIS SOME SAY IS THANELAND. The status of these lands in Holme and elsewhere is unclear. The scribe does not come to a decision, but simply says that it is at issue whether these lands lie within the jurisdiction of Wakefield, or, being thaneland, do not. See also 1W26 note.

1Y16 NORMANTON. This entry is substantially repeated, with some modifications and additions in 1W25.

1Y17 KING EDWARD. *Edw.* for Edward above the line.

1Y18 CLARETON. Subsequent to 1285 part of Coneythorpe township (LVY 234).

'HILTON'. DG 497 identifies DB *Hiltone* with Hilton, which it places to the south-east of Copgrove (DG map 59, I7). The place does not appear on the modern 6 in. OS map, so the name has been given here as lost. 'Hilton' is given here as a berewick of Aldborough in the WR and is recorded under 'Burghshire' (Claro) Wapentake in the Summary (SE,Bu14), so it cannot refer to the Hilton in the extreme north of the NR.

THIS JURISDICTION. *H* for *haec* 'this' written as a capital. Jurisdiction as 1Y8 note.

ELLENTHORPE (HALL), MILBY. Listed in DB under the WR, but now in the NR. DG 493 Ellenthorpe. The full modern name is Ellenthorpe Hall. On the shrunken vill centre see LVY 298.

FELLISCLIFFE. Felliscliffe only survives today as the name of the township, not as a settlement name, on the 6 in. OS map, and a four-figure grid reference only has therefore been given in the index.

CLIFTON. This does not occur as a settlement name on either the modern 6 in. or 1st ed. 6 in. OS map (sheets 153, 170); only as part of the township name, Clifton with Norwood. Names relating to Norwood occur in the southern half of the township, suggesting that Clifton vill was probably located in the northern half, in the area of SE 20 52/SE 21 53 (see also 2W4 note).

TIMBLE. DG 495 Great Timble. The modern form of the name of the vill centre is simply Timble, the township being Great Timble.

WHIPLEY (HALL). DG 512 Whipley. The full modern name is Whipley Hall.

(SOUTH) STAINLEY. Underlined (DF V), which is the equivalent of crossing out. If this was the intention, the correction was presumably made some time after the first writing since the land totals, including (South) Stainley, correctly add up to the 21 carucates given.

1Y19   OUTLIERS. The extents of individual outliers are entered above the relevant place-names.

WALKINGHAM (HILL). DG 511 Walkingham. The full modern name is Walkingham Hill, an extra-parochial area. The earthwork remains of the depopulated medieval settlement were destroyed in 1946 (LVY 236).

FERRENSBY, 3 CARUCATES LESS 1 BOVATE. Thus DB (DF V). Farley erroneously '3 carucates less 2 bovates'.

BESTHA(I)M. In its first occurrence in this entry Farley reads *Besthaim* (DF V) incorrectly as *Besthann*, although he reads the second occurrence correctly as *Bestham*. *Bestha(i)m* was located somewhere in Fewston township (DG 487); perhaps in the northern part and possibly even extending northwards into Menwith township, as PNWR v, 122-3 points out that in 1613 *Beeston Leaz* was described as being near Watling Street and that in 1320 *Bestaynmor* was associated with the bank of the River Nidd.

42 CARUCATES OF LAND, LESS A HALF. The addition is wrong. The individual amounts add up to 39 carucates 3 bovates only.

1N1   NORTH RIDING. The entries for the King's land in the North, East and West Ridings which follow are written in a very curtailed form. This contrasts significantly with both the preceding form and also the form used for most of the major landholders' lands.

LANGBARGH WAPENTAKE. Named from the meeting place, a hill called Langbargh in Great Ayton in the centre of the wapentake. By the early 14th century part of the wapentake had been taken to form the wapentake of Whitby Strand, and the remainder, which is now generally known as Cleveland, was subsequently divided into the two divisions of Langbargh West and Langbargh East (PNNR 111, 128).

M. The letter *M* in the margin stands for *manerium* 'manor'. When a number is written above it, it means more than one manor.

1N2   MARGINAL CROSS. This shows that Dunsley (1N20) should have followed at this point.

1N3   T.R.R. This is clearly an error. The standard form is *T.R.E.* for *tempore regis Edwardi* 'in the time of King Edward', meaning before 1066.

1N5   LOFTUS. This has the equivalent of underlining in the text (DF V). Only a few of the entries in this section are underlined and there is no obvious reason why (cf. 1N8,9 notes).

1N6   'STAINTON'. DG 534 reports DB *Steintun* as Stainton in Stanghow, whereas PNNR 270 gives it as Stainton in Downholme; the DG identification has been followed here. The name does not appear on either the modern 6 in. or the 1st ed. 6 in. OS map (sheet 18) and has therefore been treated here as lost.

1N7   LAND FOR 2 OXEN. This is not a common usage. Although it is found at various times in the Yorkshire section, the arable capacity of the land is normally indicated in terms of ploughs and not of plough-beasts.

8S. This is written at the extreme right-hand end of the line of the preceding entry.

1N8	(KILTON) THORPE. See 1N5 note.
1N9	KILTON. See 1N5 note.
1N10	PLOUGH. Written at the extreme right-hand end of the line of the preceding entry.
1N12	*WESTUDE* (KIRKLEATHAM). *Westude* is now known as Kirkleatham, the *kirkja* 'church' element, referring to its early church, displacing the 'west' element, referring to its position in relation to Upleatham, in the later 12th century (PNNR 155).
1N13	3½ CARUCATES. Thus DB (DF V). Farley erroneously '4½ carucates'. The ½, *dim.* for *dimidium* 'half', is written above the line.
1N14	UPSALL (HALL). DG 537 Upsall. The full modern name is Upsall Hall at NZ 544 158, to the west of the depopulated probable original vill centre at NZ 560 160 (LVY 307). The name also survives in that of the township, Upsall.
1N15	(PINCHIN)THORPE (HALL). DG 532 reports DB *Torp* as Pinchingthorpe. The full modern form of the name is Pinchinthorpe Hall (at NZ 576 140), to the south of the now-depopulated vill centre at NZ 578 142 (LVY 304).
1N16	ALDRED. The regularised West Saxon form for DB *Aldred* would be OE *Ealdraed* (PNDB 241), which has here been regularised to the OE Northumbrian form *Aldred*.
1N18	JURISDICTION. Although there is no distinguishing *tre.* (for *terrae* 'of land') after the abbreviation *car.*, it is clear that 'carucate' is intended. See 1Y6 note.
1N19	MORTON (GRANGE). DG 528 Morton. The full modern name is Morton Grange. The exact location of the depopulated vill centre is uncertain (LVY 303). (NUN)THORPE. Written in capitals above Morton Grange (DF V). ALFRED. The regularised West Saxon form for DB *Aluret* should be OE *Aelfraed* (PNDB 175), but the modern form Alfred has been used throughout this edition. There was in fact also an Old Breton form *Alfred, Alfret, Alfrit* (PNDB 176), although this is unlikely to be involved in the Yorkshire names.
1N20	DUNSLEY. The marginal cross matches that next to Roxby (1N2), indicating that Dunsley should have followed Roxby, but was omitted and inserted later.
1N21	MARGINAL CROSS. This shows that Tunstall (1N29) should have been inserted at this point.
1N22	10S. In this entry, as with the others in this column and the rest of this section, the land values are written somewhat to the right of the main body of the text (DF V, VI, VII, VIII). Farley exaggerates the distance, although in the lands of the East and West Ridings (DF VII, VIII) the distance between the text and the land value given is much more distinct. The arrangement gives the impression that the land values were added after the main part of the text was written. See 1N66 note.
1N23	EASBY. This has the equivalent of underlining in the text (DF V). Normally Farley draws attention to this by printing the word in capitals. In this case he omits to do so. The omission is significant since few places in this section are underlined.
1N25	MARTON (IN CLEVELAND). DG 528 Marton. The full modern name is Marton in Cleveland.
1N26	NEWHAM (HALL). DG 530 Newham. The full modern name is Newham Hall.
1N27	TOLLESBY. The earthworks of the depopulated vill centre are visible to the west of the stream and of Gunnergate Hall (LVY 307).
1N28	ACKLAM. DG 538 West Acklam. The modern name is simply Acklam. 3 CARUCATES. 2 of these were in Middlesbrough and 1 in Airsholme (VCH 200 note 23).
1N29	IN TUNSTALL (FARM). The marginal cross indicates that Tunstall should have followed Thornaby (1N21). See 1N20 note. The name survives today as an area name in Nunthorpe township and in that of Tunstall Farm. As the location of the original vill centre is uncertain (LVY 307), the grid reference for Tunstall Farm (NZ 527 120) has been used in the index.
1N31	*BERGULUESBI.* Lost in Seamer township (DG 516; PNNR xlv).
1N32	SKUTTERSKELFE (HALL). DB *Codreschelf* (DF V), Farley erroneously *Godreschelf.* DG 534 reports Skutterskelf. The full modern name is Skutterskelfe Hall (see also LVY 305); the name also survives as that of the township, Skutterskelfe.
1N33	THORALDBY (FARM). DG 536 Thoraldby. The full modern name is Thoraldby Farm.
1N34	AELFHERE. The DB form *Aluer* could represent either ON *Alfarr* or OE *Aelfhere*, from which *Alfarr* was derived (PNDB 143, cf. 1N104 note *infra*). The form *Aelfhere* has been used in this edition as being closer to the DB form. In her study of the Scandinavian personal-names of Yorkshire, Dr. G. Fellows Jensen did not find any certain instances of ON *Alfarr* (personal communication 27.10.81).
1N35	*CAMISEDALE.* Lost in Ingleby Greenhow (DG 517).

1N36   (GREAT) BROUGHTON. DG 522 Great Broughton. The main settlement at NZ 547 063 is now called simply Broughton, while the township is now known as Great and Little Broughton. To avoid confusion the DG ascription has been used in this edition.
SIWARD. DB *Siuuard* should represent ON *Sigvarthr* or OE *Sigeweard*, but the form *Siward* has been used in this edition, as that in which the name of Earl Siward is usually cited in modern historical writings; it is impossible to distinguish when the reference in the DB entries is definitely to the Earl and when not.

1N39   GOULTON (GRANGE). DG 522 Goulton. The full modern name is Goulton Grange.

1N42-57 [*DIC* (PICKERING LYTHE) WAPENTAKE]. Although recorded under the general heading of Langbargh Wapentake, these places are all located in *Dic* Wapentake in the Summary. From the 12th century onward the wapentake was known as Pickering Lythe. There are a considerable number of dykes, assumed to be Iron Age in date, in the wapentake, one of which was probably the meeting place and gave its name to the DB wapentake.

1N43   MARTIN (GARTH). DG 528 identifies the *Martun* of this entry with Marton near Middlesbrough, i.e. Marton in Cleveland (see 1N25 note). But it is here linked with *Wicham*, i.e. Wykeham near Scarborough (DG 539), so is more likely to refer to Martin Garth in Wykeham township (see 1Y3 note), which is earlier similarly linked with Wykeham (1Y3).

1N45   TROUTSDALE. The DB name survives in that of Troutsdale township. The only surviving settlement name is Troutsdale Low Hall, whose grid reference has been used in the index, although it may not be the original vill centre.

1N47   LOFT MARISHES. The DB name survives as an area name centred on SE 873 798. The original vill centre may have been at Marishes Lodge (SE 884 792), but this cannot be proved, so its grid reference has not been used in the index.

1N50   (LOW) DALBY. DG 519 Dalby. The full modern name is Low Dalby.

1N51   'KETTLETHORPE'. DG 526 reports Kettlethorpe, but the name does not occur on either the modern 6 in or the 1st ed. 6 in. OS map (sheets 75, 76) and has been treated here as lost.

1N56   IN THESE 2 MANORS. *his* 'these' is given a capital letter by Farley. This does not appear in the text (DF V). The phrase can be taken to mean either that Cropton is itself 2 manors – in which case the number '2' has been omitted from above the initial *M* – or that the 2 manors in question are Cropton itself and Cawthorn, the preceding manor, which Gospatric also previously held.

1N57   *BASCHEBI*. DG 515 reports DB *Baschebi* lost in 'Lastington' township, presumably an error for Lastingham, as no Lastington appears on the modern map nor in PNNR; DG map 63, N5, plots *Baschebi* and 'Lastington' close together just east of Hutton le Hole, i.e. in the correct position for Lastingham. The name Lastingham is omitted from the map, although indexed DG 526 following Lartington. The juxtaposition may have inspired the error.

1N58-84 [*MANESHOU* (RYEDALE) WAPENTAKE]. Although recorded under the general heading of Langbargh Wapentake, these places are all located in *Maneshou* Wapentake in the Summary. In the 12th century the name of the wapentake was changed to Ryedale. The name, 'the *haugr* of one Mann (OE) or Mani (ON)', refers to the unidentified hill or tumulus where the wapentake would have met (PNNR 42).

1N58   THORNTON (RISEBOROUGH). The vill centre is now depopulated (LVY 307).

1N59   6 CARUCATES. The scribe originally wrote *iiii* carucates, which he then crossed out with a v-shaped stroke, presumably in an attempt to change it to *vi*. He also wrote *sex* 'six' in spidery characters above (DF V). Farley reproduces the written '6' but also gives the numeral as *vi*.

1N60   2S. Thus DB (DF V). Farley erroneously 3s.

1N61   EARNE. DB *Eadne* may be an error for *Earne* (PNDB 233), representing an anglicised form of ON *Arni*. *Arni* is quite a common personal-name, while *Earne* is very rare (PNOE 122; personal communication from Dr. G. Fellows Jensen, 27.10.81). *Earne* has, however, been preferred in this edition, being closer to the DB form.

1N66   5S. Written at the end of the following line. Since the value is not the last item in the entry, this arrangement suggests that it may have been inserted later. See 1N22 note.

1N67   2 BOVATES. Written above the line.

1N72   (NORTH) HOLME (HOUSE). DG 531 North Holme. The full modern name is North Holme House, the two farms here possibly representing a formerly larger settlement (LVY 300).

1N75	(WEST) NEWTON (GRANGE). DG 538 West Newton. The full modern name is West Newton Grange, sited immediately adjacent to the original vill centre (LVY 304).
1N76	WOODLAND PASTURE ... 10S. Written at the end of the preceding line.
1N77	2 BOVATES. Written above the line.
1N78	GRIFF (FARM). See 1N23 note (DF VI). DG 523 Griff. The full modern name is Griff Farm. The earthworks of the original vill centre are just to the north-west of the farm (LVY 299).
1N79	STILTONS (FARM). DG 535 Stiltons. The full modern name is Stiltons Farm.
1N80	LAND [FOR] 2 PLOUGHS. The form normally used is *terra ad ... carucam/s* 'land for ... ploughs'. In this case the *ad* has been omitted, but clearly the sense is as usual.
1N82	RICCAL (HOUSE). DG 532 Riccall. The name is now preserved only in the names of the River Riccal, and Riccal Moor and Riccal House on its north bank in the south-east of Harome township (PNNR 5). The form Riccal House has been adopted for use throughout this edition. The original vill centre may have been located at SE 674 806 where Nunnington Lane crosses the River Riccal (LVY 304).
1N85-106	[*BOLESFORD* (BULMER) WAPENTAKE]. Although recorded under the general heading of Langbargh, these places are all located in *Bolesford* Wapentake in the Summary. After the 12th century the wapentake was known as Bulmer. The DB wapentake was named from a lost *Bulford*, probably a ford across the River Foss somewhere in Strensall parish in the centre of the wapentake and the place where the wapentake would have met (PNNR 8).
1N85	(LOW) HUTTON. Thus DG 527. PNNR 40,41, prefers to divide the DB *Hotun* forms between High Hutton and Low Hutton.
1N86	DALBY. Farley gives Dalby a capital *D* which it does not have in the text (DF VI). *S*. The letter *S* in the margin stands for *soca* 'soke', i.e. 'legal jurisdiction' (see Appendix).
1N89	WIGANTHORPE (HALL). DG 539 Wigganthorpe. The full modern name is Wiganthorpe Hall in Terrington with Wiganthorpe township.
1N90	HILDENLEY (HALL). DG 524 Hildenley. The full modern name is Hildenley Hall; the name also survives in that of the township, Hildenley.
1N91	4 M. The 4 is written as 2 sets of *II*, one above the other (DF VI). (WEST) LILLING. DG 520, 538, does not distinguish which *Lilinge* of fols. 300c (300b in DG numbering) and 381a (381 in DG) is East Lilling and which is West Lilling, nor which *Lilinga* of fol. 306a (306 DG) is which. As the two vills are immediately adjacent to each other, and the other places mentioned in the clauses in which they occur are distributed around them, there is no certain way of distinguishing between them. If the *Lilinga* of 5N61, where the Count of Mortain holds 2 bovates, is arbitrarily identified with West Lilling and the *Lilinga* also of 5N61, where he holds 1 carucate 4 bovates, is arbitrarily identified with East Lilling, then the *Lilinge* of SN,B9, where the Count holds 2 bovates, would be West Lilling, and the *Lilinge* of SN,B14-15, where he holds 1 carucate 2 bovates, would be East Lilling, although with a difference of 2 bovates between the recorded holdings. The equation with the holdings of the King is more difficult to establish. According to the Summary, the King would then have 3 carucates in West Lilling (SN,B9) and 1 carucate 6 bovates in East Lilling. In fo. 300c, in the record of the King's lands, the main text ascribes 14 bovates (i.e. 1 caruate 6 bovates) in 1N100 to *Lilinge*, which would therefore equate with East Lilling, and 4 carucates in 1N91 to *Lilinge*, which by elimination should be West Lilling, but with a difference of 1 carucate between the amounts given in the main text and in the Summary. The issue is also complicated by a further 14 bovates ascribed to Ulfr, one of the King's Thanes, in 29N11. Usually the lands held by his thanes in the main text are ascribed to the King himself in the Summary, but the lands of his thanes are not usually duplicated in the main text entries of the King's lands. So either there is a further 14 bovates unaccounted for, or else the entry of 29N11 is an erroneous duplication of the entry in 1N100, which would then make the entry in 29N11 relate to East Lilling. On the depopulation of East Lilling village see LVY 302-3.
1N92	VALUE 2S. Written in the margin to the left of the entry (DF VI).
1N93-4	NOW 8S. Written in the space at the end of the first line of the entry for Claxton. In this position it could be the completion of the entry for Harton, which ends 'T.R.E. 40s', or it could be the completion of the entry for Claxton itself which ends similarly 'T.R.E. 10s'. There is no hard and fast rule about where such completions should go, and examples are found in this same column of their being on the line above the entry being completed and on the line below. The problem here is that both entries are incomplete, but the 8s presumably refers to only one of them. There seems stronger reason to regard it as the

completion of Harton, since Claxton is the last entry in the column and there would have been room for the scribe to run on below had he wished to complete this entry. A degree of ambiguity remains, however, and therefore 8s has been added for Claxton in brackets as a possible reading.

1N96   DICHE. Lost in Haxby (DG 520). The name is derived from OE *dic*, i.e. 'at the ditch'.

1N97   CALDENESCHE. Lost in Huby (DG 517). The name is apparently a hybrid place-name from OE *cald* and ON *eski*, i.e. 'at the cold ash-wood'.

1N98   AEGELFRIDE. The regularised West Saxon form for DB *Aifride* would be the OE female personal-name *Egelfride* (PNDB 245), which has here been regularised to the OE Northumbrian form *Aegelfride*.

1N100   (EAST) LILLING. See 1N91 note.

1N102   FOR 2 PLOUGHS. Written at the end of the preceding line.

1N104   ALUERLE. PNDB 154 suggests that this strange personal-name form may represent *Aluer* (for ON *Alfarr* or OE *Aelfhere*; see 1N34 note above), with -*le* added by mistake. The nature of the mistake is not obvious: formally it could be a scribal error for *Alueric* or *Aluerie* for OE *Aelfric* (PNDB 143) or OG *Alberic* (masculine), *Alberia* (feminine) (Forssner 18); or a miscopied by-name compound such as *Alfer Erle*, containing a byname OE *eorl*, ON *jarl* 'earl' (OEB 250; JMcND).

        LAND FOR 1½ PLOUGHS. Written at the right-hand end of the space left free above this entry.

1N106   BRAFFERTON. This entry is repeated in the list of Gospatric's lands (28W34), except that the value there is given as 2½s.

1N107- [GERLESTRE (BIRDFORTH) WAPENTAKE]. Although recorded under the general
112   heading of Langbargh, these places are all located in *Gerlestre* Wapentake in the Summary, which later came to be known as Birdforth Wapentake. In the post-Conquest reorganisation the wapentake court switched to meeting at the village of Birdforth, whereas the court of the North Riding continued to meet at the old wapentake meeting centre of *Yarlestre*, possibly named from OE *eorles-treow* 'earl's tree'. This would have been a tree at which the wapentake met, although its location is now lost (PNNR 179).

1N107   OULSTON. This entry is repeated in the list of Gospatric's lands (28W35).

1N108   THORPE (LE WILLOWS). The township descended from the DB vill of *Torp* is now known as Thorpe le Willows; there is no settlement of the name and the grid reference used in the index for the vill centre is that of Thorpe Hall. This vill was probably held by Gospatric from the King, at least when the Summary was compiled (see SN,B20 note).

1N110   NEWSHAM. The depopulated vill centre is located at SE 379 848, just to the east of the road junction (LVY 303).

        2½ CARUCATES. '½' is added above the line.

1N113- [ALLERTON WAPENTAKE]. Although recorded under the general heading of
137   Langbargh, these places are all located in Allerton Wapentake in the Summary. The wapentake takes its name from Northallerton, the county town (PNNR 204).

1N115   HUTTON (BONVILLE). Only the church and hall survive at the depopulated vill centre (LVY 301).

1N116   (LITTLE) SMEATON. See 1Y2 note.

        5 CARUCATES. VCH 203 note 47 suggests that 4 of these carucates were probably in Hornby and only 1 in Little Smeaton proper.

1N118   ANOTHER (LOW) WORSALL. The scribe wrote *alio* 'another' here. He normally wrote *alia*, which is feminine, whereas *alio* is masculine. It makes no difference to the sense.

1N121   YARM. DB *Iarun* (DF V). Farley erroneously *Larun*.

1N122   (CASTLE) LEAVINGTON. The name survives in that of the township. The site of the depopulated vill centre is at NZ 461 103, adjacent to the castle on Castle Hill (LVY 302).

1N123   6 CARUCATES. The number is very difficult to read. The unclarity is possibly the result of a correction on an earlier figure (DF VI).

1N124   (WEST) HARLSEY. See 1Y2 note.

1N126   MORTON (GRANGE). DG 529 Morton (in East Harlsey). The full modern name is Morton Grange.

1N128   ARNCLIFFE (HALL). DG 514 Arncliffe. The full modern name is Arncliffe Hall.

1N129   'BORDELBY' (MOUNT GRACE). DB *Bordlebi* is now known as Mount Grace (DG 516), the last recording of the old name being in the early 16th century (PNNR 214). The new French name *Monte Grace* first appears in the early 15th century (PNNR 214) for a Carthusian priory set up here in 1396 (LVY 295).

1N133	SOWERBY (UNDER COTCLIFFE). See 1Y2 note.
1N134	CROSBY (GRANGE). See 1Y2 note.
1N136	DALE (TOWN). The DB vill was subsequently amalgamated with Hawnby township and the vill centre was depopulated in the Tudor period (LVY 297).
	ASKETILL. The first 3 letters of this word are obliterated by a blot (DF VI), although the top of an *s* can be seen. Farley reads the name as *Aschil*.
	RQ. Farley prints *rq* for *require* 'enquire further'. There is no evidence of this in the Facsimile (DF VII); this may be because it is obscured in the binding.
1E1	EAST RIDING. See 1N22 note on values.
1E2	BELBY (HOUSE). DG 467 Belby. The full modern name is Belby House, this being the only surviving building at the vill centre (LVY 58).
	BASING. DB *Basin* could represent ON *Basing* or *Basinc*, derived from *Basing* (PNDB 192-3; SPN 49-51). *Basing* is used here as being the original form.
1E3	CLEAVING (GRANGE). DG 470 Cleaving. The full modern name is Cleaving Grange. The vill centre appears to have been depopulated at an early date (LVY 59).
	LAND FOR 4 OXEN. It is unusual to describe the arable capacity of the land in terms of plough beasts rather than ploughs. This form appears more often in the King's lands in the East Riding than anywhere else in the county.
1E5	(OLD) SUNDERLANDWICK. On the deserted vill centre of Old Sunderlandwick see LVY 68.
1E6	LAND FOR 4 OXEN. See 1E3 note.
1E7	*TORP*. Lost in Tibthorpe (DG 481).
1E11	YAPHAM. DB *Iapun* (DF VII), Farley erroneously *Lapun*.
	6 BOVATES. '6 bovates' is written clearly as part of the text with there being no question of its being deleted (DF VII). Farley, however, first printed these words in larger type and then deleted them by putting a line through. His reason for doing this is not apparent.
1E11a	BIELBY and STILLINGFLEET. These place-names are written in the margin next to the entry for Yapham. No details accompany them.
1E12,13	*R*. Farley prints *r* for *require* 'enquire further' in the margin between the entries for Bridlington and Auburn.
1E13	AUBURN. The vill centre of Auburn, which was subsequently amalgamated with Carnaby vill, has now been almost entirely lost to the sea by coastal erosion (LVY 57).
1E14	EASTON. See 1Y11 note.
	4 OXEN. See 1E3 note.
1E15	AND KNUTR. This is added above the line.
1E21	4 OXEN. See 1E3 note.
1E22	*LEDEMARE*. Lost in Fordon (DG 475).
	OUTLIER. *B.* for *berewicus* 'outlier' is written above *Ledmare*.
1E23	BURTON (FLEMING). DG 477 reports North Burton or Burton Fleming; the affix 'Fleming', the surname of the family who held Burton at the time, first appears in the 12th century, while the affix 'north' first appears in the late 14th century (PNER 112). It is more normally known as Burton Fleming nowadays.
1E26	ARGAM. The site of the depopulated vill centre of Argam is located at TA 112 710 (LVY 57).
	IT LIES IN BURTON (FLEMING). This means that Argam is an outlier attached to the manor of Burton Fleming.
1E29	4 THANES. The 4 is written as 2 sets of *II*, one above the other.
	3 CARUCATES. Thus DB (DF VII). Farley erroneously '4 carucates'.
1E32	(LOW) CAYTHORPE. DG 469 Caythorpe. The full modern name is Low Caythorpe. The vill was subsequently subsumed into Rudston. The original vill centre lies just to the west of the present village (LVY 59).
1E33	KETILBJORN. DB *Chilbertus*. The name is underlined in the text (DF VII), which is the medieval equivalent of crossing out.
	2 BOVATES. This is written above the line.
1E34	*FORNETORP*. Lost in Thwing (DG 472).
1E35	OCTON. On the depopulated vill centre see LVY 66.
	IT LIES IN THWING. See 1E26 note.
1E37	SUTTON (GRANGE). DG 480 Sutton. The full modern name is Sutton Grange.
1E38	IT LIES IN NORTON. See 1E26 note.
1E40	TOWTHORPE. On the earthworks of the depopulated vill centre see LVY 69. DG 481 reports this as in Fimber township, but Towthorpe is in fact still a township in its own right in Buckrose Wapentake.

	FOR 2 PLOUGHS. This is written at the end of the preceding line.
1E42	BURDALE. On the shrunken vill centre see LVY 58.
	4 OXEN. See 1E3 note.
1E45	AND KNUTR. This is written above the line.
	5 CARUCATES. Originally '3', altered to '5' (DF VII).
	3 PLOUGHS. Originally '2', altered to '3' (DF VII).
1E48	EDDLETHORPE. The vill was subsequently subsumed into Westow, and the site of the

1E42 BURDALE. On the shrunken vill centre see LVY 58.
4 OXEN. See 1E3 note.

1E45 AND KNUTR. This is written above the line.
5 CARUCATES. Originally '3', altered to '5' (DF VII).
3 PLOUGHS. Originally '2', altered to '3' (DF VII).

1E48 EDDLETHORPE. The vill was subsequently subsumed into Westow, and the site of the vill centre is now shrunken (LVY 61). The name also survives in Eddlethorpe Mill (SE 770 664) and Eddlethorpe Grange (SE 782 668).

1E52 4 M. The '4' is written as 2 sets of *II*, one above the other.

1E54 WHARRAM (PERCY). On the site of the depopulated vill centre of Wharram Percy, which has in recent years been the site of extensive archaeological excavations, see LVY 70 and J. G. Hurst *et al, Wharram: a Study of Settlement on the Yorkshire Wolds*, Society for Medieval Archaeology Monograph Series, 8 (1979).

1E56 RAISTHORPE. The vill was subsequently subsumed into Wharram Percy township; the vill centre is now depopulated (LVY 67).

1E58 CROOM (HOUSE). DG 470 Croom. The full modern name is Croom House. The vill centre is now depopulated (LVY 60). Farley gives the reading of the place-name as *Crogun*. There is a gap in the Facsimile where the letter *g* would have been (DF VII).

1E60 COWLAM. The vill centre had been depopulated by the 18th century (LVY 60). The site is located at SE 965 655 (not SE 965 555 as given in LVY 60).

1W1 WEST RIDING. See 1N22 note on land values.
RAWCLIFFE. Listed in DB under the WR, but is now in the NR. In the Summary it is in a separate section, before the WR (SN,Y6).

1W2 SKELTON. Listed in DB under the WR, but later in the NR. In the Summary it is in a separate section, before the WR (SN,Y7).

1W3 WOTHERSOME. By the 19th century the only dwelling left in Wothersome township was Wothersome Grange (SE 399 425); the medieval centre of the vill was probably represented by the earthworks identified by Professor Beresford in Old Hall Pasture (LVY 238; WYAS 573).

1W5 MORTON. See SW,Sk11 note.

1W6 RIDDLESDEN. The vill was subsequently subsumed into the township of Morton (1W5), but as Morton and Riddlesden did not survive as independent hamlet divisions, the boundary between the original DB vills cannot be determined (WYAS 460).

1W7 MARGINAL CROSS. Clear in DF VII, but not always or clearly reproduced by Farley especially on this page. The significance of the marginal marks in this section is not always apparent.

1W8 *MORTUNE*. DG 502 reports lost in East Keswick, presumably on the basis that it comes after Shadwell (1W7) and before Harewood (1W9), although East Keswick is actually to the east of Harewood and does not occur until 1W10 in the text. PNWR iv, 184 locates it in Harewood, although with the proviso that its location is unknown. In view of the number of other DB vills which were subsequently subsumed into Harewood (WYAS 387-8), the PNWR identification seems the more likely. WYAS 232-3 identifies this *Mortune* with the *Mortun* recorded in the Summary (SW,Sk11), which is in fact Morton near Keighley in the western part of Skyrack Wapentake (see SW,Sk11 note), and attempts to locate it on that basis, but this is in fact the only entry for *Mortune*.
MARGINAL CROSS. See 1W7 note. The amounts of land in the text and the Summary differ.

1W9 HAREWOOD. The medieval township of Harewood was formed by the amalgamation of the DB vills of Harewood, Lofthouse, *Newhall* and Stockton. It is not possible to determine the boundaries between these individual DB vills (WYAS 386).
WITH ITS OUTLIER. This is written above the line.

1W11 MARGINAL CROSS. See 1W7 note.
STOCKTON. The vill centre is still represented by a shrunken settlement (WYAS 388).

1W12 *NEWHALL*. The DB vill of *Niuiehalle* was subsequently part of Harewood. The general area of the vill centre is indicated by *Newhall Field* and *Little Newhall Field* centred at SE 323 454 on an estate map of *c*.1698 (WYAS 388), which is the last recording of the name.
JURISDICTION. There is a gap in the text after the word soke where the name of the manor to which the jurisdiction of *Newhall* belonged might have been expected to be.

1W13 WIKE. The township lies partly in the ecclesiastical parish of Harewood and partly in the parish of Bardsey; Gluniairnn's manor probably consisted of the Harewood part of the vill and Ligulfr's of the Bardsey part (WYAS 563).

1W14 LOFTHOUSE. The earthworks of the deserted settlement of the vill centre are in Harewood Park at SE 323 433 (WYAS 387).

1W15 STUB HOUSE. The DB vill was subsequently subsumed into Weardley township. The original vill centre was probably Stone Close (SE 302 435) to the south of Stub House Farm (WYAS 552-3).

1W16 ALWOODLEY. The present settlement is located at SE 311 411, but LVY 237 suggests that the original depopulated vill centre may now be covered by the nearby reservoir.

1W17 THREE THANES. On the three landholders in 1066 (who may well have been Gamall, Gluniairnn and Sandi) and 1086, see WYAS 404-5.

1W18 LAND FOR 2 PLOUGHS. See 1N80 note.

1W19 YEADON. DB *Iadun* (DF VII), Farley erroneously *Ladun*. The township of Yeadon contains two main settlements – Upper Yeadon and Nether Yeadon; the grid reference given for the vill centre in the index is that for Upper Yeadon, which appears to be the primary centre.

1W20 SPROTBROUGH. No value is given for this manor.

1W21 MARGINAL CROSS. See 1W7 note.

1W22 *(WALDER)SHELF*. Probably for OE **Scelf(e)-feld* 'open ground at a shelving terrain' i.e. 'at (a place called) *Shelve*', from OE *scelf* and *feld*; the loss of *l* in the DB spelling is seen in the instance of Shelley, Suffolk, DB *Sceueleia* (fo. 287a,b) (JMcND). DG 511 identifies DB *Sceuelt* as *Waldershelfe* (correct spelling *Waldershelf*). PNWR i, 257 observes, not quite accurately, that this form cannot be reconciled with the other early forms of the name and etymology of *Waldershelf* ('Waldhere's *scelf*', from OE *scelf* and the personal-name *Waldhere*), and suggests, rather against the run of forms, that *Sceuelt* would be appropriate for Sheffield (otherwise *(E)scafeld*, with *-a*), so that this 1 carucate of land would be located in Sheffield. This carucate is, however, described by DB fo. 301 (1W22) as being located in *Sceuelt* and Onesacre, which is adjacent to *Waldershelf*, and in DB fo. 379b (SW,Sf35-6) *Scafeld* (Sheffield) and *Sceuelt* are listed next to each other as separate places. In view of the common element in the names *Sceult* and *Waldershelf*, and given that the former occurs in DB and the latter not until 1190, it is not impossible that the two names refer to one place and that 'Waldhere's *Shelf*' was formerly '*Shelf*-field'; so this identification has been followed in this edition (JMcND). *Waldershelf* itself no longer appears on the modern 6 in. OS map, but on the 1st ed. 6 in. OS map (sheet 281) the township is called Westnall with Waldershelf, while sheet 287 shows one house at Waldershelf at SK 269 962, with Waldershelf Wood to its south, i.e. just to the north-west of Ewden village which did not exist at the time of the 1st ed. OS map.

1W23 MARGINAL CROSS. See 1W7 note. In this case the cross is possibly connected with the fact that this land is recorded identically in Ilbert's land (9W71), except that there it is described as waste.
PENISTONE. Alric's 10 bovates were subsequently granted to Ilbert de Lacy and are also recorded in the main text in the list of his landholdings (9W71).

1W24 MARGINAL CROSS. As 1W23 note (see 9W73).
DARTON. Arnbjorn's 1 carucate was subsequently granted to Ilbert de Lacy and is also recorded in the main text in the list of his landholdings (9W73).

1W25 *R*. This is written in the margin for *require* 'enquire further'. It is possibly connected with the fact that this is a repeat entry of 1Y16, but with important modifications and additions.
A CHURCH. This was probably held by Ilbert de Lacy (EYC viii, 226; WYAS 464).

1W26 MARGINAL CROSS. See 1W7 note. Here the cross is possibly connected with the fact that this is almost a duplicate entry of 1Y15. On the question of the status of the land, see *INLAND* below.
2 CARUCATES. Although ascribed here to Holme, they included land in Austonley, Upperthong and Yateholme (see 1Y15 above: WYAS 403).
INLAND. Compare this with 1Y15 where land in Holme (with land in Austonley, Upperthong and Yateholme) was the subject of doubt about whether it was thaneland or soke of Wakefield. Here the doubt is about whether this land is *inland*. The land in question is probably the same land. For the kinds of interest described see Appendix.

1W27 MARGINAL CROSS. See 1W7 note. The cross might refer to the fact that this place is recorded in the Summary (SW,M12), but not in the text, as being part of the manor of Wakefield.
(OLD) LINDLEY. The vill was subsequently amalgamated with Stainland to form an enlarged township of Stainland, although the original DB boundaries survived as those of hamlet divisions within the new township (WYAS 520).

1W28   MARGINAL CROSS. As 1W27 note (SW,M12).

1W29   MARGINAL CROSS. See 1W7 note.
IN (BISHOP)THORPE. No value is given for this manor.
(BISHOP)THORPE. PNWR iv, 226, following Skaife 27, note 22 identifies DB *Badetorpes* with Middlethorpe, which DG 501 identifies with the *Torp* of DB fos. 321, 327, 379 (11W2). DG 487, on the other hand, identifies DB *Badetorpes* with Bishopthorpe, which has been followed in this edition. The affix *biscop* only appears in the 13th century, following the purchase of the manor of *Thorpe c.*1225 by the Archbishop of York (PNWR iv, 225).

1W31   (LITTLE) OUSEBURN. See 25W21 note.
INLAND. See Appendix.

1W35   (GREAT AND LITTLE) RIBSTON. DG 504 puts all the DB entries (1W35, 13W19, 16W2, 24W9, SW,Bu9) together under Great and Little Ribston, whereas PNWR v, 19, 31, ascribes the *Ripestan* (16W2, SW,Bu9) and *Ripestain* (1W35, 24W9) forms to Great Ribston and the *Ripestain* (1W35, 24W9) and *Ripesten* (13W19) forms to Little Ribston. As the Summary entry (SW,Bu9) makes it obvious that the 1½ carucates of the King (1W35), the 1½ carucates of William of Percy (13W19), the 4 carucates of Ralph Paynel (16W2) and the 2 carucates of Erneis de Burun (24W9) were all located in the same vill, the DG ascription has been followed in this edition.
      The settlement of Great Ribston, which has long been depopulated, was probably situated in Ribston Park (LVY 235).

1W37   ALLERTON (MAULEVERER). The vill centre is now represented only by the church and hall (LVY 233).

1W41   4 OXEN. See 1N7 note; 1E3 note.

1W42   R. This stands for *require* 'enquire further'. It is possibly there because Gospatric, in the list of his lands, 28W19, is shown holding 3 carucates and 2 ploughs here, which is presumably his former share of the land.
POPLETONE. Lost in Fountains Earth township (DG 504). Its precise position is not known, but it was included in the land of Covell Houses in 1540 (PNWR v, 203).
4 CARUCATES. Of the 4 carucates here, 3 were held by Gospatric and 1 by Gamalbarn, Gospatric's 3 carucates being also recorded in the section on his holdings (28W19) and under his name in the Summary (SW,Bu25).
LAND FOR 2 PLOUGHS, 30S. Although this is written at the end of the line for Aldfield, 1W40 two lines above, it belongs to *Popletone*. The entry for *Popletone* was unfinished, but there was no room for additions on either the line immediately above it or the line immediately below it. The entry was therefore completed in the nearest available space. No value is given for Aldfield, but the 30s here is clearly not intended to apply to it as there is a separation mark between the entry for Aldfield and this later addition (DF VIII).

1W45   BEAMSLEY. DB *Bomeslai* (DF VIII). DG 486 erroneously *Bedmeslei*.

1W46   ADDINGHAM. The main text ascribes to the King 1 carucate here and a further 2 carucates under the heading Craven (1W73), and 2 carucates to Gilbert Tison (21W5), but the Summary describes Gilbert Tison's holding, recorded under 'Burghshire', as only 1 carucate (SW,Bu32). It seems likely that the duplication of the Addingham entries is because one pair relates to Addingham as a manor and the other to Addingham as soke of Bolton (WYAS 297).

1W50   SICKLINGHALL. The *n* in *Sidingale* is written above the line.

1W52   D. *d* is written in the left-hand margin (DF VIII). Its meaning is not apparent.
ROSSETT (GREEN). DG 505 Rossett. The full modern name is Rossett Green.

1W53   R. This *r* stands for *require* 'enquire further'. It is not apparent why it is there.
MARGINAL CROSS. Marginal cross (DF VIII). This is not reproduced by Farley. See 1W7 note.
AELFLED. The regularised West Saxon form for DB *Elflet* would be *Alflaed* (PNDB 144), which has here been regularised to the OE Northumbrian form *Aelfled*.
WILLIAM OF PERCY. *Pci.* for *Perci* 'Percy' is written above 'William'.
VOUCH WARRANTY. This is a medieval use of *advocare*.
VALUE. There is a gap where the pre-1066 value could have been expected. A figure which looks like *X* (10) was originally entered but subsequently obliterated (DF VIII). Farley does not indicate this.

1W54   R. For *require* 'enquire further' is in the margin. This may be because Gospatric is recorded as holding 6 carucates here in the list of his own lands (28W22), as he also is in the Summary (SW,H6).

MARGINAL CROSS. Marginal cross with dots between the arms (DF VIII). This is not reproduced by Farley.

KIRBY (HILL). Listed in DB under the WR, but subsequently in the NR.

6 CARUCATES. The 6 carucates here are also recorded as held by Gospatric in the section on his holdings (28W22).

1W55 BRAMPTON (HALL). DG 516 Brampton. The full modern name is Brampton Hall.

1W56 IN CRAVEN. No values are given for any of the King's manors here.

CRAVEN. The DB wapentake of Craven approximated to the later wapentake of Staincliffe east of the River Ribble, together with a small part of Lancashire. The area is now generally known as the Dales. The name, which appears to be Celtic and related to Welsh *craf* 'garlic', survived as a suffix in many Dales place-names and as the name of an archdeaconry.

1W59 (HIGH AND LOW) BRADLEY. DG 488 reports High and Low Bradley, which has been followed in this edition. The township itself is known as Bradleys Both.

1W62 EASTBURN. See 21W15 note.

2 CARUCATES OF LAND. This is written above the line.

1W63 WILLIAM. The regularised form for DB *Wills* (i.e. *Willelmus*) should be OG *Willelm* (PNDB 415), but the modern form William has been used throughout this edition.

1W64 KEIGHLEY. The later medieval township of Keighley was formed by the amalgamation of the DB vills of Keighley, Laycock, Newsholme, Oakworth and Utley. It is not possible to determine the original boundaries between the various vills (WYAS 416).

6 CARUCATES TAXABLE. This is written at the end of the previous line.

1W65 3 CARUCATES AND ... There is a gap in the text at this point. Something, either half a carucate or a number of bovates, seems to have been written here since a contraction mark is still discernible (DF VIII), but the actual word has been obliterated or has faded beyond recognition.

1W66 MARGINAL CROSS. See 1W7 note.

OAKWORTH. There is now no main settlement called Oakworth. Oakworth Hall is located at SE 033 388, but the original medieval settlement was probably situated at Oakworth Farm, whose grid reference has been given as that of the vill centre in the index (WYAS 419, note 4).

1W67 NEWSHOLME. Now in the modern township of Oakworth. Oakworth was originally part of the medieval vill of Keighley (see 1W64 note), so Newsholme has been indexed in this edition as being in Keighley township.

1W70 MARGINAL CROSS. See 1W7 note.

1W70-1L8 IN MELLING [L]. As north-western England had not yet been divided into counties at the time of DB, some vills subsequently in northern Lancashire, Westmorland and Cumberland were included in the survey of Yorkshire. This section has already been published in this series in DB Cheshire, some details of which are revised in this volume (see 1L1 note, 1L2 note, 1L3 note, 1L4 note, 1L5 note, 1L6 note, 1L7 note, 1L8 note, 23N22 note, 30W38 note, 30W39 note, 30W40 note), in addition to some revisions in DB Leicestershire.

1W71 MARGINAL CROSS. See 1W7 note.

1W72 MARGINAL CROSS. See 1W7 note.

(NETHER AND OVER) BURROW. DB Cheshire distinguishes between the *Borch* of this entry, which it identifies with Nether Burrow (Y1), and the *Borch* of 1L3, which it identifies with Over Burrow (Y4), whereas VCH Lancs 288 gives this entry as (Over ?) Burrow. As it does not seem possible to distinguish between Nether Burrow (SD 613 752) and Over Burrow (SD 616 759) as the vill centre, both have been used in this edition, following DG 210, although Over Burrow contains the site of the Roman fort alluded to in the OE *burh* 'fortification' element in the name (JMcND).

1W73 SKIBEDEN. On the shrunken vill centre see LVY 238.

(LOW) SNAYGILL. DG 507 reports Snaygill. The full modern name is Low Snaygill.

THORLBY. DB *Toredderebi* (DF VIII). DG 509 erroneously *Toreilderebi*.

HOLME (HOUSE). DG 497 Holme (near Gargrave). The full modern name is Holme House (now in Stirton township).

(LITTLE) STAINTON. DG 507 Stainton. The full modern name is Little Stainton. It is now in Bank Newton township.

ADDINGHAM. DB *Odingehem* (DF pl VIII). DG 484 erroneously *Odingehen*. See also 1W46 note. This is written at the end of the 4th line, to which it does not belong. It is either a continuation of line 3 or of line 5. It is attributed here to line 3 since this would mean that all the outliers had been completed without running on to another line. Since the list of sokelands continues into line 6 there seems no good reason why Addingham should not have been included there if it had itself been sokeland.

1L1   AMOUNDERNESS. This was originally the district approximately between the Ribble and the Cocker, with the Yorkshire fells forming the eastern boundary. The name means 'the *nes* of Agmundr'; the *nes* 'headland, promontory' referring either to Rossall Point or to the whole of Amounderness (PNL 139).

PRESTON. The amounts of land in the various places are entered above the relevant place-names.

SALWICK (HALL). DG 215 and DB Cheshire report Salwick. The full modern name is Salwick Hall at SD 467 323 (not SD 51 31 as given for DB Cheshire Y2).

TREALES. The vill centre for Treales is located at SD 437 328 (not SD 36 34 as given for DB Cheshire Y2).

(GREAT AND LITTLE) PLUMPTON. DG 211 and DB Cheshire Y2 report Field Plumpton (at SD 38 33) and VCH Lancs 288 as Fieldplumpton. The township was formerly known as Fieldplumpton (to distinguish it from Woodplumpton:PNL 151), and has now been amalgamated with Westby to form the township of Westby with Plumptons. It is impossible to distinguish between Great Plumpton (SD 384 332) and Little Plumpton (SD 379 327) as the vill centre, so both have been used in this edition.

PREESE (HALL). DG 214 and DB Cheshire Y2 report Preese. The full modern name is Preese Hall.

WARTON. Warton near Preston at SD 410 284 (not SD 49 72 as given for DB Cheshire Y2).

ROSSALL. DG 215 and DB Cheshire Y2 report DB *Rushale* as Rossall, the latter with an erroneous grid reference SD 37 45 in the index. The name survives as that of a public school on the site of Rossall Hall (SD 312 449), and in Rossall Point, the north-west tip of Amounderness.

BURN (HALL). DG 210 and DB Cheshire Burn. The full modern name of the vill centre is Burn Hall (SD 333 454), an ancient house recently demolished by an adjacent factory.

SOWERBY (HALL). DG 215 and DB Cheshire Y2 Sowerby near Preston. The full modern name of the vill centre is Sowerby Hall.

ASCHEBI. Lost in Myerscough (SD 49 39) (DG 209; PNL 148).

(ST) MICHAEL'S (ON WYRE). DG 215 erroneously as St Michael on Wyre.

WHITTINGHAM (HALL). DG 217 and DB Cheshire Y2 as Whittingham. the full modern name of the vill centre is Whittingham Hall; the township name is Whittingham.

BARTON, 4 CARUCATES. Thus DB (DF VIII). Farley erroneously '3 carucates'.

HAIGHTON (HALL). DG 212 and DB Cheshire Y2 Haighton, which is the name of the township; the full modern name of the vill centre is Haighton Hall at SD 575 352. The name also survives in Haighton Green (SD 566 346) and Haighton House (SD 567 349).

THRELFALL'S (FARM). DG 216 erroneously Threfall, DB Cheshire Y2 correctly as Threlfall. The full modern name is Threlfall's Farm, whose grid reference is used in the index for the vill centre, although White Chapel (SD 559 412) may alternatively have been the vill centre.

AIGHTON. The name of the DB vill of *Actun* survives in that of the township of Aighton, Bailey and Chaigley; there is no settlement of the name on the modern 6 in. OS map, nor on the 1st ed. 6 in. OS map, sheets 46 (the area shown on DG map 28) or 54 (the area of SD 67 39 given in the index to DB Cheshire).

FISHWICK. The grid reference for the vill centre of Fishwick is SD 562 293 (not SD 56 24 as indexed in DB Cheshire Y2).

DILWORTH (HOUSE). DG 211 and DB Cheshire Y2 Dilworth. The full modern name is Dilworth House, whose grid reference of SD 611 372 has been used for the vill centre in the index, although it may not have been the medieval vill centre, being on the extreme edge of the township.

'SWAINSEAT'. DG 216 and DB Cheshire Y2 Swainseat, but this name does not occur on the modern 6 in. OS map, nor on the 1st ed. 6 in. OS map (sheet 35), so the name has been treated here as lost. The vill centre was probably in the area of Swainshead Hall (SD 539 528), which PNL 172 links with *Suenesat*.

(GREAT AND LITTLE) CRIMBLES. DG 210 and DB Cheshire Y2 Crimbles, but there are now two settlements of the name – Little Crimbles at SD 462 507 and Great Crimbles at SD 456 503 (not SD 45 57 as indexed in DB Cheshire).

(UPPER) RAWCLIFFE. DG 216 and DB Cheshire Y2 give DB *Rodeclif* as Upper Rawcliffe, which is the name of the township. The vill centre of Upper Rawcliffe is obliged by geography to have been in the area SD 43 41 to SD 45 41, and the grid reference used in the index is that of the 1-km square containing White Hall (SD 432 412).

RAWCLIFFE (HALL). DG 213 reports DB *alia Rodeclif* as Middle Rawcliffe; its omission from DB Cheshire Y2 is rectified in DB Leicestershire. The name does not occur on the modern 6 in. OS map; the area concerned related to the demesnes of Rawcliffe Hall (SD 416 417) in Out Rawcliffe township.

(OUT) RAWCLIFFE. The omission of this name from DB Cheshire Y2 is rectified in DB Leicestershire.

1L2 IN HALTON. See 1L1 note on land quantities.

(UPPER AND LOWER) THURNHAM. DG 216 and DB Cheshire Y3 report Thurnham. In Thurnham township there are two settlements of the name – Upper Thurnham (SD 459 544) and Lower Thurnham (SD 459 549), and a manor-house, Thurnham Hall (SD 463 545).

HILLAM. DG 212 incorrectly reports Hillham (so also DB Cheshire map key).

'KIRK LANCASTER'. DG 213 and DB Cheshire Y3 Kirk Lancaster (see PNL 174). The name, which presumably denoted the estate of the predecessor of St Mary's Priory (beside the castle at SD 474 619), is recorded only in DB, so is here treated as lost.

'HUTTON'. DG 212 and DB Cheshire Y3 Hutton, but PNL 173 reports the name as already lost by 1922, and it has been so treated in this edition.

'NEWTON'. DG 214 reports Newton in Lancaster and DB Cheshire index places the centre at SD 50 64; as the name does not appear on the modern 6 in. OS map nor on the 1st ed. 6 in. OS map (sheet 30) it has been treated here as lost.

HEATON. The grid reference for Heaton (see DG map 28) is SD 443 602 (not SD 40 11 as given in DB Cheshire Y3).

HEYSHAM. DG 212 and DB Cheshire Y3 Heysham. The settlement of Heysham is divided into Lower Heysham (SD 411 616) and High Heysham (SD 413 605), but it appears to constitute all one settlement, with the focus at Heysham Old Hall (SD 415 610).

OXCLIFFE (HALL). DG 214 and DB Cheshire Y3 Oxcliffe. The full modern name of the vill centre is Oxcliffe Hall (SD 450 619).

POULTON (HALL). DG 214 and DB Cheshire Y3 Poulton le Sands. This name does not occur on the modern 6 in. OS map, the township of *Poulton le Sands* having been developed as a seaside resort and renamed Morecambe in the 19th century (JMcND; PNL 176). The grid reference for the vill centre given in the index is that for Poulton Hall.

(NETHER AND OVER) KELLET. DB Cheshire Y3 Kellet, but there are two centres in the township – Nether and Over Kellet – and it is not possible to distinguish which might have been the original centre, so DG 212 has been followed in this edition.

'STAPLETON TERNE'. DG 215 and DB Cheshire Y3 Stapleton Terne. The vill was subsequently subsumed into the township of Slyne with Hest (PNL 186) and the name does not appear on the modern 2½ in. or 6 in. OS maps, so it is here treated as lost.

'NEWSHAM'. DG 214 reports DB *Neuhuse* as Newsham in Skerton, while PNL 177 reports it as lost in Skerton; as the name does not appear on the modern 2½ in. OS map, nor on the 1st ed. 6 in. OS map (sheet 30), it has been treated as lost in this edition. DB Cheshire places this Newsham at SD 51 36 in the index, but at *c*.SD 48 64 (i.e. adjacent to Skerton) on the map of places in Halton Hundred (no. 7). The SD 51 36 grid reference is obviously a duplication of that for Newsham near Preston, the preceding entry in the index.

1L3 IN WHITTINGTON. See 1L1 note on land quantities.

CANTSFIELD, 4 CARUCATES. Thus DB (DF VIII). Farley erroneously '3 carucates'.

(NETHER AND OVER) BURROW. DG 210 identifies DB *Borch* in this entry as Broughton in Furness, whereas DB Cheshire Y4 reports it as Over Burrow and VCH Lancs 289 has (Nether ?) Burrow. As all the places in this entry relate to the area around Whittington, the DB Cheshire location is preferable. See also 1W72 note.

(LOWER) LECK. DG 213 and DB Cheshire Y4 Leck; the township contains Over Leck (SD 651 770), Leck Hall (SD 651 768) and Lower Leck (SD 643 766), the last of these being taken as the vill centre.

CASTERTON. DG 444 erroneously as Castleton.

THIRNBY (WOOD). DG 216 and DB Cheshire Y4 Thirnby. It is not possible to be certain of the location of the original vill centre as the name only survives now as Thirnby Wood (SD 610 777), whose grid reference has therefore been used in the index to this volume.

THIRNBY (WOOD), 2 CARUCATES. Thus DB (DF VIII). Farley erroneously '6 carucates'.

1L4 *HELDETUNE*. A lost vill not recorded subsequent to 1086 (PNWR vi, 237). It is associated in DB with Clapham and Austwick, and it is impossible to decide whether

PNWR vi, 237, which places it in Clapham, or DG 497, which places it in Austwick, is correct.

MIDDLETON (HALL). DG 445 Middleton in Lonsdale, whereas DB Cheshire Y5 reports it at SD 62 86, the rather scattered hamlet of Middleton. In this edition Middleton Hall (SD 626 874) in Middleton with Lonsdale township has been taken as the vill centre.

MANSERGH. DG 445 and DB Cheshire Y5 Mansergh. Mansergh Hall (SD 607 817) is situated in the southern extremity of the township of Mansergh, with the church located on its own at SD 602 826. The main settlement appears to be at Old Town (SD 595 829), whose grid reference is used for the vill centre in the index.

PRESTON (PATRICK). DG 445 reports the DB *Prestun* of this entry as Preston Patrick and Richard, whereas VCH Lancs 369 and DB Cheshire distinguish between Preston Patrick in Y5 (i.e. this entry; given as plain Preston in the DB Cheshire translation but as Preston Patrick in the index and the map and map keys) and Preston Richard in Y13 (30W40 of this edition). As the Preston of this entry is linked with Austwick whereas that in 30W40 is linked with Beetham, the VCH Lancs and DB Cheshire identification has been followed in this edition. Old Hall (SD 533 844) in Preston Richard has been used as the vill centre in the index and Preston Patrick Hall (SD 544 837) as the vill centre of Preston Patrick vill.

HOLME. DG 444 reports incorrectly as Holm.

BURTON. DG 444 and PNW i, 57, report Burton in Westmorland, whereas DB Cheshire Y5 gives it as Burton in Yorkshire (i.e. Burton in Lonsdale). As this entry lists *Bortun* as being in Austwick and between Holme (Westmorland) and Priest Hutton (Lancashire), the geographical situation of Burton (Westmorland) makes the DG identification preferable.

1L5 (HIGH) BENTHAM. DG 486 and DB Cheshire Y6 Bentham. The full modern name of the vill centre is High Bentham (SD 667 692).

1L6 IN MILLOM. See 1L1 note on land quantities.

HOUGUN (MILLOM). It seems likely that *Hougun* ('at the mounds' from ON *haugr*) is the earlier name for Millom, which is not recorded until *c.* 1180 (EPNS xxi, 414).

'KILLERWICK'. DG 212 and DB Cheshire Y7 report DB *Chilvestreuic* as Killerwick at SD 21 75 (the approximate vill centre for Elliscales). The name is last recorded in the early 16th century and is now lost (PNL 205). Subsequent to 1086 it had become part of Elliscales, which is not recorded until 1211-22 (PNL 206), so Elliscales may have replaced 'Killerwick' as the name of the vill. The modern map marks Elliscales Farm in Dalton in Furness township at SD 225 746, which has been taken as the grid reference for the vill centre; on the 1st ed. 6 in. OS map (sheet 16), this is given simply as Elliscales.

'KILLERWICK', 3 CARUCATES. It looks as if 3 carucates was intended here. In the Facsimile (DF VIII), only 2 strokes are discernible, but these are placed so as to give the impression that there ought to be another stroke between them. Farley reads 3 carucates.

SOWERBY (HALL). DB *Sourebi* is reported as Sowerby in Dalton in Furness by DG 215 and DB Cheshire Y7, the latter incorrectly at SD 18 71. The modern name of the vill centre is Sowerby Hall at SD 198 724, with Sowerby Wood at SD 196 733.

HIETUN (HAWCOAT). DG 212 and DB Cheshire Y7 report DB *Hietun* as Heaton in Dalton in Furness at SD 22.75. PNL 203 cites no *Hietun* spellings after DB and suggests that this was an earlier name for Hawcoat.

'WART'. DG 216 and DB Cheshire Y7 report Wart at SD 24 75 and VCH Lancs 289 Wart in Dalton. The name is lost and its location is unknown (PNL 241).

(HIGH) NEWTON. DG 214 and DB Cheshire Y7 Newton in Cartmel. The full modern name of the vill centre is High Newton.

WALTON (HALL). DG 216 and DB Cheshire Y7 Walton. The full modern name of the vill centre is Walton Hall.

SUNTUN. Lost in Barrow in Furness (DG 216).

SUNTUN, 5 CARUCATES. The figure is unclear (DF VIII), but it looks more like *v* (5) than the *ii* (2) which Farley reads.

'FORDBOTTLE'. DG 211 and PN Cheshire Y7 Fordboole, but the name is now lost. PNL 202 prefers the form 'Fordbottle', which is closer to the original name, and this form has therefore been used in this edition.

HART (CARRS). DG 212 and DB Cheshire Y7 report Hart, but the grid reference of SD 26 67 given by the latter should be SD 25 69. PNL 208 reports the name as Hart Carrs near Leece, and this appears as an area name centred at SD 255 694 on the 1st ed. 6 in.OS map (sheet 22), immediately to the south of Hart Carrs Beck. By the time of the modern 6 in. map, only the stream name survived on the map.

ANOTHER LEECE. The DB vill of *alia Lies* appears subsequently to have been amalgamated with Leece to form one township. As it is impossible to be certain which of the two vill centres is represented by the modern Leece, the same grid reference has been used for both in the index.

'CRIVELTON'. DG 211 and DB Cheshire Y7 report Crivelton, which the latter places at SD 20 71 and DG map 28 at about SD 22 71. No such name appears on the modern 2½ in. or 6 in. OS maps, and PNL 202 reports this as a lost name, location unknown. It was subseqently merged with Newton (SD 229 716), whose name displaced that of 'Crivelton' for the township (PNL 202). If, as PNL proposes, the name means '*tun* of the cliff-dwellers', the site might be sought about 1 km east of Furness Abbey and immediately under Newton (JMcND).

ORGRAVE. DB *Ouregrave* is reported as Orgrave by DG 215 (map 28 locates it at approximately SD 23 75) and DB Cheshire Y7 (indexed at SD 24 76). PNL 207 reported that the name was preserved in Orgrave Mill Cottages on Poaka Beck near Tytup Hill (SD 236 759), and the 1st ed. 6 in. OS map (sheet 16) shows Orgrave Mill Iron Works at SD 2337 7595. The name now only survives in that of Orgrave Villa at SD 2342 7598.

MARTIN. DB Cheshire Y7 note states that the name of this place was traditionally spelt Martin, although the Ordnance Survey spells it Marton. The old spelling has been followed in this edition.

GERLEUUORDE (KIRKBY IRELETH). The DB form *Gerleuuorde* is not recorded after 1086, but it has been suggested that it is to be identified with Kirkby Ireleth (PNL 220). There is today no settlement of the name, only the township being so called. Kirkby Hall is situated at SD 235 835 and the village of Ireleth at SD 223 774, but PNL 220 suggests that the original vill centre was at the church at Beckside (SD 233 822).

BROUGHTON (IN FURNESS). DG 210 Nether and Over Burrow. Since all the places in this entry relate to the area around Millom, the identification as Broughton in Furness in DB Cheshire Y7 has been preferred in this edition.

WHICHAM, 2 CARUCATES. Thus DB (DF VIII). Farley erroneously '4 carucates'.

HOUGENAI (MILLOM CASTLE). EPNS xxi, 414-5 explains that Millom was formerly *Hougun* (see 1L6 note) and that *Hougenai* is that place-name with affixed OE *eg* 'island, dry ground in a marsh, water-meadow, marshland'. The 'marshland of *Hougun*' might well be Millom Marshes (SD 18 82) in the township of Millom Without, adjacent to Millom Castle.

1L7   STRICKLAND (ROGER). DG 445 and DB Cheshire Strickland. There is now no settlement of this name: DB Cheshire index places the vill centre at SD 50 97, while DG map 65 places it at about SD 499 978, which is the location of Godmond Hall. The township is known as Strickland Roger, and it is this form which has been adopted in this edition.

KIRKBY (KENDAL). DG 444 and DB Cheshire Y7 report DB *Cherchebi* as Kirkby Kendal, although the latter indexes it under Kendal. The affix Kendal was added to distinguish *Cherchebi* from Kirkby Lonsdale and Kirkby Stephen, and by the 18th century had displaced the original form, so that only the name Kendal now survives (EPNS xlii, 115).

HELSINGTON. DG 444 and DB Cheshire Y8 Helsington, the name of the township, which has been followed in this edition. Although the name also survives in Helsington Barrows and Helsington Laithes (SD 506 907), it cannot be shown that either was the vill centre.

'BOTHELFORD'. A lost vill which subsequently became part of the township either of Helsington or of Natland; the ford of the name was probably across the River Kent on the boundary between the two later townships (EPNS xlii, 113), i.e. *c.*SD 51 89.

DALTON. The township of Dalton was originally in Lancashire, not in Westmorland, although in the ecclesiastical parish of Burton (Westmorland) (EPNS xlii, 57).

PATTON (HALL). DG 445 and DB Cheshire Y8 Patton. The full modern form of the name of the vill centre is Patton Hall.

1L8   *CHERCHEBI* (CARTMEL). DG 210 reports DB *Cherchebi* as Cartmel, while DB Cheshire reports it as 'Kirkby' (Cartmel). *Cherchebi* would seem to be the earlier form of the name *Churchtown*, an alternative for Cartmel (PNL 196).

BOLTON (FARM). DG 210 Bolton in Urswick; DB Cheshire Y9 simply Bolton, but in the index erroneously as Bolton le Moors with grid reference SD 26 73. Bolton le Moors is at SD 71 09, and cannot be the Bolton in question, as all the other places in this entry are located in Cartmel. There is no township or settlement called Bolton (PNL 210); the name is preserved in Bolton Farm, adjacent to the site of Bolton chapel, the probable original vill centre, at SD 259 729.

2A1-4	LAND OF THE ARCHBISHOP OF YORK. 4 entries are found under this heading on this folio (302b). The heading is then repeated on the next folio (302c).
2A1	PATRINGTON WITH ITS 4 OUTLIERS. The distribution of the block of land recorded here was 15 carucates 2 bovates in Patrington, 7½ carucates in Winestead (SE,Th10), 7 carucates 2 bovates and 2 parts of 1 bovate in Halsham, 3 carucates in *Welwick Thorpe* (Thorpe Hill) (SE,Th11), and 2 carucates 6 bovates in 'Tharlesthorpe' (SE,Th12).

(WELWICK) THORPE (THORPE HALL). DB *Torp*, subsequently *Welwick Thorpe* (DG 482), is now only represented by the name Thorpe Hill (PNER 23). The name is written above the line.

'THARLESTHORPE'. The DB vill of *Toruelestorp* subsequently became part of Patrington township; in the periods 1286-1310 and 1353-6 the settlement of *Tharlesthorpe* suffered inundations of the Humber and, despite the construction of floodgates in 1356, again in 1393, as a result of which the grange was abandoned. It was completely covered by the Humber a few years later, although the name survived as that of the manor for some time thereafter (PNER 24, note 1; 25, note 1).

2A2	4 OUTLIERS. These were North Skirlaugh (9 bovates), Marfleet (1 bovate), Sproatley (1 bovate) and Danthorpe (1 carucate) (SE,Th13).

THERE ARE 10 CARUCATES. *sunt* 'there are' is written above the line.

2A3	VALUE BEFORE 1066 ... Space was left for the pre-1066 value, but it was never filled in.
2B1	LAND OF THE ARCHBISHOP OF YORK. The heading is repeated here (see 2A1-4 note).

SHERBURN (IN ELMET) WITH ITS OUTLIERS. An estate based on Sherburn in Elmet was granted in 963 by King Edgar to Aslakr (EYC i, no. 6), but at some date later in the 10th century passed into the hands of the Archbishop of York (for a full discussion see S. Keynes, 'The surveys of the archiepiscopal estates', in *The York Gospels*, Roxburghe Club facsimile (forthcoming)). The survey of the estate at the end of the York Gospels, probably compiled in the early 11th century by Archbishop Wulfstan, records the estate as comprising land in Cawood, Wistow, Over Selby, Flaxley, Barlow, Brayton, Burn, Burton, Gateforth, the two Thorpes, the two Hirsts, Birkin, Sutton, Byram, Brotherton, Fairburn, Ledsham, Newthorpe, Micklefield, Hillam, Fryston, Lumby, Steeton, Milford, Fenton, Barkston, Lotherton, *Hehferthehegthe* and Huddleston (EYC i, no. 7). VCH 210, note 4 suggests that the outliers in this entry were Barkston (4 carucates 2 bovates), Burn (4 carucates), Burton Salmon (4 carucates), Byron (4 carucates), Cawood (1 carucate), Church Fenton (2 carucates 5 bovates), Flaxley (2 bovates), Monk Fryston (4 carucates), Gateforth (4 carucates), Grimston (1 carucate 5 bovates), Hillam (3 carucates), Huddleston (8 carucates), Lennerton (7 carucates), Lotherton (8 carucates), Lumby (4 carucates), Micklefield (6 carucates), South Milford (3 carucates), Pool (4 carucates), Little Selby (3 carucates), Steeton Hall (3 carucates), Sutton (7 carucates) and Thorpe Willoughby (2 carucates 2 bovates), leaving 8 carucates in Sherburn itself; it is not stated on which document this is based.

THE ABBOT OF SELBY HAS 7 CARUCATES. In Monk Fryston and Little Selby (VCH 210, note 5).

OF THAT SAME LAND. *de ipsa terra* literally means 'from the land itself' or 'from the very land', but the meaning is best translated as given.

2B2	15 CARUCATES. VCH 210, note 6 states that this was the district known as Bishop Fields on the west side of the city adjacent to the River Ouse and lying in Ainsty Wapentake, possibly including Dringhouses, although no reference is given for this.
2B3	WAULDBY. On the shrunken vill centre see LVY 69.

ARCHBISHOP. *Arch.* 'Archbishop' written above the names of Aldred and Thomas (the 1066 and 1086 archbishops) throughout this section.

2B4	1 BOVATE. Written above the line.
2B9	TOWTHORPE. The earthworks of the depopulated vill centre of Towthorpe in Londesborough township are extremely well preserved (LVY 69).

17 CARUCATES. The precise distribution of these lands is shown in the Summary (SE,Wei4-6).

2B11	THERE ARE 1½ CARUCATES. Literally *est* 'there is'. The scribes normally used the singular for anything below 2, rather than our usage which is to pluralise anything above 1.
2B12	ST. PETER'S OF YORK. *Eboraci* 'of York' written above the line.
2B13	BARMBY (MOOR). See 1Y10 note.
2B15	(LOW) CAYTHORPE. See 1E32 note.
2B17	COTTAM. On the depopulated vill centre see LVY 59.

2B18	OUTLIERS, JURISDICTION. The amounts of land belonging to each place, both outliers and jurisdiction, are entered above the relevant place-names.
	WITH THESE OUTLIERS. *cum berwicis bis*, a scribal error for *cum berewicis his* 'with these outliers' (DF XI). Farley correctly reproduces this error.
	(LOW) MOWTHORPE. DG 476 Mowthorpe. The full name is Low Mowthorpe; the earthworks of the depopulated vill centre are still visible (LVY 65).
	(NORTH) GRIMSTON. DB *Grimstone* (DF XI); DG 477 erroneously *Grimestone*.
	3½ C. *d.* 'half' is usually abbreviated *dim.* for *dimidium* 'half'.
	SUTTON (GRANGE). See 1E37-8 note.
	BIRDSALL. The present settlement of Birdsall is located at SE 818 653, but this appears to represent a move out of the park, and the earthworks of the original vill centre are located at SE 815 649 (see LVY 58).
	CROOM (HOUSE). See 1E58 note.
	THIRKLEBY (MANOR). DG 481 Thirkleby. The full modern name is Thirkleby Manor. The vill centre is now depopulated, but is probably represented by the Chapel Garth at SE 920 687 (LVY 68). See also SE,Th5 note.
	ULCHILTORP. A lost vill subsequently part of West Lutton township (DG 482).
	COWLAM. See 1E60 note.
2B19	MEADOW, 8 ACRES. *Tbi sunt*, a scribal error for *Ibi sunt* 'here there are' (DF XI). Farley correctly reproduces this error.
2N7-14	BETWEEN THEM ALL. Assuming the addition to be correct, this means Old Malton, Wombleton, Pockley, Ampleforth, Flaxton, Murton Farm, Baxby and Carlton Husthwaite.
2N12	MURTON (FARM). See 1Y1 note.
2N13-14	BAXBY. The depopulated vill centre is adjacent to Husthwaite village (LVY 295).
2N15	STONEGRAVE. This entry continued onto a second line (DF XI), which was subsequently erased. Farley indicates this only by a space between the entries.
2N16	BELTHORPE. On the shrunken vill centre, now in Bishop Wilton township, see LVY 58.
2N18	WARTHILL. Although this entry has the equivalent of underlining (DF XI), Farley reproduces it in lower case. Normally he indicates underlining by using upper case. The place-names which are the main subject of the entry are normally written in capitals in the text (although there are exceptions to this).
2N19	CARLTON (FARM). DG 518 Carlton (in Stockton on the Forest). The full modern name is Carlton Farm. The shrunken vill centre now consists of just one farm (LVY 296).
	BETWEEN THEM ALL. Assuming the addition to be correct this means Belthorpe, Helmsley, Warthill and Carlton.
	ST. PETER'S OF YORK. *Eborac.* for *Eboraci* 'of York' written above the line.
	VALUE. The figures are all clear in the Facsimile (DF XI). However, there is a stated reduction of 3 ploughs between 1066 and 1086, and the land is said to be waste, yet the value given has apparently increased. It is difficult not to suspect a scribal error here.
2N24	50S; NOW 40. Presumably 40s. The scribe normally wrote £, s. or d. after the figures. In this case he omitted to do so (DF XI).
2N25	YOULTON. DB *Loletune* (DF XI). DG 539 incorrectly *Ioletune*. The DB scribe presumably miscopied an *L* for the correct *I*, which is found in SN,B23.
	WIDE OPEN (FARM). DG 539 Wide Open. The full modern name is Wide Open Farm in Skelton township.
	2 BOVATES. Written above the line.
2N29	FROM ST. PETER'S. Written at the end of the following line.
2N30	'CORBURN'. DG map 63 places the vill centre of DB *Coteborne* at about SE 570 596, which is the location of Hall Moor Farm, and this grid reference has therefore been used in this edition. The only apparent survival of the DB name is Corban Lane at SE 578 590.
2W1	WARMFIELD. The Summary states that the 9 carucates included land in an outlier (SW,Ag1) which VCH 212, note 16 identifies, although without reference, as Sharlston.
2W2	NOW 18S. 8D. *modo* 'now' written above the line.
2W4	OTLEY. On the history and composition of the Archbishop of York's Otley estate see WYAS 188-9, 472.
	STUBHAM. Subsequently absorbed into Middleton township (see PNWR v, 66; WYAS 451-2). The grid reference given in the index for the vill centre is that for Low Hall. The name survives in Stubham Wood.
	CLIFTON. See WYAS 462 on distinguishing Clifton (SE 192 482: 2W4; SW,Sk2), which was subsequently amalgamated with the vill of Newall (not Newhall as given in DG 491), from Clifton (*c.*SE 20 53: 1Y18; SW,Bu29), which was similarly amalgamated with

Norwood to form the township of Clifton with Norwood, also in Claro wapentake and immediately to the north.

BICHERTUÑ. A lost vill which subsequently became part of Newall with Clifton township (DG 487; PNWR v, 56).

(NETHER) TIMBLE. DG 500 Little Timble. The modern name for the vill centre is Nether Timble. Little Timble is the township name.

ECTONE. A lost vill which subsequently became part of Lindley township (DG 493; PNWR v, 60).

('LITTLE') HAWKSWORTH. DB *alia Henochesuurde* is 'Little' Hawksworth, whose name was later changed to Thorpe (WYAS 391), not Hawksworth Mill as given in DG 496.

BURLEY (IN WHARFEDALE). DG 489 Burley. The full modern name is Burley in Wharfedale.

2W6   ULLESKELF WITH ITS OUTLIERS. VCH 214, note 19 identifies, although without reference, the outliers as Kirkby Wharfe (2 carucates 4 bovates) and Ouston (2 carucates 3 bovates).

2W7   ST. WILFRID'S TERRITORY. Literally 'St. Wilfrid's League'. The meaning is ambiguous, for, although we are told (line 5) that this is an area of 1 league circumference around the church, the word also carries connotations of distinct authority and jurisdiction. This is not the ordinary jurisdiction expressed usually as soke, but is rather nearer in meaning to that conveyed by the medieval liberty or franchise.

'EASTWICK'. DB *Estuinc*, probably for *Estuuic* (cf. SW,Bu45). A lost vill, the name not recorded subsequent to DB. It cannot be located exactly but it has been assumed from its name to have lain across the River Ure east of Westwick. As Newby (centred on Newby Hall at SE 347 675), the adjacent township immediately to the east of Westwick, is not recorded until 1170-80, it seems likely that the name Newby displaced 'Eastwick' as that of the vill some time after 1086.

WESTWICK. The name Westwick survives at SE 349 663, but LVY 236 places the original vill centre immediately to the east at Westwick Hall (SE 355 664).

WILSILL. DG 511 identifies DB *Wifleshalle* as Warsill, but the early forms for Warsill are consistently different from those in DB. PNWR v, 186 identifies it with Wilsill, also in Lower Claro Wapentake, which is preferable. Wilsill subsequently became part of the township of High and Low Bishopside.

'KNARESFORD'. A lost vill located in the area of Skelding township; its name survives as a field-name, Knayser (SE 213 697), on the hill near High Skelding (PNWR v, 198). The name Skelding is not recorded until 1154-91, and it seems likely that it displaced *Kenaresforde* as the name of the vill some time after 1086.

(HIGH) GRANTLEY. DG 495 reports DB *Grentelaia* as Grantley, but the full modern name for the vill centre is High Grantley (SE 232 709). Low Grantley is a very small settlement at SE 237 702; Grantley Hall is at SE 241 692.

'HERLESHOW' (HOW. HILL). The DB vill of *Erlesholt* (12th-century *Herleshow*) subsequently became part of the township of Markington. The *-how* (OE *hoh* 'hill') of the name is How Hill (SE 276 670), on which stands the chapel of St. Michael built by Fountains Abbey *c.*1200 (PNWR v, 159).

2W8   ('EAST') STAINLEY. DB *Estanlai* probably formed part of the later township of North Stainley with Sleningford (PNWR v, 159).

SLENINGFORD. The vill centre was depopulated first by the 14th century and again by the 17th; its site is marked on the 6 in. OS map, but the grounds for this are uncertain. The chapel is visible on aerial photographs (LVY 235).

SUTHEUUIC. DG 508 suggests that this lost vill might be located in Bridge Hewick township, but although it is associated with Bridge Hewick and Copt Hewick, its exact location is unknown (PNWR v, 155).

2W9   RAINALD. In this edition the DB forms *Rainald, Ragenal* and *Ragenald* in entries relating to 1066 have been regularised to ON *Ragnaldr* (PNDB 346; SPN 213) and DB *Rainald* in entries relating to 1086 has been regularised to the Continental form *Rainald* (Forssner 208; PNDB 346).

2W10-11 (BRIDGE) HEWICK and (COPT) HEWICK. DG 488, 491 ascribes the DB form *Hauuinc* of 2W10 to Copt Hewick and the DB form *Hadewic* of 2W11 to Bridge Hewick, whereas PNWR v, 155, 156 vice- versa. Both names have been taken to be pre-Conquest *heah-wic* by Smith (PNWR v, 155, 156), who, however, did not analyse the fact that in DB the two Hewicks have different names. DB *Hauuinc* (earlier probably **Hau-uic<*Hauu-uic*) probably has as its first element OE *haga* 'hedge' because of the *-a-* vowel, although OE *heah, *hæh* 'high' is also possible (JMcND). The first element of DB *Hadewic* cannot, however, be *heah* and the rest of the spelling tradition does not support a derivation from *hæth* 'heath'. *Hade-* probably represents an early ME form of OE **hæged* (cf. *Hadepole* (EPNS xliv, 124) from *hegod*) meaning 'hedged about, with a hedge around it'. This conjecture is corroborated to some extent by the subsequent introduction of the affix in the name Copt Hewick of OE *coppod* (ME *copt*) 'polled, cropped', which could refer to the pollarding, reduction or cutting down of an ancient quickset hedge grown into an ancient shaw,although the alternative derivation proposed in PNWR v, 157 from OE *coppede* 'having a top or head, with a hill' should also be considered (JMcND). Thus *Hadewic* (2W11; SW, H2) would be Copt Hewick, and *Hauuinc/Hauuic* (2W10; SW,H3) would be Bridge Hewick. It has also been suggested that *Carlewic* recorded in 1030 but not in DB might be an earlier name for DB *Hauuinc* and that *Sutheuuic* might also be associated with it (see PNWR v, 155). As *Sutheuuic* is recorded as a separate vill containing 5 carucates from the two Hewicks in DB (2W8; SW,H1) it cannot be identified with either of them, although it may have subsequently formed part of one or the other (see 2W8 note). Neither can *Carlewic* be an earlier form for *Hauuinc*: the 1030 list of the vills making up the archbishop of York's estate records that *Carlewic* contained 5 hides and *Heawic* a further 5 hides (EYC i, no. 7). DB on the other hand attributes 3 carucates to *Hauuinc* and 2 carucates to *Hadeuuic* both here and in the Summary (SW, H2-3). As the hide and the carucate appear to have been interchangeable in the North in the 11th century, this suggests that the 1030 *Heawic* represented both Hewicks rather than just Copt Hewick (as suggested by PNWR v, 156) and that *Carlewic* was therefore a separate entity from these.

2W12   GIVENDALE. The earthworks of the depopulated vill centre are still visible (LVY 234).

2W13   HOWGRAVE. In the WR in DB, now in the NR. On the site of the vill centre see LVY 300.

    HUTTON CONYERS. In the WR in DB, now in the NR.

    HASHUNDEBI. DG 484, 496 considers that the *Hashundebi* of 2W13 and SW,H2 is a lost vill located in Sharow township, while DB *Asmundrebi* (13W21; SW,Bu19) is to be identified with Aismunderby. PNWR v, 168 puts all these forms together under Aismunderby. JMcND observes that the form *Hashundebi*, which is unintelligible as it stands, is not likely to represent **Asmundebi* (for Aismunderby) as it is to represent a miscopying from an earlier record of the name **Hamundebi* (from the ON personal name *Hamundr*) in miniscules where a badly written *m* with extended strokes for the first two minims has been read by the DB scribe as *sh*. The DG identification has therefore been followed in this edition.

2E1   ST. JOHN'S CARUCATE. This seems similar in meaning to St. Wilfrid's League. See 2W7 note.

    3 SOLDIERS, 3 CARUCATES. This is a difficult passage with ambiguities. The abbreviations *c.* and *car.* could represent either *caruca* 'plough' or *carucata* 'carucate', there being no distinguishing *terrae* 'of land' which would make it clear (see 1Y6 note). While *xx villanos* '20 villagers' is clearly accusative, it is not clear whether *tres milites* '3 soldiers' is nominative or accusative, and *iiic.* '3 ploughs/carucates' could be nominative, accusative or ablative. The entry thus could read 'The Canons have there in lordship 4 ploughs/carucates and [they have] 20 villagers with 6 ploughs/carucates and 3 soldiers with 3 ploughs/carucates'. Since the Canons clearly have the land, the intention is probably to indicate the number of their ploughs, and since villagers are never mentioned as landholders, ploughs are probably meant here. Soldiers, however, are more often than not said to hold land, and thus *c.* has been translated here as carucates, although it must be stressed that whether they held land or ploughs must remain an open question.

    THE CANONS. As this entry is dealing with the land of St. John's of Beverley, these must be the canons of that house, not of St. Peter's of York.

2E3   (EAST AND WEST) FLOTMANBY. Flotmanby now contains two centres – East Flotmanby at TA 079 798 and West Flotmanby at TA 073 795. As it is impossible to determine whether one was originally more important than the other, both have been used in this edition (see also LVY 61).

2E5   10S NOW 8. Presumably 9S. See 2N24 note.

2E7   RAVENTHORPE. The site of Raventhorpe village in Cherry Burton township is still known at TA 050 425, but it is depopulated (LVY 67; PNER 191, note 2).

2E8   6 BOVATES. Written above the line.

2E11   KIPLING COTES. DG 475 Kiplingcotes. The modern form of the name is Kipling Cotes. The village of Kipling Cotes, now in Middleton on the Wolds township, is depopulated (LVY 64). Cf. 5E20.

2E18   HOLDERNESS. The name of the south-eastern peninsula of the ER, which constituted a wapentake. As well as Holderness its three hundreds, *Uth Hundret* (south), *Mith Hundret* (middle) and *Nort Hundret* (north) are also mentioned in DB (2E23; 2E27; 2E36; SE,Sol;

SE,Mid1; SE,No1), although many places are not ascribed to a specific hundred but only to Holderness.

OUTLIERS. *Ber.*, *berewici* 'outliers'. Farley reproduces *BER.* with an R. In fact the scribe incorrectly wrote *BEB.* (DF XIII). What follows is a list of those outliers which the Archbishop had in the area.

2E19 LAND FOR 6 OXEN. References to oxen are interspersed with references to ploughs throughout this list of outliers. There is no apparent reason why. See 1N7 note; 1E3 note. 1 PLOUGH. *una. car* for *unam carucam* '1 plough' written at the end of the preceding line.

2E20 ½ PLOUGH. *dim. car.* for *dimidiam carucam* 'half a plough' written at the end of the following line.

2E21 ESKE. The vill centre for Eske at TA 060 433 is now depopulated, but is clearly visible on aerial photographs (LVY 61).

2E22 IN STORK(HILL). In *Estorch* the *r* is inserted above the line.
STORK(HILL). On the earthworks of the depopulated vill centre see LVY 68; PNER 201.
THIS IS NOT IN HOLDERNESS. *Haec non est in Heldernesse* inserted at the end of the previous line. It is emphasised by being written in capitals and being (effectively) underlined (DF XIII).

2E23 SOUTH HUNDRED. See 2E17 note.

2E24 GRIMSTON. DG 473 Grimston Garth. The modern name is simply Grimston. The vill centre at TA 290 350 was depopulated in the early 16th century and part of the earthworks has now been lost to the sea by coastal erosion (LVY 62).

2E25 MONKWITH. DG 476 Monkwick, the form used down to the 17th century. The modern name is Monkwith. The settlement of Monkwith is now depopulated (LVY 65; PNER 57).

2E27 MIDDLE HUNDRED. See 2E17 note.
5 OXEN. *5 bov.* for *5 boves* '5 oxen' written at the end of the preceding line (DF XIII). Farley prints it so as to make it seem more as if it was simply written above the line.

2E28 BURTON (CONSTABLE). The present church and building of the name are located at TA 188 367, but the earthworks of the original vill centre are still visible just to the east at TA 190 368 (LVY 59).

2E30 1 PLOUGH. *1 car.* for *1 caruca* '1 plough' written at the end of the preceding line (DF XIII). Farley prints it so as to make it seem more as if it were written above the line.

2E31 DANTHORPE. On the shrunken vill centre see LVY 60.

2E32 MEADOW, 20 ACRES. *ac. pti.* for *acrae prati* 'acres of meadow' written at the end of the following line.

2E33 TOOK AWAY. DB *aufert* (DF XIII). Farley wrongly reproduces this with a capital *A*.
DROGO. This must be Drogo de Bevrere, who held land in Routh (14E6) and is recorded in the Claims section as being in dispute with St. John's (CW39).

2E35 SOUTHCOATES. On the 1st ed. 6 in. OS map, sheet 226, the township is still called Southcoates and the vill centre (at TA 124 303) is represented by a cluster of buildings surrounded by fields. Southcoates has now been absorbed into the outer suburbs of Kingston upon Hull.

2E36 NORTH HUNDRED. See 2E17 note.
(GREAT) COWDEN. See 14E5 note.

2E37 This entry added in at the end of the line completing the entry for Great Cowden (2E36).

2E39 4 SMALLHOLDERS. Written at the end of the following line.

3Y1 THE BISHOP OF DURHAM. In this section and elsewhere, the entries and holdings referred to are those of the office of Bishop of Durham, as opposed to individual bishops. For clarity, entries relating to the holdings of the Bishop in the time of King Edward have been recorded in the Index of Persons under the name of Bishop Alwine, who was Bishop in 1066. Entries relating to the holdings of the Bishop in the time of King William have been indexed under the name of Bishop William, who was Bishop in 1086 (on the form of his name see 1W63 note).
OUTLIERS, JURISDICTION. See 2B18 note.
HUNSLEY. The vill centre is now depopulated (LVY 63), but the name survives at SE 953 350.
YOKEFLEET (GRANGE). DB *Iugufled* (DF XIV). Farley erroneously *Lugufled*. Yokefleet was subsequently subsumed into Gilberdyke township and is now represented by Yokefleet Grange (SE 817 321) and Yokefleet Lodge (SE 824 316).
BRANTINGHAM (THORPE). Later also known as *Thorpe juxta Brantyngham* and *Thorpe Brantingham* (PNER 222; LVY 69).
SCORBOROUGH. On the shrunken vill centre see LVY 67.
NEWTON (GARDHAM). Subsequently subsumed into Cherry Burton township together with Gardham (DB *Gerdene*). When the settlement of Gardham was depopulated, its name

was transferred to the settlement of *Newton*, whose own name then fell into disuse (LVY 61; PNER 191).

3Y2-3   LUND. PNER 163 identifies all occurrences of *Lont* in DB with Lund township in the Bainton Beacon Division of Harthill Wapentake, whereas DG 476 divides them between Lund township (3Y2-3; SE,We12) and Lund in Bubwith (15E5; 21E5; CE14; SE,He8). The latter is now represented only by the names Lund Lane and Lund Closes (SE 706 333) immediately to the south of Breighton (DGNE 173) in Breighton township (now the civil parish of Bubwith).

3Y3   *PERSENE*. A lost vill subsequently part of Scorborough township (DG 478).

3Y4   OUTLIERS, JURISDICTION. See 2B18 note.

OWSTHORPE. On the shrunken vill centre see LVY 66.

CAVIL. The depopulated site of Cavil at SE 770 305 lies immediately to the north-east of the present farm of the name (LVY 59).

BELBY (HOUSE). See 1E2 note.

YOKEFLEET. DB *Iucufled* (DF XIV). Farley erroneously *Lucufled*. DG 483 locates this Yokefleet in Blacktoft township, but it is actually a township in its own right.

COTNESS (HALL). DG 470 Cotness. The full modern name is Cotness Hall. Only the hall survives at the vill centre (LVY 59).

BARNHILL (HALL). DG 467 Barnhill. The full modern name is Barnhill Hall.

51 CARUCATES AND 6 BOVATES. If the addition is correct, the carucate contains 7 bovates. The 'and' has been partially obliterated but can still be seen (DF XIV).

19 CARUCATES, 6 BOVATES. Here, if the addition is correct, the carucate contains 8 bovates.

3Y7   *NEWTON* (GARDHAM). See 3Y1 note.

3Y8   HOLME (ON THE WOLDS). See 2N18 note.

NIGEL. DB does not specify whether this undertenant of the Bishop of Durham is Nigel Fossard, Nigel of Muneville or another Nigel. Elsewhere it can be shown that the scribe meant Nigel Fossard when he did not specify which Nigel was intended (see 5N1 note; CE2 note), so possibly this is also the case here, but it is impossible to be certain.

3Y9   HOWGRAVE. See 2W13 note.

NORTON (CONYERS). On the shrunken vill centre see LVY 304.

TORP. A lost vill subsequently part of Pickhill township (DG 537).

3Y10   BISHOP ALWINE. *Eps.* for *Episcopus* 'Bishop' is written above the line.

3Y12   *HOREBODEBI*. A lost vill in the vicinity of Sessay, possibly between Sessay and Topcliffe (DGNE 486-7). PNNR 280 incorrectly identifies this with Hornby near Appleton Wiske in Gilling East Wapentake.

3Y18   WINTON. On the earthworks of the shrunken vill centre see LVY 308.

4N1   SNEATON. *berewica* 'outlier' is written above this place-name.

EARL SIWARD. *com.* for *comes* 'earl' is written above Siward's name.

EARL HUGH. *com.* for *comes* 'earl' is written above Hugh's name.

WILLIAM OF PERCY. This is the William referred to throughout.

JURISDICTION. See 1Y8 note.

£112. Literally '£100 and £12'.

FYLING (OLD HALL) AND FYLING THORPE. PNNR 116, 117 identifies DB *Figelinge* with Fyling Thorpe and *Nortfigelinge* with Fylingdales, whereas DG 522 identifies the former with Fyling Old Hall and the latter with Fyling Thorpe. The DG identifications have been followed in this edition.

'PRESTBY'. A lost vill subsequently part of Whitby township (PNNR 127).

'SOWERBY'. A lost vill subsequently part of Whitby township (DG 534; PNNR 128).

'BRECK'. A lost vill subsequently part of Whitby township (PNNR 127).

BALDEBI. A lost vill subsequently part of Whitby township (PNNR 127).

FLOWER(GATE). The DB vill of *Florun* was subsequently subsumed into Whitby township, but the name survives in Flowergate, a main street in the southern part of the town of Whitby running from NZ 8969 1100 to NZ 8985 1106.

(HIGH) STAKESBY. DB *Staxebi* was subsequently subsumed into Newholm township (PNNR 125). It is now represented by High Stakesby (DG 524) at NZ 885 107. Low Stakesby is at NZ 890 107.

NEWHOLM. DG 530 Newholme. The correct form of the name is Newholm.

4N2   EARL SIWARD. See 4N1 note.

'ROSKELTHORPE'. A lost vill subsequently part of Loftus township (PNNR 141).

LIVERTON, 7 CARUCATES. The number is not very clear in the text (DF XV) and could be either '6' or '7'. '7' has been preferred here, although Farley reads it as '6'.

RAWCLIFF (BANKS). The name today occurs as Rawcliff Banks Cottages at NZ 6379
1642, but on the 1st ed. 6 in. OS map (sheet 17) there are no cottages and the area is
called simply Rawcliff Banks.
MARSKE (BY THE SEA). DG 528 reports DB *Mersc* as Marske, but the full modern name
is Marske by the Sea.
WESTLIDUM (KIRKLEATHAM). See 1N12 note.
46½ CARUCATES. The amounts of land are written above the relevant place-names;
they produce a total of 35½ carucates and 22 bovates. For this to amount to 46½
carucates the carucate here must be the equivalent of 2 bovates, which looks much too
low. The addition might well be in error, but other similarly small carucate sizes do seem
to appear from time to time (14E4;5;7).

4N3   ACKLAM. See 1N28 note.
ENGLEBI (BARWICK), INGLEBY (HILL). DG 515, 525 identifies the first *Englebi* of this
entry with Barwick and the second *Englebi* with Ingleby Hill, both subsequently located in
Ingleby Barwick township. LVY 301 and PNNR 170 prefer to identify both entries with
Ingleby and it is certainly surprising, if the DG identification is correct, that Barwick
should be called *Englebi* in this entry but *Beruuic* in SN,L35. LVY 301 locates the vill centre
of Ingleby at Ingleby Close (NZ 432 132) rather than at Ingleby Hill; it is possible that in
the 11th century there were two adjacent vills of *Englebi* with the first *Englebi* of this entry
being centred on Ingleby Close and the second on Ingleby Hill, but as this is not at
present capable of proof, the DG identifications have been followed in this edition.
ENGLEBI (BARWICK). *Ber.* for *berewicus* 'outlier' is written above this place-name.
EARL SIWARD. See 4N1 note.
COULBY. On the depopulated vill centre see LVY 296.
STAINSBY (HALL). The DB vill of *Steinesbi* was subsequently subsumed into Stainton
township. The name survives in a cluster of names, including Stainsby Hall (NZ 464 151),
used in this edition as the vill centre, Stainsby Grange Farm (NZ 464 158), Stainsby Hall
Farm (NZ 470 152) and Stainsby Hall Farm (NZ 468 165), which indicate the general area
of the original vill.
25 CARUCATES. The amounts of land are written above the relevant place-names. As
given they add up to only 24 carucates.

4E1   EARL HAROLD. See 4N1 note.
4E2   SEWERBY. On the location of the vill centre see LVY 68
(HIGH AND LOW) CATTON. DG 469 reports DB *Cattune* as Catton, but on the modern
2½ in. OS map the church is located in Low Catton, and Hall Hill, probably
representing the site of the hall, in High Catton, so both names have been used in this
edition.
40 CARUCATES. VCH 219, note 10 suggests that this included land in Catton and
Stamford Bridge (12 carucates), Kexby (6 carucates), Full Sutton (6 carucates),
Wilberfoss (6 carucates), North or Cherry Burton (3 carucates 2 bovates), Gate Helmsley
(6 bovates) and Newton upon Derwent (6 carucates).
EARL HAROLD. See 4N1 note.
WILLIAM. This is probably William of Percy as he holds from Earl Hugh elsewhere in
this section. In the Summary these 40 carucates are attributed direct to Earl Hugh
(SE,P4).

5N1   COUNT OF MORTAIN. *Comes* is normally translated into English as 'Earl', but here
'Count' is retained since this is a French title where Count is the appropriate usage.
NIGEL. Throughout this section on the holding of the Count of Mortain, Nigel is named
as an undertenant (5N1-8; 22-3; 27; 30; 32; 53-4; 58-61; 66. 5E1; 3-11; 15; 17-19; 21-5; 29
44; 58-9; 68-9; 71-3. 5W6-8; 11; 13; 15; 30-1; 35), but which Nigel is not specified. The
references in the Claims section to Nigel Fossard in relation to many of these places
(CN5; CE1-4; 8; 10-11; 13; 18-21; 27. CW11-14; 18; 21; 37) make it obvious that it is Nigel
Fossard who is the Count's undertenant.
5N1a   GARTON (ON THE WOLDS), BENTLEY. These two entries are added in the
right-hand margin at the top of this section.
5N4   (MUL)GRAVE CASTLE. DG 529 Mulgrave. The full modern name is Mulgrave Castle,
which is applied both to the modern settlement (NZ 847 126) and the original castle site
at NZ 839 116. The latter has been used for the vill centre in the index as it is the castle
not the modern settlement which is situated in the steep-sided valley which gave its name
to the DB vill of *Grif* (from *gryfja* 'valley': PNNR 137).
5N8   ROXBY. *Ber.* for *berewicus* 'outlier' is written above this place-name.
40S. Farley accurately transcribes *xxls* from the text (DF XV). This is probably an error
since this numerical formation does not formally exist. Consequently it has been

assumed here that the scribe wrote two *xxs* by mistake and *xl* is the figure intended. Another interpretation is possible, which is that the scribe intended that 20 (*xx*) should be deducted from 50 (*l*). This would give 30s. It is, however, a most unusual formulation if it is the case.

5N9   RICHARD OF SOURDEVAL. 'of Sourdeval' is written in an abbreviated form above his name.

5N10   *GRIMESBI*. A lost vill subsequently part of Borrowby township in Langbargh East Wapentake (DG 523; LVY 299).

5N11   SEATON (HALL). DG 533 Seaton. The full modern name is Seaton Hall.
RICHARD. The Richard named throughout the section on the holdings of the Count of Mortain is probably Richard of Sourdeval as he is named in full in 5N9 and the shortened form of his name has obviously been used to save space. This is confirmed by the entry in 5E27 where Richard is stated to hold 3 carucates 6 bovates from the Count in Middleton on the Wolds and it is added that the Count's predecessor did not have it. This resulted in disagreement over who should hold it, so this vill is recorded in the Claims, where it is stated specifically that it is Richard of Sourdeval who holds the 3 carucates 6 bovates in Middleton on the Wolds (CE7).

5N12   'STAINTON'. See 1N6 note.
5N16   COUNT ROBERT. DB *Com. R.* for *Comes Robertus* 'Count Robert'.
5N17   MARSKE (BY THE SEA). See 4N2 note.
5N19   'MIDDLETON'. A lost vill located near Guisborough in Langbargh East Wapentake (DG 528).

5N20   TOCKETTS (FARM). DB *Toscotun* (DF XVI). DG 536 erroneously *Toscutun* and reports it as Tocketts. The full modern name is Tocketts Farm. On the shrunken vill centre see LVY 307.

5N21   *WESTLIDUN* (KIRKLEATHAM). See 1N12 note.
5N24   WALTHEOF. The regularised form for DB *Waltef* should be ON *Valthjolfr*, but in this edition the form *Waltheof* is used as this is the form by which the name is generally known to modern historians.

5N26   BARNABY. On the medieval grange site see LVY 294.
5N28   13 CARUCATES. Made up of 2 carucates in Tanton and 11 carucates in Seamer (SN,L38), the latter probably including 2 carucates in Newby and 1 carucate in Braworth (VCH 221 note 16)

5N29   SKUTTERSKELFE (HALL). See 1N32 note.
BLATEN (CARR). PNNR 169 reports this as shown on the 6 in. OS map, but it does not appear in the area where it is located by DG map 62 nor on 1st ed. 6 in. OS map (sheets 28, 42), nor on the tithe award for Great Busby township (PRO IR 29/42/62), and so has been treated in this edition as lost.
WHORLTON. The vill centre is now depopulated and the castle and church are in ruins (LVY 308).
GOULTON (GRANGE). See 1N39 note.
20 CARUCATES. VCH 221, notes 17, 18 suggests that these 20 carucates were distributed as 3 carucates 1 bovate in Rudby, 4 bovates in Skutterskelfe Hall, 2 carucates 3 bovates in *Blaten Carr*, 8 carucates in Whorlton, 5 carucates in Goulton Grange and 1 carucate in Crathorne, although without giving a reference.

5N30   GREAT BROUGHTON. See 1N36 note.
5 CARUCATES. The scribe originally wrote '4' and then crossed it out, substituting '5' (DF XVI).
ULFKETILL 1 MANOR. This is written above the line.

5N32   *STEMANESBI*. A lost vill subsequently part of Scalby township (DG 535). This entry is probably a duplicate of that given in the holdings of the King's Thanes (29N10).
NOW NIGEL HAS [IT] FROM THE COUNT. In the section on the holdings of the King's Thanes, 2 carucates of land in *Stemanesbi* are ascribed to Uhtred (29N10), who according to this entry had been the predecessor of the Count of Mortain in this vill. In the Summary the 2½ carucates of this entry are also ascribed to the Count (SN,D3), not to Uhtred. Possibly Uhtred's original holding was 4½ carucates.
ARE 1½ CARUCATES. Literally 'is'. See 2B11 note.
FALSGRAVE. *regis est* 'it is the King's' is written above the place-name.

5N33   LOFT MARISHES. See 1N47 note.
5N34   *GHIGOGESMERSC*. Thus DB (DF XVI). DG 518 erroneously *Chigogesmersc*. On the location of this vill see 1Y4 note.

5N36   NEWSHAM. These 1½ carucates are entered in the Summary under the name of Amotherby (SN,Ma4).

5N37   ODFRIDA. DB *Oudfrida* could represent either OG *Odfrida* or OG *Otfrida* (PNDB 334). The former is used in this edition as being closer to the DB form.

5N45	IN BARTON (LE STREET). There was a further entry following this which was subsequently erased (DF XVI). Skaife 55 reads this as a total. He appeared to be able to discern 'In all, for geld, there are' but added that the total itself was illegible. He produced a total of 23 carucates 6 bovates by adding up the separate items. If Skaife's reading is accepted, the missing line reads 'In all, 23 carucates, 6 bovates taxable'. Nothing of this is visible in the Facsimile.
5N47	NUNNINGTON. This is added in small, tight lettering at the foot of the column.
5N48	IN SLINGSBY. This is added in small, tight lettering at the foot of the column.
5N49	STILTONS (FARM). See 1N79 note.
5N53	STITTENHAM. LVY 306 locates the earthworks of the original vill centre adjacent to the present farms.
5N54	The amounts of land are written above the relevant place-names.
	GANTHORPE. This is added to Welburn, above the line. Together they comprise 5 carucates.
5N55	WIGANTHORPE (HALL). See 1N89 note.
5N57	GODRED. DB *Godred* could represent either ON *Guthrothr* (SPN 111) or OE *Godred* (JMcND). The latter is used in this edition as being closer to the DB form.
5N59	*FORNETORP*. PNNR 30 places DB *Fornetorp* in Dalby township, but the medieval sources refer to it as a hamlet of Butterwick; they also refer to *South Fornythorpe* in Cornbrough (LVY 299). DG 522 places it as a lost vill in Farlington, but this is presumably on the basis that it is linked in this entry with Farlington (DGNE 89). Cornbrough lies just to the east of Farlington, while Butterwick is some distance to the north-east. It may well be that there were two places of the name, one in the vicinity of Butterwick and the other of Cornbrough, which eventually required to be distinguished by the use of the affix 'south'. In this case the *South Fornythorpe* (Cornbrough township) would seem the more likely candidate for DB *Fornetorp*, being close to Farlington, but in view of the uncertainty the DB form has been used in this edition.
5N60	CORNBROUGH (HOUSE). DG 519 Cornbrough. The full modern name for the vill centre is Cornbrough House. *Corlebroc* was subsequently amalgamated with Sheriff Hutton to form the township of Sheriff Hutton with Cornbrough, although the boundaries of the original vill survived until the 19th century (LVY 296).
5N61	IN WEST LILLING. The amounts of land are written above the relevant place-names. (WEST) LILLING, (EAST) LILLING. See 1N91 note. 9½ CARUCATES, 2 BOVATES. 2 bovates has been added above the line. Assuming that the addition is correct, the carucate contained 8 bovates.
5N62	A PRIEST AND A CHURCH. *pbrm.*, *presbyterem* 'priest' and *ecclesia.*, *ecclesiam* 'church' are in the accusative. This would include them in the list of the lord's possessions. Normally they are in the nominative.
5N64	SVARTHOFUTH. DB *Sorthoued* (DF XVII), representing ON *Svarthofuth* 'black-head' (SPN 275). Farley erroneously *Sorchoued*.
5N65	4 CARUCATES. The actual totals are 2½ carucates and 16 bovates. 16 bovates thus makes 1½ carucates, which would make the carucate contain, on average, 10.6 bovates.
5N66	A PRIEST AND A CHURCH. See 5N62 note.
5N68	*WARUELESTORP*. A lost vill subsequently part of Tollerton township (DG 538).
5N69	4½ CARUCATES. *dimid.* for *dimidium* 'half' is written above the line.
5N71	BRECKENBROUGH. On the depopulated vill centre see LVY 295.
5N72	(NORTH) KILVINGTON. See 1Y2 note. WALTHEOF. His name is written above the line.
5N73	LEAKE. See 1Y2 note. 12 PLOUGHS ARE POSSIBLE. This is the only part of the line which is still legible (DF XVII). Skaife 58 assumes that it totals the lands in the previous 5 entries, which does not seem unlikely. This interpretation would give '[In all 23½ carucates taxable] and 12 ploughs are possible'.
5N75	(NORTH) KILVINGTON. See 1Y2 note. HUNDULFTHORPE (FARM). DG 425 Hundulfthorpe. The full modern name is Hundulfthorpe Farm in North Kilvington township (SE 4385 8568).
5E1	ULFR. The Claims identify the Ulfr holding land in North Cave in this entry as Ulfr the Deacon (CE13).
5E3	IN THESE. That is, presumably, in North Ferriby and Anlaby.
5E7	EARNWINE. The Claims identify the man holding land in Aughton as Earnwine the Priest (CE18).
5E7	3 [PLOUGHS] POSSIBLE. Literally *et iii poss. e.e.* for *et iii possunt esse* 'and 3 possible. As this is such a standard phrase 'ploughs' is clearly omitted by accident.
5E8	IN SPALDINGTON. The amounts of land are written above the relevant place-names. 10 CARUCATES. The individual amounts add up to 8½ carucates and 17½ bovates. If the addition is correct and these comprise 10 carucates, then the carucate contains 11.6

bovates on average, which looks too high. If, however, there were 8 bovates to the carucate the final total would be 10½ carucates. Compare this with the figure given in the Summary.

5E9   7 BOVATES. The Summary gives the Count of Mortain's holding in Brantingham as 1 carucate 6½ bovates (SE,We16). VCH 224, note 34 suggests that possibly the land of Northmann son of Ulfr recorded in the Claims (CE13) might have made up the balance. *TOSCHETORP*. A lost vill subsequently part of Brantingham township (DG 481).

5E10   IN LORDSHIP. Farley reads the *I* in *In* as a lower case *i* with a long stem, which he reproduces as *j*. It appears more like a capital *I* in the text (DF XVIII), but the distinction is not significant.

5E11   THERE WERE 2 MANORS. The text is very curtailed at this point. It reads literally 'there were 2 manors, 5 brothers, of 7 carucates and 5 bovates taxable'. The sense is as translated.

5E12   1½ CARUCATES. This entry of the 1½ carucates with jurisdiction in Howden is duplicated in the 14 bovates (1 carucate = 8 bovates) recorded in 5E26.
JURISDICTION IN HOWDEN. This is written above the line.

5E13   2 BOVATES. This is written above the line.

5E15   OSGODBY. See 2N18 note (DF XVIII).
2½ CARUCATES AND ½ BOVATE. Both ½s are written above the line.
MARGINAL CROSS. See 1W7.

5E18   6 BOVATES. This is written above the line.

5E19   EASTHORPE. The earthworks of the depopulated vill centre of Easthorpe, now part of Londesborough township, are still clearly visible (LVY 61).

5E20   KIPLING COTES. See 2E11 note.

5E22   ⅓ OF 1 BOVATE. *iii parte, tercia parte* 'one third'. ¾ or 3 parts would have been *tres partes*.

5E23   AND 10S. RENT. This is one of those unfortunate places where abbreviated Latin is inevitably obscure. The problem is whether *redd.* in *x sol. redd.* is a verb (*reddere* 'to render/pay rent) or a noun (*redditio, redditus, reddita* 'a rent'). If it is a verb *x sol. redd.* means 'paying 10s' or '10s being paid'. This could refer either to:
a) the villagers paying this to Nigel, although this is unlikely in view of the 'and' sign in between, or
b) Nigel paying it to someone who is unnamed.
If, however, it is a noun, *x sol. redd.* means '10s rent', i.e. that the rent is an appurtenance of the manor just as the villagers and the ploughs are. This latter reading has been preferred here since it reads better with the sense of the entry, which seems to be listing Nigel's assets, not his obligations.

5E25   IN HOWDEN. The scribe wrote the *i* in *in* with rather a long stroke (DF XVIII). Farley reproduces this as a *j*. It is not significant.

5E26   IN (NORTH) DUFFIELD. This line is written in a very cramped style and may well have been inserted afterwards (DF XVIII).
14 BOVATES. See 5E12 note.

5E27   ALDGYTH. In this entry the name of the landholder in Middleton on the Wolds in 1066 is given as *Eddid*, whose regularised OE form would be *Eadgyth* (PNDB 231), whereas in the Claims her name is given as *Eldid* (CE6). The regularised West Saxon form of this would be *Ealdgyth* (PNDB 240), whose regularised OE Northumbrian form would be *Aldgyth*. As the amount of land concerned in each entry is 3 carucates 5 bovates, it must be the same woman in both cases. The *Eddid* form of this entry could well be a miswritten *Ealdid*, given Carolingian miniscules *al* and *d* and supposing a West Saxon spelling of the personal name *Eald* for Northumbrian *Ald-*, so the form *Aldgyth* has been used in this edition.
RICHARD. See 5N11 note.
THE COUNT'S PREDECESSOR. *Antecessor* here simply means whoever came before, i.e. predecessor. It has no connotation of family connection or formal inheritance. The meaning essentially is 'former holder' and, far from having implications of structured descent, the 'former holders' referred to are usually dispossessed English.

5E30   ALDWIF. The regularised West Saxon form for DB *Elduif* would be OE *Ealdwif* (PNDB 242), which has here been regularised to the OE Northumbrian form *Aldwif*.
30S; NOW 6. Presumaby 6s (DF XVIII). See 2N24 note.

5E31   [ONE MANOR]. As the sentence reads in the text, it does not make sense. It literally reads 'Gamall had of 3 carucates taxable'. It appears that the scribe missed the words referring to the manor/s which Gamall held from the usual formula. Most entries refer to one manor, which has been assumed here, but it remains no more than an assumption.
JURISDICTION. Farley gives this in capitals although in the text it is written in normal miniscule without the equivalent of underlining (DF XVIII).

5E32	GAMALL ... (JOINTLY) 1 MANOR. The word used is *quisque* which literally means 'each'. 'everyone'. The meaning, however, is not that they each had a manor of 9½ carucates, but that they all shared this one manor of 9½ carucates. Consequently *quisque* is better translated as 'jointly'.
5E34	*STEITORP*. A lost vill subsequently part of Etton (DG 480).
5E36	RAVENTHORPE. See 2E7 note.
5E39	DRIFFIELD HUNDRED. The later wapentake of Harthill was made up of nine DB hundreds – Driffield, Warter, Pocklington, Weighton, Cave, *Sneculfscros*, Welton, Hessle and Howden (PNER 152-3). Driffield Hundred corresponded closely to the DB soke of Driffield and comprised the north-eastern area of the later Bainton Beacon Division of Harthill (PNER 152-3).
	CRANSWICK AND HUTTON (CRANSWICK). DG 474 Hutton. The vill was subsequently combined with that of Cranswick to form Hutton Cranswick township, but both names are still in use separately at the two ends of the village.
5E40	NESWICK (HALL). DG 477 Neswick. The full modern name for the vill centre is Neswick Hall. The earthworks of the depopulated settlement are still visible (LVY 65).
5E41	*NEUSON*. A lost vill subsequently part of Leconfield township (DG 477; PNER 190), although LVY 65 has found no evidence for its location. It is recorded here under Driffield Hundred but under *Sneculfscros* in the Summary (SE,Sn6).
	NIGEL HAS (IT). *habet* 'he has' is written at the end of the preceding line.
5E42	NORTHMANN, GAMALL. Here and in 5E44 the amounts of land held by the former holders are entered above their names.
5E43	WARTER HUNDRED. The DB hundred of *Wartre* was named from Warter. It comprised the north-western part of the Bainton Beacon Division of Harthill Wapentake and the north-eastern part of the Wilton Beacon Division of Harthill, together with a detached portion in the north of Ouse and Derwent Wapentake (PNER 153).
5E44	POCKLINGTON HUNDRED. The DB hundred of *Poclinton* was named from Pocklington. It comprised the north-western part of the Wilton Beacon Division of Harthill Wapentake and the middle part of Ouse and Derwent Wapentake (PNER 153).
	SUTTON (UPON DERWENT). See 5E42 note.
	7 CARUCATES. The amounts of land given here add up to 6 carucates only. The Summary gives 6 carucates as the total (SE,P3-4).
5E45	HUNTOW HUNDRED. The DB hundred of *Hunthou* comprised the eastern part of the wapentake of Dickering. The name survives in that of Huntow (TA 158 725) in Buckton township (PNER 85-6), possibly the wapentake meeting place.
	SEWERBY. See 4E1 note.
5E46	COUNT ROBERT HAS (IT). This is written above the line.
5E53	BRIGHAM. In Hunthow Hundred here but in *Turbar* Hundred in the Summary (SE,Tu5-6).
	3½ CARUCATES. '½' is written above the line.
5E54	BURTON HUNDRED. The DB wapentake of Burton was named from Burton Agnes (TA 102 632). It comprised the western and central part of the later wapentake of Dickering (PNER 86).
5E55	*TORBAR* HUNDRED. The DB hundred of *Torbar* or *Turbar* comprised the northern part of the later wapentake of Dickering. The name is probably a compound of an OS personal name *Thur* and *beorg* 'hill'; it does not survive as a place-name so the hill from which it was named cannot be identified (PNER 86).
5E57	BINNINGTON. Under *Turbar* Hundred here, but in Burton Hundred in the Summary (SE,Bt9).
5E58	*SCARD* HUNDRED. The later wapentake of Buckrose was made up of three DB hundreds – the south-western part represented by Acklam Hundred, the central part by *Scard* Hundred and the eastern by *Toreshou* Hundred. It is possible that Scar Dale (SE 898 726) in Wintringham township may preserve the name of *Scard* (PNER 120), from ON *skarth* 'cleft in the hills'.
	BIRDSALL. See 2B18 note. This is one of the rare cases in the Yorkshire section of DB proper (as opposed to the Bruce account where it is common), where the name is given in a latinised form, *Briteshala*.
5E60	MARGINAL CROSS. See 1W7 note.
	TOWTHORPE. See 1E40 note.
5E60	KIRKHAM. DB *Cherchan* is probably an erroneous expansion of *Cherchā* (for *Chercham*). See also 5E66 note.
5E63	ACKLAM HUNDRED. The DB hundred of *Hacle*, named from Acklam (SE 782 616), comprised the south-western part of the later wapentake of Buckrose.
5E64	BARTHORPE (GRANGE). DG 467 Barthorpe. The vill centre is now represented only by Barthorpe Grange (LVY 57).

5E65 AN OUTLIER, *SUDNICTON. Ber.* for *berewicus* 'outlier' is written above this place-name. *SUDNICTON.* A lost vill subsequently part of Westow township (DG 480 an obsolete form *Wistow*). The DB forms *Sudnicton* and *Sudcniton* (SE,Ac9) are probably a misspelling of **Sudincton* 'southern farmstead, settlement in the south of a district' (JMcND).

5E66 KIRKHAM. DG 475 expands the DB form *Chercā* to *Cherchan*, as this is the form in which it occurs earlier in this folio (5E62) and in fo. 382a (SE,Ac9) (personal communication, 13.4.85, I. S. Maxwell), otherwise the expansion to *Chercam* might have been preferred, as the final element is OE *ham* 'village, village community, manor, homestead' (PNER 143-4).

5E67 JURISDICTION. See 5E31 note (DF XIX).

5E68 'THORSHOWE' HUNDRED. The DB hundred of *Toreshou* 'Thor's *haugr* or mound' comprised the eastern part of the later wapentake of Buckrose. The mound from which it was named has not been identified (PNER 120).

THIRKLEBY (MANOR). See 2B18 note. This holding is described in the Summary as 'another Thirkleby' (see SE,Th5 note).

5E71 (LOW) MOWTHORPE. See 2B18 note.

5E72 THORFINNR. The scribe originally wrote *Chitelbertus* 'Ketilbjorn', but deleted this by the usual method of underlining and inserting the correct name, *Torfin*, i.e. Thorfinnr, above (DF XX).

4 PLOUGHS. This is written as two sets of *iis*, one above the other.

5E73 CROOM (HOUSE). See 1E58 note.

5W1 [SKYRACK WAPENTAKE]. The places listed in 5W1-5 are recorded under Skyrack Wapentake in the Summary. Its name originally may have meant 'bright oak' but it came to be thought of as meaning 'shire oak' and by tradition its meeting place is believed to have been at the oak tree in the centre of Headingley (see further PNWR iv, 88-9). The wapentake occupied the area between the Aire and the Ouse.

ALWEARD. The DB form *Aluuard* could represent either OE *Alweard* (PNDB 155) or ON *Hallvarthr* (SPN 129). The OE form is used in this edition as being closer to the DB form. 2½ BOVATES. '½' is written above the line.

5W2-5 ADEL. The DB vills of Adel, Cookridge and Eccup, together probably with Burden, were subsequently amalgamated to form the enlarged township of Adel cum Eccup. The original vill boundaries, however,survived as those of hamlets within the township. The vill centre appears never to have been nucleated; the church is at the northern end of a scatter of dispersed settlement (see further Faull; WYAS 298).

5W4 BURDEN (HEAD). DG 489 Burden. The full modern name is Burden Head. *Burghedurum* probably formed part of the later township of Adel cum Eccup (WYAS 299).

5W6 BARKSTON (ASH) WAPENTAKE. The DB wapentake of *Barcheston(e)* was named from Barkston (SE 491 361) and from the 16th century on from Barkston Ash in Barkston township, presumably the wapentake meeting place, at the west of the village (PNWR iv, 1).

5W7 JURISDICTION. See 1Y8 note.

MONK HAY (STILE). DG 502 reports DB *Monechet* as Monkton, a lost DB vill east of Thorner and south-west of Bramham (DG map 59,J7). *Monechet* represents OE *muneca-haeth* 'the monks' heath' and *Monuchetone* (SW,Ba3) represents OE *munecahaeth-tun* 'farm or township at the monks' heath' (JMcND). PNWR iv, 108 identifies it with Monk Hay Stile (SE 410 405) in Bramham township, with which it is linked here and in the Summary. There is no documentary or tenurial evidence to support this identification WYAS 233), only the place-name, which tallies, and so has been used in this edition. Monk Hay Stile is *Munkheyth* in 1246.

1C. The number of carucates in each soke of Bramham is written above their place-names.

TOULSTON. The earthworks of the original vill centre are visible south of the farm (LVY 233).

OGLETHORPE (HALL). DB *Ocelestorp* (DF XX). Farley erroneously *Occlestorp*. DG 503 reports as Oglethorpe but the full modern name is Oglethorpe Hall. The medieval vill centre is probably represented by earthworks to the east of the hall (LVY 233; WYAS 332).

5W8 [STRAFFORTH WAPENTAKE]. The places listed in 5W8-31 are recorded under Strafforth Wapentake in the Summary (see SW,Sf1 note). The wapentake comprised the southern part of the WR extending from the lower Don and Thorne along the borders with Derbyshire and Cheshire. It was possibly named from *Strafford Sands* in Mexborough township which may have been its meeting place (PNWR i, 1), although as *Strafford Sands* is not recorded until later than the wapentake (PNWR i, 78) the place may have been named from the wapentake and not vice-versa. It was subsequently divided into the wapentakes of Lower Strafforth and Upper Strafforth.

EARL TOSTI. See 4N1 note.

SHUTTLEWORTH (LITTLEWORTH). The DB vill of *Scitelesuuorde* was subsequently subsumed into Rossington township, and the name *Shuttleworth* was eventually displaced by Littleworth (PNWR i, 49).

5W10   BARNBY (DUN). Also sometimes known as Barnby upon Don (PNWR i, 17).

5W12   BUGA. The DB form *Bugo* could represent OE *Buga* (personal communication G. Fellows Jensen) or ON *Buggi* (SPN 68). The OE form is used in this edition as being closer to the DB form.

5W14   HOOTON (PAGNELL) AND BILHAM (HOUSE). In the Summary these 10 carucates are ascribed to Hooton Pagnell alone (SW,Sf28).
       BILHAM (HOUSE). DG 487 Bilham. The full modern name is Bilham House. On the further history of the site see LVY 239. The name is written above the line.
       EARL EDWIN. See 4N1 note.

5W15   PICKBURN. This is written above the line.

5W18   JURISDICTION. See 1Y8 note.
       DEIGHTONBY (FIELDS). DG 492 reports DB *Dictenebi* as Deightonby, but PNWR i, 91 gives the name current locally as Deightonby Fields. The name does not occur on the modern 6 in. OS map, nor on the 1st ed. 6 in. OS map (sheet 275), but is given as *Little Deightonby, Near Deightonby* and *Far Deightonby* on the Tithe Award for Thurnscoe township (PRO IR 29/43/409, fields nos. 231, 261, 264), centred on SE 4615 0615. By the middle of this century the group of fields had come to be known simply by the collective Deightonby Fields. The area of any possible settlement has now largely been covered by modern housing and the railway line.
       CLAYTON. Formerly Clayton in the Clay (PNWR i, 89).

5W19   HANDSWORTH. 'Jurisdiction, 4½ carucates' is written above this place-name. It is presumably not included in the total of 5 carucates given for the manor as a whole.

5W20   IN TREETON. On the former landholders see 5E42 note.

5W21   IN AUGHTON (HALL). On the former landholders see 5E42 note.

5W21;24   AUGHTON (HALL). DG 485 Aughton. The full modern name is Aughton Hall.

5W27   WHEATLEY. *Ber.* for *berewicus* 'outlier' is written above this place-name. Although it is in capitals in the text, and has the equivalent of our underlining, Farley fails to represent this by using upper-case type as is his usual custom. However, the whole entry is also actually underlined in the text, which is the method of showing that the entry as a whole should be deleted (DF XXI).

5W28;29   LANGTHWAITE. The DB name today only survives in that of Langthwaite Lane. The original vill centre is represented by Radcliffe Moat and the Castle Hills motte and bailey at *c.*SE 554 069 (LVY 239).

5W30   *SCINESTORP*. A lost vill subsequently part of Sprotbrough township. It was located somewhere between Cusworth, a DB vill which also became part of Sprotbrough, and Newton. LVY 239 places it at about SE 344 036, which must be an error for SE 544 036.
       JURISDICTION. See 5E31 note.
       DONCASTER, 3 BOVATES. The scribe originally wrote '6', but underlined it to indicate a deletion, and inserted the correct figure '3', above.
       4 CARUCATES. The totals amount to 2 carucates and 13 bovates. 13 bovates thus makes 2 carucates if the addition is correct.

5W31   OSGOLDCROSS WAPENTAKE. Named apparently from *Osgold Cross* in Pontefract where the wapentake presumably met; the cross was near Pontefract Market Place (PNWR ii, 79). The wapentake is situated between Lower Strafforth to the south and the Aire to the north and extended westwards from the lower Ouse to Castleford and South Kirkby (PNWR ii, 1).

5W32   STAINCROSS WAPENTAKE. Named apparently from Staincross (SE 331 104), the wapentake presumably meeting at the 'stone cross' (PNWR i, 317). The wapentake lies to the north of Upper Strafforth Wapentake and occupies the upper valleys of the Don and the Dearne (PNWR i, 261).

5W35   AINSTY WAPENTAKE. Named from Ainsty Cliff (SE 528 460) in Bilbrough where the wapentake met (PNWR iv, 235). The wapentake occupies the land along the Ouse adjoining York and between the lower reaches of the Rivers Wharfe and Nidd (PNWR iv, 216).
       (PALLA)THORPE. The vill centre is now represented by the moated site in Bolton Percy township (see further LVY 232, but note that the correct grid reference is SE 515 427).

5W36   'BURGHSHIRE' (CLARO) WAPENTAKE. The DB wapentake of *Bargescire, Borgescire* was named from Aldborough (SE 406 664), the *burh* of whose name refers to the fortifications of the Roman site of *Isurium Brigantum* (PNWR v, 80). The name of the wapentake was changed after the Conquest to Claro, from Claro Hill where the wapentake now presumably met. The wapentake is situated in the north of the West Riding (PNWR v, 1).

Some places in the south-western part of the wapentake are described in the Summary as being within *Gereburg* wapentake (see SW,Sk2 note).

5W37 INGMANTHORPE (HALL). DG 498 Ingmanthorpe, but the name does not survive simply in this form. *Gemunstorp* was subsequently subsumed into Kirk Deighton township, but the general area of the original vill is indicated by the names Ingmanthorpe Hall (SE 423 501), Ingmanthorpe House (SE 423 511), Ingmanthorpe Hill (SE 419 509) and Ingmanthorpe Grange (SE 418 508). It is not certain which of these represents the vill centre, so the grid reference for Ingmanthorpe Hall has been adopted.

IN INGMANTHORPE (HALL). This entry is added at the end of the last line of the previous entry. It is, presumably, a jurisdiction of Hunsingore.

5W38 HALIKELD WAPENTAKE. Although considered part of the WR in DB, Halikeld Wapentake was subsequently part of the NR. It lies to the north of the River Ure. PNNR 218-19 suggests that it was named from Hallikeld Spring, first recorded in 1202, which was presumably the wapentake meeting place. There are now two springs of the name shown on the 6 in. OS map in Hutton Conyers township – at SE 3403 7556 and SE 3427 7514.

NORTON, LECKBY (PALACE). *'ber.* and *berew.* for *berewicus* 'outlier' are written above these place-names.

JURISDICTION. See 1Y8 note.

LECKBY (PALACE). DG 526 Leckby. The full modern name of the vill centre is Leckby Palace. Only a few scattered farms now represent the original settlement (LVY 302).

BRAMPTON (HALL). See 1W55 note.

(EAST) TANFIELD. The earthworks of the vill centre survive at SE 289 799 (LVY 306).

CALDEUUELLE. A lost vill subsequently part of Marton le Moor township.

6N1 COUNT ALAN. See 5N1 note.

(SOUTH) COWTON. The name of DB *Cudtun* survives in that of South Cowton township. The vill centre is now depopulated but the earthworks are still visible at NZ 294 022 (LVY 297), near to the church (NZ 293 026) and Cowton Castle (NZ 293 023).

GODRIC THE STEWARD. *dapifer* 'steward' is written above his name.

OUTLIERS, JURISDICTION. See 2B18 note.

OUTLIERS. Farley correctly reproduces *Bereuuite* (DF XXIII).

BARFORTH (HALL). DG 515 Barforth. The full modern name is Barforth Hall.

CLIFFE (HALL). DG 518 Cliffe. The full modern name is Cliffe Hall.

CARLTON. On the shrunken vill centre see LVY 296.

GIRLINGTON (HALL). DG 522 Girlington. The full modern name is Girlington Hall. The hall is all that survives of the original vill centre (LVY 299).

WYCLIFFE. VCH 231, note 1 states that this appears to have included 3 carucates in Thorpe and 3 carucates in Little Hutton, although without reference.

THORPE (HALL). DG 536 Thorpe (near Wycliffe). The full modern name is Thorpe Hall (in Wycliffe township). On the shrunken vill centre see LVY 307.

MORTHAM (TOWER). DG 529 Mortham. The full modern name is Mortham Tower, apparently on the site of the original vill centre, depopulated as a result of the early 14th-century Scottish raids (LVY 303).

EGGLESTONE (ABBEY). DG 529 Egglestone. The full modern name is Egglestone Abbey.

BRIGNALL. DB *Bringhenale* (DF XXIII). DG 516 erroneously *Bringenhale*.

BRIGNALL, 12 CARUCATES. VCH 231, note 2 states that this appears to have comprised 6 carucates in Brignall, 3 carucates in East Layton, 1 carucate in Cliffe on Tees and 2 carucates in Atley Cowton, although without reference.

6N1;8 STANWICK, ANOTHER STANWICK. There is now only one township of Stanwick, known in full as Stanwick St. John. This has no nucleated settlement within it of the name, the church being located at NZ 1854 1148 at Kirkbridge with the site of Stanwick Hall to the south at NZ 184 114. Presumably the original two DB vills were later amalgamated into the single township. The substantial earthworks and fortifications of the Late Iron Age hill-fort, which gave the vill its name 'stone walls' (PNNR 297), occupy the southern part of the township, including much of Stanwick Park. Although there is no proof of this, the northern line of the earthworks, along Forcett Gill, might have provided the boundary between the two DB vills.

6N2 THE WHOLE MANOR. *maneriū* for *manerium* 'manor' is written above the line.

6N3 UHTRED. The scribe originally began this line with something else, presumably a different name, which was subsequently erased. Farley indicates this by a blank space.

6N4 KNEETON (HALL). See 2N18 note. DG 526 Kneeton. The full modern name is Kneeton Hall. On the depopulated vill centre see LVY 302.

6N7	TAXABLE. *ad gld.* for *ad geldum* 'taxable' is written above the line.
6N9	(OVER) DINSDALE (GRANGE). See 1Y2 note.
	JURISDICTION. See 5E31 note.
6N14	CARLTON. See 6N1 note.
6N15	IN LORDSHIP. See 5E10 note.
6N16	... HAD A MANOR THERE. *Ibi hb i maneriu.* for *Ibi habuit unum manerium* literally 'there he had one manor'. In the standard form a personal name follows *habuit* 'he had' to show who it was who previously held the manor. In this case it has been omitted.
	MANOR. In the text this is written in two parts, *man eriu.* for *manerium* (DF XXIV). Farley does not reproduce this gap. It is not significant.
	NOW ENISANT. The text literally reads *nc. Enisan. de* for *nunc Enisant de* 'now Enisant from'. *Habet* 'he has' normally goes before the person's name to show who it is who is now holding the land. The scribe has omitted this also, as understood.
6N17	*TORP.* A lost vill subsequently part of Croft township (DG 537).
6N18	STARTFORTH. On the former landholders see 5E42 note.
6N19	*HINDRELAG* (RICHMOND). DB *Hindrelag* was subsequently renamed following the construction by Count Alan of the castle called Richmond on the eminence above the River Swale (PNNR 287).
	5 CARUCATES. There is a gap in the text between '5' and 'carucates' which Farley reproduces (DF XXIV).
6N20	EASBY. On the shrunken vill centre see LVY 298.
6N23	*NEUTONE.* A lost vill subsequently part of Scorton township (DG 530).
	EACH OF THE TWO. That is Skeeby and *Neutone.*
6N24	BOLTON (UPON SWALE). DG 516 Bolton on Swale. The full modern name is Bolton upon Swale.
6N26	(LITTLE) LANGTON. PNNR 277 ascribes all the DB *Langetun* and *Langeton* forms to Great Langton, whereas DG 527 identifies the *Langeton* of 6N26 and SN,CtA13 with Little Langton. The DG identification has been followed in this edition.
	(LITTLE) LANGTON. On the former landholders see 5E42 note.
6N26;31	(KIRKBY) FLEETHAM. The two separate DB vills of *Cherchebi* and *Fleteham* were subsequently amalgamated to form the township of Kirkby Fleetham (PNNR 29), the name by which the main settlement (SE 2851 9438) is now known. All that survives of *Cherchebi* is the name Kirkby Hall for the hall and church at SE 2810 9573 (see also LVY 302).
6N27	GRIMR AND KETILL. The amounts of land these held are entered above their names. But there is a *B* by Grimr's name and an *A* by Ketill's. This has been taken to mean that the amounts of land have been entered in the wrong order, and that Grimr in fact had 7 bovates, whilst Ketill had 1 carucate 1 bovate.
	PICOT. This is likely to be the same man as the Picot described in 6N58 as a man of Count Alan.
	16 NOW 16S. Presumably shillings. See 2N24 note.
6N28	SOLBERGE. The name Solberge survives today on the modern map to describe the moated remains of the deserted settlement at SE 3540 8920 (on the desertion see LVY 305), immediately adjacent to Sowber Hill Farm.
	IN SOLBERGE. On the former landholders see 5E42 note.
6N30	ULFKETILL. His land is entered above his name.
	SIWARD. His name is entered above the line over Gamall.
6N31	GRIMR. He held 2 carucates, entered above the line, over his name (line 5 of the Latin).
6N34	AINDERBY (STEEPLE). On the former landholders see 5E42 note.
	3 CARUCATES. This is written above *soca* 'jurisdiction'.
6N37	LANDRIC. This is likely to be the same man as the Landric described in the preceding entry as a man of Count Alan.
6N43	COTHERSTONE. DG 519 Cotherston. The correct modern spelling is Cotherstone.
6N44	ROKEBY (HALL). DG 532 Rokeby. The full modern name is Rokeby Hall, which is located just to the south-west of the site of the church at NZ 084 144 (LVY 305).
	THORFINNR HAD THESE. *H. habuit Torfin nc. ht. Bodin et wasta sun.* for *Haec maneria habuit Thorfinnr nunc habet Bodin et wasta sunt* 'Thorfinnr had these, now Bodin has [them] and they are waste'. Since the word for 'these' is only indicated by *H.* it could have been *hoc* 'this'; however, it is clearly plural since the verb at the end of the line *sunt* 'they are' is plural. The matter is important because it is a question of whether Thorfinnr held simply Rokeby or the 3 manors mentioned before it, i.e. Hunderthwaite, Lartington and Cotherstone as well. It appears that the intention was to show that Thorfinnr held these manors as well, not only because of what is said in this entry, but also because no details of ownership are given in the entries relating to them.

6N45   BROUGHTON (HOUSE). On the former landholders see 5E42 note.
        BROUGHTON (HOUSE). DB *Broctun* has been considered to be a lost vill located in
        Newsham township (Gilling West Wapentake) and last recorded in 1289 as *Broghtonlyth(e)*
        (DG 516; PNNR 291). LVY 297, however, suggests that it may have been located 1½
        miles from Dalton Hall, i.e. at Broughton House (NZ 1055 0975) in the south-eastern
        corner of Newsham township. The name Broughton House has therefore been used in
        this edition for *Broctun*.
6N47   IN DALTON. On the former landholders see 5E42 note.
6N47-8 DALTON and ANOTHER DALTON. The two DB vills of *Daltun* and *alia Daltun* were
        apparently subsequently amalgamated to form one single vill, although not before yet a
        third Dalton had appeared within the area of the later township (LVY 297; PNNR 290).
        There is now only one vill centre, known simply as Dalton, at NZ 1152 0839, and this has
        been used as the grid reference for the vill centre for both the DB vills.
6N50   DIDDERSTON (GRANGE). DG 520 Didderston. The full modern name is Didderston
        Grange (PNNR 298). The name no longer appears on the map, and the vill centre whose
        grid reference is given in the index is Grange Castle (NZ 1840 0761), just to the south-
        east of Diddersley Hill, whose name contains the same first element as the DB name
        (PNNR 298). The 1st ed. 6 in. OS map (sheet 25), also shows Diddersley Grange at NZ
        179 082 (by the time of the modern 6 in. OS map this had been renamed High Grange,
        obviously in relation to Low Grange at NZ 184 085).
        DIDDERSTON (GRANGE). See 2N18 note. *Berewic.* for *berewicus* 'outlier' is written above
        this place-name (DF XXV). Farley reproduces this as *Bereuuit*.
6N52   OUTLIERS. See 1Y9 note.
        KILLERBY (HALL). DG 526 Killerby. The full modern name is Killerby Hall. The castle
        at the vill centre was built in 1291 (LVY 301).
        AINDERBY (MIRES). DG 513 Ainderby Miers, which is the name of the modern
        township. The settlement is called Ainderby Mires (SE 2563 9275). On the shrunken vill
        centre see LVY 294.
        10 PLOUGHS POSSIBLE. This is inserted above the line over '11 carucates'.
6N54   IN LORDSHIP. See 5E10 note.
6N55   KIRKBY (HALL). See 6N26 note.
6N56   (KIRKBY) FLEETHAM. See 6N26 note.
        (GREAT AND LITTLE) FENCOTE. In both entries where they occur, Great Fencote
        and Little Fencote are linked – in 6N56 as 'two outliers called *Fencotes*' and in SN,CtA21
        as 'the two Fencotes'. They still survive as separate entities, although only 500 yards
        apart, with Great Fencote at SE 2839 9369 and Little Fencote at SE 2840 9320, both
        within Kirkby Fleetham township.
        UNMEWED HAWK. *sor. accipitre* for *sorum accipitrem*. *Sorus* is 'sore' or 'unmewed', that is
        untrained. *Accipiter* is 'hawk' generally rather than any particular kind, but the word is
        very often used with reference to sparrowhawks.
6N57   ASKE (HALL). DG 523 reports DB *Hasse* as lost in Kirkby Fleetham township, but LVY
        294 and PNNR 286 identify it with Aske Hall.
6N58   IN SCRUTON. On the former landholders see 5E42 note.
6N59-60 ODO. This is likely to be the same man as the Odo described in the preceding entry as a
        man of Count Alan.
6N60   IN HACKFORTH. On the former landholders see 5E42 note.
        GEOFFREY. DB *Goisfridus*; see Forssner 125-6, OG *Gosfrid*, ME *Geoffrey*.
        3 PLOUGHS. *car.* for *carucae* 'ploughs' is written above the line.
6N61   HORNBY. The earthworks of the village depopulated by Lord Conyers in 1517 are still
        visible (LVY 300).
6N62   HOLTBY (HALL). DG 524 Holtby. The full modern name for the vill centre is Holtby
        Hall, in Ainderby Miers township. The earthworks of the original settlement are visible
        on aerial photographs (LVY 300).
6N63   (EAST) APPLETON. Also known in the Middle Ages as *Parva* ('Little') Appleton (LVY
        294; PNNR 242).
6N64   BROUGH (HALL). DG 517 Brough. The full modern name is Brough Hall.
6N69   *HINDRELAGHE* (RICHMOND). Probably for *Hindrelache* for OE *Hinderlace* (JMcND). See
        6N19 note.
6N71   ELLERTON (ABBEY). The original vill centre appears to have been adjacent to the
        abbey (LVY 298).
6N76   *DENTONE*. A lost vill subsequently part of Low Abbotside township (DG 520).
6N77   BROUGH (HILL). PNNR 273 identifies DB *Borch* with Brough in Reeth township (in
        Swaledale), DG 514 with Aldbrough in Bainbridge township (in Wensleydale). Either is
        possible, as this section of DB deals with places in both Swaledale and Wensleydale.
        Aldbrough House is located at SD 9430 8961, ¾ mile south-east of Bainbridge, but if the

DG identification is correct, it seems more likely that *Borch* should be identified with Brough Hill, immediately to the east of Bainbridge. The *burh* referred to in the name is the Roman fort (possibly *Virosidum*; PNRB 506). As Bainbridge is not itself recorded in DB, it seems likely that the original name of the vill was *Borch*, named from the substantial Roman remains here, and that the name of the settlement, Bainbridge, subsequently displaced *Borch* as the vill name.

6N78 FORS (ABBEY). The DB vill of Fors subsequently became part of Low Abbotside township. The Cistercian abbey built within the vill was later moved to Jervaulx and the name Fors passed out of use (PNNR 260), but the name is still shown at SD 9368 9080 on the 6 in. OS map.

6N81 TUROT. PNDB 390 suggests that DB *Turot* represents an OE short form of one of the personal name compounds in *Thor-*, but it is more likely an AN -*ot* derivative (PNDB 125-6) of an OE name *Thor* (PNDB 390) or ON *Thorr* (SPN 295).

6N83 CROOKSBY (BARN). DG 519 Crooksby. The full modern name is Crooksby Barn on the 6 in. OS map at SD 980 851.

3 CARUCATES. *iii car.* for *iii carucatae* 'three carucates' is written above the line.

6N87 (CASTLE) BOLTON. DG 518 and PNNR 256 identify DB *Bodelton* with Castle Bolton (named from the castle built here in 1379), so also this edition. LVY 295, however, points out that *Bodelton* could be represented by the farm at Low Bolton (SE 041 909), medieval *East Bolton*.

6N88 BALD. The regularised West Saxon form for DB *Balt* would be OE *Beald* (PNDB 193), which has here been regularised to the OE Northumbrian form *Bald*.

6N89;92 THORESBY. The name of the DB vill survives at High Thoresby (SE 025 900) and Low Thoresby (SE 036 904), but the site of the original vill centre is located midway between them at SE 030 900 (LVY 306).

6N91 PRESTON UNDER SCAR. DG 532 Preston upon Scar. The correct name is Preston under Scar.

6N92 (EAST) WITTON and (WEST) WITTON. DG 520, 539 does not distinguish which *Witun* in this entry or in SN,CtA28 is East Witton and which West Witton. As the outliers recorded are all to the west of East Witton, an arbitrary decision has been made to ascribe the first *Witun* to East Witton and the second, i.e. one of the outliers, to West Witton.

12 CARUCATES. Including 2 carucates in Ulshaw (VCH 237, note 19).

OUTLIERS. See 1Y·19 note.

WENSLEY AND ANOTHER WENSLEY. Both here and in SN,CtA29 the two vills called *Wensley* are linked. There is today only one main settlement in Wensley township, suggesting that the two vills were subsequently amalgamated.

6N93 CARLTON. PNNR 253 Carlton in Coverdale. DG 517 and the modern OS maps have the shorter form Carlton used here.

THE SAME. DB *idem*. See 5E25 note.

6N95 THE SAME. DB *idem*. See 5E25 note.

6N100-1 WIUHOMARCH. This is likely to be the same man as the Wiuhomarch described in 6N57 as a man of Count Alan.

6N107 (WEST) HAUXWELL. On the shrunken vill centre see LVY 300.

6N111 *ASCAM*. A lost vill subsequently part of East Witton township (DG 514).

6N113 (HIGH) ELLINGTON. DG 521 Ellington. The full modern name is High Ellington.

6N114 'SWARTHORPE'. The name is no longer in use. The site of the original vill centre can be localised to the earthworks at SE 203 832 by the Tithe Award field-name *Swartrups* (LVY 307; PNNR 231-2).

INLAND OF MASHAM. Usually *inland* is written as a single word. Here, however, it is written as two words, *land* having a capital L (DF XXIX).

6N116 FEARBY. DB *Federbi* (DF XXIX). DG 521 erroneously *Fedebi*.

6N118 OUTLIERS. See 1Y19 note.

'TWISLEBROOK'. A lost vill subsequently part of Swinton township (near Masham) in Hang East Wapentake. The name does not appear on the 1st ed. 6 in. OS map (sheet 101), nor on the Swinton Tithe Award (PRO IR 29/42/362). PNNR 234 states that its original centre can be located fairly accurately from a 17th-century list of field-names, but unfortunately does not specify the archive source or give a grid reference.

6N119 CLIFTON (ON URE). DG 518 Clifton upon Ure, which is the name of the modern township, but the modern name of the vill centre is Clifton on Ure or Clifton Castle. On the shrunken vill centre see LVY 296.

6N120 OUTLIERS. See 1Y19 note.

(HIGH) BURTON. PNWR ii, 245 incorrectly identifies this *Burtone* with High Burton in Kirkheaton township in the WR, but it lies in the Honour of Richmond and earlier identifications with High Burton in Burton on Ure township are preferable (WYAS 420), although the earlier identification in PNNR 230 with Burton on Ure itself must also be considered (LVY 296; WYAS 420).

OPETONE. A lost vill subsequently part of Snape township (DG 531).

ACHEBI. A lost vill subsequently part of Snape township (DG 513).

6N121   FIRBY. On the shrunken vill centre see LVY 298.

6N125-6   THORNTON (WATLASS) and (THORNTON) WATLASS. DB *Torretun* (Thornton) and *Wadles* (Watlass) were separate DB vills amalgamated in the 13th century (PNNR 235). There is now only one major settlement called Thornton Watlass, but the occurrence of the names *Watlass Cover* (woodland) at SE 241 851 and Watlass Lane just to its north on the 1st ed. 6 in. OS map (sheet 85), suggest that Watlass lay to the south of Thornton. Watlass Moor, centred at SE 241 836, lies in Snape township.

6N127   THORP (PERROW). DG 536 Thorpe Perrow. The modern spelling of the name is Thorp Perrow. On the shrunken vill centre see LVY 307.

6N128   *THORNTON* (COWLING). In order to distinguish this Thornton from others in the NR, a manorial affix Cowling was added to the name. Eventually the original part of the double name was lost leaving the affix to serve as the place-name.

     EDWIN. It is possible that this could be Earl Edwin, who is named in earlier entries as a predecessor of Count Alan (6N1;52); see C36 note.

     ROBERT. This is likely to be the same man as the Robert described in 6N147 and 6N151 as a man of Count Alan.

6N129   IN LORDSHIP. See 5E10 note.

6N131   LANDRIC. An OG personal name (Forssner 173). This is likely to be the same man as the Landric described in 6N36 and 6N53 as a man of Count Alan.

6N135   HE HIMSELF HAS. i.e. Bodin.

6N136   3 SOLDIERS. *Milites* 'soldiers' is written above the line.

6N137   ... At this point part of the entry as originally written has been erased. From its location in the text it can be assumed that it was concerned with previous landholders, and the material was possibly inaccurate or copied wrongly. Farley represents the erasure simply as a blank, but is very precise as to its extent on each line (DF XXX).

6N139   (EAST) TANFIELD. See 5W38 note.

6N141   WOODLAND PASTURE. *Silva past.* for *silva pastilis* 'woodland pasture'. Farley makes a rare typographical error here, detaching the end *a* of *silva* to stand on its own.

6N142   HOWGRAVE. See 2W13 note.

6N148   YARNWICK. The modern 6 in. OS map marks 'medieval village of YARNWICK (site of)' at SE 314 817, in the area where the 1st ed. 6 in. OS map (sheet 86) shows foundations and earthworks (unnamed). The 1st ed. map shows Yarwick [*sic*] Garth just to the north-west of Kirklington. See also LVY 309.

     ROBERT. See 6N128 note.

6N149   *NORMANEBI*. A lost vill subsequently part of Carthorpe township (DG 531).

6N151   NEWTON ('PICOT'). DG 530 Newton Picot, but the name of the DB vill of *Neutone* only survives in the name of the township of Exelby, Leeming and Newton. The site of the original centre of the DB vill, later medieval *Newton Picot* or *Scabbed Newton* (PNNR 227), is uncertain, but is thought to be about SE 312 895 (LVY 304; YASI 4014).

     OUNESBI. A lost vill subsequently part of Gatenby township (DG 531).

     40 CARUCATES TAXABLE. There is an erasure between *Ounesbi* and *ad. gld.* for *ad geldum* 'taxable'. The scribe had, in fact, written *ad. gld.* twice, and half-erased the first one.

     40. The scribe originally wrote '32', which he then underlined to indicate cancellation, and wrote the correct figure, '40', above. In fact, however, 40 is not the correct total; the amounts add up to 40½.

6N152   (LOW) SWAINBY. DG 535 Swainby. The full modern name is Low Swainby, at SE 339 856, assumed in this edition to be the vill centre; the deserted site of Swainby Abbey is located at SE 336 855 (see also LVY 306).

6N153   ALLERTHORPE (HALL). DG 514 Allerthorpe. The full modern name is Allerthorpe Hall. This probably represents the site of the grange left when the priory established here in 1190 moved to Coverham in 1215 (LVY 294).

6N154   *SEUENETORP*. A lost vill subsequently part of Swainby township (DG 533).

6N155   THE COUNT HAS THEM. *Com. ht.* for *comes habet* 'the Count has [them]' is written above the line.

6N158   ROBERT. See 6N128 note.

6N160   *ASEBI*. A lost vill subsequently part of Baldersby township (DG 515; LVY 298).

6N161   TOGETHER 50 CARUCATES. This is the combined total from the last 9 manors inclusive. The correct total is 48 carucates.

6W2   OVERTON AND SKELTON. Listed in DB in the WR but subsequently in the NR.

	IN OVERTON AND SKELTON. See C32 note and C33 note. These entries here substantially repeat those in the earlier section.
	SKELTON. *Berew.* for *berewicus* 'outlier' is written above this place-name.
6W3	6S 8D. The 8d is written at the end of the following line.
6W4	STOCKTON (ON THE FOREST). Listed in DB in the WR but subsequently in the NR.
6W5	(GATE) FULFORD. Listed in DB in the WR but subsequently in the ER. See also C28 note. This entry substantially repeats the earlier one (C28).
	STILLINGFLEET. Listed in DB in the WR but subsequently in the ER.
	EAST RIDING. This is written below the last full line. It is in capitals in the text (DF XXXI).
6W6	CLIFTON. Listed in DB in the WR but subsequently in the NR. See also C30 note. This entry partly reproduces the earlier entry, except that here it gives only Count Alan's holdings. Between this entry and the next heading there are two lines which have been erased.
6E1	JURISDICTION. See 1Y8 note.
	('WATER') FULFORD. See C28 note.
	CHETELSTORP. A lost vill subsequently part of Escrick township (DG 470).
	LANGWITH (LODGE). DG 475 Langwith. The full modern name is Langwith Lodge, which has been used as the vill centre in this edition. The general area of the DB vill, which was subsequently subsumed into Heslington township, is indicated by the names Langwith Common (SE 663 477) and Langwith Great Wood (SE 652 471).
	MOREBY (HALL). DG 476 Moreby. The full modern name is Moreby Hall.
	15 CARUCATES LESS 1 BOVATE. The amounts add up to 17½ carucates and 5 bovates.
	4 FREEMEN. Thus DB (DF XXXI). Farley erroneously '3 freemen'. The initial stroke of the '4' (*iiii*) is very faint, which perhaps accounts for this error.
7E1	LAND OF ROBERT OF TOSNY. There is an 'f' to the upper left of the heading. It is not clear what it means. It is not reproduced by Farley.
8N1-2	KIRBY (MISPERTON). The three separate DB vills of *Chirchebi, alia Chirchebi* and *Mispeton* were subsequently amalgamated to form the township of Kirby Misperton (DG 526, 529; PNNR 75), the name by which the main settlement (SE 7792 7954) is now known. There is no evidence for the boundaries or approximate locations of the three component vills, so this grid reference has been used as the vill-centre location for all three.
8N1	LAND FOR 2 PLOUGHS. Throughout this section the scribe either omitted to enter the number of ploughs the land could support, or the information was not to hand. The information was therefore written into the text later, and is usually placed above the line at the point where the number of carucates is stated. Where there is room at the end of the line, for example East Ayton (8N11) and the following entries, the information is inserted there (DF XXXIII).
8N2-5	THE ABBOT. In the Summary the places listed here are also stated to be held by either the Abbot or by Berenger of Tosny with the Abbot holding from him (SN,D20; Ma1-2; 13; B2). It seems likely that the abbot concerned is the Abbot of York, rather than the Abbot of Selby, as the Abbot of York is named as holding from Berenger in 8N1 and the 'of York' was presumably just assumed in order to save time in following entries. Furthermore, all these places are in the NR, well removed from Selby and more likely to be held by the Abbot of York.
8N3	1 CARUCATE OF LAND. *tre.* for *terrae* 'of land' is written above the line.
8N5	*FORNETORP.* See 6N59 note.
8N6	MANOR. From this entry, and for the rest of the text, there is a marginal abbreviation indicating whether the land is a manor, jurisdiction or outlier, normally *M*, *S* and *B* respectively. These abbreviations were found above (fols. 300, 301, 302, 304), in part of the section on the King's land, and in part of the section on the Archbishop's land. There is no apparent reason why they should so suddenly recommence here, especially mid-way through a section.
8N7	*LEIDTORP.* A lost vill subsequently part of Wilton township in Pickering Lythe Wapentake (DG 527).
8N8	14S. In the text this amount is rather ill-written (DF XXXIII). The first stroke after the *x* in *xiiii* is at an angle, and it appears as if the scribe had been about to write *v* (which would have made the number 18, *xviii*), but left it as a single stroke to leave the number as *xiiii*. Farley reproduces this rather confusingly by amalgamating the *x* with a *v*.
8N9	(LOW) HUTTON. See 1N85 note.
	5½ CARUCATES. '½' is written above the line
8N10	HENDERSKELFE. The name of the DB vill survives as that of the township. The original vill centre (at SE 719 700), just to the north of the site of Henderskelfe Castle, has now been absorbed into the grounds and lakes of Castle Howard (LVY 300).

8N11-21   GAMALL. Named as the 1066 landholder in 8N11 and again in 8N21, where it is stated that 'he had all these lands', i.e. that he had held the places named in 8N12-20 for which no 1066 landholder is named individually.

8N14   'LITTLE MARISH'. DG 527 reports DB *in parvo Mersc* as Little Marish, but this name does not appear on the modern map, so has been taken here as lost. It is possible that Marishes Lodge may have been the vill centre for Loft Marishes vill (see 1N47 note), but it would be dangerous to assume that the Marishes Grange on the modern map (SE 864 793) could represent the vill centre for 'Little Marish', because on the 1st ed. 6 in. OS map (sheet 108), this is called Newstead Grange.

8N18   (NORTH) HOLME (HOUSE). See 1N72 note.

8N20   2 OXEN. See 1N7 note.

8N21   WIGANTHORPE (HALL). See 1N89 note.

8N23   LITTLE EDSTONE. On the shrunken vill centre see LVY 298.

8N23-8   THORBRANDR. Although no individual landholder is named in 8N24-7, it is obvious that the statement in 8N28 that Thorbrandr had these lands, applies to 8N24-8, not just to 8N28.

8N27   'WALTON'. A lost vill subsequently part of Welburn township in Ryedale Wapentake (PNNR 66)

8W1   LAND FOR 5 PLOUGHS. See 8N1 note.

8W2   CRAVEN. See 1W56 note.

8W3   BROUGHTON. This is written above the line.

8E1   BUCKTON (HOLMS). The original vill centre seems to have been located at SE 843 695 (YASI 10398), now called Kirk Hill.
LAND FOR 10 PLOUGHS. See 8N1 note.
CROOM (HOUSE). See 1E58 note.
COWLAM. See 1E60 note.

8E4   VALUE 10S. This is clearly current value, since *valet* 'it is worth' is present tense. When the previous value is given the form is normally *T.R.E. val.* for *tempore regis Edwardi valuit* 'in the time of King Edward it was worth'.

8E5   HEATHFIELD. DG 496 and PNWR v, 215 both identify DB *Higrefelt* with Heathfield in the northern part of the WR, although PNWR suggests some misgiving. *Higrefelt* is listed under the ER in this DB entry and it is possible that it represents a lost vill somewhere on the north-western Wolds where the other places given in this section are all located. In the absence, however, of any alternative identification, the DG attribution has been followed in this edition.

9W1   SKYRACK WAPENTAKE. See 5W1 note.
KIPPAX. On the estate of Ilbert de Lacy and his subsequent development of the castle and church at his manorial centre of Kippax see WYAS 212, 420, 735.
LEDSTON. It is possible that this entry refers only to that part of Ledston township which lay in the ecclesiastical parish of Kippax, and that the greater part of the township, which lay in Ledsham parish, is omitted (WYAS 425).
THREE CHURCHES. For discussion of the location of these three churches see WYAS 212.
(GREAT AND LITTLE) PRESTON. The DB vill of *Prestune* is now represented by the township of Great and Little Preston which contains two main settlements – Great Preston at SE 402 296 and Little Preston at SE 388 302 (see WYAS 383-4), and it is impossible to distinguish which may have been the main centre in 1086.
SWILLINGTON. Although there is now a village of Swillington, in the 19th century Swillington church stood in isolation and there was no main settlement in the township, which had a non-nucleated pattern of settlement. The grid reference given in the text for the vill centre is that of the church.
SKELTON (GRANGE). Skelton Grange (SE 332 313) is usually considered to be the centre of the Osmondthorpe hamlet division of Temple Newsam township. As Osmondthorpe is not recorded in DB, it seems likely that its territory was part of Skelton vill in 1086 (WYAS 530).
COLDCOTES. By the early 14th century Coldcotes had been subsumed into Seacroft township (WYAS 493-4). The area about the centre of the vill, now part of the suburbs of Leeds, is indicated by street-names such as Coldcotes Drive, Coldcotes Grove, Coldcotes Crescent, etc, centred on SE 335 348.
KIDDAL (HALL). DG 499 Kiddal. The full modern name is Kiddal Hall; on which see WYAS 317.
GIPTON. Now located within Potter Newton township, which is not mentioned in DB (WYAS 479-80), suggesting that Gipton may have been the earlier name for the township. The vill centre of Potter Newton has therefore been used as the grid reference for Gipton in the index.

PARLINGTON. The site of the depopulated lost vill centre has yet to be located. LVY 238 suggests that it was *c.* SE 422 360, but aerial photographs taken in 1974 show a bank running south-west from SE 4277 3617, which may be the southern boundary bank of the village, and medieval pottery has been found to its north-west at SE 4251 3605. It was probably depopulated between *c.*1770-1817 (WYAS 475).

CUFFORTH (COWTHWAITE). The DB vill of *Cuford* was subsequently part of Aberford township, with which it is probably to be equated, as Aberford does not occur in DB. The name survived in field-names until the 19th century, after which it was changed to Cowthwaite (WYAS 294).

9W4   SHIPPEN (HOUSE). DG 506 Shippen. The full modern name is Shippen House. The centre of the DB vill is represented by the shrunken settlement at SE 389 345 in the township of Barwick in Elmet (WYAS 319).

RALPH. There has been some discussion whether the Ralph named in this section as the undertenant of Ilbert de Lacy (9W4-5;46;54;58;140) was Ralph Paynel or Ralph Grammaticus, but it seems likely on charter evidence that it was Ralph Paynel (WYAS 525). The modern name Ralph represents the DB names *Radulf*, *Ranulf* and *Rannulf*.

9W5   40S. *sol.* for *solidi* 'shillings' is written at the end of the following line.

9W6-8   LEEDS, HEADINGLEY, SAXTON. These entries are written in cramped lettering at the foot of the page, the entries running across both columns. They were possibly added after the initial compilation of this section and therefore fitted in where there was room.

9W8   SAXTON. Recorded in Skyrack Wapentake in DB but in Barkston Ash in the Summary. 4 OUTLIERS. These were Stutton, Grimston Grange, Towton and Kirkby Wharfe (SW,Ba5).

¾ OF 1 CHURCH. VCH 244, note 7 suggests that this represents the advowson of three-fourths of the church of Kirkby Wharfe, one of the berewicks of Saxton.

9W11   NIVELUNG. The DB form *Niuelig* could be from either OG *Nivelung* or OG *Neveling* (PNDB 331). The former is used in this edition as being closer to the DB form.

9W12   10S. *x sol.* for *x solidi* '10 shillings' is written below the line.

9W13   BIRKBY (HILL). DG 487 Birkby. The full modern name is Birkby Hill.
'WHEATCROFT'. DB *Watecroft* lay somewhere in the ecclesiastical parish of Thorner, but its location has yet to be established. It is perhaps Roundhay Grange (SE 346 378) (WYAS 232).

9W14   6 CARUCATES. Including 2 carucates in Lofthouse (VCH 245, note 11).

9W15   COLTON. See 2N18 note.
A CHURCH. Whitkirk church (SE 3635 3357), situated within Colton hamlet (the successor to Colton vill) in Temple Newsam township (WYAS 529).

9W16   (TEMPLE) NEWSAM. LVY 238 locates the depopulated vill centre at *c.* SE 355 320, i.e. at the preceptory of the Templars at Temple Thorpe Farm to the south of Temple Newsam House, but WYAS 530 argues that it was at Newsam Green, whose grid reference has been used in this edition.

9W17   THORPE (STAPLETON). LVY 238 locates the shrunken vill centre at *c.* SE 350 310, pointing out that it has been absorbed by the expansion of Leeds. The original vill centre is in fact located to the south-west of this at SE 341 306 (WYAS 540), and is now part of the power-station complex.
GILBERT. DB *Gislebertus*, the latinised form of OG *Gislebert* (Forssner 115-16). The modern form Gilbert (from the OF variant *Gilbert*) has been used in this edition.

9W18   *SNITERTUN*. DG 507 reports DB *Snitertun* lost in Bingley township, relying presumably on earlier identifications of *Snitertun* with Priest Thorpe in Bingley township. This is now unacceptable (see WYAS 327-8). It is possible only to say that *Snitertun* must have lain in the eastern part of Skyrack Wapentake, and probably in the neighbourhood of Leeds (WYAS 233).

9W19   [BARKSTON ASH WAPENTAKE]. Although recorded under the general heading of Skyrack Wapentake (9W1), the places listed in 9W19-31 and 9W33 are given under Barkston Ash Wapentake in the Summary. On Barkston Ash see 5W6 note.
LEAD. The church of Lead is located in total isolation at SE 464 369, and this has been taken as the grid reference for the vill centre in the index. Although there is no documentary evidence that this was the vill centre (LVY 232), there are earthworks in the adjacent field. The name also survives in Low Lead (SE 468 376) and Lead Hall (SE 462 368).
WILLIAM. It is likely that the William of this and subsequent entries in this section is the same man as the William described in 9W2 as a man of Ilbert de Lacy.

9W20   BURTON (HALL). This entry is added at the head of the column. Although the name of the chief place is in capitals, it lacks the red underlining which the other entries have.
BURTON (HALL). DG 489 Burton, in Gateforth township. The full modern name is Burton Hall.

BRAYTON, THORPE WILLOUGHBY. *B.* for *berewicus* 'outlier' is written above these place-names.

9W21   *HUNCHILHUSE.* A lost vill subsequently part of Sherburn in Elmet (DG 498). Probably named from its tenant, Hunchil (i.e. Unnketill).
LAND FOR HALF A PLOUGH. *Tra. dim. car.* for *terra dimidiae carucae* 'land for half a plough' is written above the line.

9W22   LAND FOR HALF A PLOUGH. See 9W21 note.
THE SAME. *simil.* for *similiter* 'likewise', is written at the end of the following line.

9W23   (CHURCH AND LITTLE) FENTON. In the Middle Ages, Church Fenton and Little Fenton were separate townships. It is possible that the two at the time of DB formed one vill and were only subsequently split to form two townships. PNWR iv, 63 identifies DB *Fentun* with Church Fenton, whereas DG 494, followed here, identifies it with Church Fenton and Little Fenton, because it is impossible to distinguish which one is meant.
LAND FOR HALF A PLOUGH. See 9W21 note.

9W27   NEWTON ('WALLIS'). DB *Niuueton* was later subsumed into Ledsham township and came to be known as Newton 'Wallis'. The settlement of Newton 'Wallis' is now represented only by the ruined medieval moated house known as Newton Abbey (WYAS 424-5).

9W29   GRIMSTON (GRANGE). DG 495 Grimston. The full modern name is Grimston Grange (SE 489 417). This has been regarded here as the vill centre, but a possible alternative is Little Grimston (SE 484 417). No earthworks are visible (LVY 232).

9W31   *NIUUEHUSUM.* A lost vill subsequently part of Ulleskelf township (DG 502).

9W32   WHITWOOD. Recorded here under the heading Skyrack Wapentake, but under Agbrigg Wapentake in the Summary and also in 9W99.
WHITWOOD. As 9W20 note. There are more details on Whitwood in 9W99.

9W33   (NORTH) MILFORD (HALL). DG 503 North Milford. The full modern name is North Milford Hall (SE 505 395).

9W34   [STRAFFORTH WAPENTAKE]. Recorded here under the heading Skyrack Wapentake, but the places in this entry are under Strafforth in the Summary (see SW,Sf1 note). On Strafforth Wapentake see 5W8 note.
FRICKLEY. The original vill centre is now represented by the isolated church and hall (LVY 239).

9W35-64   [OSGOLDCROSS WAPENTAKE]. Recorded here under the heading Skyrack Wapentake, but the places in 9W35-64 are under Osgoldcross in the Summary. On Osgoldcross Wapentake see 5W31 note.

9W36   2½ CARUCATES. '½' is written above the line.
9W37;39   WILLIAM. See 9W19 note.
SKELLOW. PNWR ii, 34 gives the grid reference for Skellow as SE 10 52 in error for SE 52 10; the vill centre is at SE 530 103.

9W39   LAND FOR 3 PLOUGHS. *tra. iii car.* for *terra iii carucae* is written above the line.
9W41   'NEWSHAM'. DG 502 identifies DB *Neuuose* with Newsham, which it locates (DG map 61) to the east of Burghwallis, presumably in Roos townshp. No such name appears on the modern 6 in. OS map nor on the 1st ed. 6 in. OS map (sheets 264, 265), so it has been treated as lost in this edition.
SUTTON. DG 508 locates DB *Sutone* in Norton township (Osgoldcross Wapentake), but it is in fact a township in its own right just to the south of Norton.

9W43   HAMPHALL (STUBBS). Also known as Stubbs Hall. It would appear that Ilbert de Lacy's part of Hampole (DB *Honepole*: 10W32; SW,Sf28) included Stubbs, which was simply called *Hanepol* to distinguish it from Stubbs Walden which he also held (PNWR ii, 44). Subsequently it was known variously as Stubbs, Stubbs Hall or Hamphall Stubbs. On the shrunken vill centre see LVY 239.

9W45   ROGERTHORPE (MANOR). DG 505 Rogerthorpe. The full modern name is Rogerthorpe Manor.

9W47-8   (KIRK AND LITTLE) SMEATON. DB records just one vill of *Smedtone* where there are today two separate townships of Kirk Smeaton and Little Smeaton; the DB vill may have subsequently been divided into two. The two settlements of Kirk Smeaton (SE 520 166) and Little Smeaton (SE 522 168) are almost adjacent. As it is impossible to ascertain which was the original DB vill centre, both have been used in this edition. Alternatively, as *Smedtone* occurs in two successive entries, Kirk Smeaton may have been intended in one and Little Smeaton in the other.

9W48   5 MANORS. The scribe originally wrote '2' and then corrected it to '5' (DF XXXVII).
GAMALL, ULFKETILL, MORCAR. These names are written above the line.
9 CARUCATES. The scribe originally wrote *iii* (3), and then corrected it to *ix* (9). The abbreviation above is *ve.* for *novem* 'nine' (DF XXXVII), not, as Farley gives, *us.*

13 PLOUGHS. The scribe originally wrote what looks as if it might have been *vii* (7), and then altered it to *xiii* (13), by changing the original *v* into *x* and adding an extra stroke at the end.

9W50   STAPLETON. The vill centre is indicated by the place-name Stapleton Cottages at SE 514 197.

9W52   ACKWORTH. There are two main settlements in Ackworth township, of which the larger, High Ackworth, has been used for the grid reference for the vill centre in the index.

9W54   NOSTELL. DG 503 Nostell. The full modern name is Nostell Priory from the priory founded here in 1121 (PNWR ii, 91). Nostell vill subsequently became an extra-parochial area in Foulby township (WYAS 376).

        TWO CHURCHES. Those of Featherstone and Wragby (WYAS 212).

9W56   WHELDALE. On the shrunken vill centre see LVY 237.

        (WATER) FRYSTON. DG 494 reports DB *Fristone* as Ferry and Water Fryston, but it is in fact to be identified with Water Fryston alone (WYAS 372) which, together with Wheldale, was subsequently subsumed into Ferry Fryston township.

9W57   FERRY (FRYSTON). DG 494 reports DB *Fereia* as Ferrybridge, but it is in fact Ferry Fryston (WYAS 372).

9W61   ROALL (HALL). DG 505 Roall. The full modern name is Roall Hall.

9W64   TANSHELF. On the pre-Conquest royal manor of Tanshelf see WYAS 528. Subsequent to the Norman Conquest a number of new townships were created out of the territory of Tanshelf, including that of Pontefract, which usurped the status of Tanshelf. As Pontefract did not exist as a separate vill in 1086, the DB vill centre of Tanshelf was probably that of Pontefract itself (SE 458 221), whereas the centre of the later township of Tanshelf following the subdivision was located at SE 451 220 (WYAS 529). On the importance of Tanshelf see WYAS 190.

        16 CARUCATES. In the Summary these 16 carucates, together with the 2 carucates in Barnby Hall and 1½ carucates in Silkstone later in this entry, are assigned to the King (SW,015; SW,St1-2), who subsequently granted them to Ilbert de Lacy.

        ALMS OF THE POOR. This is presumably land to provide alms for the poor. In the Summary this is said to be 2 carucates.

        BARNBY (HALL). DG 486 Barnby. The full modern name is Barnby Hall.

9W65   STAINCROSS WAPENTAKE. See 5W32 note.

9W70   *CLACTONE*. A lost vill subsequently part of Oxspring township (DG 490).

9W71   PENISTONE. See 1W23 note. The King is said to hold this land in the list of the King's land (1W23) and no holder is given in the Summary (SW,St5).

        1 PLOUGH. The text reads literally *1 car. tre.* which is the normal abbreviation for *1 carucata terrae* '1 carucate of land', 'of land' being there to indicate that it is a carucate and not a plough. In this case, however, it is clearly a plough which is intended, and the *terrae* has been inserted in error.

9W73   DARTON. See 1W24 note; 9W71 note.

9W75   BEFORE 1066. The scribe wrote *To.R.E.* instead of the usual *T.R.E.*, *tempore regis Edwardi* 'in the time of King Edward'.

9W76   CARLTON. DG 489 reports this as located in Barnsley, but in fact it survives as an independent township in Staincross Wapentake.

9W78   JURISDICTION. Farley reproduces *soca* in upper case, although it has neither the equivalent of underlining nor is it written in capitals in the text (DF XXXIX).

9W79   STAINBOROUGH (CASTLE). DG 507 Stainborough. The full modern name is Stainborough Castle (SE 315 030). The name also survives in that of the township and in Stainborough Fold (SE 311 023) and Stainborough Lane Farm (SE 313 020).

9W80   KERESFORTH (HALL). DG 499 Keresforth. The full modern name is Keresforth Hall.

        5 CARUCATES TAXABLE. There is a gap between '5 carucates', and 'taxable', which is reproduced by Farley (DF XXXIX).

        1 VILLAGER. *un.* for *unus* 'one' is written above the line.

9W83   CHEVET. The vill centre of Chevet township is the deserted village of Chevet where there are now only earthworks. It was probably deserted as a result of emparking in the later 15th or early 16th century (WYAS 341; see also LVY 238).

9W84   (COLD) HIENDLEY. On the territory of the vill of Cold Hiendley, later part of the township of Havercroft with Cold Hiendley see WYAS 390.

9W85   HUNSHELF (HALL). DG 498 Hunshelf. The full modern name is Hunshelf Hall.

9W86   ALRIC. On the likelihood that Alric continued to have an interest in this holding, even though DB does not name the mesne tenant in 1086, see WYAS 354.

9W87   (UPPER AND LOWER) DENBY. DG 492 Denby (near Penistone), but on the modern map the township of Denby contains two settlements of the name – Upper Denby (SE 229

074) and Lower Denby (SE 238 075). WYAS 358 prefers to regard Upper Denby as the original vill centre, but as there is no proof of this, both names are used in this edition. 1½ PLOUGHS. '½' is written above the line.

9W88 (UPPER) CUMBERWORTH. See 1Y15 note. Farley correctly reproduces the gaps in the text on lines one and two (DF XXXIX).

9W91 (ROUGH)BIRCHWORTH. DG 505 erroneously attributes this entry of *Bercewrde* (fo. 317) to fo. 317b

9W94 AGBRIGG WAPENTAKE. Named from Agbrigg ('Aggi's bridge') at the eastern end of the wapentake at SE 351 194. The bridge over *Aggebriggbrook* was the wapentake meeting place (PNWR ii, 117). The wapentake comprises lower and middle Calderdale and the upland country south of Huddersfield (PNWR ii, 99).
METHLEY. There is no record of any medieval settlement known as Methley, the principal settlement in Methley township in the medieval and post-medieval periods having been Mickletown, whose grid reference is given in the index as the centre for Methley vill.

9W95 WILLIAM. See 9W19 note.
NOW THE SAME. *similiter* literally 'likewise' is written at the end of the following line.

9W96 'WESTERBY'. DB *Westrebi* is a lost vill listed in the Summary between Ackton and Normanton. It is possible that it is an earlier name for Altofts township (vill centre at SE 375 238: WYAS 303), which is located in the right general area and which is not recorded in DB, but this still awaits proof (WYAS 233).

9W99 VALUE. There is no obvious reason for the gap between *T.R.E.* for *tempore regis Edwardi* 'in the time of King Edward' and *val.* for *valuit* 'it was worth'. Farley correctly reproduces this gap (DF XL).

9W100 FLOCKTON. This entry probably refers to only part of the vill (WYAS 375).

9W101 (UPPER) DENBY. DG 492 Denby, in Upper Whitley township. The full modern name is Upper Denby. The grid reference given in the index for the vill centre is that for Upper Denby (SE 236 165), although this is by no means certain to be the original vill centre, as the establishment of Denby Grange in the late 12th century (WYAS 545) may have resulted in disruption of the previous settlement pattern; Lower Denby is situated at SE 240 168.

9W104 DALTON. According to a footnote in the Facsimile (DF XL) this entry was originally a marginal note which was obliterated with a solution of nutgall. The stain from this is still visible. The present text, which is fragmentary, is given by Farley (whose version is quoted in the footnote in the Facsimile). It can only be assumed that the entry was obliterated after Farley took his reading from it, but no explanation is given for this. See also Dalton at 9W117.

9W107 COLA. The DB form *Cola* could represent either OE *Cola* (PNDB 217) or ON *Kolr* (SPN 176-7). The OE form has been used in this edition as being closer to the DB form.

9W108 HOPTON. The DB vill of *Hoptone* was subsequently subsumed into Mirfield township. On the likely boundary between the DB vills of Mirfield and Hopton see WYAS 455.

9W110 BRADLEY. The DB vill of Bradley was subsequently subsumed into Huddersfield township, although it survived as a separate hamlet unit with its own boundaries (WYAS 408).

9W111- LINDLEY and QUARMBY. These two DB vills were subsequently amalgamated to form
12 the township of Lindley cum Quarmby, although their original boundaries survived as those of hamlets within the township (WYAS 430).

9W114 (SOUTH) CROSLAND. See 1Y15 note.

9W116 (LOWER) WHITLEY. On the territory of the DB vill of Lower Whitley see WYAS 441. There is no apparent reason for the irregular line beginning here, which Farley correctly reproduces (DF XL).
VALUE. There is no figure given for the current value.

9W117 DALTON. Cf. 9W104.

9W118 MORLEY WAPENTAKE. Named from Morley, although the wapentake meeting place may have been at Tingley at SE 281 261 at the cross-roads (PNWR ii, 175). The wapentake comprised the area of the Upper Calder valley, Bradford Dale and much of Airedale south of the Aire (PNWR iii, 1).
MORLEY. Although recorded in DB as lying in Morley Wapentake, some time after 1610 Morley township was transferred to Agbrigg Wapentake (PNWR ii, 99) and was thus not in the wapentake to which it had given its name. The vills recorded in 9W119-20 were also at a later date in Agbrigg Wapentake.

9W119 LOFTHOUSE, CARLTON. The DB vills of Lofthouse and Carlton were subsequently amalgamated to form the township of Lofthouse with Carlton. The original vill boundaries survived as those of hamlets within the new township (WYAS 438).

MIDDLETON. DG 501 locates it in Leeds township, but it is in fact a township in its own right in Agbrigg Wapentake.

24 CARUCATES AND 1 BOVATE. *1 bo.* for *1 bovata* '1 bovate' is written above the line. VCH 251, note 40 states that this included 3 carucates in Oulton and 3 carucates in Woodlesford, although without reference. The amounts held by Harold and others are written above their names. Since Harold and Barthr held 21½ carucates between them, the 21 bovates held by Alric and Steinulfr were the equivalent of 2½ carucates 1 bovate. This would make the carucate 8 bovates here.

HAROLD. The regularised OE form for DB *Harold* should be *Haraldr*, but as it is impossible to distinguish when the reference is definitely to Earl Harold and when not, the modern form Harold has been used throughout this edition.

HALLS THERE. On these see WYAS 196.

9W120   (EAST) ARDSLEY. DG 485 ascribes all entries in DB for *Erdeslauue* to East and West Ardsley jointly, but in fact the entries in 9W120 and SW,M1 relate to East Ardsley and the entry in SW,M12 relates to West Ardsley (WYAS 361, note 1).

9W121   REESTONES. The DB vill of *Ristone* subsequently came to be known as Wortley. The name survived in the field-names Long Reestones and Great Reestones recorded on the Tithe Award at SE 276 321 (WYAS 572).

9W123   BRAMLEY. DG 488 locates DB *Brameleia* in Leeds, but in fact it survived as an independent township until the 19th century (WYAS 334), when it became part of Armley township.

9W126   CALVERLEY, FARSLEY. The DB vills were subsequently amalgamated to form the township of Calverley with Farsley, although their original boundaries survived as those of hamlets within the township (WYAS 335).

9W129   GOMERSAL. The Summary ascribes the 14 carucates here to Gomersal and its two outliers (SW,M5); VCH 252, note 42 identifies the berewicks with 3 carucates in Heckmondwike and 3 carucates in Farnley, although without reference.

9W130   SIX OUTLIERS. The identity of the six berewicks is uncertain, although they almost certainly included the later townships of Horton and Manningham (WYAS 331). VCH 252 note 43 suggests that they were probably Haworth (4 bovates), Heaton (2 carucates), Horton (4 carucates), Idle (3 carucates), Manningham (6 bovates) and Oxenhope (1 carucate).

9W131   BOLTON. This large manor was later subsumed into the manor of Bradford (WYAS 330). This entry for the manor of Bolton is duplicated in 9W144.

CHELLOW (GRANGE). DG 490 Chellow. The full modern name is Chellow Grange. It is possible that Chellow is the original name for Heaton township, within which Chellow Grange is located, as Heaton is not recorded in DB (WYAS 397). Cf. 9W144 note.

WIBSEY. At an early date after this, Wibsey became part of North Bierley township. On the probable boundary between the two DB vills see WYAS 464.

ALLERTON. The exact vill centre of Allerton is uncertain, although it may have been at Allerton Lanes (WYAS 300).

9W134   (NORTH) BIERLEY. DG 487 Bierley. The full modern name is North Bierley.

9W138   MIRFIELD. See 9W108 note.

9W140   LIVERSEDGE. There is no record of any settlement called Liversedge. The principal settlement in the township is Hightown, whose grid reference has been given in the index as that for the vill centre.

9W142   3½ CARUCATES OF LAND. *tre.* for *terrae* 'of land' is written above the line.

9W143   (SOUTH)OWRAM. DG 503 reports DB *Overe* (9W143), *Oure* (SW,M10) and *Ufrun* (SW,M11) all as North and South Owram, but in fact *Overe/Oure*, held by Ilbert de Lacy, is Southowram and *Ufrun*, held by the King, is Northowram (WYAS 467,517).

9W144   CHELLOW (GRANGE). According to a footnote in the Facsimile (DF XLI), this entry was originally below Southowram, but was obliterated with a solution of nutgall. The stain can still be seen. Farley gives the present text, but his source is unclear. If the text was obliterated after Farley made his transcript, one apparent reason for the obliteration – that is that this entry was already present under Bolton near Bradford (9W131) – cannot hold. If, however, the obliteration was made before Farley transcribed his text, it is difficult to determine how he derived the text of this entry or that of Dalton (9W116). Apparently the text was partially obscured by Farley's day, from his handling of the place-name Wibsey *(Wi)betes(e)* as *(.)bet(.)es*. Compare 9W144 with 9W131 on this.

CHELLOW (GRANGE). See 9W131 note.

ALLERTON. See 9W131 note.

WIBSEY. See 9W131 note.

10W1   [STRAFFORTH WAPENTAKE]. See 5W8 note.

NEWHALL (GRANGE). DG 502 Newhall. The full modern name is Newhall Grange.

IN LORDSHIP. See 5E25 note.

10W2   24 [VILLAGERS]. There is obviously a word missed out after '24'. This is probably 'villagers', since people are listed by status in the same order throughout the text, villagers always come before smallholders.

10W3   DADSLEY. The DB vill name *Dadesleia* now only survives in that of Dadsley Well at SK 5890 9433 and of the adjacent Dadsley Well Farm, just under a mile to the north of Tickhill Castle (built by Roger de Busli). The manor of Dadsley, together with 57 other manors, formed his honour of Tickhill. As with Tanshelf *vis à vis* Pontefract (see 9W64 note), the main centre of Dadsley vill was probably in the vicinity of Tickhill and its castle; so the grid reference given for the vill centre in the index is that for the castle.

10W3-4   STAINTON, HELLABY. These two DB vills were subsequently amalgamated to form the township of Stainton with Hellaby, but Hellaby was later transferred to Bramley township (PNWR i, 135).

10W6   AESTAN. The DB form *Estan* could represent either ON *Steinn* (SPN 263) or OE *Aestan* (PNDB 182). The OE form is used in this edition as being closer to the DB form.

10W11   *GRIMESHOU*. DG 495 places the lost DB vill of *Grimeshou* in Rawmarsh township, but PNWR i, 210-11 prefers the vicinity of Grimesthorpe (SK 37 90) in Sheffield township. The latter would seem more acceptable on tenurial grounds because Roger de Busli held land in this area.

2 PLOUGHS. Thus DB (DF XLIII). Farley omits the number, as the plural verb shows.

10W12   WITH 3 PLOUGHS. The text literally reads *vi vill. et vi bord. cu. iii bord.* for *vi villani et vi bordarii cum iii bordarii* '6 villagers and 6 smallholders with 3 smallholders'. From the usual form of entries it can be inferred that this is a mistake and that the scribe repeated 'smallholders' in error. The normal form would give the number of ploughs these people held at this point, and that has been assumed here.

IN MALTBY. See 5E25 note.

10W13   3 [MANORS]. The '3' stands alone with no *M* for manors. The *M* was probably omitted accidentally. The '3' is very clear (DF XLIII), and there is no possibility that it was an ill-written *M* indicating the one manor only.

10W15   BILHAM (HOUSE). See 5W14 note.

10W16   ALMER. The regularised West Saxon form for DB *Elmar* would be OE *Almaer* (PNDB 147), which has here been regularised to the OE Northumbrian form *Almer*.

10W18   2 CARUCATES. It is supposed that the scribe has omitted *terrae* 'of land' after the first *car.*, taken for *carucatae* 'carucates', otherwise the text would read that 2 ploughs were taxable and two ploughs were possible, which is not the usual formula. See 1Y6 note.

10W19   JURISDICTION. See 1Y8 note.

TOFTES. Skaife 119 identifies *Toftes* with Altofts, but this is not possible as *Toftes* lay in the manor of Wombwell, so the DG 510 and PNWR i, 106 location of it somewhere in Wombwell township is to be preferred.

10W20   (HIGH) MELTON. Formerly known as Melton on the Hill (PNWR i, 76).

10W21   WILDTHORPE. A lost vill in Sprotbrough township. The name of the vill survives in the names Wildthorpe Field and Wildthorpe Cliff at *c.* SE 510 010 (LVY 240; PNWR i, 66).

10W29   ½ CARUCATE. *terrae* 'of land' is omitted after *car.* for *carucata* 'carucate'. The meaning is none the less quite clear. See 1Y6 note.

(SOUTH) BRAMWITH. Formerly known as *Sand Bramwith* (PNWR i, 13).

10W30   BARNBY (DUN). See 5W10 note.

10W31   12 SMALLHOLDERS ... There is a gap in the text immediately after this (DF XLIV).

10W32   HAMPOLE. See 9W43 note.

10W33   FRICKLEY. See 9W34 note.

STOTFOLD. See 5W18 note.

10W34   BRODSWORTH. The Summary ascribes the 5½ carucates here jointly to Brodsworth and Pickburn (SW,Sf29).

10W41-2   HALLAM. The DB vill name *Hallun* survives today in that of Hallam Head (SK 305 866), but there is little evidence for the existence of a settlement called Hallam in this area. It seems likely, as the manor measured 10 leagues by 8 leagues, that *Hallun* was a regional name, similar to the Hallamshire named from it (PNWR i, 101). It has been argued that Waltheof's hall was probably located on the site of the castle in Sheffield, which was part of the *inland* of Hallam manor (see further PNWR i, 194-5).

10W41   16 OUTLIERS. VCH 256, note 11 states that most of these may be tentatively identified by reference to the extents and rentals of Hallamshire, and that they probably included most of the hamlets of Midhope, Wightwizle, Bolsterstone, Oughtibridge, Onesacre, Bradfield, Wadsley, Owlerton, Stannington, Upperthorpe, Ecclesall, Heeley, Grimesthorpe, *Osgotthorpe* or *Osgerthorpe*, Skinnerthorpe, Brightside, Birley and Aldwark.

10W43   SCAWSBY. The present settlement of the name is located at SE 548 045, with Scawsby Hall to the west at SE 539 051. LVY 239 prefers the latter as the original vill centre, but

provides no proof that this was the case, so the grid reference of the present settlement
has been preferred in this edition.
BRODSWORTH. DG 489 omits to list this reference (fo. 320a) to *Brodesuurde*.

11E1 WELTON HUNDRED [CAVE HUNDRED]. Welton Hundred, named from Welton,
which was presumably the hundred meeting place (PNER 219), comprised the central
and southern parts of the later Hunsley Beacon Division of Harthill Wapentake (PNER
153). Although recorded here under Welton, the places in 11E1-6 are in fact given under
Cave Hundred in the Summary. This hundred was named from North Cave (PNER 224),
and comprised the western part of the Hunsley Beacon Division of Harthill Wapentake as
well as a detached part in the west of the Holme Beacon Division (PNER 153).

11E1 (NORTH) CAVE. On the former landholders see 5E42 note.
7 CARUCATES, 2 BOVATES. If the arithmetic is correct then the carucate in North
Cave was the equivalent of 8 bovates.

11E3 DREWTON. On the shrunken vill centre see LVY 60.

11E4 (KETTLE)THORPE. On the shrunken vill centre see LVY 64.

11E5 YOKEFLEET (GRANGE). DB *Iugufled* (DF XLVI). Farley erroneously *Jugufled*. See also
3Y1 note.

11E6-9 HOTHAM, HOUGHTON, SANCTON, BURNBY. These entries are written in the
margin.

11E6 HOTHAM, 1 CARUCATE. Thus DB (DF XLVI), Farley omits the '1', confusing it
(presumably) with the long tail of the initial *I* in *In*.

11E7 HOUGHTON. See 1Y6 note. In the Summary Houghton is listed under Weighton
Hundred (SE,Wei3).

11E8 SANCTON. In the Summary listed under Weighton Hundred.

11E9 BURNBY. In the Summary listed under Pocklington Hundred.
POCKLINGTON. DB *Poclinton* (DF XLVI). Farley erroneously *Poclintun*.

11N1 LANGBARGH WAPENTAKE. See 1N1 note.

11N3 (PINCHIN)THORPE (HALL). See 1N15 note.

11N4 THORARNA. The DB form *Turorne* could represent the ON female name *Thorarna* (SPN
300) or the ON male name *Thorormr* (SPN 313). The former has been used in this edition
as being closer to the DB form.

11N6 MARTON (IN CLEVELAND). See 1N25 note.

11N7 NEWHAM (HALL). See 1N26 note.
10S. *x sol.* for *x solidi* '10 shillings' is written at the end of the following line.

11N8 TOLLESBY. See 1N27 note.
MARTON (IN CLEVELAND). See 1N25 note.

11N9 ACKLAM. See 1N28 note.

11N11 THORNABY. DG 536 does not distinguish which *Tormozbi* of fol. 320b is which. From the
wapentake headings given in DB, the first entry must be Thornaby and the second
Thormanby.
1½ CARUCATES. Thus DB (DF XLVI). Farley erroneously 2½ carucates.

11N14 *MANESHOU* (RYEDALE) WAPENTAKE. See 1N58 note.

11N15 *BOLESFORDE* (BULMER) WAPENTAKE. See 1N85 note.
10S. See 11N9 note.

11N16 *GERLESTRE* (BIRDFORTH) WAPENTAKE. See 1N107 note.
THORMANBY. See 11N11 note.
GAMALL HAD ½ CARUCATE. *terrae* 'of land' is omitted after *car.*, *carucata* 'carucate'.
This does not alter the sense since the entry is clearly talking about land held in the vill.
See 1Y6 note.

11N18 *BERNEBI*. A lost vill subsequently part of Birdforth township (DG 516).

11N19 *HORENBODEBI*. A lost vill subsequently part of Hutton Sessay township (DG 524).

11N20 ALLERTON WAPENTAKE. See 1N113 note.

11N22 DALE (TOWN). See 1N136 note.

11N24 ... AND IN THESE 20 PLOUGHS. The first part of this sentence has been obliterated
(DF XLVI). It is impossible to tell to what it refers.

11W1 SKYRACK WAPENTAKE. See 5W1 note.
(EAST) CARLTON. DG 490 Carlton. The full modern name of the vill centre is East
Carlton; the township itself is simply Carlton.

11W2 (MIDDLE)THORPE. See 1W29 note.

11W2-4 (MIDDLE)THORPE, ACASTER (MALBIS), ACASTER (SELBY). Listed here under
Skyrack Wapentake, but recorded under Ainsty Wapentake in the Summary.
CHRIST CHURCH. VCH 303, note 31 identifies the references to Christ Church (11W2;
22W1-3; 22W5; SW,An1; SW,An8; SW,An13-14; SW,An16) as relating to the district
belonging to Holy Trinity, Micklegate, York, although does not state the basis for the

identification. Holy Trinity, Micklegate, was from 1089 to 1426 part of the Priory of the Holy Trinity, a cell of the Abbey of Marmoutier outside Tours.

NOW 3S. *m. iii s.* for *modo iii solidi* 'now 3 shillings' is written at the end of the following line.

12W1 [STRAFFORTH WAPENTAKE]. See 5W8 note.

JURISDICTION. See 1Y8 note.

BILHAM (HOUSE). See 5W14 note.

WILSIC (HALL). PNWR i, 131 reports DB *Wilseuuice* as Wilsick Hall, DG 512 as Wilsic; the correct modern name is Wilsic Hall.

AUGHTON (HALL). See 5W21 note.

TUDWORTH (GREEN). DG 510 Tudworth; the name now survives in those of Tudworth Hall (SE 689 109), Grange (SE 691 108) and Green (SE 687 102), the latter indexed as the vill centre here.

STREETTHORPE (EDENTHORPE). The name *Streetthorpe* was replaced in the 19th century by Edenthorpe (PNWR i, 22).

86 CARUCATES AND 15 ACRES. '15 acres' is written above the line. In the text after 'carucates' there were several words which were subsequently erased. This might be significant in that the Summary gives a different total for the land in this manor. As far as the figure given here is concerned, the individual amounts add up to 83 carucates and 23 bovates. If the final total is correct then 23 bovates make 3 carucates. This is almost 8 bovates to the carucate.

12W7 BILHAM (HOUSE). See 12W1 note.

12W8 WILSIC (HALL). See 12W1 note.

12W9 HARTHILL. This is called Harthill and Kiveton in the summary of soke-lands given above (12W1).

12W10 WOODLAND PASTURE. The amount of this is written at the end of the preceding line.

12W12 WOODLAND PASTURE. See 12W10 note.

12W14 WOODLAND PASTURE. See 12W10 note.

12W16 AUGHTON (HALL). See 5W21 note.

WOODLAND PASTURE. See 12W10 note.

12W17 WOODLAND PASTURE. The amount of this is written at the end of the succeeding line.

12W18 16 VILLAGERS. The text literally reads *i soch. et iii vill. et xvi vill.* for *i socheman et iiii villani et xvi villani* '1 freeholder and 4 villagers and 16 villagers'. It might be assumed that the second 'villagers' is a scribal error for smallholders, which class of tenants always follows 'villagers' in the list of tenants. There is no apparent reason why the scribe should distinguish 2 separate lots of villagers in this way, but it should be noted that the same formation is found in the entry for Fishlake (12W23). The same error either occurs twice, or the scribe did intend a distinction. If the latter, the reason for it is unknown.

12W19 WOODLAND PASTURE. See 12W17 note.

12W20 MARGINAL CROSS. This cross at the foot of 321b is there to show that the rest of the entries for William de Warenne's land which should have been inserted in column 321a, left blank at the end of Robert Malet's lands, should follow on from here. It is matched in 321a by an identical cross at the entry for Stainforth, the next entry (DF XLVII). In the MS these are upright crosses with dots between the arms (DF XLVII). Farley, however, reproduces them as saltires, although retaining the dots.

12W22 WOODLAND PASTURE. See 12W10 note.

12W23 7 VILLAGERS. This is possibly an error for 7 smallholders (see 12W18 note).

12W25 TUDWORTH (GREEN). See 12W1 note.

12W27 *STREETTHORPE* (EDENTHORPE). See 12W1 note.

13W3 HAZELWOOD (CASTLE). DG 496 Hazelwood. The full modern name is Hazelwood Castle. No earthworks are visible on the aerial photographs of the vill centre (LVY 232).

GAMALL AND ULFR. In the Claims (CW2) it is stated that in Hazelwood Castle there were 12 bovates of land of Gamall son of Asmundr's land, presumably to be equated with the Gamall of this entry, which would then leave 1 carucate 4 bovates for Ulfr. The Claims (CW2) also states that there was 1 carucate of land held by Arnketill and his brother; nowhere in the main text is Arnketill stated to hold land in Hazelwood Castle, and it is not at present possible to show that Ulfr was Arnketill's brother.

VALUE BEFORE 1066. There is no figure given in the text.

13W4 *SAXHALLA*. A lost vill, located in Lead township by DG 505 and in Tadcaster by PNWR iv, 76, which points out that in the Summary it is placed between Hazelwood and Stutton. P. Thornborrow has suggested to us (personal communication 15.5.85) that the place name Kettleman Bridge, *Ketilbarnbrigg* (1432) 'Ketilbjorn's bridge' (PNWR iv, 78), may preserve the name of the Ketill who was said to have held 1 carucate in *Saxhale* in 1066 (CW3). Kettleman Bridge (SE 492 424) is located in Tadcaster West township and so in the correct general area, but the lateness of the first date of recording of the place-name (1432) and the fact that *Ketill* and derivatives such as *Ketilbjorn* were popular names amongst the Anglo-Scandinavian population of Yorkshire should be borne in mind.

13W7   JURISDICTION. See 1Y8 note.

STEETON (HALL). DG 508 Steeton. The full modern name is Steeton Hall. On the depopulated settlement adjacent to the hall see LVY 232. It is surprising that the jurisdiction of Steeton Hall, which is in Ainsty Wapentake, should lie in Bolton upon Dearne in Strafforth Wapentake. The Summary records 1 carucate of land held by Earnwine in Steeton Hall (SW,Ån5), but no holding by William de Warenne, so this may be the same land as in 13W7. Steeton Hall occurs in the preceding entry in the Summary (SW,An4) together with Bolton Percy, and it is possible that the jurisdiction actually lay in Bolton Percy, not Bolton upon Dearne.

13W8   BARNBY (DUN). See 5W10 note.

13W9   (OLD) EDLINGTON. DG 493 Edlington, the name of the township. The full modern name of the vill centre is Old Edlington.

13W13 (PALLA)THORPE. See 5W35 note.

13W14 OUSTON (FARM). DG 503 Ouston. The full modern form of the name is Ouston Farm at SE 500 424. LVY 231 notes ridge and furrow adjacent to the farm, but incorrectly gives a grid reference of SE 500 415, which would put it south of the River Wharfe.

13W15 IN 'MALKTON'. This would appear to be a contradictory entry. The land would probably have been either waste or worth the same as before 1066. There is no way of determining which is the (apparent) error, although the lack of inhabitants would tend to suggest that it is the 20s. value in 1086 which is inappropriate.

'MALKTON'. DG 501 Malkton; PNWR iv, 240 as lost in Tadcaster East township. As no such name appears on the modern 6 in. OS map, nor on the 1st ed. 6 in. OS map (sheet 190), it has been treated as lost in this edition.

13W16 'HAGGENBY'. The lost DB vill of *Haghedenebi* is placed in Tadcaster East township by DG 496 and PNWR iv, 239, although LVY 233 puts it near *Easedike*. A map of 1636, however, shows a block of fields called *Hackerby* at SE 483 452 ('A plott and survey of Healaugh and Catterton', Leeds City Library HE/62), which places it in Healaugh township (we are grateful to Mr. B. J. D. Harrison and Mr. P. H. Thornborrow for this information).

ARNKETILL. In the Claims, the Arnketill holding land in 'Haggenby' is identified as Arnketill son of Ulfr (CW25).

3 CARUCATES. In the Summary this land is ascribed jointly to 'Haggenby' and Healaugh (SW,An7).

13W17 HORNINGTON (MANOR). DG 498 Hornington. The full modern name is now represented by Hornington Grange (SE 509 421) and Hornington Manor (SE 515 417) in Bolton Percy township (see also LVY 231). The manor has been used as vill centre in this edition.

GODFREY. The DB form *Godefrid* is the original OG form. The modern form Godfrey is used in this edition.

6 FURLONGS LONG AND 6 WIDE. The scribe originally omitted the 'and' sign. He therefore drew an oblique line between the word 'long' and the letter '6' (DF XLIX). Farley simply reproduces this as an 'and' sign.

13W19 'BURGHSHIRE' (CLARO) WAPENTAKE. See 5W36 note.

(GREAT AND LITTLE) RIBSTON. See 1W35 note.

13W20 MARKENFIELD (HALL). DG 501 Markingfield. The full modern name for the settlement is Markenfield Hall; that for the township is Markingfield Hall.

13W21 AISMUNDERBY. See 2W13 note. The medieval successor to the DB vill of *Asmundrebi* survived to be recorded on the 1st ed. 6 in. OS map (sheet 119), as the township of Aismunderby with Bondgate. Its territory has now become largely part of Littlethorpe township. The original vill centre, which is now depopulated (LVY 233), is located at SE 307 686, in Littlethorpe township (not in Ripon as erroneously stated in PNWR v, 168).

13W22 LEODWINE. PNDB 310 derives DB *Leduin* from the rare OE *Leodwine*, which has been followed here. DTL, however, points out that in Lincolnshire, DB *Leduinus* and DB *Leuuinus*, derived from the much more common *Leofwine*, appear to be variants of the name of the same man. It should therefore be borne in mind that this *Leduin* could have the same name as the *Leuuin* of 5E51, 5W33, 9W55 and 9W88.

13W24 2 PLOUGHS CAN BE. *car. poss. e.e.* for *carucae possunt esse* 'ploughs can be' is written at the end of the preceding line.

13W27 KEARBY (TOWN END). DG 498 Kearby. The full modern name is Kearby Town End.

13W28 'TIDOVER'. The DB vill of *Todoure* was subsequently subsumed into the township of Kirkby Overblow, but the name survived as Tetherfield late enough to be recorded on the Tithe Award map at SE 335 491 (Jones 49-53; PNWR v, 43).

WALTON (HEAD). DG 511 Walton, in Kirkby Overblow township, but the full modern name is Walton Head. This now only survives in the name of the lane running west from Kirkby Overblow, but on the 1st ed. 6 in. OS map (sheet 171), Walton Head is shown as an area extending from SE 301 508 to SE 315 508.

13W29 MANOR. The marginal heading is *M* for 'manor' although the entry in fact relates to jurisdiction.

BARROWBY (GRANGE). DG 486 Barrowby. The full modern name is Barrowby Grange, now in Kearby township.

13W31 PLOMPTON (HALL). DG 504 Plompton. The full modern name of the probable vill centre is Plompton Hall (SE 357 540).

13W32 'GREAT' BRAHAM. The differentiation between *Michelbram* ('Great' Braham) and *Litelbran* ('Little' Braham) is found only in DB, after which there was just one vill of Braham (PNWR v, 33). The vill centre is now represented only by Braham Hall in Spofforth township, which has been used as the vill centre for both in the index. This manor also included a moiety of Follifoot and Aketon (VCH 261, note 7).

13W34 *CRADEUUELLE*. A lost vill, location uncertain; listed here between Spofforth and Linton and later associated with Stockeld (Spofforth township), so probably located somewhere in the later township of Spofforth (PNWR v, 34). Skaife 134 identifies it with Stockeld Park.

13W35 BJORR. DB *Ber* could represent ON *Bjorn* or ON *Bjorr* (SPN 54). The latter has been used in this edition as being closer to the DB form.

13W37 IN WHIXLEY. See 5E25 note.

13W38 HALIKELD WAPENTAKE. See 5W38 note.

13W39 CRAVEN. See 1W56 note.

CROOKS (HOUSE). DG 492 Crooks. The full modern name is Crooks House.

(LITTLE) MIDDOP. DG 501 Middop, the name of the township. The full modern name for the vill centre is Little Middop.

STRATESERGUM. A lost vill subsequently part of Gisburn township (DG 508).

13W40 RAYGILL (MOSS). DG 504 Raygill. The full modern name is Raygill Moss, now in the township of Bolton by Bowland.

HOLME. DG 500 reports DB *Holme* as Long Holme (now Long Holme Row at SD 803 480 in Sawley township), but the earliest other recorded forms for Long Holme are 17th century according to PNWR vi, 183. PNWR vi, 186 identifies the DB vill with Holme (SD 7740 5283) in Bolton by Bowland township. In this entry it is linked with Bolton by Bowland and Raygill Moss, so the latter identification has been preferred.

13W45 *CHELDIS*. A lost vill which seems subsequently to have become part of Glusburn township (DG 490; PNWR vi, 18). Skaife 135 suggests that it might be identified with Malsis Hall in the adjacent township of Sutton, but this does now appear to be likely (PNWR vi, 26).

13E1 WEIGHTON HUNDRED. Named from Market Weighton (DB *Wicstun*), it comprised the eastern part of the later Holme Beacon Division and part of the Hunsley Beacon Division of Harthill Wapentake (PNER 153).

13E2 EASTHORPE. See 5E19 note.

13E3 KIPLING COTES. See 2E11 note.

JURISDICTION. See 5E25 note (DF L).

13E4 *SNECULFCROS* HUNDRED. Named from a lost place 'Snecolf's cross', presumably a cross at which the hundred met. It comprised the south-east part of the later Hunsley Beacon Division of Harthill Wapentake (PNER 153).

13E5 SCOREBY (MANOR). DG 479 Scoreby. The full modern name of the vill centre is Scoreby Manor, on which see LVY 68.

MANORS. *m* for *manerium* 'manor' is written above the first 3 personal names.

13E6 *IANULFESTORP*. A lost vill subsequently part of Dunnington township in Ouse and Derwent Wapentake (DG 474). DB *Ianulfestorp* (DF L). Farley erroneously *Janulfestorp*.

CLIFTON. In the NR.

1 PLOUGH POSSIBLE. *e.e.* for *esse* 'be' is written at the end of the following line.

13E9 WARTER HUNDRED. See 5E43 note.

13E10	POCKLINGTON HUNDRED. See 5E44 note.
13E15	*TURBAR* HUNDRED. See 5E55 note.
13E16	POCKTHORPE. The vill centre has now been depopulated but the earthworks are still clearly visible (LVY 66).
13N1	LANGBARGH WAPENTAKE. See 1N1 note.
	FYLING (OLD HALL). See 4N1 note.
13N3	*ARNODESTORP.* A lost vill subsequently part of Hinderwell township (DG 514).
13N4	MARSKE (BY THE SEA). PNNR 293 identifies the DB *Mersche* of this entry with Marske in Gilling West Wapentake, but as DB locates it in Langbargh Wapentake, the DG 528 identification with Marske by the Sea (see 4N2 note) in Langbargh East Wapentake is more likely to be correct.
13N5	*WESTLIDE* (KIRKLEATHAM). See 1N12 note.
13N6	MARSKE (BY THE SEA). See 4N2 note.
13N7	*DIC* (PICKERING LYTHE) WAPENTAKE. See 1N42 note.
13N8	KILLERBY (HALL). DG 526 Killerby, but the full modern name is Killerby Hall, in Cayton township. Only the hall and grange survive at the original vill centre (LVY 301). BLAEC. DB *Blac* could represent either ON *Blakkr* (SPN 56) or OE *Blaec* (PNDB 203); the latter has been used here as it is closer to the DB form. But note, however, that the Blakkr of 13N10, only two entries after this and also of 13N12 and 13N14, could be the same man.
13N9	4 PLOUGHS. Thus DB (DF LI). Farley misreads this as '3 ploughs'.
13N10	'THORPEFIELD'. DG 536 Thorpefield, near Scarborough, but the name does not appear on the modern 6 in. OS map nor on the 1st ed. 6 in. OS map (sheet 93), so it has been treated here as lost.
13N11	HILLGRIPS. The 1st ed. 6 in. OS map (sheet 93) shows Hillgrips Plantation at SE 999 867.
13N13	ST. HILDA'S LAND. Land belonging to the important religious house at Whitby, founded in the seventh century by St. Hilda.
13N15	'INGLETHWAITE'. The DB vill of *Inguluestuet* was subsequently subsumed into the township of Easingwold and the name is now lost (PNNR 25). Recorded here under *Dic* Wapentake but under Bulmer in the Summary. FULCHER. DB *Fulcher* (here and 23N29) is from either Old Danish/Old Swedish *Folkar* or OG *Fulcher* (PNDB 256); whereas DB *Fulcho, Fulco* and *Fulk* (10W27;33;39. 13W12; 13N14) are from OG *Fulco, Folco* (Forssner 98). In this edition the first has been regularised to *Fulcher* and the second group to *Fulco* (except for Fulk of Lisors, as this is the form in which his name is usually known to modern historians). It should, nevertheless, be appreciated that DB scribes were not always consistent in their renderings of personal names, and that the *Fulcher* of 13N15 could be the same person as the *Fulco* of 13W13 and 13N14.
13N16	*GERLESTRE* (BIRDFORTH) WAPENTAKE. See 1N107 note.
	BERGHEBI. A lost vill subsequently part of Topcliffe township (DG 516).
13N17	CRAKEHILL. On the shrunken vill centre see LVY 297. DALTON. DV *Deltunae* (DF LI). DG 519 erroneously *Deltune.*
13N18	RAINTON. The DB text reads *Ranevvat* ('Raegen's ford', from ON *vath* and the OE personal name *Raegen*) with *uel* ('or') *Rainincton* ('*tun* called after Raegen') superscribed, both names referring to Rainton (PNNR 184-5).
13N19	WULFGRIM. PNDB 399 derives DV *Vlgrim* from ON *Ulfgrimr*, but DTL has shown that a more likely derivation is from Continental Germanic *Wulfgrim*, which has been followed here.
14E1	LAND OF DROGO DE BEVRERE. There is no landholder numbered 14 in the DB text. In this edition the numbering has been maintained as a continuous sequence, but with the DB chapter number given in square brackets at the head of each page. OUTLIERS. See 1Y19 note. NUTHILL. On the depopulated vill centre see LVY 66. TOGETHER 4 CARUCATES. The correct addition is not 4 carucates, but 5 carucates 6 bovates. Throughout this section the addition is poor. [ ] PLOUGHS. The scribe omitted to enter the number. There is no gap in the text (DF LII). SKECKLING. The vill centre was depopulated, but was resettled in the 19th century (LVY 68). CAMERTON (HALL). DG 469 Camerton. The full modern name is Camerton Hall. The hall marks the site of the settlement, once larger than now (LVY 59).

(LELLEY) DYKE. On the depopulated vill centre see LVY 60.

14E2   KILNSEA. The settlement name Kilnsea is now located at TA 411 158, but the original vill centre is at TA 422 159.

13½ CARUCATES. The 'half' seems to have been added later. It is squashed at the end of the line.

IBI. Line 2, *Ibi* (DF LII). Farley omits the *I*. Although the letter is somewhat smudged, it is nevertheless clearly there.

ROOS 3C. [AND 3] AND ⅓ C. The scribe seems to have intended initially to write *et iii pars i car.*, *et tertia pars unius carucatae* 'one third of a carucate' above the 3 carucates. He began to write *iii* but crossed it out with a large zig-zag stroke and wrote the whole in the margin. Farley reproduces this stroke as a small *z* but does not make it clear that the scribe intended this as a deletion mark.

TANSTERNE. On the shrunken vill centre see LVY 68.

ETHERDWICK. On the shrunken vill centre see LVY 61.

RINGBROUGH. The present-day settlement of Ringbrough is situated at TA 272 373, adjacent to the original vill centre at TA 273 375, which has suffered considerably from coastal erosion (LVY 67).

FOSTUN. A lost vill subsequently part of Humbleton township (DG 472).

14E4   JURISDICTION. See 1Y8 note.

ANDREBI. A lost vill subsequently part of Roos township (DG 467).

DANTHORPE. See 2E31 note.

GRIMSTON. See 2E24 note.

(OW)THORNE. The present village of Owthorne, whose grid reference has been given for Owthorne in the index, is not actually in Owthorne township (see PNER 28).

REDMERE. DG 478 reports DB *Rotmare* as Redmere, Skaife 145 gives it as Redmere Field, and PNER 28 describes the name as 'local'. The name does not appear on the modern 6 in. OS map, nor on 1st ed. 6 in. OS map (sheets 242, 243), nor is it listed in the Tithe Award for Owthorne township (PRO IR 29/41/147), so it is not possible to give a grid reference although it obviously did survive as a field-name into modern times.

32 CARUCATES. The individual amounts total 23 carucates 25 bovates. This means that 25 bovates comprise 9 carucates, which would mean that the carucate contained only 2.75 bovates on average. This looks much too low, but if there is an error here it is impossible to tell where it would be. It also should be noted that the entries for Mappleton and Hornsea (14E5;7) suggest a similarly small carucate size.

14E5   JURISDICTION. See 1Y8 note.

ROLSTON. The form given on modern maps; also known as Rowlston (the form given in DG 479).

ARNESTORP. A lost vill subsequently part of Hatfield township (DG 467).

(LITTLE COWDEN). DB *Coldun* survives today in Little Cowden (TA 230 404) and Cowden Parva (TA 245 407), but neither of these represent the original vill centre. This was at TA 242 420 and has now been lost to the sea, as also was the church at Great Cowden *c.*1690.

14E6   GOXHILL. On the shrunken vill centre see LVY 62.

AND ¾ OF 1 BOVATE. *et iii parte. i bovatae, et tres partes unius bovatae* 'and ¾ of 1 bovate' is entered after the list of named soke lands, all of which have their individual amounts entered above the place-names. Exactly where this minute amount of land belongs is not clear.

26 CARUCATES. The totals given actually add up to 25 carucates, 2¾ bovates. If 26 carucates is correct, then 2¾ bovates make 1 carucate. This looks much too low, but compare it with Withernsea (14E4 note) and Hornsea (14E7 note).

14E7   JURISDICTION. See 1Y8 note.

(SOU)THORPE. The site of the depopulated settlement of Southorpe is located at TA 196 463 on the modern 2½ in. OS map (see also LVY 68).

(HIGH) SKIRLINGTON. DG 480 Skirlington. The full modern name is High Skirlington (TA 180 525), now in Atwick township (LVY 68).

11½ CARUCATES. The individual totals add up to 5½ carucates and 17 bovates. If 11½ carucates is correct then 17 bovates would make 6 carucates, which would give an average of 2.8 bovates to the carucate. This looks much too low, but compare it with Withernsea (14E4 note) and Mappleton (14E5 note).

14E8   CLEETON. The name Cleeton now applies to the eastern end of Skipsea village (at TA 169 552), but the original vill centre was at TA 182 550, now lost to the sea (LVY 59; PNER 82).

14E9   RINGBROUGH. See 14E2 note.

BALDWIN. This is likely to be the same man as the Baldwin described in 14E48 as the man of Drogo de Bevrere.

14E10 DIMLINGTON. DB *Dimelton* (DF pl LIII). DG 470 erroneously *Dimeltun*.
       VALUE. Presumably the figure here refers to both Easington and Dimlington.
14E11 JURISDICTION. See 1Y8 note.
       (SOUTH) SKIRLAUGH, DOWTHORPE (HALL). The scribe omitted to specify
       whether the lands of these places were carucates or bovates (DF LIII). Farley inserts *c.* for
       carucates. The matter is not resolvable through arithmetic since neither an assumption
       that they were carucates, nor an assumption that they were bovates, nor an assumption
       that one was carucates and the other bovates in whatever order, produces a total which
       agrees with the 41 carucates given by the scribe. Presumably Farley inserted carucates
       because they are said to be carucates in the Summary (SE,Hol16;17).
       TOTLEYS (FARM). DG 481 Totleys. The full modern name is Totleys Farm. The vill
       may have been absorbed into Burstwick township when the park was created (LVY 69).
       MEAUX. The original vill centre of Meaux prior to the estabishment of the abbey lay in
       the area around the later North Grange at TA 096 403 (LVY 64).
       BENNINGHOLME (HALL). DG 467 Benningholme. The full modern name of the vill
       centre is Benningholme Hall; the earthworks of the settlement are around the hall (LVY
       58).
       ROWTON (FARM). DG 479 Rowton. The full modern name is Rowton Farm. The
       deserted medieval site is on the opposite side of the road from the farm (LVY 67).
       DOWTHORPE (HALL). DG 471 Dowthorpe. The full modern name is Dowthorpe Hall.
       On the shrunken vill centre see LVY 60.
       FOSHAM. On the depopulated vill centre see LVY 61.
       BEWICK (HALL). DG 468 Bewick. The full modern name is Bewick Hall, in Aldbrough
       township. On the history of the vill see LVY 58.
       2 SMALLHOLDERS. Thus DB (DF LIII). Farley misreads this as '3 smallholders'.
14E12 WHO HAVE 3 PLOUGHS. Of this phrase only 'ploughs' can be read clearly in the
       Facsimile (DF LIII); 'who have' can be deduced from the text, but Farley's reasons for
       giving '3' are not clear.
14E14 ... PLOUGHS. The number is illegible (DF LIII).
       GUNNARR. The DB form *Gumar* is probably a scribal error for *Gunar*, the regularised
       form of which is ON *Gunnarr* (SPN 113).
14E15 (GREAT AND LITTLE) NEWSOME. DG 477 Newsome; but there are now settlements
       of Great Newsome (TA 308 265) and Little Newsome (TA 303 269). It is not possible to
       be certain which was the original vill centre (see also LVY 66, but note that the grid
       reference given there, TA 205 268, is incorrect).
       [9] VILLAGERS; [1] WIDE. The figures are illegible in the Facsimile (DF LIII). Farley
       gives them as 9 and 1 respectively.
14E16 BALDWIN. See 14E9 note.
14E18 REDMERE. See 14E4 note.
14E19 ODDI. The Claims (CE49) identify the Oddi holding land in Holmpton as Oddi the
       Priest.
14E19;22 WALTER. It is likely that this Walter is the man described in 14E42 as a man of Drogo de
       Bevrere.
       HWELP. DB *Welp* could represent either ON *Hvelpr* (SPN 147) or OE *Hwelp* (PNDB 297).
       The OE form is used in this edition as being close to the DB form.
14E19 AETHELSTAN. PNDB 153, 188 derives DB *Alestan* of this entry from OE *Aelfstan*,
       Aethelstan, **Ealdstan* or *Ealhstan* and the *Adestan* of 21W2 and CE48 from *Aethelstan*. As CE48
       is dealing with 8 carucates of land in Holmpton, as in this entry, the *Adestan* of that entry
       must be the same man as the *Alestan* of 14E19, so his name must be derived from
       Aethelstan. The probable development of the name was from a form of **Adel-, *Adle-stan* to
       Adestan/Alestan. This use of the two forms of the name for the same man is also found in
       DB Lincolnshire (DTL).
14E22 '(NOR)THORPE'. DG 477 reports DB *Torp* as Northorpe, which it locates (DG map
       57K8) off the southern coast of the ER and to the east of Easington. No such name
       appears on the 1st ed. 6 in. OS map (sheet 257), nor on the modern 6 in. OS map, so the
       name must be assumed to be lost. The only Northorpe given in PNER (65) is located in
       Hornsea township at TA 195 490, but the earliest recording given for this name is 1198
       when it was already *Nortorp*. In this entry and in the Summary (SE,Hol20) *Torp* is recorded
       in relation to places in both the South Hundred and the Middle Hundred of Holderness,
       so either location would be possible. In view of the uncertainty as to the identification,
       the DG ascription has been accepted in this edition.
       THORGAUTR. In this entry Thorgautr (DB *Turgot*) is named as the man who held these
       3 carucates before Drogo de Bevrere, whereas in the Claims (CE51) he is called
       Grimketill (DB *Grinchel*). Neither name is a by-name, so it is unlikely that the one man

was called both Thorgautr and Grimketill. Nor is the discrepancy likely to represent a change in tenants between the compilation of the main text and the Claims, as this is the 1066 landholder not the man in occupation in 1086. Possibly the land had changed hands about 1066 and so was known indiscriminately as that of Grimketill or of Thorgautr, although it should be noted that Thorgautr is in fact named as the 1066 holder of the land in Rysome Garth in the previous entry in the Claims (CE50) to that naming Grimketill. Alternatively one of the entries may represent a scribal error.

14E24   JURISDICTION. See 1Y8 note.
'WINKTON'. Depopulated in the 16th century; the site seems to have been lost to the sea (LVY 70; PNER 83).
(NUN)KEELING. On the depopulated vill centre see LVY 63.

14E27   EREMBALD. DB *Erenbald* represents OG *Erembald* (Forssner 77).

14E28   BALDWIN. See 14E9 note.

14E30   ARRAM. The depopulated vill centre of Arram lies near Arram Hall (LVY 57).

14E32   DROGO'S MAN. DB *homo Drogonis* (DF LIV). The word is written no differently here than the other entries on the page, but Farley prints Drogo with a lower case *d*.

14E33   CATFOSS (HALL). DG 469 Catfoss. The full modern name is Catfoss Hall.

14E35   *CHENECOL*. A lost vill subsequently part of Long Riston township (DG 470).

14E38   WASSAND (HALL). DG 482 Wassand. The full modern name is Wassand Hall.

14E41   LANGTHORPE (HALL). DG 475 Langthorpe. The full modern name is Langthorpe Hall.

14E42   DROGO'S MAN. The text literally reads *Walter. ht. Drg. ht.* for *Walterus habet Drogonis habet* 'Walter has [it] of Drogo has [it]'. The first *ht.* is clearly an error for *ho.*, *homo* 'man'. This is the common form throughout this section. With this reading the sense would then be 'Walter, Drogo's man, has'.
7 VILLAGERS. The text literally reads *viii vill. et vii vill.* for *viii villani et vii villani* '8 villagers and 7 villagers'. It can be assumed that the second *vill.* is an error for *bord.* for *bordarii* 'smallholders', who normally follow villagers in the list of tenants. Note, however, that a similar form is found in Warmsworth and Fishlake (12W18; 12W23).

14E43   FRANI. The Claims identify the holder of the land in Ellerby as Frani son of Thorr (CE41), and there he alone is said to hold the 4 carucates listed here.
MAN. DB *Man* could represent either ON *Man* (SPN 194) or OE *Mann* (PNDB 324). The ON form is used in this edition as it is the same as the DB spelling.

14E44   FRUMOLD. An OG masculine personal name (Forstemann 546). Note that Forssner 96 erroneously gives the name as *Frumond* not *Frumold*.

14E45   ALBERT. An OG masculine personal name of the same form as the modern name (Forssner 19).

14E48   FRANI. The Claims identify the holders of 16 carucates of land in Preston (although only 10 carucates 2 bovates are given here) as Frani and his brother (CE45), so one of the other men named here was probably Frani's brother.
MACCUS. DB *Macus* could represent either ON *Magnus* (SPN 192) or Old Irish *Maccus* (PNDB 323). In Ireland this is also the form taken by ON *Magnus*, so the DB *Macus* could have been a Scandinavian who had been named in Ireland. The Old Irish form is used in this edition as being closer to the DB form.

14E49   SOUTHCOATES. See 2E35 note.
ODDI. DB *Ote* could represent either ON *Oddi* or ON *Otti* (SPN 202, 208). It is, however, stated in the Claims regarding this land in Southcoates that the land had belonged to *Ode* (i.e. Oddi) the Deacon (CE52), so the form concerned here is Oddi; and 'the Deacon' is understood after his name.

14E54   WILSTHORPE. There is no obvious reason for the different layout of this entry. See also 1Y11 note.
CLEETON. See 14E8 note.

15E1   HESSLE HUNDRED. Named from Hessle (PNER 215). It comprised the southern part of the later Hunsley Beacon Division of Harthill Wapentake together with a detached part of the south of the Holme Beacon Division (PNER 153).

15E2   OUTLIERS. See 1Y19 note.
WAULDBY. See 2B3 note.
RIPLINGHAM. The earthworks of the depopulated vill centre are still visible (LVY 67).
TOTFLED. A lost vill subsequently part of Hull township (DG 481).
'MYTON'. A lost vill subsequently part of Hull township (PNER 213). The name survives today in the Hull street-name Myton Gate 'street leading to Myton' (PNER 211).
6½ CARUCATES. Since the amounts given add up to 5 carucates and 12 bovates it can be assumed that 8 bovates make 1 carucate.
HESSLE. The second mention of this place is written in minuscules (DF LV), correctly reproduced by Farley.

15E3	OF THIS LAND. *de hac terra* 'of this land' is written above the line.
	JURISDICTION. See 1Y8 note.
	WRESSLE. DG 483 Wressell. The modern spelling of the name is Wressle.
15E5	LUND. See 3Y2 note.
15E6	FOGGATHORPE. Recorded under Hessle Hundred here but under Cave Hundred in the Summary.
	JURISDICTION. See 1Y8 note.
15E7	*CHETELESTORP*. A lost vill subsequently part of Storwood township (DG 470). DB *Chetelestorp* (DF LV). DG 470 erroneously *Chetelstorp*.
	WASTE. This is written at the end of the preceding line.
15E8-9	MELBOURNE, THORNTON. Recorded here under Hessle Hundred, but under Cave Hundred in the Summary.
15E10	*SCARD* HUNDRED. See 5E58 note.
15E11	SUTTON (GRANGE). See 1E37 note.
15E12	WITH 6 PLOUGHS. *cu. vi car.* for *cum vi carucis* 'with 6 ploughs' is written on the line below, which is the last line of the page (DF LVI).
15E14	KNAPTON. DB *Cnapeton* (DF LVI). DG 475 erroneously *Cnateton*.
15E14-15	KNAPTON, THIRKLEBY (MANOR). Recorded here under *Scard* Hundred, but under Cave Hundred in the Summary.
15E15	THIRKLEBY (MANOR). See 2B18 note; SE,Th5 note.
15E16	DALBY. Although recorded here under *Scard* Hundred in the ER, Dalby is in the NR and is recorded under Bulmer Wapentake in the Summary.
15E17	GILLING (EAST). Although recorded here under *Scard* Hundred in the ER, Gilling East is in the NR and is recorded under *Manshowe* Wapentake in the Summary.
16E1	IN THORGANBY. There is an 'f' in the margin to the left of the entry. It is not clear what it means. It is not reproduced by Farley.
16E4	NEWTON. On the depopulated vill centre see LVY 65.
	1½ LEAGUES LONG. '½' is written above the line. There are gaps in the text on lines 2 and 3 (DF LVI). Farley reproduces the first of these but not the second, which occurs between *val* for *valuit* 'it was worth' and '£4'.
16N1	JURISDICTION. See 1Y8 note.
	(EAST) NESS. DG 529 Ness Hall. The hall (SE 695 789) is located immediately to the west of the settlement of East Ness (SE 696 788), with West Ness just to the west again at SE 688 792. As the settlement-name East Ness is the same as that of the township (see further PNNR 51), this has been regarded in this edition as the vill centre.
	10 CARUCATES. If the addition here is correct, 8 bovates make 1 carucate.
16N2	*TORESBI*. A lost vill subsequently part of Newton upon Ouse township (DG 537).
16W1	DRAX. Place-names which are the main subject of the entry are normally written in capitals with the equivalent of underlining. In this case Drax is not (DF LVI). Farley correctly shows this.
16W2	(GREAT AND LITTLE) RIBSTON. See 1W35 note.
16W5	(KIRK AND NORTH) DEIGHTON. DG 492 puts all the DB *Distone* forms (16W5; 24W20; SW,Bu43) together under Kirk Deighton and North Deighton, although in the Middle Ages these were separate townships (PNWR v, 23, 25). It may be that some of the DB references are to Kirk Deighton and some to North Deighton, but this cannot be determined at present.
16W6	THORPE (UNDERWOOD). The inhabitants of the vill centre were removed in 1175 when a grange of Fountains Abbey was established there (LVY 236).
18W3	TWO WIGHILLS. DG 512 suggests that the two Wighills are Wighill itself (SE 475 469) and Wighill Park (SE 468 486).
19W1;3	THORIR. PNDB 393 and SPN 307-9 derive DB *Tori* of 19W1 from ON *Thorir* or a side-form, *Thori*, while DB *Stori* of 19W3 should derive from ON *Stori*. DTL has shown, however, that these two entries must refer to the same man. Either an inorganic initial *S*- was prefixed to an AN *Tori*, derived from an original *Thorir*, to give the form in 19W3, or else in 19W1 the more common name *Tori* has been substituted for the rare *Stori*. As DTL argues that the former is the more likely, the form *Thorir* has been used in this edition.
19W2	*TOFTES*. See 10W10 note.
20E3	*RICSTORP*. A lost vill subsequently part of Muston township (DG 478).
	JURISDICTION. See 1Y8 note.
	SCOLFSTONA. A lost vill subsequently part of Muston township (DG 479).
	(EAST AND WEST) FLOTMANBY. See 2E3 note.
	14 CARUCATES. The correct addition is 13 carucates.
21E4	*CHRACHETORP*. A lost vill subsequently part of Hessle township (DG 470).
21E5	WRESSLE. See 15E3 note.
	SIUUARBI. A lost vill subsequently part of Wressle township (DG 479).

LUND. See 3Y2 note.

TO THE SAME MANOR BELONGS ANOTHER (JURISDICTION). Literally *ad eund. m. p.tinet alia* for *ad eundum manerium pertinet alia* 'to the same manor belongs another'. There is no subject noun and the substantive adjective requires a nominative singular feminine antecedent, *soca*. Since the text says 'other', it might be assumed that this is other jurisdiction, since *alia* also agrees with *soca* 'jurisdiction'. However, the marginal heading *M. & B.* for *manerium et berwicus/i* 'manor and outlier/s' implies that there ought to be some outlier/s listed as part of the entry. For *alia* to be appropriate 'outlier' would need to be neuter, *berewicum* (which is unusual, though not impossible, as it is given in the text variously as masculine and feminine), and it would have to be plural. The amounts of land concerned are given above the place-names.

21E6 GUNBY. On the shrunken vill centre see LVY 63.

21E9 HOLME (UPON SPALDING MOOR). The present village of the name is situated at SE 804 383, but the church at SE 820 389 is more likely to be on the original settlement site, as the area was formerly very marshy and Church Hill would have provided a well-drained site. Moreover the *holmr* of the name of the vill (PNER 234) clearly refers to the island formed by the hill in the marshland.

21E11 HOUGHTON.See 1Y6 note.
½ CARUCATE. *terrae* 'of land' is omitted after *car.* for *carucata* 'carucate'. It is obviously an amount of land which is intended, however, since the entry goes on to say how many ploughs it could support. See 1Y6 note.

21E12 THORPE (LE STREET). See 1Y7 note.

21W4 BEAMSLEY. The mark ⱱ before this entry indicates that it is intended to stand separately. However, it has not got the equivalent of underlining, which most individual entries have.
BEAMSLEY. DB *Bomeslai* (DF LVIII). DG 486 erroneously *Bemeslai*.

21W5 ADDINGHAM. See 1W46 note.

21W7 BRIMHAM (HALL). DG 488 Brimham. The full modern name is Brimham Hall.

21W9 BECKWITH (HOUSE). There is now no settlement called Beckwith, although the name survives in that of Beckwith House at SE 280 524 and as an area name on the 6 in. OS map extending from SE 280 520 to SE 282 523 and centred on SE 281 522; the church is situated at Beckwithshaw at SE 268 531 with Beckwith Head at SE 281 529.

21W10 ROSSET (GREEN). See 1W52 note.

21W11 PAYS 3S. *redd.* is repeated twice in this sentence. Depending on whether it is used as a noun or a verb (see 5E23 note), this either reads *reddit 3s redditum* 'pays 3s rent', which leaves the word 'rent' rather superfluous, or else it is simple scribal error, the word *reddit* 'it pays' being duplicated unnecessarily.

21W13 PLOMPTON (HALL). See 13W31 note.

21W14 'GREAT' BRAHAM. See 13W32 note.

21W15 CRAVEN. See 1W56 note.
GRASSINGTON. None of the names in Craven have the equivalent of underlining, and the amounts of land are all written above the relevant place-names.
EASTBURN, STEETON. By the late 13th century these two DB vills had been amalgamated to form the combined township of Steeton with Eastburn. The original boundary between them may have been Steeton Beck (WYAS 524).
GILBERT TISON. *Tison* is written above the line.

21W16 *CHELCHIS.* See 13W45 note.
3 CARUCATES. *terrae* 'of land' is omitted after *car.* for *carucata* 'carucate'. However, there is no reason to believe that the scribe has suddenly stopped recording amounts of land held, and for this one entry alone records the holding in terms of ploughs. See 1Y6 note.

21W17 OAKWORTH. See 1W66 note.
1 CARUCATE. As above, 21W16 note.

22W1 [AINSTY WAPENTAKE]. See 5W35 note.
(MIDDLE)THORPE. See 1W29 note.

22W1-3 CHRIST CHURCH. See 11W2 note. In these entries and 22W5 the Latin is sometimes a nominative *christi ecclesia* and sometimes a genitive *christi ecclesiae*, as if a manorial affix to the place-name.

22W3 9 CARUCATES. *terrae* 'of land' is omitted after *car.* for *caruata* 'carucate'. An amount of land is obviously intended since the entry goes on to record how many ploughs it could support. See 1Y6 note.
6 FURLONGS (LEAGUES) LONG. 'leagues' is added after 'furlongs' (DF LIX). Obviously it is either one or the other, and 'leagues' is most likely to be the error, since the manor could not contain such an amount of woodland pasture within its stated extent.

	NOW 20S. *xx sol.* for *xx solidi* '20s.' is written at the end of the following line.
22W4	2 CARUCATES. As 22W3 note.
22W5	CHRIST CHURCH. See 11W2 note; 22W1-3 note.
	3 CARUCATES. As 22W3 note.
22W6	½ A CARUCATE. As 22W3 note.
23N1	WEST RIDING. Although this section is headed 'West Riding' in DB, all the places listed are in fact in the NR, as is indicated by the wapentake subheading, so it has been numbered 23N not 23W.
	GERLESTRE (BIRDFORTH) WAPENTAKE. See 1N107 note. This rubric heading is as inaccurate as that of the riding, for in the Summary, Ampleforth (23N1), Cawton (23N4), Walton (23N20), Harome, Nawton, Great Barugh, Normanby, Ryton and Little Barugh (all 23N21) are recorded as being in *Manshowe* Wapentake; Kepwick (23N8), Ravensthorpe Manor (23N12), Cowesby (23N15) and Ellerbeck (23N16) are in Allerton Wapentake, Crunkly Gill (23N17), Danby, Lealholm, Great Broughton and *Camisedale* (all 23N18) are in Langbargh Wapentake, Welburn (23N21) is in Bulmer and Marton (23N21) is in *Dic.*
	IN *IRETONE*. The amounts of land in the vills are entered above the relevant place-names.
	IRETONE. A lost vill, which DG 525 suggests subsequently became part of Thornton on the Hill, whereas PNNR 193 places it in Yearsley. There is insufficient evidence on which to make a definite ascription.
	OSGOODBY (HALL). DG 531 Osgoodby. The full modern name is Osgoodby Hall.
23N1	BAXBY. See 2N13 note.
	20 CARUCATES LESS 1 BOVATE. If the addition is correct the carucate here is the equivalent of 7 bovates.
23N3	WILDON (GRANGE). DG 539 Wildon. The full modern name is Wildon Grange.
23N4	GERARD. This is likely to be the same man as the Gerard described in 23N9-11;13;15-16 as a man of Hugh son of Baldric.
23N6	THORPE(FIELD). On the identification of this vill see DGNE 488.
	NEWSHAM. See 1N110 note. DB *Neuhusu.* (DF LIX). Farley correctly expands to *Neuhusum*; DG 530 *Neuhusu*, omitting the abbreviation mark.
23N8	OUTLIERS. See 1Y19 note.
	KIRBY (KNOWLE). DG 526 Kirkby Knowle. The modern spelling of the name of both the settlement and the township is Kirby Knowle.
	ISLEBECK (GRANGE). DG 525 Islebeck. The full modern name of the settlement, now in Sessay township, is Islebeck Grange, representing a grange of Byland Abbey (LVY 301). The Isle Beck stream forms the southern boundary between the townships of Sessay and Dalton.
	SUTTON (UNDER WHITESTONE CLIFFE). DG 535 Sutton under Whitestone Cliff. The modern spelling of the name is Sutton under Whitestone Cliffe.
	ARDEN (HALL). DG 514 Arden, the name of the township. The full modern name of the vill centre is Arden Hall.
23N9-11	GERARD. See 23N4 note.
23N10	MARDERBY (HALL). DG 528 Marderby. The full modern name is Marderby Hall; the settlement at the vill centre had been depopulated by the early 16th century (LVY 303).
	WITHOUT PASTURE. *sine* 'without' is written above the line.
23N11-12	*FRIDEBI* (FELIXKIRK). DG 522 reports DB *Fridebi* as lost in Felixkirk, but PNNR 199 suggests that *Fridebi* may have been the earlier name for Felixkirk.
23N12	RAVENSTHORPE (MANOR). See 1Y2 note.
23N13	AND NOW [.?.]. The text simply reads *T.R.E. val. xx sol. et m.*, *tempore regis Edwardi valuit xx solidi et modo* 'value before 1066 20s. and now'. A figure representing the 1086 value has possibly been omitted, but the text may have been intended to read 'value before 1066 20s., now also'.
23N13; 15;17	GERARD. See 23N4 note.
23N17	HUGH SON OF BALDRIC. *F B* for *filius Baldrici* 'son of Baldric' is written above Hugh's name.
23N17-18	IN CRUNKLY (GILL). The entry for this manor is duplicated in 23N34-5.
23N18	DANBY. The present settlement of the name is located at NZ 707 084, but LVY 297 places the original depopulated vill centre adjacent to the now-isolated church at NZ 696 062.
	LEALHOLM. DG 526 Lealholme. The correct modern spelling is Lealholm.
	(GREAT) BROUGHTON. See 1N36 note.

(GREAT) BROUGHTON. Ill-written in the text. DB *Brocastvn* (DF LX). Farley erroneously *Broctun*.

CAMISEDALE. See 1N35 note.

23N19-21 KIRBY (MOORSIDE). DG 526 Kirkby Moorside, the spelling of the name of the township. The name of the vill centre is spelt Kirkby Moorside.

23N19 HUGH SON OF BALDRIC. See 23N17 note.

A PRIEST AND A CHURCH. The church concerned is situated not in Kirby Moorside itself but at Kirkdale, where the church had 1 carucate of land geld-free (VCH 275, note 7). St. Gregory's Minster, Kirkdale, is an important surviving Anglo-Saxon church (Taylor & Taylor 357-61). A carved panel set in the south wall above the doorway states that 'Ormr son of Gamall (*ORM GAMAL SVNA*) bought St. Gregory's Minster when it was completely broken and collapsed, and had it built anew from the ground to Christ and St. Gregory in the days of Edward the King and the days of Tosti the Earl', thus dating it to A.D. 1055-65, when Tosti was Earl of Northumbria. The Ormr son of Gamall will be the Ormr of this entry.

23N20 'WALTON'. See 8N27 note.

'HOVETON'. DG 525 Hoveton, but no such place appears on the modern 6 in. OS map and PNNR 66 gives no forms subsequent to the 13th century, so the name has been treated here as lost. LVY 300 locates it at *c.* SE 675 860 based on the description in the *Rievaulx Cartulary.*

23N21 *MIDDLEHAM.* A lost vill subsequently part of Muscoates township (DG 528).

MISPERTON. See 8N1 note.

27½ CARUCATES. *terrae* 'of land' is omitted after *car.* for *carucata* 'carucates'. It is obviously an amount of land which is intended as the entry goes on to state how many ploughs it could support.

23N22 CRAVEN. This is written at the end of the last line of the previous entry (23N21). See 1W56 note. This rubric heading applies only to the first entry, after which the text returns to the NR.

HOLKER AND BIRKBY (HALL). Both these places are in Lancashire (see 1W70 note), and this section has also been published in DB Cheshire Y9. These two places form a totally detached portion of Craven, some 30 miles to the north-west of the rest of Craven.

BIRKBY (HALL). The name of the DB vill survives in Middle Birkby at SD 374 774 and Lower Birkby at SD 377 779, but Professor G. R. J. Jones informs us that the original vill centre is located at Birkby Hall at SD 376 771.

23N23 HUGH SON OF BALDRIC. See 23N17 note.

23N24 WATH. On the shrunken vill centre see LVY 308.

HOWTHORPE (FARM). DG 525 Howthorpe. The full modern name is Howthorpe Farm, the sole survivor of the original medieval vill centre (LVY 300).

HAWADE. A lost vill perhaps subsequently part of Wath township. As the name Wath (ON *vath* 'ford') refers to the point where the Roman road crossed the Wath Beck, and *Hawade* (ON *har vath*) means 'high ford', it has been suggested (PNNR 52) that the name refers to a ford in Wath Wood higher up Wath Beck (centred *c.* SE 671 742).

GRIMSTON. DG 523 Grimston, the name of the township. The identification of the vill centre is problematical. LVY 299 suggests that it might have been located *c.* SE 604 740, i.e. at Grimston Grange, although in the absence of earthworks, Grimston Manor (SE 619 751) might be an equally valid candidate.

(EAST) NESS. See 16N1 note.

WOODLAND, ... THE WHOLE ... The scribe clearly left room for these details to be filled in later.

23N25 LAYSTHORPE (LODGE). DG 526 Laysthorpe. The full modern name is Laysthorpe Lodge (see also LVY 302).

HUGH SON OF BALDRIC. See 23N17 note.

23N26 HUGH SON OF BALDRIC. See 23N17 note.

23N27 BRANDSBY. The present village is located at SE 589 725, but the original vill centre was adjacent to Brandsby Hall at SE 598 719 (LVY 295).

HUGH SON OF BALDRIC. See 23N17 note.

23N28 BEFORE 1066. Only the beginning of the usual phrase is given here. Possibly the scribe left room for the former value and the current value to be inserted later. See 23N24 note.

23N29 HUGH SON OF BALDRIC. See 23N17 note.

23N32 BARNBY (HOUSE). DG 515 Barnby. The full modern name is Barnby House. There are no earthwork remains of the original depopulated settlement (LVY 294).

BOSSALL. The depopulated vill centre is located north-west of the church (LVY 295).

BUTTERCRAMBE. All that is visible in the Facsimile is *Butec*, the remainder of the word being obliterated by a blot (DF LX). Farley reads the word as *Buttecrame* (spelt this way 23N29, but *Butecram* 23N33). There seems no reason to doubt the identification.

23N33   HUGH SON OF BALDRIC. See 23N17 note.

23E1   EAST RIDING. 23N33-36 follow at the foot of fol. 328b, after 23E1-19.

23N34-5   IN CRUNKLY (GILL). See 23N17-18 note.

23E1   HESSLE HUNDRED. See 15E1 note. This hundred rubric applies only to 23E1, the places in 23E2-19 being recorded under a variety of other hundreds in the Summary.

23E2   PILLWOODS (FARM). DG 478 Pillwoods. The full modern name is Pillwoods Farm.
MILL/S. The number is blotted in the text and is illegible (DF LXI). Farley gives no reading for this.
AND 1 WIDE. *et 1 lat.* for *et 1 latitudine* 'and 1 wide' (DF LXI). Farley omits these words.

23E3   NORTH CAVE. This is written above the line. It does not have the equivalent of underlining (DF LXI).
2 BOVATES. This is written above the line.

23E4   HUNSLEY. See 3Y1 note.

23E7   *TORP.* A lost vill subsequently part of Etton township (DG 481).

23E8   HUTTON (CRANSWICK). See 5E39 note.

23E9   ... S. The figure for the current value has been obliterated by a blot (DF LXI).

23E10   BEFORE 1066. *T.R.E.* for *tempore regis Edwardi* 'in the time of King Edward' is inserted superfluously at the end of line 2. It is directly above the correct entry of the abbreviation, and this error may have occurred through space being left for the value to be added later and the scribe mistakenly commencing on the wrong line. This process of later insertion is compatible with the observations made in 23N24 note and 23N28 note.

23E12   MOREBY (HALL). See 6E1 note.

23E13   SHERBURN. DB *Schirebur* (DF LXI). DG 479 erroneously *Schiresbur.*

23E14   BURDALE. See 1E42 note.
RAISTHORPE. See 1E56 note.
GEOFFREY. VCH 277, note 25 suggests that this might be Geoffrey de Stutevill, although without reference.

23E16   BUCKTON (HOLMS). See 8E1 note.

23E19   (BISHOP)THORPE. See 1W29 note.

23N34-36   NORTH RIDING. These three entries at the foot of col. 328b are separated from the rest of the 23N series by 23E1-19.

23N34   LEALHOLM. See 23N18 note.
DANBY. See 23N18 note.

23N35   *CAMISEDALE.* See 1N35 note.

23N36   HEWORTH. See C26 note.

24W1   SKYRACK WAPENTAKE. See 5W1 note. This wapentake rubric applies only to 24W1, the places in 24W2-3 being in Ainsty Wapentake in the Summary.
BINGLEY. In this entry DB states that Bingley with its soke of Baildon, Cottingley, Eldwick, Micklethwaite, Marley and 'Halton' lies in Skyrack Wapentake, but in 24W21 it locates the manors and berewicks of Marley, 'Halton', Cottingley, Cullingworth and Hainworth in Craven. All these places are ascribed to Skyrack Wapentake in the Summary, apart from Cullingworth and Hainworth, which are omitted from the Summary. It seems likely that Cullingworth and Hainworth lay in Craven and also formed part of the manor of Bingley, while the others were probably in Skyrack Wapentake (see also WYAS 323). Bingley, Eldwick, Cottingley, 'Halton', Micklethwaite, Marley and Hainworth were subsequently amalgamated to form a greatly enlarged township of Bingley (for the history of these vills and the probable boundaries between them see WYAS 323-7).
JURISDICTION. See 1Y8 note.
'HALTON'. The name of DB *Hateltun* (given in DG 496 as *Hathelton*) was subsequently changed to Harden. The name of Harden Grange (SE 093 389), the vill centre, was changed to St. Ives in the 19th century by the Ferrand family. The present Harden Grange (SE 095 382) was originally called St. Ives (see WYAS 325).

24W2   2 CARUCATES AND 2 BOVATES. *terrae* 'of land' is omitted after *bo.* for *bovatae* 'bovates'. An area of land is clearly intended, however, since the number of ploughs it can support follows in the text.

24W4   'BURGHSHIRE' (CLARO) WAPENTAKE. See 5W36 note.
(UPPER AND LOWER) DUNSFORTH. In the Middle Ages these were separate townships. An original single vill of Dunsforth may have been divided subsequent to 1086 or some of the DB references may be to one and some to the other. PNWR v, 83 ascribes all the DB references to Lower Dunsforth, but DG 493 ascribes them to the two combined.

24W6   '(LITTLE) CATTAL' (OLD THORNVILLE HALL). The name of the DB vill of *Cathale* appears to have been changed in the 18th century to Thornville (PNWR v, 9, 17). The vill centre is Old Thornville Hall (see LVY 236).
3 CARUCATES. As 24W2 note.

24W9	(GREAT AND LITTLE) RIBSTON. See 1W35 note.
	2 CARUCATES. As 24W2 note.
	5S 4D. In the Facsimile the pence figure appears to be written oddly as *ii.j*. This could be interpreted as '3d' or '4d'. Farley gives '4d' and this is much the more likely.
24W11	LOFTUS (HILL). DG 500 reports DB *Lotes* as Loftus. The full modern name is Loftus Hill. The territory of the vill was subsequently divided between the townships of Staveley and Arkendale, that part in Arkendale being known as *Arkendale Loftus* (see further PNWR v, 89, 104-5).
24W13	BRIMHAM (HALL). See 21W7 note.
	3 CARUCATES AND 6 BOVATES. As 24W2 note.
24W14	WHIPLEY (HALL). See 1Y18 note.
	ERNEIS HAS IT. Only 4 bovates of this were actually held by Erneis, as Gospatric retained the rest as King's Thane (28W20; SW,Bu26).
24W16-17	'LITTLE' BRAHAM, 'GREAT' BRAHAM. See 13W32 note.
24W18	NEWSOME (FARM). DG 502 Newsome. The full modern name is Newsome Farm, now in Spofforth township.
	4 ACRES LONG. Woodland is normally found in larger amounts; 'acres' is quite clear in the text however (DF LXII).
24W20	JURISDICTION. See 1Y8 note.
	BARROWBY (GRANGE), See 13W29 note.
	(KIRK AND NORTH) DEIGHTON. See 16W5 note.
	INGMANTHORPE (HALL). See 5W37 note.
	8½ CARUCATES. As 24W2 note.
24W21	IN CRAVEN. See 1W56 note; 24W1 note.
	MARLEY. The amounts of land are entered above the relevant place-names.
	'HALTON'. See 24W1 note.
	CULLINGWORTH, HAINWORTH. DB does not state who held these two vills in 1066, but it was probably Gospatric, the lord of Bingley (WYAS 323).
	6½ CARUCATES. The correct addition is 7½ carucates.
24E1	CAVE HUNDRED. See 11E1 note. This hundred rubric applies only to 24E1, Stillingfleet in the following entry being in Pocklington Hundred in the Summary.
24E2	STILLINGFLEET. A line has been erased below this entry (DF LXII). Since it is at the foot of a column it is not discernible in Farley, who normally indicates deletions by leaving a space.
	2 CARUCATES. As 24W2 note.
25W1	AINSTY WAPENTAKE. See 5W35 note.
	STEETON (HALL). See 13W7 note.
	ARNKETILL. The Claims identify the Arnketill who held land in Steeton Hall as Arnketill son of Wulfstan (CW24).
	GODWINE. The Claims identify the person who held 13 bovates of land in Colton and Steeton Hall as Godwine son of Eadric (CW27). He was presumably one of the two men called Godwine recorded amongst others as holding 6 carucates of land in Steeton Hall (25W1) and 4½ carucates in Colton (25W3).
25W3	ARNKETILL. The Claims identify the Arnketill who held land in Colton as Arnketill son of Wulfstan (CW24). His father may well be the Wulfstan named in this entry.
	GODWINE. See 25W1 note.
	WULFSTAN. The Claims identify the Wulfstan who held land in Colton as Wulfstan the Priest (CW29).
	4½ CARUCATES. As 24W2 note.
	RODOUUELLE. DG 505 identification with Rothwell in Morley Wapentake in the honour of Pontefract is unlikely geographically as all the other places listed in this section are in Ainsty Wapentake, and it would seem better to regard *Rodouuelle* as a lost vill somewhere in Ainsty.
25W4	(PALLA)THORPE. See 5W35 note.
25W6	FIVE THANES. The Claims identify Arnketill son of Wulfstan as holding land in Catterton which was subsequently held by Osbern de Arches (CW24). The fact therefore that one of these five thanes can be identified as Arnketill increases the likelihood that the five thanes are Arnketill and the four men linked with him in 25W3, i.e. Godwine, Godwine, Thorr and Wulfstan. It seems probable that the scribe simply assumed that it would be obvious who was meant and so did not bother to write out all the names again.
	2 CARUCATES OF LAND. *t.re* for *terrae* 'of land' is written above the line.
25W7	HORNINGTON (MANOR). See 13W17 note.
25W11-12	(LONG) MARSTON, (HUTTON) WANDESLEY. The vill centres of Long Marston and Hutton Wandesley are now contiguous, with the township boundary, on which the

church (SE 505 507) is located, running between them. The boundary kinks at this point as if the church, which is now in Long Marston township, was once in Hutton Wandesley township; in medieval documents the parish is sometimes called Hutton Wandesley and sometimes Long Marston (Skaife Papers, Yorkshire Archaeological Society MD 216). This was not, however, the original position of the church: in 1400-1 Richard le Scrope, Archbishop of York, granted a petition to move the church from its inconvenient position on Chapel Hill, a little under a mile to the south, and to rebuild it on its present site, then occupied by a chapel of ease (Skaife Papers, Yorkshire Archaeological Society MD 216). The first church was close to the boundary between Hutton Wandesley and Angram, another constituent township of the ecclesiastical parish. It seems likely that Hutton Grange (SE 512 489), immediately adjacent to the former church site, may represent the site of an earlier settlement of Hutton, and that it was a shift in settlement prior to 1400 which necessitated the transfer of the church (we are grateful to Professor M. W. Beresford for drawing to our attention these references and the unusual situation here described).

25W11   11 CARUCATES. *terrae* 'of land' is omitted after *car.* for *carucatae* 'carucates'. Land is clearly intended, however, as jurisdiction would not be exercised over things but over areas, and the locations are mentioned. See 1Y6 note.

WILSTROP (HALL). DG 512 Wilstrop, the name of the township. The full modern name of the vill centre is Wilstrop Hall. On the shrunken vill centre see LVY 232.

25W13   EARNWINE. In the Claims this Earnwine is identified as Earnwine Catenase (CW32), but it is also stated there that Earnwine Catenase held 6½ carucates in the two Poppletons (i.e. Upper and Nether Poppleton). This implies that in the Claims he was attributed the land in Nether Poppleton attributed in this section (25W14) to Oddi the Deacon.

25W14   ODDI THE DEACON. *diac.* for *diaconus* 'deacon' is written above Oddi's name.

25W16   SCAGGLETHORPE. The name of the DB vill survives today in Scagglethorpe Bridge (SE 537 549) and Scagglethorpe Moor (centred SE 53 55). The present-day Red Hall has been identified with the Scagglethorpe manor-house, locating the original vill centre at *c.*SE 540 550 (LVY 232).

EARNWINE. The Claims identify the man holding land in Scagglethorpe as Earnwine the Priest (CW32).

25W17   RAGENOT. DB *Ragenot* represents an AN derivative (PNDB 125-6) of the ON personal name *Ragni* (PNDB 347; SPN 215).

25W20   'BURGHSHIRE' (CLARO). See 5W36 note.

25W21   KIRBY (HALL). In the 12th century DB *Chirchebi* was known as *Kirby Ouseburn*, which led to some confusion with the adjacent township of Little Ouseburn (DB *Useburne*: 1W31; 29W14; SW,Bu3). Kirby was in the ecclesiastical parish of Little Ouseburn, although the church, which presumably gave Kirby its name, lies outside the township boundary of Kirby. The church is probably one of the two ascribed to Whixley in 25W22 (PNWR v, 4). There is no indication where the vill centre of *Kirby Ouseburn* was located; LVY 234 suggests that the original settlement may lie beneath the parkland of Kirby Hall, whose name preserves that of the DB vill (but note that the grid reference given in LVY 234 should be SE 458 610 not SE 485 610).

25W22   2 CHURCHES. At Whixley and Kirkby, near Ouseburn (VCH 281, note 19).

25W23   6 CARUCATES. Thus DB (DF LXIV). Farley erroneously '5 carucates'.

25W26   SUSACRES. This is one of the rare instances in the Yorkshire section of DB proper (as opposed to the Bruce account; see 31E1 note) of the name being given in a latinised form, *Sosacra*.

MARGINAL CROSS. A highly decorative cross in the margin matches that next to Cattal at the foot of the page (DF LXIV). This shows that Cattall should have followed at this point.

25W27   MARGINAL CROSS. A marginal cross matching that at 25W26 shows that Cattal should have followed at that point.

25W28   BARKSTON (ASH) WAPENTAKE. See 5W6 note.

2 SMALLHOLDERS WITH 1 SMALLHOLDER. Literally *ii bord. cu. i bord.* for *ii bordarii cum i bordarius* '2 smallholders with 1 smallholder'. The form is unusual, and it is possible that there is an error in this entry. However, since 'smallholder' is usually last in the list of persons it is not possible to argue that the word was a repeat in mistake for the next category (see 12W18 note; 12W23 note), and it does not seem to be a simple repeat since the number of persons concerned is different. If it was an error the nature of the error cannot be determined, and it is quite possible that the entry was intended to read as it does, in which case the reason for there being two kinds of smallholders is not apparent.

25W29   TOULSTON. See 5W7 note.

OGLETHORPE (HALL). See 5W7 note.

25W29-30	FOUR THANES, FIVE THANES. In these entries in the section dealing with the lands of Osbern de Arches, the thanes who held a total of 10 carucates 7 bovates in Toulston, Newton Kyme and Oglethorpe Hall in 1066 are not named. In the Claims, however, it is stated that William Malet had 1 carucate of the land of Grimr and Asgeirr in Oglethorpe Hall (CW2), 1 carucate of the land of Thorketill in Toulston (CW3) and 2 carucates of the land of Ligulfr and Thorn in Newton Kyme (CW3), giving a total of 4 carucates. Despite the discrepancy in the amounts of land recorded in the dispute, it seems likely Grimr, Asgeirr, Thorketill, Ligulfr and Thorn are the five thanes referred to in 25W29-30. Elsewhere in DB proper Ligulfr alone is named as the predecessor of the Count of Mortain in these three vills (5W7).
25W31	CRAVEN. See 1W56 note.
	MARGINAL CROSS. There is a marginal cross at this point. Its purpose is not clear.
26E1	IN BUGTHORPE. There is an 'f' in the margin to the left of the entry. It is not clear what it means. It is not reproduced by Farley.
26E2	BARTHORPE (GRANGE). See 5E64 note.
26E4	FRIDAYTHORPE. VCH 282, note 24a suggests that this probably included part of Fimber, which was assessed at about 8 carucates of land. 13 CARUCATES/18½ CARUCATES. The scribe originally wrote '13 carucates'. Later '18½ (carucates)' was added above the line, but '13' was not deleted. *R.* In the margin, not reproduced by Farley, is *r.* for *require* 'enquire further' (DF LXIV). The uncertain amount of land might well have been the cause of this enquiry. The exact amount in question, however, remains unresolved. The Summary (SE,Ac10-11) is no help, since this merely records Odo's land in Fridaythorpe as being 7½ carucates.
26E7	RAISTHORPE. See 1E56 note.
26E8	*SCRADIZTORP.* A lost vill subsequently part of Skirpenbeck township (DG 479).
26E8;10	FORNI. The men holding land in *Scradiztorp* and Skirpenbeck in 1066 are named here as Ormr and *Forne*, the regularised form of which would be *Forni* (PNDB 252), but in the Claims (CE32) they are stated to have been Ormr and *Bunde*, the regularised form of which would be *Bondi* (PNDB 206). The discrepancy is unlikely to represent a change in tenants as they are the 1066 landholders, not those in occupation at 1086. It may simply be a scribal error or Forni may also have been known as Bondi, from ON *bondi* 'peasant', either as his by-name or as a designation of his social status (JMcND).
26E9	SWAYTHORPE. The site of the depopulated vill centre is marked on the modern 6 in. OS map as the earthworks are still visible (LVY 68).
26E11	(HANGING) GRIMSTON. On the shrunken vill centre see LVY 62.
28W2	*CADRETONE.* A lost vill, which DG 489 locates in Allerton Mauleverer township. PNWR v, 14 points out that the exact location is uncertain, but *Cadretone* must be located somewhere in that area as it is grouped with Allerton Mauleverer and Marton in 'Burghshire' Wapentake.
28W3	ALLERTON (MAULEVERER). See 1W37 note. IN THESE. The land for 1 plough is the ½ carucate in *Cadretone* and Allerton Mauleverer.
28W5	THORNBOROUGH. DG 509 Thornbrough. The correct modern spelling is Thornborough.
28W6	19S. The figure is ill-written in the text, but appears nearer to *xix* '19' (DF LXV). Farley reads it as '20'.
28W8	CLARETON. See 1Y18 note. IN CLARETON. There is an 'f' in the margin to the left of this entry. It is not clear what it means. It is not reproduced by Farley.
28W9	2½ CARUCATES. As 24W2 note.
28W15	BRAMLEY (GRANGE). DG 488 Bramley. The full modern name is Bramley Grange.
28W19	*POPLETONE.* See 1W42 note.
28W20	BRIMHAM (HALL). See 21W7.
28W22	KIRBY (HILL). Listed in DB under the WR, but subsequently in the NR. See also 1W54 note.
28W25	*HEUUORDE.* A lost vill subsequently part of Conistone township (DG 497). *HEUUORDE.* This is repeated in the land of the King's Thanes (29W49).
28W26	(OLD) SUNDERLANDWICK. Listed here under the WR, but subsequently in the ER. See also 1E5 note.
28W27	SNAINTON. Listed here under the WR but subsequently in the NR.
28W28	NOW 10S. *mo. x sl.* for *modo x solidi* 'now 10s' is written at the end of the following line.
28W30	WEARDLEY. This reference to Weardley in fol. 330b is omitted from DG 511 (DG numbering fol. 330). The grid reference given in the index for the vill centre of Weardley is that for Low Weardley (WYAS 552).

28W31-6 (LANG)THORPE, THORNTON (BRIDGE), (HUM)BURTON, BRAFFERTON, OULSTON. The places in these entries are listed here under the WR but were all subsequently in the NR.

28W32 THORNTON (BRIDGE). The DB vill survives as a separate township, but the vill centre appears to have been depopulated by the 16th century (LVY 306).

28W33; 36 (HUM)BURTON. In the Middle Ages, as part of the manor of Aldborough, it is usually listed in documents under the WR, as here, although actually part of the NR. The earthworks of the depopulated vill centre are located to the north-west of the present farm (LVY 301).

28W34 BRAFFERTON. This is a repeat of the entry in the section on the King's lands, 1N106 (see 1N106 note), except that the value is given here as 2½s.

28W35 OULSTON. This is a repeat of the entry in the King's lands, 1N107 (see 1N107 note).

28W36 2 CARUCATES *INLAND*. This is written above '4 carucates'.
4 CARUCATES. As 24W2 note.

28W39 'MIDDLETON'. DG 528 Middleton, in Appleton Wiske township (NR), but no such name appears on the modern 6 in. OS map, nor on the 1st ed. 6 in. OS map, sheet 41, so the name has been treated here as lost.

28W40 SLEDMERE. Listed here under the WR, but subsequently in the ER.
IN SLEDMERE. In the Summary the 9 carucates of land here are assigned to the King (SE,Th7), not to Gospatric.

28W41 'KNARESFORD'. See 2W7 note.

29W1 SKYRACK WAPENTAKE. See 5W1 note. Despite the DB rubric, of the places listed in this section only East Rigton (29W24) is given as being in Skyrack Wapentake in the Summary.

29W2 GRUCAN. DB *Grucan* (DF LXVI). Farley erroneously *Crucan*. PNDB 276 suggests that this name may be Irish in origin, although the etymology is uncertain.
EARNWINE THE PRIEST. *prb.* for *presbyter* 'priest' is written above Earnwine's name throughout this section.

29W4, 29W5 (WEST) MELTON. This is written above the line in capitals.
(WEST) MELTON WITH 4 OUTLIERS. *cu.* for *cum* 'with' is written above the line. VCH 285, note 4 suggests that the outliers were Hoyland Swaine (4 bovates), Thorpe Hesley (3 bovates), Wentworth (2 bovates) and Brampton Bierlow (3 bovates).

29W6 3 OUTLIERS. VCH 285, note 5 suggests that the outliers were West Melton (3 bovates), Wentworth (6 bovates) and *Eldeberge* (4 bovates).

29W7 4 OUTLIERS. VCH 285, note 6 suggests that the outliers were West Melton (1 carucate 5 bovates), Brampton Bierlow (included with West Melton in the heading for the entry), Thorpe Hesley (5 bovates) and *Eldeberge* (half a carucate). Brampton is written here above the line in capitals. *cu.* for *cum* 'with' is also written above the line.
ARNTHORR THE PRIEST. *pbr.* for *presbyter* 'priest' is written above Arnthorr's name.
6 CARUCATES AND 2 BOVATES. The scribe originally wrote '6½ carucates'. He deleted the '½' by underlining it (the normal method of indicating a deletion) and inserted the corrected figure, '2 bovates', above.

29W8 BILLINGLEY. This entry has been added in the margin.
ARNTHORR. It is likely that the Arnthorr of this entry is the Arnthorr the Priest of the previous entry, as the DB scribe frequently gives names in a shortened form in entries immediately succeeding those in which the names are given in full. His name here has been inserted above the line.

29W9 EARNWINE. As 29W2 note.

29W11 *MULEDE*. A lost vill subsequently part of Bishopthorpe township (DG 502).

29W12 (BISHOP)THORPE. See 1W29 note. There are marginal marks of what look like *f*s down the dividing space between the 2 columns on this page (DF LXVI). Presumably they apply to entries in the right-hand column, that is Bishopthorpe onwards, and they continue through the entries for the ER, which are in this column, and on to the left hand column of the next folio (DF LXVII), but are not found for the NR, which is the right-hand column of that page. These marks are found next to all entries in this column (DF LXVI) except Allerton Mauleverer, East Rigton, North Dalton and Flamborough. It is not clear what they mean. These marks are not reproduced by Farley.
LAND FOR 2 OXEN. See 1N7 note.

29W13 10 FURLONGS. The '10' is somewhat ill-written. It looks as if the scribe started to write *v* (5) and adapted it into an *x* (10). The intention of 10 seems clear enough, and Farley also reads it this way (DF LXVI).

29W15   HOPPERTON. DG 498 omits this reference to *Homtone* in fol. 330d (DG numbering fol. 330b).

29W16   ALLERTON (MAULEVERER). See 1W37 note.

29W17   LOFTUS (HILL). See 24W11 note.

          IT PAYS 5S. *redd.* for *reddit* 'it pays' is written at the end of the following line.

29W19   *(SCOTTON) THORPE.* The DB vill of *Torp* was subsequently subsumed into Scotton township and came to be known as *Scotton Thorpe.* The name is now lost (PNWR v, 92).

29W20   WULFRIC. His name is written above the line.

29W21   WIDDINGTON (HALL). DG 512 Widdington. The full modern name is Widdington Hall.

29W24   (EAST) RIGTON. DG 505 Rigton (near Bardsey). The full modern name is East Rigton. This distinguishes it from North Rigton in Rigton township (Upper Claro Wapentake). By the latter half of the 12th century Rigton vill had been amalgamated with Bardsey vill to form the township of Bardsey cum Rigton (WYAS 313-14).

          A PRIEST. This entry might be assumed to indicate the existence of a church, but no church is known in the vill. Rigton is part of the ecclesiastical parish of Bardsey, which contains an important Anglo-Saxon church (Taylor and Taylor 39-40). It may be that the priest recorded here lived in Rigton but served at Bardsey church (WYAS 222, note 28).

29E1   HESSLE HUNDRED. See 15E1 note. The DB rubric applies only to the first entry in this section, the places listed in 29E2-26 being recorded under a variety of hundreds in the Summary.

29E7   EARNWINE. As 29W2 note.

          HAS [IT] ... WASTE. *ht. mo. et waste. e.* for *habet modo et wasta est* 'has [it] and it is waste' is written at the end of the previous line.

29E8   MARTON. The marginal marks referred to above (29W12 note) are found in this column also (DF LXVI). The only entries without this marginal mark are Wharram Percy, West Heslerton, Walkington and Watton. Farley does not reproduce them.

29E9   HILDERTHORPE. See 1Y11 note.

          LAND FOR 2 OXEN. See 1N7 note.

          VALUE 10S. *x sol.* for *x solidi* '10s' is written at the end of the following line.

29E12   EARNWINE. As 29W2 note.

29E13   NORTHMANN. This is written above the line.

          4 CARUCATES. This is written as 2 sets of *II*s one above the other.

29E15   BIRDSALL. See 2B18 note.

          SUTTON (GRANGE). See 2B18 note. This is written above the line. Farley reproduces it accurately in lower-case lettering.

29E16   (HANGING) GRIMSTON. See 26E11 note. DB *Grimstone* (DF LXVII). DG 473 erroneously *Grimestone.*

29E17   SIWARD, 1 CARUCATE. This is written above the line, over Arngrimr and his land.

29E19   3 CARUCATES. The scribe originally wrote 6 carucates. He deleted the 6 by the normal method of underlining it and inserted the correct figure of 3 carucates above.

29E19   GARROWBY (HALL). DG 472 Garrowby. The full modern name is Garrowby Hall; the depopulated settlement at the vill centre is adjacent to the hall (LVY 610).

29E20   THORALBY (HALL). DG 481 Thoralby. The full modern name is Thoralby Hall (see also LVY 69).

29E21   WHARRAM (PERCY). See 1E54 note.

29E26   MARGINAL CROSS. The marginal cross at the end of this entry shows that Sewerby and the next 3 entries (29E27-30) should follow at this point. The cross is more decorative than Farley's reproduction.

29N4   UPSALL (HALL). See 1N14 note.

          LAND FOR 1 PLOUGH. *t.ra ad i car.* for *terra ad i carucam* 'land for 1 plough' is written at the end of the preceding line.

29N6-7 MARTON (IN CLEVELAND). See 1N43 note.

29N7   TOLLESBY. See 1N27 note.

29N9   JURISDICTION. See 1Y8 note.

29N9   SKUTTERSKELFE (HALL). See 1N32 note.

          THORALDBY (FARM). See 1N33 note.

          (LITTLE) BROUGHTON. There is no longer a settlement by the name of Little Broughton; the name survives in that of the township of Great and Little Broughton and as the name of an area centred on NZ 560 074 and in the name Little Broughton Bridge (NZ 560 068), which is where the medieval settlement was probably located (LVY 296). The 2½ in. OS map marks 'foundations and medieval pottery found' on the railway line just to the north, centred on NZ 560 070.

KIRKBY. DG 526 Kirby, in Stokesley township. The spelling on the modern 2½ in. OS map is Kirkby. This is a township in its own right, whose vill centre is also called Kirkby, in Langbargh Wapentake to the south-east of Stokesley township.

DROMONBY (HALL). DG 520 Dromonby. The full modern name is Dromonby Hall, adjacent to the depopulated vill centre (LVY 298).

(LITTLE) BUSBY. The name survives only as a township name, not as the name of a settlement. It is likely that the depopulated vill centre is adjacent to Busby Hall (LVY 296).

34½ CARUCATES. ½ is written above the line. The figure is incorrect. The actual total is 34½ carucates and 2 bovates.

29N10	*STEMANESBI*. See 5N32 note.
29N11	(EAST) LILLING. See 1N91 note.
	14 BOVATES. See 1N100 note.
29E27	ALSO IN THE EAST RIDING. This entry and the matching marginal cross by Sewerby show that these entries should follow on from the others in the ER (29E26). They were presumably entered here because the ER entries filled the whole of the previous column, leaving no room for them to be added there (DF LXVII). The additions continue at the top of the next folio.
	SEWERBY. See 4E1 note.
29E28	13 CARUCATES. Including 1 carucate in Auburn (VCH 287, note 27).
29E29	ACKLAM. This continues the entries for the ER. See 29E27 note.
	MARGINAL MARKS. See 29W12 note. These marks are found for both columns of this folio, and occur against all places except Hensall, Wortley, Bishopthorpe and Acaster Selby in the left hand column; and Kilnsey, *Heuurde* and Coniston in the right hand column (DF LXVIII). Farley does not reproduce these marks.
	LAND FOR 4 PLOUGHS. *T.ra ad iiii car.* for *terra ad iiii carucas* 'land for 4 ploughs' is written above the line.
29W25	WEST RIDING. The entries for the West Riding recommence here.
	HENSALL. Compare this with 1Y12 and SW,O16.
29W27	(BISHOP)THORPE. See 1W29 note.
	2 OXEN. See 1N7 note.
29W29	2 OXEN. See 1N7 note.
29W30	(UPPER AND LOWER) DUNSFORTH. See 24W4 note.
	THE SAME MAN. The regular form *idem* 'the same man' is derived from a combination of the demonstrative pronoun *is* with the intensive suffix *-dem*, and means 'that same man'. The form *isdem* which appears in this section bears the same meaning as *idem* but represents a transitional stage of phonetic development.
29W31-3	THE SAME MAN. See 29W30 note.
29W34	WHIPLEY (HALL). See 1Y18 note.
	LAND FOR 2 OXEN. See 1N7 note.
	THE SAME MAN. See 29W30 note.
	[NOW] 2S. There is a gap in the text as reproduced by Farley between 2s 8d and 2s (DF LXVIII). The intention was probably to indicate that 2s was the current value.
29W36	(DUN)KESWICK. On the ecclesiastical and tenurial status of Dunkeswick later in the Middle Ages see WYAS 360.
	THE SAME MAN. See 29W30 note.
29W37	THE SAME MAN. See 29W30 note.
29W38	THE SAME MAN. See 29W30 note.
29W39	IN CRAVEN. See 1W56 note. There is a cross with dots between the arms to the left of the heading. Its purpose is not clear. It is not reproduced by Farley.
29W42	THORPE. The township immediately adjacent to Burnsall, with which it is linked in this entry. It has been suggested that the *thorp* place-name element 'outlying or dependent settlement' may refer to its dependence on Burnsall (PNWR vi, 960).
	THE SAME MAN. See 29W30 note.
29W43-4	THE SAME MAN. See 29W30 note.
29W46-7	*HOLEDENE*. A lost vill subsequently part of Hartlington township (DG 497).

29W48	KILNSEY. DG 499 incorrectly refers this entry to fol. 332 instead of fol. 331d (fol. 331b in DG numbering).
29W49	*HEUURDE*. See 28W25 note.
30W1	LAND OF ROGER OF POITOU. There is no number in DB against Roger's name; according to the DB numbering it would have been 41.
	OUTLIERS. See 1Y19 note.
	LAND OF ROGER OF POITOU. There is a cross with dots between the arms to the left of the heading. Its purpose is not clear. It is not reproduced by Farley.
30W2	WILLIAM OF PERCY. *p.ci* for *Perci* 'of Percy' is written above William's name.
30W4	LONG PRESTON. The amounts of land in each vill are written above the relevant place-names.
	CROOKS (HOUSE). See 13W39 note.
30W5	½ CARUCATE. This is written above the line over Hubberholme and Starbotton.
30W6	3 CARUCATES. This is written above the line over Settle.
30W7	WINTERBURN. See 30W4 note.
	WINTERBURN, FLASBY. Two DB vills subsequently amalgamated to form the township of Flasby with Winterburn.
	LEUETĀT. A lost vill subsequently part of Winterburn (DG 500).
30W8	IN THE SAME PLACE. It is not certain whether this applies to all the vills listed in 30W7 or just the last mentioned. In the index it has been assumed that it applies only to Selside.
30W9	RATHMELL. See 30W4 note.
	HELLIFIELD. DB *Helgeflet* (DF LXIX). DG 496 omits this form for Hellifield.
30W10	ARNFORD. See 30W4 note.
	CARETORP. A lost vill subsequently part of Wigglesworth township.
30W11	PAYTHORNE. DG 504 *Pathorme*: Farley *Pahtorme*. The DB scribe originally wrote *Patorme* and then inserted *h* immediately above the *t* (DF LXIX). Thus technically either reading would be possible, although the DG form is the more probable.
	GAMALBARN. The DB scribe originally wrote *Gameltorp*, presumably in anticipation of the *torp* element in the next place-name, and then corrected it to *Gamelbar* by inserting *bar* above *torp* (DF LXIX).
30W21	ANOTHER EARBY. Subsequent to DB there was only one vill of Earby, which was itself eventually subsumed into the township of Thornton in Craven. It is therefore not possible to discover the location of *alia Eurebi* within Earby vill, and both have been given the same grid reference in the index.
30W25	STAINTON. See 1W73 note. DB *Stainton* (DF LXIX). Farley *Stamton*. The DB manuscript is difficult to read at this point.
30W26	(EAST AND WEST) MARTON. The DB vill of *Martun* is now represented by the township of Martons Both, containing the settlements of West Marton and East Marton; as it is not possible to distinguish which may have been the original vill centre, both names have been used in this edition. West Marton is at SD 893 504 and East Marton is now at SD 905 510, but the church is located to the south-east at SD 908 506 and the site of the old hall south of that at SD 908 505, so the original settlement of East Marton may have been in the area around the church and hall.
30W27	INGTHORPE (GRANGE). DG 498 Ingthorpe. The full modern name is Ingthorpe Grange.
30W30	ERNEIS. This is probably Erneis de Burun, the only Erneis mentioned elsewhere in the Yorkshire section of DB.
	BUT NOW IT IS IN ROGER'S CASTLERY. *S. mo. e. in castell. Rog.* for *sed modo est in castello Rogeris* 'but now it is in Roger's castlery' is written at the end of the following line.
30W36	HAWKSWICK. After this entry there was a section of 2 or 3 lines which has been erased (DF LXIX).
30W37	GRINDLETON. See 30W4 note.
	BASHALL (EAVES). The DB vill of *Baschelf* is now represented by the township of Bashall Eaves. The settlement named Bashall Eaves is at SD 696 433, but it seems likely that the original vill centre was at Bashall Town (SD 711 420).
	HAMMERTON (HALL). DG 496 Hammerton. The full modern name of the now-depopulated vill centre (see LVY 238) is Hammerton Hall.
	BATTERSBY (BARN). DG 486 Battersby, located just to the west of Slaidburn (DG map 58B8); PNWR vi, 204 gives the form of the name as Battersby Farm, but the only name surviving on the OS maps here is Battersby Barn at SD 705 520. LVY 238 identifies *Badresbi* with Beatrix (SD 665 514), 2½ miles to the west, but this is in fact the site of the medieval settlement of *Batherarghes*, first recorded in 1343 (PNWR vi, 211).

NEWTON. DG 502 Newton on Hodder, which PNWR vi, 206 describes as simply Newton, but formerly called *Newton in Bowland*. The name on the modern 2½ in. OS map is Newton.

BOGEUURDE. DG 486 Barge Ford, but no such name appears on the modern 2½ in. OS map; PNWR vi, 203 and DGNE 12 report the name as lost.

SOTLEIE. A lost vill subsequently part of Bowland Forest township (DG 507).

30W38-40 IN 'LONSDALE' [L] AND COCKERHAM [L]. These places are in Lancashire and Westmorland (see 1W70-1L8 note).

30W38 'LONSDALE'. DG 213 reports DB *Lanesdale* as Lonsdale near Cockerham and DB Cheshire gives the grid reference in the index as SD 43 54. The name at first meant 'the Lune valley', but in the 12th century began to be used of the entire hundred (PNL 167). As it does not appear on the modern 6 in. OS map, nor on the 1st ed. 6 in. OS map (sheet 34) as a settlement, it has been given here as lost. Here the reference may be to that part of Lonsdale Hundred adjacent to Cockerham, south of River Lune, and next to the Amounderness boundary.

30W39 ASHTON (HALL). DG 209 and DB Cheshire Y12 report DB *Estun* as Ashton (near Lancaster), but the full modern name is Ashton Hall; the township is Ashton with Stodday.

MACHERN. The origins of the DB personal name *Machern* are obscure (PNDB 323).

30W40 IN BEETHAM. On the amounts of land see 30W4 note.

EARNWINE THE PRIEST. See 29W2 note.

YEALAND (CONYERS AND REDMAYNE). DG 217 and DB Cheshire Y14 report DB *Ialant* as Yealand, but the name does not now survive simply in this form but in the names Yealand Conyers (SD 507 748), where the church is located, and Yealand Redmayne (SD 502 755). As it is impossible to be certain which settlement was the vill centre, both names have been used in this edition. In the text the name has a capital *I* (DF LXIX). Farley reproduces it with a lower-case *j*. The sense is the same.

PRESTON (RICHARD). See 1L4 note.

BORWICK, 1 CARUCATE. Thus DB (DF LXIX). Farley erroneously '2 carucates'.

HEVERSHAM (HEAD). DG 444 and DB Cheshire Y13 report Heversham. The full modern name is Heversham Head.

31E1 THIS IS THE HOLDING OF ROBERT OF BRUS. See Appendix.

THE BOOK OF WINCHESTER. Domesday Book.

EAST RIDING. In the Bruce account, the name appears as *Oustredinc* with the ON adjective *austr*, whereas in DB proper it always has the form *East* or *Aest* with the OE adjective *east*. Also in the Bruce account form the final *g* has been unvoiced to *c* (Jensen 11,16).

BURTON (AGNES). DB proper *Burton(e)* (1Y14; SE,Bt1); Bruce account *Bortona*. Throughout the Bruce account, unlike in the Yorkshire section of DB proper, a large proportion of the names are given with latinised second elements. These are latinised as if the second element were of the feminine first declension regardless of the original gender of the OE or ON element involved. Thus where DB has forms in *-ton* (for OE *tun*) and *-bi* (for ON *by*), the Bruce account has forms in *-tona* and *-bia* (see further Jensen 13-15).

HARPHAM. DB proper *Arpen* (1Y14; 29E12; SE,Bt1); Bruce account *Harpein*. In a number of cases in the Bruce account names are given in a scandinavianised form in comparison with the English forms which appear in DB proper (see further Jensen 11-12).

GRANSMOOR. The form of the name in the Bruce account shows substitution or restoration of OE genitive *-es* for the Scandinavian genitive *-s* which is found in DB proper (Jensen 13).

HAISTHORPE. The form of the name in the Bruce account, with initial *h*, is closer to the original form of the name than that used in DB proper, *Aschel-*, *Aschiltorp* (Jensen 11).

THORNHOLME. DG 481 reports DB *Tirnu'* on fol. 322 b in error for fol. 332b.

31E2 THIS SAME THWING. *h* for *hoc* 'this' is written above the line. It is is not strictly necessary.

RUDSTON. DB proper *-stan* scandinavianised to *-stein* (see 31E1 note).

(EAST AND WEST) HESLERTON. Bruce account latinised form *in duabus Haselintonis* (see 31E1 note).

SCAMPSTON. Bruce account latinised *Scamestona* (see 31E1 note).

31E3 (KIRK)BURN. See 1Y8 note.

TIBTHORPE. The variation of spelling of the Bruce account *Tipetorp* from *Tibetorp* in DB proper probably represents a phonetic variation rather than a change of name.

31E4 (NORTH) CAVE. Bruce account latinised *Caua* (see 31E1 note). DG 469 does not give the form *Caua* nor record any entry in this folio for North or South Cave, but this entry is normally taken as referring to North Cave (Jensen 14; PNER 224).

HOTHAM. The form of the name in the Bruce account, *Hodhu.*, is closer to the original form of the name than that used in DB proper, which only has forms in -*e* (Jensen 10).

31E5 KILNWICK (PERCY). See 1Y10 note.

MILLINGTON. Bruce account latinised *Milletona* (see 31E1 note).

31E6 BIRDSALL. See 2B18 note. Bruce account latinised *Brideshala* (see 31E1 note), as it also has in DB proper *Briteshala* (5E58).

GARROWBY (HALL). See 29E19 note.

EDDLETHORPE. See 1E48 note. The variation of spelling of *Eduardestorp* in the Bruce account from the form *Ged-*, *Guduualestorp* in DB proper probably represents a phonetic development rather than a change of name (Jensen 10).

31E7 THORNTHORPE. Not in DB proper, only in the Bruce account; subsequently part of Burythorpe township. The vill centre is now depopulated (LVY 69).

31E8 FIRBY. Not in DB proper, only in the Bruce account. Latinised *Friebia* (see 31E1 note).

(NORTH) GRIMSTON. Bruce account latinised *Grimetona* (DF pl LXX: see 31E1 note). DG 477 erroneously *Grimestona*.

BURYTHORPE. Unlike spelling in DB proper, *Bergetorp*, the spelling *Berguetorp* in the Bruce account, with -*gu*-, indicates French as opposed to Norman influence (Jensen 16).

31W1 WEST RIDING. Unlike in DB proper, where it appears as *West Reding*, in the Bruce account the final *g* of the name has been unvoiced to *c* to give *Westredinc* (Jensen 16).

THE SAME ROBERT. The scribe wrote the *i* in *ide.* for *idem* 'the same' with rather a long stroke (DF LXX). Farley reproduces it as a *j*. It is not significant.

ALLERTON (MAULEVERER). See 1W37 note. Bruce account latinised *Aluretona* (see 31E1 note).

31W2 WIDDINGTON (HALL). See 29W21 note. Bruce account latinised *Widetona* (see 31E1 note).

HOPPERTON. The form of the name in the Bruce account, *Hopretone*, is more accurate than DB proper (Jensen 11).

31W3 (UPPER AND LOWER) DUNSFORTH. See 24W4 note. Unlike the *Dunesford(e)* forms found in DB proper, the form in the Bruce account omits the genitive -*s* and also substitutes *o* for *u* to avoid minim confusion (Jensen 10, 11).

BRANTON (GREEN). Bruce account latinised *Brantona* (see 31E1 note).

GRAFTON. Bruce account latinised *Graftona* (see 31E1 note).

(SCOTTON) THORPE. See 29W19 note.

SCOTTON. Bruce account latinised *Scotona* (see 31E1 note).

SUSACRES. In the Bruce account form *Sotesac* the OE genitive -*es* has been substituted or restored from the Scandinavian -*s* found in the DB forms *Sosacra*, -*acre* (Jensen 13), i.e. an OE genitive '*Sotres* acre' as opposed to DB ON genitive '*Sotrs* acre'.

LAVERTON. Bruce account latinised *Lauretona* (see 31E1 note).

31W4 HORSFORTH. The variation in spelling in the Bruce account, *Hoseforde*, from that in DB proper, *Horseford(e)*, probably represents a phonetic process rather than a change of name (Jensen 10).

31W5 CARLTON. Bruce account latinised *Carletona* (DF LXX; see 31E1 note). DG 490 erroneously *Carletone*.

CAMBLESFORTH. The variation of spelling in the Bruce account, *Gamesford*, from the form in DB proper, *Camelesford(e)*, *Canbesford*, probably represents a phonetic process rather than a change of name.

31N1 APPLETON (WISKE). Bruce account latinised *Apeltona* (see 31E1 note).

31N2 HORNBY. Not in DB proper, only in the Bruce account, with latinised *Hornebia* (see 31E1 note). PNNR 280 omits this DB reference to Hornby (see also 3Y12 note).

(LOW) WORSALL. Bruce account latinised *Wercheshala* (see 31E1 note).

YARM. The -*ou* ending of the Bruce account form *Gerou* is probably a scribal error for the late OE dative plural -*on* (JMcND).

31N3 (SOUTH) OTTERINGTON. Bruce account latinised *Otrintona* (see 31E1 note); the name also shows AN sound-substitution of -*in* for -*ing* (Jensen 16).

WELBURY. Bruce account latinised *Welberga* (see 31E1 note).

31N4 (KIRK) LEAVINGTON, (CASTLE) LEAVINGTON. Bruce account latinised *Leuetona* (see 31E1 note). The form of the name in the Bruce account is also closer to the original form (derived from the river-name Leven) than that used in DB proper (Jensen 11-12).

(CASTLE) LEAVINGTON. See 1N122 note.
MORTON (GRANGE). DG 529 gives DB *Mortona* (31N4; 31N6) in fol. 332d (332b in DG numbering) as respectively Morton, in East Harlsey, and Morton, near Guisborough, but does not distinguish which entry on this folio refers to which place. The forms of the names in the two entries are identical and the landholder is the same man in both cases, but it seems likely that the *Mortona* of 31N6 is Morton Grange near Guisborough (i.e. Morton township in Langbargh West Wapentake), as it is linked with Newton, Upsall Hall and Pinchinthorpe Hall. This would mean that the Morton of 31N4 is Morton Grange in East Harlsey township; it is linked in this entry with Kirk Leavington and Castle Leavington, which lie about 7 miles to the north.
MORTON (GRANGE). See 1N126 note.

31N5   'BORDELBY' (MOUNT GRACE). See 1N129 note. Bruce account latinised *Bordelbia* (see 31E1 note).
ARNCLIFFE (HALL). See 1N128 note. The DB form of the name *Gerneclif* (1N12) indicates that in 1086 the OE initial diphthong æ still survived, whereas the Bruce account form *Ernecliue* suggests a change in pronunciation to an initial *e* (Jensen 13).
INGLEBY (ARNCLIFFE). Bruce account latinised *Englebia* (see 31E1 note).
(LITTLE) BUSBY. See 29N9 note. Bruce account latinised *Buschebia* (see 31E1 note).
CRATHORNE. Bruce account latinised *Cratorna* (see 31E1 note).
FOXTON. The form of the name in the Bruce account, *Foxtun*, is more accurate than that of DB proper, which appears to have corrupt spellings (Jensen 11).
HILTON. Bruce account latinised *Hiltona* (see 31E1 note).
THORNABY. Bruce account latinised *Tormozbia* (see 31E1 note).
MARTON (IN CLEVELAND). See 1N25 note. Bruce account latinised Martona (see 31E1 note).
NEWHAM (HALL). See 1N26 note.
TOLLESBY. See 1N27 note. The Bruce account form of the name with a single -*l*- is closer to the original form of the name than that used in DB proper with a double -*ll*- (Jensen 11).
ACKLAM. See 1N28 note.
FACEBY. In the Bruce account form, *Foitesbi*, the OE genitive -*es* has been substituted or restored from the Scandinavian -*s* found in the DB form *Fe(i)zbi* (Jensen 13). The unvoiced [*s*] represented in the -*c*- spelling, however, may well be due to the Scandinavian inflexion: the OE genitive -*es* would probably have given [z] (JMcND). The -*oi* spelling suggests a French as opposed to a Norman scribe (Jensen 15).
TANTON. Bruce account latinised *Tametona* (see 31E1 note).
GOULTON (GRANGE). See 1N39 note. Bruce account latinised *Goltona* (see 31E1 note). The form in the Bruce account with -*ol*- is closer to the original form of the name than that used in DB proper where there has been AN pre-consonantal vocalisation to give -*ou*- (Jensen 11).
BERGOLBI. See 1N31 note.

31N6   MORTON (GRANGE). See 1N19 note; 31N4 note.
NEWTON. Bruce account latinised *Nietona* (see 31E1 note).
UPSALL (HALL). See 1N14 note. The form of the name in the Bruce account, *Upesale*, is closer to the original form of the name than that in DB proper, *Upeshale* (29N4; SN,L26), although in one entry (1N14) DB also has *Upesale* (see Jensen 11).
(PINCHIN)THORPE (HALL). See 1N15 note. In DB proper Pinchinthorpe Hall appears as simply *Torp*, but by the time of the Bruce account it had become *Oustorp* 'east thorp'; Jensen 9 suggests that this was in relation to neighbouring Newton, but Newton is in fact to the south of Pinchinthorpe Hall. The adjective may have been added to distinguish it from Nunthorpe (also *Torp* in DB), whose vill centre is only 2¼ miles due west of Pinchinthorpe Hall.

31N7   KILDALE. Bruce account latinised *Childala* (see 31E1 note).
ORMESBY. Bruce account latinised *Ormesbia* (see 31E1 note).
LAZENBY. Bruce account latinised *Laisinbia* (see 31E1 note); the name also shows AN sound-substitution of -*in* for -*ing* (Jensen 16).
GUISBOROUGH. The form of the name in the Bruce account, *Gisborne*, already shows that simplification of the consonant group found in *Ghiges-, Gighes-, Chigesburgh, -burch, -borc* in DB proper which led eventually to the modern form of the name (Jensen 13).

31N8   'STAINTON'. See 1N6 note. Bruce account latinised *Esteintona* (see 31E1 note); the name also shows the addition of AN prosthetic *E*- not present in the DB form *Steintun* (Jensen 16).

CAWTHORN. Bruce account latinised *Caltorna* (see 31E1 note).

AMOTHERBY. Bruce account latinised *Edmundrebia* (see 31E1 note). The variation in spelling from the form in DB proper, *Aimundrebi, Andebi, Eindebi*, probably represents a phonetic process rather than a change of name.

(LOW) HUTTON. See 8N9 note.

GANTHORPE. Possibly because it was preceded by *Hotun* and followed by *Brunetona*, the scribe of the Bruce account accidentally wrote *-tona* instead of the *-torp* forms given in DB proper and in all subsequent recordings of the name. The Bruce account form *Galme-* is, however, closer to the original personal name *Galmr* from which the place-name was formed, than the form *Gamel-* given in DB proper, where there has been confusion with ON *Gamall* (PNNR 34; SPN 89).

BROMPTON. Bruce account latinised *Brunetona* (see 31E1 note). Note that Jensen 13 incorrectly ascribes this name to Potter Brompton in the ER, although it is definitely listed here under the NR in a list of other NR places.

THORNTON (DALE). Bruce account latinised *Torentona* (see 31E1 note).

31N9   CAYTON. Bruce account latinised *Caimtona* (see 31E1 note). The variation in spelling from the DB form with *Calve-* probably represents a scribal error rather than a change of name (Jensen 10).

31N10   HARPHAM, GRANSMOOR. Although listed here under the NR, both these places were in the ER. They are in fact listed in the ER earlier in the Bruce account (31E1), where they are given in a list of the places in Burton Agnes and its jurisdiction in which Robert held 44 carucates of land.

HARPHAM. See 31E1 note.

EXCHANGED. *cambiavit* 'he exchanged' (DF LXXI). Farley erroneously gives this a capital *C*.

GRANSMOOR. See 31E1 note. Unlike in its first recording in the Bruce account, here given in latinised form *Grentesmora* (see 31E1 note).

IN ESKDALE. The *i* in *in* has rather a long stroke, which Farley reproduces as a *j*. It is not significant.

ESKDALE(SIDE). Omitted from DG. Bruce account latinised *Eschedala* (see 31E1 note). Not in DB proper, only in the Bruce account. The vill was subsequently amalgamated with Ugglebarnby to form the township of Eskdaleside cum Ugglebarnby. The original vill centre is uncertain; the grid reference given in the index is that for Esk Hall.

12 CARUCATES, 2 BOVATES. Assuming the addition is correct, the carucate here contains 8 bovates.

NAMELY IN. DB *scili. in* for *scilicet in* 'namely in' (DF LXXI). Farley omits the *in*.

DANBY. See 23N18 note. Bruce account latinised *Danebia* (see 31E1 note).

CRUNKLY (GILL). Bruce account latinised *Crubecliva*. This reference to Crunkly Gill is omitted from DG 519.

TWO HANGTONS. Not in DB proper, only in the Bruce account, where the name has a latinised form (see 31E1 note). DG 523 gives Bruce account *in duabus Hanechetonis* as Hangton and Hangton Hill, but only Hangton Hill appears on the modern 6 in. OS map and on the 1st ed. 6 in. OS map, sheets 31, 45, in Glaisdale township at NZ 762 062, so 'Hangton' has been treated here as lost.

LEALHOLM. See 23N18 note. The variation of the spelling in the Bruce account, *Laclum*, from the form in DB proper, *Lelun*, probably represents a corruption rather than a change of name (Jensen 10).

CN1   CLAIMS OF YORKSHIRE. See Appendix. Throughout this section Farley tends to reproduce *i* as *j*. This is not significant.

LANGBARGH WAPENTAKE. See 1N1 note.

FYLING (OLD HALL). DB *Figelinge* (DF LXXVII). Farley erroneously *Figelingae*.

CN2   *MANESHOU* (RYEDALE) WAPENTAKE. See 1N58 note. This rubric heading does not apply to the places in CN4-5, which are in *Bolesford* (Bulmer) Wapentake in the Summary.

CN3   YORKSHIRE. DB *eurvicsyre* (DF LXXVII). Farley erroneously *euruicscyre*.

CN4-5   (SAND) HUTTON, (SHERIFF) HUTTON. DG 533 gives Bruce account *Hotone, -tun(e)* as both Sand Hutton and Sheriff Hutton but does not distinguish which is which on fol. 373a. As the land in *Hotune* of CN5 is stated to be that of Thorulfr, Thorketill and Thorsteinn, and these men held land in Sheriff Hutton (1N87), the reference in CN5 must be to Sheriff Hutton, and in CN4 to Sand Hutton.

CN5   SHERIFF HUTTON. This is written above the line.

CE1   1 MANOR. This is written above the line.

(SOUTH) CLIFFE. DG 470, 480 gives DB *Cliue* as Cliffe (near Hemingbrough) and South Cliffe, but does not distinguish which is which on fol. 373a. As the land in the *Cliue* of CE21 is linked with Osgodby, this must be Cliffe, and so the entry in CE1 must refer to South Cliffe.

CE1-4;8   NIGEL. This is obviously Nigel Fossard, who is given with his full name in the preceding entry, CN5, the shortened form being used by the scribe to save space.

CE6   ALDGYTH. See 5E27 note.

CE10   CROOM (HOUSE). See 1E58 note.
'THORSHOWE' WAPENTAKE. See 5E68 note.

CE11   NIGEL FOSSARD. 'Fossard' is written above the line.

CE12   BELBY (HOUSE). See 1E2 note.

CE13   BRANTINGHAM. See SE,We12 note.
NIGEL FOSSARD. 'Fossard' is written above the line.

CE14   LUND. See 3Y2 note.

CE16   BURLAND (HOUSE). Not in DB proper, only in the Claims and the Summary. DG 469 Burland. The full modern name is Burland House.

CE17   BELBY (HOUSE). See 1E2 note.

CE18   COUNT ROBERT. 'Robert' is written above the line.

CE19   NORTH DUFFIELD. DB *Nortdufelt* (DF LXXVII). Farley *Nort dufelt*.

CE19-21   NIGEL. This is obviously Nigel Fossard (see CE1 note).

CE20   YORK. DG 539 omits this reference to York.

CE21   CLIFFE. See CE1 note.

CE24   *NEWTON* (GARDHAM). See 3Y1 note.

CE25   *IANULFESTORP*. See 13E6 note. Farley erroneously *Lanulfestorp* (DF LXXVII).

CE26   SCOREBY (MANOR). See 13E5 note.
THAT IS. There is a blot in the text at this point (DF LXXVII). Farley represents this by dots, but it is clear that *id est* 'that is' was written.
IANULFESTORP. See 13E6 note. Farley erroneously *Lanulfestorp* (DF LXXVII).

CE27   NIGEL. This is obviously Nigel Fossard (see CE1 note).
EARNWINE THE PRIEST. See 29W2 note.

CE28   THORPE (LE STREET). See 1Y7 note.
GILBERT TISON'S. 'Tison' is written above the line.

CE30   CLIFTON. This is in the NR.
IN LORDSHIP. *In dnio* for *in dominio* 'in lordship' is written above the line.

CE32   *SCARDIZTORP*. See 26E8 note.
BONDI. See 26E8 note.

CE33   AFTER 1066. In the text *T.R.W.* for *tempore regis Willelmi* 'in the time of King William'.

CW1-3   ILBERT. This is Ilbert de Lacy, who held these places as part of the honour of Pontefract.

CW1   ILBERT'S CASTLE. A reference to the honour of Pontefract, administered from Pontefract Castle, as Thorner was part of the honour (WYAS 532-3). See Appendix.

CW2   WILLIAM MALET. There is a small blot after his name. It is unlikely that it conceals anything (DF LXXVIII).
YEADON. DB *Iadon* (DF LXXVIII). Farley erroneously *Ladon*. Yeadon remained outside Ilbert de Lacy's honour of Pontefract, as half lay in the Percy fee and half in the Meschin fee (WYAS 575-6). In this section the number of manors is written above the relevant place-names.
OGLETHORPE (HALL). See 5W7 note.
BRAMHAM. There is a gap in the text after this place-name.

CW2-3   HAZELWOOD (CASTLE). See 13W3 note.

CW3   STUTTON. The number of manors is written above the relevant place-names.
(NORTH) MILFORD (HALL). See 9W33 note.
NEUHUSE. See 9W31 note.
TOULSTON. See 5W7 note.
SAXEHALE. Thus DB (DF LXXVIII). DG 505 erroneously *Saxehala*.
THE CASTLE. Pontefract Castle, the administrative centre of Ilbert de Lacy's honour of Pontefract. See CW1 note.
LEAD. See 9W19 note.

CW6   WEARDLEY. See 28W30.
(EAST) RIGTON. See 29W24 note.
COMPTON. Not in DB proper, only in the Claims. The territory of the vill of Compton seems subsequently to have been known as Collingham, with Compton surviving as the name of a minor settlement within Collingham township (see WYAS 350).

CW10   WILSIC (HALL). See 12W1 note.
        BELONGS TO IT. *ad* 'to' is written above the line.

CW11   SOTAKOLLR. The name *Sotecol* has been written above the phrase '1 church'. SPN 259 considers that the name may be an AN formation, whereas Skaife 285 regards the man of this entry as the same person as the *Scotcol, Scotecol* (i.e. Skotakollr) of 5W11 and 9W40. The SPN attribution has been followed in this edition.

CW12-
14   NIGEL. This is obviously Nigel Fossard (see CE1 note).

CW13   TUDWORTH (GREEN). See 12W1 note.

CW14   *STREETTHORPE* (EDENTHORPE). See 12W1 note.

CW16   LOVERSALL. The unusual arrangement of this entry is as Farley reproduces it (DF LXXVIII).

CW18   WADWORTH. Manors. See CW3 note.
        STANCIL. Not in DB proper, only in the Claims. DG 508 reads the DB form of Stancil as *Steineshale*, whereas Farley reads it as *Stemeshale*. It is impossible to tell from the Facsimile (DF LXXVIII) which the scribe intended as the minims are so close together that the reading could be either -*in*- or -*m*-. The scribe of this section normally leaves a space between -*i*- and the following letters, so that Farley's reading is perhaps the more logical; but in view of the likely derivation of the name from ON *steinn* or OE *stan* (PNWR i, 60), the DG reading seems the more likely. On the depopulated vill centre of Stancil see LVY 239.

CW19   WADWORTH. DB *Wadeuorde* (DF LXXVIII). DG 511 erroneously *Wadewrde*.

CW20   HOUGHTON. Manors. See CW3 note.

CW21;23 NIGEL. This is obviously Nigel Fossard (see CE1 note).

CW23   ST. MARY'S CHURCH ... IN MORLEY WOOD. Woodkirk church (WYAS 222, note 28), situated at SE 2719 2504 in West Ardsley township, which formed part of the King's manor of Wakefield. Ilbert de Lacy's interest in the church, as lord of the honour of Pontefract, may have been through his ownership of East Ardsley (which appears originally to have been part of Woodkirk ecclesiastical parish) or his being lord of Morley (WYAS 361, 554).

CW24   AINSTY. There is a gap between 'men' and 'Ainsty' in the text as reproduced by Farley (DF LXXVIII).
        2 MANORS. Farley's reproduction of '2' is rather obscure because he attached a penstroke of the scribe to the first figure. Despite this penstroke '2' is clear in the Facsimile (DF LXXVIII).
        STEETON (HALL). See 13W7 note.
        ARNKETILL SON OF WULFSTAN. *fil Ulstan* for *filius Ulstani* 'son of Wulfstan' is written above the line.

CW25   'HAGGENBY'. See 13W16 note.

CW26   THE SAME WILLIAM. *eiusdem* 'of the same' is written above the line. As this section of the Claims (CW25-30) is dealing with lands which should be held by William Malet, it seems likely that the William of this entry is also William Malet.

CW27   OSBERN DE ARCHES. *Arcis* 'of Arches' is written above the line.
        STEETON (HALL). See 13W7 note.

CW30   (PALLA)THORPE. See 5W35 note.
        MULEHALE. See 29W11 note.

CW31   HORNINGTON (MANOR). See 13W17 note.
        MALET. As William Malet is referred to with his full name in the preceding entry, this is probably William Malet, with his Christian name being assumed, rather than Robert Malet.

CW32   SCAGGLETHORPE. See 25W16 note. The number of manors is written above the place-names (see CW3 note).

CW34   HEALAUGH. DB *Hailage* (DF LXXIX). DG 496 erroneously *Hailaga*.

CW37   STEETON (HALL). See 13W7 note.
        STEETON. This entry begins abruptly. Furthermore it lacks the marginal mark which indicates the commencement of the other entries. In this context it may be significant that there is a gap between this entry and the previous one, sufficient for 1 line of text (DF LXXIX). It is possible that there was originally some text before Ulfketill's name which the scribe either could not read from the draft or omitted for some other reason.
        HORNINGTON (MANOR). See 13W17 note.
        (PALLA)THORPE. See 5W35 note.

CW38   'BURGHSHIRE' (CLARO) WAPENTAKE. See 5W36 note.

CW39   DROGO. This must be Drogo de Bevrere as he is the only major landholder of that name recorded in the Yorkshire section of DB and, in view of his extensive landholdings in Holderness, is the most likely person to be in dispute with St. John's of Beverley.

THE CANONS. As this entry deals with the land claimed for St. John's of Beverley, the Canons must belong to that house, not to St. Peter's of York.

CE34-52 [HOLDERNESS]. See 2E17 note. All the places listed in this section are recorded as being in Holderness in the Summary.

CE36   *LUUETOTHOLM*. Not in DB proper, only here in the Claims. A lost vill subsequently part of Leven township (DG 476).

LOVETTOT. PNDB 322 considers that the origins of this name are obscure, but it seems likely that it is derived from the AN personal name *Lovett, Luuet, Louet* (see DB Herts 39,2,8; DB Leics 13,58;27; DB Staffs 12,13; PNDB 322), wth an *-ot* diminutive suffix (PNDB 125-6); an interesting duplication of the diminutive. The name is probably masculine, although it could be feminine (we are grateful to JMcND for his comments on this form). It is striking that the vill named in this entry appears to contain the same personal name as the holder of the land in 1066, suggesting that it may have been named from its holder; an example of the type of name which changes each time the holder of the land changes. This hypothesis is perhaps strengthened by the fact that this appears to be the only recording of the place-name.

CE37   *CHENUTHESHOLM*. See 14E35 note. As with the previous entry (see CE36 note), this may be a case of a place named temporarily from its holder.

CE38   CATFOSS (HALL). See 14E33 note.

CE41   SON. DB *f.* for *filius* 'son' (DF LXXIX). Farley erroneously prints this in upper case.

CE42   LANGTHORPE (HALL). See 14E41 note.

CE45   HIS BROTHER. See 14E48 note.

CE46   *ANDREBI*. See 14E4 note.

CE48   REDMERE. See 14E4 note.

CE49   5 MANORS. The text is not clear at this point and the figure could be '6'. The interpretation depends on whether the characters are read as *.v.* (Farley) or *.vi* (Skaife 208). The third character certainly looks more like a minim than a dot (DF LXXIX) but, on the other hand, were it intended to be a minim, a dot would be expected to follow it to give *.vi*. The matter must remain unresolved, but Farley's reading seems preferable, and is followed here.

SIWARD. Is written above the line at the end of the entry.

CE51   GRIMKETILL. See 14E22 note.

CE52   SOUTHCOATES. See 2E35 note.

DROGO. This is Drogo de Bevrere, who is recorded in DB proper as holding this land (14E49).

CW40   HEALAUGH. The earlier entries relating to Healaugh and its jurisdiction end at CW37.

'HAGGENBY'. See 13W16 note.

OUSTON (FARM). See 13W14 note.

CW42   COUNT ALAN. *Com.* for *comes* 'count' is written above the line.

SN,Y1   THE SUMMARY. See Appendix for discussion of this.

IN THE CITY OF YORK. The capital *I* in *In* is missing from the text (DF LXXXI).

SN,Y2   MURTON. DG 529 reports DB *Mortune* as *Morton* (in Skelton) and *Murton* (near York), but does not distinguish which entry on fol. 379 is which. As the *Mortune* of this entry is linked with Osbaldwick, it is likely to be Murton township in Birdforth Wapentake near York, and the entry in SN,Y8 must be *Mortun* in Skelton township, especially as it is there linked with Wigginton.

SN,Y3   SANDBURN (HOUSE). See C25 note.

SN,Y4   (GATE) FULFORD. See C28 note.

SN,Y8   *MORTUN*. See C34 note; SN,Y2 note.

SW,Sk1 SKYRACK WAPENTAKE. See 5W1 note.

SW,Sk1-
2   OTLEY. See 2W4 note.

SW,Sk1 MANOR. *M.* for *manerium* 'manor' is written above Otley.

('LITTLE') HAWKSWORTH. See 2W4 note.

BURLEY (IN WHARFEDALE). See 2W4 note.

SW,Sk2 *GEREBURG* WAPENTAKE. Mentioned only in the Summary, not in DB proper, where the vills concerned are included in 'Burghshire' Wapentake (see 5W36 note). It consisted of the western part of the later wapentake of Upper Claro and comprised those berewicks of the Archbishop of York's Otley estate which were west of the River Washburn and north of the River Wharfe as far west as Middleton. This is the only recording of the

name, which probably means 'earthwork, or fort, in the triangular corner of land' (PNWR
v, 1). So the wapentake meeting place was probably at a yet-to-be-identified fortified site.
STUBHAM. See 2W4 note.
(NETHER) TIMBLE. See 2W4 note.
ESTONE. DG 485, 493 does not distinguish which *Estone* of fol. 379 is the lost vill *Estone*
and which is Aston. This *Estone*, which the Archbishop of York holds as an outlier of
Otley, must be the lost *Estone*, which is similarly an outlier of the Archbishop's Otley
estate in DB proper (2W4). On this see 2W4 note. The *Estone* of SW,Sf33 must then be
Aston.
CLIFTON. See 2W4 note.
BICHERUN. See 2W4 note.
IN ALL 20 ... The entry was left incomplete (DF LXXXI). Possibly 20 carucates was
intended.

SW,Sk3   (EAST) RIGTON. See 28W24 note.
WEARDLEY. See 28W30 note. DB *Wartle* (DF LXXXI). Farley erroneously *Warde.*
GOSPATRIC. His name is continued above the line.

SW,Sk4   ILBERT. The Summary lists only tenants-in-chief, so here and in subsequent entries
references to Ilbert are to Ilbert de Lacy, who holds these lands in DB proper as part of
the honour of Pontefract.
KIPPAX. See 9W1 note.
LEDSTON. See 9W1 note.
ALLERTON (BYWATER). DG 484, 490 does not distinguish which *Alretune* of fol. 379 is
Allerton Bywater and which is Chapel Allerton. As the *Alretune* of this entry comes
between Ledston and Great and Little Preston, it must on geographical grounds be
Allerton Bywater. The *Alretune* of SW,Sk9, there linked with Gipton and Colton, must be
Chapel Allerton.
(GREAT AND LITTLE) PRESTON. See 9W1 note.

SW,Sk4   COLDCOTES. See 9W1 note.
GIPTON. See 9W1 note.

SW,Sk4-   SWILLINGTON. See 9W1 note.
5   SKELTON (GRANGE). See 9W1 note.
SW,Sk   KIDDAL (HALL). See 9W1 note.
4;6   PARLINGTON. See 9W1 note.
SW,Sk6   SHIPPEN (HOUSE). See 9W4 note.
SW,Sk7   *CUFFORTH* (COWTHWAITE). See 9W1 note.
SW,Sk8   BIRKBY (HILL). See 9W13 note.
'WHEATCROFT'. See 9W13 note. DB *Watecroft* (DF LXXXI). Farley erroneously
Watecrost.

SW,Sk9   (CHAPEL) ALLERTON. See 9W14 note; SW,Sk4 note.
GIPTON. See 9W1 note.

SW,Sk10   (TEMPLE) NEWSAM. See 9W16 note.
THORPE (STAPLETON). DG 501, 509 does not distinguish which *Torp* of fol. 379 is
Middlethorpe, Thorpe Hesley, Thorpe Salvin, Thorpe Stapleton or Thorpe Willoughby,
but as the *Torp* of this entry is linked with Temple Newsam, it must be Thorpe Stapleton,
the adjacent vill (on Thorpe Stapleton see 9W17 note). The *Torp* of SW,BA5, linked there
with Brayton, must be Thorpe Willoughby, as they are adjacent vills. The *Torp* of SW,Sf2,
which is linked with North Anston and South Anston, must be Thorpe Salvin, as they are
adjacent townships. The *Torp* of SW,Sf16, which is linked with Wentworth, must be
Thorpe Hesley, as they are adjacent townships.

SW,Sk11   MORTON. DG 502 reports Morton (near Keighley), whereas WYAS 232-3 identifies
with the *Mortune* of 1W8 (see further 1W8 note). The main text ascribes 4 carucates in
Mortune to the King (1W5) and a further 3 carucates to him in a second *Mortune* (1W8).
The *Mortun* of this entry, where the King has 4 carucates, is more likely to be identified
with the *Mortune* of 1W5 in view of the coincidence of the amounts of land involved. In the
main text the *Mortune* of 1W5 is linked with Riddlesden, thus identifying it as Morton
near Keighley in the west of Skyrack Wapentake. WYAS 232-3 considers that the *Mortun*
of SW,Sk11 should be located in the eastern part of Skyrack because it is listed after
Leeds and Headingley (SW,Sk11) and before *Snitertun,* Wothersome and Bardsey
(SW,Sk12). But the geographical order generally followed in the Summary is not a
conclusive argument, as *Redelesdene* (SW,Sk13), which must be Riddlesden in western
Skyrack, is similarly listed in the Summary amongst a group of eastern Skyrack vills,

being preceded by Bardsey (SE,Sk12) and followed by Harewood and *Newhall* (SW,Sk13). The DG identification has therefore been followed in this edition.

MORTON, 4 CARUCATES. '4' is written as 2 sets of *II*s one above the other.

SW,Sk12 *SNITERTUN*. See 9W18 note.

WOTHERSOME. See 1W3 note.

SW,Sk13 RIDDLESDEN. See 1W5 note.

HAREWOOD. See 1W9 note.

SW,Sk
13-14 *NEWHALL*. See 1W12 note.

SW,Sk14 STOCKTON. See 1W11 note.

SW,Sk15 LOFTHOUSE. See 1W14 note.

STUB HOUSE. See 1W15 note.

ALWOODLEY. See 1W16 note.

SW,Sk16 WIKE. See 1W13 note.

(EAST) CARLTON. DG 490 does not distinguish which *Carletun* of fol. 379 is Carlton near Otley and which Carlton near Snaith. As this *Carletun* is recorded under Skyrack Wapentake and as held by Robert Malet, it must be East Carlton near Otley in Skyrack, which is similarly held by Robert Malet in DB proper (11W1; see also 11W1 note). The *Carletun* of SW,BA7 listed under Barkston Ash Wapentake must be Carlton township near Snaith in Barkston Ash.

SW,Sk17 HORSFORTH. See 1W17 note.

YEADON. DB *Iadun* (DF LXXXI). Farley erroneously *Ladun*.

SW,Sk18 BINGLEY. See 24W1 note.

ELDWICK. See 24W1 note.

'HALTON'. See 24W1 note.

ERNEIS. The Summary lists only tenants-in-chief, so this is Erneis de Burun, who holds these lands in DB proper (24W1).

ADEL. See 5W2 note.

SW,Sk20 BURDEN (HEAD). See 5W4 note.

SW,BA1 BARKSTON (ASH) WAPENTAKE. See 5W6 note.

SHERBURN (IN ELMET) WITH ITS OUTLIERS. See 2B1 note.

SW,BA2 ULLESKELF WITH ITS OUTLIERS. See 2W6 note.

SW,BA3 MONK HAY (STILE). See 5W7 note.

TOULSTON. See 5W7 note.

OGLETHORPE (HALL). See 5W7 note.

HAZELWOOD (CASTLE). See 13W3 note.

SW,BA4 *SAXHALE*. See 13W4 note. DB *Saxhale* (DF LXXXI). DG 505 erroneously *Saxhala*.

SW,BA5 GRIMSTON (GRANGE). See 9W29 note.

TOWTON. Not in DB proper, only in the Summary.

LEAD. See 9W19 note.

BURTON (HALL). See 9W20 note.

THORPE (WILLOUGHBY). See SW,Sk10 note.

HUNCHILHUSES. See 9W21 note.

SW,BA6 (CHURCH AND LITTLE) FENTON. See 9W23 note.

SW,BA7 CARLTON. See SW,Sk16 note.

EARNWINE. DB proper identifies the man holding this land in Camblesforth as Earnwine the Priest (29W2).

SW,BA8 NEWTON ('WALLIS'). See 9W27 note.

TOULSTON. See 5W7 note.

OGLETHORPE (HALL). See 5W7 note.

7 CARUCATES AND 7 BOVATES. DB *vii c.* and *vii b.* (DF LXXXI). Farley erroneously '7 carucates and 6 bovates'.

GRIMSTON (GRANGE). See 9W29 note.

NEUHUSE. See 9W31 note.

SW,BA9 (NORTH) MILFORD (HALL). See 9W33 note.

SW,BA
10-13 FAIRBURN, LEDSHAM, TADCASTER, NEWTON (KYME). These 4 entries have been added in the margin.

SW,Sf1 [STRAFFORTH WAPENTAKE]. See 5W8 note. Although a space has been left by the DB scribe between the list of places in Barkston Ash Wapentake and those in Strafforth (DF LXXXI), he appears to have omitted to write in the rubric for Strafforth Wapentake.

ITS OUTLIERS. For a list of the berewicks of Conisbrough see 12W1, where the total land is given as 86 carucates and 15 acres.

SW,Sf2   (SOUTH) ANSTON. DG 507 reads the DB form as *Litelanstan*, whereas Farley gives it as *Titelanstan*. The actual DB form (DF LXXXI) is difficult to read and could be either; it appears to be closer to a *T* than to an *L*, although an *L* is to be expected and the form earlier in the main text is *Litelastone* (10W1).

       THORPE (SALVIN). See SW,Sk10 note.

       (SLADE) HOOTON. DG 498, 508 does not distinguish which *Hotone* of fol. 379b (fol. 379 in DG numbering) is Hooton Levitt and which Slade Hooton, both located in Strafforth Wapentake and less than 2 miles apart. As the *Hotone* of this entry is held by Roger de Busli it must be Slade Hooton, similarly held by Roger de Busli in DB proper (10W1). The *Hotone* of SW,Sf24, held by the Count of Mortain, must be Hooton Levitt, which is held by the Count in the main text (5W12).

       NEWHALL (GRANGE). DG 502 does not distinguish which *Neuhalle* of fol. 379b (fol. 379 in DG numbering) is Newhall and which Newhill. Both are held by Roger de Busli, but the *Neuhalle* of this entry, linked with the townships around Laughton en le Morthen, must be Newhall Grange (on which see 10W1 note). The *Neuhalle* of SW,Sf8, linked with Hooton Roberts and Denaby, must be Newhill.

SW,Sf4   DADSLEY. See 10W3 note.

SW,Sf4-5   HELLABY. See 10W3 note.

SW,Sf7   *GRIMESHOU*. See 10W11 note.

SW,Sf8   NEWHILL. See SW,Sf2 note.

       HOOTON (ROBERTS). DG 498 does not distinguish which *Hotun* of fol. 379b (fol. 379 in DG numbering) is Hooton Pagnell and which Hooton Roberts, both in Strafforth Wapentake. As the *Hotun* of this entry is linked with Denaby, the adjacent township to Hooton Roberts, and is held by Roger de Busli, who holds Hooton Roberts in DB proper (10W12), it must be Hooton Roberts. The *Hotun* of SW,Sf28, which is linked with Hampole, the adjacent township to Hooton Pagnell, and is held by the Count of Mortain, who holds Hooton Pagnell in the main text (5W14), must be Hooton Pagnell.

SW,Sf9   ADWICK (UPON DEARNE). DG 484 does not distinguish which *Adeuuic* of fol. 379b (fol. 379 in DG numbering) is Adwick upon Dearne and which Adwick le Street. This *Adeuuic*, which is linked with Barnbrough and in which Roger de Busli holds 2½ carucates, should be Adwick upon Dearne, in which Roger de Busli holds 2½ carucates in DB proper (10W14). The *Adeuuic* of SW,Sf34 should be Adwick le Street, as it is linked with Doncaster and places to its north and is held by the Count of Mortain, who holds this estate in the main text (5W30). The *Adeuuic* of SW,O2 is also probably Adwick le Street, as it is mentioned in the same clause as Norton, which lies 4 miles to the north of Adwick le Street. Although listed there under Osgoldcross Wapentake, whereas in SW,Sf34 under Strafforth Wapentake, Adwick le Street is on the northern boundary of Strafforth Wapentake with Osgoldcross and part of the vill may have extended into Osgoldcross. According to SW,O2 Roger de Busli held 7 carucates and 2 bovates in *Adeuuic*, while the Count of Mortain had 2 bovates; the main text does not tell us how much land the Count held there, but Roger is stated to have 6 bovates (10W39). Nevertheless Adwick le Street appears to be the best candidate in this case.

       BILHAM (HOUSE). See 5W14 note.

SW,Sf11   (WEST) MELTON. DG 497, 512 does not distinguish which *Medeltone* of fol. 379b (fol. 379 in DG numbering) is High Melton and which is West Melton, in two entries the land being held by Roger de Busli (SW,Sf11 and SW,Sf14) and in the third by the King (SW,Sf16). As the *Medeltone* of this entry is linked with *Toftes* and Wombwell, just to the west of West Melton, which is linked also with these two places in entries in the main text (10W19; 29W4), it must be West Melton, while the *Medeltone* of SW,Sf14, which is linked with Cadeby, should be High Melton, the adjacent township. The *Medeltone* of SW,Sf16 should be West Melton, which occurs twice elsewhere in that clause and is linked with places located in the area of West Melton, although the King is not recorded in the main text as holding land in West Melton.

       TOFTES. See 10W19 note.

SW,Sf
13;15   COUNT AUBREY. Aubrey of Coucy, who holds these lands in DB proper (27W1-2).

SW,Sf13   DARFIELD, 4 CARUCATES. 4 is written as 2 sets of *II*s one above the other.

SW,Sf14   (HIGH) MELTON. See 10W20 note; SW,Sf11 note.

       WILDTHORPE. See 10W21 note.

SW,Sf15   SPROTBROUGH, CUSWORTH AND BALBY. There is a large *r* in the margin beside this entry, standing for *require* 'enquire further'. This may be because these 3 places do not have a tenant indicated.

SW,Sf16   (WEST) MELTON. See SW,Sf11 note.

THORPE (HESLEY). See SW,Sk10 note. Not in DB proper, only in the Summary.

SW,Sf16-17 BRAMPTON (BIERLOW). DG 488 does not distinguish which *Brantone* of fol. 379b (fol. 379 in DG numbering) is Brampton Bierlow, Brampton en le Morthen or Branton. Since the *Brantone* of these entries is linked with Wentworth, Wath upon Dearne and Thorpe Hesley, it is likely to be Brampton Bierlow, as they are adjacent townships; the King is not recorded in DB proper as holding Brampton Bierlow directly but it is held by one of his thanes, Arnthorr (29W7), and such holdings are ascribed directly to the King in the Summary. The *Brantone* of SW,Sf21 should be Branton as it is linked with Cantley, the adjacent vill into which it was subsumed subsequent to DB, and it is recorded there as being held by Geoffrey Alselin who holds Branton and Cantley in the main text (18W1). The *Brantone* of SW,Sf33 should be Brampton en le Morthen as it is linked with Ulley, the adjacent township, and is held by the Count of Mortain, who also holds Brampton en le Morthen in DB proper (5W25).

SW,Sf16-17 *ELDEBERGE*. Lost in Brampton Bierlow (DG 493). *Eldeberge* only occurs in these two entries in the Summary, not in DB proper.

SW,Sf21 *SHUTTLEWORTH* (LITTLEWORTH). See 5W8 note.

LOVERSALL. Farley reads the DB form as *Iuureshale*, whereas DG 500 and PNWR i, 34 read it as *Luureshale*. The cross-stroke of the bottom of the initial letter is extremely short (DF LXXXI) and the Farley reading would appear to be correct, although in view of the *L* in two of the earlier recordings in DB and also in later documents, an *L* would seem more likely. Possibly the DB scribe miscopied an *L* as *I*.

AUCKLEY AND AUCKLEY. DG 485 and PNWR i, 44 concur in ascribing both the *Alceslei* and the *Alchelie* forms of this entry to Auckley. The entry in DB proper for the manor of Hexthorpe records only one entry for Auckley, but the carucage given there is 15 (5W8), whereas 22½ carucates are recorded here; possibly the Count of Mortain had two separate holdings in Auckley so it was entered twice, and part of the second holding may account for some of the missing carucates.

BRANTON. See SW,Sf16 note.

SW,Sf22 EARNWINE. The main text identifies the man holding land in Armthorpe as Earnwine the Priest (29W9).

SW,Sf23 BARNBY (DUN). See 5W10 note.

SW,Sf24 HOOTON (LEVITT). See SW,Sf2 note.

SW,Sf25 (OLD) EDLINGTON. See 13W9 note.

SW,Sf28 HAMPOLE. See 9W43 note.

FRICKLEY. See 9W34 note.

SW,Sf 28;30 STOTFOLD. See 5W18 note.

SW,Sf28 HOOTON (PAGNELL). See SW,Sf8 note.

SW,Sf29 BRODSWORTH AND PICKBURN. See 10W34 note.

SW,Sf30 CLAYTON. See 5W18 note.

DEIGHTONBY (FIELDS). See 5W18 note.

SW,Sf32 AUGHTON (HALL). See 5W21 note.

SW,Sf33 ASTON. See SW,Sk2 note.

BRAMPTON (EN LE MORTHEN). See SW,Sf16 note.

SW,Sf34 ADWICK (LE STREET). See SW,Sf9 note.

SCINESTORP. See 5W30 note.

LANGTHWAITE. See 5W28 note.

BENTLEY. Although recorded here under Strafforth Wapentake, of which it continued to be a part, Bentley is also recorded in the Summary under Osgoldcross Wapentake (SW,O1), together with Arksey, which was also subsequently part of Strafforth Wapentake, as it was subsumed into Bentley township. Bentley lies on the northern boundary of Strafforth with Osgoldcross; it may be that it was Arksey which was originally in Osgoldcross, which is why Bentley is recorded in Osgoldcross in the linked entry.

SW,Sf35 HALLAM. See 10W41 note.

SW,Sf36 *(WALDER)SHELF*. See 1W22 note.

SW,Sf37 (SOUTH) ELMSALL. DG 503, 507 does not distinguish which *Ermeshale* of fol. 379c (fol. 379b in DG numbering) is North Elmsall and which is South Elmsall, both being held in the Summary by Ilbert de Lacy. As this *Ermeshale* is linked with the same places as South Elmsall in DB proper (9W34), it should be South Elmsall. The *Ermeshale* of SW,O13 should be North Elmsall, which is there linked with Kellington and which comes directly after Kellington in the main text (9W63).

FRICKLEY. See 9W34 note.

(MOOR)THORPE. DG 502, 504, 509 does not distinguish which *Torp* of fol. 379c (fol. 379b in DG numbering) is Moorthorpe, Pallathorpe, Thorp Arch, Thorpe Audlin, Thorpe Hill or Thorpe on the Hill. The *Torp* of SW,Bu1 should be Thorpe Hill in Upper Claro Wapentake, as it is listed there under 'Burghshire' Wapentake. The *Torp* recorded under Morley Wapentake in SW,M2 should be Thorpe on the Hill, now in Agbrigg Wapentake, but in the 11th century located in Morley Wapentake (see 9W118 note). Of the two held by Ilbert de Lacy, both in the Summary and in the text proper, the *Torp* of SW,Sf37 can be identified with Moorthorpe as it is linked with South Elmsall, Frickley, and South Kirkby, as is Moorthorpe in DB proper (9W34), leaving the other *Torp* (SW,O6), which is recorded under Osgoldcross Wapentake, as Thorpe Audlin in Osgoldcross; in the Summary this *Torp* comes in the entry before that for Badsworth, Upton and Rogerthorpe, which it follows in DB proper (9W46). Of the three entries under Ainsty Wapentake in the Summary, the *Torp* of SW,An5 with land held by Percy and Osbern de Arches should be Pallathorpe, where William of Percy holds land in the main text (13W13). The *Torp* of SW,An8 is held by Osbern de Arches, who had land in both Pallathorpe (25W4) and Thorp Arch (25W8) – however, the 2 bovates recorded as held by Osbern in Pallathorpe in SW,An5 are probably the 2 bovates recorded in 25W4, which leaves Thorp Arch as the *Torp* of SW,An8, especially as it comes in the entry after that for Hornington Manor, as it also does in DB proper in 25W8. This only leaves the *Torp* of SW,An1 where Richard son of Arnfastr is recorded as holding 2 carucates of land; although DG does not report any entries for Middlethorpe in fol. 379c (fol. 379b in DG numbering), it seems likely that this is Middlethorpe, where Richard held 2 carucates according to DB proper (22W1).

(SOUTH) KIRKBY. DG 499, 507 does not distinguish which *Chirchebi* of fol. 379c (fol. 379b in DG numbering) is Kirby Hall and which is South Kirkby, but this *Chirchebi* should be South Kirkby, now in Osgoldcross Wapentake, but originally in Strafford (WYAS 515), as it is here recorded under Strafforth. The *Chirchebi* of SW,Bu2 should be Kirby Hall in Upper Claro Wapentake, as it is there recorded under 'Burghshire' Wapentake.

SW,O1	OSGOLDCROSS WAPENTAKE. See 5W31 note.
	ARKSEY, BENTLEY. See SW,Sf34 note.
SW,O2	ADWICK (LE STREET). See SW,Sf9 note.
SW,O3	SCAWSBY. See 10W43 note. There is an *r* in the margin beside this entry, standing for *require* 'enquire further'. The reason for this enquiry is not apparent.
SW,O4	SKELLOW. See 9W39 note.
SW,O5	'NEWSHAM'. See 9W41 note.
	HAMPHALL (STUBBS). See 9W43 note.
SW,O6	THORPE (AUDLIN). See SW,Sf37 note.
SW,O7	ROGERTHORPE (MANOR). See 9W45 note.
SW,O8	(KIRK AND LITTLE) SMEATON. See 9W47 note.
SW,O9	STAPLETON. See 9W50 note.
SW,O10	ACKWORTH. See 9W52 note.
	FERRY (FRYSTON). See 9W57 note.
SW,O11	NOSTELL (PRIORY). See 9W54 note.
SW,O12	WHELDALE. See 9W56 note.
	(WATER) FRYSTON. See 9W56 note.
SW,O13	(NORTH) ELMSALL. See SW,Sf37 note.
SW,O14	ROALL (HALL). See 9W61 note.
	EGGBOROUGH. This is written above the line.
SW,O15	TANSHELF. See 9W64 note.
SW,O16	HENSALL. See 1Y12 note.
SW,St1	STAINCROSS WAPENTAKE. See 5W32 note.
	BARNBY (HALL). See 9W64 note.
	IN KINSLEY. There is a 'c' in the margin to the left of this entry. Its meaning is not clear. It is not reproduced by Farley.
SW,St7	*SACTUN*. See 1Y13 note.
	CARLTON. See 9W76 note.
SW,St10	STAINBOROUGH (CASTLE). See 9W79 note.
	HUNSHELF (HALL). See 9W85 note.
	3 CARUCATES. '3 carucates' is written at the end of the preceding line.
SW,St11	(ING)BIRCHWORTH. DG 498, 505 does not distinguish which *Berceuuorde* of fol. 379c (379b in DG numbering) is Ingbirchworth and which is Roughbirchworth, both of which are held by Ilbert de Lacy. This *Berceuuorde* should be Ingbirchworth as it is linked here

with Thurlstone and Skelmanthorpe, as is Ingbirchworth in DB proper (9W86). The *Berceuuorde* of SW,St13 should be Roughbirchworth as it is linked with Oxspring, as is Roughbirchworth in the main text (9W91).

(UPPER) CUMBERWORTH. See 1Y15 note.

SW,St12 (UPPER AND LOWER) DENBY. DG 492 does not distinguish which *Denebi* of fol. 379c (fol. 379b in DG numbering) is Upper and Lower Denby and which is Upper Denby, both held by Ilbert de Lacy and both containing 3 carucates of land. It seems likely that this *Denebi* is Upper and Lower Denby in Staincross Wapentake, as it is entered here under Staincross and follows the entry for Thurlstone, Ingbirchworth and Skelmanthorpe, as is also the case with Upper and Lower Denby in DB proper (9W87). On Upper and Lower Denby see 9W87 note. The *Denebi* entered under Agbrigg Wapentake in SW,Ag5 would be Upper Denby in Agbrigg.

SKELMANTHORPE. See 9W86 note.

SW,St13 (MONK) BRETTON. DG 501, 511 does not distinguish which *Brettone* of fol. 379c (fol. 379b in DG numbering) is Monk Bretton and which is West Bretton. As this *Brettone* is entered here under Staincross Wapentake and is held by Ilbert de Lacy it should be Monk Bretton, in Staincross, which is also held by Ilbert in DB proper (9W90). The *Brettone* entered under Agbrigg Wapentake in SW,Ag10 and held by the King, must be West Bretton in Agbrigg, which is also held by the King in the main text (1Y15).

(ROUGH)BIRCHWORTH. See SW,St11 note.

SW,St15 KERESFORTH (HALL). See 9W80 note.

CHEVET. See 9W83 note.

SW,St16 (COLD) HIENDLEY. See 9W84 note.

SW,Ag1 AGBRIGG WAPENTAKE. See 9W94 note.

WARMFIELD AND ITS OUTLIER. See 2W1 note.

METHLEY. See 9W94 note.

SW,Ag2 'WESTERBY'. See 9W96 note.

SW,Ag3 WALTON. Not in DB proper, only in the Summary.

8 CARUCATES. '8' is written as *vii* with *i* added above it.

SW,Ag4 FLOCKTON. This entry probably refers to only part of the vill (WYAS 375).

SW,Ag5 (UPPER) DENBY. See 9W101 note; SW,St12 note.

SW,Ag6 (LOWER) WHITLEY. See 9W116 note.

SW,Ag8 SHEPLEY. DG 506 does not distinguish which *Scipelei* of fol. 379c (fol. 379b in DG numbering) is Shepley and which is Shipley, both being held by Ilbert de Lacy. As this *Scipelei* is entered under Agbrigg Wapentake it should be Shepley, in Agbrigg, while the *Scipelei* entered under Morley Wapentake in SW,M8 should be Shipley, in Morley Wapentake.

SW,Ag9 WAKEFIELD. VCH 302, note 26, although without giving any supporting reference, apportions the land involved here as 8 carucates 3⅓ bovates in Wakefield, 6 carucates in Sowerby, 4 carucates in Warley, 6 carucates in *Feslei*, 4 carucates in Midgley, 4 carucates in Wadsworth, 2 carucates in Cruttonstall, 4 carucates in Longfield and 2 carucates in Stansfield. This is, however, on the erroneous assumption that the *Werlafeslei* of 1Y15 represents two places, Warley and *Feslei*, rather than in fact being the full form of the name of Warley (see 1Y15 note).

1 CARUCATE AND 2 BOVATES. '2 bovates' is written at the end of the previous line.

SW,Ag10 (WEST) BRETTON. See 1Y15 note; SW,St13 note.

(EARLS)HEATON. See 1Y15 note

SW,Ag11 STANLEY. See 1Y15 note.

SHITLINGTON. See 1Y15 note.

SW,Ag12 (YATE)HOLME. See 1Y15 note.

(UPPER)THONG. See 1Y15 note.

(LOWER) CUMBERWORTH. See 1Y15 note.

SW,Ag13 (NORTH) CROSLAND. See 1Y15 note.

(UPPER) HOPTON. See 9W108 note.

SW,Ag14 CARTWORTH. See 1Y15 note.

HEPWORTH, WOOLDALE, FULSTONE, THURSTONLAND. Not in DB proper, only in the Summary.

SW,Ag15 BRADLEY. See 9W110 note.

LINDLEY. See 9W111 note.

QUARMBY. See 9W111 note. DB *Cornelbi* (DF LXXXII). Farley erroneously *Cornesbi*.

SW,Ag16 (SOUTH) CROSLAND. See 1Y15 note.

SW,M1 MORLEY WAPENTAKE. See 9W118 note.

SW,M1-
2   MORLEY. See 9W118 note.
SW,M1   (EAST) ARDSLEY. See 9W120 note.
SW,M2   CARLTON, LOFTHOUSE. See 9W119 note.
           THORPE (ON THE HILL). See SW,Sf37 note.
           MIDDLETON. See 9W119 note.
SW,M3   REESTONES. See 9W121 note.
           ·BRAMLEY. See 9W123 note.
SW,M4   CALVERLEY, FARSLEY. See 9W126 note.
SW,M5   GOMERSAL AND ITS TWO OUTLIERS. See 9W129 note.
SW,M6-   BOLTON. The vills listed in SW,M7 formed part of the large manor of Bolton (see
7   9W131 note).
SW,M6   SIX OUTLIERS. The identity of these six berewicks is uncertain (see 9W130 note).
SW,M7   CHELLOW (GRANGE). See 9W131 note.
           ALLERTON. See 9W131 note.
           WIBSEY. See 9W131 note.
SW,M8   SHIPLEY. See SW,Ag8 note.
           (NORTH) BIERLEY. See 9W134 note.
SW,M9   MIRFIELD. See 9W108 note.
SW,M10   LIVERSEDGE. See 9W140 note.
SW,M
10-11   (SOUTH)OWRAM, (NORTH)OWRAM. See 9W143 note.
SW,M11   HIPPERHOLME, (NORTH)OWRAM, SHELF, STAINLAND. Not in DB proper, only in
           the Summary.
SW,M12   (OLD) LINDLEY. See 1W27 note.
           FIXBY. Not in DB proper, only in the Summary. The location of the original vill centre,
           which was probably depopulated by emparking, is not known (WYAS 374). The name of
           the DB vill survives in that of Fixby Hall, whose grid reference has been used in the index.
           ECCLESHILL. Not in DB proper, only in the Summary.
SW,M13   FARNLEY. Not in DB proper, only in the Summary. DG 494 reports it as in Leeds, but it
           is actually now part of Armley township, although it survived as an independent township
           until the 19th century (WYAS 369).
           (WEST) ARDSLEY. See 9W120 note. Unlike East Ardsley, West Ardsley is not recorded
           in DB proper, only in the Summary. 'St. Mary's Church which is in Morley Wood',
           recorded in the Claims section of the main text (CW23) is, however, to be identified with
           Woodkirk church (SE 2719 2504), which is situated within West Ardsley township (CW23
           note; WYAS 222, note 28).
           GREETLAND. Not in DB proper, only in the Summary. This is the only evidence for the
           existence of Greetland as an independent vill, and it had certainly become part of the
           later township of Elland cum Greetland by the 14th century (WYAS 364). In fact its
           omission from DB proper is probably because it had been amalgamated with Elland
           between the composition of the Summary and that of the main text: the Summary records
           Ilbert de Lacy as holding 3 carucates in Elland (SW,M10) and half a carucate in
           Greetland (SW,M13), but the total 3½ carucates are ascribed to Elland alone in the
           main text (9W142).
              Greetland does not appear to have had a nucleated centre bearing the name, which
           always functioned purely as an area name until the 19th century. On the 1st ed. 6 in. OS
           map (sheet 246), Greetland Chapel is shown at SE 0881 2129 and Greetland Edge centred
           at SE 085 213. Along Greetland Edge are a row of houses called Mount Pleasant, just to
           the west of the settlement now called Greetland.
SW,M14   (HANGING) HEATON. See 1Y15 note. Not in DB proper, only in the Summary.
SW,An1   AINSTY WAPENTAKE. See 5W35 note.
           (BISHOP)THORPE. See 1W29 note.
           (MIDDLE)THORPE. See 1W29 note; SW,Sf37 note.
           ROBERT MALET. This section is inserted at the end of the following line.
SW,An2   COPMANTHORPE. DB *Copeman Torp* (DF pl LXXXII). DG 491 erroneously *Copemantorp*.
           COUNT W. *co. W.* only in the text (DF LXXXII). The *co.* for *comes* obviously stands for
           'Count' or 'Earl', but the significance of the *W.* is unclear. Presumably it stands for
           William (although there are other names beginning with 'W', William was by far the most
           common at this time and the one most likely to be abbreviated to a single *W*), but the only
           Count or Earl William holding land in Yorkshire was William de Warenne, and he did
           not hold land in Copmanthorpe according to the statement of his lands in the text. The 3
           carucates 6 bovates in Copmanthorpe here attributed to Count W do not seem to be
           recorded in DB proper, which only ascribes 2 carucates 2 bovates to Erneis de Burun

(24W2). VCH 303, note 30 suggests restoring *Comes W[illelmus]*, to be identified with the King's son, later William II (Rufus), but this is purely conjectural.

SW,An4 STEETON (HALL). See 13W7 note.

SW,An5 (PALLA)THORPE. See 5W35 note; SW,Sf37 note.

SW,An6 OUSTON (FARM). See 13W14 note.

'MALKTON'. See 13W15 note.

SW,An7 'HAGGENBY'. See 13W16 note.

HORNINGTON (MANOR). See 13W17 note.

SW,An8 CHRIST CHURCH. See 11W2 note.

THORP (ARCH). See SW,Sf37 note.

SW,An9 TWO WIGHILLS. See 18W3 note.

SW,An
10 WILSTROP (HALL). See 25W11 note.

SW,An (HUTTON) WANDESLEY. See 25W12 note.
11 ASKHAM (RICHARD). DG 485 does not distinguish which *Ascham* of fol. 379d (fol. 379b in DG numbering) is Askham Richard and which is Askham Bryan. This *Ascham* must be Askham Richard as it is held by Osbern de Arches who holds Askham Richard in DB proper (25W15). The *Ascham* of SW,An18 must be Askham Bryan as it is held by Count Alan who holds Askham Bryan in the main text (6W1).

SW,An
12 SCAGGLETHORPE. See 25W16 note.

SW,An
13-14;16 CHRIST CHURCH. See 11W2 note.

SW,An
16 *MULHEDE*. See 29W11 note.

SW,An *BITHEN*. Not in DB proper, only in the Summary. A lost vill in Middlethorpe township
17 (DG 487).

SW,An
18 ASKHAM (BRYAN). See SW,An11 note.

SW,Bu1 'BURGHSHIRE' (CLARO) WAPENTAKE. See 5W36 note.

THORPE (UNDERWOOD). See 16W6 note.

THORPE (HILL). See SW,Sf37 note.

SW,Bu2 WIDDINGTON (HALL). See 29W21 note.

KIRBY (HALL). See 25W21 note; SW,Sf37 note.

SW,Bu3 (UPPER AND LOWER) DUNSFORTH. See 24W4 note.

SW,Bu6 ELWICKS. Not in DB proper, only in the Summary. The name occurs as an area name centred at SE 448 595 on both the modern 2½ in. OS map and the 1st ed. 6 in. OS map (sheet 155), but there is no settlement of the name.

SW,Bu7 '(LITTLE) CATTAL' (OLD THORNVILLE HALL). See 24W6 note.

SW,Bu9 (GREAT AND LITTLE) RIBSTON. See 1W35 note.

SW,Bu10 ALLERTON (MAULEVERER). See 1W37 note.

SW,Bu11 CLARETON. See 1Y18 note.

SW,Bu12 LOFTUS (HILL). See 24W11 note.

SW,Bu14 STAVELEY. DG 503, 507, 508 does not distinguish which *Stanlei* of fol. 380 is North Stainley, South Stainley or Staveley. This *Stanlei* should be Staveley as it is here held by Gospatric, who holds Staveley in DB proper (28W6). The *Stanlei* of SW,Bu18 should be South Stainley, as it is held by the King, who holds land in South Stainley in DB proper (1Y18-19). The *Stanlei* of SW,H9 should be North Stainley, as it is held by the Count of Mortain, who holds land in North Stainley in DB proper (5W38).

'HILTON'. See 1Y18 note.

SW,Bu15 *(SCOTTON) THORPE*. DG 495, 500, 506, 526, 537 does not distinguish which *Torp* of fol. 380 is Grewelthorpe (WR), Langthorpe (NR), Littlethorpe (WR), *Scotton Thorpe* (WR) or *Torp* (NR). The *Torp* of SW,Bu23 is entered twice with 5 carucates and 2 carucates and held by Gospatric, which should equate with the 7 carucates held in Grewelthorpe by Gospatric in DB proper (28W11). The *Torp* of SW,H5, where the Bishop of Durham is recorded with 1 carucate, should equate with the 1 carucate held by the Bishop in the lost *Torp* in Pickhill township in the main text (3Y9), while the 6 carucates recorded for Gospatric in *Torp* in SW,H6 should be the 6 carucates ascribed to him in the main text in Langthorpe (28W31). The Archbishop of York is ascribed 4 carucates of land in

Littlethorpe in DB proper (2W7), which must be the 4 carucates held by the Archbishop in *Torp* in SW,Bu45. This only leaves the 2 carucates of the King in *Torp* in this entry (SW,Bu15), which should be the same 2 carucates recorded in the main text as held in *Scotton Thorpe* by Rafnketill and Thorketill, the King's Thanes (29W19), obviously as mesne lords with the King as tenant-in-chief. On *Scotton Thorpe* see 29W19 note.

SW,Bu16 WALKINGHAM (HILL). See 1Y19 note.

SW,Bu18 (SOUTH) STAINLEY. See SW,Bu14 note.

SW,Bu19 CAYTON. DB *Chettone* (DF LXXXIII). Farley erroneously *Cheitone*.
MARKENFIELD (HALL). See 13W20 note.
AISMUNDERBY. See 13W21 note.

SW,Bu23 (GREWEL)THORPE. See SW,Bu15 note.

SW,Bu24 BRAMLEY (GRANGE). See 28W15 note.

SW,Bu25 *POPLETONE*. See 1W42 note.
WHIPLEY (HALL). See 1Y18 note.
THE KING, IN THE SAME PLACE. This section is written at the end of the following line.

SW,Bu26 BRIMHAM (HALL). See 21W7 note.

SW,Bu28 *BESTHAIM*. See 1Y19 note.

SW,Bu29 'ELSWORTH'. Not in DB proper, only in the Summary. DG 493 Elsworth, but the name is lost in Norwood township (PNWR v, 124).
CLIFTON. See 1Y18 note.
TIMBLE. See 1Y18 note.

SW,Bu30 FELLISCLIFFE. See 1Y18 note.

SW,Bu31 BEAMSLEY. DB *Bemeslai* (DF LXXXIII). DG 486 erroneously *Bomeslai*.

SW,Bu32 NESFIELD, 2 CARUCATES. DB '2' (DF LXXXIII). Farley erroneously '3'.
ADDINGHAM. See 1W46 note.

SW,Bu35 (DUN)KESWICK. See 29W36 note.
KEARBY (TOWN END). See 13W27 note.
BARROWBY (GRANGE). See 13W29 note.

SW,Bu36 WALTON (HEAD). See 13W28 note.
'TIDOVER'. See 13W28 note.

Sw,Bu38 BECKWITH (HOUSE). See 21W9 note.
ROSSETT (GREEN). See 1W52 note.

SW,Bu40 PLOMPTON (HALL). See 13W31 note.
'LITTLE' BRAHAM. See 13W32 note.

SW,Bu41 'GREAT' BRAHAM. See 13W32 note.

SW,Bu42 *CALDEUUELLE*. DG 492, 517 does not distinguish which *Caldeuuelle* of fol. 380 is lost in Spofforth and which is lost in Marton le Moor. The *Caldeuuelle* of this entry, where William of Percy has 2 carucates, must be the *Cradeuuelle* of DB proper (13W34), i.e. lost in Spofforth, as William also had 2 carucates there. The *Caldeuuelle* of SW,H9, where the Count of Mortain holds 4 carucates should be the *Caldeuuelle* of 5W38, i.e. lost in Marton le Moor, where the Count is similarly recorded as having 4 carucates.
IN *CALDEUUELLE*. What appears to be 'cra' is written in the margin to the left of this entry. It is not reproduced by Farley. It might be thought possibly to stand for Craven, except that none of the three places listed here are in Craven.
NEWSOME (FARM). See 24W18 note.

SW,Bu43 (KIRK AND NORTH) DEIGHTON. See 16W5 note.

SW,Bu44 INGMANTHORPE (HALL). See 5W37 note.

SW,Bu45 IN RIPON. The amounts of land are written above the relevant place-names.
(LITTLE)THORPE. See SW,Bu15 note.
'EASTWICK'. See 2W7 note.

SW,Bu46 IN WESTWICK. As SW,Bu45 note.
WESTWICK. See 2W7 note.

SW,Bu47 IN SAWLEY. As SW,Bu45 note.
WILSILL. See 2W7 note.

SW,Bu
47;49 'KNARESFORD'. See 2W7 note.

SW,Bu48 (HIGH) GRANTLEY. As SW,Bu45 note; see also 2W7 note.
'HERLESHOW' (HOW HILL). See 2W7 note.
('EAST') STAINLEY. DG 493, 507 does not distinguish which *Stanlai* of fol. 380 is 'East' Stainley and which is South Stainley. The *Stanlai* of SW,H3 should be South Stainley as it is stated there that the Archbishop of York has 1 carucate in Markington and *Stanlai*, and

in DB proper the Archbishop holds 1 carucate in Markington and South Stainley (2W13). That the *Stanlai* of SW,Bu48 is then 'East' Stainley is supported by its association here with Sutton Grange, North Stainley and Sleningford with which, amongst others, it is also linked in the main text (2W7). On 'East' Stainley see 2W8 note.

SLENINGFORD. See 2W8 note.

SW,H1   HALIKELD WAPENTAKE. See 5W38 note. The amounts of land are written above the relevant place-names throughout this section.

SUTHAUUIC. See 2W8 note.

GIVENDALE. See 2W12 note.

SW,H2   (COPT) HEWICK. See 2W10 note.

HASHUNDEBI. See 2W13 note.

SW,H3   HUTTON (CONYERS). See 2W13 note.

(SOUTH) STAINLEY. See SW,Bu48 note.

(BRIDGE) HEWICK. See 2W10 note.

SW,H4   NORTON (CONYERS). See 3Y9 note.

HOWGRAVE. See 2W13 note.

SW,H5   *TORP.* See 3Y9 note; SW,Bu15 note.

SW,H6   (LANG)THORPE. See SW,Bu15 note.

THORNTON (BRIDGE). See 28W32 note.

(HUM)BURTON. See 28W33 note.

SW,H7   ELLENTHORPE (HALL). See 1Y18 note.

SW,H7-8 BRAMPTON (HALL). See 5W38 note.

SW,H8   LECKBY (PALACE). See 5W38 note.

SW,H9   CUNDALL. This is written at the end of the preceding line.

(NORTH) STAINLEY. See SW,Bu14 note.

(EAST) TANFIELD. See 5W38 note.

CALDEUUELLE. See 5W38 note; SW,Bu42 note.

SW,Cr1-5   CRAVEN. See 1W56 note. No landholder is recorded for the vills listed here under Craven, but the main text shows that they belonged to the King (1W73).

SW,Cr2   SKIBEDEN. See 1W73 note.

(LOW) SNAYGILL. See 1W73 note.

SW,Cr3   ADDINGHAM. See 1W46 note.

HOLME (HOUSE). See 1W73 note.

SW,Cr4   (LITTLE) STAINTON. See 1W73 note.

SN,L1   LANGBARGH WAPENTAKE. See 1N1 note.

FYLING (OLD HALL), FYLING (THORPE). See 4N1 note.

SN,L2   'PRESTBY'. See 4N1 note.

SN,L3   NORMANBY. DG 530 does not distinguish which *Normanebi* of fol. 380c (fol. 380b in DG numbering) is Normanby near Eston in Langbargh East Wapentake, Normanby in Fylingdales township, or Normanby near Thornton Riseborough in Ryedale Wapentake. The *Normanebi* of this entry, in which the King is given as holding 2 carucates, should be Normanby in Fylingdales township, as according to 1N1 in DB proper the King had 2 carucates there. The *Normanebi* of SN,L25, where the Count of Mortain holds 7 carucates, should be Normanby near Eston, as the main text records the Count as having 7 carucates there (5N25). The *Normanebi* of SN,Ma14, also held by the King but with 3 carucates, should be Normanby near Thornton Riseborough where DB proper ascribes 3 carucates to the King (1N74), but see further SN,Ma14 note.

SN,L4   'SOWERBY'. See 4N1 note.

'BRECK'. See 4N1 note.

BALDEBI. See 4N1 note.

FLOWER(GATE). See 4N1 note.

SN,L5   (HIGH) STAKESBY. See 4N1 note.

NEWHOLM. DG 530 does not distinguish which *Neuham* of fol. 380c (fol. 380b in DG numbering) is Newholm and which is Newham Hall. This *Neuham*, where Earl Hugh holds 4 carucates must be Newholm, where he also holds 4 carucates in DB proper (4N1). On Newholm see 4N1 note. The *Neuham* of SN,L31, where Robert Malet holds 2 carucates and 2 bovates, should be Newham Hall, as Robert is recorded in DB proper (11N7) as holding 10 bovates (presumably here 4 bovates = 1 carucate) there. These 2 carucates and 2 bovates eventually became part of the holding of Robert of Brus (31N5).

SN,L6   HUTTON (MULGRAVE). DG 525, 533 does not distinguish which *Hotone* of fol. 380c (fol. 380b in DG numbering) is Hutton Mulgrave and which is Sheriff Hutton. This *Hotone*, where the Count of Mortain has 3 carucates, should be Hutton Mulgrave, where the Count is recorded as holding 3 carucates in DB proper (5N2). The *Hotone* of SN,B3 where the Count has 11 carucates and the King 4 carucates, must be Sheriff Hutton, as in the main text the Count is recorded as having 11 carucates there (5N54) and the King 4 carucates (1N87).

SN,L7 (MUL)GRAVE CASTLE. DG 523, 529 does not distinguish which *Grif* of fol. 380c (fol. 380b in DG numbering) is Griff Farm and which is Mulgrave Castle. This *Grif*, where the Count of Mortain holds 6 carucates, should be Mulgrave Castle, where the Count is similarly recorded holding 6 carucates in DB proper (5N4). On Mulgrave Castle see 5N4 note. The *Grif* of SN,Ma17, in which the Count and the King each have 2 carucates, should be Griff Farm, where the King is stated in the main text to have 2 carucates (1N78); the 2 carucates held there by the Count of Mortain according to the Summary do not appear to be recorded in DB proper.

(EAST AND WEST) BARNBY. Not in DB proper, only in the Summary. DG 515 Barnby, but Barnby township today contains two settlements of the same size bearing the name – East Barnby at NZ 827 127 and West Barnby at NZ 819 125 – so both names have been used in this edition.

SN,L9 *GRIMESBI*. See 5N10 note.

ROXBY. DG 532, 533 does not distinguish which *Rozebi* of fol. 380c (fol. 380b in DG numbering) is Roxby near Loftus and which is Roxby Hill in Thornton Dale township. This *Rozebi*, where the Count of Mortain holds 3 carucates and the King 1 carucate, should be Roxby near Loftus, as the main text records the King as having 1 carucate there (1N2) and the Count of Mortain as holding 6 carucates in Roxby and Borrowby (5N8), although the total for Roxby and Borrowby given in the Summary amounts in fact to 8 carucates. The *Rozebi* of SN,D12, where the King is recorded as having 37 carucates in a number of vills, should be Roxby Hill, as the places listed all occur together with Roxby Hill in a list of places belonging to the King according to the main text (1Y4).

SN,L10 'ROSKELTHORPE'. See 4N2 note.
SN,L11 *ARNODESTORP*. See 13N3 note.
SN,L12 SEATON (HALL). See 5N11 note.
SN,L14 LEALHOLM. See 23N18 note.
DANBY. See 23N18 note.

SN,L15 'STAINTON'. DG 534 does not distinguish which *Steintun* of fol. 380c (fol. 380b in DG numbering) is 'Stainton' in Stanghow township, Stainton near Thornaby on Tees or Staintondales. This *Steintun*, where the Count of Mortain holds 7 bovates and the King 1 bovate, should be 'Stainton', as the main text states that the Count of Mortain has 7 bovates there (5N12) and the King 1 bovate (1N6). On 'Stainton' see 1N6 note. The King's 1-bovate holding eventually passed to Robert of Brus (31N8). The *Steintun* of SN,L34, where Earl Hugh and Robert Malet both hold 2 carucates, should be Stainton near Thornaby upon Tees, as DB proper ascribes 2 carucates here to Earl Hugh (4N3) and a further 2 carucates to Robert Malet (11N10). The *Steintun* of SN,D2, belonging to the King, should be Staintondale, as the four vills listed in this entry occur in the same order, including Staintondale, in the list of the vills in the King's manor of Falsgrave and Northfield Farm (1Y3).

SN,L16 (KILTON) THORPE. DG 526, 532, 536 does not distinguish which *Torp* of fol. 380c (fol. 380b in DG numbering) is Kilton Thorpe, which Nunthorpe, which Pinchinthorpe Hall and which 'Thorpefield'. This *Torp*, where the Count of Mortain holds 1½ carucates and the King 2½ carucates, should be Kilton Thorpe, as according to DB proper the Count holds 1½ carucates in Kilton Thorpe (5N15) and the King 2½ carucates (1N8). The *Torp* of SN,L27, where Robert Malet and the King both hold 3 carucates, should be Pinchinthorpe Hall, as the main text states that Robert Malet holds 3 carucates there (11N3), as does the King (1N15). The *Torp* of SN,L29 should be Nunthorpe: according to the main text the King holds 9 carucates in Nunthorpe and Morton Grange (1N19) – the 6 carucates ascribed to the King in *Torp*, combined with the 3 carucates ascribed to him in Morton Grange in the Summary (SN,L29), give the requisite 9 carucates. The *Torp* of SN,D6 should be 'Thorpefield' as the Summary ascribes 4 carucates to *Torp* and Irton, held by William of Percy, and these equate with the 4 carucates of William in 'Thorpefield' and Irton in the main text (3N10); the holding of Richard son of Arnfastr in 'Thorpefield' (23N6) does not appear to be recorded in the Summary.

SN,L18 'MIDDLETON'. See 5N19 note.

HUTTON (LOWCROSS). DG 525, 527 does not distinguish which *Hotun* of fol. 380c (fol. 380b in DG numbering) is Hutton Buscel, Hutton Lowcross, Hutton Rudby or Low Hutton. The *Hotun* of this entry, which states that the Count of Mortain has 25 carucates in *Hotun* and two other vills, must be Hutton Lowcross, as the Count is recorded in DB proper (5N19) as holding 25 carucates in these same three vills, including Hutton Lowcross. The *Hotun* of SN,L42, where the Count holds 6 carucates, equates with Hutton Rudby, where the Count similarly holds 6 carucates according to the main text (5N29). The *Hotun* of SN,D7, belonging to the King, should be Hutton Buscel, as it is listed together with the other three vills of this entry in the same order in the account of the King's holdings in the main text (1Y3). The *Hotun* of SN,B1, where Berenger of Tosny holds 5½ carucates and the King 8½ carucates, should be Low Hutton as, according to DB proper, the King has 8½ carucates in Low Hutton (1N85) and Berenger 5½ carucates (8N9); only 3 carucates in Low Hutton, presumably from the King's estate, remained in the holding of Robert of Brus (31N8).

SN,L19   RAWCLIFF (BANKS). See 4N2 note.

SN,L20   TOCKETTS (FARM). See 5N20 note.

SN,L21   MARSKE (BY THE SEA). See 4N2 note.

        WESTLID (KIRKLEATHAM). See 1N12 note.

SN,L22   WILTON. DG 538 does not distinguish which *Wiltune* of fol. 380c (fol. 380b in DG numbering) is Wilton near Eston in Langbargh West Wapentake and which is Wilton near Pickering in Lythe Wapentake. The *Wiltune* of SN,D12 should be Wilton near Pickering, as it occurs with a list of vills belonging to the King, and these vills, including Wilton near Pickering, are all listed together under the King's holdings in DB proper (1Y4). This then would leave Wilton near Eston for the *Wiltune* of this entry, although there is a discrepancy between the holdings recorded: according to the Summary the King has 4½ carucates in *Wiltune* (SN,L22) and the Count of Mortain a further 4½ carucates (SN,L23), but in the main text the Count of Mortain has only 4 carucates (5N22). The King's land here is recorded under the holdings of his thanes, Halldorr having 3 carucates 6 bovates (29N1), with a further carucate in Wilton and Lazenby (29N2). The King also has a further 3 carucates in Lazenby (1N13), giving the King a total of 8 carucates 2 bovates in Wilton and Lazenby combined, which equals the total holding in those two vills in the Summary (SN,L22-3). This only leaves half a carucate in the Count of Mortain's holding in the Summary unaccounted for.

SN,L25   NORMANBY. See SN,L13 note.

SN,L26   UPSALL (HALL). See 1N14 note.

        BARNABY. See 5N26 note.

SN,L27   (PINCHIN)THORPE (HALL). See 1N15 note; SN,L16 note.

        (LITTLE) AYTON. DG 520, 527 does not distinguish which *Atun* of fol. 380c (fol. 380b in DG numbering) is East Ayton and which is Little Ayton. The *Atun* of SN,D7, in which William of Percy has 6 carucates of land should be East Ayton, as he is recorded as holding 6 carucates there in DB proper (13N12); the 2 carucates which Berenger of Tosny holds there in the main text (8N11) do not appear to be mentioned in the Summary. The *Atun* of this entry (SN,L27) and of SN,L29 should be Little Ayton, as the 2 carucates ascribed in SN,L27 to the King are probably those ascribed to him in the main text in Little Ayton (1N17). It is stated in SN,L27 that Robert Malet has 3 carucates there and in SN,L29 that he has a further 2 carucates; according to DB proper Robert has only 4 carucates in Little Ayton, so either there is an error here or else Robert had 1 carucate less when DB was compiled than at the time of the Summary. The 4 carucates held by the Count of Mortain in the main text (5N7) in Little Ayton do not appear to be recorded in the Summary.

SN,L28   MORTON (GRANGE). See 1N19 note.

SN,L29   (NUN)THORPE. See SN,L16 note.

        (LITTLE) AYTON. See SN,L27 note.

SN,L31   MARTON (IN CLEVELAND). DG 528 does not distinguish which *Martun* of fol. 380c (380b in DG numbering) is Marton in Cleveland near Middlesbrough, Marton near Pickering or *Martune*, lost in Hutton Buscel (but actually Martin Garth in Wykeham township: see 1N43 note). As the *Martun* of this entry is located by the Summary in Langbargh Wapentake and is listed here with Newham Hall, it is likely to be Marton in Cleveland, although there is some discrepancy in the landholdings between the Summary and DB proper. In this entry Robert Malet has 5 carucates of land, as he does in the main text (11N6), but the King here has 4½ carucates, whereas in the main text he himself has 1 carucate (1N25) and Arnketill, one of his Thanes, has a further 3 carucates (29N6), leaving a shortfall of half a carucate. On Marton in Cleveland see 1N25 note. The other two examples of *Martun* in this folio are both located in the same wapentake. The *Martun* of SN,D8 is probably Martin Garth as it is here held by the King and linked with

Wykeham; in the main text Martin Garth is twice linked with Wykeham (1Y3; 1N43), the first time also with Ruston, and both times held by the King. This then leaves the *Martun* of SN,D21 as Marton near Pickering; according to the Summary the Abbot holds 5 carucates there, whereas in DB proper Marton is a berewick of Hugh son of Baldric's Kirby Moorside estate (23N1), while Berenger of Tosny also has 5 carucates there (8N16) – elsewhere in the Summary it is stated that the Abbot holds land from Berenger (e.g. SN,Ma1), so it is probably Berenger's 5 carucates which are recorded both in the main text and in the Summary in SN,D21.

NEWHAM (HALL). See 1N26 note; SN,L5 note.

SN,L32   TOLLESBY. See 1N27 note.

ACKLAM. See 2N28 note.

SN,L33   COULBY. See 4N3 note.

SN,L34   STAINTON. See SN,L15 note.

THORNTON. DG 536 does not distinguish which *Torentun* of fol. 380c (fol. 380b in DG numbering) is Thornton (in Stainburn township, near Thornaby on Tees) and which is Thornton Dale. This *Torentun*, in which Earl Hugh holds 3 carucates and Robert Malet 1 carucate, should be Thornton, as DB proper states that Earl Hugh has 3 carucates there (4N3) and Robert Malet 1 carucate (11N12). This would leave the *Torentun* of SN,D15 as Thornton Dale: the Summary states that Berenger of Tosny holds 1 carucate of land there, and Berenger similarly holds 1 carucate of land in Thornton Dale in DB proper (8N15). The other landholder in Thornton Dale in the main text is the King with 2 carucates (1N48); it is difficult to tell from SN,D15 whether the landholder to whom the 5 carucates there listed are ascribed is the Count of Mortain or the King, but it is probably the King, even though the two amounts of land do not tally.

SN,L35   INGLEBY (HILL). DG 525 does not distinguish which *Englebi* of fol. 380c (fol. 380b in DG numbering) is Ingleby Hill and which is Ingleby Greenhow. This *Englebi*, in which Earl Hugh holds 6 carucates, should be Ingleby Hill, as the main text ascribes 6 carucates in Ingleby Hill to him (4N3)..On Ingleby Hill see 4N3 note. The *Englebi* of SN,L40, where the King has 7 carucates, should equate with the 7 carucates held in Ingleby Greenhow by Uhtred, one of the King's Thanes, according to DB proper (29N9).

BARWICK. See 4N3 note.

SN,L37   STAINSBY (HALL). See 4N3 note.

TUNSTALL (FARM). See 1N29 note.

SN,L38   SEAMER. DG 533 does not distinguish which *Semer* of fol. 380c (fol. 380b in DG numbering) is Seamer near Scarborough and which is Seamer near Stokesley. This *Semer*, in which the Count of Mortain holds 11 carucates, should be Seamer near Stokesley, as the main text states that the Count has 13 carucates in Seamer and Tanton (5N28), and the 11 carucates here, combined with the 2 ascribed to Tanton in this entry, give the requisite 13. The *Semer* of SN,D6, where William of Percy holds 6 carucates, should be Seamer near Scarborough, as this is the same number of carucates ascribed to William there in DB proper (13N9).

BERGULUESEBI. See 1N31 note.

SN,L39   MIDDLETON (UPON LEVEN). DG 528 does not distinguish which *Mideltun* of fol. 380c (fol. 380b in DG numbering) is Middleton near Pickering and which is Middleton upon Leven. This *Mideltun*, where the Count of Mortain holds 8 carucates, should be Middleton upon Leven, in which the main text states the Count similarly holds 8 carucates (5N28). The *Mideltun* of SN,D18, where the King has 5 carucates, should be Middleton near Pickering, as in the main text Middleton is listed amongst the berewicks of the King's manor of Pickering (1Y4).

THORALDBY (FARM). See 1N33 note.

SN,L40   INGLEBY (GREENHOW). See SN,L35 note.

CAMISEDALE. See 1N35 note.

SN,L41   (LITTLE) BROUGHTON. DG 517, 527 does not distinguish which *Broctun* of fol. 380c (fol. 380b in DG numbering) is Broughton near Malton and which is Little Broughton. This *Broctun*, where the King has 8 carucates, should be Little Broughton, as in DB proper 8 carucates in Little Broughton are held by Uhtred, one of the King's Thanes (29N9). The *Broctun* of SN,Ma6, in which the King has 8 carucates 2 bovates and Berenger of Tosny 1 carucate, should be Broughton near Malton, as the main text states that in Broughton the King has 8 carucates 2 bovates (1N67) and Berenger 1 carucate (8N17).

(LITTLE) BROUGHTON, (GREAT) BROUGHTON. See 1N36 note; 29N9 note.

SN,L42   KIRKBY. DG 526 does not distinguish which *Cherchebi* of fol. 380c (fol. 380b in DG numbering) is Kirby Misperton and which is Kirby in Stokesley (actually Kirby near

Stokesley: see 29N9 note). This *Cherchebi*, where the King has 3 carucates, should be Kirkby, as in DB proper 3 carucates are ascribed to Uhtred, the King's Thane, in Kirkby (29N9). The *Cherchebi* and *alia Cherchebi* of SN,Ma1, where Berenger of Tosny holds 7 carucates, are the *Chirchebi* of DB proper (8N1), in which Berenger holds 2 carucates 6 bovates, and the *alia Chirchebi* (8N2), in which he holds 4 carucates 2 bovates, giving the requisite total of 7 carucates (8 bovates = 1 carucate). On these two vills which, together with DB *Mispeton*, make up the modern township of Kirkby Misperton, see 8N1 note.

DROMONBY (HALL). See 29N9 note.

HUTTON (RUDBY). See SN,L18 note.

SN,L43   (LITTLE) BUSBY. See 29N9 note.

SN,L44   *BLATEN (CARR)*. See 5N29 note.

GOULTON (GRANGE). See 5N29 note.

GOULTON (GRANGE), CRATHORNE. These names are written above the line.

WHORLTON. See 5N29 note.

SN,D1   *DIC (PICKERING LYTHE) WAPENTAKE*. See 1N42 note.

NORTHFIELD (FARM). See 1Y3 note.

SN,D3   CLOUGHTON, 4 CARUCATES. This is ill-written in the text. The scribe wrote the first minim too long, with the result that the numeral looks to be *liii* '53'. However the scribe also wrote *or.* above the numeral to make it *iiii or.* for *quattuor* 'four' (DF LXXXIV).

STEMAINESBI. See 5N32 note.

SN,D4   'SCAWTHORPE'. See 1Y3 note.

GRISTHORPE. The name is written above the line.

ROUDELUESTORP. See 1Y3 note.

ETERSTORP. See 1Y3 note. The name is written above the line.

FILEY. DB *Fiuelace* (DF LXXXIV). Farley erroneously *Fuielac*.

SN,D5   KILLERBY (HALL). See 13N8 note.

'BURTON (DALE)'. See 1Y3 note.

(HIGH, MIDDLE AND LOW) DEEPDALE. See 1Y3 note.

SN,D6   SEAMER. See SN,L38 note.

'THORPEFIELD'. See 13N10 note; SN,L16 note.

HILLGRIPS. See 13N11 note.

SN,D7   (EAST) AYTON. See SN,L27 note.

'NEWTON'. See 1Y3 note.

PRESTON (HILL). See 1Y3 note.

HUTTON (BUSCEL). See SN,L18 note. The name is written above the line.

SN,D8   MARTIN (GARTH). See 1N43 note; SN,L31 note.

SN,D10   'LITTLE MARISH'. See 8N14 note.

SN,D11   (HIGH) BLANDSBY. See 1Y4 note.

EASTHORPE (HOUSE). See 1Y4 note.

SN,D12   *OUDULUESMERSC, ASCHELESMERSC, CHILUESMERSC, MAXUDESMERSC*. These four vills, all held by the King and lost in Pickering Marishes (1Y4 note), are apparently the same as the *Odulfesmare, Aschilesmares, Chiluesmares* and *Maxudesmares* held by the King in DB proper (1Y4). In the Summary, which is the earlier survey, all four names have OE *mersc* 'marsh' as their final element, whereas by the time of DB proper, the final element has been influenced by OF *mareis* (PNNR 84).

FARMANBY. See 1Y4 note.

KINGTHORPE (HOUSE). See 1Y4 note.

WILTON. See SN,L22 note.

ROXBY (HILL). See 1Y4 note; SN,L9 note.

6 BOVATES. This is written above the line.

SN,D13   TROUTSDALE. See 1N45 note.

SN,D14   LOFT MARISHES. See 1N47 note.

SN,D15   *CHIGOMERSC*. See 1Y4 note.

THORNTON (DALE). See SN,L34 note.

SN,D16   *LIEDTORP*. See 8N7 note. DB *Liedtorp* (DF LXXXIV). DG 527 erroneously *Leidtorp*.

(LOW) DALBY. DG 519 does not distinguish which *Dalbi* of fol. 380d (fol. 380b in DG numbering) is Low Dalby in Thornton Dale township and which is Dalby near Whenby. This *Dalbi*, where the King has 2 carucates, should be Low Dalby, as DB proper ascribes 2 carucates there to the King (1N50). On Low Dalby see 1N50 note. The *Dalbi* of SN,B2, in which the Abbot holds 3 carucates of land from Berenger of Tosny, should be Dalby near Whenby, as the main text states that Berenger holds 3 carucates in Dalby (8N5). The 1 carucate held in Dalby by Ralph of Mortemer (15E16) does not appear to be mentioned in the Summary.

SN,D17   'KETTLETHORPE'. See 1N51 note.

SN,D18   MIDDLETON. See SN,L39 note.

SN,D20-1   THE ABBOT. This is the Abbot of York, rather than the Abbot of Selby (see L4 note; 8N2 note).

SN,D20   *BASCHESBI*. See 1N57 note.

SN,D21   APPLETON (LE MOORS). Not in DB proper, only in the Summary, where it is listed once under *Dic* Wapentake (SN,D21) and once under *Manshowe* (SN,Ma14). It was subsequently in Ryedale Wapentake, the successor to *Manshowe*. See also L4 note.

    MARTON. See SN,L31 note.

SN,Ma1   *MANSHOWE* (RYEDALE) WAPENTAKE. See 1N58 note.

    THORNTON (RISEBOROUGH). See 1N58 note.

    KIRBY (MISPERTON) AND ANOTHER KIRBY (MISPERTON). See 8N1 note; SN,L42 note.

    THE ABBOT. This is the Abbot of York, who is recorded as holding this land in DB proper (8N1), not the Abbot of Selby.

SN,Ma2   *SALESCALE*. Not in DB proper, only in the Summary. Lost in Ryton township (DG 533).

SN,Ma4   AMOTHERBY. See 5N36 note.

SN,Ma6   BROUGHTON. See SN,L41 note.

SN,Ma7   SALTON, 9 CARUCATES. A capital *I*, reproduced by Farley, follows '9 carucates' in this entry (DF LXXXIV). There is also what appears to be the start of another letter, possibly an *n*. In this case it can be assumed that the scribe began to write *In*, but then changed his mind and began on a new line.

SN,Ma9   (LITTLE) EDSTONE. See 8N23 note.

SN,Ma 10   (NORTH) HOLME (HOUSE). DG 531, 534 does not distinguish which *Holm* of fol. 380d (fol. 380b in DG numbering) is North Holme and which is South Holme. This *Holm*, in which the King and Berenger of Tosny each hold 1½ carucates, should be North Holme House, as DB proper states that the King has 1½ carucates there (1N72), as also does Berenger (8N18). On North Holme House see 1N72 note. The *Holm* of SN,Ma22, where Ralph Paynel holds 1 carucate, should be South Holme, where the main text similarly states he holds 1 carucate (16N1). The berewick of Hovingham in South Holme held by Hugh son of Baldric (23N24) does not appear to be mentioned in the Summary.

SN,Ma 12   WELBURN. DG 538 does not distinguish which *Wellebrune* of fol. 380d (fol. 380b in DG numbering) is Welburn near Bulmer and which is Welburn near Kirby Moorside. This *Wellebrune*, in which Berenger of Tosny and the King each have 1 carucate, should be Welburn near Kirby Moorside, as DB proper ascribes 1 carucate each in Welburn to Berenger (8N26) and the King (1N73); the berewick of Kirby Moorside in Welburn held by Hugh son of Baldric (23N21) does not appear to be recorded in the Summary. The *Wellebrune* of SN,B4, where the Count of Mortain holds 3½ carucates, should be Welburn near Bulmer, as in the main text this Welburn is included in the lands of the Count of Mortain (5N54), who holds 5 carucates in Welburn and Ganthorpe; the 2 carucates recorded for Ganthorpe in the Summary (SN,B4) means that there is a difference of 1 carucate between the holdings recorded in these two vills for the Count in the Summary and the main text.

SN,Ma 13   'WALTON'. See 8N27 note.

    THE ABBOT. This is probably the Abbot of York, rather than the Abbot of Selby (see L4 note; 8N2 note).

SN,Ma 14   APPLETON (LE MOORS). See SN,D21 note.

    THE ABBOT. This is likely to be the Abbot of York, rather than the Abbot of Selby (see 8N2 note).

    IN NORMANBY. See SN,L3 note. This entry ascribes 3 carucates in Normanby to the King and a further 3 carucates to the Abbot of York, held from the King. The Normanby berewick of Kirby Moorside held by Hugh son of Baldric according to the main text (23N21) is not recorded in the Summary, but DB proper ascribes a total of only 3 carucates in Normanby to the King (1N74). Although the record of the lands of the Abbot of York is omitted from the main text, VCH 311, note 58 suggests that the lands here ascribed to the Abbot are those in 1N74, formerly held by Gamall, whose other lands were given to St. Mary's of York.

SN,Ma 16	(WEST) NEWTON (GRANGE). See 1N75 note.
SN,Ma 17	GRIFF (FARM). See 1N78 note; SN,L7 note.
SN,Ma 18	STILTONS (FARM). See 1N79 note.
SN,Ma 20	RICCAL (HOUSE) See 1N82 note.
SN,Ma 21	(EAST) NESS. See 16N1 note.
SN,Ma 22	(SOUTH) HOLME. See SN,Ma10 note.
SN,B1	*BOLESFORD* (BULMER) WAPENTAKE. See 1N85 note.
	(LOW) HUTTON. See 8N9 note; SN,L18 note.
	HENDERSKELFE. See 8N10 note.
SN,B2	*DALBY.* See SN,D16 note.
	THE ABBOT. This is probably the Abbot of York, rather than the Abbot of Selby (see 8N2 note).
SN,B3	STITTENHAM. See 5N53 note.
	(SHERIFF) HUTTON. See SN,L6 note.
SN,B4	WELBURN. See SN,Ma12 note.
SN,B6	WIGANTHORPE (HALL). See 1N89 note.
SN,B7	HILDENLEY (HALL). See 1N90 note.
SN,B8	*FORNETORP.* See 5N59 note.
	CORNBROUGH (HOUSE). See 5N60 note.
SN,B9	(WEST) LILLING. See 1N91 note.
SN,B9- 10	THORNTON (LE CLAY). DG 537 does not distinguish which *Torentun* of fol. 381 is Thornton le Clay and which is Thornton le Street. This *Torentun,* where the Count of Mortain holds 3 carucates and Count Alan 2 carucates, should be Thornton le Clay, as the main text ascribes 3 carucates there to the Count of Mortain (5N61) and 2 carucates to Count Alan (6N162); 2 carucates there are also attributed to Robert Malet in DB proper (11N15), and these are probably the further 2 carucates recorded in SN,B10 without the landholder specified. The *Torentun* of SN,A1, in which it is listed as a berewick of Northallerton belonging to the King, should be Thornton le Street, which appears in a similar role in DB proper (1Y2).
SN,B10	IN THE SAME PLACE, 2 CARUCATES. The scribe omitted to include the name of the landholder here.
	BARTON (LE WILLOWS), 8 CARUCATES. The '8' is written as *vi* (6) with *ii* (2) over it.
SN,B12	*DIC.* This is written without a capital *D* in the text (DF LXXXV). Farley erroneously prints it in capitals. On *Dic* see 1N96 note.
SN,B14	CARLTON (FARM). See 2N19 note.
	(EAST) LILLING. See 1N91 note.
	1 CARUCATE, 6 BOVATES. See 1N100 note.
SN,B18	WHENBY. Not in DB proper, only in the Summary.
SN,B19	MOXBY (HALL). See 1Y1 note.
	MURTON (FARM). DG 529 does not distinguish which *Mortun(e)* of fol. 381 is Morton Grange in East Harlsey, Morton upon Swale, Murton near Cold Kirby or Murton Farm in Sutton on the Forest. This *Mortun,* in which the Archbishop holds 2½ carucates and the King 2 carucates, should be Murton Farm in Sutton on the Forest, as DB proper ascribes 2½ carucates there to the Archbishop (2N12) and 2 carucates to the King (1Y1) – a difference of half a carucate, but the equation should be correct, as the list of names in SN,B19 and SN,B20 occur in the same order as they do in 1Y1. On Murton Farm see 1Y1 note. The *Mortune* of SN,A7, where the King has 3 carucates, should be Morton Grange in East Harlsey township, as the main text states that the King has 3 carucates there (1N126); it was presumably these 3 carucates which eventually passed to Robert of Brus (31N4). The *Mortun* of SN,A10 where Robert Malet holds 6 carucates, should be Murton near Cold Kirby, as the main text ascribes 6 carucates there to Robert (11N21). The *Mortune* of SN,CtA14, in which Count Alan holds 11 carucates, equates with Morton upon Swale, in which DB proper records that Count Alan holds 11 carucates (6N31).
SN,B20	THORPE (HILL). DG 536 does not distinguish which *Torp* of fol. 381 is Thorpe Hill in Sutton on the Forest, Thorpe Hall near Wycliffe, Thorpe le Willows, Thorp Perrow or *Torp,* lost in Croft. This *Torp* should be Thorpe Hill in Sutton on the Forest as it is held by

the King and occurs in a list of names in the same order as is given in the main text for the King's manor of Easingwold (1Y1). On Thorpe Hill see 1Y1 note. The *Torp* of SN,Bi1, in which Gospatric holds 3 carucates, is probably Thorpe le Willows: in DB proper these 3 carucates appear to be listed under the lands of the King (1N108), but the four vills before Thorpe le Willows.in this section are given as held by Gospatric from the King (1Y104-7) and it seems likely that this was also the case with Thorpe le Willows, at least at the time when the Summary was compiled. The *Torp* of SN,CtA5, in which Count Alan holds 3 carucates, should equate with Thorpe Hall in Wycliffe township, in which the main text states the Count holds 3 carucates (6N1). The *Torp* of SN,CtA11, in which the Count holds 2 carucates, should be the *Torp* lost in Croft where he similarly holds 2 carucates in the main text (6N17), while that in SN,CtA36, in which the Count has 4 carucates, should be Thorp Perrow, where DB states he has 6 carucates (6N127).

KELSIT (GRANGE). See 1Y1 note.

SN,B21 'CORBURN'. See 2N30 note.

SN,B22 NEWTON (UPON OUSE). DG 530 does not distinguish which *Neuton* of fol. 381 is Newton le Willows, Newton Morrell or Newton upon Ouse. This *Neuton*, which together with *Toresbi* makes up 9 carucates held by Ralph Paynel, should be Newton upon Ouse, as Ralph Paynel is ascribed 9 carucates in Newton upon Ouse and *Toresbi* in DB proper (16N2). The *Neuton* of SN,CtA1, where Count Alan holds 6 carucates of land, should be Newton Morrell, as the main text attributes 6 carucates there to the Count (6N1). The *Neuton* of SN,CtA27 should be Newton le Willows, where DB proper states the Count holds 12 carucates (6N134), as in the Summary.

TORESBI. DG 536, 537 does not distinguish which *Toresbi* of fol. 381 is the vill lost in Newton upon Ouse and which is Thoresby. This *Toresbi* where, together with Newton upon Ouse, Ralph Paynel holds 9 carucates must be the lost *Toresbi* (see 16N2 note; and previous footnote). The *Toresbi* of SN,CtA28, in which Count Alan holds 2 carucates, should be Thoresby as the main text ascribes 2 carucates there to Count Alan as part of his manor of East Witton (6N92); a further carucate held by the Count in Thoresby (6N89) appears not to be recorded in the Summary.

TORESBI. In the text there is a gap between the first 2 letters and the rest of the word (DF LXXXV). This is not reproduced by Farley.

'INGLETHWAITE'. See 13N14 note.

SN,B23 HAXBY. Except for Haxby, refer all places to SW,Bu45 note.

YOULTON. DB *Ioletun* (DF LXXXV). Farley erroneously *Loletun*.

SN,B24 IN THOLTHORPE. The amounts of land are written above the place-names.

WIDE OPEN (FARM). See 2N25 note.

THESE [ARE] THE ARCHBISHOP'S. This refers not only to Tholthorpe and Wide Open Farm, but also to the last 4 places in the previous entry.

SN,B27 (LOW) MOWTHORPE (FARM). Not in DB proper, only in the Summary. The DB vill of *Muletorp* was subsequently subsumed into Terrington vill, but the group of Mowthorpe names in the south-eastern corner of the modern township of Terrington with Wigganthorpe, e.g. Mowthorpe Mill at SE 676 690, with Mowthorpe Wood to its south at SE 677 688, indicate the area originally occupied by the vill. There is no nucleated settlement of the name and LVY 303 locates the vill centre at *c.* SE 685 690, immediately adjacent to Low Mowthorpe Farm.

SHIPTON. Not in DB proper, only in the Summary.

BOSSALL. See 23N32 note.

SN,Bi1 *GERLESTRE* (BIRDFORTH) WAPENTAKE. See 1N107 note.

SN,Bi2 BAXBY. See 2N13 note.

CARLTON (HUSTHWAITE). DG 518 does not distinguish which *Carletun* of fol. 381 is Carlton Miniott and which is Carlton Husthwaite. This *Carletun*, in which the Archbishop holds 4½ carucates, should be Carlton Husthwaite, as DB proper ascribes 4½ carucates there to the Archbishop (2N14). The *Carletun* of SN,Bi6, where the King has 4 carucates, should be Carlton Miniott, as the main text states that he has 4 carucates there (1N109). The 3 carucates held by Hugh son of Baldric (23N8) do not appear to be recorded in the Summary.

THORPE (LE WILLOWS). See 1N108 note; SN,B20 note.

SN,Bi3 *BERNEBI*. See 11N18 note.

SN,Bi4 *HORENBODEBI*. See 3Y12 note.

4 OUTLIERS. '4' is written above the line.

SN,Bi5 *BERGEBI*. DG 516 does not distinguish which *Bergebi* of fol. 381 is the lost vill in Topcliffe township and which is Borrowby near Northallerton. This *Bergebi*, in which William of

Percy holds 8 carucates of land, should be the lost vill, as DB proper ascribes 8 carucates in *Berghebi* to William of Percy (13N16). The *Bergebi* of SN,A1, part of the King's manor of Northallerton, should be Borrowby near Northallerton, as the main text also records Borrowby as part of the King's Northallerton manor (1Y2).

SN,Bi6   CARLTON (MINIOTT). See SN,Bi2 note.

(SAND) HUTTON. DG 525, 533 does not distinguish which *Hotune* of fol. 381 is Hutton Bonville, Hutton Hang, Hutton Magna or Sand Hutton (near Thirsk). The situation is complicated by the fact that in both SN,Bi6 and SN,A2 the King is stated to have 6 carucates in *Hotune*. As, however, the *Hotune* of this entry is dealt with in the same clause as the King's land in Carlton Miniott and Thirsk, it seems likely that it is Sand Hutton near Thirsk, in which the King has 6 carucates according to DB proper (1Y1). The *Hotune* of SN,A2 would then be Hutton Bonville, where the main text ascribes 6 carucates to the King; in SN,A2 *Hotune* occurs in the same clause as Romanby, and in DB proper Hutton Bonville is recorded in the clause following that dealing with Romanby. The *Hotune* of SN,CtA8, in which Count Alan holds 6 carucates, should be Hutton Magna, where the main text states that he similarly holds 6 carucates (6N2). The *Hotune* of SN,CtA37, where 5 carucates are ascribed to Count Alan, would be Hutton Hang, where he is also listed as holding 6 carucates in DB proper (6N131).

BRECKENBROUGH. See 5N71 note.

THIRSK, 8 CARUCATES. The '8' is as SN,Ma10 note.

SN,Bi7   NEWSHAM. DG 530 does not distinguish which *Neuhuse* of fol. 381 is Newsham Grange in Brompton township and which is Newsham near Kirby Wiske. This *Neuhuse*, where the King has 2½ carucates, should be Newsham near Kirby Wiske, as DB proper ascribes 2½ carucates in Kirby Wiske to the King (1N110); the 8 carucates which Hugh son of Baldric is stated to hold according to the main text in Thorpefield and Newsham do not appear to be recorded in the Summary. On this Newsham see 1N110 note. The *Neuhuse* of SN,A1, making up part of the King's manor of Northallerton, should equate with Newsham Grange in Brompton township, which is described in the main text as similarly forming part of the King's Northallerton manor (1Y2).

SN,Bi8   (NORTH) KILVINGTON. See 1Y2 note; 5N72 note.

UPSALL. DG does not distinguish which *Upsale* of fol. 381 is Upsall near Kirby Knowle and which is Upsland. This *Upsale*,where, together with North Kilvington and Hundulfthorpe, the Count of Mortain holds 13 carucates, should be Upsall near Kirby Knowle as, according to the main text, the Count had land as a block in these three vills – the amount given is only 11 carucates (5N75), but in the next clause in the main text it is further stated that in Upsall there are three villagers with a plough and that Richard has it from the Count, so possibly there were an additional 2 carucates held by Richard. The *Upsale* of SN,CtA39, where Count Alan holds 3 carucates, should be Upsland, as DB proper states that the Count holds 3 carucates in Upsland (6N141).

HUNDULFTHORPE (FARM). See 5N75 note.

SN,A1   ALLERTON WAPENTAKE. See 1N113 note.

BIRKBY. See 1Y2 note.

SOWERBY (UNDER COTCLIFFE). See 1Y2 note.

KIRBY (WISKE). DG 526 does not distinguish which *Cherchebi/ Chirchebi* of fol. 381 is Kirby Wiske and which is Kirkby Hall in Kirkby Fleetham township. This *Cherchebi*, which forms part of the King's manor of Northallerton, should be Kirby Wiske, which according to DB proper was also part of the royal manor of Northallerton (1Y2). The *Chirchebi* of SN,CtA13, where Count Alan holds 8 carucates, should also be Kirby Wiske, as the main text ascribes 8 carucates there to the Count (6N30). The *Chirchebi* of SN,CtA20, where the Count holds 3 carucates, should be Kirkby Hall in Kirkby Fleetham township, where the main text states the Count holds 3 carucates (6N55).

LANDMOTH. See 1Y2 note.

THORNTON (LE BEANS). DB *Gritorentun* (DF LXXXV). Farley erroneously *Griftorentun*; DG 536 erroneously *Gristorentun*.

(GREAT) SMEATON ... YAFFORTH. The names of the last 6 places in this list have been added above the line.

(LITTLE) SMEATON. See 1Y2 note.

BORROWBY. See SN,Bi5 note.

YAFFORTH (first entry). DB *Iaforde* (DF LXXXV). Farley erroneously *Laforde*.

NEWSHAM (GRANGE). See 1Y2 note; SN,Bi7 note.

(WEST) HARLSEY. See 1Y2 note.

'WESTHOUSE'. See 1Y2 note.

(KIRBY) SIGSTON. See 1Y2 note.

YAFFORTH (second entry). DB *Iaiforde* (DF LXXXV). Farley erroneously *Laiforde*.

LEAKE. See 1Y2 note.

LAZENBY (HALL). See 1Y2 note. DB *Leisinghi* (DF LXXXV). DG 526 erroneously *Leisenghi*.

RAVENSTHORPE (MANOR). See 1Y2 note.

(OVER) DINSDALE (GRANGE). See 1Y2 note.

THORNTON (LE STREET). See SN,B9 note.

CROSBY (GRANGE). See 1Y2 note.

(NORTH) OTTERINGTON. DG 531, 534 does not distinguish which *Otrintune* of fol. 381 is North Otterington and which is South Otterington. This *Otrintune*, which forms part of the King's manor of Northallerton, should be North Otterington, which is listed as part of the same manor in DB proper (1Y2). On North Otterington see 1Y2 note. The *Otrintune* of SN,A2, where the King has 6 carucates, should be South Otterington, where the King also has 6 carucates in DB proper (1N113); it was presumably these 3 carucates which eventually passed to Robert of Brus (31N3).

IRBY (MANOR). See 1Y2 note.

SN,A2   (SOUTH) OTTERINGTON. See SN,A1 note.

HUTTON (BONVILLE). See 1N115 note; SN,Bi6 note.

SN,A3   (LITTLE) SMEATON. See 1Y2 note.

SN,A4   (CASTLE) LEAVINGTON. See 1N122 note.

SN,A5   YARM. DB *Iarun* (DF LXXXV). Farley erroneously *Larun*.

SN,A6   WINTON. See 3Y18 note.

WINTON, FOXTON. The amounts of land are written above the place-names.

BROMPTON. Farley made a most uncharacteristic error here. He prints '14 carucates' above Brompton, whereas in the text the scribe omitted to include the amount of land at all (DF LXXXV). Farley no doubt obtained his figure of 14 from the main text (3Y15), but it is most unusual for him to amend the original in this way.

SN,A7   MORTON (GRANGE). See 1N126 note; SN,B19 note.

ARNCLIFFE (HALL). See 1N128 note.

'BORDELBY' (MOUNT GRACE). See 1N129 note.

SN,A8   (NETHER) SILTON. Not in DB proper, only in the Summary.

SN,A9   SOWERBY (UNDER COTCLIFFE). See 1Y2 note.

CROSBY (GRANGE). See 1Y2 note.

LEAKE. See 1Y2 note.

SN,A10   MURTON. See SN,B19 note.

DALE (TOWN). See 1N136 note.

SN,CtA1   [LAND OF] COUNT ALAN. The vills in SN,CtA1-44 both here and in DB proper are given not by wapentake but recorded as *Terra Alani Comitis*, comprising virtually the western half of the NR, i.e. the area making up the medieval wapentakes of Gilling East, Gilling West, Hang East, Hang West and part of Halikeld (see Appendix; DGNE 87, 149). The amounts of land are written above the place-names throughout this section.

NEWTON (MORRELL). See SN,B22 note.

SN,CtA2   (SOUTH) COWTON. See 6N1 note.

SN,CtA3   BARFORTH (HALL). See 6N1 note.

SN,CtA4   CLIFFE (HALL). See 6N1 note.

CARLTON. See 6N1 note. DB *Cartune* (DF LXXXV). DG 518 erroneously *Cattune*.

SN,CtA5   BARFORTH (HALL). See 6N1 note.

GIRLINGTON (HALL). See 6N1 note.

WYCLIFFE. See 6N1 note.

THORPE (HALL). See 6N1 note; SN,B20 note.

SN,CtA6   MORTHAM (TOWER). See 6N1 note.

EGGLESTONE (ABBEY). See 6N1 note.

BRIGNALL. See 6N1 note.

SN,CtA7   THE TWO STANWICKS. See 6N1 note.

SN,CtA8   KNEETON (HALL), See 6N4 note.

SN,CtA9   STANWICK. See 6N1 note. This entry obviously refers to both the Stanwicks as it gives the amount of land involved as 4 carucates, whereas 6N1 ascribes 3 carucates to Stanwick and 1 carucate to another Stanwick. This entry may be a duplicate of that in SN,CtA7.

(OVER) DINSDALE GRANGE. See 1Y2 note.

SN,CtA 10   (GREAT) LANGTON. DG 523, 527 does not distinguish which *Langeton* of fol. 381b (fol. 381 in DG numbering) is Little Langton and which is Great Langton, both being held by

Count Alan. This *Langeton*, in which he holds 9 carucates of land, should be Great Langton, as DB proper similarly attributes 9 carucates to him in Great Langton (6N11). The *Langeton* of SN,CtA13, where he holds 7½ carucates, should be Little Langton, as the main text states that he held 7½ carucates there (see 6N26 note).

CARLTON. See 6N1 note.

SN,CtA 11 *TORP*. See 6N17 note; SN,B20 note.

INDRELAGE (RICHMOND). See 6N19 note.

EASBY. See 6N20 note.

SN,CtA 12 BROMPTON (ON SWALE). DG 517, 532 does not distinguish which *Brunton* of fol. 381b (fol. 381 in DG numbering) is Brompton on Swale and which is Patrick Brompton, both being held by Count Alan. This *Brunton*, in which he holds 10 carucates, should be Brompton on Swale, in which he also holds 10 carucates according to DB proper (6N21). The *Brunton* of SN,CtA38, in which he holds 13 carucates, should be Patrick Brompton, where the main text similarly ascribes 13 carucates to him (6N137).

NEUTONE. See 6N23 note.

BOLTON (UPON SWALE). See 6N24 note.

SN,CtA 13 (LITTLE) LANGTON. See 6N26 note; SN,CtA10 note.

SOLBERGE. See 6N28 note.

KIRBY (WISKE). See SN,A1 note.

SN,CtA 14 MORTON (UPON SWALE). See SN,B19 note.

SN,CtA 15 DANBY (WISKE). DG 520 does not distinguish which *Danebi* of fol. 381b (fol. 381 in DG numbering) is Danby Wiske and which is Danby in Thornton Steward township, both being held by Count Alan. This *Danebi*, where the Count holds 10 carucates, should be Danby Wiske, as DB proper ascribes 10 carucates there to the Count (6N36). The *Danebi* of 6N103, where he holds 4 carucates, should be Danby in Thornton Steward, as the main text states that the Count holds 4 carucates there (6N103).

MICKLETON. DG 528 *Micleton*. Farley *Mideton*. The original (DF LXXXV) is difficult to read as the ascender touches the right-hand side of the left-hand letter, and so could be read either as *d* or as *cl*. In view of later forms of the name (PNNR 309) and its occurrence earlier in the text as *Micleton* (6N39), the DG reading is probably to be preferred.

SN,CtA 16 COTHERSTONE. See 6N43 note.

ROKEBY (HALL). See 6N44 note.

SN,CtA 17 BROUGHTON (HOUSE). See 6N45 note.

DALTON, ANOTHER DALTON. See 6N48 note.

SN,CtA 18 DIDDERSTON (GRANGE). See 6N50 note.

SN,CtA 19 KILLERBY (HALL). See 6N52 note.

SN,CtA 19-20 AINDERBY (MIRES). See 6N52 note.

SN,CtA 20 KIRKBY (HALL). See 6N26 note; SN,A1 note.

(KIRKBY) FLEETHAM. See 6N26 note.

ASKE (HALL). See 6N57 note.

SN,CtA 21 TWO FENCOTES. See 6N56 note.

SCRUTON, 14 CARUCATES. This is written as *xii* (12) with *ii* (2) above it.

SN,CtA 22 HORNBY. See 6N61 note.

HOLTBY (HALL). See 6N62 note.

(EAST) APPLETON. See 6N63 note.

BROUGH (HALL). DG 514, 517 does not distinguish which *Burg* of fol. 381b (fol. 381 in DG numbering) is Aldbrough in Bainbridge (i.e. Brough Hill) and which is Brough Hall. This *Burg*, in which Count Alan holds 9 carucates, should be Brough Hall, where he is similarly described as holding 9 carucates in DB proper (6N64). On Brough Hall see

6N64 note. The *Burg* of SN,CtA25, where the Count holds 3 carucates, should be Brough Hill (identified by DG 514 with Aldbrough: see 6N77 note), as he is ascribed 3 carucates there in the main text (6N77).

SN,CtA *INDRELAGE* (RICHMOND). See 6N19 note.
24 ELLERTON (ABBEY). See 6N71 note.
SN,CtA *DENTON*. See 6N76 note.
25 BROUGH (HILL). See 6N77 note; SN,CtA22 note.
FORS (ABBEY). See 6N78 note.
SN,CtA .
26 CROOKSBY (BARN). See 6N83 note.
SN,CtA (WEST) BURTON. DG 524, 538 does not distinguish which *Burton* of fol. 381b (fol. 381 in
27 DG numbering) is High Burton and which is West Burton. This *Burton*, in which Count Alan holds 6 carucates, should be West Burton, in which he is similarly described as holding 6 carucates in DB proper (6N85). The *Burton* of SN,CtA34, in which the Count holds 4 carucates, should be West Burton, as the main text similarly ascribes 4 carucates to him there (6N85).
(CASTLE) BOLTON. See 6N87 note.
SN,CtA
27-8 THORESBY. See 6N89 note; SN,B22 note.
SN,CtA PRESTON (UNDER SCAR). See 6N91 note.
28 (EAST) WITTON, (WEST) WITTON. See 6N92 note.
SN,CtA THE TWO WENSLEYS. See 6N92 note.
29 CARLTON. See 6N93 note.
SN,CtA
31 DANBY. See SN,CtA15 note.
SN,CtA (WEST) HAUXWELL. See 6N107 note.
32 *ASCHAM*. See 6N111 note. DB *Ascham* (DF LXXXV). DG 514 erroneously *Ascam*.
SN,CtA (HIGH) ELLINGTON. See 6N113 note.
33 'SWARTHORPE'. See 6N114 note.
(HIGH) SUTTON. DG 523, 535 does not distinguish which *Sutone* of fol. 381b (fol. 381 in DG numbering) is High Sutton and which is Sutton Howgrave. This *Sutone*, in which Count Alan holds 1 carucate, should be High Sutton, in which DB proper states he has 1 carucate (6N115). The *Sutone* of SN,CtA39, where the Count holds 5 carucates, should then be Sutton Howgrave, although in the main text only 4 carucates are ascribed to him there (6N143).
FEARBY. DB *Federbi* (DF LXXXV). DG 521 erroneously *Fedebi*.
SN,CtA 'TWISLEBROOK'. See 6N118 note.
34 CLIFTON (ON URE). See 6N119 note
SN,CtA (HIGH) BURTON. See 6N120 note; SN,CtA27 note.
35 *OPETUNE*. See 6N120 note.
ACHEBI. See 6N120 note.
FIRBY. See 6N121 note.
SN,CtA THORNTON (WATLASS), (THORNTON) WATLASS. See 6N125 note.
36 THORP (PERROW). See 6N127 note; SN,B20 note.
THORNTON (COWLING). See 6N128 note.
SN,CtA HUTTON (HANG). See SN,Bi6 note.
37 NEWTON (LE WILLOWS). See SN,B22 note.
SN,CtA (PATRICK) BROMPTON. See SN,CtA12 note.
38 (EAST) TANFIELD. See 5W38 note.
SN,CtA UPSLAND. See SN,Bi8 note.
39 HOWGRAVE. See 2W13 note.
SUTTON (HOWGRAVE). See SN,CtA33 note.
SN,CtA
40 YARNWICK. See 6N148 note.
SN,CtA
41 *NORMANEBI*. See 6N149 note.
SN,CtA NEWTON ('PICOT'). See 6N151 note.
42 *OUNESBI*. See 6N151 note.
(LOW) SWAINBY. See 6N152 note.

SN,CtA   ALLERTHORPE (HALL). See 6N153 note.
43   *SEUENETORP.* See 6N154 note.
SN,CtA
44   *ASEBI.* See 6N160 note.
SN,CtA   200 MANORS, LESS 1. The addition is incompatible with this figure. 108 manors waste,
45   plus 133 in the hands of sub-tenants, makes 241.
SE,He1   HESSLE HUNDRED. See 15E1 note.
    CRACHETORP. See 21E4 note.
SE,He5   WAULDBY. See 2B3 note.
    'MYTON'. See 15E2 note.
    RIPLINGHAM. See 15E2 note.
    2 BOVATES. 'Bovates' is written above the line.
SE,He6   *TOTFLED.* See 15E2 note.
    WRESSLE. See 15E3 note.
    IN WRESSLE 14 CARUCATES. This was made up of 8 carucates in Wressle and *Siuuarbi*
    and 6 carucates in Spaldington according to the main text (21E5).
SE,He7   1½ BOVATES. 'Bovates' is written above the line.
SE,He8   LUND. DG 476 does not distinguish which *Lont* of fol. 381c (fol. 381b in DG numbering)
    is Lund near Beverley and which is Lund in Bubwith township (in fact Breighton
    township: see 3Y2 note). This *Lont*, in which Gilbert Tison holds 1½ carucates and
    Ralph of Mortemer holds 2½ carucates, should be Lund in Breighton township, as DB
    proper states that Gilbert Tison holds 1½ carucates there (21E5) with Ralph of
    Mortemer holding 2½ carucates (15E5); according to the Claims 3½ bovates there
    were also claimed by Ralph of Mortemer but it was considered that they should belong to
    Gilbert Tison (CE14). On this Lund see 15E5 note. The *Lont* of SE,We12, where the
    Bishop of Durham holds 18 carucates, should then be Lund near Beverley, although the
    main text ascribes only 12 carucates there to the Bishop (3Y2).
SE,He9   GUNBY. See 21E6 note.
SE,He11   WILLERBY. Not in DB proper, only in the Summary.
SE,Wel1   WELTON HUNDRED. See 11E1 note.
    BRANTINGHAM, WALKINGTON. These have their land written above their names.
SE,Wel2   IN LUND. The amounts of land are written above the relevant place-names.
    LUND. See 3Y2 note; SE,He8 note.
    BRANTINGHAM (THORPE). DG 468 does not distinguish which *Brentingham* of fol.
    381c (381b in DG numbering) is Brantingham and which is Brantingham Thorpe; the
    situation is complicated by the apparent lack of correspondence between the amounts of
    land recorded in DB proper for these places and in the Summary. According to the
    Summary, the Bishop of Durham holds 2 carucates in Brantingham (SE,Wel1) and a
    further 2 carucates 7 bovates in *Brentingham* (SE,Wel12), while the Count of Mortain holds
    1 carucate 6½ bovates and Ralph of Mortemer holds 2 carucates 7½ bovates in
    Brentingham in SE,We16. DB proper records that in Brantingham the Bishop of Durham
    holds 2 carucates (3Y1) and the Count of Mortain 7 bovates (5E9), while in Brantingham
    Thorpe the Bishop of Durham holds 5 bovates (3Y1). In 3Y1, under the lands of the
    Bishop of Durham, Brantingham Thorpe, with 5 bovates, comes immediately after
    Brantingham with 2 carucates, and it seems possible that a similar order was used in this
    section, which would make the *Brentingham* of SE,Wel2 Brantingham Thorpe (on which
    see 3Y1 note). The *Brentingham* of SE,Wel6 would then be Brantingham, although the
    holdings recorded for the Count of Mortain here and in 5E9 do not tally, and the main
    text does not record any holding by Ralph of Mortemer in the vill. There was also some
    dispute over land in Brantingham held by Nigel Fossard but claimed to be part of the
    lands of William Malet (CE13); neither of these men appear in either DB proper or in the
    Summary as holding land in Brantingham, and this land (the amount is not specified)
    may account for the discrepancies between the quantities in the main text and the
    Summary.
    THE BISHOP OF DURHAM (HAS) ALL THESE. i.e. Brantingham, Walkington, Lund
    and Brantingham Thorpe.
SE,Wel4   ELLOUGHTON, WAULDBY. These have their land written above their names.
    WAULDBY. See 2B3 note.
SE,Wel5   WALKINGTON. The amounts of land are written above the relevant place-names.
    THE ARCHBISHOP. Holds these and Elloughton and Wauldby.
SE,Wel6   BRANTINGHAM. See 5E9 note; SE,Wel6 note.
SE,Wel7   PILLWOODS (FARM). See 23E2 note.

SE,C1   CAVE HUNDRED. See 11E1 note.
SE,C2   EVERTHORPE. Not in DB proper, only in the Summary. The holder and the amount of land are both written above the place-name.
SE,C3   DREWTON. See 11E3 note.
         HUNSLEY. See 3Y1 note.
SE,C4   (KETTLE)THORPE. DG 478, 481 does not distinguish which *Torp* of fol. 381c (fol. 381b in DG numbering) is Kettlethorpe, Ousethorpe Farm, Thorpe Lidget, *Torp* (lost in Etton) or *Torp* (lost in Tibthorpe). This *Torp*, in which Robert Malet holds 3 carucates, should be Kettlethorpe, as DB proper records that in Kettlethorpe Robert Malet holds 2 carucates which had formerly been held by Ketill and 1 carucate which had been held by Thorthr (11E4). On Kettlethorpe see 11E4 note. The *Torp* of SE,How4, in which the Bishop of Durham holds 1½ carucates, should be Thorpe Lidget, as the main text ascribes 1½ carucates there to the Bishop (3Y4). The *Torp* of SE,Sn5 where Hugh son of Baldric holds 1 carucate, should be the *Torp* lost in Etton, as DB proper states that Hugh holds 1 carucate there (23E7). The *Torp* of SE,Dr6 where the King has 2 carucates, should be the *Torp* lost in Tibthorpe, where the main text ascribes 2 carucates to the King (1E7). The *Torp* of SE,Wa4, where the King has 3 carucates, should be Ousethorpe Farm, as DB proper states that he has 3 carucates there (1Y10).
SE,C5   (SOUTH) CLIFFE. DG 470, 480 does not distinguish which *Cliue* of fol. 381c (fol. 381b in DG numbering) is Cliffe near Hemingbrough, North Cliffe or South Cliffe. The *Cliue* of SE,How7, in which the Count of Mortain holds 3 carucates, should be Cliffe near Hemingbrough, as DB proper ascribes 3 carucates there to the Count (5E14); the further 3 carucates in Cliffe which are stated to be held by Nigel Fossard, but are claimed to belong to the lands of William Malet (CE21), do not seem to be recorded in the Summary. The *Cliue* of SE,Wei1, where the King has 1 carucate, and of SE,Wei3, where he has a further 1 carucate, are probably both North Cliffe: in the main text, 1 carucate is listed under the King's own holdings (1Y6) and a second carucate is recorded as held by Northmann, one of the King's Thanes (29E25). This would then leave the *Cliue* of this entry (SE,C5) as South Cliffe: according to the Summary the Bishop of Durham holds 3½ carucates in this vill and the King a further 2 carucates. The main text ascribes 4 carucates in South Cliffe to the Bishop, with nothing to the King, but it is stated in the Claims that Nigel Fossard has relinquished 2 carucates which are in the King's hands (CN5-CE1), which should be the 2 carucates ascribed to the King in the Summary. Later Robert of Brus held only 2 bovates in South Cliffe (31E5), unless 'bovates' is a scribal error for 'carucates'.
SE,C10   YOKEFLEET (GRANGE). DB *Iugufled* (DF LXXXVI). Farley erroneously *Lugufled*. DG 483 does not distinguish which *Iugufled* of fol. 381c (fol. 381b in DG numbering) is Yokefleet in Blacktoft (although actually Yokefleet is a township in its own right: see 3Y4 note) or Yokefleet Grange in Gilberdyke township. This *Iugufled*, where the Bishop of Durham holds 1½ carucates and Robert Malet 1 carucate, should be Yokefleet Grange, as DB proper ascribes 1½ carucates there to the Bishop (3Y1) and 1 carucate to Robert Malet (11E5). The *Iugufled* of SE,How2 where the Bishop of Durham holds half a carucate, should be Yokefleet near Blacktoft, as the Bishop similarly holds half a carucate there according to the main text (3Y4).
SE,How1 HOWDEN HUNDRED. The DB hundred of *Hoveden* was named from Howden, presumably the hundred meeting place (PNER 250-1). It was the predecessor of the medieval wapentake of Howdenshire, except that it also included the southern part of the later wapentake of Ouse and Derwent (PNER 244).
         IN HOWDEN. The amounts of land are written above the relevant place-names.
         OWSTHORPE. See 3Y4 note.
         PORTINGTON. DB *Portinton* (DF LXXXVI). DG 478 erroneously *Portiton*.
SE,How2 BURLAND (HOUSE). See CE16 note.
         CAVIL. See 3Y4 note.
         YOKEFLEET. See 3Y4 note; SE,C10 note. DB *Iugufled* (DF LXXXVI). Farley erroneously *Lugufled*.
SE,How3 COTNESS (HALL). See 3Y4 note.
         BARNHILL (HALL). See 3Y4 note.
SE,How4 BELBY (HOUSE). See 1E2 note.
         THORPE (LIDGET). See SE,C4 note.
SE,How
5;7;9   BRACKENHOLME. Not in DB proper, only in the Summary. On the shrunken vill centre see LVY 58.

SE,How5 HAGTHORPE. Not in DB proper, only in the Summary.
BOWTHORPE. Not in DB proper, only in the Summary,
SE,How6 THE BISHOP OF DURHAM. The Bishop holds all the lands in the first 6 entries.
SE,How7 BELBY (HOUSE). See 1E2 note.
CLIFFE. See SE,C5 note.
SE,How8 HAGTHORPE. See SE,How5 note.
SE,How
10 HEMINGBROUGH. See 1Y5 note.
SE,Wei1 WEIGHTON HUNDRED. See 13E1 note.
SHIPTON(THORPE). See 1Y6 note.
THE KING OR ROBERT MALET. There is a contraction mark between the two names, rather inadequately reproduced by Farley, the meaning of which is not clear. Both Skaife (Skaife 240) and Farrer (VCH 319) prefer the reading 'or', which is the one given here, but it should be noted that this contraction could possibly mean 'and'. Possibly the DB scribe was uncertain as to whom these 3½ carucates belonged, and in fact there is no holding of 3½ carucates recorded in this vill in DB proper. The 4½ carucates of the King in Houghton recorded in SE,Wei3 are presumably the 4½ carucates in Houghton listed amongst the King's holdings in DB proper (1Y6), and the half carucate of Gilbert Tison in SE,Wei3 would be the half carucate there ascribed to Gilbert Tison in the main text (21E11). According to the main text Robert Malet had 4½ carucates in Houghton (11E7) and, as no other holding in this vill is recorded for Robert elsewhere in the Summary, it may be these 4½ carucates which are recorded as 3½ in this entry.
SE,Wei
1;3 HOUGHTON. See 1Y6 note.
SE,Wei
1;3 (NORTH) CLIFFE. See SE,C5 note.
SE,Wei2 HOLME (UPON SPALDING MOOR). See 21E9 note.
SE,Wei5 EASTHORPE. See 5E19 note.
SE,Wei6 TOWTHORPE. See 2B9 note.
TORPI. See 1Y7 note.
CLEAVING (GRANGE). See 1E3 note.
SE,Wei7 KIPLING COTES. See 2E11 note.
(BISHOP) BURTON. DG 468,470 states that Bishop Burton occurs in fol. 381d (fol. 381b in DG numbering) as _Burtone_ and Cherry Burton in the same folio as _Burton(e)_. In fact in both occurrences on this folio the name has the form _Burton_, and it is difficult to distinguish which of the two vills is meant in the two cases. In this entry it is stated that the Archbishop has 17 carucates in _Burton_ while in SE,Sn7 14 carucates 2 bovates are ascribed to the Archbishop and 1 carucate to the King. None of these figures bear much resemblance to those recorded in DB proper. In the main text 31 carucates belonging to St. John's of Beverley in Bishop Burton and Skidby are recorded under the holdings of the Archbishop (2E1), and in the same section 12 carucates 6 bovates, similarly held by St. John's of Beverley, are recorded in Cherry Burton (2E8). Also in Cherry Burton is 1 carucate held by Nigel Fossard but which he was relinquishing to the Count of Mortain (5E37); it is probably this carucate which is recorded in the Claims as being relinquished by Nigel, although there it is given as a manor of St. John's of Beverley. It is therefore necessary to turn to their geographical locations of these two vills. The hundreds to which they are assigned are not here helpful, as Weighton and _Sneculfcros_ hundreds are adjcacent and the two vills occur on the boundary close to each other. It seems more likely, however, that the _Burton_ of SE,Sn7, i.e. in _Sneculfcros_, is Cherry Burton, as this would give a compact block of vills in this hundred; it would then follow that the _Burton_ of SE,Wei7 would be Bishop Burton, which would form a detached part of Weighton Hundred to the east of the main part of the hundred. This distribution of the vills concerned is in fact that followed on fig. 40 in DGNE 165.
SE,Sn1 _SNECULFCROS_ HUNDRED. See 13E4 note.
SE,Sn2 BRACKEN. Not in DB proper, only in the Summary. On the depopulated vill centre see LVY 58.
SE,Sn4 _PERSENE._ See 3Y3 note.
SE,Sn4-5 SCORBOROUGH. See 3Y1 note.
SE,Sn5 ETTON, 8 CARUCATES. The '8' is written _vi_ (6) with _ii_ (2) written above it.
TORP. See 23E7 note;SE,C4 note.
STEINTORP. See 5E34 note.
SE,Sn6 _NEUSON._ See 5E41 note.
SE,Sn7 RAVENTHORPE. See 2E7 note.
(CHERRY) BURTON. See SE,Wei7 note.

SE,Sn8   *NEWTON* (GARDHAM), GARDHAM. See 3Y1 note.
           NEWTON (GARDHAM), 1 CARUCATE. This entry was added in the margin.
           NEWTON (GARDHAM), 3 CARUCATES. The '3' is rather ill-written. The scribe seems
           initially to have written *.ii.* (2) and then altered it to '3' by elongating the initial dot (DF
           LXXXVI). There is no reason to doubt the intention, however, and Skaife reads this as
           '3' (Skaife 241).
           MOLESCROFT. DB *Molecroft* (DF LXXXVI). DG 476 erroneously *Molescroft.*
SE,Sn9   SCOREBY (MANOR). See 13E5 note.
           IANULFESTORP. Thus DB (DF LXXXVI). Farley erroneously *Lanulfestorp.*
           DUNNINGTON, 4 CARUCATES. The '4' is written as 2 sets of *II*s, one above the other.
SE,Dr1   DRIFFIELD HUNDRED. See 5E39 note.
SE,Dr2   (GREAT) KENDALE. See 1Y8 note.
           EASTBURN. See 1Y8 note.
           (KIRK)BURN. See 1Y8 note.
SE,Dr4   ROTSEA. Not in DB proper, only in the Summary. On the shrunken vill centre see LVY
           67, but note that the grid reference given there should be TA 064 516.
           NESWICK (HALL). See 5E40 note.
SE,Dr5   HUTTON (CRANSWICK). See 5E39 note.
SE,Dr6   (OLD) SUNDERLANDWICK. See 1E5 note.
           TORP. See 1E7 note; SE,C4 note.
SE,Wa1   WARTER HUNDRED. See 5E43 note.
SE,Wa3   EARNWINE. The main text identifies the man holding land in Huggate as Earnwine the
           Priest.
SE,Wa4   KILNWICK (PERCY). See 1Y10 note.
           (OUSE)THORPE FARM. See 1Y10 note; SE,C4 note.
SE,Wa5   YAPHAM. DB *Iapun* (DF LXXXVI). Farley erroneously *Lapun.*
           (LITTLE) GIVENDALE. Not in DB proper, only in the Summary. On the shrunken vill
           centre see LVY 62.
SE,Wa6   GRIMTHORPE (MANOR). See 1Y10 note.
           ('WATER') FULFORD. See C28 note.
SE,Wa8   LANGWITH (LODGE). See 6E1 note.
SE,P1   POCKLINGTON HUNDRED. See 5E44 note.
SE,P2   WAPLINGTON (HALL). See 1Y10 note.
SE,P3   THORPE (LE STREET). See 1Y7 note.
SE,P4   (HIGH AND LOW) CATTON. See 4E2 note.
SE,P5   STILLINGFLEET. DB *Steflingefeld* (DF LXXXVI). Farley erroneously *Steslingefeld*, DG 480
           erroneously *Steflingefled.*
SE,P6   MOREBY (HALL). See 6E1 note.
           CHETELSTORP. See 6E1 note.
           BISHOP WILTON, 15 CARUCATES. This number is very ill-written. It appears that the
           scribe originally wrote *xii* (12) and subsequently altered the last 2 minims to *v* to make *xv*
           (15). Traces of the original number are still discernible (DF LXXXVI).
SE,P8   GOWTHORPE. DB *Geutorp* (DF LXXXVI). DG 473 erroneously *Guetorp.*
SE,P9   BELTHORPE. See 2N16 note.
           BARMBY (MOOR). See 1Y10 note.
SE,Hu1   HUNTHOW HUNDRED. See 5E45 note.
SE,Hu1-
2   SEWERBY. See 4E1 note.
SE,Hu3   HILDERTHORPE. See 1Y11 note.
           WILSTHORPE. See 1Y11 note.
SE,Hu4   DROGO. Drogo de Bevrere, who is also recorded as holding these 2 carucates in DB
           proper (14E54).
SE,Hu5   AUBURN. See 1E13 note.
           EASTON. See 1Y11 note.
SE,Hu6   BEMPTON. DB *Benton* (DF LXXXVI). DG 467 erroneously *Bentone.*
SE,Hu7   BUCKTON. DG 469 does not distinguish which *Bocheton* of fol. 382a (fol. 382 in DG
           numbering) is Buckton and which is Buckton Holms. This *Bocheton*, in which the King has
           5 carucates 6 bovates and the Count of Mortain 3 carucates 6 bovates, should be Buckton,
           as DB proper ascribes 5 carucates there (a shortfall of 6 bovates) to the King (1Y11) and 3
           carucates 6 bovates to the Count of Mortain (5E51). The *Bocheton* of SE,Sc5, in which
           Berenger of Tosny holds 22 carucates 6 bovates and Hugh son of Baldric holds 3
           carucates, should be Buckton Holms: the main text states that Berenger holds 10
           carucates there (8E1: a difference of 12 carucates 6 bovates) and Hugh son of Baldric 3
           carucates (23E16), as in the Summary.

SE,Hu8   STAXTON. DB *Stacstone* (DF LXXXVII). DG 480 erroneously *Stactone*.

FOXHOLES, 8 CARUCATES. This is written as *vii* (7) with *i* (1) above it.

SE,Tu1   *TURBAR* HUNDRED. See 5E55 note.

RICSTORP. See 20E3 note.

SE,Tu2   *SCLOFTONE*. See 20E3 note.

SE,Tu2-3   (WOLD) NEWTON. DG 477, 483 does not distinguish which *Neuton* of fol. 382a (fol. 382 in DG numbering) is Wold Newton and which is Newton in Wintringham township. The *Neuton* in SE,Th1, in which Ralph Paynel holds 18 carucates, should be Newton, as DB proper ascribes 18 carucates there to Ralph (16E4). The *Neuton* of SE,Tu3, where the King has 4 carucates, should be Wold Newton in which the main text states he has a total of 4 carucates (1E20-1). The *Neuton* of SE,Tu1, in which Gilbert of Ghent holds 3 carucates, is probably also Wold Newton; as Gilbert holds no land in Newton but does have 7 carucates, a shortfall of 4 carucates, in Wold Newton in the main text (20E4).

SE,Tu2   (EAST AND WEST) FLOTMANBY. See 2E3 note.

SE,Tu4   *LEDEMARE*. See 1E22 note.

BURTON (FLEMING). DG 469, 477 does not distinguish which *Burton* of fol. 382a (fol. 382 in DG numbering) is North Burton (or Burton Fleming) and which is Burton Agnes. This *Burton*, in which the King has 16 carucates, should be Burton Fleming, as DB proper states that he has 14½ carucates (1E23) and 1½ carucates (1E24) in Burton Fleming. On Burton Fleming see 1E23 note. The *Burton* of SE,Bt1, in which the King has 12 carucates, should then be Burton Agnes: the main text does not specify exactly how much land the King has in Burton Agnes, but states that he has a total of 25 carucates in Burton Agnes together with its three berewicks (1Y14).

SE,Tu5   ARGAM. See 1E26 note.

SE,Tu6   *ESTOLF*. See 1Y11 note.

SE,Tu7   POCKTHORPE. See 13E16 note.

SE,Tu8   ELMSWELL. DG 471 incorrectly attributes the *Helmesuuelle* of fol. 382a (fol. 382 in DG numbering) to fol. 381c/d (fol. 381b in DG numbering).

ELMSWELL, 9 CARUCATES. DB '9' (DF LXXXVII). Farley erroneously '10'.

SE,Bt1   BURTON HUNDRED. See 5E54 note.

BURTON (AGNES). See SE,Tu4 note.

HARPHAM, 4 CARUCATES. The 4 is written as 2 sets of *II*s one above the other.

SE,Bt1-2   EARNWINE. DB identifies the man holding land in Gransmoor, Harpham and Kilham as Earnwine the Priest (29E12).

SE,Bt3   THORPE (HALL). DG 477, 480, 481, 482 does not distinguish which *Torp* of fol. 382a (fol. 382 in DG numbering) is 'Northorpe', Southorpe, Thorpe in Rudston township, Thorpe Bassett or *Welwick Thorpe*. The *Torp* of SE,Sc9, in which the King has 5 carucates and the Count of Mortain 6 bovates, should be Thorpe Bassett, as DB proper ascribes 5 carucates there to the King (1E45); the land held by the Count of Mortain does not appear to be recorded in the main text. The *Torp* of SE,Th11, in which the Archbishop of York holds 3 carucates, should be *Welwick Thorpe*, which according to the main text is held by the Archbishop as a berewick of Patrington (2A1); DB proper does not state how much land the Archbishop has in *Welwick Thorpe*, but the identification is confirmed by its association there with the same places as in the Summary. The *Torp* of SE,Hol12, which is associated with Hornsea and Hornsea Burton, should be Southorpe, which is also associated with these places in its only recording in the main text (14E7); there Drogo de Bevrere holds 1½ carucates, which should probably equate with the 1½ carucates listed in the Summary where no landholder is given. This is also the case with the *Torp* of SE,Hol20; the 3 carucates are listed after Rysome Garth and before Lissett, as are the 3 carucates of Drogo in Northorpe in the main text (14E21-3), so this *Torp* should be identified with Northorpe. This then leaves the *Torp* of this entry (SE,Bt4) as Thorpe (in Rudston township), which is not recorded in DB proper, only in the Summary. The vill centre is now depopulated, but the name survives in that of Thorpe Hall at TA 109 676. LVY 69 locates the settlement at TA 110 680, the grid reference used for the vill centre in the index in this edition, although LVY 69 also describes the site as west of Thorpe Hall, whereas the grid reference places it north-north-east of the hall.

SE,Bt5   13 CARUCATES. See 29E28 note.

(LOW) CAYTHORPE. See 1E32 note.

SE,Bt7   SWAYTHORPE. See 26E9 note.

FORNETORP. See 1E34 note.

OCTON. See 1E35 note. The name is written above *Fornetorp*.

BUTTERWICK. Not in DB proper, only in the Summary.

SE,Sc1   *SCARD* HUNDRED. See 5E58 note.

BIRDSALL. See 2B18 note.

SE,Sc1-2 SUTTON (GRANGE). See 2B18 note.

SE,Sc5 BUCKTON (HOLMS). See 8E1 note; SE,Hu8 note.

(NORTH) GRIMSTON. DG 473, 477 does not distinguish which *Grimston* of fol. 382a (fol. 382 in DG numbering) is Grimston Garth, in Garton township (in fact now simply Grimston: see 2E24 note), Hanging Grimston or North Grimston. The *Grimston* of SE,Ac3, where the King has 4½ carucates and Odo the Crossbowman a further 4½ carucates, should be Hanging Grimston, as DB proper states that Odo holds 4½ carucates in Hanging Grimston (26E11) and that Osweard and Rothmundr, the King's Thanes, hold 4 carucates (29E16), a shortfall of half a carucate from that ascribed to the King in the Summary. The *Grimston* of SE,So2, in which the Archbishop holds 2 carucates, should be Grimston in Garton township, as the main text states that the Archbishop holds 2 carucates there (2E24); so also should be the *Grimston* of SE,Ho18, as 4 carucates are ascribed to Drogo de Bevrere in Grimston in the main text (14E4). This then leaves the *Grimston* of this entry (SE,Sc5), where the King has 4 carucates 2 bovates, as North Grimston: in DB proper only 4 carucates are recorded in the King's hands (1E53), although later Robert of Brus, who usually holds land which was in the King's hands at the time of DB proper, holds a full 4 carucates 2 bovates (31E8), so possibly 2 bovates were omitted accidentally from the main text. The 2 carucates 2 bovates held by Hugh son of Baldric (23E17) and the 3½ carucates held by the Archbishop (2B18) in the main text do not appear to be recorded in the Summary.

SE,Sc7 BURDALE. See 1E42 note.

SE,Sc8 LINTON. Not in DB proper, only in the Summary. The site of the original vill centre is now depopulated (LVY 64), but the name survives on the modern 2½ in. OS map at SE 909 707.

SE,Sc9 THORPE (BASSETT). See SE,Bt4 note.

SE,Ac1 ACKLAM HUNDRED. See 5E63 note.

EDDLETHORPE. See 1E48 note.

SE,Ac2 KIRBY (UNDERDALE). DG 475 does not distinguish which *Chirchebi* of fol. 382a (fol. 382 in DG numbering) is Kirby Grindalythe and which is Kirby Underdale. This *Chirchebi*, in which the King has 6 carucates, should be Kirby Underdale: DB proper ascribes 4 carucates 2 bovates in Kirby Underdale to the King himself (1E50) and 1 carucate 6 bovates to his Thanes Arngrimr and Siward (29E17), giving the total for the King of the 6 carucates of the Summary (1 carucate = 8 bovates). The *Chirchebi* of SE,Th6, in which the Count of Mortain holds 16½ carucates and the King 1½ carucates, should then be Kirby Grindalythe, although there is some discrepancy between the carucage given in the Summary and in DB proper, which records only half a carucate for the King in Kirby Grindalythe (1E57), but does record that the Count holds one manor of 4½ carucates there (5E69) and a second manor of 12 carucates (5E70), giving the requisite total of 16½ carucates.

GEOFFREY MAMINOT. His name is written at the end of the previous line.

SE,Ac3 (HANGING) GRIMSTON. See 26E11 note; SE,Sc5 note.

ODO ..., IN THE SAME PLACE, 4½ CARUCATES. The 4 is written as 2 sets of *II*s one above the other.

SE,Ac4 GARROWBY (HALL). See 29E19 note.

SE,Ac5 ANOTHER LEAVENING. Not in DB proper, only in the Summary. Leavening itself appears in both the main text (29E3) and here in the Summary, on both occasions with 5 carucates. There is no evidence as to the vill centre of the second Leavening, which was probably subsumed into Leavening at an early date.

HOWSHAM, 8 CARUCATES. '8' is written as *vi* (6) with *ii* (2) above it.

SE,Ac6 THORALBY (HALL). See 29E20 note.

SE,Ac8 *SCRADIZTORP*. See 26E8 note.

BARTHORPE (GRANGE). See 5E64 note.

SE,Ac9 LEPPINGTON. Not in DB proper, only in the Summary.

SUDCNITON. On this vill see 5E65 note.

KIRKHAM. DB *Chirchan* (DF LXXXVII). DG 475 erroneously *Chercan*. See also 5E66 note.

SE,Ac10 WHARRAM (PERCY). See 1E54 note.

SE,Ac11 FRIDAYTHORPE. See 26E4 note.

SE,Ac12 RAISTHORPE. See 1E56 note.

SE,Th1 'THORSHOWE' HUNDRED. See 5E68 note.

NEWTON. See 16E4 note; SE,Tu2 note.

NEWTON, 18 CARUCATES. This is written as *xvi* (16) with *ii* (2) above it.

SE,Th3 KNAPTON. DB *Cnapetone* (DF LXXXVII). DG 475 erroneously *Cnatetone*.

SE,Th5 THIRKLEBY (MANOR), ANOTHER THIRKLEBY (MANOR). See 2B18 note. The first
Turgislebi of this entry, in which Ralph of Mortemer holds 8 carucates, is the Thirkleby
Manor recorded in DB proper with 8 carucates under the lands of Ralph of Mortemer
(15E15). The second *Turgislebi*, where the Count of Mortain holds 4 carucates, is the
Thirkleby Manor recorded as containing 4 carucates held by the Count in the main text
(5E68). Both have therefore been given the same grid reference in the index. The single
carucate here which the main text ascribes to the Archbishop of York (2B18) does not
seem to be recorded in the Summary.
TURODEBI. See 1Y7 note.

SE,Th6 KIRBY (GRINDALYTHE). See SE,Ac2 note.
(LOW) MOWTHORPE. See 2B18 note.

SE,Th7 THE COUNT OF MORTAIN, IN THE SAME PLACE, 1 CARUCATE. DB '1 carucate'
(DF LXXXVII). Farley erroneously '2'.
IN SLEDMERE. See 28W40 note.

SE,Th7;9 COWLAM. See 1E60 note.

SE,Th8 CROOM (HOUSE). See 1E58 note.
COTTAM. See 2B17 note.

SE,Th [HOLDERNESS]. The places recorded in this section are all in Holderness, on which see
10-14 2E17 note.

SE,Th11 *(WELWICK) THORPE* (THORPE HALL). See 2A1 note; SE,Bt4 note.

SE,Th12 'THARLESTHORPE'. See 2A1 note.

SE,Th
13-14 IN (NORTH) SKIRLAUGH. The amounts of land are written above the place-names.

SE,Th13 DANTHORPE. See 2E31 note.

SE,Th14 ESKE. See 2E21 note.
STORK(HILL). See 2E22 note. The name is written at the end of the following line.

SE,So1-2 SOUTH HUNDRED. As with the entries under the heading Middle Hundred (SE,Mid1-
3) and North Hundred (SE,No1-2), only a few vills are recorded in this division of
Holderness, although it is obvious from the map that the places listed simply under
Holderness (SE,Hol1-26) must also have been allocated to one of the three divisions. It is
uncertain what determined whether a place was specifically allocated to a hundred as
opposed to the wapentake in general. On Holderness see 2E17 note. For all entries in this
section, the amounts of land are written above the relevant place-names. No landholder is
named for the vills in this section, but the Archbishop, who is named in the preceding
entry (SE,Th14), is obviously assumed as the holder, and he in fact holds all these places
in DB proper.

SE,So2 GRIMSTON. See 2E24 note; SE,Sc5 note.
MONKWITH. See 2E25 note.

SE,Mid MIDDLE HUNDRED. See SE,So1 note. No landholder is named for the vills in this
1-3 section, but it is obviously assumed, as with the preceding two entries, that it is the
Archbishop, who in fact holds all these places in DB proper. For all entries in this section,
the amounts of land are written above the relevant place-names.

SE,Mid1 BURTON (CONSTABLE). See 2E28 note.

SE,Mid2 DANTHORPE. See 2E31 note.

SE,Mid3 SOUTHCOATES. See 2E35 note.

SE,No1- NORTH HUNDRED. See SE,So1 note. For all entries in this section, the amounts of land
2 are written above the relevant place-names.

SE,No1 (GREAT) COWDEN. See 14E5 note.
RISE. DG 478, 479 does not distinguish which *Rison* of fol. 382b (fol. 382 in DG
numbering) is Rise and which is Rysome Garth. This *Rison*, in which the Archbishop
holds half a carucate, should be Rise as DB proper ascribes half a carucate there to the
Archbishop (2E37). The *Rison* of SE,Hol20, where there are 2 carucates, should be
Rysome Garth, where, according to the main text, Drogo de Bevrere holds 2 carucates
(14E21). The *Rison* of SE,Hol23, in which there are 3 carucates, should equate with Rise,
although in DB proper Drogo holds 5½ carucates there. In addition to these lands, the
Claims state that there are a further 7½ carucates in Rise which are held by William
Malet (CE34;39) and 2 carucates in Rysome Garth, also held by William Malet
(CE34;50); these lands do not appear to be recorded in the Summary.

SE,No2 BRANDESBURTON, LEVEN. No landholder is named for these vills, but the
Archbishop, who is named in the preceding entry (SE,No1), is obviously assumed as the
holder, and he in fact holds these places in DB proper.

SE,Hol1-   HOLDERNESS. See 2E17 note. No landholder is named for this section, but the vills
26   listed here are all held by Drogo de Bevrere in DB proper. But note the mention of St.
          John's, Beverley, in SE,Hol12. For all entries in this section, the amounts of land are
          written above the relevant place-names.

SE,Hol2   NEWTON (GARTH). DG 477, 478 does not distinguish which *Niuueton* of fol. 382b (fol.
          382 in DG numbering) is Newton Garth and which is Out Newton. This *Niuueton*, where
          there is 1 carucate, should be Newton Garth, in which DB proper states that Drogo de
          Bevrere holds 1 caruate (14E1). The *Niuueton* of SE,Hol20, in which there are 5 carucates,
          should be Out Newton, as the main text ascribes 5 carucates there to Drogo (14E20).
          NUTHILL. See 14E1 note.
          SKECKLING. See 14E1 note.
          CAMERTON (HALL). See 14E1 note.

SE,Hol3   (LELLEY) DYKE. See 14E1 note.
SE,Hol4   KILNSEA. See 14E2 note.
SE,Hol5   TANSTERNE. See 14E2 note.
SE,Hol6   ETHERDWICK. See 14E2 note.
          RINGBROUGH. See 14E2 note.
          FOSTUN. See 14E2 note.
          FLINTON, 4½ CARUCATES. DB '4½' (DF LXXXVII). Farley erroneously '3½'.
SE,Hol7   *ANDREBI.* See 14E4 note.
          BURTON (PIDSEA). DG 468, 469, 474 does not distinguish which *Bortun* of fol. 382b (fol.
          382 in DG numbering) is Brandesburton, Burton Pidsea or Hornsea Burton. This *Bortun*,
          where there are 7 carucates, should be Burton Pidsea, as the main text states that Drogo
          de Bevrere holds 7 carucates there (14E4). The *Bortun* of SE,Hol12, where there are 2
          carucates, should be Hornsea Burton, as DB proper ascribes 2 carucates there to Drogo
          (14E7). The *Bortun* of SE,Hol22, where there are 12½ carucates, should equate with
          Brandesburton, where Drogo is stated to hold 12½ carucates in the main text (14E31).

SE,Hol8   DANTHORPE. See 2E31 note.
          GRIMSTON. See 2E24 note; SE,Sc5 note.
SE,Hol9   (OW)THORNE. See 14E4 note.
          REDMERE. See 14E4 note.
SE,Hol   ROLSTON. See 14E5 note.
10   *ARNESTORP.* See 14E5 note.
          (LITTLE) COWDEN. See 14E5 note.
          (HORNSEA) BURTON. See SE,Hol7 note.
SE,Hol   ST. JOHN'S. St. John's of Beverley presents an exception to Drogo de Bevrere's holding.
12   (SOU)THORPE. See 14E7 note; SE,Bt4 note.
SE,Hol   (NORTH) SKIRLAUGH. DG 477, 480 does not distinguish which *Schirelai* of fol. 382b
13   (fol. 382 in DG numbering) is North Skirlaugh and which is South Skirlaugh. This
          Schirelai, where there are 6 bovates, should be North Skirlaugh, as DB proper ascribes 6
          bovates there to Drogo de Bevrere (14E7); the 9 bovates in North Skirlaugh held by the
          Archbishop according to the Summary (SE,Th13) do not appear to be recorded in the
          main text. The *Schirelai* of SE,Hol15 should be South Skirlaugh: according to the
          Summary there are 1½ carucates in East Newton, 1 carucate in *Schirelai* and 2 bovates in
          Totleys Farm, giving a total of 2 carucates 6 bovates (1 carucate = 8 bovates), which is the
          total amount of land attributed to Drogo's holding in these three vills in the main text
          (14E11).
          (HIGH) SKIRLINGTON. See 14E7 note.
          CLEETON. See 14E8 note.
SE,Hol
14   RINGBROUGH. See 14E2 note.
SE,Hol   (SOUTH) SKIRLAUGH. See SE,Hol13 note.
15   TOTLEYS (FARM). See 14E11 note.
          MEAUX. See 14E11 note.
SE,Hol   BENNINGHOLME (HALL). See 14E11 note.
16   ROWTON (FARM). See 14E11 note.
          DOWTHORPE (HALL). See 14E11 note.
SE,Hol   FOSHAM. See 14E11 note.
17   BEWICK (HALL). See 14E14 note.
          RINGBROUGH. See 14E2 note.
SE,Hol
18   TOTLEYS (FARM). See 14E11 note.

SE,Hol	(GREAT AND LITTLE) NEWSOME. See 14E15 note.
19	REDMERE. See 14E4 note.
SE,Hol20	(OUT) NEWTON. See SE,Hol2 note.
	RYSOME (GARTH). See SE,No1 note.
	'(NOR)THORPE'. See SE,Bt4 note.
SE,Hol	
21	'WINKTON'. See 14E24 note.
SE,Hol	
21-2	(NUN)KEELING. See 14E24 note.
SE,Hol	ARRAM. See 14E30 note.
22	(BRANDES)BURTON. See SE,Hol7 note.
	CATFOSS (HALL). See 14E33 note. DG 469 fails to record this entry in fol. 382b (fol. 382 in DG numbering).
SE,Hol	*CHENUCOL*. See 14E35 note.
23	RISE. See SE,No1 note.
	WASSAND (HALL). See 14E38 note.
SE,Hol	LANGTHORPE (HALL). See 14E41 note.
24	(LITTLE) HATFIELD, 3 CARUCATES AND 2 PARTS OF 1 CARUCATE. The scribe had originally written just '1 carucate', but '2 carucates and 2 parts' has been added above the line.
SE,Hol	SOUTHCOATES. See 2E35 note.
25	

INDEX OF PERSONS

The personal-names given in the Yorkshire section of DB have been regularised in this edition from the forms in which they occur in DB. This is necessary because the same personal-name referring to the same individual may occur with different forms at different points in the manuscript, e.g. the ON name *Sveinn* has the forms *Suen, Suuan* and *Suuen*. In general the OE names have been regularised to the West Saxon forms given in PNDB. Northumbrian OE, which was the dialect used by the English recorded in this section of DB, varied in certain vowels and diphthongs from West Saxon, and, where different, the Northumbrian forms of the personal-names have been used, e.g. the regularised West Saxon form for DB *Aldred* would be *Ealdraed* (PNDB 241), but the regularised Northumbrian form *Aldred* is used here. The forms used for names of ON origin follow those given in SPN. In some cases it is impossible to ascertain whether a name is of OE or ON origin, e.g. DB *Brun* could be ON *Brunn* or OE *Brun(a)*. In such cases the form closest to that found in DB is used. If either would be possible, an arbitrary decision has been taken to use the ON rather than the OE form, as the dialect of 11th-century Yorkshire was Anglo-Scandinavian; it should be borne in mind throughout that in such instances the OE form is equally possible. All such cases are discussed in the notes. In the spelling of the names the OE letters *thorn* ($\flat$) and *eth* ($\eth$) have been given as 'th' and *ash* (α) as 'ae'.

It should be emphasised that this is essentially an index of personal-names not of persons. It is probable that in the case of some entries of simple names, more than one person bearing the same name has been included, as DB does not in general give patronymics; names such as *Grimr* were common in the Yorkshire area in the 11th century and could have been borne by a number of different men. In some cases it is possible to identify people more closely from information given in the Claims, or vice-versa, e.g. the Arnketill of 13W16 is identified as Arnketill son of Ulfr in CW25; where an individual has been so identified, the reference is given in brackets in this index. All such cases are discussed in the notes. As it would appear that holdings were allocated to the new Norman lords not by geographical distribution, but by the transfer of the lands of individual English landholders, a series of references to the same name as that of the 1066 holder in the list of the lands of an individual Norman 1086 landholder is likely to relate to the same person, e.g. the Knutr of 1N59-60;68-69;85;89-90;103. 1E15;45. 1W25 is probably the same man, but this is much less certain where the same name occurs as the 1066 holder of the lands of a number of different 1086 Norman landholders. Conversely, on occasion, variations in the forms recorded in DB can result in different regularised forms for the name of what in fact may be the same person, e.g. the Blaec of 13N8 may well be the same man as the Blakkr of 13N10;12;14. Likewise, a person who elsewhere bears a title or byname may be represented under a single name, e.g. some of the references to Edwin may be to Earl Edwin.

Regularisation of the Norman-French personal-names is a greater problem, because much less research has been carried out on the subject. Only a limited range of personal names was in use amongst the new lords, most of which survive in modern English today. The modern, not the 11th-century forms, have been used in this edition. In general the rule has been followed in this edition that the majority of the surnames of the Norman lords relate to known places in France, mainly in Normandy, and that the 11th-century surnames functioned as true descriptive terms of the individuals concerned, described by reference to their points of origin, rather than to hereditary surnames. Therefore, surnames such as *de Tosny* have been modernised as 'of Tosny'. Unfortunately certain prominent landholders are already well known to historians of the period with names varying from the strictly regularised forms. It has been decided in these cases to use the commonly known rather than the regularised forms; thus Ilbert de Lacy not Ilbert of Lassy. Similarly, the current rather than the regularised forms have been used for influential Anglo-Saxon landholders, e.g. Earl Harold (i.e. Harold Godwinson) not Earl Haraldr. Where the same name occurs without title, the modern form has also been used in case it is the same person.

The definite article is used before bynames where there is a probability that they describe the individual rather than his or her ancestors. The chapter numbers of listed landholders are printed in italics. Female landholders have been indicated by 'f' in brackets following their names in the index.

Adelo	9W39
Aegelfride (f)	1N98, note
Aelfhere	1N34, note
Aelfled	1W53, note
Aelfric	9W26;78
Aestan	10W6, note
Aethelhelm	14E17
Aethelstan	14E19, note. 21W2. CE49
Aethelwulf	13E14
Agmundr	10W8
Count Alan	6. *SN,CtA*. C24;28;30;32–33. CW42. SN,Y4–7. SW,An3; 18. SN,B6;10;16–18;27. SE,Wa7–8. SE,P4–6
Albert, Drogo de Bevrere's man	14E45, note
Alcolm	30W19–21
Aldgyth (f)	5E27, note. CE6
Aldred	1N16, note. 6N55;95;116. 11E2. 11N4;13. 13W30–31. 25W15;17
Archbishop Aldred of York (1066)	C1a, note. C1b;21. 2A1–3. 2B1;3–7;9–11;13;18. 2W4; 6–7. 2E1–2;12. CE33. CW22;39
Aldwif (f)	5E30, note. CE35;40
Aldwulf	C11, note. 25W19
Alfgrimr	C10
Alfketill	6N26. 9W25. 14E26
Alfred	1N19, note. 1E59. 1W30. 5W38. 9W40. 29W21
Alhmund	C18, note
Almer	10W16, note
Almund	29W39–40. 30W10
Alric	1W23. 5W32;34. 9W60;63;67;70–71;76;85–88;100;108; 116–117;119–120. 29W10;26
Alsige	C12. 1N117. 1W14. 6N9. 9W35–36;39;41;44;46;51;63; 65;76;89;141. 10W3–4;16;31;34;43. 11W3. 18W2. 29W3. CW15
Aluerle	1N104, note
Alweard	5W1, note. 5W2–5. 9W12;27;53;98
Alwine	C7;13;15. 1W53. 5W35. 9W42. 13E5. 21E1–2;5–7;9;12. 25W2–2;11–12;18–19. CE14. CW11;31
Bishop Alwine of Durham (1066)	3Y9–10;16–18
Arnbjorn	1E55. 1W24. 9W72–73;77;98;102;115–116;120;138; 140–141
Arnbrandr	30W26;28
Arnfastr, Richard son of. See Richard son of Arnfastr	
Arngeirr	1N94
Arngrimr	1N101. 29E17–18
Arnketill	C3;34. 1N31;33;38–39;45;47;132;135. 1E15. 1W8;59; 61. 5N65. 5E43. 5W30. 6N60–62;72;77;79;117;134; 137;139;141;144–145;149–150;159. 9W24;34;44;121; 123;126;131;144. 10W8;39. 11N15. 11W1. 13W2;22; 26. 13N18. 23N2. 24W9. 28W33;37–38. 29N6. 29W34– 35;37–38;50. 30W15–16;18;26–27;29;32–33. CW2. SN,Y8
Arnketill son of Ulfr	(13W16, note). CW25
Arnketill son of Wulfstan	(25W1, note. 25W3, note. 25W6, note). CW24
Arnketill, brother of	13W3 note. CW2
Arnthorr	5W25. 9W48. 27W1
Arnthorr the Priest	29W7. (29W8, note)
Arulf	5W28
Asa (f)	13E5;10–11. 29E13. CE15;31
Asfrithr	9W16
Asfrothr	23N28
Asgautr	9W43
Asgeirr	(25W29–30, note). CW2

Asi	5W15
Asketill	1N136. 6N34;100;152–154. 11N5;14;16–19;21–22
Asmundr	9W23
Asmundr, Gamall son of. See Gamall son of Asmundr	
Asulfr	5E55. 6N133–134. 9W52;75;94. 10W15;24;26;28;38. 13W8
Atsurr	14E19
Aubrey of Coucy	27. SW,Sf13, note. SW,Sf15
Authbjorn	29E3
Authhildr (f)	6N26
Authulfr	C10. 1N84. 1E48. 6N100
Authvithr	6N121. 29E16
Bald, four sons of	6N88, note
Baldric, Hugh son of. See Hugh son of Baldric	
Baldwin, Drogo de Bevrere's man	(14E9, note. 14E16;28). 14E48
Barkr	1E27. 23N26
Barn	CE2
Barthr	1Y12. 1E9. 9W20;38;48;50–51;58–62;119. 25W22. 29W25
Basing	1E2, note. 3Y7. 5E1. 11E2;5. 14E48;52. 29W27. CE1; 12;17
Berenger of Tosny	8. C15. 7E1–2. 30W3. SW,Bu27;33. SN,L6. SN,D7;10; 13;16;20–21. SN,Ma1;6;9–13;15;20. SN,B1–2;5–6;8. SE,Sc4–6;10. SE,Ac1–3. SE,Th2;8–9
Bergulfr	9W12
Bjarni	1W53
Bjornulfr	C10, note. C18. 6N53;83–84;93;120;129. 13W20–21; 25;44. 13E2–3;11–12. 13N17;19. CE15
Bjorr	13W35, note
Blaec	13N8, note
Blakkr	13N8 note. 13N10;12–14
Bodin	6N7;11;18;38–40;44–47;49–51;67;73;75–76;78;80;91; 122;135
Bondi	C19. 14E26. 26E8 note. CE32
Boso, Osbern son of. See Osbern son of Boso	
Brandulfr	CE47
Brunn	1N76. 1E4. CW8
Brunn the Priest	C16, note
Brunn the priest, mother of	C16
Buga	5W12, note
Bui	30W6
Clibert	2B19. 29E6;8–9;27. 30W39
Cola	9W107, note
Crin	6N74
Dolgfinnr	1W40. 9W110. 29W39–41
Domnall	6N119
Drengr	25W32–33
Drogo de Bevrere	14. 2E33, note. (CW39, note. CE52, note. SE,Hu4)
Dubhan	1L8
Dubhghall	1N133
Dunning	10W16
Dunstan	C10. 1W26. 9W3;16;113;118;122;128–129;136;139. 13W1. CW5
Eadgifu (f)	15E1–4;7–10;12;14–16. CE14
Eadmund	11N3–4;6–7;9–11;20
Eadric, Godwine son of. See Godwine son of Eadric	
Eadweard	9W44
Eadwulf	5E39. 9W52;87
Eardwulf	1W5–6. 13N18
Earne	1N61, note. 24W18
Earnwine	C2, note. C12. 9W2;4;25;67;97. 13W12. 14E15;31. SW,An5. SE,How9

Earnwine, another	C12
Earnwine Catenase	(25W13, note). CW32
Earnwine the Priest	(5E7, note. 25W16, note). 29W2;9. 29E7;12. 30W40. CE18;27. CW32. (SW,BA7, note. SW,Sf22, note. SE,Wa3, note. SE,Bt1-2, note)
Earnwulf	1L8. 9W54
Eburhard	13W16;26;35
Eburhard, William of Percy's man	1W53. SW,Bu49
Ecgbeorht	C10
Ecgfrith	1E30-32. CE42
King Edward	C1a;2;20;36-37. 1Y15;17-19. 3Y4;6. 9W64. CW39
Edwin	C36, note. 2B8. 6N128, note
Earl Edwin	C36 note. 1Y2. 1W73. 5W14. 6N1;52. 6W1. 9W1. 10W1
Egbrand	1W49-50. 6N98. CE17
Egelfride (f)	1N113. 23N33
Eilafr	C17. 1N131. 1E14. 14E43
Einulf	C7
Enisant	6N5-6;8;12-13;15-21;23-25;64;66;68;86;104;109;146
Erembald	14E27
Ermenfrid, Osbern de Arches' man	25W13;16
Ernegis	6N118
Erneis de Burun	24. C13. (30W30, note. SW,Sk18, note. SE,An2-3. SW,Bu3-5;7-14;25-26;28;31;35;40-44. SE,C9. SE,Sn2. SE,Wa7)
Esbjorn	1N71
Fargrimr	13E5
Farthegn	25W2
Feigr	30W1;31
Finnghall	6N11
Flotmann	1W41. 6N143;157
Forni	C17. 1E1;4. 9W30. 13E5. 14E52. 26E1-2;4;8-10, note. 26E12. 29E4
Franco, Drogo de Bevrere's man	14E33;37;47;51
Frani	14E45;48, note. CE45
Frani, another	14E48
Frani, brother of	(14E48, note). CE45
Frani, son of Thorr	(14E43, note). CE41
Frithgestr	1N79;101;123;136-137
Frumold, Drogo de Bevrere's man	14E44, note
Fulcher	13N15, note. 23N29
Fulco	10W27;33;39. 13W13. 13N14
Fulco, Drogo de Bevrere's man	14E53
Fulco, Gilbert Tison's man	21E4
Fulco, Osbern de Arches' man	25W6;29-30
Fulcric	23E12
Fulk of Lisors	CW14, note
Gamalbarn	C10, note. 1W42-46;56-57;62;65-66. 13W13;17;24; 28;30-33. 21W5;8-15;17. 30W11-12
Gamalkarl	C15
Gamall	C3. 1N3;32;57-58;67-68;72;74;82-83;86;88. 1E16;45. (1W17, note). 1W18-19;39;59-60. 2N5. 5N63;73. 5E4; 21;29;31;32;42;44;67. 6N30;56;71;90;103;105;107; 132. 8N2-7;11. (8N12-20). 8N21-22. 8W2. 8E2;4-5. 9W24;26;47-48;56;65-66;76-78;100;103;112;115-116;129-130;138;142-143. 11E1. 11N16. 11W2. 13W4-5;25;45. 13N15. 14E35;48. 21W16. 23N10-11; 15-16. 23E2-6;8-10;13;15-17. 24W11. 25W24-25. 26E4-5;12. 29E2;13;19-20;24. 29N11. 29W48. 30W3; 13-14;36. CE33. CW2. SN,Bi1
Gamall, brother of	29E20
Gamall, mother of	29E20

Gamall, sons of	6N103
Gamall, son of Asmundr	(13W3, note). CW2
Gamall, son of Osbert	C36
Geoffrey	6N60, note. 6N82;85;108. 13E2;7;9
Geoffrey, the Archbishop's man	2A3
Geoffrey, Gilbert Tison's man	21E9
Geoffrey, Hugh son of Baldric's man	23E14, note
Geoffrey Alselin	*18.* CW16;19;33–34. SW,Sf21. SW,An9
Geoffrey Bainard	1Y14
Geoffrey of Beauchamps	CE9. SE,Ac2
Geoffrey of la Guerche	*17.* SW,St2
Gerard, Hugh son of Baldric's man	(23N4, note). 23N9–11;13;15–16
Gerbodo	9W56;98
Gerbodo, Drogo de Bevrere's man	14E36
Gernand	6N26;58;148
Gilbert	9W17, note. 9W50
Gilbert Maminot	C14
Gilbert of Ghent	*20.* CW4. SE,Tu1–2
Gilbert Tison	*21.* CE14;16;28. SW,Sk16. SW,Sf27. SW,Bu17;26;31–32; 34;37–41. SE,He1–3;6;8–9;11. SE,C7–8. SE,How7–9. SE,Wei2–3. SE,P3
Gilleandrais	13N12
Gillebride	29E30
Gillemicel	1N135. 1L7. 30W39
Gillepatric	6N28;87;90;94;99;102
Gilli	1E46. 6N29;131;137–138
Gluniairnn	C12. 1W13. (1W17, note). 1W18–19;29. 6N92. 9W14;16; 39–40. 10W39. 30W30
Godelind (f)	C10
Godfrey	13W17–19;32;37
Godhyse	5W17. CW20
Godred	5N57, note
Godric	1W22;25. 2N29. 9W4;42–43;74;82;87. 10W7;10;16;37
Godric the Steward	6N1
Godwine	1W27–28. 2B3. 6W3. 9W106;109–112. 25W8. CW34
Godwine son of Eadric	(25W1, note. 25W3;6, note). CW27
Gospatric	*28.* C11;13;18. 1N42;46;48–51;53–56;93–96;104–107. 1W42;54. 5N28–29. 6N31–32;47–48;61–62;65;67;70; 72;79;89;112–113;116–118;135;139;149–150. 9W15. 24W1–2;4–7;12–16. 29E22. 29W47;49. 30W22–23;30. SW,Sk3. SW,An17. SW,Bu2;4–6;11–12;14–15;20–26; 30;32;34;37;49. SW,H6. SN,Bi2–3. SE,D6
Grimketill	C12. 1E33. 9W5. 14E19;22 note. 14E46. CE51
Grimr	C12–13. 1N73;75;78. 1E10;56. 1W9. 5W21. 6N27;31. 13W20–21. 24W3. (25W29–30, note). CW2
Grucan	29W2, note
Gunnarr	1W35;37. 6N106–107. 9W19. 14E14, note
Gunnvor (f)	5N31;53–54
Guntard	14E16
Guthrithr (f)	29E16
Gytha (f)	5E35–36
Hakon	5W13
Halfdan	C12. 1E19. 9W77;86;96;101;115;138. 10W6;35–36. 13W17. 13E6–7. 14E45;47. 22W4. CE26. CW31
Halldorr	1N113;117. 5N74. 6N28–29. 25W24. 29N1
Hamelin	C7. 9W57. CE5
Harold	9W119, note. 14E8;54
Earl Harold	C36. (C37–39). 4E1–2. 12W1
Havarthr	1N22–24;118;120–122. 29N8. CN3
Heardwulf	29W42
Hedned	C11, note

Henry	14E13
King Henry I	31N10
Herewig	6N11;35. 9W42
Hubert of Mont-Canisy	C19
Hubert, Ralph Paynel's man	16N3
Hugh	9W24. 13E15
Hugh, Osbern de Arches' man	25W20
Earl Hugh	4. C2;10. CN1. SN, L1-5; 10; 12-13; 19-24; 33-37. SE,P4. SE,Hu1;8
Hugh son of Baldric	23. C11;26. SW,An1. SW,Bu1. SN,L14;41. SE,He4. SE,Wel3;7. SE,C2-3. SE,How9. SE,Sn5. SE,Dr4-5. SE,Wa7-8. SE,P4-6. SE,Sc1-7. SE,Ac7;12. SE,Th1-2;8
Hugh, Hugh son of Baldric's man	23E6
Hugh son of Northmann	4N3. 4E1
Humphrey	9W27;52;97
Humphrey, Erneis de Burun's man	24E2
Humphrey, Gilbert Tison's man	21E11
Hundigrimr	1N42. 6N27
Hundingr	1E56
Hundingr, three sons of	1W17
Huni	14E36
Hwelp	14E19, note
Ilbert	2W1
Ilbert de Lacy	9. (CW1-3, note. CW23. SW,Sk4-12, note. SW,BA5-11. SW,Sf37. SW,O2-14;16. SW,St1;3-8;10-16. SW,Ag1-8; 13;15-16. SW,M1-10)
Ingifrithr (f)	1E42
Ingirithr (f)	1E10. 29E7
Ingjaldr	C36
John, Erneis de Burun's man	24W18
John, Osbern de Arches' man	25W24
Joli	1Y9
Countess Judith (f)	10W41. SW,Sf35
Kalmann	1W38
Karli	1N41. 1E12-13;17-18;22-23;25-26;41;54. 1W15. 5E45-46. 13E15-16. 13N9-11;19. 14E18. 20E1. 29E5; 10. 30W9
Ketilbjorn	1E20;24;32-33, note. 1E60. 5E57-59;68-69;71;72, note. 9W77. 10W19;21;30. 20E2. 29W3. 29E21;28
Ketilbjorn, brother of	1E60
Ketilfrothr	1N4. 14E29;31;39
Ketilfrothrs, two	14E28
Ketill	1W7;37;48. 1L5. 2E11. 6N27. 9W31;105;110. 11E3-4. 21E1-2;7-8. 23E1. 29W15;28;45-46;50. 30W22. CW3
Ketill the Priest	C6
Ketill, brother of	CW3
Killi	13E5
Knutr	C36. 1N59-60;62;68-69;85;89-90;103. 1E15;45. 1W25. 5E10;39. 6N58;82;119. 9W94. 13N16. 14E33;37. 21E1;3-4. 23N27. CE37-39
Kofsi	C36, note. 6N36. 23N1
Kolbrandr	1N66. 29E30
Kolgrimr	5E18-20;44
Lagmann	1E40;54
Lanbert, Drogo de Bevrere's man	14E46
Landric	29W27-28. CW30
Landric, Count Alan's man	6N36. (6N37, note). 6N53. (6N131, note)
Landric the Carpenter	C20
Leodwine	13W22, note
Leofing	9W113
Leofing the Priest	C3

Robert of Brus	*31*
Robert of Tosny	7. SE,Wa1–2
Roger	9W96;99
Roger, Drogo de Bevrere's man	14E52
Roger de Busli	*10.* CW7;15;19. SW,Sf2–11;14;18–20;22–23;27–29;34; 36. SW,O1–3
Roger of Poitou	*30.* 1L1
Rossketill	1W11;14;16. 6N144;147. 9W24. 13W35
Rothmundr	29E16
Rozelin	13W6;10–12
Saexfrith	2N26–30. 29N13. SN,Y6
Saexfrith the Deacon	C31, note. C35
Saksulfr	9W22. 28W30
Salomon	23N4
Sandi	1W17 note. 1W18
Selakollr	C10
Sigrithr (f)	6N126. 13E12
Sigvarthbarn	17W1
Sindi	9W132
Siward	1N36, note. 1N63;65. 1E5. 1W21. 5N6. 5E2–3;23;36. 6N30;35. 9W63;66. 10W2–3;5. 14E19;26. 29E17;29. 29N13. CW7;18. CE49
Earl Siward	1N36 note. 4N1–3
Skammketill	5N63
Skelfr	9W137
Skjaldfrithr (f)	23E18
Skotakollr	5W11. 9W40
Skuli	29E1
Slettan	2B8
Snaebjorn	29W33
Snarri	C3
Sotakollr	CW11, note
Sprottr	1E49. 1W9. 5E32. 6N26;46;155;158. 13N8. 23N30. 29E30. CN4
Steinn	6N125. 30W25
Steinulfr	6N130. 9W11;119;122;127;134–135;139
Sterri	C3;6
Sudan	6N156
Sumarfugl	23N13
Sumarlithi	1N92
Suneman	1W33
Sunnifa (f)	C10
Sunnulfr	1E40. 5E38;56. CE27
Sunnulfr the Priest	C3
Svartgeirr	14E32;53
Svarthofuth	5N64, note
Svartkollr	1N77;81. 1W20. 25W15. 30W24;34
Svartr	C10
Sveinn	5N1–8;10. 9W34;57;69;74;91;96;105–107;114;117; 120. 10W20;22–23;25;29;32–33;39;42. 14E31;34;38; 50–51. 27W1–2. 29W5. CW14
Sveinn of Adwick le Street	CW22
Sveinnbrothir. See Ulfketill Sveinnbrothir	
Theodbald, Drogo de Bevrere's man	14E43
Tholfr	1E16
Archbishop Thomas of York (1086)	*2.* C1a, note. C21–22;30;37. 6N142. CE25;28;33. SN,Y1–3;5;7–8. SW,Sk1–2. SW,BA1–2. SW,Ag1. SW,An12;15;18. SW,Bu5;20;45. (SW,Bu46–48). SW,H1–3. SN,Ma5;7–8;11–12;15;19;21–22. SN,B13–14;17–19;23–25. SN,Bi2. SE,Wel4–5. SE,C2;4. SE,How11. SE,Wei4–7. SE,Sn1;3–5;7–9. SE,Dr1. SE,Wa3–7. SE,P2–3;6–9. SE,Hu2;6. SE,Tu3–4;6;8.

SE,Bt3–5;8. SE,Sc1;3;6. SE,Ac6;10. SE,Th1;4;6–7;
10–14. (SE,So1–2, note. SE,Mid1–3). SE,No1. (SE,No2,
note)

Thorarna (f)   11N4, note

Thorbjorn   C31;33. 1W1–2;36–37. 9W92. 13W19;34. 14E43;48.
29N12. 29W30–32

Thorbrandr   1N48. 1W30. 8N1;8–10;23. (8N24–27). 8N28. 8W1;3.
8E1;3–4;6. 13N12. 23N4

Thorfinnr   C3;29. 1E18. 1L4. 5N33–34;67;71. 5E70;72. 6N7;11;
18;38–40;44;47;49–51;58;67;73;75–76;78;80;91;
135–137;141. 30W7–8;35. SN,Y8

Thorfrothr   14E12;44;48. 29E4. CE44
Thorgautr   7E1–2. 14E21–22, note. 24W9. CE50
Thorgautr Lagr   C36, note
Thorgrimr   1W37
Thorir   19W1, note. 19W3
Thorketill   C8;11;29. 1Y13. 1N8–9;64–65;85;87. 1E3;8;51. 1W58–
59. 2N27. 5N56;63;66. 5E1–2;5;23;25;29;32;34;36;
45;47;49;56. 5W19. 6N34;37;63;85;96;108;113–114;
120;134;140;160–161. 13W1;12;38. 14E13;17;26–27;
29–30. 21E11. 23N31. 23E9;18. 25W24;28. (25W29–
30, note). 29W12;19. 29E1;4. 29W29. CN5. CE9. CW3;
5. SN,Y8

Thorlaug (f)   1N77
Thormothr   5N66
Thorn   5N67. 13N19. (25W29–30, note). CW4
Thorr   1N41;48;134. 1W9–10;55. 6N2;5–6;8;11–13;15;18–21;
23–25;30;57;64;66;68–69;86;98;101;104;109;122;
145–146;155. 14E13;17;40–41;48;52. 23N5. 25W3.
(25W6, note). 25W8. 29W4

Thorr, Frani son of. See Frani son of Thorr
Thorsteinn   1N87. 9W33;124. 11E2. 14E27. CN5. CE43
Thorsteinn, Drogo de Bevrere's man   14E38
Thorsteinn, Erneis de Burun's man   24W12
Thorthr   11E2;4. 23E7. 29E26
Thorulfr   1N20;87. 1E34. 1L8. CN5
Toki   5E17. 9W37. 10W2. 18W1;3. CW16;19
Toki son of Ottarr   C36
Toli   1W64
Tonni   25W2. 29W29
Tosti   1Y3;5
Earl Tosti   1L1–3;6. 5W8. 14E1. 30W37;40
Tumi   C12
Turot   6N81, note
Uglubarthr   1E57;59
Uhtred   C2, note. C10. 1N96. 1E28. 5N9;11–21;25–26;32;38–
42;49–50;52. 5E32;40–41. 6N3–4;56;59–60. 9W18.
29E10;14;22. 29N8;10;12. 30W27;33

Ulfketill   C10. 1N10–11;15;17;21;25;28;35;52;109;133. 1E38–
39;45. 1W32;64. 5N30;35. 5E9. 5W9–10;20;25;29.
6N30;34;45–46;133;138. 9W9;12;40;47–48;50;68;
111. 10W8;12–13;27. 13W25;35. 13E8;14. 14E31.
21W1;6. 21W1;6. 29W1;9;13;16;20;22. 29E15. 29W36;
47. 30W15. CE29. CW12–13. CE35

Ulfketill, another   10W12–13
Ulfketill, wife of   29W36
Ulfketill Sveinnbrothir   CW37
Ulfr   1N40;44;59;100;136. 1E7;11;15;49. 1W52;70. 2B16–
17. 2N2–4;6–15. 5E44. 6N1;3–4. 9W12;66. 11N22–
23. 13W3;35. 14E11;23–25;31–32;36. 21W10. 29N11.
29W26;48. 30W4–5;38. CN2. CE2. CW4. CE35

Ulfr, another   14E31
Ulfr, brother of   CE35
Ulfr the Deacon   (5E1, note). CE13. CW28

Wulfgeat	2E8;14–15. 11E2. 13E4
Wulfgrim	13N19, note
Wulfheah	9W68. 10W11–14;16
Wulfmaer	9W11;90. CW14
Wulfric	1W50. 24W31. 29W20
Wulfsige	5W26;30. 9W29. 29W6
Wulfstan	1E11. 5E32. 9W12;33. 10W27. 11W4. 13W2. CW3
Wulfstan the Priest	(25W3, note. 25W6, note). CW29
Wulfstan, Arnketill son of. See Arnketill son of Wulfstan	
Wulfweard	6N125
Wulfwine	13W23

CHURCHES AND CLERGY

Beverley (St. John's)		C37. 2E1–2, note. 2E15–17;22;33. CE11;33. CW39. SE,Sn10. SE,Ho112
	Canons	(2E1). CE24. (CW39)
	Clergy	2E3
Christ Church		11W2, note. 22W1–3;5. SW,An1;8;13–14;16
Coutances, Bishop		C9;16
Durham (St. Cuthbert's)		C2;37. 3Y11;13;15
	Bishop. See Bishop Alwine; Bishop William; Bishop Walcher
Holy Trinity's		C37
Ripon (St. Wilfrid's)		C37. 2W7, note. SW,Bu45
St. Everilda's		25W14
Selby, Abbot		2B1
York (St. Peter's)		C30–31;33;35;37. 2B12;15–17;19. 2N1–6;14–15;19–30. 2W1–3;13. CN2
	Abbot	4N1. 8N1. (8N2–5, note. SN,D20–21, note. SN,Ma1, note. SN,Ma13–14, note. SN,B2, note).
	Archbishop. See Archbishop Aldred; Archbishop Thomas
	Canons	(C1a, note. C2;21;23–25;30). 2B4–8. (2W5;7)
deacons		Oddi; Ulfr
priests		Arnthorr; Brunn; Earnwine; Ketill; Leofing; Oddi; Sunnulfr; Wulfstan

UNNAMED LANDHOLDERS

brothers, two		5W24. 9W45;103
brothers, five		5E11
burgesses, of:	Bridlington	1Y11
	Dadsley	10W3
	Pocklington	1Y10
	York	C1a;2;22;40
burgesses, lesser, of Tanshelf		9W64
cleric, one		2E40
clerics, two		2A1. 2B1;9
drengs, four		C3
Englishmen, three		9W138
Freemen, three		5W21
Freemen, five		2W4
Freemen, seven		8E1
Frenchmen		C1b
judges, four		C1a
man, of Osbern de Arches		25W9
marshalls, two		CW17
men, of Count Alan		SN,CtA45
men, of the Count of Mortain		SE,Sn1
men, of Drogo de Bevrere		14E6

INDEX OF PLACES

As in most counties, some wapentake rubrics are missing from the main text. Others seem to be wrongly entered or to refer to only the entry immediately below the rubric. In the Summary, however, the vills are entered under their respective wapentake or hundred divisions, not by landholder, and it is therefore possible to correct the rubrics given in the main text or to insert rubrics where these are omitted. The only omission in the Summary is the rubric for Strafforth Wapentake (SW,Sfl), and there the DB scribe had in fact left a space for it.

WAPENTAKES AND HUNDREDS
In northern England, much of the area was administered on the basis of wapentakes, rather than of the earlier hundreds which were still the main administrative subdivision of southern England. Thus in Yorkshire the divisions used in DB in the NR and WR are wapentakes not hundreds. In the WR these are substantially the same as the later wapentakes of the High Middle Ages — Agbrigg (Ag), Ainsty (An), Barkston Ash (BA), Morley (M), Osgoldcross (O), Skyrack (Sk), Staincross (St), and Strafforth (Sf); Halikeld (H), later in the NR, was included in the WR in DB, and Claro is called 'Burghshire' (Bu). Only Craven (Cr), uniquely not referred to in DB as a wapentake but by the formula *in Crave*, was represented subsequently by the medieval wapentakes of East Staincliffe, West Staincliffe and part of Skyrack. The Summary also includes a number of places under *Gereburg* (Ge) which are in the main text allocated to 'Burghshire'. In the NR the units involved are geographically almost identical with the later wapentakes but with a number of name changes. Allerton (A) and Langbargh (L) survived with their names intact, but *Bolesford* (B) had its name changed to Bulmer, *Dic* (D) to Pickering Lythe, *Gerlestre* (Bi) to Birdforth and *Maneshou* (Ma) to Ryedale. The order in which the vills are entered in the Summary suggests that Allerton, *Bolesford*, *Dic* and *Maneshou* each had a two-fold internal subdivision and that Langbargh had a three-fold internal subdivision (see also DGNE 87). The western third of the NR appears not yet to have been divided into wapentakes at the time of DB, which records the area subsequently occupied by the wapentakes of Gilling East, Gilling West, Hang East, Hang West and part of Halikeld simply as 'lands of Count Alan' (CtA). Only in the ER did the earlier hundreds survive. These were much smaller areas of land than the later wapentakes and the post-1086 reorganisation of the ER into wapentakes involved a complex regrouping with hundreds being divided between up to three different wapentakes. The areas constituting each of the hundreds are discussed in detail in the notes on each of the hundreds: Acklam (Ac; see 5E63 note), Burton (Bt; 5E54 note), Cave (C; 11E1 note), Driffield (Dr; 5E39 note), Hessle (He; 15E1 note), Howden (How; SE,How1 note), Hunthow (Hu; 5E45 note), Pocklington (P; 5E44 note), *Scard* (Sc; 5E58 note), *Sneculf(s)cros* (Sn; 13E4 note), 'Thorshowe' (Th; 5E68 note), *Turbar* (Tu; 5E55 note), Warter (Wa; 5E43 note), Weighton (Wei; 13W1 note) and Welton (Wel; 11E1 note). But the reorganisation to wapentakes had already begun in the ER, as Holderness is given as a wapentake, although still retaining its three-fold hundredal division into North Hundred (No), Middle Hundred (Mid) and South Hundred (So). Most places in the wapentake were not, however, allocated specifically to one of the hundreds but simply to Holderness in general (see 2E17 note); it is unclear what determined the allocation but it may relate to the nature of the earlier documents available to the compilers of DB. Finally, the Yorkshire folios of DB also included a section dealing with some lands lying in what became the later counties of Cumberland, Lancashire and Westmorland; these lands all lay within the wapentake of Amounderness (Am), which also included some places in the WR. Subsequently the name Amounderness was applied simply to one of the Lancashire hundreds. Although in its arrangement into manors, DB implies some degree of territorial subdivision of Amounderness (see DB Cheshire), this is nowhere explicitly stated in the text. On the maps in this volume the only divisions shown are those definitely given in DB; thus no subdivisions within the NR wapentakes nor within Amounderness are shown. For the possible line of the NR subdivisions see DGNE fig. 21 and for the Amounderness subdivisions see DB Cheshire maps of Mid Lancashire, and North Lancashire with Westmorland and Cumberland.

IDENTIFICATION OF PLACES

In general the identifications of places in this edition follow those given in DG, with all variations being discussed in the relevant notes. There is, however, one major difference, in that the names given in DG are those of the townships which were the successors of the DB vills, whereas the names used in this edition are those of the settlement centres of the townships concerned. The names given in the DB text are actually the names of vills, later townships, not of settlements. These vills were areas of land, roughly the equivalent in size of modern civil parishes, which were the basic units of organisation of the farming landscape at the peasant level. Within each township were areas of arable land, common grazing, common meadow and common woodland which were generally available for the use only of people living within the township concerned. In many cases, especially in the upland moorland and Pennine areas of the NR and WR, the pattern in the High Middle Ages was one of dispersed settlement, i.e. a large number of small scattered settlements within each vill, rather than one large nucleated settlement per vill, as is more usual in southern England. This pattern is already apparent when the first documents from which settlement patterns can be deduced become available in about the mid-13th century (see WYAS), but it is extremely likely that it was already in existence in 1086 and also in the preceding Anglo-Saxon period. Conversely, as DB and other early documents do not record individual settlements, only vill areas, it is impossible to be certain that the settlements of the same names as those of the vills given in DB were already in existence in 1086; it is probable that the great majority of these settlements were in fact already there, but in view of evidence for settlement mobility at other times in history, this caveat should be borne in mind when looking at any individual example.

In this edition, the settlement rather than the township names have been used in order to relate the names concerned to the grid references given in the index, which are those of the settlement centres. In many cases the township and settlement names are the same, but in cases where there are variations, it is the settlement name which is used, e.g. the township is Ainderby Miers, whereas the settlement-name, used in this edition, is Ainderby Mires. All such examples of variation of the settlement name from the township name given in DG are observed in the notes, although for brevity using the abbreviated formula of, for example, 'DG 523 Griff, but the full modern name is Griff Farm', i.e. the vill name was Griff but the modern settlement is Griff Farm. In some cases where there is no settlement known of the same name as the township, the name used is that of the township, but the grid reference given in the index is that of the main settlement in that township, e.g. the reference of SD 999 284 given in the index for Wadsworth is that of Old Town, the main settlement. All such cases are discussed in the relevant note. In other cases the present settlement of the name is not located in exactly the same location as its medieval predecessor. Where this can be ascertained, the grid reference given in the index is that of the medieval, not the modern centre.

The locations in the index are given as six-figure grid references, derived, except where stated otherwise, by reference to the modern 2½-inch OS map (1:25,000). In some cases places are small enough to enable eight-figure grid references to be given in the notes, but these have been changed to six figures in the index for consistency. It has sometimes been necessary, as stated in the notes, to refer to the 6-inch OS map (1:10,000) for very small places, or to the 1st ed. 6-inch OS maps (cited by county sheet number) or the tithe award apportionments and maps (cited by Public Record Office reference number) for places which are no longer recorded on modern maps. The point chosen to cite for the grid reference of larger settlements is in each case the church. Where no church exists, the grid reference used is that of the hall, or failing that, the crossroads. A grid reference for the approximate geographical centre point is given for names surviving only as area names not settlements.

The name of each place is followed by (i) its pre-1974 riding (for places in Yorkshire); (ii) the abbreviated name of its wapentake (for places in the NR and WR, Cumberland, Lancashire and Westmorland) or hundred (for places in the ER) and its location on the map in this volume; (iii) its National Grid reference; (iv) chapter and section references in DB. References to notes dealing with specific places are given in the form '23N4, note', where the place occurs in that entry in DB and there is also a note on it; the form '23N4 note' indicates that the place is discussed in the note to 23N4. Unidentifiable places are given in DB spelling in italic print, e.g. *Chetelestorp*; names which survived late enough for it to be possible to ascertain the likely eventual form of the name are given in that form in inverted commas, e.g. 'Kettlethorpe'. In the text place-names are given with the part of the name derived from the DB form given in upper case, with later additions to the name given in brackets in lower case, e.g. (Low) DALBY. Places whose names have changed since 1086 are given with the original name in italics followed by the new name (both in upper case in the text), e.g. *Hindrelaghe* (Richmond). The National Grid reference system is explained on all Ordnance Survey maps, and in the Automobile Association Handbooks; the figures reading from left to right are given before those reading from bottom to top of the map. Where DB does not differentiate between what are now two distinct places, e.g. North and South Newbald, both sets of grid references are given, bracketed in the index, and both places are plotted on the maps with a linking line between them. Places of the same name have not been differentiated in the text or notes, but may be easily distinguished from each other by reference to the entries in the index. In the index places of the same name located in the same county or riding are distinguished by either the township in which they were later located, if subsequently subsumed into another vill, e.g. Newsham (in Amotherby), or, if surviving as an independent township name, by reference to a well-known adjacent township, e.g. Newton (near Guisborough). Where there are today two or more places of the same name in the same riding or county, only one of which is recorded in DB, the DB example is not specifically distinguished in the index, as which place is involved is apparent from the maps at the end of this volume and the grid references given below. In the text places in counties outside Yorkshire are identified by the use of the following abbreviations in square brackets following the names concerned: [C] Cumberland; [L] Lancashire; [W] Westmorland. In the index, but not in the text, the pre-1974 (not the DB) ridings are given in brackets after each name using the following abbreviations: ER, East Riding; NR, North Riding; WR, West Riding. The places in each hundred or wapentake are listed after the index, adjacent to the maps on which they are plotted. Some places are given in both the main text and in the Summary under two different wapentakes or hundreds, presumably because, as also at a later period, the wapentake or hundred boundary ran through the vill instead of following the vill boundary. Such places have been given in the map keys under both wapentakes or hundreds.

	Map	Grid	Text
YORKSHIRE			
Acaster Malbis (WR)	An22	SE 588 451	11W3. SW,An3
Acaster Selby (WR)	An38	SE 574 409	6W3. 11W4. 24W3. 29W28-29. CW40. SW,An3-4
Achebi (NR)			6N120, note. SN,CtA35
Acklam (ER)	Ac10	SE 782 616	5E63. 29E29. SE,Ac4
Acklam (NR)	L18	NZ 486 170	1N28, note. 4N3. 11N9. 31N5. SN,L32-33
Ackton (WR)	Ag5	SE 412 219	9W95. SW,Ag2
Ackworth (WR)	O20	SE 441 180	9W52, note. SW,O10
Acomb (WR)	An8	SE 572 514	2W3. 29W13. SW,An15
Addingham (WR)	Bu85; Cr99	SE 085 497	1W46, note. 1W73. 21W5. SW,Bu32. SW,Cr3
Addlethorpe (WR)	Bu117	SE 348 486	1W49. 28W21. SW,Bu37
Adel (WR)	Sk38	SE 276 403	5W2, note. SW,Sk18
Adlingfleet (WR)	St13	SE 844 210	17W1. SW,St2
Adwick le Street (WR)	O40; Sf5	SE 540 085	5W30-31. 10W39. CW22. SW,Sf9 note. SW,Sf34. SW,O2
Adwick upon Dearne (WR)	Sf61	SE 470 015	10W14. SW,Sf9, note
Agglethorpe (NR)	CtA105	SE 087 864	6N96. SN,CtA29
Aike (ER)	Sn13	TA 049 458	2B14. 5E33. SE,Sn4
Ainderby Mires (NR)	CtA120	SE 256 927	6N52-53, note. SN,CtA19-20
Ainderby Quernhow (NR)	CtA183	SE 349 809	6N157. SN,CtA43
Ainderby Steeple (NR)	CtA128	SE 334 920	1Y2. 6N34. SN,A1. SN,CtA14
Little Airmyn (WR)	BA34	SE 723 252	16W1. SW,BA9

	Map	Grid	Text
Airton (WR)	Cr34	SD 901 592	30W28
Airy Holme (NR)	L59	NZ 578 115	1N16. SN,L27
Aiskew (NR)	CtA134	SE 270 884	6N123. SN,CtA36
Aislaby (near Pickering) (NR)	D19	SE 774 857	1N53. SN, D18
Aislaby (near Whitby) (NR)	L75	NZ 857 085	5N9. SN,L10
Aismunderby (WR)	Bu23	SE 305 686	2W13 note. 13W21, note. SW,Bu19
Aldborough (WR)	Bu36	SE 406 664	1Y18. 1W30. 21W3. 24W10. 25W27. 28W36. SW,Bu13
Aldbrough (ER)	Mid28	TA 244 387	14E11. SE,Hol14
Aldbrough (NR)	CtA32	NZ 201 113	6N13-14. SN,CtA10
Aldfield (WR)	Bu18	SE 263 693	1W40. 2W8. 28W38. SW, Bu20
Aldwark (NR)	B9	SE 467 633	5N70. SN,B26
Allerston (NR)	D31	SE 878 829	1Y4. 1N46. SN,D12;14
Allerthorpe (ER)	P24	SE 785 444	1Y10. SE,P3
Allerthorpe Hall (NR)	CtA151	SE 320 868	6N153, note. SN,CtA43
Allerton (WR)	M8	SE 113 339	9W131, note. 9W144. SW, M7
Allerton Bywater (WR)	Sk69	SE 418 275	9W1. SW,Sk4, note
Allerton Mauleverer (WR)	Bu74	SE 415 579	1W37, note. 28W3. 29W16; 31W1. SW, Bu10-11
Chapel Allerton (WR)	Sk56	SE 307 370	9W14. SW,Sk4 note. SW,Sk9
(North)allerton. See Northallerton			
Almondbury (WR)	Ag30	SE 168 150	9W105. SW,Ag7
Alne (NR)	B10	SE 495 653	2N24. SN,B23
Alwoodley (WR)	Sk39	SE 311 411	1W16, note. SW,Sk15
Amotherby (NR)	Ma59	SE 750 734	1N62. 5N36 note. 23N24. 31N8. SN,Ma3-4
Ampleforth (NR)	Ma27	SE 583 786	2N10;14. 23N1. SN,Ma22
Andrebi (ER)	So4	*c.* TA 29 33	14E4, note. CE46. SE,Hol7
Anlaby (ER)	He14	TA 036 288	1E1. 5E2. 15E2. 21E3. 29E1. SE,He2-3
Anley (WR)	Cr16	SD 815 618	1W73. 30W6. SW,Cr4
North Anston (WR)	Sf16	SK 528 844	10W1. 12W1;20. SW,Sf2
South Anston (WR)	Sf117	SK 517 838	10W1. SW,Sf2, note
Appleton le Moors (NR)	Ma5	SE 734 880	SN,D21, note. SN,Ma14
Appleton le Street (NR)	Ma58	SE 734 735	1N69. SN,Ma7
Appleton Roebuck (WR)	An37	SE 554 422	25W2. CW36. SW,An4
Appleton Wiske (NR)	A9	NZ 389 047	1N119. 31N1. SN,A4
East Appleton (NR)	CtA78	SE 235 957	6N63, note. SN,CtA22
Appletreewick (WR)	Cr27	SE 054 601	29W41;45
Arden Hall (NR)	Bi1	SE 522 905	23N8
East Ardsley (WR)	M55	SE 304 251	9W120, note. SW,M1
West Ardsley (WR)	M52	SE 287 254	9W120 note. SW,M13, note
Argam (ER)	Tu9	TA 112 710	1E26, note. SE,Tu5
Arkendale (WR)	Bu42	SE 388 609	1W38. 24W11. SW,Bu12
Arksey (WR)	O41	SE 579 069	10W37. SW,Sf34 note. SW,O1
Armley (WR)	M16	SE 274 335	9W121. SW,M3
Armthorpe (WR)	Sf40	SE 621 048	29W9. SW,Sf22
Arncliffe (WR)	Cr8	SD 933 719	30W35
Arncliffe Hall (NR)	A20	NZ 452 002	1N128, note. 31N5, note. SN,A7
Arnestorp (ER)	No3	*c.* TA 18 42	14E5, note. SE,Hol10
Arnford (WR)	Cr40	SD 837 562	30W10
Arnodestorp (NR)			13N3, note. SN,L11
Arram (ER)	No15	TA 165 493	14E30, note. SE,Hol22
Arthington (WR)	Sk5	SE 274 447	5W1. SW,Sk19
Asc(h)am (NR)			6N111, note, SN,CtA32

	Map	Grid	Text
Aschelesmersc, Aschilesmares (NR)			1Y4, note. SN,D12, note
Asebi (NR)			6N160, note. SN,CtA44
Asenby (NR)	Bi40	SE 398 753	13N17
Aske Hall (NR)	CtA53	NZ 177 034	6N57, note. SN,CtA20, note
Askham Bryan (WR)	An19	SE 552 484	6W1. CW42. SW,An11 note. SW,An18
Askham Richard (WR)	An18	SE 537 480	25W15. CW28. SW,An11, note
Askrigg (NR)	CtA94	SD 947 910	6N79. SN,CtA25
Askwith (WR)	Bu87	SE 169 484	8W2. 13W25. 28W28. SW,Bu32–33
Asselby (ER)	How16	SE 718 280	3Y4. 5E25. SE,How4;7
Aston (WR)	Sf111	SK 468 852	5W22. 12W1;11. SW,Sk2 note. SW,Sf33
Attercliffe (WR)	Sf93	SK 378 888	10W42. SW,Sf35
Auburn (ER)	Hu19	TA 170 628	1E13, note. SE,Hu5
Auckley (WR)	Sf43	(SE 650 011	5W8. SW,Sf21, note
Auckley, another (WR)	Sf43	(	SW,Sf21
Aughton (ER)	C6	SE 701 386	5E7;24. CE18. SE,C8
Aughton Hall (WR)	Sf110	SK 455 867	5W21, note. 5W24. 12W1; 16. SW,Sf32
Austerfield (WR)	Sf45	SK 661 946	5W8. SW,Sf21
Austhorpe (WR)	Sk62	SE 370 338	9W1. SW,Sk4
Austonley (WR)	Ag48	SE 114 073	1Y15. SW,Ag12
Austwick (WR)	Am76	SD 767 684	1L4
Aysgarth (NR)	CtA99	SE 004 884	6N82. SN,CtA26
East Ayton (NR)	D42	SE 991 849	8N11. 13N12. SN,L27 note. SN,D7
Great Ayton (NR)	L58	NZ 563 107	11N5. SN,L29
Little Ayton (NR)	L60	NZ 570 101	1N17–18;22. 5N27. 11N4. SN,L27–29, note. SN,L29
West Ayton (NR)	D41	SE 987 847	1Y3. SN,D7
Azerley (WR)	Bu9	SE 259 742	28W14. 29W23. 31W3. SW,Bu23–24
Babthorpe (ER)	How12	SE 690 299	3Y4. SE,How5
Badsworth (WR)	O28	SE 463 149	9W45. SW,O7
Bagby (NR)	Bi20	SE 463 806	23N7–8
Baildon (WR)	Sk34	SE 156 397	2W4. 24W1, note. SW,Sk1; 18
Bainton (ER)	Dr14	SE 965 523	5E42. 23E9. SE,D5
Balby (WR)	Sf48	SE 561 012	5W8. 10W23. SW,Sf15–16; 21
Baldebi (NR)			4N1, note. SN,L4
Baldersby (NR)	CtA180	SE 355 786	6N159. SN,CtA44
Barden (NR)	CtA85	SE 146 936	6N105. SN,CtA31
Bardsey (WR)	Sk13	SE 363 430	1W4. SW,Sk12
Barforth (Hall) (NR)	CtA17	NZ 163 167	6N1, note. SN,CtA3;5
Barkston (WR)	BA17	SE 491 361	9W22. SW,BA5
Barlby (ER)	How6	SE 632 340	3Y4. 16E3. SE,How6;10
Barlow (WR)	BA30	SE 642 287	16W1. SW,BA9
Barmby (Moor) (ER)	P10	SE 776 489	1Y10, note. 2B13. SE,P9
Barmby on the Marsh (ER)	How15	SE 690 284	3Y4. SE,How5
Barmston (ER)	No2	TA 156 588	14E26. SE,Hol21
Barnaby (NR)	L28	NZ 570 160	5N26, note. SN,L26
Barnbrough (WR)	Sf54	SE 484 032	10W15. 12W1;5. CW9–10. SW,Sf9
Barnby Dun (WR)	Sf31	SE 614 097	5W10, note. 10W30. 13W8. SW,Sf23
Barnby Hall (WR)	St20	SE 292 081	9W64, note. SW,St1
Barnby House (NR)	B50	SE 725 609	23N32, note

	Map	Grid	Text
[East and West] Barnby (NR)	L66 L65	(NZ 827 127 (NZ 819 125	SN,L7, note
Barnhill Hall (ER)	How17	SE 734 288	3Y4, note. SE,How3
Barningham (NR)	CtA13	NZ 085 104	6N1;6. SN,CtA7;9
Barnoldswick (in Burton in Lonsdale) (WR)	Am73	SD 665 718	1L3
Barnoldswick (near Gisburn) (WR)	Cr83	SD 877 467	30W3
Barnsley (WR)	St31	SE 343 066	9W80. SW,St15
Barrowby Grange (WR)	Bu116	SE 334 478	13W29, note. 24W20. SW,Bu35
Barthorpe Grange (ER)	Ac22	SE 770 595	5E64, note. 26E2. SE,Ac8
Barton (NR)	CtA47	NZ 230 089	6N1. SN,CtA4
Barton le Street (NR)	D56; Ma57	Se 721 742	1Y4. 5N45. SN,D11;19. SN,Ma14
Barton le Willows (NR)	B43	SE 714 633	5N63. SN,B10
Barugh (WR)	St19	SE 314 086	9W72. SW,St5
Great Barugh (NR)	Ma39	SE 747 790	1N70. 2N4. 23N21. SN,Ma8
Little Barugh (NR)	Ma40	SE 761 797	1N71. 2N4. 23N21. SN,Ma8-9
Barwick. See *Englebi*			
Barwick in Elmet (WR)	Sk47	Se 399 373	9W1. SW,Sk4
Basche(s)bi (NR)			1N57, note. SN,D20
Bashall Eaves (WR)	Cr64	SD 711 420	30W37, note
Batley (WR)	M48	SE 242 243	9W139. SW,M9
Battersby (NR)	L100	NZ 595 075	1N24. SN,L30
Battersby Barn (WR)	Cr58	SD 705 520	30W37, note
Baxby (NR)	Bi35	SE 512 752	2N13, note. 2N14. 23N1. SN,Bi2
Beadlam (NR)	Ma9	SE 651 847	5N41;52. SN,Ma19
Beal (WR)	O6	SE 534 253	9W59. SW,O13
Beamsley (WR)	Bu84; Cr98	SE 082 524	1W45;73. 21W4. 24W14. SW,Bu31. SW,Cr3
Beckwith House (WR)	Bu91	SE 280 524	21W9, note. SW,Bu38
Bedale (NR)	CtA135	SE 265 884	6N122. SN,CtA35
Beeford (ER)	No7	TA 128 543	14E24. SE,Hol20
Beeston (WR)	M18	SE 287 308	9W124-125. SW,M1
Belby House (ER)	How23	SE 771 290	1E2, note. 3Y4-5. CE12; 17. SE,How4;7
Bellerby (NR)	CtA86	SE 115 927	6N104. SN,CtA31
Belthorpe (ER)	P4	SE 780 541	2N16, note. SE,P9
Bempton (ER)	Hu8	TA 191 720	5E52. SE,Hu6
Beningbrough (NR)	B73	SE 529 577	23N28
Benningholme Hall (ER)	Mid8	TA 128 390	14E11, note. SE,Hol16
High Bentham (WR)	Am74	SD 667 692	1L5, note
Bentley (ER)	Wel3	TA 019 359	2E17. 5N1a. SE,Wel5
Bentley (WR)	O42; Sf27	SE 572 050	5W30. 10W38. SW,Sf34, note. SW,O1
Berg(h)ebi (NR)			13N16, note. SN,Bi5, note
Bergolbi, Berguluesbi (NR)			1N31, note. 31N5. SN,L38
Bernebi (NR)			11N18, note, SN,Bi3
Bessingby (ER)	Hu16	TA 158 659	1Y11. SE,Hu4
Bestha(i)m (WR)			1Y19, note. SW,Bu28
Beswick (ER)	Sn8	TA 012 481	1Y9. 5E31. SE,Sn3
Beverley (ER)	Sn21	TA 037 392	2E1;3;17. CE33. SE,Sn10
Bewerley (WR)	Bu27	SE 157 647	24W15. SW,Bu28
Bewholme (ER)	No13	TA 165 500	14E29. SE,Hol22
Bewick Hall (ER)	Mid15	TA 233 395	14E11, note. SE,Hol17
Bicher(t)un (WR)			2W4, note. SW,Sk2
Bickerton (WR)	An14	SE 451 505	28W37. SW,An17
Bielby (ER)	P25	SE 788 437	1Y10. 1E11a. SE,P1
North Bierley (WR)	M21	SE 179 295	9W134, note. SW,M8

	Map	Grid	Text
Bilbrough (WR)	An26	SE 530 464	22W2. SW,An8
Bilham House (WR)	Sf18	SE 484 064	5W14, note. 10W15. 12W1; 7. SW,Sf9
Billingley (WR)	Sf15	SE 436 047	10W25. 29W8. SW,Sf17;19
Bilton (ER)	Mid38	TA 156 327	2E27. 14E47. SE,Mid1. SE,Hol25
Bilton (near Harrogate) (WR)	Bu78	SE 315 576	21W11. 29W38. SW,Bu39
Bilton (near Wetherby) (WR)	An16	SE 476 500	25W10. SW,An10
Bingley (WR)	Sk31	SE 105 395	24W1, note. SW,Sk18
Binnington (ER)	Bt2	SE 996 787	5E57. SE, Bt9
(Ing)birchworth. See Ingbirchworth			
(Rough)birchworth. See Roughbirchworth			
Birdsall (ER)	Sc17	SE 815 649	2B18, note. 5E58. 29E15. 31E6. SE,Sc1
Birkby (NR)	A12	NZ 330 025	1Y2, note. SN,A1
Birkby Hill (WR)	Sk41	SE 358 395	9W13, note. SW,Sk8
Birkin (WR)	BA25	SE 530 265	9W26. CW4. SW,BA7
Birstwith (WR)	Bu52	SE 238 594	1W43. 28W23. SW,Bu30
Bishopthorpe (WR)	An21	SE 591 476	1W29, note. 23E19. 29W12;27. SW,An1
Bithen (WR)			SW,An17, note
High Blandsby (NR)	D21	SE 827 875	1Y4, note. SN,D11
Blaten Carr (NR)			5N29, note. SN,L44
Bogeuurde (WR)			30W37, note
Boltby (NR)	Bi5	SE 490 866	23N13–14
Bolton (ER)	P9	SE 771 522	2B11. 29E5. SE,P7
Bolton (WR)	M41	SE 168 350	9W131, note. SW,M6, note
Bolton Abbey (WR)	Cr97	SE 072 538	1W73. SW,Cr1;5
Bolton by Bowland (WR)	Cr70	SD 786 494	13W40
Bolton Percy (WR)	An36	SE 531 412	13W7 note. 13W12. CW33; 35;40. SW,An4
Bolton upon Dearne (WR)	Sf55	SE 455 025	10W26. 13W7, note. SW,Sf19
Bolton upon Swale (NR)	CtA69	SE 252 991	6N24, note. SN,CtA12
Castle Bolton (NR)	CtA89	SE 032 918	6N87, note. SN,CtA27
West Bolton (NR)	CtA90	SE 020 909	6N88. SN,CtA27
'Bordelby' (Mount Grace) (NR)	A25	SE 449 985	1N129, note. 31N5. SN,A7
Bordley (WR)	Cr17	SD 941 649	30W34
Borrowby (near Loftus) (NR)	L33	NZ 770 155	5N8. SN,L9
Borrowby (near Northallerton) (NR)	A47	SE 427 892	1Y2. SN,Bi5 note. SN,A1
Bossall (NR)	B51	SE 718 607	23N32, note. SN,B27
Old Boulby (NR)	L15	NZ 760 183	1N4. 4N2. SN,L12
Bowling (WR)	M13	SE 174 322	9W132. SW,M6
Bowthorpe (ER)	How9	SE 697 330	SE,How5, note
Boynton (ER)	Hu14	TA 136 679	1Y11. 1E15. 5E49. SE,Hu5
Boynton Hall (ER)	Hu15	TA 138 678	1Y11
Boythorpe (ER)	Bt6	SE 997 719	1Y14. SE,Bt8
Bracewell (WR)	Cr78	SD 863 484	30W15
Bracken (ER)	Sn5	SE 981 505	SE,Sn2, note
Brackenholme (ER)	How13	SE 700 300	SE,How5, note. SE,How7;9
Bradford (WR)	M12	SE 167 333	9W130, note. SW,M6, note
West Bradford (WR)	Cr66	SD 743 445	30W37
Bradley (WR)	Ag11	SE 172 205	9W110, note. SW,Ag15
[High and Low] Bradley (WR)	Cr92 Cr103	(SE 003 494 (SE 005 483	1W59, note
Brafferton (NR)	B3	SE 436 701	1N105–106, note. 5N74. 28W34. SN,B26
'Great' Braham (WR)	Bu95	SE 357 526	13W32, note. 21W14;17. SW,Bu41
'Little' Braham (WR)	Bu96	SE 357 526	13W32 note. 24W16–17. SW,Bu40
Braithwell (WR)	Sf78	SK 529 947	12W1;4. 13W9. SW,Sf25

	Map	Grid	Text
Bramham (WR)	BA5	SE 428 429	5W7. CW2. SW,BA3
Bramhope (WR)	Sk19	SE 249 433	21W1. SW,Sk16
Bramley (near Leeds) (WR)	M7	SE 247 350	9W123, note. SW,M3
Bramley (near Rotherham) (WR)	Sf98	SK 490 923	12W1;15
Bramley Grange (WR)	Bu3	SE 203 769	28W15, note. SW,Bu24
Brampton Bierlow (WR)	Sf58	SE 414 017	29W7. SW,Sf16, note. SW,Sf17
Brampton en le Morthen (WR)	Sf105	SK 485 881	5W25. SW,Sf16 note. SW,Sf33
Brampton Hall (WR)	H24	SE 367 665	1W55, note. 5W38. SW,H7–8
Kirk Bramwith (WR)	Sf33	SE 620 117	10W29. 12W1;22. CW12. SW,Sf22
South Bramwith (WR)	Sf32	SE 621 114	10W29, note
Brandesburton (ER)	No16	TA 119 476	2E40. 14E31. CE35. SE,No2. SE,Hol7 note. SE,Hol22
Brandsby (NR)	B2	SE 598 719	23N27
Brantingham (ER)	Wel9	SE 941 296	3Y1. 5E9, note. 31E4. CE13. SE,Well. SE,Wel2 note. SE,Wel6
Branton (WR)	Sf41	SE 622 027	18W1. SW,Sf16 note. SW,Sf21
Branton Green (WR)	Bu39	SE 440 622	1W32. 24W5. 29W31. 31W3. SW,Bu4
Brawby (NR)	Ma38	SE 738 781	2N3. SN,Ma8
Brayton (WR)	BA29	SE 600 305	9W20. SW,BA5
Brearton (WR)	Bu56	SE 323 610	1Y19. SW,Bu18
'Breck' (NR)			4N1, note. SN,L4
Breckenbrough (NR)	Bi9	SE 384 833	5N71, note. SN,Bi6
Breighton (ER)	He2	SE 709 337	15E4-6. 21E7. SE,He8
Monk Bretton (WR)	St32	SE 363 076	9W90. SW,St13, note
West Bretton (WR)	Ag39	SE 287 137	1Y15, note. SW,St13 note. SW,Ag10
Bridlington (ER)	Hu12	TA 177 679	1Y11. 1E12. 5E47. SE,Hu2–5
Brierley (WR)	St12	SE 410 110	9W67. SW,St3
Brigham (ER)	Tu18	TA 078 537	5E53. SE,Tu5–6
Brignall (NR)	CtA12	NZ 072 123	6N1, note. SN,CtA6
Brimham Hall (WR)	Bu30	SE 221 629	21W7, note. 24W13. 28W20. SW,Bu26
Brinsworth (WR)	Sf95	SK 415 899	10W7. 13W6. SW,Sf5–6
Brodsworth (WR)	Sf7	SE 506 072	5W15. 10W34;43. SW,Sf29
Brompton (near Northallerton) (NR)	A29	SE 373 963	1Y2. 3Y15. SN,A1;6
Brompton (near Scarborough) (NR)	D35	SE 943 821	1Y4. 1N44. 8N6. 31N8, note. SN,D10
Brompton on Swale (NR)	CtA66	SE 217 996	6N21. SN,CtA12, note
Patrick Brompton (NR)	CtA137	SE 219 906	6N137. SN,CtA12 note. SN,CtA38
Potter Brompton (ER)	Bt4	SE 979 768	1Y14. SE,Bt8
Brotton (NR)	L7	NZ 691 197	5N17. SN,L17
Brough Hall (NR)	CtA67	SE 216 978	6N64, note. SN,CtA22, note
Brough Hill (NR)	CtA96	SD 937 901	6N77, note. SN,CtA22 note. SN,CtA25
(Sprot)brough. See Sprotbrough			
Broughton (NR)	Ma61	SE 767 732	1N67. 8N17. 23N24. SN,L41 note. SN,Ma6
Broughton (WR)	Cr87	SD 941 513	8W3. 30W17
Broughton House (NR)	CtA21	NZ 105 097	6N45, note. SN,CtA17
Great Broughton (NR)	L97	NZ 547 063	1N36, note. 5N30. 23N18. SN.L41–42. note

	Map	Grid	Text
Little Broughton (NR)	L98	NZ 560 068	29N9, note. SN,L41, note
Bubwith (ER)	He3	SE 712 363	21E7. SE,He9–10
Buckton (ER)	Hu7	TA 181 726	1Y11. 5E51. SE,Hu7–8, note
Buckton Holms (ER)	Sc13	SE 843 695	8E1, note. 23E16. SE,Hu8 note. SE,Sc5
Bugthorpe (ER)	Ac20	SE 772 578	2B19. 26E1. SE,Ac6
Bulmer (NR)	B53	SE 699 676	5N53;61. SN,B3
Burdale (ER)	Sc18	SE 873 624	1E42, note. 23E14. SE,Sc7
Burden Head (WR)	Sk17	SE 293 437	5W4, note. SW,Sk20
Burghwallis (WR)	O38	SE 537 120	9W37. SW,O4
Burland House (ER)	How21	SE 775 303	CE16, note. SE,How2
Burley in Wharfedale (WR)	Sk2	SE 167 464	2W4, note. SW,Sk1
(Kirk)burn. See Kirkburn			
(South)burn. See Southburn			
Burnby (ER)	P22	SE 835 463	1Y10. 2A3. 11E9. 13E10–11. SE,P2
Burneston (NR)	CtA153	SE 308 849	6N151. SN,CtA41
(Nun)burnholme. See Nunburnholme			
Burniston (NR)	D4	TA 012 929	1Y3. SN,D2
Burnsall (WR)	Cr26	SE 032 615	25W33. 29W42
Burrill (NR)	CtA147	SE 238 872	6N124. SN,CtA36
Burstwick (ER)	So9	TA 227 276	14E1. SE,Ho11
Burton Agnes (ER)	Bt17	TA 102 632	1Y14. 31E1. SE,Tu4 note. SE,Bt1
Burton Constable (ER)	Mid19	TA 188 367	2E28, note. SE,Mid1
'Burton Dale' (NR)			1Y3, note. SN,D5
Burton Fleming (ER)	Tu8	TA 083 723	1E23–24, note. 1E26, note. SE,Tu4, note
Burton Hall (WR)	BA28	SE 584 292	9W20, note. SW,BA5, note
Burton in Lonsdale (WR)	Am67	SD 651 721	1L3
Burton Leonard (WR)	Bu47	SE 326 638	1Y18. SW,Bu15
Burton Pidsea (ER)	Mid46	TA 252 311	14E4. SE,Ho17, note
Bishop Burton (ER)	Wei12	SE 990 397	2E1
Cherry Burton (ER)	Sn18	SE 992 419	2E8. 5E37. CE11
Constable Burton (NR)	CtA115	SE 165 909	6N109. SN,CtA32
High Burton (NR)	CtA168	SE 226 827	6N120, note. SN,CtA27 note. SN,CtA35
Hornsea Burton (ER)	No22	TA 207 468	14E7. SE,Ho17 note. SE,Ho112
(Kirk)burton. See Kirkburton			
West Burton (NR)	CtA101	SE 016 865	6N85. SN,CtA27, note
Burythorpe (ER)	Ac6	SE 790 646	1E49. 8E6. 31E8. SE,Ac2
Great Busby (NR)	L94	NZ 520 056	1N37. 11N13. 29N9. SN,L43
Little Busby (NR)	L93	NZ 515 042	29N9, note. 31N5. SN,L43
Buttercrambe (NR)	B62	SE 731 580	23N29;32–33
Butterwick (ER)	Bt5	SE 991 714	23N24. SE,Bt7, note
Old Byland (NR)	Bi22	SE 550 859	11N17. SN,Bi3
Cadeby (WR)	Sf51	SE 514 005	10W22. 27W2. SW,Sf14–15
Cadretone (WR)			28W2, note
Caldbergh (NR)	CtA109	SE 092 850	6N97. SN,CtA30
Caldenesche (NR)			1N97, note
Caldeuuelle (NR)			5W38, note. SW,Bu42 note. SW,H9
Caldeuuelle, Cradeuuelle (WR)			13W34, note. SW,Bu42, note
Caldwell (NR)	CtA27	NZ 162 134	6N12. SN,CtA10
Calton (WR)	Cr33	SD 909 592	30W30
Calverley (WR)	M5	SE 218 371	9W126, note. SW,M4
Camblesforth (WR)	BA31	SE 647 262	16W1. 29W2. 31W5. SW,BA7;9

	Map	Grid	Text
Camerton Hall (ER)	So15	TA 217 260	14E1, note. SE,Hol2
Camisedale (NR)			1N35, note. 23N18;35. SN,L40–41
Campsall (WR)	O34	SE 544 140	9W36;38. SW,O3
Cantley (WR)	Sf42	SE 627 021	18W1–2. CW15. SW,Sf21
Caretorp (WR)			30W10, note
Carlesmoor (WR)	Bu5	SE 193 735	28W16. SW,Bu24
Carleton (WR)	Cr90	SD 973 498	30W14
Carlton (near Middleham) (NR)	CtA107	SE 064 847	6N93, note. SN,CtA29
Carlton (in Stanwick) (NR)	CtA30	NZ 194 122	6N1, note. 6N14. SN,CtA4; 10
Carlton (near Stokesley) (NR)	L92	NZ 506 045	5N28. SN,L43
Carlton (near Barnsley) (WR)	St10	SE 366 101	9E76, note. SW,St7
Carlton (in Lofthouse) (WR)	M57	SE 338 273	9W119, note. SW,M2
Carlton (near Snaith) (WR)	BA32	SE 647 240	29W1. 31W5. SW,Sk16 note. SW,BA7
Carlton Farm (NR)	B62	SE 670 565	2N19, note. SN,B14
Carlton Husthwaite (NR)	Bi32	SE 499 767	2N14. SN,Bi2, note
Carlton Miniott (NR)	Bi11	SE 394 810	1N109. 23N8. SN,Bi2 note. SN,Bi6
East Carlton (WR)	Sk20	SE 221 432	11W1, note. SW,Sk16, note
West Carlton (ER)	Mid17	TA 219 389	14E50. SE,Hol26
Carnaby (ER)	Bt14	TA 144 655	29E28. SE,Bt5
Carperby (NR)	CtA91	SE 005 897	6N86. SN,CtA27
Carthorpe (NR)	CtA15	SE 307 837	6N150. SN,CtA41
Cartworth (WR)	Ag46	SE 142 071	1Y15, note. SW,Ag14
Castley (WR)	Bu113	SE 268 458	1W53. SW,Bu49
Catfoss Hall (ER)	No19	TA 148 463	14E33, note. CE38. SE,Hol22
Cattal (WR)	Bu100	SE 451 541	25W27. SW,Bu6
'Little Cattal' (Old Thornville Hall) (WR)	Bu101	SE 456 547	24W6, note. SW,Bu7
Catterick (NR)	CtA80	SE 240 979	6N52. SN,CtA19
Catterton (WR)	An27	SE 510 459	25W6. CW24. SW,An8
Catton (NR)	Bi18	SE 370 780	13N19. SN,Bi5
[High and Low] Catton (ER)	P6 P7	(SE 717 534 (SE 704 539	4E2, note. SE,P4
Catwick (ER)	No18	TA 130 453	2E39. 14E34. CE40. SE,No1. SE,Hol23
North Cave (ER)	C16	SE 896 327	2B5. 5E1. 11E2. 23E3. 31E4, note. CE13. SE,C1–2
South Cave (ER)	C20	SE 921 310	11E1. SE,C1
Cavil (ER)	How20	SE 770 305	3Y4, note. SE,How2
Cawthorn (NR)	D7	SE 776 890	1N55. 31N8. SN,D19
Cawthorne (WR)	St21	SE 285 079	9W70. SW,St4
Cawton (NR)	Ma34	SE 640 767	5N43. 23N4. SN,Ma23
Low Caythorpe (ER)	Bt13	TA 116 678	1E32, note. 2B15. SE,Bt5
Cayton (NR)	D51	TA 056 833	1N42. 31N9. SN,D5
Cayton (WR)	Bu49	SE 299 630	1Y19. SW,Bu19
Chelchis, Cheldis (WR)			13W45, note. 21W16
Chellow Grange (WR)	M3	SE 122 351	9W131, note. 9W144. SW,M7
Chenecol, Chenucol, Chenuthesholm (ER)			14E35, note. CE37, note. SE,Hol23
Chetelestorp (ER)			15E7, note
Chetelstorp (ER)			6E1, note. SE,P6
Chevet (WR)	St1	SE 345 155	9E83, note. SW,St15
Chigogemers, Chigomersc, Ghigogesmersc (NR)			1Y4, note. 5N34. SN,D15
Chiluesmares, Chiluesmersc (NR)			1Y4, note. SN,D12, note
Chrachetorp, Crachetorp (ER)			21E4, note. SE,He1
Clactone (WR)			9W70, note

	Map	Grid	Text
Clapham (WR)	Am75	SD 745 694	1L4
Clareton (WR)	Bu61	SE 395 593	1Y18, note. 28W8. SW,Bu11-12
Claxton (NR)	B54	SE 693 601	1N94. 5N61. SN,B11
Clayton (near Bradford) (WR)	M10	SE 119 321	9W131;144. SW,M7
Clayton (near Thurnscoe) (WR)	Sf11	SE 454 078	5W18, note. SW,Sf30
Clayton West (WR)	St15	SE 260 109	9W89. SW,St12
Cleasby (NR)	CtA34	NZ 251 130	6N15. SN,CtA11
Cleaving Grange (ER)	Wei1	TA 851 460	1E3-4, note. SE,Wei6
Cleckheaton (WR)	M42	SE 190 253	9W136. SW,M8
Cleeton (ER)	No9	TA 182 550	14E8, note. 14E54. SE,Hol13
Cliffe (ER)	How10	SE 662 317	5E14. CE1 note. CE21. SE,C5 note. SE,How7
Cliffe Hall (NR)	CtA29	NZ 207 152	6N1, note. SN,CtA4
North Cliffe (ER)	Wei14	SE 874 372	1Y6. 29E25. SE,C5 note. SE,Wei1;3
South Cliffe (ER)	C12	SE 875 362	3Y1. 31E5. CE1, note. SE,C5, note
Clifford (WR)	BA1	SE 426 441	5W6. SW,BA3
Clifton (NR)	Y1	SE 593 531	C30. 6W6. 6E1. 13E6, note. CE30. SN,Y5
Clifton (near Morley) (WR)	M40	SE 162 228	9W137. SW,M9
Clifton (in Newall with Clifton) (WR)	Ge5	SE 192 482	2W4, note. SW,Sk2
Clifton (in Conisbrough) (WR)	Sf72	SK 519 964	12W1;3. CW7-8
Clifton (in Norwood) (WR)	Bu82	c. SE 20 53	1Y18, note. SW,Bu29
Clifton on Ure (NR)	CtA163	SE 217 843	6N119, note. SN,CtA34
Clotherholme (WR)	Bu12	SE 286 722	13W23. SW,Bu20
Cloughton (NR)	D3	TA 008 942	1Y3. 5N31. 13N7. SN,D3
Colburn (NR)	CtA64	SE 198 991	6N65. SN,CtA23
Coldcotes (WR)	Sk54	SE 335 348	9W1, note. SW,Sk4
Colton (near York) (WR)	An24	SE 541 447	25W3. CW24;27;29;37. SW,An6
Colton (in Temple Newsam) (WR)	Sk63	SE 367 327	9W1;15, note. SW,Sk4;9.
Compton (WR)	Sk11	SE 395 449	CW6, note
Coneysthorpe (NR)	B32	SE 712 714	5N56. SN,B7
Conisbrough (WR)	Sf71	SK 514 988	12W1. CW9;11-14. SW,Sf1
Coniston (ER)	Mid24	TA 155 351	14E6. SE,Hol11
Coniston Cold (WR)	Cr43	SD 902 553	1W73. 13W44. 30W2. SW,Cr5
Conistone (WR)	Cr19	SD 981 674	29W50
Cononley (WR)	Cr104	SD 986 469	1W58
Cookridge (WR)	Sk37	SE 254 408	5W3. SW,Sk19
Copgrove (WR)	Bu46	SE 346 632	24W12. SW,Bu14
Copmanthorpe (WR)	An23	SE 565 468	24W2. SW,An2
'Corburn' (NR)	B71	SE 570 596	2N30. SN,B21
Cornbrough House (NR)	B25	SE 630 670	5N60, note. SN,B8
(Kipling) Cotes. See Kipling Cotes			
Cotherstone (NR)	CtA5	NZ 012 193	6N43, note. SN,CtA16
Cotness Hall (ER)	How32	SE 798 241	3Y4, note. SE,How3
Cottam (ER)	Th16	SE 993 646	2B17, note. SE,Th8
Cottingham (ER)	Wel6	TA 047 329	C36. 23E2. SE,Wel3
Cottingley (WR)	Sk33	SE 118 370	24W1, note. 24W21. SW,Sk18
East Cottingwith (ER)	C4	SE 703 424	5E10. SE,C9
West Cottingwith (ER)	C3; How2	SE 690 419	5E8. 16E2. 24E1. SE,C9. SE,How10
Coulby (NR)	L44	NZ 506 138	4N3, note. SN,L33
Coulton (NR)	Ma50	SE 635 742	1N84. 2A4. 5N51. 23N24. SN,Ma22-23
Coverham (NR)	CtA110	SE 106 863	6N98. SN,CtA30
Great Cowden (ER)	No34	TA 229 428	2E36. 14E5 note. SE,No1

	Map	Grid	Text
Little Cowden (ER)	No35	TA 242 420	14E5, note. SE,Hol10
Cowesby (NR)	A46	SE 464 899	1Y2. 23N15. SN,A1
Cowlam (ER)	Th15	SE 965 655	1E60, note. 2B18. 8E1. SE,Th7;9
Cowling. See *Thornton* (Cowling)			
Cowling (WR)	Cr106	SD 968 430	30W18
Cowthorpe (WR)	An13; Bu103	SE 426 526	13W18;37. SW,An17. SW,Bu44
Cowthwaite. See *Cufforth* (Cowthwaite)			
East Cowton (NR)	A11; CtA41	NZ 306 032	1Y2. 6N37. SN,A1. SN,CtA15
North Cowton (NR)	CtA43	NZ 283 038	6N1. SN,CtA2
South Cowton (NR)	CtA42	NZ 294 022	6N1, note. SN,CtA2
Coxwold (NR)	Bi34	SE 533 771	C36. 23N1
Crachetorp. See *Chrachetorp*			
Cradeuuelle. See *Caldeuuelle*			
Great Crakehall (NR)	CtA136	SE 244 899	6N138. SN,CtA38
Crakehill (NR)	Bi29	SE 429 735	13N17, note
Crambe (NR)	B42	SE 733 648	1N92. 5N62. 31N8. SN,B10
Cranswick (ER)	Dr15	TA 022 524	1Y8. 5E39. 23E8. SE,Dr3;5
Crathorne (NR)	L83	NZ 443 075	1N40. 5N29. 31N5. SN,L44–45
Crayke (NR)	Bi39	SE 560 706	3Y10. SN,Bi1
Crigglestone (WR)	Ag26	SE 312 162	1Y15. SW,Ag9
Croft (NR)	CtA36	NZ 288 098	6N16. SN,CtA11
Crofton (WR)	Ag24	SE 377 181	9W98. SW,Ag4
Crooks House (WR)	Cr76	SD 867 499	13W39, note. 30W4
Crooksby Barn (NR)	CtA97	SD 980 851	6N83, note. SN,CtA26
Croom House (ER)	Th13	SE 934 658	1E58–59, note. 2B18. 5E73. 8E1. CE10. SE,Th8
Cropton (NR)	D6	SE 756 892	1N56. SN,D20
Crosby Grange (NR)	A48	SE 406 886	1Y2, note. 1N134. SN,A1;9
North Crosland (WR)	Ag15	SE 135 153	1Y15, note. SW,Ag13
South Crosland (WR)	Ag33	SE 115 128	1Y15 note. 9W114. SW,Ag16
Crunkly Gill (NR)	L102	NZ 753 070	23N17;34. 31N10, note. SN,L14
Cruttonstall (WR)	M25	SD 986 260	1Y15, note
Cufforth (Cowthwaite) (WR)	Sk45	SE 424 395	9W1, note. SW,Sk7
Cullingworth (WR)	Cr117	SE 067 368	24W21, note
Lower Cumberworth (WR)	Ag41	SE 223 094	1Y15, note. SW,Ag12
Upper Cumberworth (WR)	St24	SE 211 088	1Y15 note. 9W88. SW,St11
Cundall (NR)	H12	SE 423 726	5W38. SW,H8–9
Cusworth (WR)	Sf23	SE 548 040	10W23. 12W1;14. SW,Sf15
Dacre (WR)	Bu29	SE 192 609	24W15. SW,Bu28
Dadsley (WR)	Sf76	SK 593 929	10W3, note. SW,Sf4
Dalby (NR)	B27	SE 637 712	1N86. 8N5. 15E16, note. SN,D16 note. SN,B2
Low Dalby (NR)	D22	SE 856 873	1N50, note. SN,D16, note
Dale Town (NR)	A55	SE 535 885	1N136, note. 11N22. SN,A10
Dalton (near Ravensworth) (NR)	CtA22	(	6N47, note. SN,CtA17
Dalton, another (near Ravensworth) (NR)	CtA22	(NZ 115 083 (	6N47 note. 6N48. SN,CtA17
Dalton (near Topcliffe) (NR)	Bi26	SE 435 763	13N17, note
Dalton (near Huddersfield) (WR)	Ag17	SE 172 167	9W104;117. SW,Ag7
Dalton (near Rotherham) (WR)	Sf81	SK 458 943	12W1;10. 13W11. SW,Sf26
North Dalton (ER)	Wa15	SE 934 522	5E43. 7E1. 29E3. CE8. SE,Wa2
South Dalton (ER)	Sn11	SE 967 455	2E2. SE,Sn8

	Map	Grid	Text
Danby (near Moorsholm) (NR)	L101	NZ 696 062	23N18, note. 23N34. 31N10. SN,L14
Danby (in Thornton Steward) (NR)	CtA142	SE 158 871	6N103. SN,CtA15 note. SN,CtA31
Danby Wiske (NR)	CtA72	SE 336 986	6N36. SN,CtA15, note
Danthorpe (ER)	Mid45	TA 245 326	2E31, note. 14E4. SE,Th13. SE,Mid2. SE,Hol8
Darfield (WR)	Sf14	SE 418 042	29W3. SW,Sf13
Darrington (WR)	O13	SE 486 200	9W51. SW,O9
Darton (WR)	St18	SE 310 099	1W24, note. 9W73;81. SW,St5;14
[High, Middle and Low] Deepdale	D48 D47 D50	(TA 040 857 (TA 045 853 (TA 042 841	1Y3, note. SN,D5
Deighton (ER)	P15	SE 627 441	6E1. SE,P6
Deighton (NR)	A15	NZ 381 017	3Y17. SN,A6
[Kirk and North] Deighton (WR)	Bu105 Bu106	(SE 398 505 (SE 390 517	16W5, note. 24W20. SW,Bu43
Deightonby Fields (WR)	Sf17	SE 460 066	5W18, note. SW,Sf30
Denaby (WR)	Sf70	SK 483 990	10W12. SW,Sf8
Upper Denby (WR)	Ag28	SE 236 165	9W101, note. SW,St12 note. SW,Ag5
[Upper and Lower] Denby (WR)	St23 St22	(SE 229 074 (SE 238 075	9W87, note. SW,St12, note
Denton(e) (NR)			6N76, note. SN,CtA25
Denton (WR)	Ge4	SE 144 489	2W4. SW,Sk2
Dewsbury (WR)	M49	SE 246 216	1Y17. SW,M9
Dic(he) (NR)			1N96, note. SN,B12
Didderston Grange (NR)	CtA50	NZ 184 076	6N50, note. SN,CtA18
Dimlington (ER)	So34	TA 397 207	14E10
Dinnington (WR)	Sf115	SK 525 859	10W1. 12W1;19. SW,Sf2
Over Dinsdale Grange (NR)	A2; CtA39	NZ 349 115	1Y2, note. 6N9. SN,A1. SN,CtA9
Dishforth (NR)	H10	SE 382 731	13W38
Dodworth (WR)	St30	SE 314 051	9W69. SW,St4
Doncaster (WR)	Sf26	SE 574 035	5W8;30. 13W9. SW,Sf21; 25;34
Downholme (NR)	CtA58	SE 112 979	6N70. SN,CtA24
Dowthorpe Hall (ER)	Mid12	TA 153 380	14E11, note. SE,Hol16
Draughton (WR)	Cr96	SE 038 523	1W73. SW,Cr1
Drax (WR)	BA33	SE 675 263	16W1. SW,BA9
Drebley (WR)	Cr28	SE 052 591	25W33
Drewton (ER)	C18	SE 924 332	11E3, note. SE,C3
Great Driffield (ER)	Dr4	TA 021 579	1Y8–9. 5E22;28;31. CE4–5;7. SE,Dr1;4
Little Driffield (ER)	Dr3	TA 009 577	1Y8, note
Drighlington (WR)	M20	SE 224 290	9W128. SW,M5
Dringhoe (ER)	No5	TA 150 551	14E8
Dromonby Hall (NR)	L95	NZ 534 057	29N9, note. SN,L42
Drypool (ER)	Mid41	TA 105 288	2E35. 14E49. SE,Mid3. SE,Hol25
North Duffield (ER)	How5	SE 685 368	5E13;26. 21E5. CE19. SE,How8–9
South Duffield (ER)	How8	SE 681 334	5E11–12;26. CE20. SE,How8
Duggleby (ER)	Sc15	SE 878 670	1Y7. 8E4. SE,Sc6
Dunkeswick (WR)	Bu115	SE 306 469	29W36, note. SW,Bu35
Dunnington (near Bewholme) (ER)	No11	TA 153 521	14E24. SE,Hol20
Dunnington (near York) (ER)	Sn2	SE 668 526	2B8. 13E7. CE26. SE,Sn9–10

	Map	Grid	Text
[Upper and Lower] Dunsforth (WR)	Bu38 Bu37	(SE 442 631 (SE 443 648	24W4, note. 29W30. 31W3. SW,Bu3-4
Dunsley (NR)	L70	NZ 857 111	1N20. SN,L6
Lelley Dyke (ER)	Mid35	TA 212 332	14E1, note. SE,Hol3
Earby (WR)	Cr84	(SD 908 466	30W20
Earby, another (WR)	Cr84	(	30W21
Earlsheaton (WR)	Ag10	SE 256 212	1Y15, note. SW,Ag10
Earswick (NR)	B67	SE 620 572	2N29. SN,B16
Easby (near Ingleby Greenhow) (NR)	L61	NZ 577 087	1N23. SN,L29
Easby (near Richmond) (NR)	CtA55	NZ 187 004	6N20, note. SN,CtA11
Easington (ER)	So36	TA 398 191	14E9-10. SE,Hol14
Easington (NR)	L14	NZ 744 180	4N2. SN,L13
Easington (WR)	Cr60	SD 709 506	30W37
Easingwold (NR)	B6	SE 528 696	1Y1. SN,B21
Eastburn (ER)	Dr6	SE 991 558	1Y8, note. SE,Dr2
Eastburn (WR)	Cr109	SE 020 444	1W62. 21W15, note
Easthorpe (ER)	Wei3	SE 881 454	5E19, note. 13E2. SE,Wei5
Easthorpe House (NR)	D57	SE 736 713	1Y4, note. SN,D11
Easton (ER)	Hu13	TA 152 680	1Y11, note. 1E14. SE,Hu5
Eastrington (ER)	How25	SE 796 299	3Y4. SE,How2
'Eastwick' (WR)			2W7, note. SW,Bu45
Eavestone (WR)	Bu16	SE 224 682	2W7. SW,Bu47
Ebberston (NR)	D33	SE 898 826	1Y4. SN,D12
Ecclesfield (WR)	Sf84	SK 353 942	10W16. SW,Sf10
Eccleshill (WR)	M4	SE 183 362	SW,M12, note
Eccup (WR)	Sk18	SE 289 423	5W5. SW,Sk20
Ectone, Estone (WR)			2W4, note. SW,Sk2, note
Eddlethorpe (ER)	Ac5	SE 773 661	1E48, note. 31E6. SE,Ac1
Edenthorpe. See *Streetthorpe*			
Old Edlington (WR)	Sf73	SK 532 972	13W9, note. SW,Sf25
Great Edstone (NR)	Ma13	SE 705 840	8N22. SN,Ma9
Little Edstone (NR)	Ma14	SE 715 847	8N23, note. SN,Ma9
Eggborough (WR)	O9	SE 561 233	9W61-62. SW,O14
Egglestone Abbey (NR)',	CtA8	NZ 061 150	6N1, note. SN,CtA6
Egton (NR)	L105	NZ 808 063	5N3. SN,L6
Eldeberge (WR)			SW,Sf16-17, note
Eldwick (WR)	Sk32	SE 121 401	24W1, note. SW,Sk18
E(le)stolf (ER)			1Y11, note. SE,Tu6
Kirk Ella (ER)	He12	TA 020 297	5E23. 15E1. 21E1. 23E1. SE,He3-4
Elland (WR)	M37	SE 108 212	9W142. SW,M10
Ellenthorpe (WR)	Cr72	SD 818 498	13W41. 30W11
Ellenthorpe Hall (NR)	H22	SE 412 673	1Y18, note. SW,H7
Ellerbeck (NR)	A27	SE 433 967	1N130. 23N16. SN,A8
Ellerburn (NR)	D27	SE 841 842	1Y4. 1N49. SN,D16
Ellerby (ER)	Mid20	TA 169 379	14E43. CE41. SE,Hol24
Ellerby (NR)	L36	NZ 799 145	5N6. SN,L8
Ellerker (ER)	Well1	SE 921 293	3Y1
Ellerton (ER)	C5	SE 706 398	5E24. CE2. SE,C8
Ellerton Abbey (NR)	CtA59	SE 079 973	6N71, note. SN,CtA24
Ellerton on Swale (NR)	CtA70	SE 258 974	6N29-30;32-5. SN,CtA14
High Ellington (NR)	CtA164	SE 197 832	6N113, note. SN,CtA33
Elloughton (ER)	Well2	SE 944 282	2B3. SE,Wel4
North Elmsall (WR)	O30	SE 476 127	9W63. SW,Sf37 note. SW,O13
South Elmsall (WR)	Sf3	SE 473 110	9W34. SW,Sf37, note
Elmswell (ER)	Dr2; Tu11	SE 998 581	1Y8. 29E11. SE,Dr1. SE,Tu8
Elslack (WR)	Cr86	SD 938 492	30W22
Elstronwick (ER)	Mid44	TA 233 322	14E2. SE,Hol5
'Elsworth' (WR)			SW,Bu29, note

	Map	*Grid*	*Text*
Elvington (ER)	P12	SE 701 474	13E14. CE29. SE,P7
Elwicks (WR)	Bu63	SE 448 595	SW,Bu6
Embsay (WR)	Cr94	SE 018 536	1W73. SW,Cr1
Emley (WR)	Ag38	SE 245 132	1Y15. SW,Ag5
Englebi (Barwick) (NR)	L38	NZ 432 146	4N3, note. SN,L35
Eppleby (NR)	CtA28	NZ 178 133	6N1. SN,CtA4
Eryholme (NR)	CtA38	NZ 320 090	6N1. SN,CtA2
Escrick (ER)	P18	SE 631 422	6E1. SE,P5
Eshingtons (NR)	CtA100	SE 012 875	6N85
Eshton (WR)	Cr47	SD 935 561	30W33
Eskdaleside (NR)	L106	NZ 865 078	31N10, note
Eske (ER)	Mid1	TA 060 433	2E21, note. SE,Th14
Estolf. See *Elestolf*			
Eston (NR)	L9	NZ 554 185	5N24. SN,L24
Estone. See *Ectone*			
Eterstorp (NR)			1Y3, note. SN,D4
Etherdwick (ER)	Mid29	TA 231 372	14E2, note. SE,Hol6
Etton (ER)	Sn15	SE 981 435	2E6. 5E34. 23E6. SE,Sn5-6
Everingham (ER)	P26	SE 804 423	2B9. SE,P3
Everley (NR)	D13	SE 971 889	13N13. SN,D8
Everthorpe (ER)	C21	SE 909 319	SE,C2, note
Exelby (NR)	CtA150	SE 295 870	6N151. SN,CtA41
Faceby (NR)	L91	NZ 495 030	1N38. 31N5, note. SN,L44
Fadmoor (NR)	Ma2	SE 673 895	5N46. SN,Ma17
Fairburn (WR)	BA24	SE 471 279	9W28. SW,BA10
Falsgrave (NR)	D44	TA 028 879	1Y3. 5N32. 13N13. SN,D1
Fangfoss (ER)	P8	SE 766 533	1Y10. SE,P8
Farlington (NR)	B24	SE 614 674	5N59. SN,B8
Farmanby (NR)	D24	SE 854 858	1Y4, note. SN,D12
Farnham (WR)	Bu58	SE 348 605	1Y19. 28W7. SW,Bu15
Farnhill (WR)	Cr102	SE 008 461	1W60
Farnley (in Armley) (WR)	M15	SE 251 324	SW,M13, note
Farnley (near Otley) (WR)	Ge6	SE 212 480	2W4. SW,Sk2
Farnley Tyas (WR)	Ag31	SE 165 128	9W106. SW,Ag7
Farsley (WR)	M6	SE 216 350	9W126, note. SW,M4
Fearby (NR)	CtA167	SE 193 819	6N116. SN,CtA33
Featherstone (WR)	O15	SE 423 220	9W54. SW,O11
Felixkirk. See *Fridebi*			
Felliscliffe (WR)	Bu80	SE 23 56	1Y18, note. SW,Bu30
Great Fencote (NR)	CtA123	SE 283 936	6N56, note. SN,CtA21
Little Fencote (NR)	CtA124	SE 284 932	6N56, note. SN,CtA21
[Church and Little] Fenton (WR)	BA20 BA19	(SE 514 367 (SE 521 351	9W23, note. SW,BA6
Ferrensby (WR)	Bu43	SE 369 607	1Y19. SW,Bu16
North Ferriby (ER)	He15	SE 986 262	5E3. 15E2. SE,He4
Fewston (WR)	Bu81	SE 194 541	1Y19. SW,Bu29
Filey (ER)	D55	TA 117 810	1Y3. SN,D4
Fingall (NR)	CtA140	SE 181 896	6N132. SN,CtA37
Firby (ER)	Ac1	SE 744 664	31E8, note
Firby (NR)	CtA148	SE 268 864	6N121, note. SN,CtA35
Fishlake (WR)	Sf35	SE 652 133	12W1;23. CW13
Fitling (ER)	Mid33	TA 253 347	14E4. SE,Hol8
Fixby (WR)	M38	SE 133 195	SW,M12, note
Flamborough (ER)	Hu9	TA 226 701	4E1. 29E6. SE,Hu1
Flasby (WR)	Cr46	SD 946 566	30W7
Flaxby (WR)	Bu75	SE 395 578	24W10. SW,Bu11
Flaxton (NR)	B48	SE 678 622	1N102. 2N11. 6N162. 23N33. SN,B17
Kirkby Fleetham (NR)	CtA75	SE 285 943	6N26-27, note. 6N31;56. SN,CtA20
Flinton (ER)	Mid26	TA 220 361	2E30. 14E2. SE,Mid1. SE,Hol6

	Map	*Grid*	*Text*
Flixton (ER)	Hu2	TA 041 796	1Y11. 1E17. SE,Hu8
Flockton (WR)	Ag37	SE 236 149	9W100, note. SW,Ag4, note
[East and West] Flotmanby (ER)	Tu3 Tu2	(TA 079 798 (TA 073 795	2E3, note. 20E3. SE,Tu2-3
Flowergate (NR)	L73	NZ 897 110	4N1, note. SN,L4
Foggathorpe (ER)	C9	SE 754 375	5E8. 15E6. 21E8. SE,C6-7
Folkton (ER)	Tu1	TA 053 796	1E25. SE,Tu4
Forcett (NR)	CtA26	NZ 175 122	6N1. SN,CtA3
Fordon (ER)	Tu6	TA 049 751	1E22. SE,Tu3
Fornetorp (ER)			1E34-35, note. SE,Bt7
Fornetorp (NR)			5N59, note. 8N5. SN,B8
Fors Abbey (NR)	CtA95	SD 936 908	6N78, note. SN,CtA25
Fosham (ER)	Mid16	TA 209 388	14E11. SE,Hol17
Foston (NR)	B44	SE 699 651	6N162. SN,B18
Foston on the Wolds (ER)	Tu17	TA 100 558	13E15. SE,Tu6
Fostun(e) (ER)			14E2, note. SE,Hol6
Foxholes (ER)	Hu3	TA 010 731	1Y11. 31E1. SE,Hu8
Foxton (in Crathorne) (NR)	L82	NZ 456 081	5N28. 31N5. SN,L39
Foxton (in Thimbleby) (NR)	A30	SE 420 960	3Y14. SN,A6
Fraisthorpe (ER)	Hu20	TA 154 616	5E48. 23E13. 29E10. SE,Hu4
Fremington (NR)	CtA62	SE 043 990	6N74. SN,CtA25
Frickley (WR)	Sf10	SE 466 085	9W34, note. 10W33. SW,Sf28;37
Fridaythorpe (ER)	Ac15	SE 874 592	1E55. 2B11. 26E4, note. 26E6. SE,Ac10-11
Fridebi (Felixkirk) (NR)	Bil3	SE 468 847	23N11-12, note
North Frodingham (ER)	No6	TA 097 531	14E25. SE,Hol21
Ferry Fryston (WR)	O4	SE 480 241	9W57, note. SW,O10
Water Fryston (WR)	O2	SE 469 264	9W56, note. SW,O12
Fryton (NR)	Ma53	SE 688 750	5N51. 23N24. SN,Ma24
Gate Fulford (ER)	Y4	SE 608 492	C28, note. 6W5, note. SN,Y4
'Water' Fulford (ER)	Wa2	SE 608 484	C28 note. 6E1. SE,Wa6-7
Fulstone (WR)	Ag43	SE 175 094	SW,Ag14, note
Fyling Old Hall (NR)	L81	NZ 942 026	4N1, note. 13N1. CN1. SN,L1
Fyling Thorpe. See (Fyling) Thorpe			
Ganstead (ER)	Mid23	TA 149 342	14E45. SE,Hol25
Ganthorpe (NR)	B31	SE 689 703	1N88. 5N54. 31N8, note. SN,B4-5
Ganton (ER)	Bt3	SE 990 776	1Y11. SE,Bt9
Gardham (ER) (see also *Newton*)	Sn17	SE 945 415	3Y1, note. SE,Sn8
Garforth (WR)	Sk50	SE 409 331	9W1-2. SW,Sk4-5
Gargrave (WR)	Cr50	SD 932 539	1W73. 30W7;13. SW,Cr3
Garriston (NR)	CtA84	SE 157 927	6N108. SN,CtA31
Garrowby Hall (ER)	Ac19	SE 795 574	29E19, note. 31E6. SE,Ac4-5
Garton (ER)	Mid32	TA 270 354	14E9. SE,Hol14
Garton on the Wolds (ER)	Tu10	SE 982 593	2E15. 5N1a. 5E55-56. SE,Tu8
Gatenby (NR)	CtA132	SE 325 879	6N151. SN,CtA42
Gembling (ER)	Tu16	TA 109 570	2E14. SE,Tu6
Ghigogesmersc. See *Chigogemers*			
Giggleswick (WR)	Cr14	SD 811 640	30W1
Gillamoor (NR)	Ma1	SE 684 901	23N20
Gilling (NR)	CtA52	NZ 182 051	6N1;8;50. SN,CtA1
Gilling East (NR)	Ma33	SE 615 768	15E17. 23N26. SN,Ma16
Gipton (WR)	Sk55	SE 308 367	9W1, note. 9W15. SW,Sk4;9
Girlington Hall (NR)	CtA18	NZ 128 137	6N1, note. SN,CtA5
Girsby (NR)	A4	NZ 353 083	3Y16. SN,A3
Gisburn (WR)	Cr73	SD 829 488	13W41. 30W4

	Map	Grid	Text
Givendale (WR)	H17	SE 337 691	2W12, note. SW,H1
Great Givendale (ER)	Wa6	SE 812 538	1Y10. SE,Wa5
Little Givendale (ER)	Wa11	SE 823 530	SE,Wa5, note
Glusburn (WR)	Cr107	SE 002 449	13W45. 21W16
Gnipe Howe (NR)	L78	NZ 933 085	4N1. SN,L2
Golcar (WR)	Ag14	SE 096 159	9W113. SW,Ag15
Goldsborough (NR)	L37	NZ 836 146	5N5. SN,L7
Goldsborough (WR)	Bu76	SE 384 560	16W3. SW,Bu8
Goldthorpe (WR)	Sf19	SE 465 043	1W21. 10W28. SW,Sf20;31
Gomersal (WR)	M43	SE 207 266	9W129, note. SW,M5
Goodmanham (ER)	Wei5	SE 889 431	1Y6. 2B9. 5E18. 13E1. SE,Wei2
Goulton Grange (NR)	L89	NZ 477 040	1N39, note. 5N29. 31N5, note. SN,L44
Gowthorpe (ER)	P5	SE 763 545	2B11. SE,P8
Goxhill (ER)	No26	TA 185 448	14E6, note
Grafton (WR)	Bu41	SE 416 632	1W33–34. 2W5. 24W5. 29W32. 31W3. SW,Bu5
Gransmoor (ER)	Bt22	TA 123 594	1Y14. 29E12. 31E1. 31N10, note. SE,Bt1
High Grantley (WR)	Bu14	SE 232 709	2W7, note. SW,Bu48
Grassington (WR)	Cr21	SE 003 641	1W56. 21W15
Greasbrough (WR)	Sf67	SK 419 956	10W10. 12W1;13. SW,Sf7
Greenwick (ER)	P3	SE 851 567	2B11. SE,P9
Greetland (WR)	M34	SE 085 213	SW,M13, note
Grewelthorpe (WR)	Bu2	SE 230 763	28W11. 31W5. SW,Bu15 note. SW,Bu23
Gribthorpe (ER)	C10	SE 760 355	15E3. 21E5. SE,C7
Griff Farm (NR)	Ma17	SE 587 839	1N78, note. SN,L7 note. SN,Ma17
Grimesbi (NR)			5N10, note. SN,L9
Grimeshou (WR)			10W11, note. SW,Sf7
Grimston (in Dunnington) (ER)	Sn1	SE 646 515	5E38. 13E8. CE27. SE,Sn10
Grimston (in Garton) (ER)	So1	TA 290 350	2E24, note. 14E4. SE,Sc5 note. SE,So2. SE,Hol8
Grimston (NR)	Ma49	SE 604 740	23N24, note
Grimston Grange (WR)	BA9	SE 489 417	9W29, note. SW,BA5;8
Hanging Grimston (ER)	Ac11	SE 800 608	26E11. 29E16. SE,Sc5 note. SE,Ac3
North Grimston (ER)	Sc14	SE 841 677	1E53. 2B18. 23E17. 31E8. SE,Sc5–6, note
Grimthorpe Manor (ER)	Wa10	SE 812 529	1Y10, note. SE,Wa6
Grindale (ER)	Hu6	TA 129 709	1Y11. 2B12. SE,Hu6
Grindleton (WR)	Cr67	SD 762 456	30W37
Grinton	CtA61	SE 046 984	6N73. SN,CtA24
Gristhorpe (NR)	D54	TA 087 819	1Y3. SN,D4
Guisborough (NR)	L29	NZ 616 161	1N10. 4N2. 5N19. 11N1. 31N7, note. SN,L18
Guiseley (WR)	Sk22	SE 194 422	2W4. SW,Sk1
Gunby (ER)	He1	SE 709 353	21E6, note. SE,He9
[Great and Little] Habton (NR)	Ma44 Ma43	(SE 758 762 (SE 744 772	1N59. 5N35. SN,Ma2
Hackforth (NR)	CtA119	SE 243 941	6N60. SN,CtA22
Hackness (NR)	D12	SE 967 900	13N13. SN,D9
'Haggenby' (WR)	An31	SE 483 452	13W16, note. CW25;40. SW,An7
Hagthorpe (ER)	How14	SE 701 301	SE,How5, note. SE,How8
Low Hail (NR)	CtA37	NZ 308 097	6N1. SN,CtA2
Hainworth (WR)	Cr116	SE 059 390	24W21, note
Haisthorpe (ER)	Bt15	TA 127 647	1Y14. 2E16. 31E1. SE,Bt4

	Map	Grid	Text
Hallam (WR)	Sf91	SK 305 866	10W41, note. 10W42. SW,Sf35
Halsham (ER)	So18	TA 275 269	2A1. 14E14. SE,Th11. SE,Hol18
Halton (WR)	Sk61	SE 351 335	9W10. SW,Sk7
'Halton' (WR)	Sk30	SE 093 389	24W1, note. 24W21. SW,Sk18
Halton East (WR)	Cr95	SE 043 539	1W73. SW,Cr1
Hambleton (WR)	BA26	SE 553 318	9W25. SW,BA6
Hammerton Hall (WR)	Cr57	SD 718 537	30W37, note
Green Hammerton (WR)	Bu72	SE 459 571	25W24. SW,Bu7
Kirk Hammerton (WR)	Bu102	SE 465 555	25W23. SW,Bu7
Hamphall Stubbs (WR)	O32	SE 496 111	9W43, note. SW,O5
Hampole (WR)	Sf4	SE 505 102	9W43 note. 10W32. SW,Sf28
Handsworth (WR)	Sf109	SK 410 863	5W19. SW,Sf31
'Hangton' (NR)			31N10, note
Hangton Hill (NR)	L104	NZ 762 062	31N10, note
Hanlith (WR)	Cr30	SD 903 614	1W73. SW,Cr5
West Hardwick (WR)	O17	SE 418 184	9W54. SW,O11
Harewood (WR)	Sk7	SE 322 451	1W9, note. SW,Sk13
East Harlsey (NR)	A21	SE 424 998	1N125. 31N3. SN,A5
West Harlsey (NR)	A23	SE 415 981	1Y2, note. 1N124. SN,A1;5
Harmby (NR)	CtA112	SE 128 895	6N101. SN,CtA30
Harome (NR)	Ma21	SE 647 820	1N81. 5N42. 8N28. SN,Ma19–20
Harpham (ER)	Bt21	TA 092 615	1Y14. 29E12. 31E1, note. 31N10. SE,Bt1–2
Harswell (ER)	Wei8	SE 825 408	1Y7. SE,Wei6
Hartforth (NR)	CtA51	NZ 171 063	6N1. SN,CtA1
Harthill (WR)	Sf119	SK 494 809	12W1;9
Hartlington (WR)	Cr25	SE 037 611	29W40;43
Harton (NR)	B49	SE 708 619	1N93. SN,B11
Hartshead (WR)	M45	SE 182 226	9W141. SW,M10
Hashundebi (WR)			2W13, note. SW,H2
Hatfield (WR)	Sf38	SE 663 095	12W1;26
Great Hatfield (ER)	No29	TA 188 426	14E6;39. SE,Hol23
Little Hatfield (ER)	No30	TA 173 433	14E42. SE,Hol24
East Hauxwell (NR)	CtA82	SE 168 937	6N106. SN,CtA32
West Hauxwell (NR)	CtA83	SE 165 930	6N107, note. SN,CtA32
Hawade (NR)	Ma52	SE 671 742	23N24, note
Hawkswick (WR)	Cr10	SD 955 705	30W36
Hawksworth (WR)	Sk24	SE 169 417	2W4. SW,Sk1
'Little' Hawksworth (WR)	Sk23	SE 176 422	2W4, note. SW,Sk1
Hawnby (NR)	A54	SE 542 897	1N137. 11N23. SN,A11
Hawold (ER)	Wa5	SE 821 545	1E10. SE,Wa4
Haxby (NR)	B69	SE 606 582	2N22. SN,B23
Hayton (ER)	P21	SE 820 460	1Y10. 13E10. SE,P1
Hazelwood Castle (WR)	BA7	SE 449 398	13W3, note. CW2–3. SW,BA3
Headingley (WR)	Sk57	SE 280 360	9W7. SW,Sk11
Healaugh (WR)	An17	SE 498 479	13W14;16. 18W3. CW25; 33–34;40. SW,An7;9
Heathfield (WR)	Bu28	SE 137 673	8E5, note. SW,Bu27
Hanging Heaton (WR)	M50	SE 257 232	1Y15 note. SW,M14, note
(Kirk)heaton. See Kirkheaton			
Hebden (WR)	Cr23	SE 026 629	25W32
Heldetune (WR)			1L4, note
Hellaby (WR)	Sf99	SK 506 922	10W3, note. 10W4. SW,Sf4–5
Hellifield (WR)	Cr41	SD 856 564	1W73. 13W44. 30W4;9. SW,Cr5

	Map	Grid	Text
Helmsley (NR)	Ma19	SE 611 838	1N80. 2A4. 5N50. SN,Ma18
Gate Helmsley (NR)	B57	SE 690 552	2N17. SN,B13
Upper Helmsley (NR)	B56	SE 695 570	5N61. SN,B12
Helperby (NR)	B4	SE 439 698	2N25–26. SN,B24–25
Helperthorpe (ER)	Th7	SE 952 704	2B18. SE,Th4
Hemingbrough (ER)	How11	SE 673 306	1Y5. SE,How10
Hemlington (NR)	L43	NZ 501 143	4N3. SN,L33
Hemsworth (WR)	St7	SE 428 132	9W66. SW,St1
Henderskelfe (NR)	B33	SE 719 700	8N10, note. SN,B1
Hensall (WR)	O10	SE 593 234	1Y12. 29W25. SW,O16
Hepworth (WR)	Ag45	SE 162 069	SW,Ag14, note
'Herleshow' (How Hill) (WR)	Bu25	SE 276 670	2W7, note. SW,Bu48
East Heslerton (ER)	Th3	SE 926 766	8E1. 23E14. 29E22. 31E2. SE,Th2
West Heslerton (ER)	Th2	SE 911 758	29E23. 31E2. SE,Th3
Heslington (ER)	Wa1	SE 628 505	23N29. SE,Wa7
Hessay (WR)	An3	SE 520 533	22W4. 25W17. SW,An13–14
Hesselton (NR)	CtA117	SE 198 917	6N136. SN,CtA38
Hessle (ER)	He16	TA 032 261	15E2. 21E2. SE,He1
Hessle (WR)	O19	SE 431 173	9W53. SW,O9
Hetton (WR)	Cr48	SD 961 587	30W24
Heuu(o)rde (WR)			28W25, note. 29W49
Bridge Hewick (WR)	H16	SE 340 712	2W10, note. SW,H3
Copt Hewick (WR)	H15	SE 335 702	2W10 note. 2W11. SW,H2
Heworth (NR)	Y3	SE 618 526	C26–27. 23N36. SN,Y4
Hexthorpe (WR)	Sf25	SE 564 024	5W8. 10W27. CW14;16;21. SW,Sf21
Hickleton (WR)	Sf20	SE 482 053	27W1. SW,Sf13
Cold Hiendley (WR)	St4	SE 372 142	9W84, note. SW,St16
South Hiendley (WR)	St8	SE 397 126	9W67. SW,St3
Hildenley Hall (NR)	B34	SE 748 709	1N90, note. SN,B7
Hilderthorpe (ER)	Hu17	TA 175 655	1Y11, note. 29E9. SE,Hu3
Hillgrips (NR)	D43	SE 999 867	13N11, note. SN,D6
Hilston (ER)	So2	TA 287 336	14E3. SE,Hol5
Hilton (NR)	L54	NZ 465 113	1N34. 5N28. 31N5. SN,L38
'Hilton' (WR)			1Y18, note. SW,Bu14
Hinderwell (NR)	L34	NZ 791 170	4N2. 13N2–3. SN,L11–12
Hindrelag(he), Indrelag(e) (Richmond) (NR)	CtA56	NZ 174 010	6N19, note. 6N69. SN,CtA11;24
Hipperholme (WR)	M31	SE 124 258	SW,M11, note
Hipswell (NR)	CtA65	SE 188 985	6N66. SN,CtA23
Hive (ER)	How27	SE 820 310	3Y4. SE,How1
Holdworth (WR)	Sf88	SK 286 915	10W35. SW,Sf34
Holedene (WR)			29W46–47, note
Hollym (ER)	So27	TA 344 252	14E4. SE,Hol9
Holme (NR)	H2	SE 355 822	3Y9. SW,H5
Holme (in Bolton by Bowland) (WR)	Cr56	SD 774 528	13W40, note
Holme (near Holmfirth) (WR)	Ag49	SE 108 059	1Y15. 1W26. SW,Ag12
Holme House (WR)	Cr49	SD 945 544	1W73, note. SW,Cr3
Holme on the Wolds (ER)	Sn10	SE 966 463	3Y8. SE,Sn9
Holme upon Spalding Moor (ER)	Wei9	SE 820 389	21E9, note. SE,Wei2
North Holme House (NR)	Ma23	SE 705 807	1N72, note. 8N18. SN,Ma10, note
Paull Holme (ER)	So14	TA 184 247	14E1. SE,Hol1;3
South Holme (NR)	Ma37	SE 701 775	16N1. 23N24. SN,Ma10 note. SN,Ma22
(Yate)holme. See Yateholme			
Holmpton (ER)	So28	TA 367 233	14E19. CE49. SE,Hol19
Holtby (NR)	B58	SE 675 541	1N99. SN,B12
Holtby Hall (NR)	CtA121	SE 268 922	6N62, note. SN,CtA22
Honley (WR)	Ag32	SE 138 120	9W107. SW,Ag8

	Map	*Grid*	*Text*
Hutton Buscel (NR)	D39	SE 972 840	1Y3. SN,L18 note. SN,D7
Hutton Conyers (NR)	H9	SE 323 733	2W13, note. 3Y9. SW,H3–5
Hutton Cranswick (ER)	Dr12	TA 024 533	5E39, note. 23E8. SE,Dr5
Hutton Hang (NR)	CtA141	SE 169 888	6N131. SN,Bi6 note. SN,CtA37
Hutton le Hole (NR)	Ma3	SE 704 900	23N20
Hutton Lowcross (NR)	L52	NZ 602 137	5N19. SN,L18–19, note
Hutton Magna (NR)	CtA19	NZ 126 124	6N2. SN,Bi6 note. SN, CtA8
Hutton Mulgrave (NR)	L69	NZ 835 102	5N2. SN,L6, note
Hutton Rudby (NR)	L86	NZ 469 061	5N29. SN,L18 note. SN,L42
Low Hutton (NR)	B40	SE 762 674	1N85, note. 8N9. 31N8. SN,L18 note. SN,B1
Sand Hutton (near Thirsk) (NR)	Bi10	SE 384 820	1Y1. SN,Bi6, note
Sand Hutton (near York) (NR)	B55	SE 694 585	1N95. 23N30. CN4, note. SNB11
Sheriff Hutton (NR)	B41	SE 657 662	1N87. 5N54. CN5, note. SN,L6 note. SN,B3
Ianulfestorp (ER)			13E6, note. CE25–26. SE,Sn9
Ilkley (WR)	Sk1	SE 116 478	2W4. 13W5. SW,Sk1;18
Ilton (NR)	CtA171	SE 191 781	6N117. SN,CtA33
Indrelag(e). See *Hindrelag(he)*			
Ingbirchworth (WR)	St25	SE 223 059	9W86. SW,St11, note
Ingleby Arncliffe (NR)	A19	NZ 447 009	1N127. 31N5. SN,A7
Ingleby Greenhow (NR)	L99	NZ 580 062	29N9. SN,L35 note. SN,L40
Ingleby Hill (NR)	L39	NZ 440 127	4N3, note. SN,L35, note
'Inglethwaite' (NR)			13N15, note. SN,B22
Ingleton (WR)	Am65	SD 695 722	1L3
Ingmanthorpe Hall (WR)	Bu104	SE 423 501	5W37, note. 24W20. SW,Bu44
Ingthorpe Grange (WR)	Cr80	SD 892 520	30W27, note
Irby Manor (NR)	A18	NZ 410 030	1Y2, note. SN,A1
Iretone (NR)			23N1, note
Irton (NR)	D45	TA 010 841	13N10. SN,D6
Islebeck Grange (NR)	Bi25	SE 456 778	23N8, note
Kearby Town End (WR)	Bu118	SE 346 468	13W27, note. SW,Bu35
Keighley (WR)	Cr112	SE 061 410	1W64, note
Kelbrook (WR)	Cr85	SD 902 447	13W43. 30W4
Kelfield (ER)	P19	SE 595 383	6E1. 23E10. SE,P4
Great Kelk (ER)	Tu15	TA 103 580	2E14. SE,Tu4
Little Kelk (ER)	Tu14	TA 097 595	1E28. SE,Tu5
Kelleythorpe (ER)	Dr5	TA 011 564	1Y8. 2E10. SE,Dr1–2
Kellington (WR)	O7	SE 551 249	9W60;62. SW,O13–14
Kelsit Grange (NR)	B15	SE 548 635	1Y1, note. SN,B20
Great Kendale (ER)	Dr1	TA 017 601	1Y8, note. SE,Dr2
Kennythorpe (ER)	Sc12	SE 788 660	23E14. SE,Sc1
Kepwick (NR)	A41	SE 470 909	1N135. 23N8. SN,A10
Keresforth Hall (WR)	St33	SE 334 048	9W80, note. SW,St15
East Keswick (WR)	Sk10	SE 360 445	1W10. SW,Sk14
Kettlethorpe (ER)	C17	SE 916 334	11E4, note. SE,C4, note
'Kettlethorpe' (NR)		SE 916 334	1N51, note. SN,D17
Kettlewell (WR)	Cr9	SD 971 722	30W5
Kexbrough (WR)	St17	SE 199 095	9W74. SW,St6
Kex Moor (WR)	Bu4	SE 201 750	28W17. SW,Bu25
Keyingham (ER)	So17	TA 245 255	14E12. CE44. SE,Hol18
Kiddal Hall (WR)	Sk44	SE 394 393	9W1, note. 9W9. SW,Sk4;6
Kilburn (NR)	Bi23	SE 513 796	23N2
Kildale (NR)	L62	NZ 604 095	29N5. 31N7. SN,L30

	Map	Grid	Text
Kildwick (WR)	Cr101	SE 011 459	1W61
Kilham (ER)	Bt18	TA 064 643	1Y8. 1E29. 26E12. 29E12. SE,Bt2
Killerby Hall (near Catterick) (NR)	CtA77	SE 258 960	6N52, note. SN,CtA19
Killerby Hall (in Cayton) (NR)	D52	TA 065 828	13N8, note. SN,D5
Killinghall (WR)	Bu53	SE 284 583	1Y18. 2W7. SW,Bu31;46
Kilnsea (ER)	So37	TA 422 159	14E2, note. SE,Hol4
Kilnsey (WR)	Cr18	SD 974 678	29W48, note
Kilnwick (ER)	Sn6	SE 997 495	1Y8. 5E30. SE,Sn2-3
Kilnwick Percy (ER)	Wa17	SE 825 499	1Y10, note. 31E5. SE,Wa4
Kilpin (ER)	How28	SE 772 269	3Y4. SE,How2
Kilton (NR)	L12	NZ 700 182	1N9. 5N16. SN,L17
North Kilvington (NR)	Bi7	SE 423 852	1Y2, note. 5N72;75. SN,Bi8
Kimberworth (WR)	Sf83	SK 408 930	10W31. SW,Sf27
Kingthorpe House (NR)	D23	SE 835 858	1Y4, note. SN,D12, note
Kinsley (WR)	St6	SE 417 145	9W65. SW,St1
Kiplin (NR)	CtA71	SE 289 970	6N25. SN,CtA12
Kipling Cotes (ER)	Wei4	SE 901 479	2E11, note. 5E20. 13E3. SE,Wei7
Kippax (WR)	Sk68	SE 417 302	9W1, note. SW,Sk4
Kirby Grindalythe (ER)	Th11	SE 903 676	1E57. 5E69-70. SE,A2 note. SE,Th6
Kirby Hall (WR)	Bu65	SE 458 610	25W21, note. SW,Sf37 note. SW,Bu2
Kirby Hill (NR)	H19	SE 393 685	1W54, note. 28W22, note. SW,H6
Kirby Knowle (NR)	Bi4	SE 468 872	23N8, note
Kirby Misperton (NR)	Ma42		8N1, note. SN,L42 note. SN,Ma1
Kirby Misperton, another (NR)	Ma42	SE 779 795	8N1 note. 8N2. SN,L42 note. SN,Ma1
Kirby Moorside (NR)	Ma6	SE 697 866	23N19, note. 23N20-21
Kirby Underdale (ER)	Ac17	SE 808 585	1E50. 29E17. SE,Ac2, note
Kirby Wiske (NR)	A51; CtA156	SE 376 848	1Y2. 6N30. SN,A1, note. SN,CtA13
Cold Kirby (NR)	B3	SE 533 845	1Y1. SN,B20
Kirkburn (ER)	Dr8	SE 979 550	1Y8, note. 31E3. SE,Dr2
Kirkburton (WR)	Ag36	SE 198 125	1Y15. SW,Ag13
Kirkby (NR)	L96	NZ 538 060	29N9, note. SN,L42, note
Kirkby Fleetham. See (Kirkby) Fleetham			
Kirkby Hall (NR)	CtA76	SE 281 957	6N55, note. SN,A1 note. SN,CtA20
Kirkby Malham (WR)	Cr31	SD 894 609	30W1
Kirkby Malzeard (WR)	Bu7	SE 235 745	28W10. SW,Bu23
Kirkby Overblow (WR)	Bu110	SE 324 492	13W28-29. SW,Bu36
Kirkby Wharfe (WR)	BA11	SE 506 410	6W8 note. 9W30. SW,BA5;9
South Kirkby (WR)	Sf1	SE 453 111	9W34. SW,Sf37, note
Kirkham (ER)	Ac2	SE 736 660	5E62;66, note. SE,Ac9
Kirkheaton (WR)	Ag18	SE 181 179	9W103. SW,Ag6
Kirkleatham. See Weslide			
Kirklington (NR)	CtA185	SE 318 810	6N147. SN,CtA40
Kiveton (WR)	Sf113	SK 498 834	12W1
Knapton (ER)	Th1	SE 881 758	15E14. SE,Th3
Knapton (WR)	An7	SE 560 520	22W5. 25W18. SW,An14
Knaresborough (WR)	Bu77	SE 350 568	1Y19. 1W31. 13W36. 24W8;19. SW,Bu17
'Knaresford' (WR)	Bu15	SE 213 697	2W7, note. 28W41. SW,Bu47;49
Knayton (NR)	A53; Bi2	SE 432 877	1Y2, note. 3Y13. SN,Bi7. SN,A1
Knedlington (ER)	How18	SE 731 281	3Y4. SE,How4

	Map	Grid	Text
West Lilling (NR)	B47	SE 646 651	1N91, note. 5N61. SN,B9, note
Lindley (WR)	Ag12	SE 117 184	9W111, note. SW,Ag15
Old Lindley (WR)	M36	SE 093 190	1W27, note. SW,M12
Linton (ER)	Sc6	SE 909 707	SE,Sc8, note
Linton (near Hebden) (WR)	Cr22	SD 997 627	21W15
Linton (near Wetherby) (WR)	Bu120	SE 390 467	13W35. SW,Bu42
Linton upon Ouse (NR)	B13	SE 496 606	5N67–68
Lissett (ER)	No3	TA 144 580	14E23. SE,Hol20
Littlethorpe (WR)	Bu22	SE 323 693	2W7. SW,Bu15 note. SW,Bu45
Littleworth. See *Shuttleworth*			
Litton (WR)	Cr6	SD 905 741	30W1
Liversedge (WR)	M44	SE 196 239	9W140, note. SW,M10
Liverton (NR)	L31	NZ 712 159	4N2. SN,L13
Lockington (ER)	Sn9	SE 994 475	2E5. 5E32. SE,Sn3
Lockton (NR)	D10	SE 843 900	1N52. SN,D17
Lockwood. See North Crosland			
Lofthouse (in Harewood) (WR)	Sk15	SE 323 433	1W14, note. SW,Sk15
Lofthouse (near Wakefield) (WR)	M56	SE 333 260	9W119. SW,M2
Loft Marishes (NR)	D32	SE 873 798	1N47, note. 5N33. SN,D14
Loftus (NR)	L13	NZ 718 182	1N5. SN,L14
Loftus Hill (WR)	Bu44	SE 370 615	24W11, note. 29W17. SW,Bu12–13
South Loftus (NR)	L23	NZ 723 178	4N2. SN,L13
Londesborough (ER)	Wei2	SE 868 453	2B9. SE,Wei5
Longfield (WR)	Sk27	SE 939 236	1Y15, note
Lonton (NR)	CtA1	NY 954 247	6N38. SN,CtA15
Lothersdale (WR)	Cr105	SD 963 459	30W14
Loversall (WR)	Sf47	SE 576 987	5W8. CW14;16. SW,Sf21
Lowthorpe (ER)	Bt20	TA 079 608	1E31. 2E16. 29E13. CE31. SE,Bt3
Lund (near Beverley) (ER)	Wel1	SE 970 481	3Y2–3, note. SE,He8 note. SE,Wel2
Lund (in Breighton) (ER)	He4	SE 706 333	3Y2 note. 15E5. 21E5. CE14. SE,He8, note
[East and West] Lutton (ER)	Th8 Th9	(SE 942 697 (SE 930 692	2B18. SE,Th4
Luuetotholm (ER)			CE36, note
Lythe (NR)	L67	NZ 846 130	5N1. SN,L5
Malham (WR)	Cr29	SD 900 626	1W73. 13W44. SW,Cr4
'Malkton' (WR)			13W15, note. SW,An6
Maltby (NR)	L40	NZ 466 132	4N3. SN,L35
Maltby (WR)	Sf100	SK 527 918	10W4;12. SW,Sf5
Old Malton (NR)	Ma62	SE 798 725	1N65–66. 2N7. 5N37. SN,Ma5–6
Manfield (NR)	CtA33	NZ 222 133	6N1. SN,CtA8
Manston (WR)	Sk52	SE 365 351	9W1. SW,Sk4
Mappleton (ER)	No28	TA 225 438	14E5–6. SE,Hol9
Marderby Hall (NR)	Bi14	SE 468 839	23N10, note
Marfleet (ER)	Mid42	TA 142 295	14E6. SE,Th13. SE,Hol11
'Little Marish' (NR)			8N14, note. SN,D10
Markenfield Hall (WR)	Bu24	SE 294 673	13W20, note. SW,Bu19
Markington (WR)	Bu32; H25	SE 290 652	2W7;13. SW,Bu48. SW,H3
Marley (WR)	Sk29	SE 091 406	24W1, note. 24W21. SW,Sk18
Marr (WR)	Sf21	SE 514 053	5W9;31. 10W27;40. SW,Sf20–21
Marrick (NR)	CtA60	SE 077 982	6N72. SN,CtA24
Marske by the Sea (NR)	L2	NZ 633 223	4N2, note. 5N17. 13N4;6. SN,L21
Long Marston (WR)	An11	SE 502 512	25W5;11, note. SW,An10

	Map	Grid	Text
Martin Garth (NR)	D37	SE 966 841	1Y3, note. 1N43, note. SN,L31 note. SN,D8
Marton (near Burton Constable) (ER)	Mid13	TA 180 392	14E11;51. SE,Hol16;26
Marton (in Sewerby) (ER)	Hu10	TA 203 698	1Y11. 2N20. 5E46. 29E8. SE,Hu2
Marton (NR)	D25	SE 734 832	8N16. 23N21. SN,L31 note. SN,D21
Marton (WR)	Bu40	SE 418 627	28W1. SW,Bu4
Marton in Cleveland (NR)	L26	NZ 515 158	1N25, note. 11N6;8. 29N6–7. 31N5. SN,L31, note
Marton in the Forest (NR)	B23	SE 602 682	5N58. SN,B7
[East and West] Marton (WR)	Cr81 Cr79	(SD 905 510 (SD 893 504	30W26, note
Masham (NR)	CtA169	SE 226 806	6N114;118;123;138. SN,CtA34
Maunby (NR)	A58; CtA154	SE 349 863	1Y2. 6N29. SN,A1. SN,CtA13
Maxudesmares, Maxudesmersc (NR)			1Y4, note. SN,D12, note
Meaux (ER)	Mid5	TA 096 403	14E11, note. SE,Hol15
Melbourne (ER)	C2	SE 751 440	15E8. SE,C10
Melmerby (near Hutton Conyers) (NR)	CtA179	SE 337 770	6N145. SN,CtA40
Melmerby (near Middleham) (NR)	CtA106	SE 076 853	6N95. SN,CtA29
Melsonby (NR)	CtA49	NZ 198 083	6N50. SN,CtA18
Meltham (WR)	Ag34	SE 100 106	9W107. SW,Ag8
High Melton (WR)	Sf53	SE 509 018	10W20, note. SW,Sf11 note. SW,Sf14
West Melton (WR)	Sf59	SE 425 010	10W19. 19W2. 29W4–5;7. SW,Sf11, note. SW,Sf16
Meltonby (ER)	Wa7	SE 795 525	1Y10. SE,Wa4
Menethorpe (ER)	Ac3	SE 769 675	1E47. 5E61. 8E2. SE,Ac1
Menston (WR)	Sk25	SE 168 439	2W4. SW,Sk1
Methley (WR)	Ag1	SE 397 272	9W94, note. SW,Ag1
Mexborough (WR)	Sf62	SE 472 005	10W13. SW,Sf8
Mickleby (NR)	L64	NZ 801 129	5N7. SN,L8
Micklethwaite (WR)	Sk26	SE 103 415	24W1, note. SW,Sk18
Mickleton (NR)	CtA2	NY 968 237	6N39. SN,CtA15
Middleham (NR)	CtA111	SE 128 876	6N99. SN,CtA30
Middelham (NR)			23N21, note
Middlethorpe (WR)	An20	SE 598 486	1W29 note. 11W2. 22W1. SW,Sf37 note. SW,An1
'Middleton' (in Appleton Wiske) (NR)			28W39, note
'Middleton' (in Guisborough) (NR)			5N19, note. SN,L18
Middleton (near Pickering) (NR)	D20	SE 782 854	1Y4. SN,L39 note. SN,D18
Middleton (near Ilkley) (WR)	Ge2	SE 123 493	2W4. SW,Sk2
Middleton (near) Leeds) (WR)	M53	SE 306 284	9W119, note. SW,M2
Middleton on the Wolds (ER)	Sn4	SE 947 495	2E12. 5E21–22;27–28. CE3–7. SE,Sn1
Middleton Quernhow (NR)	CtA177	SE 334 783	6N146. SN,CtA40
Middleton Tyas (NR)	CtA45	NZ 226 056	6N3. SN,CtA8
Middleton upon Leven (NR)	L55	NZ 465 099	5N28. SN,L39, note
Little Middop (WR)	Cr69	SD 841 457	13W39, note
Midgley (WR)	M28	SE 029 264	1Y15
Milby (NR)	H20	SE 403 678	1Y18. SW,H7
North Milford Hall (WR)	BA13	SE 505 395	9W33, note. CW3. SW,BA9
Millington (ER)	Wa12	SE 830 517	1Y10. 2B13. 31E5. SE,Wa6
Minskip (WR)	Bu35	SE 388 647	1W39. SW,Bu13
Minsthorpe (WR)	O31	SE 473 122	9W64. SW,O16
Mirfield (WR)	M46	SE 209 204	9W108 note. 9W138. SW,M9

	Map	Grid	Text
Misperton (NR)	Ma41	SE 779 795	8N1–2 note. 23N21
Great Mitton (WR)	Cr63	SD 715 389	30W37
Molescroft (ER)	Sn19	TA 021 408	2E9. SE,Sn8
Monk Hay Stile (WR)	BA6	SE 410 405	5W7, note. SW,BA3
Bishop Monkton (WR)	Bu33	SE 329 664	2W7. SW,Bu46
Moor Monkton (WR)	An1	SE 508 569	22W3. SW,An13
Nun Monkton (WR)	Bu68	SE 508 577	25W20. CW38. SW,Bu1
Monkwith (ER)	So3	TA 300 328	2E25, note. SE,So2
Moorsholm (NR)	L53	NZ 688 144	1N7. 5N13. 31N8. SN,L15
Little Moorsholm (NR)	L30	NZ 684 161	5N14. SN,L16
Moorthorpe (WR)	Sf2	SE 467 110	9W34. SW,Sf37, note
Moreby Hall (ER)	P16	SE 595 432	6E1, note. 23E12. SE,P6
Morley (WR)	M51	SE 263 280	9W118, note. CW23, note. SW,M1
Mortham Tower (NR)	CtA10	NZ 086 142	6N1, note. SN,CtA6
Morton (WR)	Sk27	SE 098 419	1W5. 1W6 note. 1W8 note. SW,Sk11, note
Morton Grange (in East Harlsey) (NR)	A22	SE 427 995	1N126, note. 31N4, note. SN,B19 note. SN,A7
Morton Grange (near Guisborough) (NR)	L49	NZ 555 145	1N19, note. 31N4 note. 31N6. SN,L28
Morton upon Swale (NR)	CtA129	SE 321 919	6N27;31. SN,B19 note. SN,CtA14
Mortun (NR)			C34, note. SN,Y2 note. SN,Y8
Mortune (WR)			1W8, note. SW,Sk11 note
Moulton (NR)	CtA44	NZ 237 039	6N1. SN,CtA4
Mount Grace. See 'Bordelby'			
Low Mowthorpe (ER)	Th12	SE 895 670	2B18, note. 5E71. SE,Th6–7
Low Mowthorpe Farm (NR)	B35	SE 685 690	SN,B27, note
Moxby Hall (NR)	B20	SE 596 669	1Y1, note. SN,B19
Mulgrave Castle (NR)	L68	NZ 839 116	5N4, note. SN,L7, note
Mul(h)ede, Mulehale (WR)			29W11, note. CW30. SW,An16
Murton (near Cold Kirby) (NR)	A56	SE 535 880	11N21. SN,B19 note. SN,A10
Murton (near York) (NR)	B59	SE 649 527	C23. SN,Y2, note
Murton Farm (NR)	B19	SE 606 643	1Y1, note. 2N12. SN,B19, note
Muston (ER)	Tu4	TA 096 796	1E19. 20E3. SE,Tu1;3
'Myton' (ER)			15E2, note. SE,He5
Myton on Swale (NR)	B8	SE 439 666	1N104. 2N25. 5N69. SN,B23;25
Naburn (ER)	Wa3	SE 598 453	1E8. 7E2. CE9. SE,Wa1
Nafferton (ER)	Tu13	TA 055 589	1E27. 13E16. SE,Tu7
Nappa (WR)	Cr53	SD 855 533	13W42
Nawton (NR)	Ma10	SE 654 846	2N6. 8N24. 23N21. SN,Ma11
Nesfield (WR)	Bu86	SE 094 496	13W24. SW,Bu32
East Ness (NR)	Ma36	SE 696 788	16N1, note. 23N24. SN,Ma21
Neswick Hall (ER)	Dr13	SE 974 528	5E40, note. SE,Dr4
Neuhuse, Niuuehusum (WR)			9W31, note. CW3. SW,BA8
Neuson (ER)			5E41, note. SE,Sn6
Neutone (NR)			6N23, note. SN,CtA12
[North and South] Newbald (ER)	C13 C14	(SE 912 365 (SE 911 359	2B6. SE,C4
Newhall (WR)	Sk8	SE 323 454	1W12, note. SW,Sk13–14
Newhall Grange (WR)	Sf102	SK 502 910	10W1, note. SW,Sf2, note
Newham Hall (NR)	L45	NZ 517 132	1N26, note. 11N7. 31N5. SN,L5 note. SN,L31–32

	Map	Grid	Text
Newhill (WR)	Sf64	SK 430 998	10W12. SW,Sf2 note. SW,Sf8
Newholm (NR)	L71	NZ 866 105	4N1, note. SN,L5, note
Temple Newsam (WR)	Sk64	SE 367 306	9W16, note. SW,Sk10
Newsham (in Amotherby) (NR)	Ma48	SE 748 762	1N61. 5N36, note. 23N24. 29N12. 31N8. SN,Ma3
Newsham (near Hutton Magna) (NR)	CtA20	NZ 108 100	6N46. SN,CtA17
Newsham (near Kirby Wiske) (NR)	Bi8	SE 379 848	1N110, note. 23N6. SN,Bi7, note
'Newsham' (WR)			9W41, note. SW,O5
Newsham Grange (NR)	A32	SE 384 953	1Y2, note. SN,Bi7 note. SN,A1
Newsholme (ER)	He8	SE 718 297	15E3. SE,He7
Newsholme (near Gisburn) (WR)	Cr54	SD 835 513	13W41. 30W4
Newsholme (in Keighley) (WR)	Cr114	SE 020 398	1W67, note
Newsome Farm (WR)	Bu107	SE 373 510	24W18, note. SW,Bu42
[Great and Little] Newsome (ER)	So21 So22	(TA 308 265 (TA 303 269	14E15, note. SE,Hol19
Newton (in Wintringham) (ER)	Th5	SE 887 725	16E4, note. SE,Tu2–3 note. SE,Th1
Newton (Gardham) (ER)	Sn16	SE 955 422	3Y1, note. 3Y7. CE24. SE,Sn8
Newton (near Guisborough) (NR)	L50	NZ 569 132	1N18. 31N6, note. SN,L28
Newton (near Levisham) (NR)	D8	SE 812 903	1Y4. 8N12. SN,D10–11
'Newton' (in West Ayton) (NR)			1Y3, note. SN,D7
Newton (WR)	Cr61	SD 696 504	30W37, note
Newton Garth (ER)	So12	TA 181 270	14E1. SE,Hol2, note
Newton Kyme (WR)	BA3	SE 465 448	5W7. 25W29–30. CW3. SW,BA3;8;13
Newton le Willows (NR)	CtA138	SE 215 895	6N134. SN,B22 note. SN,CtA37
Newton Morrell (NR)	CtA48	NZ 239 094	6N1. SN,B22 note. SN,CtA1
Newton Mulgrave (NR)	L35	NZ 787 156	5N8. SN,L8
Newton 'Picot' (NR)	CtA133	SE 312 895	6N151, note. SN,CtA42
Newton upon Ouse (NR)	B14	SE 510 599	16N2. 16W6. SN,B22, note
Newton 'Wallis' (WR)	BA23	SE 444 278	9W27, note. SW,BA8
Bank Newton (WR)	Cr51	SD 912 530	8W3. 30W23
East Newton (ER)	Mid30	TA 266 379	14E11. SE,Hol15;17
East Newton (NR)	Ma29	SE 644 794	1N76. 2N5. 23N24. SN,Ma15
Little Newton (WR)	Cr36	SD 851 579	30W7
Out Newton (ER)	So33	TA 382 218	14E20. SE,Hol12 note. SE,Hol20
West Newton (ER)	Mid18	TA 199 378	2E29. SE,Mid1
West Newton Grange (NR)	Ma31	SE 645 795	1N75, note. SN,Ma16
Wold Newton (ER)	Tu7	TA 045 731	1E20–21. 20E4. SE,Tu2–3, note
Nidd (WR)	Bu54	SE 301 608	2W7. SW,Bu45
Niuuehusum. See *Neuhuse*			
Normanby (near Eston) (NR)	L8	NZ 546 183	5N25. 11N2. 13N6. SN,L3 note. SN,L25
Normanby (in Fylingdales) (NR)	L79	NZ 928 061	1N1. SN,L3, note
Normanby (near Thornton Riseborough) (NR)	Ma25	SE 734 816	1N74. 23N21. SN,L3 note. SN,Ma14
Normanebi (NR)			6N149, note. SN,CtA41
Normanton (WR)	Ag4	SE 387 227	1Y16. 1W25. SW,Ag3
Northallerton (NR)	A34	SE 365 939	1Y2. 6N9. SN,A1
Northfield Farm (NR)	D15	SE 986 907	1Y3, note. SN,D1
'Northorpe' (ER)			14E22, note. CE51. SE,B4 note. SE,Hol20
Northowram (WR)	M23	SE 112 269	9W143 note. SW,M11

	Map	Grid	Text
Norton (ER)	Sc8	SE 795 714	1E38–39. 15E11. 23E15. SE,Sc3–4
Norton (WR)	O35	SE 548 152	9W35. SW,O2
Norton Conyers (NR)	H7	SE 319 762	3Y9, note. SW,H4
Norton le Clay (NR)	H14	SE 401 710	5W38. SW,H8
Nostell Priory (WR)	O18	SE 403 174	9W54, note. SW,O11
Notton (WR)	St3	SE 351 131	9W82. SW,St14
Nunburnholme (ER)	Wa18	SE 847 477	1Y7;10. 29E4. SE,Wa2
Nunkeeling (ER)	No12	TA 143 502	14E24, note. 14E28. SE,Hol21–22
Nunnington (NR)	Ma32	SE 666 790	1N83. 5N47. 16N1. SN,Ma20–21
Nunthorpe (NR)	L46	NZ 540 132	1N19. 31N5. SN,L16 note. SN,L29
Nunwick (WR)	H8	SE 321 744	2W9. SW,H1
Nuthill (ER)	So8	TA 215 299	14E1, note. SE,Hol2
Oakworth (WR)	Cr115	SE 036 388	1W66, note. 21W17
Octon (ER)	Bt8	TA 032 698	1E35, note. SE,Bt7
Odulfesmare, Ouduluesmersc (NR)			1Y4, note. SN,D12, note
Oglethorpe Hall (WR)	BA2	SE 447 442	5W7, note. 25W29. CW2. SW,BA3;8
Onesacre (WR)	Sf86	SK 297 934	1W22
Opetone, Opetune (NR)			6N120, note. SN,CtA35
Orgreave (WR)	Sf108	SK 422 868	10W9
Ormesby (NR)	L19	NZ 530 167	29N3–4. 31N7. SN,L26
Osbaldwick (NR)	B60	SE 634 518	C23. 2W1. SN,Y2
Osgodby (ER)	How7	SE 645 338	5E15;17. CE21. SE,How9
Osgodby (NR)	D49	TA 056 845	1Y3. SN,D1
Osgoodby Hall (NR)	Bi21	SE 492 809	23N1, note
Osmotherley (NR)	A26	SE 455 971	1N131. SN,A8
Ossett (WR)	Ag9	SE 278 203	1Y15. SW,Ag11
Oswaldkirk (NR)	Ma28	SE 620 788	5N38. 8N19. SN,Ma15
Otley (WR)	Sk3	SE 202 455	2W4, note. SW,Sk1–2
Otterburn (WR)	Cr35	SD 883 577	1W73. 30W12. SW,Cr4
North Otterington (NR)	A44	SE 362 897	1Y2, note. SN,A1, note
South Otterington (NR)	A50	SE 371 875	1N113. 31N3. SN,A1 note. SN,A2
Ottringham (ER)	So19	TA 267 244	2E26. 14E11;13. SE,So2. SE,Hol18
Oubrough (ER)	Mid21	TA 156 369	14E44. SE,Hol24
Ouduluesmersc. See *Odulfesmare*			
Oulston (NR)	Bi36	SE 546 775	1N107–108, note. 28W35. SN,Bi3
Ounesbi NR)			6N151, note. SN,CtA42
Great Ouseburn (WR)	Bu66	SE 449 617	1W30. 31W2. SW,Bu3
Little Ouseburn (WR)	Bu64	SE 449 607	1W31. 25W21 note. 29W14. SW,Bu3
Ousethorpe Farm (ER)	Wa9	SE 813 511	1Y10, note. SE,C4 note. SE,Wa4
Ouston Farm (WR)	An33	SE 500 424	13W14, note. CW40. SW,An6
Overton (NR)	B77	SE 553 557	C32–33. 6W2. SN,Y6
Ovington (NR)	CtA16	NZ 131 146	6N1. SN,CtA5
(North)owram. See Northowram			
(South)owram. See Southowram			
Owsthorpe (ER)	How26	SE 808 309	3Y4, note. SE,How1
Owston (WR)	O37	SE 551 111	9W40. SW,O4
Owstwick (ER)	So5	TA 269 325	14E2–3. SE,Hol5
Owthorne (ER)	So25	TA 341 281	14E4, note. SE,Hol9
Oxspring (WR)	St41	SE 271 020	9W91. SW,St13
Oxton (WR)	An32	SE 504 430	25W5. CW37. SW,An5
Painley (WR)	Cr74	SD 842 500	13W41. 30W4

	Map	Grid	Text
Painsthorpe (ER)	Ac18	SE 812 583	1E52. 29E18. SE,Ac2
Pallathorpe (WR)	An34	SE 515 427	5W35, note. 13W13. 25W4. CW30;37. SW,Sf37 note. SW,An5
Parlington (WR)	Sk48	SE 425 360	9W1, note. 9W9. SW,Sk4;6
Patrington (ER)	So29	TA 315 225	2A1. SE,Th10
Paull (ER)	So13	TA 165 264	14E1. SE,Hol1
Paythorne (WR)	Cr55	SD 829 518	13W41. 30W11, note
Penistone (WR)	St27	SE 246 033	1W23, note. 9W71. SW,St5
Persene (ER)			3Y3, note. SE,Sn4
Pickburn (WR)	Sf6	SE 512 074	5W15. SW,Sf29
Pickering (NR)	D26	SE 799 840	1Y4. SN,D11
Pickhill (NR)	CtA157	SE 347 837	6N155;161. SN,CtA42
Pilley (WR)	St36	SE 334 006	5W32. SW,St8
Pillwoods Farm (ER)	Wel5	TA 049 345	23E2, note. SE,Wel7
Pinchinthorpe Hall (NR)	L51	NZ 578 142	1N15, note. 11N3. 31N6. SN,L16 note. SN,L27
Plompton Hall (WR)	Bu94	SE 357 540	13W31, note. 21W13. SW,Bu40
Pockley (NR)	Ma8	SE 637 860	2N9. 5N40. SN,Ma19
Pocklington (ER)	P11	SE 803 489	1Y10. 11E9. 21E12. 26E3. 29E4. CE20. SE,P1
Pockthorpe (ER)	Tu12	TA 040 630	13E16, note. SE,Tu7
Pool (WR)	Sk4	SE 244 453	2W4. SW,Sk1
Popletone (WR)			1W42, note. 28W19. SW,Bu25
Nether Poppleton (WR)	An6	SE 564 550	25W14. CW32. SW,An12
Upper Poppleton (WR)	An5	SE 555 540	2W2. 25W13. CW32. SW,An11
Portington (ER)	How24	SE 788 309	3Y4. SE,How1
Potterton (WR)	Sk46	SE 406 387	9W1. SW,Sk4
'Prestby' (NR)			4N1, note. SN,L2
Preston (ER)	Mid43	TA 188 304	14E1;48. CE45. SE,Hol3;25
[Great and Little] Preston (WR)	Sk67 Sk66	(SE 402 296 (SE 388 302	9W1, note. SW,Sk4
Preston Hill (NR)	D40	SE 975 845	1Y3, note. SN,D7
Preston under Scar (NR)	CtA87	SE 069 912	6N91, note. SN,CtA28
Long Preston (WR)	Cr37	SD 832 581	30W4
Pudsey (WR)	M47	SE 219 330	9W122. SW,M4
Purston Jaglin (WR)	O16	SE 429 199	9W54. SW,O11
Quarmby (WR)	Ag13	SE 114 172	9W112, note. SW,Ag15
Radholme Laund (WR)	Cr62	SD 666 459	30W37
Rainton (NR)	Bi28; CtA181	SE 369 752	6N161. 13N18, note. SN,Bi5. SN,CtA44
Raisthorpe (ER)	Ac14	SE 855 617	1E56, note. 23E14. 26E7. SE,Ac12
Raskelf (NR)	B5	SE 489 707	1N103. SN,B21
Rastrick (WR)	M39	SE 139 217	1W28. SW,M12
Rathmell (WR)	Cr38	SD 804 599	30W1;9
Ravenfield (WR)	Sf79	SK 485 951	12W1–2
Ravensthorpe Manor (NR)	A57	SE 495 851	1Y2, note. 23N12;14. SN,A1
Ravensworth (NR)	CtA23	NZ 140 078	6N49. SN,CtA17
Raventhorpe (ER)	Sn20	TA 050 425	2E7, note. 5E36. SE,Sn7
Rawcliff Banks (NR)	L21	NZ 638 164	4N2, note. SN,L19
Rawcliffe (NR)	B78	SE 582 551	C31. 1W1, note. SN,Y6
Rawdon (WR)	Sk35	SE 218 393	1W18. 31W4. SW,Sk17
Rawmarsh (WR)	Sf68	SK 436 961	19W3. SW,Sf12
Raygill Moss (WR)	Cr71	SD 806 498	13W40, note
Redmere (ER)			14E4, note. 14E18. CE48. SE,Hol5;19
Redmire (NR)	CtA88	SE 045 912	6N90. SN,CtA28

	Map	*Grid*	*Text*
Reestones (WR)	M17	SE 276 321	9W121, note. SW,M3
Reeth (NR)	CtA63	SE 038 991	6N75. SN,CtA25
Reighton (ER)	Hu4	TA 129 751	1E16. 2E14. SE,Hu6
[Great and Little] Ribston (WR)	Bu97	(SE 392 536	1W35, note. 13W19. 16W2.
	Bu98	(SE 386 533	24W9. SW,Bu9
Riccal House (NR)	Ma22	SE 674 806	1N82, note. SN,Ma20
Riccall (ER)	How3	SE 619 378	2B7. 3Y6. SE,How6;11
Richmond. See *Hindrelag(he)*			
Ricstorp (ER)			20E3, note. SE,Tu1
Riddlesden (WR)	Sk28	SE 079 425	1W6, note. SW,Sk13
Rigton (WR)	Bu112	SE 280 491	21W8. 29W37. SW,Bu37
East Rigton (WR)	Sk12	SE 372 438	29W24, note. CW6. SW,Sk3
Rillington (ER)	Sc2	SE 852 743	1E43;46. 5E62. SE,Sc9-10
Rimington (WR)	Cr68	SD 805 458	13W39
Rimswell (ER)	So23	TA 311 287	14E16. SE,Hol19
Ringbrough (ER)	Mid31	TA 273 375	14E2, note. 14E9;11.
			SE,Hol6;14;17
Ripley (WR)	Bu50	SE 283 605	16W4. 29W35. SW,Bu27
Riplingham (ER)	He9	SE 963 320	15E2, note. SE,He5
Ripon (WR)	Bu21	SE 314 711	2W7-9. SW,Bu45
Risby (ER)	Wel4	TA 008 349	2E4. CE33. SE,Wel5
Rise (ER)	No32	TA 149 419	2E37. 14E37. CE39.
			SE,No1, note. SE,Hol23
Long Riston (ER)	No31	TA 123 427	14E7;36. SE,Hol13;23
Roall Hall (WR)	O8	SE 568-247	9W61, note. SW,O14
Rodebestorp, Roudeluestorp (NR)			1Y3, note. SN,D4
Rodouuelle (WR)			25W3, note
Rogerthorpe Manor (WR)	O27	SE 469 152	9W45, note. SW,O7
Rokeby Hall (NR)	CtA9	NZ 084 144	6N44, note. SN,CtA16
Rolston (ER)	No27	TA 214 451	14E5, note. SE,Hol10
Romaldkirk (NR)	CtA4	NY 995 221	6N40. SN,CtA15
Romanby (NR)	A35	SE 358 933	1Y2. 1N114. SN,A1-2
Rookwith (NR)	CtA145	SE 204 865	6N130. SN,CtA37
Roos (ER)	So6	TA 290 334	14E2;53. SE,Hol4;26
'Roskelthorpe' (NR)			4N2, note. SN,L10
Rossett Green (WR)	Bu92	SE 299 528	1W52, note. 21W10.
			SW,Bu38
Rotherham (WR)	Sf82	SK 438 926	5W13. SW,Sf26
Rothwell (WR)	M58	SE 345 281	9W119. 25W3 note. SW,M2
Rotsea (ER)	Dr16	TA 064 516	SE,Dr4, note
Roudeluestorp. See *Rodebestorp*			
Roughbirchworth (WR)	St42	SE 262 016	9W91. SW,St11 note.
			SW,St13
East Rounton (NR)	L88	NZ 421 033	1N41. SN,L45
West Rounton (NR)	A17	NZ 413 034	1Y2. SN,A1
Routh (ER)	Mid4	TA 091 425	2E33. 14E6. SE,Mid2.
			SE,Hol12
Rowden (WR)	Bu79	SE 257 574	1W44. SW,Bu30
Rowton Farm (ER)	Mid9	TA 138 402	14E11, note. SE,Hol16
Roxby (NR)	L32	NZ 763 160	1N2. 5N8;11. SN,L9, note
Roxby Hill (NR)	D29	SE 826 828	1Y4, note. SN,L9 note.
			SN,D12
Royston (WR)	St9	SE 364 112	9W68. SW,St3
Rudby (NR)	L87	NZ 471 066	5N29
Rudfarlington (WR)	Bu93	SE 342 543	13W30. 21W12. SW,Bu39-40
Rudston (ER)	Bt11	TA 097 677	5E54. 16E5. 29E14. 31E2.
			SE,Bt6
Rufforth (WR)	An9	SE 527 514	25W19. CW41. SW,An15
Ruston (NR)	D36	SE 957 831	1Y3. SN,D8
Ruston Parva (ER)	Bt19	TA 064 617	1E30. 2E16. SE,Bt3
Ruswick (NR)	CtA139	SE 195 894	6N133. SN,CtA37

	Map	Grid	Text
Ryhill (WR)	St5	SE 385 142	9W93. SW,St16
Rylstone (WR)	Cr45	SD 971 588	29W39;44
Rysome Garth (ER)	So32	TA 361 220	14E21. CE50. SE,No1 note. SE,Hol20
Ryther (WR)	BA21	SE 555 394	9W24. CW3. SW,BA6
Ryton (NR)	Ma45	SE 791 755	1N60. 23N21. SN,Ma3
Sactun, Santone (WR)			1Y13, note. SW,St7
Salescale (NR)			SN,Ma2, note
Saltmarshe (ER)	How31	SE 785 240	3Y4. SE,How3
Salton (NR)	Ma24	SE 716 800	2N2. SN,Ma7
Sancton (ER)	Wei11	SE 899 394	11E8. 21E10. CE22. SE,Wei3
Sandal Magna (WR)	Ag23	SE 343 182	1Y15. SW,Ag4
Kirk Sandall (WR)	Sf30	SE 610 082	5W30. 12W1;12. CW11. SW,Sf34
Long Sandall (WR)	Sf29	SE 605 069	5W11. 12W1;28. SW,Sf24
Sandburn House (NR)	B64	SE 665 591	C25, note. SN,Y3
Santone. See *Sactun*			
Sawley (WR)	Bu17	SE 248 678	2W7. SW,Bu47
Sax(e)hale, Saxhalla (WR)			13W4, note. CW3. SW,BA4
Saxton (WR)	BA16	SE 475 368	9W8, note. SW,BA5
Scackleton (NR)	B28	SE 649 726	1N86. 5N44. 23N24. SN,B2
Scagglethorpe (ER)	Sc3	SE 836 727	5E61. SE,Sc10
Scagglethorpe (WR)	An4	SE 540 550	25W16, note. CW32. SW,An12
Scalby (NR)	D16	TA 009 903	1Y3. SN,D2
Scampston (ER)	Sc1	SE 861 754	1E43–44. 15E13. 31E2. SE,Sc8–9
Scardiztorp, Scradiztorp (ER)			26E8, note. CE32. SE,Ac8
Scargill (NR)	CtA11	NZ 050 107	6N1. SN,CtA6
Scawsby (WR)	O43	SE 548 045	10W43, note. SW,O3
'Scawthorpe' (NR)			1Y3, note. SN,D4
Scawton (NR)	Ma16	SE 549 835	5N39. 11N14. SN,Ma17
Scinestorp (WR)	Sf24	SE 544 036	5W30, note. SW,Sf34
Scloftone, Scolfstona (ER)			20E3, note. SE,Tu2
Scorborough (ER)	Sn12	TA 015 453	3Y1, note. SE,Sn4–5
Scoreby Manor (ER)	Sn3	SE 698 529	13E5, note. CE26. SE,Sn9
Scorton (NR)	CtA68	NZ 252 002	6N51. SN,CtA18
Scosthrop (WR)	Cr32	SD 901 595	1W73. 30W29. SW,Cr4
Scotton (NR)	CtA81	SE 190 958	6N67. SN,CtA23
Scotton (WR)	Bu59	SE 326 593	21W3. 29W18. 31W3. SW,Bu17
Scotton Thorpe. See *(Scotton) Thorpe*			
Scradiztorp. See *Scardiztorp*			
West Scrafton (NR)	CtA108	SE 073 836	6N94. SN,CtA28
Scrayingham (ER)	Ac23	SE 732 603	23N31;33. 23E18. SE,Ac7
Scriven (WR)	Bu60	SE 348 583	1Y19. SW,Bu16
Scruton (NR)	CtA125	SE 300 925	6N58. SN,CtA21
Seacroft (WR)	Sk53	SE 359 357	9W11. SW,Sk7
Seamer (near Scarborough) (NR)	D46	TA 015 833	13N9. SN,L38 note. SN,D6
Seamer (near Stokesley) (NR)	L56	NZ 498 103	5N28. SN,L38, note
Seaton (ER)	No20	TA 162 468	14E32. SE,Hol22
Seaton Hall (NR)	L16	NZ 781 178	5N11, note. SN,L12
Seaton Ross (ER)	C8	SE 781 413	1Y7. 5E4. SE,C6
Sedbergh (WR)	Am39	SD 657 920	1L3
Selside (WR)	Cr3	SD 784 756	30W7–8, note
Sessay (NR)	Bi30	SE 457 752	3Y11–12. SN,Bi4
Settle (WR)	Cr15	SD 819 638	30W6
Settrington (ER)	Sc7	SE 839 702	8E3. SE,Sc4
Seuenetorp (NR)			6N154, note. SN,CtA43

	Map	Grid	Text
Sewerby (ER)	Hu11	TA 199 687	4E1, note. 5E45. 29E27. SE,Hu1-2
Shadwell (WR)	Sk40	SE 345 397	1W7, SW,Sk10
Shafton (WR)	St11	SE 391 110	5W18. 9W76;93. SW,St7
Sheffield (WR)	Sf92	SK 354 875	10W42. SW,Sf35
Shelf (WR)	M22	SE 125 288	SW,M11, note
Shelley (WR)	Ag40	SE 207 112	1Y15. SW,Ag8
Shepley (WR)	Ag42	SE 193 098	1Y15. SW,Ag8, note
Sherburn (ER)	Th4	SE 958 767	2B18, note. 23E13-14. SE,Th1
Sherburn in Elmet (WR)	BA18	SE 487 335	2B1. SW,BA1
Shipley (WR)	M2	SE 147 376	9W133. SW,Ag8 note. SW,M8
Shippen House (WR)	Sk51	SE 389 345	9W4, note. SW,Sk6
Shipton (NR)	B72	SE 553 589	SN,B27, note
Shiptonthorpe (ER)	Wei7	SE 852 431	1Y6, note. SE,Wei1
Shitlington (WR)	Ag27	SE 266 173	1Y15, note. SW,Ag11
Shuttleworth (Littleworth) (WR)	Sf44	SK 629 984	5W8, note. SW,Sf21
Sicklinghall (WR)	Bu119	SE 363 484	1W50. SW,Bu36
Sigglesthorne (ER)	No25	TA 154 456	2E38. SE,No1
Kirby Sigston (NR)	A36	SE 417 947	1Y2, note. SN,A1
Silkstone (WR)	St29	SE 290 058	9W64;70. SW,St2;4
Silsden (WR)	Cr100	SE 042 464	25W31
Nether Silton (NR)	A40	SE 456 923	SN,A8, note
Over Silton (NR)	A38	SE 451 932	1N132. SN,A8
Sinderby (NR)	CtA184	SE 342 818	6N156. SN,CtA43
Sinnington (NR)	D17;Ma15	SE 744 857	8N8;25. SN,D21. SN,Ma10
Sitlington. See Shitlington			
Siuuarbi (ER)			21E5, note
Skeckling (ER)	So10	TA 227 280	14E1, note. SE,Ho12
Skeeby (NR)	CtA54	NZ 201 026	6N22. SN,CtA12
Skelbrooke (WR)	O33	SE 511 120	9W42. SW,O5
Skellow (WR)	O39	SE 530 103	9W39, note. SW,O4
Skelmanthorpe (WR)	St14	SE 235 107	9W86, note. SW,St12
Skelton (ER)	How29	SE 766 256	3Y4. SE,How3
Skelton (near Saltburn) (NR)	L11	NZ 655 188	5N18. SN,L17
Skelton (near York) (NR)	B76	SE 568 565	C33, note. 1W2, note. 6W2, note. SN,Y7
Skelton (WR)	H18	SE 360 679	2W12, note. 28W24. SW,H2;6
Skelton Grange (WR)	Sk59	SE 332 313	9W1, note. SW,Sk4
Skerne (ER)	Dr11	TA 046 550	1Y8. 23E8. SE,Dr3-4
Skewsby (NR)	B22	SE 626 709	5N57. SN,B9
Skibeden (WR)	Cr93	SE 016 526	1W73, note. SW,Cr2
Skidby (ER)	Wel7	TA 015 336	2E1. SE,Wel4
Skipton (WR)	Cr89	SD 988 513	1W73. SW,Cr2
Skipton on Swale (NR)	Bi17	SE 366 798	13N17
Skipwith (ER)	How4	SE 664 385	23E5. SE,How9
North Skirlaugh (ER)	Mid10	TA 143 399	14E7. SE,Th13. SE,Hol13, note
South Skirlaugh (ER)	Mid11	TA 141 296	14E11. SE,Hol13 note. SE,Hol15-16
High Skirlington (ER)	No10	TA 180 525	14E7, note. SE,Hol13
Skirpenbeck (ER)	Ac24	SE 749 572	26E10. CE32. SE,Ac7
Skutterskelfe Hall (NR)	L84	NZ 483 071	1N32, note. 5N29. 29N9
Slaidburn (WR)	Cr59	SD 710 521	30W37
Sledmere (ER)	Th14	SE 930 645	5E72. 28W40. SE,Th7
Sleningford (WR)	Bu1	SE 277 776	2W8, note. SW,Bu48
Slingsby (NR)	Ma55	SE 696 749	5N48. 23N24. SN,Ma23
Great Smeaton (NR)	A10;CtA40	NZ 348 044	1Y2. 6N10. SN,A1 SN,CtA10

	Map	Grid	Text
[Kirk and Little] Smeaton (WR)	O25 O24	(SE 520 166 (SE 523 168	9W47, note. 9W48. SW,O8
Little Smeaton (NR)	A13	NZ 346 035	1Y2, note. 1N116. SN,A1;3
Snainton (NR)	D34	SE 919 821	1Y4. 8N13. 13N14. 28W27. SN,D13
Snaith (WR)	O11	SE 640 221	9W26. 29W10;25
Low Snaygill (WR)	Cr91	SD 994 497	1W73, note. SW,Cr2
Sneaton (NR)	L77	NZ 893 078	4N1. SN,L3
Snitertun (WR)			9W18, note. SW,Sk12
Snydale (WR)	Ag6	SE 400 215	9W97. SW,Ag3
Solberge (NR)	CtA131	SE 354 892	6N28, note. SN,CtA13
Sotleie (WR)			30W37, note
Southburn (ER)	Dr9	SE 988 544	1Y8. SE,Dr3
Southcoates (ER)	Mid40	TA 124 303	2E35, note. 14E49. CE52. SE,Mid3. SE,Hol25
Southorpe (ER)	No23	TA 196 463	14E7, note. SE,Bt4 note. SE,Hol12
Southowram (WR)	M33	SE 112 236	9W143, note. SW,M10
Sowerby (near Thirsk) (NR)	Bi16	SE 431 813	1Y1. 1N111. SN,Bi7
'Sowerby' (in Whitby) (NR)			4N1, note. SN,L4
Sowerby (WR)	M30	SE 041 233	1Y15
Sowerby under Cotcliffe (NR)	A37	SE 412 936	1Y2, note. 1N133. SN,A1;9
Spaldington (ER)	He6	SE 759 335	5E8. 15E3. 21E5. SE,He7
Spaunton (NR)	Ma4	SE 723 898	8N4. SN,Ma13
Speeton (ER)	Hu5	TA 151 749	1Y11. 5E50. SE,Hu7
Spennithorne (NR)	CtA114	SE 137 889	6N102. SN,CtA31
Spofforth (WR)	Bu107	SE 364 510	13W33. SW,Bu41
Sproatley (ER)	Mid36	TA 194 343	14E1;4;52. CE43. SE,Th13. SE,Hol3;8;26
Sprotbrough (WR)	Sf50	SE 539 020	1W20. 10W23. SW,Sf15
Sproxton (NR)	Ma20	SE 613 815	1N77. SN,Ma16
Stackhouse (WR)	Cr12	SD 814 656	30W32
Stainborough Castle (WR)	St34	SE 315 030	9W79, note. SW,St10
Stainburn (WR)	Bu90	SE 247 485	1W51. SW,Bu38
Stainforth (near Settle) (WR)	Cr11	SD 820 673	30W1;4.
Stainforth (near Thorne) (WR)	Sf34	SE 643 119	12W1;21. CW13
Stainland (WR)	M35	SE 077 193	SW,M11, note
'East' Stainley (WR)			2W8, note. SW,Bu48, note
North Stainley (WR)	Bu10; H6	SE 286 770	2W8. 5W38. SW,Bu14 note. SW,Bu48. SW,H9
South Stainley (WR)	Bu48; H26	SE 306 631	1Y18–19. 2W13. SW,Bu14 note. SW,Bu18. SW,Bu48 note. SW,H3
Stainsby Hall (NR)	L24	NZ 464 151	4N3, note. SN,L37
'Stainton' (in Stanghow) (NR)			1N6, note. 5N12. 31N8. SN,L15, note
Stainton (near Thornaby on Tees) (NR)	L42	NZ 480 140	4N3. 11N10;12. SN,L15 note. SN,L34
Stainton (WR)	Sf77	SE 555 936	10W3;5. SW,Sf3;4
Staintondale (NR)	D1	SE 990 984	1Y3, note. SN,L15 note. SN,D2
Little Stainton (WR)	Cr52	SD 891 530	1W73, note. 30W25. SW,Cr4
High Stakesby (NR)	L72	NZ 885 107	4N1, note. SN,L5
Stancil (WR)	Sf46	SK 608 959	CW18, note
Stanley (WR)	Ag3	SE 344 229	1Y15, note. SW,Ag11
Stansfield (WR)	M26	SD 946 249	1Y15, note
Stanwick (NR)	CtA31	((NZ 185 114	6N1, note. 6N8. SN,CtA7; 9, note
Stanwick, another (NR)	CtA31	(	6N1, note. SN,CtA7;9, note
Stapleton (NR)	CtA35	NZ 264 123	6N1;5. SN,CtA3;8
Stapleton (WR)	O21	SE 514 197	9W50, note. SW,O9
Starbotton (WR)	Cr7	SD 953 747	30W5

	Map	Grid	Text
Startforth (NR)	CtA7	NZ 047 159	6N18. SN,CtA11
Staveley (WR)	Bu45	SE 362 626	28W6. SW,Bu14, note
Staxton (ER)	Hu1	TA 016 790	1Y11. 1E18. SE,Hu8
Stearsby (NR)	B21	SE 611 715	23N27. SN,B26
Steeton (WR)	Cr110	SE 034 443	21W15, note
Steeton Hall (WR)	An25	SE 532 441	13W7, note. 25W1. CW24; 27;37. SW,An4–5
Stei(n)torp (ER)			5E34, note. SE,Sn5
Stema(i)nesbi (NR)			5N32, note. 29N10. SN,D3
Stillingfleet (ER)	P17	SE 593 409	1E11a. 6W5. 23E11. 24E2. SE,P5
Stillington (NR)	B75	SE 583 678	2N21. SN,B18
Stiltons Farm (NR)	Ma18	SE 598 845	1N79, note. 5N49. SN,Ma18
Stittenham (NR)	B36	SE 679 676	5N53, note. SN,B3
Stock (WR)	Cr77	SD 867 490	30W16
Stockton (WR)	Sk9	SE 335 454	1W11, note. SW,Sk14
Stockton on the Forest (NR)	B62	SE 656 560	C24. 6W4. SN,Y3
Stokesley (NR)	L57	NZ 525 085	29N8. SN,L40
Stonegrave (NR)	Ma35	SE 655 778	2N15. 16N1. CN2. SN,Ma21
Storkhill (ER)	Mid2	TA 048 420	2E22, note. SE,Th14
Stotfold (WR)	Sf18	SE 472 063	5W18, note. 10W33. SW,Sf28;30
Stratesergum (WR)			13W39, note
Streetthorpe (Edenthorpe) (WR)	Sf39	SE 621 066	12W1, note. 12W27. CW14
Strensall (NR)	B65	SE 630 607	2N27. SN,B15
Stubham (WR)	Ge3	SE 115 485	2W4, note. SW,Sk2
Stub House (WR)	Sk16	SE 302 435	1W15, note. SW,Sk15
Studley Roger (WR)	Bu20	SE 290 700	2W8. SW,Bu47
Studley Royal (WR)	Bu19	SE 277 701	13W22. 28W12. 29W33. SW,Bu21
Sturton Grange (WR)	Sk49	SE 422 332	9W4–5. SW,Sk5–6
Stutton (WR)	BA8	SE 479 414	13W2. 25W28. CW3. SW,BA4–5
Sudcniton, Sudnicton (ER)			5E65, note. SE,Ac9
Suffield (NR)	D14	SE 984 906	13N13. SN,D8
Old Sunderlandwick (ER)	Dr10	TA 010 548	1E5, note. 28W26. SE,Dr6
Susacres (WR)	Bu55	SE 308 610	1Y19. 25W26. 31W3, note. SW,Bu18
Suthauuic, Sutheuuic (WR)			2W8, note. SW,H1
Sutton (near Burghwallis) (WR)	O36	SE 550 123	9W41, note. SW,O5
Sutton (near Keighley) (WR)	Cr108	SE 007 442	1W69
Sutton Grange (ER)	Sc9	SE 794 704	1E37–38, note. 2B18. 15E11. 29E15. SE,Sc1–3
Sutton Grange (WR)	Bu11	SE 283 738	2W8. SW,Bu48
Sutton Howgrave (NR)	CtA176; H3	SE 316 791	3Y9. 6N143. SW,H2;4. SN,CtA33 note. SN,CtA39
Sutton on Hull (ER)	Mid39	TA 117 329	2E34. 14E1;46. SE,Mid2. SE,Hol1;25
Sutton on the Forest (NR)	B17	SE 583 647	1Y1. 1N97–98. SN,B12;20
Sutton under Whitestone Cliffe (NR)	Bi15	SE 481 825	23N8, note. 23N9
Sutton upon Derwent (ER)	P13	SE 705 473	5E44. 13E12. SE,P3–4
High Sutton (NR)	CtA166	SE 203 825	6N115;118. SN,CtA33, note. SN,CtA34
Low Swainby (NR)	CtA155; H1	SE 339 856	6N152, note. SN,CtA42
'Swarthorpe' (NR)	CtA165	SE 203 832	6N114, note. SN,CtA33
Swaythorpe (ER)	Bt9	TA 037 690	26E9, note. SE,Bt7
Swetton (WR)	Bu6	SE 189 732	28W18. SW,Bu24
Swillington (WR)	Sk65	SE 385 305	9W1, note. 9W3. SW,Sk4–5
Swinden (WR)	Cr42	SE 861 543	13W44
Swine (ER)	Mid22	TA 134 358	2A2. SE,Th12
Swinton (near Malton) (NR)	Ma60	SE 757 731	1N68. SN,Ma7

	Map	Grid	Text
Swinton (near Masham) (NR)	CtA170	SE 211 797	6N118. SN,CtA34
Swinton (WR)	Sf63	SK 453 991	10W17. 21W2. SW,Sf10;27
Tadcaster (WR)	BA10	SE 485 435	13W1. CW3;5. SW,BA12
East Tanfield (NR)	CtA173; H5	SE 289 779	5W38, note. 6N139. SW,H9. SN,CtA38
West Tanfield (NR)	CtA172	SE 268 790	6N140. SN,CtA39
Tankersley (WR)	St37	SK 348 997	5W33. SW,St9
Tanshelf (WR)	O14	SE 458 221	9W64, note. 9W78-84;96. SW,O15
Tansterne (ER)	Mid27	TA 222 375	14E2, note. SE,Hol5
Tanton (NR)	L48	NZ 523 106	1N30. 5N28. 29N9. 31N5. SN,L37-38
Terrington (NR)	B30	SE 672 707	5N54-55. 6N162. 8N20. SN,B5-6
'Tharlesthorpe' (ER)			2A1, note. SE,Th12
Theakston (NR)	CtA152	SE 301 856	6N151. SN,CtA41
Thimbleby (NR)	A31	SE 449 954	1Y2. SN,A1
Thirkleby (NR)	Bi24	SE 478 786	23N1
Thirkleby Manor (ER)	Th10	⎰	2B18, note. 15E15. SE,Th5, note
Thirkleby Manor, another (ER)	Th10	⎱ SE 920 687	2B18 note. 5E68. SE,Th5, note
Thirley Cotes (NR)	D2	SE 975 950	1Y3. SN,D2
Thirn (NR)	CtA162	SE 216 858	6N129. SN,CtA37
Thirsk (NR)	Bi12	SE 427 823	1N112. 23N5. SN,Bi6
Thirtleby (ER)	Mid25	TA 176 347	14E6. SE,Hol11
Thixendale (ER)	Ac12	SE 842 610	5E67. 26E5-6. SE,Ac11
Tholthorpe (NR)	B7	SE 475 669	2N25. SN,B24
(Upper)thong. See Upperthong			
Thoralby (NR)	CtA98	SE 000 867	6N84. SN,CtA26
Thoralby Hall (ER)	Ac21	SE 770 585	29E20, note. SE,Ac6
Thoraldby Farm (NR)	L85	NZ 492 072	1N33, note. 29N9. SN,L39
Thoresby (NR)	CtA102	SE 030 900	6N89, note. 6N92. SN,B22 note. SN,CtA27-28
Thorganby (ER)	How1	SE 689 416	16E1-2. SE,How11
Thorlby (WR)	Cr88	SD 966 528	1W73. SW,Cr2
Thormanby (NR)	Bi31	SE 496 749	1Y1. 11N11 note. 11N16. SN,Bi1
Thornaby (NR)	L17	NZ 450 176	1N21. 4N3. 11N11, note. 31N5. SN,L36
Thornborough (WR)	Bu62	SE 420 586	28W5. SW,Bu5
Thorne (WR)	Sf36	SE 689 132	12W1;24
Thorner (WR)	Sk42	SE 377 403	9W12. CW1. SW,Sk8
Thorngumbald (ER)	So11	TA 206 265	14E1. SE,Hol3
Thornhill (WR)	Ag21	SE 249 188	9W115. SW,Ag5
Thornholme (ER)	Bt16	TA 115 636	1Y14. 31E1. SE,Bt4
Thornthorpe (ER)	Ac4	SE 782 672	31E7, note
Thornton (ER)	C1	SE 759 452	15E9. SE,C10
Thornton (NR)	L41	NZ 478 137	4N3. 11N12. SN,L34, note
Thornton (WR)	M9	SE 101 327	9W131;144. SW,M7
Thornton Bridge (NR)	H13	SE 430 714	28W32, note. SW,H6
Thornton (Cowling) (NR)	CtA146	SE 237 876	6N128, note. SN,CtA36
Thornton Dale (NR)	D28	SE 838 831	1Y4. 1N48. 8N15. 31N8. SN,L34 note. SN,D15-16
Thornton Fields (NR)	L10	NZ 614 181	1N11. SN,L20
Thornton in Craven (WR)	Cr83	SD 901 483	13W43. 30W19
Thornton in Lonsdale (WR)	Am66	SD 679 737	1W72
Thornton le Beans (NR)	A43	SE 395 903	1Y2. SN,A1
Thornton le Clay (NR)	B45	SE 685 651	5N61. 6N162. 11N15. SN,B9-10, note
Thornton le Moor (NR)	A49	SE 389 881	11N20. SN,A9
Thornton le Street (NR)	A52	SE 414 862	1Y2. SN,B9 note. SN,A1

	Map	Grid	Text
Thornton Riseborough (NR)	Ma26	SE 747 826	1N58, note. SN,Ma1
Thornton Rust (NR)	CtA92	SD 973 888	6N81. SN,CtA26
Thornton Steward (NR)	CtA144	SE 175 870	6N110;112. SN,CtA32
Thornton Watlass (NR). See also (Thornton) Watlass	CtA161	SE 232 852	6N125, note. SN,CtA36
Bishop Thornton (WR)	Bu31	SE 263 635	2W7. SW,Bu46
Old Thornville Hall. See 'Little Cattal'			
Thorp Arch (WR)	An30	SE 437 460	25W8. SW,Sf37 note. SW,An8
Thorp Perrow (NR)	CtA149	SE 262 855	6N127, note. SN,B20 note. SN,CtA36
Thorpe (WR)	Cr24	SE 013 618	25W32. 29W42, note
Thorpe Audlin (WR)	O26	SE 480 158	9W46. SW,Sf37 note. SW,O6
Thorpe Bassett (ER)	Sc4	SE 858 734	1E45. SE,Bt4 note. SE,Sc9
'Thorpefield' (in Irton) (NR)			13N10, note. SN,L16 note. SN,D6
Thorpefield (in Sowerby) (NR)	Bi19	SE 419 794	23N6, note
Thorpe Hall (ER)	Bt12	TA 110 680	SE,Bt4, note
Thorpe Hall (NR)	CtA14	NZ 104 141	6N1, note. SN,B20 note. SN,CtA5
Thorpe Hesley (WR)	Sf66	SK 378 960	SW,Sk10 note. SW,Sf16–17, note
Thorpe Hill (ER). See Welwick Thorpe			
Thorpe Hill (in Sand Hutton near York) (NR)	B52	SE 717 595	23N29
Thorpe Hill (in Sutton on the Forest) (NR)	B18	SE 592 647	1Y1, note. SN,B20, note
Thorpe Hill (WR)	Bu70	SE 455 591	28W4. SW,Sf37 note. SW,Bu1–2
Thorpe le Street (ER)	P23	SE 837 440	1Y7 note. 21E12. CE28. SE,P3
Thorpe le Willows (NR)	Bi37	SE 573 766	1N108, note. SN,B20 note. SN,Bi2
Thorpe Lidget (ER)	How22	SE 765 297	3Y4. SE,C4 note. SE,How4
Thorpe on the Hill (WR)	M54	SE 316 269	9W119. SW,Sf37 note. SW,M2
Thorpe Salvin (WR)	Sf118	SK 520 811	10W1. SW,Sk10 note. SW,Sf2
Thorpe Stapleton (WR)	Sk60	SE 341 306	9W17, note. SW,Sk10, note
Thorpe Underwood (WR)	Bu69	SE 463 592	16W6, note. SW,Bu1
Thorpe Willoughby (WR)	BA27	SE 579 313	9W20. SW,Sk10 note. SW,BA5
Fyling Thorpe (NR)	L80	NZ 943 050	4N1, note. SN,L1
(Kettle)thorpe. See Kettlethorpe			
Kilton Thorpe (NR)	L22	NZ 692 176	1N8. 5N15. SN,L16, note
(Lang)thorpe. See Langthorpe			
(Middle)thorpe. See Middlethorpe			
(Mins)thorpe. See Minsthorpe			
(Moor)thorpe. See Moorthorpe			
(Nor)thorpe. See Northorpe			
(Nun)thorpe. See Nunthorpe			
(Ouse)thorpe Farm. See Ousethorpe Farm			
(Pains)thorpe. See Painsthorpe			
(Palla)thorpe. See Pallathorpe			
(Pinchin)thorpe Hall. See Pinchinthorpe Hall			
(Pock)thorpe. See Pockthorpe			
(Rais)thorpe. See Raisthorpe			
(Scaggle)thorpe. See Scagglethorpe			
'(Scaw)thorpe'. See Scawthorpe			
Scotton Thorpe (WR)			29W19, note. 31W3. SW,Bu15, note

	Map	Grid	Text
(Shipton)thorpe. See Shiptonthorpe			
(Sou)thorpe. See Southorpe			
(Thol)thorpe. See Tholthorpe			
(Thorn)thorpe. See Thornthorpe			
(Tib)thorpe. See Tibthorpe			
(Tow)thorpe. See Towthorpe			
Welwick Thorpe (Thorpe Hill) (ER)	So30	TA 329 218	2A1, note. SE,Bt4 note. SE,Th11
Threshfield (WR)	Cr20	SD 989 637	1W57. 21W15
Thrintoft (NR)	CtA126	SE 320 930	6N27. SN,CtA13
Throapham (WR)	Sf114	SK 529 869	10W1. SW,Sf2
Thrybergh (WR)	Sf80	SK 469 954	13W10. SW,Sf26
Thurgoland (WR)	St40	SE 290 009	9W78. SW,St10
Thurlstone (WR)	St26	SE 232 037	9W86. SW,St11
Thurnscoe (WR)	Sf16	SE 450 056	5W18. 10W28. 13W7. SW,Sf20;30
Thurstonland (WR)	Ag35	SE 164 103	SW,Ag14, note
Thwing (ER)	Bt7	TA 049 702	1Y14. 1E33;35. 31E1–2. SE,Bt6
Tibthorpe (ER)	Dr7	SE 960 555	1Y8. 1E6. 29E2. 31E3. SE,Dr3;6
Tickton (ER)	Mid3	TA 065 419	2E20. SE,Th14
'Tidover' (WR)	Bu109	SE 335 491	13W28, note. SW,Bu36
Timble (WR)	Bu83	SE 180 529	1Y18, note. SW,Bu29
Nether Timble (WR)	Ge1	SE 189 524	2W4, note. SW,Sk2
Tinsley (WR)	Sf94	SK 404 906	10W8. SW,Sf6–7
Tocketts Farm (NR)	L20	NZ 619 175	5N20, note. SN,L20
Tockwith (WR)	An12	SE 466 523	25W11
Todwick (WR)	Sf114	SK 495 846	5W16. SW,Sf30
Toftes (WR)			10W19, note. 19W2. SW,Sf11–12
Tollerton (NR)	B11	SE 509 640	2N23. SN,B23
Tollesby (NR)	L25	NZ 510 160	1N27, note. 11N8. 29N7. 31N5. SN,L32
Tong (WR)	M14	SE 219 306	9W127. SW,M4
Topcliffe (NR)	Bi27	SE 400 761	13N17. SN,Bi4
Toresbi (NR)			16N2, note. SN,B22, note
Torp (in Etton) (ER)			23E7, note. SE,C4 note. SE,Sn5
Torp(i) (in Thorpe le Street) (ER)			1Y7, note. SE,Wei6
Torp (in Tibthorpe) (ER)			1E7, note. SE,C4 note. SE,Dr6
Torp (in Croft) (NR)			6N17, note. SN,B20 note. SN,CtA11
Torp (in Pickhill) (NR)			3Y9, note. SW,Bu15 note. SW H5
Toschetorp (ER)			5E9, note
Totfled (ER)			15E2, note. SE,He6
Totleys Farm (ER)	So16	TA 239 274	14E11, note. SE,Hol15;18
Toulston (WR)	BA4	SE 452 440	5W7, note. 25W29–30. CW3. SW,BA3;8
Towthorpe (near Fimber) (ER)	Sc19	SE 901 628	1E40–41, note. 5E60. SE,Sc7
Towthorpe (in Londesborough) (ER)	Wei6	SE 867 439	2B9, note. SE,Wei6
Towthorpe (NR)	B66	SE 623 588	2N28. SN,B15
Towton (WR)	BA14	SE 484 395	SW,BA5, note
Treeton (WR)	Sf107	SK 430 878	5W20. SW,Sf32
Troutsdale (NR)	D11	SE 931 899	1N45, note. SN,D13
Tudworth Green (WR)	Sf37	SE 687 102	12W1, note. 12W25. CW13
Tunstall (ER)	So7	TA 305 319	14E2;4. SE,Hol4;9
Tunstall (NR)	CtA79	SE 217 958	6N52;54. SN,CtA19–20
Tunstall Farm (NR)	L47	NZ 527 120	1N29, note. SN,L37

	Map	Grid	Text
Turodebi (ER)			1Y7, note. SE,Th5
'Twislebrook' (NR)			6N118, note. SN,CtA34
Ugglebarnby (NR)	L76	NZ 879 071	4N1. SN,L3
Ughill (WR)	Sf89	SK 258 904	10W36. SW,Sf36
Ugthorpe (NR)	L63	NZ 798 111	1N3. SN,L10
Ulchiltorp (ER)			2B18, note
Ulleskelf (WR)	BA12	SE 519 400	2W6, note. SW,BA2
Ulley (WR)	Sf106	SK 465 875	5W24. SW,Sf33
Ulrome (ER)	No4	TA 161 567	14E27. SE,Hol21
Uncleby (ER)	Ac16	SE 811 591	1E51. 8E1. SE,Ac3
Upleatham (NR)	L6	NZ 632 194	4N2. SN,L20
Upperthong (WR)	Ag47	SE 128 084	1Y15, note. SW,Ag12
Upsall (WR)	Bi3	SE 452 872	5N75–76. SN,Bi8, note
Upsall Hall (NR)	L27	NZ 560 160	1N14, note. 29N4. 31N6. SN,L26
Upsland (NR)	CtA174	SE 304 798	6N141. SN,Bi8 note. SN,CtA39
Upton (ER)	No8	TA 143 543	14E8
Upton (WR)	O29	SE 475 132	9W45. SW,O7
Utley (WR)	Cr111	SE 053 428	1W63
Waddington (WR)	Cr65	SD 728 438	30W37
Wadsley (WR)	Sf90	SK 321 906	10W36. SW,Sf36
Wadsworth (WR)	M24	SD 999 284	1Y15, note
Wadworth (WR)	Sf74	SE 568 970	10W2. CW18–19. SW,Sf3
Wakefield (WR)	Ag8	SE 333 208	1Y15–17;25–26. CW23. SW,Ag9. SW,M14
Walden Stubbs (WR)	O23	SE 550 168	9W44. SW,O6
Waldershelf (WR)	Sf87	SK 269 962	1W22, note. SW,Sf36
Wales (WR)	Sf112	SK 477 836	5W23. 10W1. SW,Sf2;32
Walkingham Hill (WR)	Bu57	SE 347 619	1Y19, note. SW,Bu16
Walkington (ER)	Wel2	SE 996 370	2B4. 3Y1. 29E24. CE33. SE,Wel1;5;7
'Walton' (NR)			8N27, note. 23N20. SN,Ma13
Walton (near Wakefield) (WR)	Ag25	SE 354 170	SW,Ag3, note
Walton (near Wetherby) (WR)	An29	SE 442 478	25W9. CW34;41. SW,An9
Walton Head (WR)	Bu111	SE 318 496	13W28, note. SW,Bu36
Hutton Wandesley (WR)	An10	SE 509 503	25W12, note. SW,An11
Waplington Hall (ER)	P20	SE 775 465	1Y10, note. SE,P2
Warlaby (NR)	A42; CtA130	SE 349 914	1Y2. 6N35. SN,A1. SN,CtA14
Warley (WR)	M29	SE 058 248	1Y15, note
Warmfield (WR)	Ag7	SE 374 210	2W1, note. SW,Ag1
Warmsworth (WR)	Sf49	SE 543 004	5W8. 12W1;18. SW,Sf21
Warter (ER)	Wa16	SE 869 504	1Y7. 5E32. 13E3;9. SE,Wa1
Warthill (NR)	B61	SE 675 552	2N18. 5N64. SN,B13
Waruelestorp (NR)			5N68, note
Wassand Hall (ER)	No24	TA 174 461	14E38, note. SE,Hol23
Wath (near Hovingham) (NR)	Ma51	SE 677 750	23N24, note
Wath (near East Tanfield) (NR)	CtA177	SE 325 771	6N144. SN,CtA39
Wath upon Dearne (WR)	Sf60	SE 433 008	10W17. 29W6. SW,Sf10;16
Thornton Watless (NR). See also (Thornton) Watless	CtA160	SE 242 836	6N126, note. SN,CtA36
Watton (ER)	Sn7	TA 022 497	5E29. 29E26. SE,Sn2
Wauldby (ER)	He10; Wel10	SE 968 297	2B3, note. 15E2. SE,He5. SE,Wel4
Wawne (ER)	Mid7	TA 091 368	2E18. 14E11. SE,Th14. SE Hol15
Waxholme (ER)	So24	TA 327 297	14E4;11;17. CE47. SE,Hol8;17;19
Weardley (WR)	Sk6	SE 297 447	28W30, note. CW6. SW,Sk3
Weaverthorpe (ER)	Th6	SE 966 711	2B18. SE,Th4

	Map	Grid	Text
Weel (ER)	Mid6	TA 064 394	2E19. SE,Th14
Weeton (ER)	So35	TA 355 201	2E23. SE,So1
Weeton (WR)	Bu114	SE 286 468	1W48. 28W29. 29W22. SW,Bu34
Little Weighton (WR)	Wel8	SE 987 338	23E3–4. SE,Wel3
Market Weighton (ER)	Wei10	SE 877 417	1Y6. 11E6–8. SE,Wei1
Welburn (near Bulmer) (NR)	B38	SE 719 680	5N54. SN,Ma12 note. SN,B4
Welburn (near Kirby Moorside) (NR)	Ma12	SE 680 846	1N73. 8N26. 23N21. SN,Ma12, note
Welbury (NR)	A16	NZ 399 022	1N123. 31N3. SN,A5
Welham (ER)	Sc10	SE 782 696	15E10–11. 23E15. SE,Sc2
Well (NR)	CtA159	SE 268 820	6N120;127. SN,CtA35
Welton (ER)	Wel13	SE 959 273	3Y1–2;8. 5E6;16;32–33; 37. 11E6. CE11;24;33. SE,Wel1
Welwick (ER)	So31	TA 341 210	2E23. SE,So1
Wensley (ER)	CtA104	⎧SE 092 895	6N92, note. SN,CtA29
Wensley, another (NR)	CtA104	⎩	6N92, note. SN,CtA29
Wentworth (WR)	Sf65	SK 384 983	10W17. SW,Sf10;16;18
Weslide, Westlid(um), Westlidun, Westude (Kirkleatham) (NR)	L1	NZ 593 218	1N12, note. 4N2. 5N21. 13N5. SN,L21–22
'Westerby' (WR)			9W96, note. SW,Ag2
'Westhouse' (NR)			1Y2, note. SN,A1
Weston (WR)	Bu88	SE 178 470	8W1. SW,Bu33
Westwick (WR)	Bu34	SE 349 663	2W7, note. SW,Bu46
Wetherby (WR)	Bu121	SE 404 482	13W36. 24W19. SW,Bu43
Wetwang (ER)	Wa14	SE 932 590	2B10. SE,Wa3
Wharram le Street (ER)	Sc16	SE 864 659	5E59. SE,Sc4
Wharram Percy (ER)	Ac13	SE 858 646	1E54, note. 29E21. SE,Ac10
'Wheatcroft' (WR)			9W13, note. SW,Sk8
Wheatley (WR)	Sf28	SE 585 043	5W26–27;30. SW,Sf34
Wheldale (WR)	O1	SE 452 267	9W56, note. SW,O12
Wheldrake (ER)	P14	SE 682 449	13E13. CE30. SE,P7
Whenby (NR)	B26	SE 630 698	SN,B18, note
Whipley Hall (WR)	Bu51	SE 265 609	1Y18, note. 24W14. 29W34. SW,Bu25
Whiston (WR)	Sf96	SK 448 901	5W19. 12W1;17. SW,Sf31
Whitby (NR)	L74	NZ 901 112	4N1. CN1. SN,L2
Whitley (WR)	O12	SE 561 213	29W10. SW,O16
Lower Whitley (WR)	Ag20	SE 221 179	9W116, note. SW,Ag6
Whitwell on the Hill (NR)	B39	SE 724 658	5N65. SN,B14
Whitwood (WR)	Ag2	SE 403 233	9W32;99. SW,Ag2
Whixley (WR)	Bu71	SE 442 582	13W18;37. 25W22. SW,Bu6
Whorlton (NR)	L90	NZ 483 024	5N29, note. SN,L44
Wibsey (WR)	M11	SE 151 301	9W131, note. 9W144. SW,M7
Wickersley (WR)	Sf97	SK 478 916	10W6. SW,Sf4
Widdington Hall (WR)	Bu67	SE 498 598	29W21, note. 31W2. SW,Bu2
Wide Open Farm (NR)	B74	SE 579 578	2N25, note. SN,B24
Wiganthorpe Hall (NR)	B29	SE 662 723	1N89, note. 5N55. 8N21. SN,B6
Wigginton (NR)	B70	SE 599 585	C35. SN,Y8
Wigglesworth (WR)	Cr29	SD 808 568	30W4;9–10
Wighill (WR)	An28	SE 475 469	18W3, note. SW,An9
Wighill Park (WR)	An15	SE 468 486	18W3, note. SW,An9
Wike (WR)	Sk14	SE 336 424	1W13, note. SW,Sk16
Wildon Grange (NR)	Bi33	SE 516 780	23N3, note
Wildthorpe (WR)	Sf52	SE 510 010	10W21, note. SW,Sf14
Willerby (near Hull) (ER)	He11	TA 033 301	SE,He11, note

	Map	*Grid*	*Text*
Willerby (near Hunmanby) (ER)	Bt1	TA 008 791	1Y11. SE,Bt9
Willitoft (ER)	He5	SE 743 349	5E8. 15E6. 21E5. SE,He10–11
Wilsden (WR)	M1	SE 091 366	1W65
Wilsic Hall (WR)	Sf75	SK 564 959	12W1, note. 12W8. CW10
Wilsill (WR)	Bu26	SE 181 647	2W7, note. SW,Bu47
Wilsthorpe (ER)	Hu18	TA 170 640	1Y11, note. 14E54. SE,Hu3–4
Wilstrop Hall (WR)	An2	SE 484 542	25W11, note. SW,An10
Wilton (near Eston) (NR)	L5	NZ 583 197	5N22. 29N1-2. SN,L22–23, note
Wilton (near Pickering) (NR)	D30	SE 861 827	1Y4. SN,L22 note. SN,D12
Bishop Wilton (ER)	P2	SE 798 552	2B11. SE,P6
Winestead (ER)	So20	TA 298 237	2A1. 14E2. SE,Th10. SE,Hol7
Winksley (WR)	Bu13	SE 252 712	28W13. SW,Bu22
'Winkton' (ER)	No1	TA 150 590	14E24, note. SE,Hol21
Winterburn (WR)	Cr44	SD 935 586	30W7
Winton (NR)	A28	SE 410 966	3Y18, note. SN,A6
Wintringham (ER)	Sc5	SE 887 731	15E12. SE,Sc8
Withernsea (ER)	So26	TA 342 276	14E4. SE,Hol7
Withernwick (ER)	Mid14	TA 193 404	2E32. 14E5;40. SE,Mid2. SE,Hol11;24
East Witton (NR)	CtA143	SE 146 860	6N92, note. 6N111;124. SN,CtA28
West Witton (NR)	CtA103	SE 061 884	6N92, note. SN,CtA28
Wolfreton (ER)	He13	TA 036 294	15E2. SE,He6
Wombwell (WR)	Sf56	SE 396 031	10W19. 19W1. 29W4. SW,Sf11
Wombleton (NR)	Ma11	SE 669 838	2N8. SN,Ma12
Womersley (WR)	O22	SE 532 189	9W49. SW,O8
Wooldale (WR)	Ag44	SE 152 089	SW,Ag14, note
Woolley (WR)	St2	SE 319 130	1Y13
Worrall (WR)	Sf85	SK 307 921	10W36. SW,Sf36
High Worsall (NR)	A5	NZ 385 094	1N117. SN,A3
Low Worsall (NR)	A3	NZ 392 101	1N118. 31N2. SN,A3
Worsborough (WR)	St35	SE 353 035	9W77. SW,St8
Wortley (WR)	St38	SK 307 993	5W34. 29W26. SW,St8–9
Worton (NR)	CtA93	SD 955 900	6N80. SN,CtA26
Wothersome (WR)	Sk43	SE 405 426	1W3, note. SW,Sk12
Wrelton (NR)	D18	SE 766 860	1N54. SN,D19
Wressle (ER)	He7	SE 707 312	15E3, note. 21E5. SE,He6–7
Wycliffe (NR)	CtA15	NZ 116 143	6N1, note. SN,CtA5
Wyke (WR)	M32	SE 153 270	9W135. SW,M8
Wykeham (in Old Malton) (NR)	Ma47	SE 816 752	1N63. SN,Ma3
Wykeham (near Scarborough) (NR)	D38	SE 964 833	1Y3. 1N43. 31N9. SN,D8
Wykeham Hill (NR)	Ma46	SE 818 754	1N64. 2N1. SN,Ma4–5
Wyton (ER)	Mid37	TA 179 334	14E6. SE,Hol11
Yafforth (NR)	A33; CtA127	SE 344 944	1Y2. 6N33. SN,A1. SN,CtA14
Yapham (ER)	Wa8	SE 788 520	1E11. SE,Wa5
Yarm (NR)	A1	NZ 416 129	1N121. 31N2. SN,A5
Yarnwick (NR)	CtA158	SE 314 817	6N148, note. SN,CtA40
Yateholme (WR)	Ag50	SE 114 049	1Y15, note. SW,Ag12
Yeadon (WR)	Sk21	SE 207 411	1W19, note. CW2. SW,Sk17
Yearsley (NR)	Bi38	SE 585 743	23N1
Yokefleet (ER)	How33	SE 824 242	3Y4, note. SE,C10 note. SE,How2
Yokefleet Grange (ER)	C11	SE 817 321	3Y1, note. 11E5. SE,C10, note

	Map	*Grid*	*Text*
York (NR)	Y2	SE 603 521	C1–22;29;37;40. 2B2. 22W6. CE20. CW35. SN,Y1;8
Youlthorpe (ER)	P1	SE 766 556	2B11. 26E3. SE,P8
Youlton (NR)	B12	SE 490 635	2N25. SN,B23

CUMBERLAND

	Map	*Grid*	*Text*
Bootle	Am1	SD 107 883	1L6
Hougun (Millom)	Am4	SD 172 803	1L6, note
Hougenai (Millom Castle)	Am5	SD 171 813	1L6, note
Kirksanton	Am3	SD 140 808	1L6
Millom. See *Hougun*			
Millom Castle. See *Hougenai*			
Whicham	Am2	SD 134 826	1L6

LANCASHIRE

	Map	*Grid*	*Text*
Aighton	Am130	*c.* SD 67 39	1L1, note
Aldcliffe	Am98	SD 466 600	1L2
Aldingham	Am16	SD 283 710	1L8
Arkholme	Am70	SD 583 721	1L3
Aschebi			1L1, note
Ashton Hall	Am101	SD 461 573	30W39, note
Ashton on Ribble	Am167	SD 520 302	1L1
Bardsea	Am24	SD 300 745	1L6
Bare	Am91	SD 453 650	1L2
Barton	Am139	SD 515 375	1L1
Birkby Hall	Cr2	SD 376 771	23N22, note
Bispham	Am115	SD 309 401	1L1
Bolton Farm	Am19	SD 259 729	1L8, note
Bolton le Sands	Am83	SD 483 677	1L2
Borwick	Am60	SD 525 730	30W40
Broughton	Am136	SD 529 343	1L1
Broughton in Furness	Am6	SD 209 873	1L6, note
Burn Hall	Am112	SD 333 454	1L1, note
[Nether and Over] Burrow	Am62 / Am63	(SD 614 752 / (SD 616 759	1W72, note. 1L3
Cantsfield	Am68	SD 620 729	1L3
Carleton	Am116	SD 333 397	1L1
Carnforth	Am82	SD 498 705	1L2
Cartmel. See *Cherchebi*			
Caton	Am86	SD 531 645	1L4
Catterall	Am123	SD 495 426	1L1
Cherchebi (Cartmel)	Am26	SD 379 787	1L8, note
Chipping	Am126	SD 622 433	1L1
Claughton (near Garstang)	Am125	SD 530 422	1L1
Claughton (near Lancaster)	Am87	SD 566 666	1L4
Clifton	Am165	SD 467 303	1L1
Cockerham	Am106	SD 465 522	30W38
[Great and Little] Crimbles	Am109 / Am108	(SD 456 503 / (SD 461 507	1L1, note
'Crivelton'			1L6, note
Dendron	Am18	SD 246 706	1L8
Dalton in Furness	Am21	SD 231 742	1L6
Dilworth House	Am128	SD 611 372	1L1, note
Great Eccleston	Am142	SD 428 400	1L1
Little Eccleston	Am143	SD 413 398	1L1
Ellel	Am102	SD 486 560	30W39
Elswick	Am145	SD 423 382	1L1
Farleton	Am88	SD 572 671	1L5
Fishwick	Am169	SD 562 293	1L1, note
'Fordbottle'			1L6, note
Forton	Am107	SD 488 512	1L1

	Map	Grid	Text
Freckleton	Am163	SD 429 290	1L1
Garstang	Am124	SD 490 450	1L1
Gerleuuorde (Kirkby Ireleth)	Am7	SD 233 822	1L6
Gleaston	Am17	SD 255 708	1L6
Goosnargh	Am133	SD 559 369	1L1
Greenhalgh	Am153	SD 402 358	1L1
Gressingham	Am79	SD 572 699	1L3
Grimsargh	Am131	SD 584 343	1L1
Haighton Hall	Am132	SD 575 352	1L1, note
Halton	Am85	SD 503 649	1L2
Hambleton	Am118	SD 378 425	1L1
Hart Carrs	Am15	SD 255 694	1L6, note
Hawcoat. See *Hietun*			
Heaton	Am95	SD 443 602	1L2, note
Heysham	Am94	SD 415 610	1L2, note
Hietun (Hawcoat)	Am12	SD 203 720	1L6, note
Hillam	Am105	SD 452 529	1L2, note
Holker	Cr1	SD 360 772	23N22, note
Hornby	Am78	SD 585 685	1W70–71
'Hutton'			1L2, note
Inskip	Am141	SD 463 379	1L1
Ireby	Am64	SD 654 754	1L3
Kirkby Ireleth. See *Gerleuuorde*			
[Nether and Over] Kellet	Am81	(SD 505 682	1L2, note
	Am80	(SD 520 700	
'Killerwick'	Am10	SD 225 746	1L6, note
'Kirk Lancaster'. See '(Kirk) Lancaster'			
Kirkby Ireleth. See *Gerleuuorde*			
Kirkham	Am158	SD 427 323	1L1
Lancaster	Am99	SD 481 614	1L2
'Kirk Lancaster'			1L2, note
Layton	Am148	SD 320 373	1L1
Lea	Am166	SD 482 308	1L1
Lower Leck	Am51	SD 643 766	1L3, note
Leece	Am14	(SD 244 694	1L6
Leece, another	Am14		1L6, note
'Lonsdale'			30W38, note
Lytham	Am161	SD 371 271	1L1
Martin	Am8	SD 240 771	1L6, note
Marton. See Martin			
[Great and Little] Marton	Am149	(SD 328 349	1L1
	Am150	(SD 346 343	
Melling	Am71	SD 598 711	1W70–71
(St.) Michael's on Wyre. See St. Michael's on Wyre			
Middleton	Am96	SD 422 586	1L2
Mythop	Am151	SD 361 348	1L1
Newsham (near Preston)	Am137	SD 513 362	1L1
'Newsham' (in Skerton)			1L2, note
'Newton' (in Lancaster)			1L2, note
Newton (near Preston)	Am164	SD 445 306	1L1
Newton (in Whittington)	Am61	SD 598 745	1L3
High Newton	Am27	SD 401 838	1L6, note
Orgrave	Am9	SD 233 759	1L6, note
Overton	Am97	SD 434 579	1L2
Oxcliffe Hall	Am93	SD 450 619	1L2, note
Pennington	Am22	SD 262 774	1L6
[Great and Little] Plumpton	Am154	(SD 384 332	1L1, note
	Am155	(SD 379 327	
(Wood)plumpton. See Woodplumpton			
Poulton le Fylde	Am117	SD 348 394	1L1
Poulton Hall	Am92	SD 437 645	1L2, note
Preesall	Am110	SD 367 471	1L1

	Map	Grid	Text
Preese Hall	Am146	SD 377 361	1L1, note
Preston	Am168	SD 543 291	1L1
Priest Hutton	Am60	SD 530 737	1L4
Rawcliffe Hall	Am120	SD 416 417	1L1, note
Out Rawcliffe	Am119	SD 405 417	1L1, note
Upper Rawcliffe	Am121	*c.* SD 43 41	1L1, note
Ribby	Am157	SD 402 316	1L1
Ribchester	Am129	SD 649 350	1L1
Roose	Am13	SD 223 694	1L6
Rossall	Am113	SD 312 449	1L1, note
St. Michael's on Wyre	Am122	SD 461 410	1L1, note
Salwick Hall	Am158	SD 467 323	1L1, note
Scotforth	Am100	SD 480 595	30W39
Singleton	Am144	SD 383 381	1L1
Skerton	Am89	SD 472 633	1L2
Slyne	Am84	SD 477 659	1L2
Sowerby Hall (in Dalton in Furness)	Am11	SD 198 724	1L6, note
Sowerby Hall (near Preston)	Am141	SD 474 385	1L1, note
Staining	Am147	SD 346 360	1L1
Stainton	Am20	SD 248 724	1L6
Stalmine	Am111	SD 374 455	1L1
'Stapleton Terne'			1L2, note
Suntun			1L6, note
'Swainseat'			1L1, note
Tatham	Am77	SD 605 694	1L5
Thirnby Wood	Am52	SD 610 777	1L3, note
Thornton	Am114	SD 339 421	1L1
Threlfall's Farm	Am135	SD 532 357	1L1, note
[Upper and Lower] Thurnham	Am103 Am104	(SD 459 544 (SD 459 549	1L2, note
Torisholme	Am90	SD 456 637	1L2
Treales	Am159	SD 437 328	1L1, note
Tunstall	Am69	SD 607 734	1L5
Ulverston	Am23	SD 284 781	1L8
Walton Hall	Am25	SD 368 788	1L6, note
'Wart'			1L6, note
Warton (near Carnforth)	Am58	SD 498 723	1L4
Warton (near Preston)	Am162	SD 409 284	1L1, note
Weeton	Am152	SD 384 347	1L1
Wennington	Am72	SD 617 700	1W70-71. 1L5
Westby	Am156	SD 381 317	1L1
Wheatley	Am127	SD 620 398	1L1
Whittingham Hall	Am134	SD 542 360	1L1, note
Whittington	Am53	SD 601 763	1L3
Woodplumpton	Am138	SD 499 344	1L1
Yealand [Conyers and Redmayne]	Am57 Am56	(SD 507 748 (SD 502 755	30W40, note

WESTMORLAND

Barbon	Am41	SD 637 825	1L3
Beetham	Am46	SD 495 796	30W40
'Bothelford'			1L7, note
Burton	Am55	SD 530 769	1L4, note. 1L7
Casterton	Am50	SD 624 796	1L3, note
Dalton	Am54	SD 543 766	1L7, note
Farleton	Am45	SD 536 811	30W40
Helsington	Am32	*c.* SD 50 89	1L7, note
Heversham Head	Am34	SD 501 837	30W40, note
Hincaster	Am35	SD 509 847	30W40
Holme	Am47	SD 523 788	1L4, note
Hutton Roof	Am48	SD 570 783	1L3
Old Hutton	Am38	SD 564 885	1L7

	Map	Grid	Text
Kirkby (Kendal)	Am31	SD 519 929	1L7, note
Kirkby Lonsdale	Am49	SD 611 798	1L4
Levens	Am33	SD 481 867	30W40
Lupton	Am44	SD 554 811	1L4
Mansergh	Am42	SD 595 829	1L4, note
Middleton Hall	Am40	SD 626 874	1L4, note
Mint House	Am30	SD 521 943	1L7
Patton Hall	Am29	SD 547 960	1L7, note
Preston Patrick	Am43	SD 544 837	1L4, note
Preston Richard	Am37	SD 533 844	1L4, note. 30W40
Stainton	Am36	SD 523 857	1L7
Strickland Roger	Am28	SD 499 978	1L7, note

Places not in Cumberland, Lancashire, Westmorland or Yorkshire

Elsewhere in Britain
Winchester   31E1

Outside Britain
Aincourt ... Walter. Arques ... Osbern de Arches. Beauchamps ... Geoffrey. Beuvrière ... Drogo de Bevrere. Brus ... Robert. Buron ... Erneis de Burun. Bully ... Roger de Busli. Coucy ... Aubrey. Coutances ... Bishop of. Fjon ... Ulfr Fenisc. Ghent ... Gilbert. Lassy ... Ilbert de Lacy. la Guerche ... Geoffrey. Lisors ... Fulk. Mont-Canisy ... Hubert. Mortemer ... Ralph. Muneville ... Nigel. Percy ... William. Poitou ... Roger. Sourdeval ... Richard. Tosny ... Berenger; Robert. Verly ... William. Warenne ... William.

MAPS AND MAP KEYS

The boundaries of the ridings of Yorkshire (whose outer line also forms the county boundary) are marked by thick lines. Wapentake boundaries are given as dashed lines and hundred boundaries as thin lines. The only divisions shown are those definitely given in DB, whose boundaries must perforce be relatively conjectural, being based on those recorded at later dates. In view of this, varying degrees of certainty as to the lines shown have not been differentiated on these maps. Detached portions of wapentakes or hundreds are linked by arrows to the division to which they belong. Where DB does not differentiate between what are now two distinct places, both are plotted with separate numbers, but with a linking line between them and the names bracketed in the index. Places given in DB under two different wapentakes or hundreds have been given in the map keys for both divisions and are plotted using both symbols and the numbers given in the map keys, but with a linking line between them. Places marked with an asterisk in the map keys are not assigned to any individual wapentake or hundred in the text, and their allocation to a particular division has been assumed on a geographical basis. The riding ascriptions given in the map keys are those of DB, not the pre-1974 ridings as given in the index.

The letters of the National Grid 10-kilometre squares are shown on the map borders. Each four-figure square covers 1 square kilometre, or 247 acres.

MAP I

Wapentake Abbreviations

A	Allerton (NR)	L	Langbargh (NR)
Ac	Acklam (ER)	M	Morley (WR)
Ag	Agbrigg (WR)	Ma	*Manshowe* [Ryedale] (NR)
Am	Amounderness	Mid	Middle Hundred of Holderness (ER)
An	Ainsty (WR)	No	North Hundred of Holderness (ER)
B	*Bolesford* [Bulmer] (NR)	O	Osgoldcross (WR)
BA	Barkston Ash (WR)	P	Pocklington (ER)
Bi	*Gerlestre* [Birdforth] (NR)	Sc	*Scard* (ER)
Bt	Burton (ER)	Sf	Strafforth (WR)
Bu	'Burghshire' [Claro] (WR)	Sk	Skyrack (WR)
C	Cave (ER)	Sn	*Sneculf(s)cros* (ER)
CtA	land of Count Alan (NR)	So	South Hundred of Holderness (ER)
Cr	Craven (WR)	St	Staincross (WR)
D	*Dic* [Pickering Lythe] (NR)	Th	'Thorshowe' (ER)
Dr	Driffield (ER)	Tu	*Turbar* (ER)
Ge	*Gereburg* (WR)	Wa	Warter (ER)
H	Halikeld (WR)	Wei	Weighton (ER)
He	Hessle (ER)	Wel	Welton (ER)
How	Howden (ER)	Y	York
Hu	Hunthow (ER)		

MAP II

Land of Count Alan (CtA) (NR)

Achebi
105 Agglethorpe
120 Ainderby Mires
183 Ainderby Quernhow
128 Ainderby Steeple
134 Aiskew
32 Aldbrough
151 Allerthorpe Hall
78 East Appleton
Asc(h)am
Asebi
53 Aske Hall
94 Askrigg
99 Aysgarth
180 Baldersby
85 Barden
17 Barforth Hall
13 Barningham
47 Barton
135 Bedale
86 Bellerby
69 Bolton upon Swale
89 Castle Bolton
90 West Bolton
12 Brignall
66 Brompton on Swale
137 Patrick Brompton
67 Brough Hall
96 Brough Hill
21 Broughton House
153 Burneston
147 Burrill
115 Constable Burton
168 High Burton
101 West Burton
109 Caldbergh
27 Caldwell
107 Carlton (near Middleham)
30 Carlton (in Stanwick)
91 Carperby
15 Carthorpe
80 Catterick
34 Cleasby
29 Cliffe Hall
163 Clifton on Ure
64 Colburn
5 Cotherstone
110 Coverham
41 East Cowton
43 North Cowton
42 South Cowton
136 Great Crakehall
36 Croft
97 Crooksby Barn
22 Dalton
22 another Dalton
142 Danby
72 Danby Wiske
Denton(e)
50 Didderston Grange
39 Over Dinsdale Grange
58 Downholme
55 Easby
8 Egglestone Abbey
59 Ellerton Abbey
70 Ellerton on Swale
164 High Ellington
28 Eppleby
38 Eryholme
100*Eshingtons
150 Exelby
167 Fearby
123 Great Fencote
124 Little Fencote
140 Fingall
148 Firby
75 Kirkby Fleetham
26 Forcett
95 Fors Abbey
62 Fremington
84 Garriston
132 Gatenby
52 Gilling
18 Girlington Hall
61 Grinton
119 Hackforth
37 Low Hail
112 Harmby
51 Hartforth
82 East Hauxwell
83 West Hauxwell
117 Hesselton
56 *Hindrelag(he), Indrelage(e)* (Richmond)
65 Hipswell
121 Holtby Hall
118 Hornby
180 Howe
175 Howgrave
57 Hudswell
3 Hunderthwaite
116 Hunton
141 Hutton Hang
19 Hutton Magna
171 Ilton
77 Killerby Hall
71 Kiplin
156 Kirby Wiske
76 Kirkby Hall
185 Kirklington
46 Kneeton Hall
122 Langthorne
73 Great Langton
74 Little Langton
6 Lartington
25 East Layton
24 West Layton
113 Leyburn
1 Lonton
33 Manfield
60 Marrick
169 Masham
154 Maunby
179 Melmerby (near Hutton Conyers)
106 Melmerby (near Middleham)
49 Melsonby
2 Mickleton
111 Middleham
177 Middleton Quernhow
45 Middleton Tyas
10 Mortham Tower
129 Morton upon Swale
44 Moulton
Neutone
20 Newsham
138 Newton le Willows
48 Newton Morrell
133 Newton 'Picot'
Normanebi
Opetone, Opetune
Ounesbi
16 Ovington
157 Pickhill
87 Preston under Scar
181 Rainton
23 Ravensworth
88 Redmire
63 Reeth
9 Rokeby Hall
4 Romaldkirk
145 Rookwith
139 Ruswick
11 Scargill
68 Scorton
81 Scotton
108 West Scrafton
125 Scruton
Seuenetorp
184 Sinderby
54 Skeeby
40 Great Smeaton
131 Solberge
114 Spennithorne

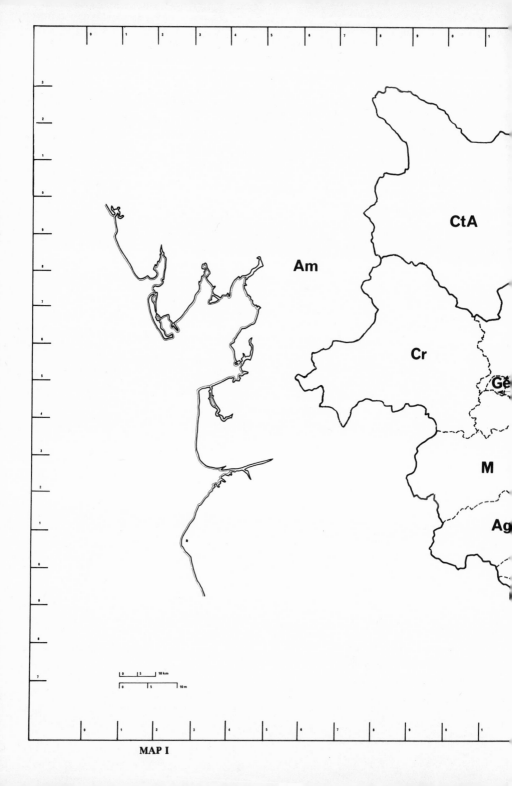

MAP I

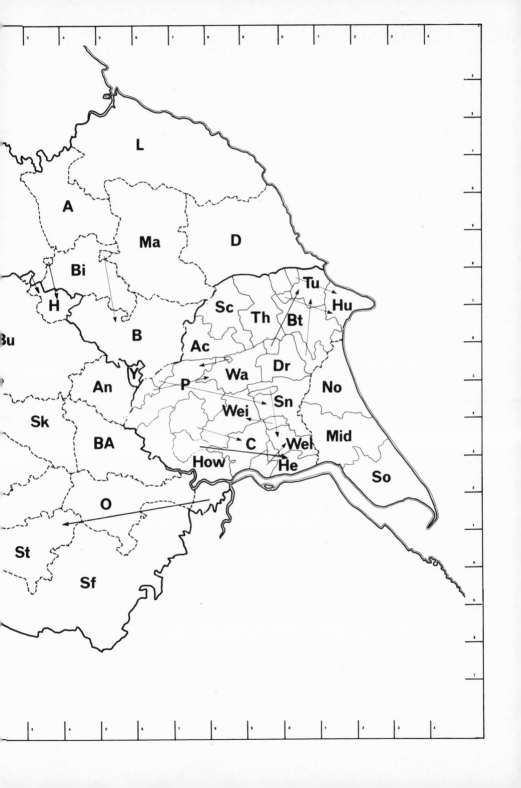

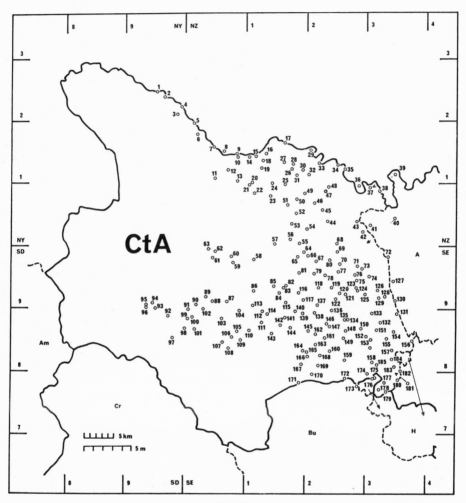

MAP II

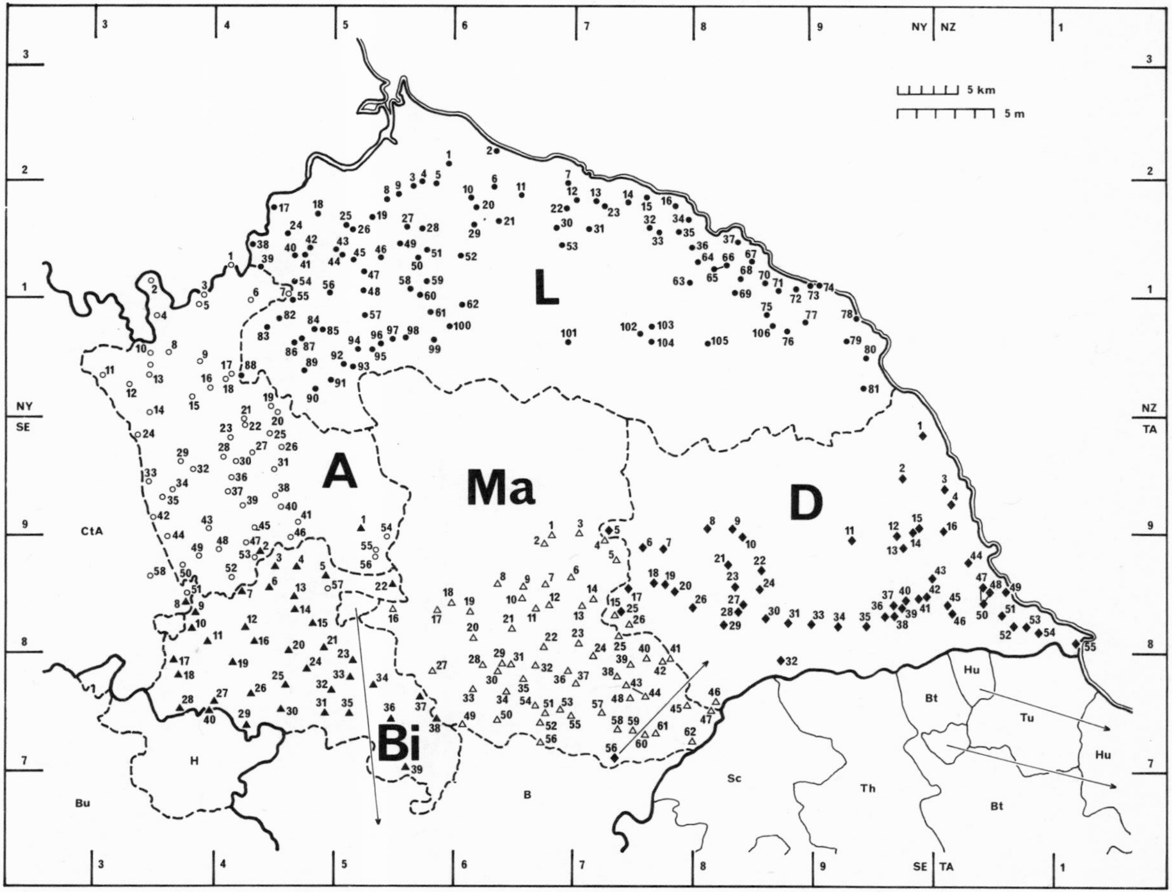

MAP III

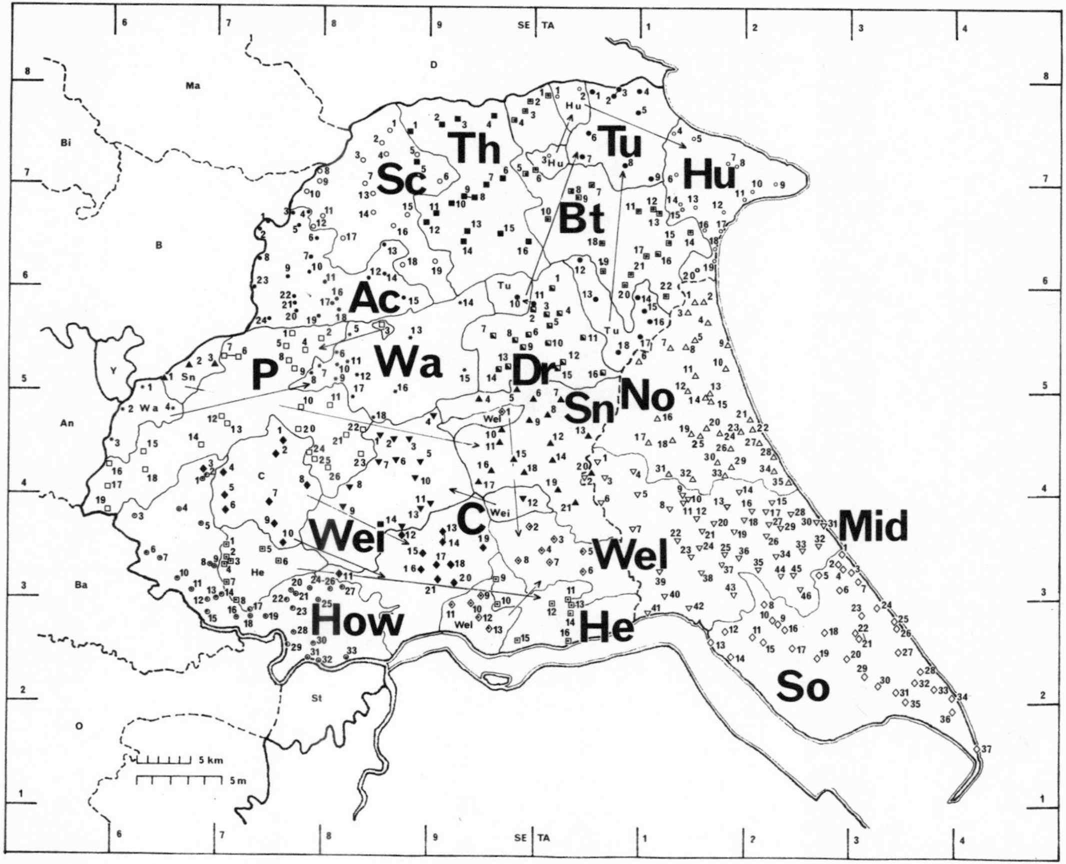

Th
Sc
Tu
Hu
Bt
Ac
Wa
P
Dr
Sn
No
C
Wei
Wel
Mid
How
He
So
Ma
Bi
B
D
Y
An
Ba
St
O
SE
TA
5 km
5 m

MAP IV

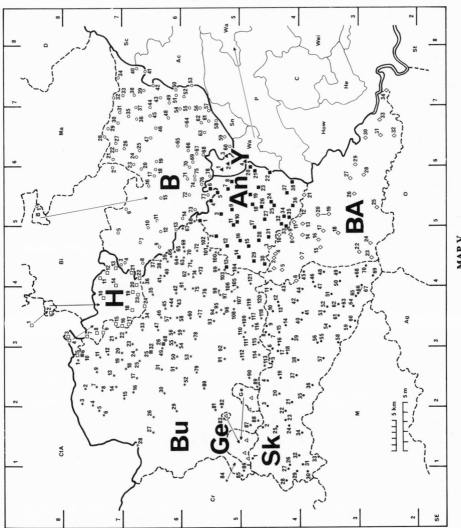

MAP V

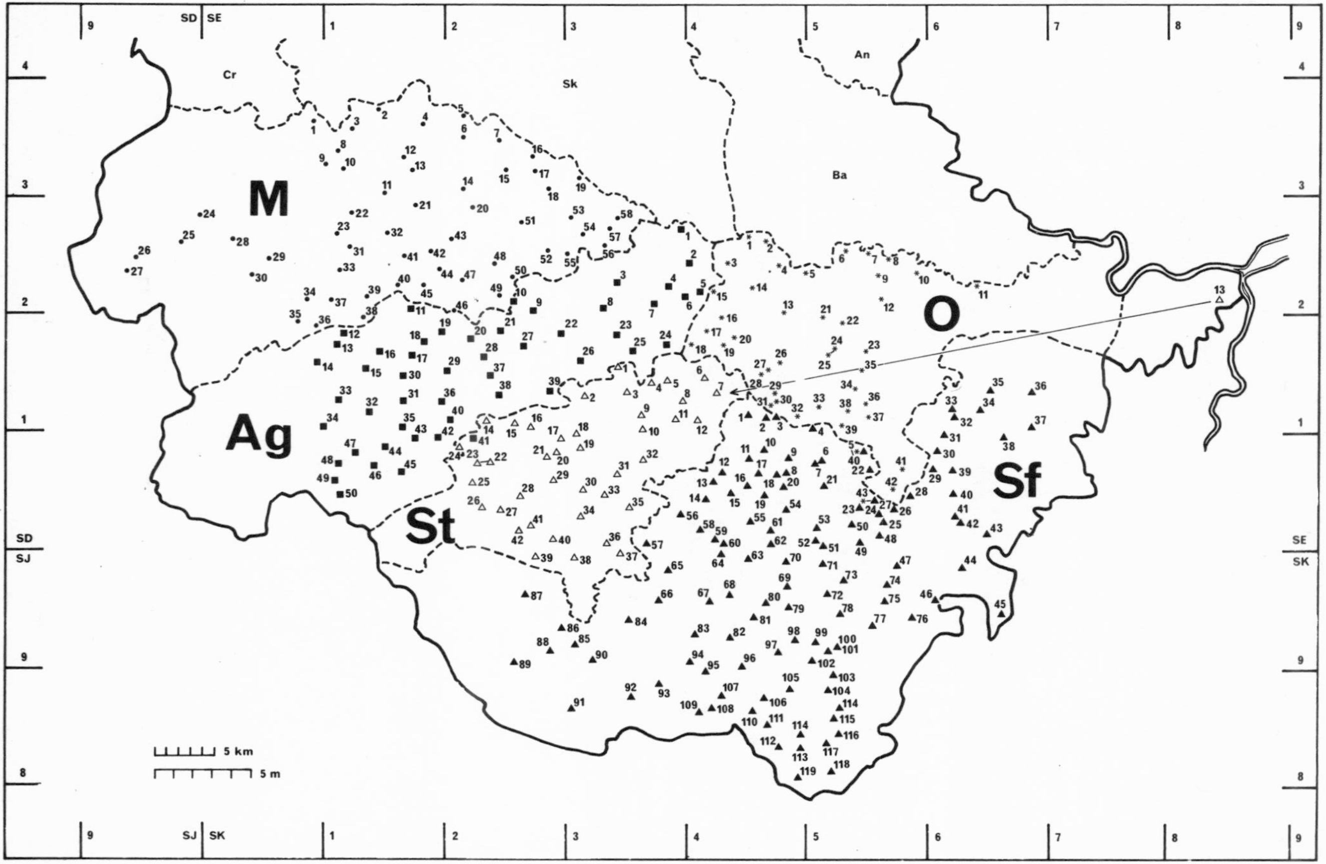

MAP VI

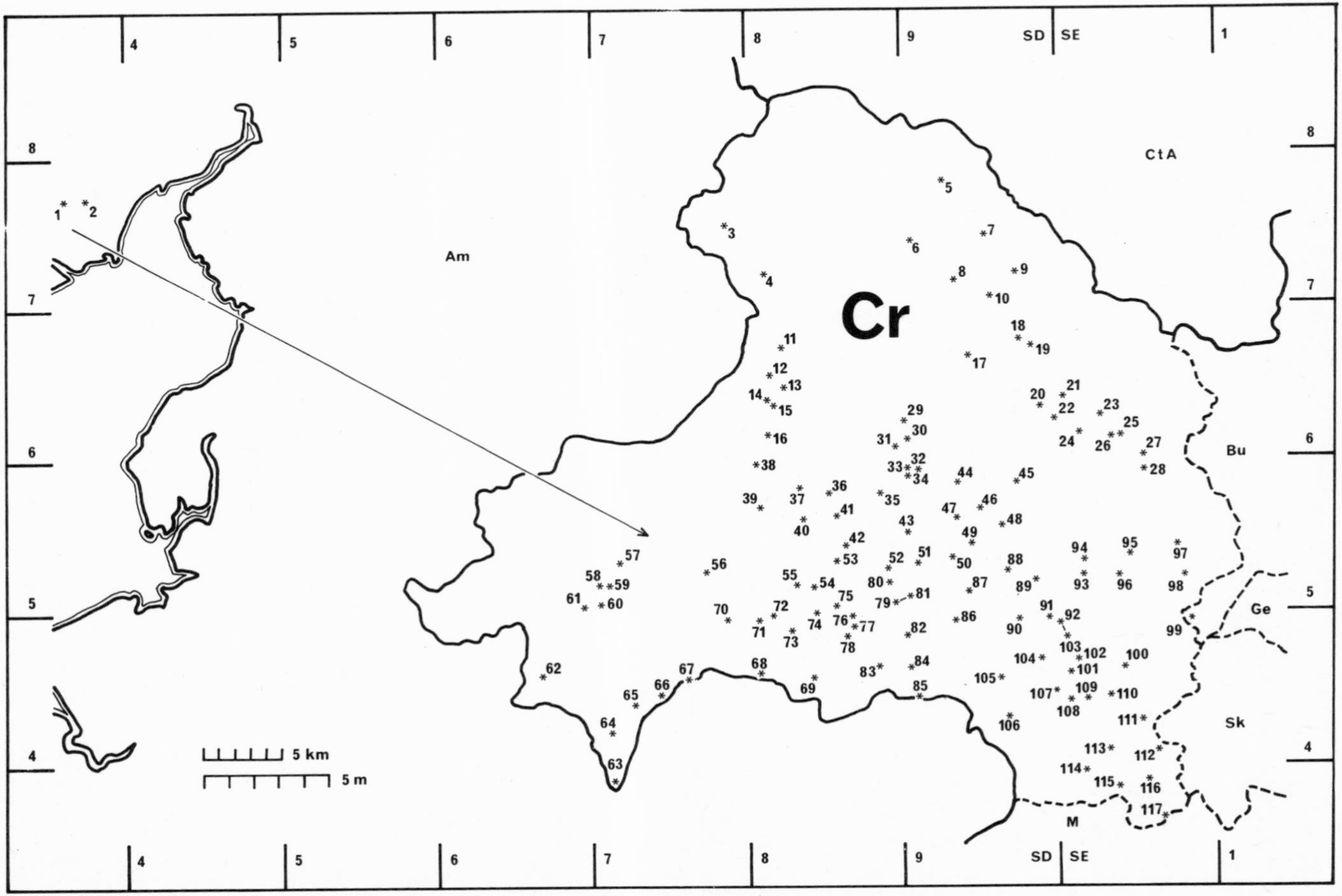

MAP VII

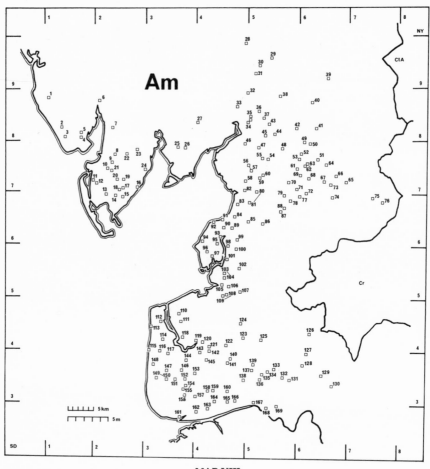

MAP VIII

MAP III

Allerton (A) (NR)
9 Appleton Wiske
20 Arncliffe Hall
12 Birkby
25 'Bordelby' (Mount Grace)
47 Borrowby
29 Brompton
46 Cowesby
11 East Cowton
48 Crosby Grange
55 Dale Town
15 Deighton
2 Over Dinsdale Grange
27 Ellerbeck
30 Foxton
4 Girsby
21 East Harlsey
23 West Harlsey
54 Hawnby
8 Hornby
14 Hutton Bonville
19 Ingleby Arncliffe
18 Irby Manor
41 Kepwick
51 Kirby Wiske
53 Knayton
39 Landmoth
24 Lazenby Hall
45 Leake
7 Castle Leavington
6 Kirk Leavington
58 Maunby
22 Morton Grange
56 Murton
32 Newsham Grange
34 Northallerton
26 Osmotherley
44 North Otterington
50 South Otterington
57 Ravensthorpe Manor
35 Romanby
17 West Rounton
36 Kirby Sigston
40 Nether Silton
38 Lower Silton
10 Great Smeaton
13 Little Smeaton
37 Sowerby under Cotcliffe
31 Thimbleby
43 Thornton le Beans
49 Thornton le Moor
52 Thornton le Street
42 Warlaby
16 Welbury
'Westhouse'
28 Winton
5 High Worsall
3 Low Worsall
33 Yafforth
1 Yarm

Birdforth (Bi) (NR)
1 Arden Hall
40*Asenby
20 Bagby
35 Baxby
Berg(h)ebi
Bernebi
5 Boltby
9 Breckenbrough
22 Old Byland
32 Carlton Husthwaite
11 Carlton Miniott
18 Catton
34*Coxwold
29*Crakehill
39 Crayke
26 Dalton
13 *Fridebi* (Felixkirk)
Hore(n)bodebi
6 Hundulfthorpe Farm
10 Sand Hutton
Iretone
25 Islebeck Grange
23 Kilburn
7 North Kilvington
4 Kirby Knowle
2 Knayton
14 Marderby Hall
Middelham
8 Newsham
21 Osgoodby Hall
36 Oulston
28 Rainton
30 Sessay
17 Skipton
16 Sowerby
15 Sutton under Whitestone Cliffe
24 Thirkleby
12 Thirsk
31 Thormanby
19 Thorpefield
37 Thorpe le Willows
27 Topcliffe
3 Upsall
33 Wildon Grange
38 Yearsley

***Dic* (D) (NR)**
19 Aislaby
31 Allerston
Aschelesmersc, Aschilesmares
42 East Ayton
41 West Ayton
56 Barton le Street
Baschebi
21 High Blandsby
35 Brompton
4 Burniston
'Burton Dale'
7 Cawthorn
51 Cayton
Chig ogemers, Chig omersc, Ghigogesmersc
Chiluesmares, Chiluesmersc
3 Cloughton
6 Cropton
22 Low Dalby
{48 High Deepdale
{50 Low Deepdale
{47 Middle Deepdale
57 Easthorpe House
33 Ebberston
27 Ellerburn
Eterstorp
13 Everley
44 Falsgrave
24 *Farmanby*
55 Filey
54 Gristhorpe
12 Hackness
43 Hillgrips
39 Hutton Buscel
45 Irton
Kettlethorpe
52 Killerby Hall
23 Kingthorpe House
5 Lastingham
53 Lebberston
Leidtorp
9 Levisham
10 Lockton
32 Loft Marishes
'Little Marish'
37 Martin Garth
25 Marton
Maxudesmares, -mersc
20 Middleton
8 Newton
'Newton'
15 Northfield Farm
Odulfesmare, Ouduluesmersc
49 Osgodby
26 Pickering
40 Preston Hill
Rodebestorp, Roudeluestorp
29 Roxby Hill
36 Ruston

MAP IV (cont'd)

North Hundred of Holderness (No) (ER)†

3 *Arnestorp*
15 Aram
2 Barmston
7 Beeford
13 Bewholme
16+Brandesburton
22 Hornsea Burton
19 Catfoss Hall
18+Catwick
   Chenecol, Chenucol,
   Chenuthesholm
9 Cleeton
34+Great Cowden
35 Little Cowden
5*Dringhoe
11 Dunnington
6 North Frodingham
26*Goxhill
29 Great Hatfield
30 Little Hatfield
21 Hornsea
14 Langthorpe Hall
17+Leven
3 Lissett
+*Luuetotholm*
28 Mappleton
12 Nunkeeling
32+Rise
31 Long Riston
27 Rolston
20 Seaton
25+Sigglesthorne
10 High Skirlington
23 Southorpe
4 Ulrome
8*Upton
24 Wassand Hall
1 'Winkton'

South Hundred of Holderness (So) (ER)††

Andrebi
9 Burstwick
15 Camerton Hall
34*Dimlington
36 Easington
1+Grimston
18 Halsham
2 Hilston
27 Hollym
14 Paull Holme
28 Holmpton
17 Keyingham
37 Kilnsea
3+Monkwith
}21 Great Newsome
}22 Little Newsome
12 Newton Garth
33 Out Newton
   'Northorpe'
8 Nuthill
19+Ottringham
5 Owstwick
25 Owthorne
29*Patrington
13 Paull
Redmere
23 Rimswell
6 Roos
32 Rysome Garth
10 Skeckling
  *'Tharlesthorpe'
11 Thorngumbald
30*Welwick Thorpe
   (Thorpe Hill)
16 Totleys Farm
7 Tunstall
24 Waxholme
35+Weeton

31+Welwick
20 Winestead
26 Withernsea

Howden (How) (ER)

16 Asselby
12 Babthorpe
6 Barlby
15 Barmby on the Marsh
17 Barnhill Hall
23 Belby House
9 Bowthorpe
13 Brackenholme
21 Burland House
20 Cavil
10 Cliffe
32 Cotness Hall
2 West Cottingwith
5 North Duffield
8 South Duffield
25 Eastrington
14 Hagthorpe
11 Hemingbrough
27 Hive
19 Howden
28 Kilpin
18 Knedlington
30 Laxton
7 Osgodby
26 Owsthorpe
24 Portington
3 Riccall
31 Saltmarshe
29 Skelton
4 Skipwith
1 Thorganby
22 Thorpe Lidget
33 Yokefleet

Hunthow (Hu) (ER)

19 Auburn
8 Bempton
16 Bessingby
14 Boynton
15 Boynton Hall
12 Bridlington
7 Buckton
13 Easton
9 Flamborough
2 Flixton
3 Foxholes
20 Fraisthorpe
6 Grindale
17 Hilderthorpe
10 Marton
4 Reighton
11 Sewerby
5 Speeton
1 Staxton
18 Wilsthorpe

Pocklington (P) (ER)

24 Allerthorpe
10 Barmby Moor
4 Belthorpe
25 Bielby
9 Bolton
22 Burnby
}6 High Catton
}7 Low Catton
Chetelstorp
15 Deighton
12 Elvington
18 Escrick
26 Everingham
8 Fangfoss
5 Gowthorpe
3 Greenwick
21 Hayton

† Places marked + are stated specifically to be in North Hundred, others are simply stated to be in Holderness and have been allocated to this hundred on a geographical basis.

†† Places marked + are stated specifically to be in South Hundred, others are simply stated to be in Holderness and have been allocated to this hundred on a geographical basis.

MAP IV (cont'd.)

Pocklington (cont'd.)
19 Kelfield
16 Moreby Hall
11 Pocklington
17 Stillingfleet
13 Sutton upon Derwent
23 Thorpe le Street
20 Waplington Hall
14 Wheldrake
2 Bishop Wilton
1 Youlthorpe

Scard (**Sc**) (**ER**)
17 Birdsall
13 Buckton Holms
18 Burdale
15 Duggleby
14 North Grimston
12 Kennythorpe
11 Langton
6 Linton
8 Norton
2 Rillington
3 Scagglethorpe
1 Scampston
7 Settrington
9 Sutton Grange
4 Thorpe Bassett
19 Towthorpe
10 Welham
16 Wharram le Street
5 Wintringham

Sneculfcros (**Sn**) (**ER**)
13 Aike
8 Beswick
21 Beverley
5 Bracken
18 Cherry Burton
11 South Dalton
2 Dunnington
15 Etton

17 Gardham
1 Grimston
10 Holme on the Wolds
Ianulfestorp
6 Kilnwick
14 Leconfield
9 Lockington
4 Middleton on the Wolds
19 Molescroft
Neuson
16 Newton (Gardham)
Persene
20 Raventhorpe
12 Scoreborough
3 Scoreby Manor
Stei(n)torp
Torp
7 Watton

Thorshowe (**Th**) (**ER**)
16 Cottam
15 Cowlam
13 Croom House
7 Helperthorpe
3 East Heslerton
2 West Heslerton
11 Kirby Grindalythe
1 Knapton
{{8 East Lutton
{{9 West Lutton
12 Low Mowthorpe
5 Newton
4 Sherburn
14 Sledmere
10 Thirkleby Manor
10 another Thirkleby Manor
Turodebi
Ulchiltorp
6 Weaverthorpe

Turbar (**Tu**) (**ER**)
9 Argam
18 Brigham
8 Burton Fleming
E(le)stolf
11 Elmswell
{{3 East Flotmanby
{{2 West Flotmanby
1 Folkton
6 Fordon
17 Foston on the Wolds
10 Garton on the Wolds
16 Gembling
5 Hunmanby
15 Great Kelk
14 Little Kelk
Ledemare
4 Muston
13 Nafferton
7 Wold Newton
12 Pockthorpe
Ricstorp
Scolf(s)tone, -tona

Warter (**Wa**) (**ER**)
15 North Dalton
2 Water Fulford
6 Great Givendale
11 Little Givendale
10 Grimthorpe Manor
5 Hawold
1 Heslington
13 Huggate
17 Kilnwick Percy
4 Langwith Lodge
7 Meltonby
12 Millington
3 Naburn
18 Nunburnholme
9 Ousethorpe Farm
16 Warter
14 Wetwang
8 Yapham

Weighton (**Wei**) (**ER**)
12 Bishop Burton
1 Cleaving Grange
14 North Cliffe
3 Easthorpe
5 Goodmanham
8 Harswell
9 Holme upon Spalding Moor
13 Houghton
4 Kipling Cotes
2 Londesborough
11 Sancton
7 Shiptonthorpe
Torp
6 Towthorpe
10 Market Weighton

Welton (**Wel**) (**ER**)
3 Bentley
9 Brantingham
9 Brantingham Thorpe
6 Cottingham
11*Ellerker
12 Elloughton
1 Lund
5 Pillwoods Farm
4 Risby
7 Skidby
Toschetorp
2 Walkington
1 Wauldby
8 Little Weighton
13 Welton

MAP V

Ainsty (An) (WR)
22 Acaster Malbis
38 Acaster Selby
8 Acomb
37 Appleton Roebuck
19 Askham Bryan
18 Askham Richard
14 Bickerton
26 Bilbrough
16 Bilton
21 Bishopthorpe
Bithen
36 Bolton Percy
27 Catterton
24 Colton
23 Copmanthorpe
13 Cowthorpe
31 'Haggenby'
17 Healaugh
3 Hessay
35 Hornington Manor
7 Knapton
'Malkton'
11 Long Marston
20 Middlethorpe
1 Moor Monkton
Mul(h)ede, Mulehale
33 Ouston Farm
32 Oxton
34 Pallathorpe
6 Nether Poppleton
5 Upper Poppleton
Rodouuelle
9 Rufforth
4 Scagglethorpe
25 Steeton Hall
30 Thorp Arch
12*Tockwith
29 Walton
10 Hutton Wandesley
28 Wighill
15 Wighill Park
2 Wilstrop Hall

Bulmer (B) (NR)
9 Aldwark
10 Alne
50*Barnby House
43 Barton le Willows
73*Beningbrough
51 Bossall
3 Brafferton
2*Brandsby
37 Bulmer
53*Buttercrambe
62 Carlton Farm
54 Claxton
32 Coneysthorpe
71 'Corburn'
25 Cornbrough House
42 Crambe
27 Dalby
Dic(he)
67 Earswick
6 Easingwold
24 Farlington
48 Flaxton
Fornetorp
44 Foston
31 Ganthorpe
49 Harton
69 Haxby
57 Gate Helmsley
56 Upper Helmsley
4 Helperby
33 Henderskelfe
34 Hildenley Hall
58 Holtby
16 Huby
68 Huntington
40 Low Hutton
55 Sand Hutton
41 Sheriff Hutton
'Inglethwaite'
15 Kelsit Grange
3 Cold Kirby
46 East Lilling
47 West Lilling
13*Linton upon Ouse
23 Marton in the Forest
**Mortun*
35 Low Mowthorpe Farm
20 Moxby Hall
59*Murton
19 Murton Farm
8 Myton on Swale
14 Newton upon Ouse
60*Osbaldwick
77*Overton
5 Raskelf
78*Rawcliffe
64*Sandburn House
28 Scackleton
72 Shipton
76*Skelton
22 Skewsby
21 Stearsby
75 Stillington
36 Stittenham
62*Stockton on the Forest
65 Strensall
17 Sutton on the Forest
30 Terrington
7 Tholthorpe
45 Thornton le Clay
18 Thorpe Hill (in Sutton on the Forest)
52*Thorpe Hill (in Sand Hutton near York)
11 Tollerton
Toresbi
66 Towthorpe
61 Warthill
Waruelestorp
38 Welburn
26 Whenby
39 Whitwell on the Hill
74 Wide Open Farm
29 Wiganthorpe Hall
70*Wigginton
12 Youlton

Barkston Ash (BA) (WR)
34 Little Airmyn
17 Barkston
30 Barlow
25 Birkin
5 Bramham
29 Brayton
28 Burton Hall
31 Camblesforth
32 Carlton
1 Clifford
33 Drax
24 Fairburn
{20 Church Fenton
{19 Little Fenton
9 Grimston Grange
26 Hambleton
7 Hazelwood Castle
Hunchilhuse(s)
11 Kirkby Wharfe
15 Lead
22 Ledsham
13 North Milford Hall
6 Monk Hay Stile
Neuhuse, Niuuehusum
3 Newton Kyme
23 Newton 'Wallis'
2 Oglethorpe Hall
21 Ryther
Saxhalla, Sax(e)hale
16 Saxton
18 Sherburn in Elmet
8 Stutton
10 Tadcaster
27 Thorpe Willoughby
4 Toulston
14 Towton
12 Ulleskelf

MAP VI

Agbrigg (Ag) (WR)
5 Ackton
30 Almondbury
48 Austonley
11 Bradley
39 West Bretton
46 Cartworth
26 Crigglestone
24 Crofton
15 North Crosland
33 South Crosland
41 Lower Cumberworth
17 Dalton
28 Upper Denby
10 Earlsheaton
38 Emley
31 Farnley Tyas
37 Flockton
43 Fulstone
14 Golcar
45 Hepworth
49 Holme
32 Honley
19 Upper Hopton
22 Horbury
16 Huddersfield
36 Kirkburton
18 Kirkheaton
29 Lepton
12 Lindley
34 Meltham
1 Methley
4 Normanton
9 Ossett
13 Quarmby
23 Sandal Magna
40 Shelley
42 Shepley
27 Shitlington
6 Snydale
3 Stanley
21 Thornhill
35 Thurstonland
47 Upperthong
8 Wakefield
25 Walton
7 Warmfield
'Westerby'
20 Lower Whitley
2 Whitwood
44 Wooldale
50 Yateholme

Morley (M) (WR)
8 Allerton
55 East Ardsley
52 West Ardsley
16 Armley
48 Batley
18 Beeston
21 North Bierley
41 Bolton
13 Bowling
12 Bradford
7 Bramley
5 Calverley
57 Carlton
3 Chellow Grange
10 Clayton
42 Cleckheaton
40 Clifton
25*Cruttonstall
49 Dewsbury
20 Drighlington
4 Eccleshill
37 Elland
15 Farnley
6 Farsley
38 Fixby
43 Gomersal
34 Greetland
45 Hartshead
50 Hanging Heaton
31 Hipperholme
19 Hunslet
36 Old Lindley
44 Liversedge
56 Lofthouse
27*Longfield
53 Middleton
28*Midgley
46 Mirfield
51 Morley
23 Northowram
47 Pudsey
39 Rastrick
17 Reestones
58 Rothwell
22 Shelf
2 Shipley
33 Southowram
30*Sowerby
35 Stainland
26*Stansfield
9 Thornton
54 Thorpe on the Hill
14 Tong
24*Wadsworth
29*Warley
11 Wibsey
1*Wilsden
32 Wyke

Osgoldcross (O) (WR)
20 Ackworth
40 Adwick le Street
41 Arksey
28 Badsworth
6 Beal
42 Bentley
38 Burghwallis
34 Campsall
13 Darrington
9 Eggborough
30 North Elmsall
15 Featherstone
4 Ferry Fryston
2 Water Fryston
32 Hamphall Stubbs
17 West Hardwick
10 Hensall
19 Hessle
3 Glass Houghton
7 Kellington
5 Knottingley
31 Minsthorpe
'Newsham'
35 Norton
18 Nostell Priory
37 Owston
16 Purston Jaglin
8 Roall Hall
27 Rogerthorpe Manor
43 Scawsby
33 Skelbrooke
39 Skellow
{25 Kirk Smeaton
{24 Little Smeaton
11*Snaith
21 Stapleton
36 Sutton
14 Tanshelf
26 Thorpe Audlin
29 Upton
23 Walden Stubbs
1 Wheldale
12 Whitley
22 Womersley

Strafforth (Sf) (WR)
5 Adwick le Street
61 Adwick upon Dearne
116 North Anston
117 South Anston
40 Armthorpe
111 Aston
93 Attercliffe
43 Auckley

MAP VIII

Amounderness (Am)†

130 Aighton (L)
98 Aldcliffe (L)
16 Aldingham (L)
70 Arkholme (L)
Aschebi (L)
101*Ashton Hall (L)
167 Ashton on Ribble (L)
76 Austwick (WR)
41 Barbon (W)
24 Bardsea (L)
91 Bare (L)
73 Barnoldswick (WR)
139 Barton (L)
46*Beetham (W)
74 High Bentham (WR)
115 Bispham (L)
19 Bolton Farm (L)
83 Bolton le Sands (L)
1 Bootle (C)
60*Borwick (L)
'Bothelford' (W)
136 Broughton in Furness (L)
6 Broughton in Furness (L)
112 Burn Hall (L)
{62 Nether Burrow (L)
{63 Over Burrow (L)
55 Burton (W)
67 Burton in Lonsdale (WR)
68 Cantsfield (L)
116 Carleton (L)
82 Carnforth (L)
50 Casterton (W)
86 Caton (L)
123 Catterall (L)
26 *Cherchebi* (Cartmel) (L)
126 Chipping (L)
75 Clapham (WR)
125 Claughton (near Garstang) (L)

87 Claughton (near Lancaster) (L)
165 Clifton (L)
106*Cockerham (L)
{109 Great Crimbles (L)
{108 Little Crimbles (L)
'Crivelton' (L)
54 Dalton (W)
18 Dendron (L)
21 Dalton in Furness (L)
128 Dilworth House (L)
142 Great Eccleston (L)
143 Little Eccleston
102*Ellel (L)
145 Elswick (L)
88 Farleton (L)
45*Farleton (W)
169 Fishwick (L)
'Fordbottle' (L)
107 Forton (L)
163 Freckleton (L)
124 Garstang (L)
7 *Gerleuuorde* (Kirkby Ireleth) (L)
17 Gleaston (L)
133 Goosnargh (L)
153 Greenhalgh (L)
79 Gressingham (L)
131 Grimsargh (L)
132 Haighton Hall (L)
85 Halton (L)
118 Hambleton (L)
15 Hart Carrs (L)
95 Heaton (L)
Heldetune (WR)
32 Helsington (W)
34*Heversham Head (W)
94 Heysham (L)
12 *Hietun* (Hawcoat) (L)
105 Hillam (L)

35*Hincaster (W)
47 Holme (W)
78 Hornby (L)
4 *Hougun* (Millom) (C)
5 *Hougenai* (Millom Castle) (C)
'Hutton' (L)
48 Hutton Roof (W)
38 Old Hutton (W)
65 Ingleton (WR)
141 Inskip (L)
64 Ireby (L)
{81 Nether Kellet (L)
80 Over Kellet (L)
10 Killerwick (L)
31 *Kirkby* (Kendal) (W)
49 Kirkby Lonsdale (W)
158 Kirkham (L)
3 Kirksanton (C)
99 Lancaster (C)
'Kirk Lancaster' (L)
148 Layton (L)
166 Lea (L)
33*Levens (W)
51 Lower Leck (L)
14 Leece (L)
14 another Leece (L)
*'Lonsdale' (L)
44 Lupton (W)
161 Lytham (L)
42 Mansergh (W)
8 Martin (L)
{149 Great Marton (L)
{150 Little Marton (L)
71 Melling (L)
96 Middleton (L)
40 Middleton Hall (W)
30 Mint House (W)
151 Mythop (L)
137 Newsham (near Preston) (L)

'Newsham' (in Skerton) (L)
'Newton' (in Lancaster) (L)
164 Newton (near Preston) (L)
61 Newton (in Whittington) (L)
27 High Newton (L)
9 Orgrave (L)
97 Overton (L)
93 Oxcliffe Hall (L)
29 Patton Hall (W)
22 Pennington (L)
{154 Great Plumpton (L)
{155 Little Plumpton (L)
117 Poulton le Fylde (L)
92 Poulton Hall (L)
110 Preesall (L)
146 Preese Hall (L)
168 Preston (L)
43 Preston Patrick (W)
37*Preston Richard (W)
60 Priest Hutton (L)
120 Rawcliffe Hall (L)
119 Out Rawcliffe (L)
121 Upper Rawcliffe (L)
157 Ribby (L)
129 Ribchester (L)
13 Roose (L)
113 Rossall (L)
122 St. Michael's on Wyre (L)
158 Salwick Hall (L)
100*Scotforth (L)
39 Sedbergh (WR)
144 Singleton (L)
89 Skerton (L)
84 Slyne (L)
11 Sowerby Hall (in Dalton in Furness) (L)
141 Sowerby Hall (near Preston) (L)
147 Staining (L)
20 Stainton (L)

† The places listed in DB under Amounderness were subsequently distributed between the medieval counties of Cumberland (C), Lancashire (L), Westmorland (W) and the West Riding of Yorkshire (WR).

MAP VIII (cont'd.)

Amounderness (cont'd.)

36 Stainton (W)
111 Stalmine (L)
    'Stapleton Terne' (L)
28 Strickland Roger (W)
    Suntun (L)
    'Swainseat' (L)
77 Tatham (L)
52 Thirnby Wood (L)

114 Thornton (L)
66*Thornton in Lonsdale (WR)
135 Threlfall's Farm (L)
{104 Lower Thurnham (L)
{103 Upper Thurnham (L)
90 Torisholme (L)
159 Treales (L)
69 Tunstall (L)

23 Ulverston (L)
25 Walton Hall (L)
58 'Wart' (L)
    Warton (near Carnforth) (L)
162 Warton (near Preston) (L)
152 Weeton (L)
72 Wennington (L)

156 Westby (L)
127 Wheatley (L)
2 Whicham (C)
134 Whittingham Hall (L)
53 Whittington (L)
138 Woodplumpton (L)
{57 Yealand Conyers
{56 Yealand Redmayne